THE GREAT AUSTRALIAN

Wine Book

TITLE PAGE: *Sheep graze in the vineyards of Coonawarra, South Australia, during autumn.*

REED

AUSTRALIA

Darwin

ALICE SPRINGS

ROMA

STANTHORPE   *Brisbane*

Perth SWAN VALLEY

SOUTH-WEST COASTAL REGION

MARGARET RIVER

MT BARKER-FRANKLAND REGION

CLARE   RIVERLAND

BAROSSA VALLEY

ADELAIDE

McLAREN VALE

LANGHORNE CREEK

COONAWARRA

GREAT WESTERN

CENTRAL VICTORIA

GOULBURN VALLEY

GEELONG

MILDURA

SWAN HILL

MUDGEE   UPPER HUNTER
          LOWER HUNTER

Sydney

GRIFFITH/LEETON M.I.A.

RUTHENGLEN

GLENROWAN/MILAWA

Melbourne

YARRA VALLEY

LAUNCESTON

HOBART

THE GREAT AUSTRALIAN Wine Book

FOREWORD BY HUGH JOHNSON

COMPILED BY ROBERT MAYNE

WITH

Len Evans • Paul Lloyd • David Dunstan • Sir James Hardy • James Halliday
Walter James • Michael Hill Smith • Brian Croser • Brenton Baker • Max Lake
Tony Hitchin • Frank Doherty • Mark Shield • Helen Guy • Robin Bradley • Samuel Cook
David Bray • David Foster • John Stanford • John Parkinson • Don Hogg • Chris Quirk

PHOTOGRAPHY BY MILTON WORDLEY · PHILIP QUIRK · ROGER GARWOOD

FRONT COVER:
Brother John May,
winemaker at the Sevenhill
winery in the Clare Valley,
South Australia. The Jesuit
Fathers had their first
vintage here in 1854,
making it the oldest winery
in the valley. One of the
winery's main activities is to
produce altar wines, some of
which are exported to a
number of countries.

BACK COVER:
Malcolm Redman (left) and
his older brother Bruce have
recently taken over the
operation of the Redman
winery at Coonawarra,
South Australia, from their
father, Owen Redman, who
is still involved in the family
winemaking concern but
who lives in Adelaide.

The Publisher acknowledges the co-operation of
the Australian wine industry in the preparation of
The Great Australian Wine Book. The assistance
given by persons too numerous to mention is
appreciated and valued.

Photography for *The Great Australian Wine Book* was
commissioned by the Publisher from the following:
Milton Wordley's work illustrates The Colours of
Wine, Grape's Progress, Wines and Wineries of
South Australia and A Day in the Life of a
Winemaker; however many photographs by Milton
were also used to illustrate other chapters.
Philip Quirk photographed Wines and Wineries of
New South Wales, Wines and Wineries of Victoria
and Camden Park Winery; other photographs by
Philip were chosen to support additional chapters.
Roger Garwood captured the activity of the industry
in the Wines and Wineries of Western Australia.
Allan Moult at the eleventh hour added his expertise
to our book with photography for the Wines and
Wineries of Tasmania.
Michael Trafford, who managed to tear himself away
from his beloved canine friends for just a little while,
photographed Len Evans for A Nose for It.
The historical photographs used in A Tradition of
Families are from the Hardy family collection and
were photographically copied by David Simpson.

First published in 1985 by
REED BOOKS PTY LTD
2 Aquatic Drive Frenchs Forest NSW 2086

© Reed Books Pty Ltd 1985

National Library of Australia
Cataloguing-in-Publication Data
The Great Australian wine book.
   Includes index.
   ISBN 0 7301 0101 0.
   I. Wine and Wine Making – Australia.
   I. Mayne, Robert. II. Title.
641.2'0994

Produced in Australia by the Publisher
Edited by Margaret Olds
Designed by Bruno Grasswill
Maps by Michael Gorman
Drawings by Sheila Sullivan Kelly

Typeset in Australia by Deblaere Typesetting Pty Ltd
Printed by Dai Nippon Printing Limited, Hong Kong

FOREWORD

For years I have wondered how the world overseas could remain as indifferent as it by and large has to the glorious individuality of the wines of Australia. Surely being different is an essential virtue in every wine we will ever respect. Alone, it is reason enough to sip and enjoy any well-made wine. When you can add exceptional value for money, and add on top of that sometimes first-division, seldom less than second-division, quality you have, I would have thought, an irresistible proposition.

Yet it hasn't been so, as far as British buyers are concerned – and the world at large has tended to imitate their inactivity. Why? A contributory reason struck me as I read the proofs of this book. I felt that almost for the first time, I was reading an objective account aimed at me, as an outsider. I was sitting at table with informed, articulate and sober (or nearly) authorities whose aim was to include me, not shut me out.

Australian wine-folk have developed a jargon based on the history of their industry (a history a surprising number know down to the last bottle-washer) which means nothing to an outsider. It is sometimes difficult even to tell what is a penetrating comment and what is the sort of raucous rubbish Australians seem to love to indulge in. (I love it, too.) So close are many Australian wine-critics to their subject (and so distant from others' views) that communication breaks down.

'Bloody Byzantine,' the poor Pom murmurs, reading of the products and the structure of an industry apparently without any central direction, or even sense of direction. We are all for freedom of speech, not to mention action, but when every release needs an interpretation longer than the Declaration of Independence – that was yours, wasn't it? – we groan; yea, do we groan.

A system? Western Australia has started a system. What will happen, though, when Croser wants 3 per cent Mt Barker riesling in his Clare and Coonawarra brew, or Tisdall looks to lace his virgin Victorian with a shot of Margaret River? Is the legislator going to say, stop: let Victoria be Victoria, and more to the point Geelong Geelong, or must every Australian wine with ambitions be a cocktail?

It comes right back to people. Australians prefer them, reasonably enough, to places. Up there in the pantheon there are the Schuberts, the Haselgroves, the Manns and Preeces. They devised their cellar styles. Are the present and future winemakers not to have the same privilege? Or must they be laced into a straitjacket of appellations? And would appellations help the consumer anyway?

I don't propose (as if I could) to dissect this can of worms – still less digest it. But it brings me to the point of a foreword, which is to urge the reader to buy, or if he has already bought, to read the pages ahead. I don't say they will answer every question. I do say they are written by a team of rightly respected wine-lovers, briefed to give their points of view on almost every aspect of Australian wine. Together they form a coherent coverage of where it's at, and where it's going. And I can understand it.

There are puzzles in it. Maybe I have harped on them too much. But above all there are vivid and enthralling prospects – of good wine and great pleasure now, and, for a wager, even better and greater to come.

Hugh Johnson

CONTENTS

Captions to all photographs written by Robert Mayne with the exception of those written by David Bray for Wines and Wineries of Queensland, and David Dunstan for The Changing Tastes.

CONTRIBUTORS

JAMES HALLIDAY is a lawyer with a lifelong love of wine. He has at various times made wine in Australia and France; been a part owner of a vineyard and winery; written eight books on wine; provided the weekly column for the *National Times* for five years before moving to the *Weekend Australian* in 1984; is a national wine show judge; and provides consultancy services to David Jones and Qantas.

MARK SHIELD is well known to Victorian wine-lovers for his idiosyncratic and amusing column called 'Noble Rot' in the *Age*, Melbourne. He is a consultant with the Australian Wine Club and produces their magazine. He lives in Melbourne and contributes to a number of other publications on wine.

HUGH JOHNSON is widely acknowledged in the world of wine as its most authoritative and stylish commentator. His book, *The World Atlas of Wine,* which was first published in 1971, has sold almost two million copies in ten languages. He has also written a number of other definitive wine books. He lives in an Elizabethan hall in Essex, England, and is also an authority on trees.

PAUL LLOYD is a senior journalist on the staff of the *Advertiser* newspaper in Adelaide. As wine columnist for the paper, and for *Home Beautiful* and *Epicurean* magazines, he is a passionate advocate of wine, its industry and its heritage. He is raising a family in Adelaide and 'mucks about' in his vineyard.

WALTER JAMES is the well-known author of many books on vines and wines, including *Wine in Australia.* For many years he wrote the lucid and charming observations on wine and associated subjects which appeared in the pages of *Australian Home Beautiful.* He lives in deserved retirement in Melbourne, from whence he was persuaded to write the perceptive essay in this book.

MILTON WORDLEY worked as a newspaper staff photographer in Adelaide and Sydney before beginning to freelance in London in 1974. His photographs have appeared in a number of magazines and books, including *A Day in the Life of Australia* and *Salute to Singapore.* He lives in Adelaide and runs his own photographic business.

JOHN STANFORD is well known in the Australian wine industry as a leading wine judge, winemaker and writer. He graduated in the outstanding class of 1947 from Roseworthy Agricultural College and worked as a winemaker at a number of wineries – including the Emu Wine Company and Rosemount – until 1974. He formed his own wine technology and marketing consultancy company, Vintech, in 1970. He has been wine columnist and adviser to the *Australian* for over ten years and contributes to wine magazines and books. He is Australia's longest serving and most experienced senior wine judge. John lives in Sydney, is President of the New South Wales Wine Press Club and Chairman of Directors of the Australian Wine Society.

DR MAX LAKE is a wine judge of international standing. He has been invited to be President of the International Wine and Spirit competition in Great Britain for 1986. He has written nine highly original books on wine. His current mission is to increase the enjoyment of life by a better appreciation of flavour. He now lives in Sydney but commutes regularly to the Hunter Valley, where his son Stephen is winemaker at Lake's Folly.

ROBERT MAYNE is now the Public Relations Manager for a large group of major Australian wine companies and he writes regularly about wine and other subjects. He was trained at the *Sydney Morning Herald* and has worked on a number of other newspapers, including *The Times,* London, and *The Sunday Times*. For five years he was National Promotions Manager of the Australian Wine and Brandy Corporation and wrote *Understanding Australian Wine* then. He lives amid the vineyards in McLaren Vale, South Australia, and when he is not flying aeroplanes he collects wine and writes.

SIR JAMES HARDY comes from one of Australia's best known wine families but is more widely known as a yachtsman – and syndicate director and back-up skipper for *Australia II*. He is Director of Sailing for the South Australian Defence of the America's Cup 1987. He is now chairman of his family's large wine company, based at Reynella, South Australia, but he lives on the shores of Sydney Harbour.

DAVID DUNSTAN was introduced to the pleasures of wine by his father, the Melbourne columnist and author, Keith Dunstan. He is a professional historian, a graduate of Monash and Melbourne Universities, who wrote weekly wine columns for the *Age* and the *Sun-Herald* for some years. He has an enduring interest in the history of wine and viticulture. He now works for the Heritage Unit of the Victorian Ministry for Planning and Environment.

LEN EVANS has one of Australia's finest palates. He is Chairman of Judges at the Sydney Wine Show and the National Wine Show in Canberra. Len is deeply involved in the wine business as Chairman of the Rothbury Estate and Petaluma Wines, and he runs Len Evans Wines, a fine wine and restaurant business in the heart of Sydney. He is also a prolific writer and broadcaster on the subject of wine and food, and is the author of the *Complete Book of Australian Wine* (first published in 1973).

ROBIN BRADLEY was one of the founders of the Expovin Wine Exhibition. He is an elegant and witty writer about wine in various forms. He compiled *Australian Wine Vintages* and his eight books include *Small Wineries of Australia*. He lives in suburban Melbourne and refuses to drink poor wine.

HELEN GUY is a former editor of *Wine and Spirit* magazine. She has been deeply involved with wine for many years, an enthusiasm she shares with her husband Colin McWilliam, who is an auctioneer with a special interest in wine. They live in Sydney.

TONY HITCHIN, English-born but now an Australian, came here as a reporter on the *Sydney Morning Herald* and now edits several magazines and publications, including *Home Beautiful* and *Epicurean,* for the Melbourne Herald group. He lives with his wife, two daughters, two large gentle dogs and a small ferocious mortgage on the shores of Port Phillip Bay.

CHRIS QUIRK is an Adelaide economist who now works for Australian National Railways. For four years he was the economist for the Australian Wine and Brandy Corporation, the Federal statutory authority responsible for the wine industry.

JOHN PARKINSON was the founding editor of the consumer magazine *Wine and Spirit Monthly*. He began his wine career working for Len Evans and has written extensively on wine for a wide range of publications. He now operates a wine consultancy business in Sydney.

MICHAEL HILL SMITH is a sixth-generation descendant of the founder of S. Smith and Son, Yalumba Wines. He is a director of that company and actively involved in the family business at management and promotional levels. Michael also is involved as a wine commentator on the A.B.C., writes a regular column for *Epicurean* magazine and is involved as an associate wine judge and as a regular wine-tasting panellist for national wine magazines.

DAVID FOSTER is a Perth-based wine writer and commentator who for four years was Secretary of the Wine and Brandy Producers' Association of Western Australia. He writes a wine column for the *Daily News* and is working on several wine publications of his own. His other activities in the wine industry include a marketing consultancy and the operation of a wine club dealing exclusively in Western Australian wines to the eastern States.

DAVID BRAY is the chief sub-editor of the *Courier Mail,* Brisbane, and writes that paper's weekly wine column. He is a former president of the Queensland Wine Press Club and is a keen collector of wine.

SAMUEL COOK is a former wine writer for the *Sydney Morning Herald,* a newspaper with which he has had a long association. A confirmed bachelor, he visits Sydney regularly from his country retreat. He never drinks more than one glass of wine a day, a habit he says that has enabled him to reach a ripe old age.

FRANK DOHERTY is an experienced journalist who, for ten years, was wine writer for the Wine Information Bureau in Victoria. He now lives in suburban Melbourne and writes about wine for a number of Australian newspapers and several magazines. It is believed he is the only professional journalist ever to have been appointed a senior wine judge.

BRIAN CROSER is the winemaker at Petaluma Wines. He is widely considered to be one of the brightest and most innovative winemakers in Australia. He was trained at Roseworthy Agricultural College, worked for Hardy's and spent a year studying oenology at the University of California's Davis campus. He lives with his family in the Adelaide Hills near the Petaluma winery.

ROGER GARWOOD was reportedly born on a Thames barge in 1945, but he is not sure how that story came about. Formerly a staff photographer on *Paris Match* he is now a naturalised Australian living with his wife, Helen, and son, Ben, in Fremantle. Freelances for several magazines including *National Geographic.* Also specialises in marine photography and is official photographer for the America's Cup Defence 1987.

PHILIP QUIRK was born in Melbourne in 1948 and studied at the Prahran College of Advanced Education. He lectured in photography at Deakin University, Melbourne, and at a number of other institutions until 1982. In 1976 he established a photographic business in Sydney, specialising in reportage and documentary photography, and his work has been shown in a large number of Australian galleries and published in many leading newspapers and magazines. His photos were included in *A Day in the Life of Australia* in 1981 and *Salute to Singapore* (1984). Philip was awarded the Lady Warwick Fairfax Award for Portraiture at the Art Gallery of New South Wales in 1984.

DON HOGG was born in New Zealand and is an experienced journalist. He worked for many years in New Guinea before returning to Australian journalism. He is the author of a number of books including one on Australian wineries. He works as General Manager of the McLaren Vale Winemakers' Association and runs their annual Bushing Festival. He says he counts many winemakers among his drinking buddies.

BRENTON BAKER is one of Australia's most talented young viticulturists. He was educated in South Australia and graduated from Roseworthy Agricultural College in 1966 and was dux in horticulture. Later in his career he undertook further studies in New South Wales. He joined the South Australian Department of Agriculture, where he worked, and got to know the Australian grape-growing business closely, for eighteen years. Since 1984 he has been Group Viticulturalist with Hardy's, based at Reynella, south of Adelaide. He is married and lives in Fair View Park, an Adelaide suburb.

Tutored wine tastings are now a part of the Australian wine scene, and many young people are enthusiastically learning about the varied pleasures of Australian wines.

THE FIRST SIP

Robert Mayne

An extraordinary social phenomenon has swept across Australia in the last decade or so: Australians turned away from their image of traditional beer drinkers, turning instead to wine.

Only an abstemious outback hermit would not have noticed the change taking place, in tandem with some other significant changes in our society. In 1974/75 Australians drank a record 187 bottles of beer each on average, and – also a record – 16 bottles of wine, more of it red wine than white wine or fortified wine. The proportions were about to change, though, and a year later white wine had surged forward to take and hold the lead over all other forms of wine. Ten years on and we were still consuming more beer than any other form of alcohol, but there had been quite a drop to an average of 160 bottles of beer, and a dramatic climb in wine, to 30 bottles a person.

Whatever the reasons for the rapid change in tastes, wine had clearly come to most levels of Australian society to stay. We took cardboard 4-litre casks of white wine to Chinese restaurants and shamelessly stood them on the Laminex tabletops. We quaffed cask wine at barbeques and at parties. One pair of academics from the University of New-

castle suggested, in a study of the white wine boom, that one of its major causes was the use of white wine as a social lubricant to get the males and females of Australia together – and they may well have been right.

The reasons for these changes to our lifestyle are complex, but two things are fairly evident. Wine has been extraordinarily cheap and it has remained an economic beverage even after the imposition of a tax on it in the 1984 Federal Budget. And a technical revolution which took effect in the 1970s started the mass production of good, fruity and clean white wines. More affluence and – undoubtedly – the effects of European living on Australians turned wine from a luxury and a curiosity into an everyday drink.

For all this, though, it seems to me that there is still a 'them and us' syndrome about wine. The 'us' side of the equation tends to drink cask wine because it is cheap (still around a dollar a litre or so), and because on the whole it is fairly clean, fresh, fruity and free of obvious winemaking faults. There's no snobbery about casks, unless it is a sort of inverse snobbery. The 'them' are the comparatively smaller segment of Australians who are somehow supposed to have the

13

Rothbury winemaker David Lowe noses a glass of a young Rothbury white wine.

apparent success has more to do with a public thirst for sensible knowledge about wine than any particular genius on the part of the author. There *is* a great curiosity in Australia to know more about our own wines in an age when we are making better wine, and more wine, than ever before – and these wines are available at reasonable cost. This book takes over where *Understanding Australian Wine* left off.

More than two dozen writers, photographers, artists and other specialists were involved in the writing, compiling, editing, design and illustration of *The Great Australian Wine Book*. We chose them from an even larger talent pool for a variety of attributes, not the least of which was knowledge of subject. They were also chosen for their ability to communicate their knowledge, ideas and images, for this was never intended to be what is derisorily – and often unfairly – described as a 'coffee table' book.

Other authors, photographers and artists could have contributed equally well, and indeed I regret that some of them could not be fitted in. Nevertheless, we have tried our level best to put into these pages an accurate series of images of Australian wines and wineries, the industry and the wine drinkers in the latter half of the 1980s. This is an overview of the Australian wine scene, though not specifically a reference book. Others have done that. This book strives to be informative, entertaining, visually exciting and educative – but above all, it aims to be a good read about the down-to-earth subject of Australian wine.

Len Evans gets to the core of it in his opening words to the next chapter. Wine *is* just a drink, though of course there is almost endless variety to it. Any reasonable interest in the subject of learning more about wine, and hence being able to enjoy it more, begins with two simple precepts. First, ask yourself whether you enjoy drinking wine (any wine at all), and whether you have ever thought to yourself, 'I don't know much about it, but I know what I like...' If the answer is yes, you are half way there. Second, if you can grasp the simple difference between *generic* wines and *varietal* wines, and you have the makings of a wine-lover.

secret key to knowing what the good stuff is and where it's buried. This last group may read wine magazines and columns and indulge – I have heard it said – in secret rituals which include sniffing and spitting.

This book is an attempt to reconcile these two groups and to prove that the secrets of Australian wine really aren't terribly secret, and certainly not hard to understand.

What is between these covers came from discussions in late 1983 between the publisher Bill Templeman and me. Three years previously we had both been involved in the production of *Understanding Australian Wine,* aimed at taking some of the nonsense out of wine and to do exactly what the title suggested. The attempt was obviously successful, because as I write this, *Understanding Australian Wine* has sold out its third big print run. I think its

Put simply, generic wines (such as claret or white burgundy) indicate by their labels only vaguely what taste experience you can expect with the first sip. With many Australian 'burgundies' you can expect a dry red wine, but the generic description tells you little more than that. A varietal description such as Rhine riesling or cabernet sauvignon, when combined with the maker's name and the growing area, gives a far better palate picture from which to make a forward judgement to taste or buy.

From there, it is a matter of tasting, trying and enjoying. As with food, the enjoyment of wine appreciation increases. You go on learning with each bottle, with each glass, you try. A healthy sense of curiosity and a willingness to ask questions also help enormously. And a browse through these pages should both stimulate that sense of inquiry and provide some advice from some of the finest palates and most enthusiastic advocates of Australian wine.

What wines are we drinking today? White wine is king, five glasses to one of red, but it has been that way for only just a decade, since mid-1975. Whites started outselling reds then, although the sales graphs had been showing rocketing sales of this type of wine for several years, while red wine sales were static.

Looking back over the decades, Australians have traditionally been beer drinkers and before that, spirit drinkers. If we drank wine at all, it was fortified wines such as sweet red (port), sherry and maybe vermouth. In the years leading up to World War II we exported quite a lot of wine, much of it going to England from companies such as the English-owned Emu Wine Company; in the peak years of our export activity we exported more wine (18 million litres) than we drank inside Australia (16 million litres); most of this wine was cheap, sweet, red fortified wine, the Empire's version of port.

The change in the Australian lifestyle has seen a swing away from beer and towards wine, especially white wine.

A leisurely lunch at The Barn, one of the best known restaurants around Adelaide. It was started as an art gallery and restaurant in 1970 at McLaren Vale, 40 kilometres south of Adelaide. Diners choose wines here before sitting down around a vine-covered courtyard surrounded by vineyards.

Dinner at the Blaxland Barn in the heart of the Hunter Valley. Owner Chris Barnes came from England to grow grapes and make wine, but then started one of the Valley's most popular restaurants.

After the war's end, as the European immigrants started to pour into underpopulated Australia, beer remained king and sales of sherry rose (mostly sweet and cream sherries), and port and brandy dominated the wine sector of the marketplace. The year 1959 was the last when fortified wines outsold table wines. Then the red wine boom began, under the enthusiastic encouragement of men like Len Evans, a Welshman who came to Australia via New Zealand and a variety of tough jobs in the Australian bush.

The red wine boom coincided with the popularity of European restaurants and food – Italian and Greek, and later French, cooking which cried out for a glass of wine. It was a short step from drinking it with meals to putting it away in cellars where, it was learnedly but falsely suggested, any red wine would improve for ever, especially if it was big, tannic, chewy and had a stewed fruit flavour that one winemaker once compared to crushed ants. It was certainly a red wine boom, though there were disappointments years later as many a proud cellarmaster pulled a mouldy cork from a bottle of red wine that had long ago shed its label, not to mention any pretensions it may have had to once tasting like grapes.

In the mid-1950s to the late 1960s a lot of winemakers in Australia were beginning to find ways to keep grape flavours in wines, especially white wines. European technology started to have an impact on Australian winemaking, with companies such as Orlando (with Barossa Rhine Riesling and Barossa Pearl) leading the way. Barossa Pearl, launched during the Melbourne Olympic Games in late 1956, perhaps did more than any other table wine to establish wine as an integral part of our society. Guenter Prass, managing director of Orlando, has this to say of his product:

We wanted a completely neutral, light delicate, fruity sparkling wine with a clean, lingering finish wihout being cloying. The acceptance of this new wine style in Australia was instantaneous, and no all-embracing marketing campaign was necessary. The message travelled like wildfire: 'You don't have to be a connoisseur of wine to order, to serve or to enjoy this wine.' Inevitably other companies joined the rush and launched similar products. One of the greatest compliments handed to any product must be its progression to become a generic term. Frequently, when someone ordered Barossa Pearl, the waiter would ask, 'But which one?' The rest is history. After the production of 10 million bottles Orlando stopped celebrating because the next million became an everyday event. After nearly three decades the product was finally put to rest, but never to be forgotten, as the beginning of a new era – wine being a part of the Australian lifestyle.

The same year Lindemans launched a still table wine called Ben Ean Moselle, which went on to even greater success. Indeed, the wine developed by Ray Kidd, now also managing director of his company, became so successful that in the mid-1980s it was being pooh-poohed by some drinkers and its sales suffered as a result. Yet it remains a fine example of how skill, technology and marketing can be combined to make an admirable, clean and world class commercial wine. Aware of its problems, under their Leo Buring label, Lindemans launched a replacement for Ben Ean, another moselle-style wine, Leibfrauwine, which has been equally successful.

A few years later another national winemaker, Thomas Hardy and Sons, rejuvenated its Siegersdorf Rhine Riesling, made in a new style by a young winemaker called Brian Croser. The 1975 vintage of Siegersdorf showed what could be done when the winemaker used the new technology at his fingertips to leave a little natural grape sugar ('residual sugar') in the finished wine. Siegersdorf set the style for the rieslings and their look-alike whites which now so commandingly dominate our wine preferences. They are wines which, whether in 750-millilitre glass bottle, flagon or bag-in-box (cardboard cask), are clean, fresh, slightly fruity and/or sweet, and which almost to a sip taste like the grapes from whence they came.

Whether it is price, quality, social change or convenience, there is no doubt that the cardboard cask has come to dominate our wine market. It is possible to argue that some drinkers may even see wine in glass bottles and wine in casks as completely different

White wines stand well in front of red wines in the sales figures in Australia today, by about five to one.

Australia, with their sprawling stainless steel tank farms. Much of the wine, even, comes from the same blend, being adjusted for sugar and acid by the winemaker depending on whether the marketing department wants 'moselle', 'riesling', 'white burgundy' or 'chablis'. Such is the flexibility of generic wine styles.

Price is the common denominator of cask wines. They are specialled in the liquor supermarkets, chains and drive-in bottle shops which have come to dominate the liquor market by the force of their combined buying power. It is Fair Average Quality wine at a dollar or so a litre – and if F.A.Q. also stands for Fair Average Quaffing, drinkers are getting just that, and they have come to appreciate it, even if they believe somehow that there are better things to be had for just a dollar more.

Here's where we hide the **ORLANDO COOLABAH**

Orlando's Coolabah casks and flagons are among the most popular branded lines in Australia today.

Stainless steel technology helps make cask and flagon wine well, and economically.

products, so totally has cask wine been accepted as an everyday beverage. Nearly half of the wine Australians drink comes from these containers, most of it packaged originally in 1 gallon plastic sacs inside the cardboard outer, now metrically reduced to 4 litres. Orlando have repeated the success of creating a generic identity for one of their products: thousands of cask drinkers just ask for 'a cask of Coolabah' now, as they might ask for a Thermos, a pack of Cellophane or fill their vehicle from a petrol Bowser.

In the latter years of the 1980s there were only two strong areas of growth in the Australian wine market: cask white wines and bottle-fermented (méthode champenoise) sparkling wine, or champagne.

The ubiquitous cask, an odd looking piece of packaging brilliance, was developed by Australians from an American milk container. It is convenience packaging at its best: cheap, transportable, convenient, disposable – and it even fits into the refrigerator. Cask wine is the *vin ordinaire* of Australia, and increasingly the package is being adopted in North America and Europe. Much of the wine sold in these packs in Australia comes from the vast 'winery refineries' of the river-irrigated areas of south-eastern

It's here, then, that any serious appreciation of Australian wine has to begin. Cask wines in Australia are good value (although there is substantial evidence to show that quality has often declined in recent years because of the savage price discounting and other competition endemic in the Australian winemaking jungle). But they have almost monotonous similarity, perhaps because many come from the same large winemaking concerns, and the flavour components are also minimal. The wines from Chateau Cardboard reflect their origins and their marketers' constant pressure for economies of production.

Good things still come in glass, and anyone looking for great Australian wines will have to look to bottled wines. Not necessarily expensive bottled wine, for there are some excellent and highly enjoyable wines in glass at reasonable prices – say below $3.50 a bottle. What then are Australians drinking from 750-millilitre bottles? Are we drinking what many of our wine writers and buffs would have us believe? Chardonnays? Cabernet sauvignon reds from small makers who drive Porches? Wood aged semillons? French Champagnes? Wines from the High Barossa Ranges or with strange sounding abbreviations like 'Cab Mac'? If you have read that we are drinking these wines (and your newspapers and magazines would certainly lead you to think this way) you would have a highly distorted view of what Australians *are* drinking. We are not drinking dry whites and reds in volume; we are drinking sweet, or at least semi-sweet. Here is a 'guesstimated' table showing in rough order of sales what we are consuming as a nation of wine drinkers, from glass bottles, in descending order of case sales.

	WINE	TYPE	SALES BY CASES	
1	Kaiser Stuhl Summerwine	Pop/fruity bubbly	430 000	↔
2	Seppelt Great Western Champagne	Champagne	420 000	↑
3	Lindemans Ben Ean Moselle	Fruity white wine	310 000	↓
4	Leo Buring Leibfrauwine	Fruity white wine	240 000	↑
5	McWilliam's Bodega	Fruity bubbly	215 000	↓
6	Wynn's Seaview Champagne	Champagne	210 000	↑
7	Penfolds Minchinbury Champagne	Champagne	195 000	↑
8	Wolf Blass Rhine Riesling	White table wine	150 000	↑
9	Houghton White Burgundy	Dry white table wine	150 000	↑
10	Miranda Golden Gate Spumante	Sweet bubbly	145 000	↓
11	Wynn's Seaview Rhine Riesling	White table wine	130 000	↑
12	Orlando Jacob's Creek Claret	Dry red table wine	125 000	↑
13	Woodley's Queen Adelaide Rhine Riesling	White table wine	120 000	↑
14	Stock Gala Spumante	Sweet bubbly	100 000	↓
15	Black Tower Moselle	Fruity white wine	100 000	↓
16	Orlando Carrington Champagne	Champagne	90 000	↑
17	Leo Buring Rinegolde	Fruity white wine	85 000	↓
18	Orlando Starwine	Fruity bubbly	85 000	↓
19	Kaiser Stuhl Rosé	Semi-sweet light red	80 000	↓
20	Don Camillo Spumante	Sweet bubbly	75 000	↓
21	Kaiser Stuhl Champagne	Champagne	75 000	↑
22	Hardy's Siegersdorf Rhine Riesling	White table wine	75 000	↑
23	McWilliam's Mount Pleasant Riesling	White table wine	75 000	↑
24	Wyndham Estate Traminer/Riesling	White table wine	60 000	↓

↑ Sales increasing
↓ Sales decreasing
↔ Sales static

In a few weeks' time this bucket of ripe shiraz grapes will be red wine.

The figures are best guesses, because the wine industry is as shy as any and probably more than most about revealing its business secrets. There are not many dry wines on the list, at least in nomenclature, if you equate the word 'riesling' with comparative sweetness or fruitiness. The only ones apparently dry in flavour are Houghton White Burgundy, from Western Australia, Jacob's Creek Claret from South Australia and McWilliam's Mount Pleasant Elizabeth Riesling from New South Wales (because its makers slyly use the word 'riesling' to mean Hunter River riesling, that is, made from the dry semillon grape, but certainly with some residual sugar in the wine).

Obviously, we are a nation of people who, if we drink wine, prefer wines which are either sweet, or bubbly, or both. Of the sale of nearly 4 million cases of wine listed above, some 54 per cent is bubbly and 66 per cent is sweet. Some are sweet and bubbly together; for example, Summerwine.

Drinkers are voting with their palates as well as their pockets. They are enjoying wines with residual sugar or lots of grape flavours. Fruitiness and sugar, by the way, are not to be confused, for they should not be. And none of this is to disparage these popular wines, because certainly they have been crafted by dedicated winemakers using high levels of skill and technology.

There is nothing wrong with things that are sweet or bubbly. Most Australians have been nurtured on these two taste sensations, whether it be with Coca-Cola or beer. But I believe one of the glories of Australian wines is the huge diversity of different flavours available. Many ordinary wines from cask, flagon and some bottles are just that: ordinary. They may be well made, but like many fast foods which are also clean and unexceptional, they are by no means memorable. Good wines, like good friends and good times, *should* be memorable. That is why breaking out of a rut – even if it is with sweet and fruity wines – is the logical beginning of an exploration into the wonderful world of Australian wine.

Some general rules for entering the wine maze may be appropriate before you take the second sip of this book. Even though the Australian wine industry is trying – or is having forced upon it – rationalisation of one form or another, there are still far too many labels on our market. It is and will remain for some years a bewildering maze. There are probably some 450 Australian wineries, with Lord knows how many thousand labels pouring from them each vintage.

It is confusing, but some pointers may help. When starting to buy wine, either for cellaring or for drinking in a restaurant, buy cautiously. That's easily said, of course, so let me be more explicit. Don't hesitate at first to buy well-known brands, drink them curiously and compare your taste sensations with the label or back label notes, and store your opinions away for next time. Learn a little about varietal wines, whether by reading books or going to wine appreciation courses. Try as many wines as you reasonably can. Be careful about buying from small winemakers, not because they necessarily make bad wines (some certainly do) but because their styles tend often to be individualistic and highly variable from vintage to vintage. They cannot always sell, blend or distill their mistakes. The time to experiment with the fascinating range of wines from smaller makers is further down the palate path, when you are more sure of your likes, dislikes and cellar needs.

When storing wines in a cellar, whatever form that cellar takes, from under-the-bed to under-the-house, buy sparingly at first. Everyone makes mistakes when they start to collect wines; I certainly did, and you may have to cook with your errors, if not worse. Certainly try your cellared wines regularly to see how they are going.

This century will surely be the one in which wine quality took its greatest leap forward in the long, long history of wine in our world. Australians have been a part of that progress and we are living in the Golden Age of wine. I have no doubt of that. We may get better wines, though I suspect that wine quality will not take so dramatic a leap forward as it has in the past couple of decades. Progress will surely be slower, though there is plenty of room left for advances in our vineyards, where wine quality is born.

Barossa grapegrower, Leo Pech.

One thing is certain: wines will not get cheaper. Competition will remain fierce from within Australia and from overseas, where there is an ocean of wine lying unwanted. Another factor, introduced in late 1984, was a Federal tax. Few believe that fair-minded governments (Federal or State) will lighten that load; it is more likely that they will, acting out of the need for revenue and under the lobby of various pressure groups, increase wine taxes and impose other restrictions.

Our choice of wines will diminish, which some believe to be A Bad Thing. I do not, for there are far too many labels around, and too many mediocre wines. There will be a lot more takeovers of middle and large sized wine companies, and a number of small ones will vanish. But at the end of it, in a few decades when things balance out, we will be left with some big companies making large quantities of good to excellent wines at reasonable prices, a few middle sized companies, and a goodly range of small to very small makers, making specialised and innovative wines such as those described later by Robin Bradley. There will be plenty of choice for wine lovers – the innate fascination with wine will always ensure that.

So, at the end of the beginning, the outlook for wine drinkers is encouraging. There are some great wines around, waiting for us to pull the cork, and take the first sip...

Len Evans noses some young chardonnays at the Sydney Wine Show judging.

A NOSE FOR IT

Len Evans

The first thing that must be understood is that wine is a drink. That is the justification of it. Above all else, it is something to be enjoyed. If it is not enjoyed, there is no point in wine.

The level of enjoyment varies from person to person. Most people who enjoy wine do not know very much about it, and though they may sometimes wish they knew more, they don't really care; certainly not enough to do something about it. Even those who do care have different levels of discernment. I have a friend who is a tremendous wine enthusiast. I have never heard him criticise a single wine. Simply, some are better than others. From every wine he drinks he appears to receive great enjoyment. Sometimes I envy him.

The second thing to understand is that wine is beset by snobs, poseurs, 'would-bes', pretenders, label-readers and half-baked knowledges. There seems nothing so rigid as a recent wine affectation. There is also the earnest student syndrome, wherein, it seems, the facts and figures of the wine are more important than the wine itself. 'What is the pH, the v.a. level, the alcohol? Has the malolactic taken place?' And what side did the winemaker get out of bed that morning and was his wife speaking to him?

The third thing to understand is that in most cases, discernment and knowledge heighten enjoyment. Although wine is just a drink, to most people who become enthusiasts, it is something more. It is a grace of life, to many a way of life. It has an amazing depth of interest. What other food lasts so long? What other food improves on initial quality for such a long time? And what other food provides such an endless topic of conversation?

There is no question that the more one knows about wine, the more one realises just how much there is to know. A great violinist once complained that, after fifty years of practice and performance, he had begun to understand how many lifetimes would be needed to learn to play the violin properly. So it is with wine; the professional, after many many years in the business, realises that it would simply not be possible to fully understand the world of wine in one lifetime. But, I must remind you, it is still just a drink.

A wine enthusiast does not need to have a vast knowledge to be able to discriminate. After all, it's all in the sight, the smell and the taste. I believe that an awareness of what one is about is very important.

Frank Stone, a visiting American wine expert, pours a glass of red for a visitor to Sydney's Expovin wine fair.

The mere quaffer of any wine will always remain so. So it is vitally important to give thought to the process, and to understand certain principles. Equally, one must have some level of sensory perception. Most people have a fairly strong sense of smell, so there is no reason why they shouldn't be able to discriminate between good and bad.

Obviously, the enthusiast must indulge in the most necessary of requirements – drinking the stuff. Practice may not make perfect, but it's a hell of a lot of fun trying. A golf immortal was once asked three ways to improve a golfer's ability. He answered, 'By playing golf, playing golf, playing golf.' So it is with wine. The interested person sharing a bottle a day will learn more about wine than the one trying a bottle a week.

The principles which may be observed are simple.
★ Wine should always be enjoyed in moderation. It is a grace of life, not an abuse of it. Most wines of the world have a 'place' in the normal order of daily living. Most table wine is enjoyed in conjunction with food. It enhances food flavours just as food flavours may enhance those of wine. Three glasses of sherry on an empty stomach can befuddle the tongue. A bottle of wine over a long, leisurely dinner can cause no problems at all. Enjoy wine for its stimulation of the senses, the mind and the tongue, but don't ever let any part of these faculties be in any way out of control.

★ All wine is made to be consumed. *All* of it. But most of it, good sound beverage wine (bag-in-box and flagon in Australia) is not made to be other than quaffed. I once dined with a Federal Minister who derided winemanship. 'Good old flagon stuff is good enough for me,' he proclaimed. Fair enough, so why did he carefully decant his flagon into a decanter? 'I believe it shows the wine off so much better.'

★ Only some wine deserves all the talk, tasting and dedication that goes into it. The top wines of France comprise less than 1 per cent of all of that country's wine production. All the other wines of note would comprise less than 20 per cent of the total. In Australia some 80 per cent of our table wine is sold in cask, flagon and bulk. The remainder includes those popular lines which sell in the hundreds of thousands of cases and yet feature but rarely in wine conversation and writing. Probably less than 2 per cent of all of our wine is the stuff of dreams, those wines which command the most attention. To reinforce this, consider that those wines which sell really well around the world – Portuguese Rosés, German generics, Italian light slightly sweet reds, French commercials and so on – have features in common, their safeness, soundness and lack of real individuality. These are the superior quaffing wines, whatever the advertisements say, wines to be enjoyed but not dwelt upon.

★ One sips and tastes the good wines, not quaffs them, because of all the inherent pleasures of sight, smell and taste. These good wines are often bought through the recommendation of writer, merchant or maker, and need not be tasted beforehand to be bought. I have a surprising number of friends who drink only good wine yet who do not have a cellar or even a small store of wine. They buy a dozen or so bottles every so often and replace them like tins of beans.

★ When one starts to lay down a cellar, more thought and application is required. Obviously the greater financial involvement demands this. Wherever possible, one should taste before buying. Most makers provide excellent tasting facilities, most merchants encourage their regular customers into tastings. The planning of a cellar is very important and is directly related to consumption. I know of vast cellars full of wine which cannot possibly be consumed by the owners, families or friends. Equally, headstrong buying often leads to unwanted wines which just sit in the cellar. Careful cautious tasting is necessary and a lot of common sense must be applied.

★ To be an adequate professional one must have the ability to taste wine young and be able to evaluate its future. For years I've been amused at the attitude shown by people when I've picked a masked wine on the dot. Yet that is not so difficult for the really experienced, to get at least somewhere near. The hard thing is to spot, among hundreds of samples, the young wine with the great potential. Needless to say, with often hundreds of thousands of dollars involved, one would not be doing it for long if the ability wasn't there.

The urge to taste and learn about Australian wine is growing. Graham Wiltshire, of Heemskerk vineyard in Tasmania (at left), shows some of his wines to the public.

In suburban Adelaide, a party of enthusiastic home bottlers can't resist the opportunity to taste what is being drained from the 200-litre drum of red wine.

THE SIGHT, SMELL AND TASTE OF WINE

In the judging system which is largely used in Australia, 3 points is the maximum which may be given for colour and condition, 7 for nose (aroma and bouquet) and 10 for palate (flavour, balance and finish). Judging is covered later, but the points roughly indicate the relative importance of each sense. Interestingly, since the 10 points available to palate include so many aspects of each wine, it could be stated that the 'nose' is probably the single most important element in the whole process. Certainly, I believe so. Obviously sight is extremely necessary and important. Too few people really look at a wine before drinking it. Yet there is tremendous pleasure to be obtained from the colours of the wine spectrum

Good, bright colour gets a maximum of 3 points.

and one can certainly learn a lot even before touching the glass.

All table wines should be brilliant in condition. Only aged wines are permitted some cloudiness, and even this can be avoided by careful decanting. All wines should be true to the colour of their style or variety. How often at shows do we see almost crystal clear whites without almost any colour at all, or insipid reds that 'stand alone and pale'. These wines may be dismissed almost at once, for rarely have I seen one which smelt and tasted better than it looked.

The colour of a vigorous young red is purple, or at least ruby with purple overtones. This colour softens with age into ruby, then a little garnet may appear. A wine may have this common garnet hue for quite a while before a little brick appears – not a brown, but a colour which owes something to both red and brown. An old wine which is brick in colour might hold this for some time and yet be in splendid order.

Tawny is the next shade of development, and at this stage, though a wood-matured dessert wine may be just hitting its straps, most red table wine is on the way out. Finally very old red wine achieves a pale, light gemstone shade which is almost an amber. If the wine has anything left at this stage, then you're lucky.

The colours of white wine vary considerably from variety to variety and even region to region. However, because of the narrowness of the range, it takes a really experienced eye to be able to sort things out.

French Chablis and Hunter Valley semillon often have a same hue, a gorgeous green-gold which deepens with age but which doesn't lose its greenness. Chardonnay may have this touch of green but more often it veers towards the gold, sometimes, dare I say it, even with a drop of browning which has come from maturation in new wood vessels. Riesling has a lighter colour, a straw yellow which, when intensely hued, can be quite beautiful. Blanquette has a plain colour ('send in a plain brown wrapper' springs to mind), sauvignon blanc a touch of green in straw yellow, and so on. All browning, even that mentioned before, shows some kind of oxidation. Too much of this can ruin a wine, but I will deal with that in 'faults'.

The nose, to me, is terribly important. There are all sorts of views expressed but I must speak for myself. When my nose is not functioning properly I don't function properly as a taster. There are two chief points to nose of a wine: aroma and bouquet, though these are often confused and used the wrong way round.

Aroma is the essence, so to speak, of the initial fruit character. The floweriness of Rhine riesling, the herbaceous almost sharp smell of sauvignon blanc, the rich tropical fruit characters of chardonnay. Bouquet is the development of this and the other characters given by soil, region, wood and maker. The statement, 'Oh, the fruit of such and such a wine has really grown in the bottle,' is often heard. The aromatic fruit character cannot grow. What actually happens is one of the great delights of wine and one of the major reasons for the interest that lies in it.

Once in the bottle a decomposition takes place. At best this is very slow. During this decomposition, this slow oxidation, the fruit and other characters meld and soften, developing unique flavours. This build up of flavour may be compared to the eighteen-month maturation of a hard cheese, or the three-day, rather more obvious process with a piece of fish. As various substances in these foods break down, so flavour grows. Wine is the most magic of all of them, for in some cases wines have improved in flavour for over thirty years and then held such flavour for many years after.

The nose is a very important part of the process of tasting wine. Some famous international tasters preach that nose should be inhaled but lightly and almost fleetingly, that first impressions are always best. Others recommend a deep inhalation, with the glass being swirled around to release all the esters and aromas, great concentration being given to the various characters.

I am of the latter school, and believe that most of what is to be learnt of any wine is there, 'on the nose'. There are other factors, to be sure, but in the judgement of wine I have rarely seen a good wine emerge from one which had no nose, and I have never seen a great wine which didn't impress greatly before it was tasted.

If I could give any advice to the intending wine judge , it would be to pay great attention to this aspect of tasting. I have watched thousands of wine enthusiasts drink wine, and nearly all of them have given but cursory attention to the aroma and bouquet.

As for the various smells themselves, I have never been able to do justice to the endless wine vocabulary available overseas. The French talk of all sorts of flowers – violets, marigolds, roses – of various aromatic characters of mints, nuts, trees, herbs, berries and fruits. I have neither the range nor the inclination to adopt it (though I once described Grange Hermitage of tasting of raspberries, strawberries, truffles and old boots). Perhaps I've been tasting too long. But to me wine smells of itself. A rose is a rose is a rose. Cabernet from Coonawarra smells like cabernet from Coonawarra. And if you say to yourself, 'Well, that's not a very satisfactory explanation,' I challenge you to describe the smell of strawberries or bananas. We've eaten these fruits since our first memories and they smell like themselves. So it is with wine. The enthusiast has to train and work at these individual characters as hard as possible. As I've said, practice will never make perfect, but we'll have an awful lot of fun along the way.

One of the most interesting aspects of nosing wine is a test I have given to children. I have ranged a top French red alongside a good Australian red and a

Blind tasting. Usually this means tasting from masked bottles. But this time the taster himself is masked — a formidable sensory challenge.

A master winemaker at work: Max Schubert blending wines in his workroom at Penfolds' Grange winery.

flagon red. I've asked the children to tell me what is the best wine. Invariably they get them in the right order, without the slightest knowledge of what they are drinking. This proves, to me at least, that there is no great endless mystery in wine. If the kids can get it right, so can everyone.

The taste of wine in the mouth may be split into three parts, with various side-effects.

The fore palate is when the wine initially hits the front of the tongue, the first impression of actual contact after the nosing. The tastebuds on the tip of the tongue are sensitive to sweetness, and the flavours, particularly with young wine, are quite pronounced at this stage. Many tasters keep the wine at the front of the mouth for quite a while, using the tongue as a sort of plunger and drawing in air through their pursed mouth, aerating the wine. Very useful, but not recommended at a dinner party, unless you are all in the same wine boat.

The middle palate has various uses. Sweetness, sourness, saltiness may all be detected as the wine passes over the tongue and is milled around in the mouth. At this stage we detect the body (strength and alcohol) of the wine, the complexity and the intensity of the flavours. To me, the greatest wines are not heavy or too strong, but verging on lightness. They have finesse, that mysterious word which means so much and is so difficult to describe. And they have great depth of flavour, an intensity which reminds one of the subtlety of an expensive perfume, a lightness and a deftness with great strength.

There are two expressions which the French use for sensations on the middle palate which could be used with purpose in Australia. These are fleshiness and suppleness, which are allied but which don't necessarily mean the same thing. I like fleshy wines, especially reds, which fill the mouth with generous flavour yet which are soft and easy on the palate. Perhaps the celebrated Château Petrus of Pomerol is the fleshiest of all great reds. If you can afford it, it is mandatory that you should taste for yourself. The top Hermitage reds of the Rhône have this quality, as do their counterparts, at best, from the Hunter Valley. Suppleness is a soft richness, and integration of all parts of the palate without any edges or corners. It's surprising just how much excessive acid and tannin can disturb the palate of a wine, and not just on the finish.

The finish, is, of course, immensely important, for what seems to be a great wine can be down-graded here. The finish on the back of the palate, followed by the aftertaste, should perfectly extend the wine to its ultimate conclusion. Too tannic a wine leaves the mouth puckered and astringent. Too acidic a wine leaves the mouth sour and reactive. A wine can be bitter, almost nasty. Or it may be deficient, flat and coarse. The French use the terms 'long' and 'short'. Length is the sustainment of the flavours of the wine through to the end and after, when a lingering taste stays in the mouth. Short is obviously the converse when the wine leaves the mouth abruptly, offering no sustained pleasure. The good and great wines are balanced with each part of the palate offering part of the whole, all characters of nose and palate and finish coming together as one harmonious whole. Top wines are complete wines, no one part dominating any other.

To learn to taste to extract the maximum enjoyment, considerable application is necessary. Yet, as I've mentioned, there is no great mystery to it, it is just a matter of using the senses and applying oneself. There is no short cut.

Years ago a wealthy young man-about-town asked me how much it would cost him to become a 'wine-man', to be knowledgeable enough to be totally at ease in any wine situation, and, dare I suggest it, probably to be in a position to preach to his peer group. I told him that a working knowledge of the great wines of the world would cost about $25 000.

'That's fine,' he said.

I added, 'Spent over five years.'

'Oh,' he replied, 'I haven't got the time.' He didn't enquire whether or not I had the time, assuming, I suppose, that my sale of the appropriate wines would be enough. Some years later, when he had become a nicer man, we were talking of this.

'Now I understand what a fool I was,' he said. 'I didn't realise how kind you were being. If I had taken

you up on it I know you couldn't have resisted the challenge, and I'd be a good wine-man now.'

'Yes,' I said. 'And today it would cost you $75 000.'

That, however, is in the realms of all the greatest of the world's wines. It is not necessary to go to those lengths to become accomplished in wine. All it requires beyond the normal faculties is thought, application, and dedication.

Practice will lead to an understanding of the major faults of wine. How often people who should have more courage will put up with a poor wine at a tasting or in a restaurant, simply because they're frightened of making fools of themselves. What nonsense. Poor wine tastes poor to a child, and should be discarded. Even the best wines may suffer from a fault which occurs in one bottle only. The same wines stored differently over a period of time may taste quite different. Australian wine should be more fault free than it sometimes is, for it appears that some makers become 'cellar bound' and learn to tolerate faults which stand out to others.

His palate is a winemaker's best friend. Hardy's winemaker Bill Hardy — great-great-grandson of his company's founder — 'looks at' (a winemaker's term meaning 'to taste') a red wine straight from oak barrels at Hardy's Tintara winery, McLaren Vale.

slight amount can spoil the freshness and flavour in any wine.

★ Acetification. A vinegary smell on the nose, a vinegary taste on the back of the tongue. It comes from excessive acetic acid, which is present, in small amounts, in almost any wine. Since this acid is highly volatile, it is often called v.a. (volatile acidity). The v.a. of a white can show at only 0.5 a gram per litre. A soft red with a v.a. of 0.6 to 0.7 g/l can be tainted by it, yet a robust, big flavoured red will not be so affected. Grange Hermitage 1971 for example, one of the top of the series, had a v.a. of over a gram per litre, yet it is still a marvellous wine.

★ Oxidation. A flatness, coarseness, and downright nastiness coming from the wine being contaminated, at winemaking, maturation, or in bad storage conditions, by too much oxygen. There are different oxidised flavours but there seems no point in discussing them here. It is sufficient to say that a white wine will dull and brown; a red will develop colours premature for its age, the nose will be flat and dull, the palate flat and flabby and the finish coarse and hard.

★ Corked. Simply a nasty taste, bitter, acrid, and totally unfruitlike, which comes from one diseased cork. You can buy ten dozen of a wine and only one bottle may be corked. If this is excessive the wine will dull and brown, but even small amounts are obvious. Once an experienced taster shares a corked bottle with you and declares the taste, you should never forget it.

★ Dirty wood. Some wines are stored badly during wood maturation and various 'dirty' flavours may emerge. V.a. is one problem. A flavour not unlike corked character (caused by old, diseased wood) is another. Some casks have water stored in them and develop a 'bilgey' character, redolent of old stagnant water. In others this is less obvious, yet a 'water-butt' taste may emerge, not quite bilgey but reminiscent of rain water stored in old barrels. Again, it's a matter of experience.

Finally, the palate. The taste of wine gets a maximum of 10 out of the 20 points from wine judges. Colour and condition get 3 and nose (aroma and bouquet) a top of 7.

The main faults are easy to spot.

★ Excessive sulphur dioxide. SO_2 is used in wine-making as an anti-oxidant. If there is too much of it, it smells sulphury, like hot mineral springs. Since free sulphur will diminish once the bottle is opened, often leaving the bottle for a while or pouring it from glass to glass will help. But if there's too much of it avoid the winemaker in future.

★ Hydrogen sulphide. H_2S, the dreaded fault, with its offshoot, mecaptan. Smells like burnt rubber or animal dung, and also prevails on the palate. Even a

SHOW JUDGING

I began my show judging career in the early Sixties. I didn't quite understand what I was doing then, and after twenty-plus years of it I'm still learning.

The show judging system receives a fair bit of criticism, much of which is nothing to do with the judges and the judging. Each State Council of the various Royal Agricultural Societies runs the shows, and they are not part of the wine industry. They seek wine judges to participate in each wine section. Naturally, many of these people come from the industry, but this is not mandatory. Each council is a separate entity. It's their show and they can do what they want with it. Consequently, although various wine industry companies or factions will do what *they* want to do – argue, support, not enter, feature medal winners as *they* see fit – this is not the business of the councils.

Simply, each show is a sovereign affair, the council appointing a committee which recommends a schedule and appoints a number of judges. Once they make their awards, these are in the public domain, and much of the criticism which ensues should be levelled at those who use such awards to their commercial advantage.

Having got that off my chest (all judges work on an honorary basis, receiving but bare expenses) I should outline the systems used in Australia. There are but two, and one predominates.

This is the 3-7-10 system I mentioned earlier, judged on a comparison basis. A gold must score 18½, a silver 17-18, a bronze 15½-16½. Therefore there is little room for error. A typical gold score would be 3/3 for Colour and Condition, 6½/7 for Nose, 9/10 for Palate; just 1½ points lost to achieve 18½ out of 20 and so a gold medal. Hence a *non*-award winner could score 3/3, 5/7, 7/10, a total of 15, not a bad figure, yet still miss out on a medal.

Most judging takes place between 13½ and 18½, a wine having to be very poor to score 13 or less, and extremely good to do better than 18½. This is a narrow range, and requires great concentration from the judge in question. It is so easy to push wine into certain pigeonholes, and much harder to sense and look for perhaps hidden qualities or faults which will raise or lower the points awarded.

The comparison category must be understood. There are various classes of different styles and varieties of wine, of different years and availabilities (sixty-seven in the Sydney Wine Show alone). There may be as many as eighty wines in any one class. In Brisbane, a difficult show, there are often over a hundred wines in a single class, judged by two-man panels, a further difficulty. Most shows use three-man panels, with a senior judge being identified in each. It is his job to hold the panel together, totalling points, trying to settle differences, calling the chairman when required.

The chairman is a highly experienced judge who has been through the mill for years. He runs the organisation of the judging itself, though there are several other formalities which are the responsibility of the wine committee of the show, who generally sit

Spitting it out after tasting is not compulsory, just sensible. Years of tasting experience have made Len Evans one of the best palates in the wine business — and one of the best spitters.

Wine judges often use tasting boards like these marked only with numbers, and upon which sit 'nosing' glasses.

outside and do not intrude into the judging arena. The chairman is there to establish, with the senior judges, the various judging criteria. Probably the most important single job of the chairman is to adjudicate when judges are not necessarily disagreeing, but are having trouble agreeing. Often, for example, three or four wines will emerge as the best of the class, but each of the three judges will prefer one to another. The chairman settles the dispute in two ways. In some cases, when called, he simply nominates his choice or choices, and the top awards are then made following his resolution.

I prefer another method. As Chairman of the R.A.S. Sydney Show and the National Wine Show in Canberra, I prefer to discuss the qualities and faults of the final selection with the judges, in an attempt to persuade them to change their minds voluntarily. It may amount to the same thing, but I believe this method promotes greater discussion and analysis of the wines and it also helps the associate judges learn more of their seniors' thinking.

Associate judges are generally selected from the wine industry, though they may be from the ranks of 'gifted amateurs'. The late, great Rudy Komon, the art dealer, was one of the most able and experienced wine judges in Australia, for example, and he was a 'stylist' judge, not a technocrat. Probably he knew less about the faults of wine than many technically apt wine judges but no one was better than he in determining the final qualities of the top few in each class.

It is the responsibility of the chairman and the senior judges to see that the associates are schooled. They judge as each panel does, their points being considered but not counting in the final compilation. Associates generally serve from three to six years before being asked to judge.

Interestingly, behind the associates are another group, the pourers, the people who assemble each class and pour the wines. (All bottles are under a code number and judges are not even allowed to look at the bottle, let alone the code labels.) In some cases, these pourers will become associates, to become judges, to become senior, maybe to chair a show. A long and dedicated application, all done on an honorary basis.

Jim Roberts (in checked shirt), owner of Belbourie Wines in the Hunter Valley, New South Wales, lets the public be their own judge at a Sydney wine fair.

There is much argument regarding the difference between the comparison method, in which wines are lined up in one class, and the international method, in which wines are judged one at a time by each panel. The international method, using the same scoring system has its points. It is fast, and wines can be recalled when the views differ. I would like to try an extension of both methods: to judge by the international method and then to re-pour the top dozen or so wines of each class, to judge comparatively. That would appear to me to satisfy all demands.

There are generally three panels of three judges to a show, with from two to nine associates, depending on the space available and the attitude of the committee. Since some shows have well over two thousand entries, judges may be called upon to taste over seven hundred wines during the week. A top panel, being attended to properly by efficient pourers, and not having too many prolonged discussions, may taste up to two hundred wines a day. This may seem a large number to a lot of people, but there is a trick to it.

The morning may start at 8.30 with a range of one-year-old Rhine rieslings, followed by a class of older vintage wines of the same variety. Then a class of young cabernet sauvignons before a break for lunch. After this rest, a smaller class of museum reds may be judged, then sweet table wines, a fino sherry class, a tawny port class and finally the muscats. Thus through the day the flavours mount, the variety in fact helping to prevent the judges' palates becoming dull and tired. Sometimes I suggest that the younger people present go back to taste the young whites after the muscat. Most agree that it would be impossible to judge them fairly.

The show system does very well for the Australian wine industry. It allows exhibitors to compare their

Each year during their Bushing Festival the winemakers of McLaren Vale judge one wine to be the best of the area — and its maker to be the Bushing King. In 1984 Geoff Merrill, winemaker at Chateau Reynella, was crowned for the second time.

wines against others. It enables the exhibitor to have his wines judged by the highest standards available so that he or she may learn from the decisions made. And it allows the successful exhibitor to tell the world of success. Many a company has established their destiny by winning a couple of golds at an early stage.

I am a great supporter of the Australian show system, in spite of its failings and the abuse of it. Yet once I judged a show which made me wonder if we do it the right way. This was at Tournus in central France. The occasion was the Tasse d'Or, a gold cup being awarded to the winners of each of four categories: best red Burgundy, best white Burgundy, best Beaujolais (red), best Maconnais (white). I was on the Super Jury, and found I wasn't required until the evening. What was happening?

In the morning the growers and winemakers, the exhibitors, were the judges. They were seated eight to a table, were served eight wines, and had to find the best two. They drank and didn't spit. In the afternoon these selections were examined by an intermediate jury who passed their selections on to jury. They didn't spit, either.

In the early evening the jury passed on to us about twenty-four wines, six in each category. It was our job to select the best in each case. As we did our job, bands were playing, the early judges were singing, shouting and talking and everyone was making a tremendous din. Finally, the winners were announced to a huge applause and everyone went off and had a drink or two to celebrate.

This was in the heart of a country which has had vineyards for over two thousand years. They enjoy their wine enormously, and don't get too technically wrapped up in it, as, say, some Americans do.

For, as I've said, it is just a drink.

The Colours of Wine

*M*ilton Wordley's close-ups of a range *of wines show the incredible differences in colours in wines, which Len Evans refers to. The best place to look for clues about a wine's age, condition and make-up is at the 'meniscus', the centimetre or less at the very edge of a tilted, clear glass containing 50 to 100 millilitres of wine. The colour of healthy wines should also be clear and bright, showing that they are in good condition, like these wines. The 'browning' effect starts to show with the older wines. The glasses used in the illustrations here are the XL-4 wine judging glass, approved for wine judging by the International Standards Organisation.*

Young rosé (one year)
*Houghton Cabernet Rosé 1984
(Moondah Brook, W.A.)*

Light red (one year)
*Len Evans Light Dry
Red 1984 (shiraz,
Hunter Valley, N.S.W.)*

Young red (three years)
*Orlando Jacob's Creek
Claret 1982 (S.A.)*

Old red (eighteen years)
*McWilliam's OP & OH
Hermitage 1967 (Hunter
Valley, N.S.W.)*

Young Coonawarra cabernet (one year)
Mildara Coonawarra
Cabernet Sauvignon 1984 (S.A.)

Young cabernet (three years)
Cape Mentelle Cabernet
Sauvignon, 1982 (Jimmy Watson
Trophy 1983, Margaret River, W.A.)

Mid aged cabernet (five years)
Petaluma Coonawarra 1980
(88 per cent cabernet,
12 per cent shiraz, S.A.)

Blended red (ten years)
Wolf Blass Jimmy Watson
Cabernet/Shiraz 1975 (S.A.)

Blended red (fifteen years)
Brown Brothers Shiraz,
Mondeuse & Cabernet 1970
(Milawa, Vic.)

Shiraz (eight years)
Penfolds Grange Hermitage
1977 (Barossa, S.A.)

WHITE WINES

Young riesling (one year)
Yalumba Pewsey Vale Rhine
Riesling 1984 (S.A.)

Aged riesling (ten years)
Hardy's Barossa/McLaren Vale Rhine
Riesling 1975 (S.A.)

Young sauvignon blanc (one year)
Katnook Coonawarra Sauvignon
Blanc 1984 (S.A.)

Mid aged semillon (nine years)
The Rothbury Estate
Individual Paddock Semillon
1976 (Hunter Valley, N.S.W.)

Aged semillon (seventeen years)
Lindemans Hunter
River White Burgundy Bin 3470
1968 (N.S.W.)

Old semillon (average age thirty years)
McWilliam's Mount Pleasant
Sauternes 1946 & 1966
(Hunter Valley, N.S.W.)

Young chardonnay (one year)
Lindemans Padthaway Chardonnay
1984 (S.A.)

Mid aged chardonnay (six years)
Tyrrells Vat 47 Pinot Chardonnay
1979 (Hunter Valley, N.S.W.)

Botrytis affected (three years)
De Bortoli Sauternes/Semillon
1982 (Griffith, N.S.W.)

SPARKLING WINES

Young champagne (two years)
Tyrrells Pinot Noir
1983 (Hunter Valley, N.S.W.)

Mid aged champagne (five years)
Wynn Edmond Mazure
Méthode Champenoise 1980 (S.A.)

Aged champagne (thirteen years)
Seppelt Great Western
Show Champagne 1972 (Vic.)

FORTIFIED WINES

Young vintage port
(eight years)
Chateau Reynella 1977
(Reynella, S.A.)

Tawny port
(twelve years average)
Hardy's Show Port
(McLaren Vale, S.A.)

Old liqueur muscat
(average age thirty years)
Morris Liqueur Muscat
(Rutherglen, Vic.)

Vintage port
(nineteen years)
Hardy's 1956 Vintage Port
(McLaren Vale, S.A.)

Very old port
(one hundred years)
Seppelt Para Liqueur Port 1885
(Seppeltsfield, S.A.)

Fino sherry
Seppelt DP 117 Show Fino
(Seppeltsfield, S.A.)

Amontillado sherry
Mildara Amontillado
(Mildura, Vic.)

Going Underground

I don't know many people with cellars. Most of my friends buy wine as they need it, or keep a few shelves full of bottles picked up in moments of bibulous extravagance in the Hunter Valley.

I'm not a heavy drinker. My needs could easily be filled by a visit every couple of months to one of the many excellent vintners in the city.

So my reasons for building a cellar were a little more complex than they seemed on the surface. Admittedly, I have always had an interest in wine — an interest initiated by my father and greatly stimulated by 'Mechanical'

Mayne himself when, a couple of years ago, I produced a film for the Wine Board during his celebrated tenure as Promotions Manager.

I travelled around the country during pre-production for the film and was intoxicated, literally and figuratively, with the romance of wine. And I returned with cases of the stuff which I laid down under the stairs in our two-storey house.

I was very unhappy with that arrangement. Paddington houses are fine, but temperature control is impossible. In winter, it often falls below 15°C and in summer it can climb into the 30s. Under the stairs, I mean.

There isn't much point in hanging onto bottles for a long time if you can't cellar them properly. Better to forget the cost advantages of daring raids on discount liquor shops and buy what you want when you are ready to drink it. But that's too rational for me.

I wanted a cellar. Or to be more precise, a cave. The French, whom I esteem above all races, have the right word. 'Cave' is redolent with atmosphere, mystery, even danger. Perhaps it echoes antediluvian longings deep in the psyche. Or perhaps it is nostalgia for childhood expeditions into the bush when a cave was full of heartstopping possibilities.

Anyway, the desire was there and, when the time came to replace the decrepit shed in the back yard with something more substantial, the idea struck. Underneath the new brick studio/laundry/extra bathroom I would build my cellar.

The idea was greeted, naturally, with assorted reactions. Amused tolerance from my wife, astonishment from some friends, bewilderment in others. And consternation from architects and builders. But it was designed and a builder found: a great, good-natured fellow called David Brown who was quite happy to take the risk of demolishing the

neighbour's house, if I was.

Building my cellar was one of the most enjoyable things I've done. Sort of like building a pyramid or a tree house. A piece of folly, folie de grandeur if you like. The back yard looked like a bomb site, the house was reduced to chaos. Sand was tramped into the carpets and blown into cupboards and drawers. My wife's good humour evaporated. But it was fun.

It's been finished for six months. And it's there to stay. It measures around 2.5 metres square and can easily hold a couple of thousand bottles — far more than I intend to own. The walls are more than a third of a metre thick, and a heavy concrete slab sits on top. Entry is by a steep flight of wooden stairs, through a steel trapdoor.

The cost would have kept me and several friends drunk for years but I rationalise it by telling myself too much alcohol is bad for you, and the cellar has added not only value to the house but an irresistible selling point.

The reactions of friends are wonderful to behold. Their faces light up with happy surprise. Is it because the idea of a cave touches us all? And what can you do with a cave but store wine in it? There's great pleasure to be had in the contemplation of bottles lying peacefully in carefully sorted rows.

I've learned one thing. It's a waste of time and money cellaring mediocre wines. Better to buy half as much at twice the price. A cellar should be full of treasures, not plonk.

My advice, for what it's worth, is to buy whites you know will last a long time and improve with age: Leo Buring's rhine rieslings, for example, Hunter River semillons and good chardonnays. And resist the temptation of buying too many cheap reds. Go for ones that are really going to benefit from resting under your watchful eye for several years.

You can't lose.

GRAPE'S PROGRESS

Paul Lloyd

I am Grape. Some call me humble fruit, but no — I may boast — what other fruit offers so much? Look again, at Milton Wordley's photographic attempt to bare my essence, and say that this shows something simple! Ah, but though he tenderly stripped me naked, I revealed not all to him.

Me. This shot from the family album was taken after I had been cut in half. Here I am a red grape, though of course I can also be white. In almost all cases, however, my flesh is pale green.

Some seek me historically. My plant, botanically named **Vitis vinifera,** *commonly known as the grapevine, originated in the vicinity of ancient Persia — call it the Garden of Eden, if you like — and spread across the temperate zones of the world, only by the hands of fascinated Man. I am known in 5000 variations, although only some hundreds are used for making wine. But the vine is merely my mother, to be tended with love in order that I, Grape, might flourish.*

Some seek me through science. Callow students learn that in Australia I come to maturity between January and May depending on the region, and they take measuring devices to my physical structure, height, weight, colour and so forth. What do they find? Nought but skin, pulp, pips and juice. Scientists take this vulgarity further by spending millions in taxpayer monies on all manner of sophisticated computerised chromatography, digital refractometry and spectrographic analysis.

And what do they find? That my juice consists of water, of course; of the sugars glucose and fructose (8 to 13 per cent); three organic acids, tartaric (0.2 to 1 per cent), malic (0.1 to 0.8 per cent) and citric (0.01 to 0.05 per cent); the tannins, catechol, chlorogenic acid, caffeic acid (0.01 to 1 per cent); nitrogenous compounds including amino acids and proteins (0.03 to 0.17 per cent); traces of such other minerals as phosphorus and sulphates; the B-group vitamins, thiamine, riboflavin, pyridoxine and nicotinic acid; traces of ascorbic acid, which is to say, vitamin C; volatile aroma constituents; and colour components. Ho-hum. One boffin pompously proclaimed that he had identified over 500 components. How I laughed for I had not revealed all even to him.

Some seek me in art, music, literature, and I must sniff at writers such as Daisy Ashford for coining the phrase 'sour grapes' in The Young Visitors *and Julia Howe for 'the grapes of wrath' in* The Battle Hymn of the Republic. *As for Keats and Wordsworth and their wimpish mates, I sport with the poets and let them have their fun. I don't pretend to be a great literary critic, but I was a bit touched by Edward FitzGerald's translation of* Rubaiyat of Omar Khayyam *which sang of the 'Grape that can with Logic absolute the two-and-seventy jarring Sects refute'. And Shakespeare wasn't a bad writer, with that little ditty in* Antony and Cleopatra:

Come, thou monarch of the vine,
Plumpy Bacchus, with pink eyne!
In thy fat our cares be drown'd,
With thy grapes our hairs be crown'd.
  Cup us, till the world goes round,
  Cup us, till the world goes round!

Some seek me through mysticism and religion. 'Of all the ineffable mysteries of horticulture,' wrote Australian essayist Paul Lloyd, 'none so affects human happiness as the magic of the Grape.' The Christian Bible makes frequent mention of me, sometimes with choice allegory, and St Matthew did ask: 'Do men gather grapes of thorn, or figs of thistles?' Worth thinking about.

Some seek me through gastronomy. And here, finally, is where they are most likely to succeed. For it is not until yeasts transform my sugars into alcohol that my juice becomes wine. And then, only through all the finest senses of eyes, nose, mouth, indeed, the whole body, may Man understand the essence of Grape.

Come with me through the next few pages, with photographer Milton, and follow my progress from vine to you. See for yourself, and scoff not at the amazing adventures, by which I, Grape, aspire to immortality through wine.

*Early days. This is bud-
burst, as the young leaves
emerge from the grapevine's
canes in spring.*

*Every year, as the warm sun
hits me, I push out these
leaves.*

*The leaves grow quickly to
nourish me and protect my
fruit . . .*

*My fruit starts its life as tiny
grape berries like this bunch.*

Viticulture is the cultivation of the vine — to produce fruit for the table, for drying, or for making wine. Above: *a tiny cluster of grape berries waits for the vine to pump water and nutrients in and the sun to help them ripen.* Right: *halfway there, the berries are green and hard, high in acid and low on sugar.* Far right: *nearly ripe, the acid level is falling and the sugar rising as vintage approaches.*

Ripe grapes in the South Australian Riverland.

Winemaker Brian Croser. Grapes and good wine are as much a part of civilisation as great works of literature, music and art.

MAKING WINE

A PERSONAL PERSPECTIVE

Brian Croser

Only God knows where it all began; undoubtedly in the cradle of human development because the same plant has been used for centuries for the same purposes in Asia, Arabia and Europe. Those parts of the globe not planted with the vine in ancient times have been since planted by the efforts of the European settlers in the new world. As a result of his determination to cultivate the grapevine, it is the most ubiquitous and productive agricultural plant used by man.

Rejoicing in the rather bookish name *Vitis vinifera,* the one species produces fruit of pale green colour to blushing pink through to a semi-translucent blue grey to a lustrous black.

The flavours are equally diverse; it is difficult to conceive that the same parents gave issue to both the power of the muscat frontignan which can fill the airspace of a dining room with floral aromatics and to the subtle dusty green, herbaceous characters of cabernet sauvignon, which have to be teased out of the glass by the nose.

The selective force which has created this collection of varieties of one plant has been man himself. To some extent convenience of cultivation in the difficult and varied environments of northern Europe, has favoured the choice of cabernet sauvignon in the Bordeaux region, pinot noir in Burgundy and Rhine riesling on the banks of the Rhine in Germany.

But the disparate flavours and qualities of the wines made from these varieties has also been the object of human preference. The subtleties of wine style and quality are as diverse as the range of human appreciation and preference in the same way as musical tastes range from Beethoven to the Rolling Stones, or artistic tastes from Michaelangelo to Picasso. Grapes and wine are as much part of the wardrobe of human civilisation as great works of literature, music and art. Wine has the additional feature that is an accepted social drug, necessary to oil the wheels of a society operating under pressure and generally used in moderation, and accompanied by food.

Enough of this speculation and philosophising. How is this substance made?

Winemaking is a seasonal activity punctuated by the deciduous nature of the vine. For the vine the trigger for budburst is the disappearance of the

53

Old vines, new shoots.

begin to fall off the flowers, exposing the sexual machinery of the grape. The yellow pollen on its fibrous supports suddenly breaks the camouflage of green foliage and the flowers become apparent as miniature bottle brushes. The air at this time is pervaded by a subtle sweet aroma which is very difficult to describe, but almost narcotic in its effect on the paternal vigneron as he watches the birth of the child of his labours. The interference of bad weather, rain, wind or hail in this delicate and private process can result in the barren flowers shattering onto the ground, leaving the vigneron no choice but to wait for the seasonal cycle to turn once more.

The relief of a successful flowering is followed by a period of vigilance as the vigneron watches for any natural disaster which might interfere with the development of his crop. His responsibility as nursemaid is to keep the vine healthy and acting as a factory, providing the substances of berry growth, as well as sugar, colour and flavour. Continued spray protection against the earlier feared fungus diseases, and protection against snails, caterpillars, grasshoppers, domestic animals and birds are some of the battles the vigneron fights in defence of his crop.

The grape berries expand from a pinhead size to pea size very rapidly from November to mid-January. At this stage they are green, hard and fibrous with a high acid content and little or no sugar and flavour – not at all appetising. The heat of summer then induces a dramatic and critical change which sends the winemaker scurrying to ensure his equipment is clean and ready for the frantic period of vintage.

The lovely French word *veraison* meaning 'the turn' describes a biological change akin to puberty in humans. The green bullet of the immature grape begins to soften, the skin changes from an opaque, intense, leaf green to a transluscent yellow green, the first blush of red colour appears in red grapes. Accompanying these visible changes a chemical process begins inside the berry as the acids of immaturity reduce and are replaced by sugar from the factory like leaves. The flavour characteristic of a variety begins to become apparent and the expectant vigneron chews the occasional berry on his patrols of vigilance.

winter chill, in Australia usually in September. Then begins a period of anxiety for the vigneron as each bud unfurls into a tender miniature shoot, at the mercy of late frosts, hail and wind. Remarkably early in this process the tiny shoot displays the miniature inflorescences which will, with luck and good management, become a plump and flavoursome bunch of grapes. The rate of growth of these shoots accelerates dramatically as the weather warms to the season and at peak growth in November these shoots are growing at a rate of 5-6 centimetres a day. A constant war of preventive measures is waged at this time to keep the rapidly growing leaves and shoots covered with a veneer of the time-honoured copper and sulphur sprays which prevent the growth of destructive fungi. A combination of inattention to this spraying programme and warm wet conditions can see a fungus such as downy mildew rage through the vineyard in a matter of days, defoliating the vines just as surely as a bushfire.

With crossed fingers and a feeling of helplessness, the anxious vigneron prays for calm warm weather in mid- to late November as the flowers expand into the intricate skeleton of a full-sized bunch. The caps

The birds also begin to experiment with the ripening grapes. The twittering and fluttering in the dense vine canopy can drive the vigneron to distraction. The peace of the dewy vineyard morning is shattered by the sound of explosions from shotguns and bird scaring devices. Fake hawks hover on the top of poles, scarecrows flap, aluminium foil tinkles and glitters, and the recorded hunting cries of predator birds shriek weirdly across the vineyards.

In the same few weeks as this rowdy and gaudy 'star wars' is waging, the acid and sugar of the grape move slowly towards a balance and the varietal flavour begins to dominate the green character of unripeness. The skill and experience of the winemaker is exposed to no more severe test than in this decision of when the flavour and composition of his grapes are optimal for their intended wine style.

In the cool, strained sunlight of the early morning a motley and colourful collection of chattering pickers kick the dust, discuss the excesses of the night before and finger their snips, before they are unleashed on the vineyard. The threat of rains over this man's vineyards would galvanise a new and accelerated picking plan, even then the chances of predicting and winning against nature rely more on the kindness of the season than on the vigneron's actions.

Cloud bursts on vineyards loaded with ripe grapes are the stuff of the winemaker's nightmare. Bedraggled, unhappy pickers, bogged tractors, desperation and helplessness are his dread. Under these conditions the vines, against the will of the season and the winemaker, pump the excess ground water into the already plump and tense bunches of berries. Finally the pressure is too much and like an overblown balloon first one berry and then another will split their skins and leave the sugary, nutrient-rich juice seeping out over the bunch. Encouraged by the warm, wet conditions and fuelled by the available nutrient, moulds will proliferate and the bunches take on the appearance of the bottom of a mouldy fruit bowl.

Scarecrows, silhouettes of hawks and birdguns try to keep the birds at bay until the pickers get to the ripe grapes.

Red grapes from a mechanical harvester are carried into a bin ready for transporting to the winery, and fermentation.

Fortunately this does not happen this vintage, as the monsoons obligingly peter out on the north-east and north-west of the continent of Australia.

The lever is pushed and the first grapes of the season tumble out of the vineyard bin with initial dull thuds, then a sigh as the momentum of the grape mass takes over. The gleaming, stainless steel receiving bin has stood empty for the past nine months, and now with the stab of a switch, the auger in the bottom shudders into action. The fruit is pushed gently and slowly by this giant horizontal corkscrew toward a hole at the end of the receiving bin, which is the start of the winemaking process itself.

Anxiously standing by his controls the winemaker opens a small valve and a fine mist of preservative coats the first bunches as they chatter into the crusher beneath the receiving bin. This is the signal for more action and the complicated, almost Heath Robinsonish contraption called the crusher whirrs, clanks and roars into life, drowning out all competing sounds. Stainless steel fingers smash the berries off the stalks and fling them through a revolving screen into the blurred teeth of two competing rollers meshing at high speed. Plump grape berries bounce momentarily on top of these rollers until, grabbed by the teeth, they disappear between.

A puree of seeds, skins, pulp and juice begins to accumulate in the tray beneath, and with the flick of another switch the winemaker starts the big pump attached to the bottom aperture of the sump. An invisible suction force begins to collapse the mound of sticky mash in the sump and finally reaches agreement with the splattering mash dropping from the rollers above. The pump warms to its task, as the outlet hose fills with an extrusion of this grape mixture. This is called the *must,* it carries on into the serpentine stainless steel tube known as the must cooler. With the flick of another switch, a huge amount of very cold, refrigerated liquid is pitched into the outside tube of the device, surrounding and moving contrary to the advancing grape must in the inner tubes. Within seconds of being crushed the temperature of the grape must has been dropped from the warm vineyard temperature of 20°C to a handnumbing 5°C.

It is with a sense of growing relief and satisfaction that the winemaker springs up on the side of the horizontal cylindrical barrel of his press to see the first sausage of cold juice, skins and seeds spew out of the delivery hose and slowly, like a green mud flow, begin to move down the length of the press chamber. The must's low temperature protects the precious liquid from the damage which can be wrought by flavour changing air and stray germs.

The first press is filled to brimming with the precious green mixture, the door is sealed down and the winemaker prepares himself for the first taste of the season's quality. The press is revolved until the drainage ports point to the sky. As the caps which have until now held the juice in are removed, juice barely dribbles over the top. With one quick half turn these ports are rotated to the bottom and with a gush reminiscent of a fire hose the juice eagerly separates itself from the skins and seeds inside the press and floods into a tray under the press. Immediately a pump springs into action to handle the tidal wave of juice and pump it away into a clean stainless steel vault which has stood empty for the past few months. The first juice separates readily but finally the flow

White grapes pour into the crusher, which turns the grapes into 'must' ready for fermentation.

Insulation around the tank holds the juice at the required temperature.

from the press slows and dies to a dribble. The reluctant juice left in the skin mass in the press is flavoursome, and needed to make a complete wine. By repeatedly inflating a rubber balloon inside the press, the juice can be teased away from the skins and joins the earlier liquid in the tank. Finally the spent skins are dumped out of the press.

The tank in which this juice is collected acts like a Thermos flask. The cold juice from the press is further chilled in this tank by an inbuilt refrigeration system and the insulation around the tank protects it from the warming effect of the hot summer sun. There the juice sits quietly at -2°C, shut away from heat, light and disturbance as the activity of vintage continues around it. The frantic process which led to the filling of this tank will be repeated out in the vineyard and winery, by an increasingly tired band of pickers and winemakers, as many as fifty times.

For this juice the first steps of vintage are complete and it will wait patiently, slowly depositing on the bottom of the tank bits of grape seed, skin and pulp which have escaped the pressing operation.

Meanwhile out in the vineyard the picking crews have gleaned the last of the early ripening varieties,

In the laboratory at Arrowfield in the Hunter Valley.

chardonnay, pinot noir and merlot from the cooler areas such as Piccadilly and Coonawarra. The Rhine riesling from Clare, a relatively warm area, is also safely in tank. With another roll of the sleeve and hitch of the belt, flagging energies are mustered to begin the final lap of vintage: the cabernet, shiraz and malbec from Coonawarra. To the outside observer very little of the initial picking and delivering routine alters from the inexorable pattern already established – except that the pickers' hands, the bins and the receivable bin are stained with the blue/black red, the trademark of the noble cabernet grape.

But the winemaker has other problems. Some of the earliest juice from the vineyard has been put through gleaming filters, and all of the natural germs have been removed by this process. This juice has been stored in special vessels and has received, by the surgically clean hand and technique of the

Fermenting red wine in
concrete open vats.

winemaker, the seed of a yeast culture. This sparkling clear grape juice turns milkily turbid as the original added cells multiply slowly at first, then very rapidly. The winemaker, peering down his microscope, decides that his culture is free of other germs and is healthy, strong and ready for action.

The first major point of departure from the process which yielded the chilled white grape juice in tank, is about to be made in the handling of the Coonawarra cabernet sauvignon. As these ripe, stalky, berry-smelling grapes are being pumped away from the crusher — a steady but small stream of the milky liquid yeast culture is trickled into the collecting tray under the crusher. Pumped through the heat exchanger but cooling to only 10°C, the grape must and yeast mixture spews into a cone bottomed stainless steel tank which resembles a coffee pot. This is suspended on steel frames above the presses which have squashed the last drop of white juice for the season out of the last white skins.

The supercharged yeast cells, able to be seen only by microscope, are immediately enriched by the nutrient of the grape juice and multiply rapidly and begin to digest the sugar of the grape, converting it to alcohol and carbon dioxide. The latter causes a plum-red froth to rise to the surface of the tank. The agitation of the escaping carbon dioxide boiling out of the liquid and the design of the fermenter combine to keep the flavour and colour containing skins in contact with the increasingly coloured juice.

The fermentation on skins takes a week, by which time all the colour and flavour have been extracted from the skins into the juice and all of the sugar has been converted to alcohol. The red wine is then drained away from the spent skins to another tank and the soggy mass of skins and seeds settle in the cone of the fermenter. To extract the last precious drops of highly coloured wine from these skins they are dropped from the cone into the presses and the same squashing and teasing principle is applied as had been applied in the extraction of white grape juice. The difference is that the white grape juice had not undergone the yeast fermentation and therefore retained all of its sugar when collected in tank. The

Cool and even temperatures in underground 'drives' like this one enable premium wines to mature properly for years.

red liquid drained off the fermenter and press has completed the fermentation and therefore contains no sugar and has the alcohol content of a finished wine.

The last gasps of vintage are completed in mid-April and each tank in the winery is full of either sparkling clear white grape juice sitting over the amassed sludges of settled grape solids or of clear red wine over the grape solids and dead yeast cells produced during fermentation in the presence of skins.

But there is no rest for the wicked. It's time for a change of clothes, a long night of 'end of vintage'

celebration and back to the fermentation of the white juices. The white juices are carefully separated from their deposited sludges, warmed from -2°C to 10°C and a yeast culture prepared with equal care to those produced for the reds is added. For 2 to 3 weeks the yeast digests the sugar of the white juices and produces carbon dioxide gas and alcohol. Finally all of the sugar has gone and the tank can be once again cooled to settle out a new batch of deposits including the yeast of fermentation.

The clear wine from Rhine riesling grapes is placed immediately in bottle to capture behind glass and cork the fresh, floral fruit characters of the ripe berries on the vine. The clear white wine of chardonnay and the clear red wine of cabernet are put in new oak barrels for one year to give additional flavours and maturity before they are consigned to the protection of the bottle.

By the time the clear wine has been put in bottle and barrel, nature's clock has turned to another phase in the vineyard. The last decorative leaves have fallen off the vines in July in response to the hoary breath of winter.

However, the whippy and winter-hardened canes that were last year's fragile green shoots so anxiously nurtured by the vigneron already contain the miniature structures of next year's shoots complete with leaves and flowers. The cycle is set to turn another revolution.

Standing in the pristine white tasting room looking at the products of the last and previous vintage displaying their varied hues, the winemaker reflects with satisfaction on the year's work. The hurly-burly of the vintage seems aeons behind as the ripe fig and melon of a Piccadilly chardonnay fills the nostrils. Has it had enough oak? Does it require some Coonawarra for body? When should I bottle it? These are some of the questions filling his thoughts as the vineyard manager breaks his reverie with the observation that budburst has just begun again.

When the sun starts warming the vines in spring, budburst again brings on the shoots of new leaves, which will eventually help nourish the grapes for the next year's wines.

MAKING WHITE WINE

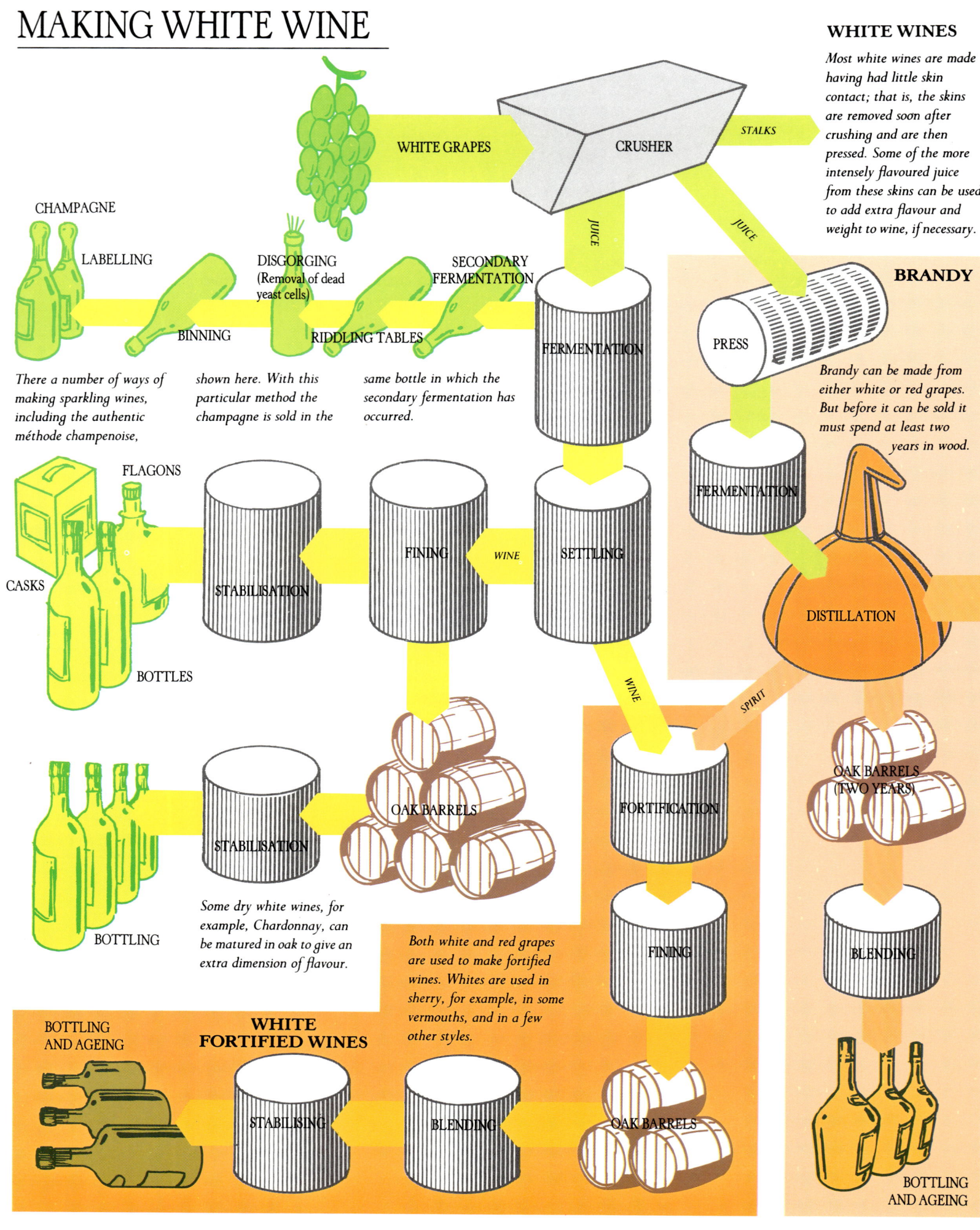

WHITE GRAPES

CRUSHER

STALKS

JUICE

JUICE

WHITE WINES

Most white wines are made having had little skin contact; that is, the skins are removed soon after crushing and are then pressed. Some of the more intensely flavoured juice from these skins can be used to add extra flavour and weight to wine, if necessary.

CHAMPAGNE

LABELLING

DISGORGING (Removal of dead yeast cells)

SECONDARY FERMENTATION

BINNING

RIDDLING TABLES

FERMENTATION

PRESS

BRANDY

Brandy can be made from either white or red grapes. But before it can be sold it must spend at least two years in wood.

FERMENTATION

There a number of ways of making sparkling wines, including the authentic méthode champenoise,

shown here. With this particular method the champagne is sold in the same bottle in which the secondary fermentation has occurred.

FLAGONS

CASKS

FINING

WINE

SETTLING

STABILISATION

DISTILLATION

BOTTLES

SPIRIT

WINE

OAK BARRELS (TWO YEARS)

STABILISATION

OAK BARRELS

FORTIFICATION

BOTTLING

Some dry white wines, for example, Chardonnay, can be matured in oak to give an extra dimension of flavour.

Both white and red grapes are used to make fortified wines. Whites are used in sherry, for example, in some vermouths, and in a few other styles.

FINING

BLENDING

BOTTLING AND AGEING

WHITE FORTIFIED WINES

STABILISING

BLENDING

OAK BARRELS

BOTTLING AND AGEING

62

MAKING RED WINE

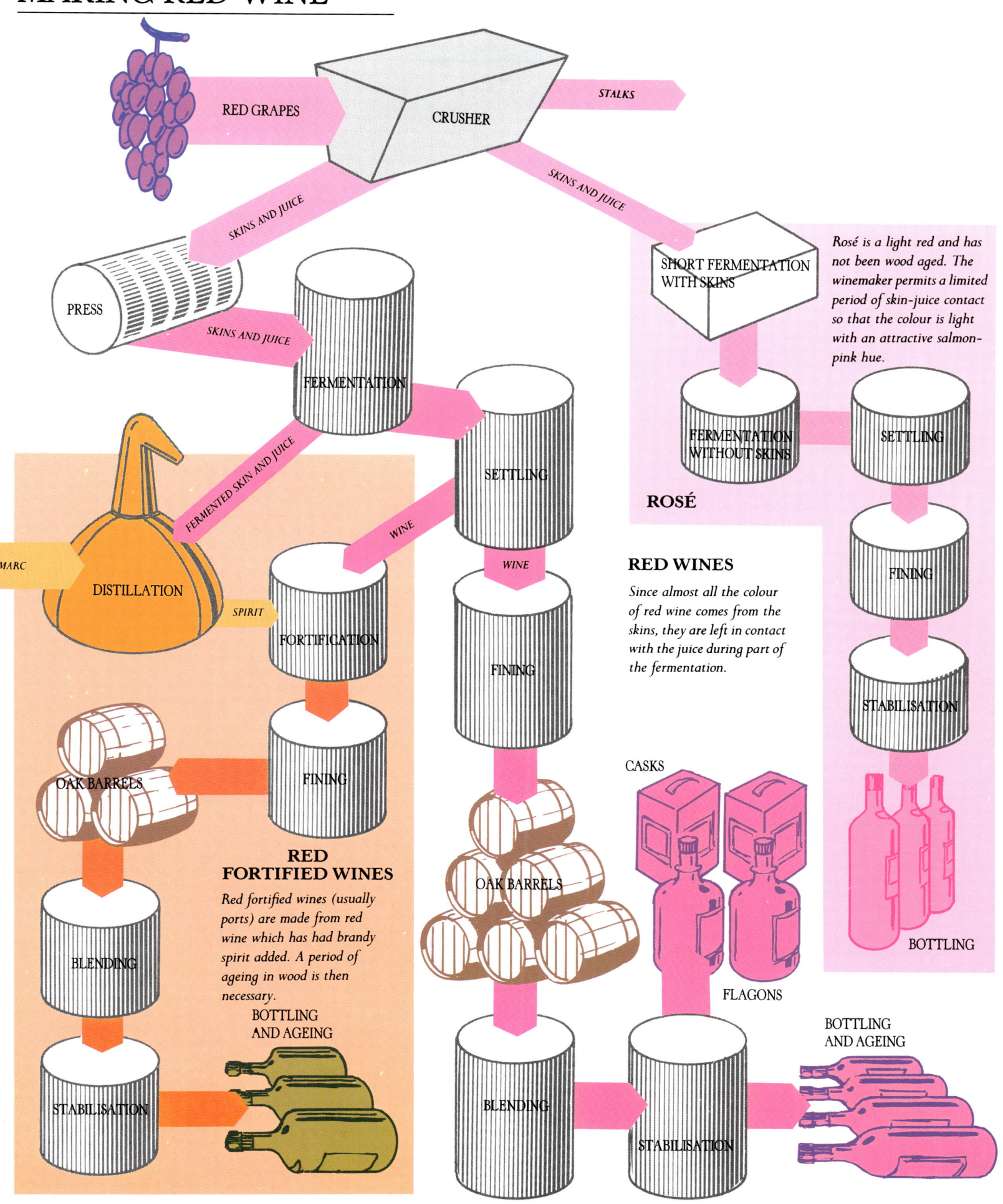

RED GRAPES

CRUSHER

STALKS

SKINS AND JUICE

SKINS AND JUICE

PRESS

SKINS AND JUICE

FERMENTATION

FERMENTED SKIN AND JUICE

MARC

DISTILLATION

SPIRIT

FORTIFICATION

OAK BARRELS

FINING

BLENDING

STABILISATION

RED FORTIFIED WINES

Red fortified wines (usually ports) are made from red wine which has had brandy spirit added. A period of ageing in wood is then necessary.

BOTTLING AND AGEING

SETTLING

WINE

WINE

FINING

OAK BARRELS

BLENDING

STABILISATION

CASKS

FLAGONS

BOTTLING AND AGEING

SHORT FERMENTATION WITH SKINS

Rosé is a light red and has not been wood aged. The winemaker permits a limited period of skin-juice contact so that the colour is light with an attractive salmon-pink hue.

FERMENTATION WITHOUT SKINS

SETTLING

ROSÉ

RED WINES

Since almost all the colour of red wine comes from the skins, they are left in contact with the juice during part of the fermentation.

FINING

STABILISATION

BOTTLING

The cooperage at Seppeltsfield, around 1890. Large Australian wineries once maintained cooperages as a matter of course. With the advent of stainless steel storage and modern transport the numbers of coopers have been greatly reduced.

THE CHANGING TASTES

WINE IN A NEW LAND

David Dunstan

G rapevines were part of the promise European civilisation brought to Australia. They accompanied the First Fleet which landed at Port Jackson on 26 January 1788. Together with livestock and other essentials of life, they had been obtained the previous November at the Cape of Good Hope, and were planted at Farm Cove – which later became Sydney's Botanic Gardens – and their progress was, for a time, carefully observed.

It would be nice to think that these were a beginning – either real or symbolic – for the Australian wine industry, but they were not. Like many other vines imported into the colony in those years they suffered from a form of blight which destroyed the young shoots and leaves. At the time this was thought to be caused by the effects of the hot Australian winds on plants more suited to a temperate climate, but the likely cause was probably a fungoid disease called 'Black Spot' or 'Anthracnose' which was, however, almost certainly made much worse by the subtropical humidity of the Sydney Harbour area. Gradually they ceased to attract much interest. The 3 acres (about 1.2 hectares) of vines that Captain Phillip reported in 1791 appear to have been neglect-

ed, and the initial optimism that inspired the cartage of seedlings of 'the Claret grape' – possibly cabernet sauvignon – half way around the world was dissipated as settlers were forced to confront the bare necessities of life in a struggle for survival amidst unfamiliar surroundings.

Gradually circumstances improved, but although the introduction of the plants, livestock and agricultural traditions of the Old World was an ambition of early settlers in almost all of the Australian colonies it was not until well into the nineteenth century that anything like a viable Australian wine industry was to develop, with buoyant local and export markets sustaining skilled producers with an economic return on their investment. Even then it was not to be anything like a rival to the chief staples of wheat and wool. Considered in the overall scheme of things, wine has mainly been a minor industry. Indeed it is still so today compared to the massive output in other realms of agricultural produce, but this has long been belied by its somewhat exotic and colourful character.

It is curious that wine production has been an eccentric and mainly experimental pursuit in Australia, given what might seem to be the country's

Fallon's Vineyard, Albury. Romantic scenes of cellars and vineyards such as this one that appeared in Cassell's Picturesque Atlas of Australasia *(1889) were as much the expression of an ideal as evidence of lasting achievement in the Australian wine industry. (National Library of Australia.)*

almost natural affinity for its production. Even more puzzling is the history of the industry which, over the years, has experienced severe fluctuations. We have seen the decimation of whole viticultural areas, and the loss of much in the way of painstakingly accrued expertise and technology. The efforts of a great many dedicated and talented people have come to naught. To the historian who scans the endeavour of the past the sight is not an altogether comforting one, as it presents little in the way of a story of steady progress, but rather one of bursts of development and disastrous collapse.

Is the past a useful guide to Australian wine? Of what relevance are learned and discursive forays into the distant past when it is a fact that it is only in very recent times that Australians have become wine drinkers *en masse,* literally in the last couple of decades? One might argue forcefully that there are few active traditions in the industry today that extend back more than a generation or two, and most of them have had to be learnt from scratch by a new generation. Despite the historical public relations gloss of some wine companies the industry is a very modern one. If anything, the emphasis in Australian wine is on the new and what may yet be achieved – with the latest yeast strain, an exciting new variety, or viticultural or winemaking technique. This fits the industry's popular image of itself and accords with the style of most of its wine, which is not intended for maturation over time but rather for speedy consumption. The heroic figure of the modern scene is not the hoary old cellar hand or winemaker – the heir to the wisdom and traditions of the past – but the brilliant young technocrat, straight out of college and sharp as a tack but sometimes also as green as a bud in spring.

It is commonplace to hear observations that our greatest vineyards are yet to be planted and that, *ipso facto,* our greatest wines are yet to be made. This sort of thinking denies the past, its wines, and its lessons. It is indeed something of a paradox that so many of our so-called innovations seem to follow on the examples of previous generations. An instance of this can be seen in the 'trail-blazing' of modern winegrowers who are developing vineyard sites in regions

Grapes and vines in nineteenth-century Australia did not always mean wine. Kitchen gardens were common and many vignerons who did make wine also cultivated dual-purpose varieties. The predominantly Anglo-Saxon and Celtic population probably appreciated the fresh fruit more than they did table wine. (State Library of Victoria.)

that, for one reason or another, were abandoned as such last century. Many of them seem quite determined to repeat the mistakes of the past without ever wishing to learn from them.

This cult of youth is perhaps appropriate to a country that still sees itself as young, but Australia has a history of winemaking quite as old as the modern industries of Europe which have themselves strayed from their more ancient traditions. The truth is that we are perhaps obsessed more with promise than performance, and do not properly understand what we have achieved, or failed to achieve. We tend to hide behind the seemingly endless opportunities offered by the future, but a thorough investigation of the past may reveal that we have wasted more opportunities than we have capitalised on.

An adequate history of the Australian wine industry has yet to be written, although there have been some worthy efforts in this direction. When, and if, an adequate work is published it is not likely that it will be a simple story of success building on success, for that would not be a true account. Equally, it will not simply be an investigation of the past affairs of existing commercial operations, for there were vast concerns that have left virtually no present-day heirs. All of which begs the question: what role can the past play in introducing a volume like this? By focusing on a handful of selected figures tucked away in our wine industry's past we can perhaps glimpse some of the more specific problems of former times and also the aspirations of a more perennial nature. We can perhaps identify some of the forces which both favoured and discouraged individual endeavour, and even go some way to reminding enthusiasts of the present that they are not the first to feel the way they do.

THE BEGINNINGS

James Busby (1801-1871), Australia's first prophet of the vine. In the space of a few years in the 1820s and 1830s Busby wrote and published textbooks on viticulture and winemaking, toured the great vineyards and nurseries of Europe, and introduced a comprehensive collection of grape varieties into the new land. (Mitchell Library, State Library of New South Wales.)

From the earliest times colonial officials and well-to-do citizens were disposed to look favourably on viticulture and winemaking, in spite of rebuffs from both man and nature. The sunny climates of the Australian colonies seemed to beg for the cultivation of the vine, and there were rolling hills that appeared only to need to be so clothed to remind homesick exiles of altogether more European aspects. Here also was something Australia could do for the Mother Country, in that it obviously had the capacity to produce what the parent society – with its cold northern European climate – could not. This sentiment was shared by the French botanist François Péron, who was attached to the explorer Baudin's expedition of 1800-04. He believed that Australia would eventually enable England to stop buying wine from Spain, Portugal and France, and it remains a pertinent question to ask why – given so many opportunities – Australia did not achieve a stranglehold on the British wine market.

Did it have something to do with the culture of the people themselves? As early as 1830 James Busby, one of Australia's early prophets of the vine, certainly thought so:

Had New South Wales been settled by a Colony from France, or any other country whose climate is favourable to the growth of the vine, we should at this day have seen few corn fields without their neighbouring vineyards; and the poorest settler, aye, and his meanest servant, would daily have regaled their palates and invigorated their bodies with this first of the blessings which nature bestows upon the more genial climates of the earth.

As the settlement developed, with many former convicts being released on tickets-of-leave, but forbidden ever to return to England, there were more immediate reasons for encouraging interest in vines and winemaking. It was hoped that this might undermine the unhealthy interest in spirits – both in their

consumption and as a means of exchange – that had sprung up. Late in 1800 Acting Governor King indicated that this was the thinking that lay behind the decision to secure the services of two French prisoners of war, who were believed to be expert vignerons, to cultivate vineyards and to make wine.

By 1802 they had planted upwards of 1200 vines on the side of a hill at Parramatta, and in 1803 they made some wine. King also attempted to promote viticulture and winemaking among the settlers, and in 1803 the *Sydney Gazette* carried information on pruning and the preparation of red and white wines and brandy. Soon afterwards he announced his intention of planting a large vineyard at Castle Hill, but was discouraged by the poor quality of the wine the Frenchmen had already produced. In this instance he displayed little patience, and in March 1804 announced the cessation of the project. It was the two foreigners who were blamed, King considering that they 'knew very little of the business'. They had made wine from the best grapes available but King, although he informed his superiors back home of the exercise, declined to send them any as it was so bad.

The Frenchmen may have considered themselves unlucky to have been so hastily dealt with, but the problem was that what little success had been met with in no way compensated for the drain on time and resources. Besides, it seemed a folly to be engaging in the difficult and exacting business of making wine in a strange and unfamiliar land when it could so easily be obtained by other means. This was seen in 1808 when a large quantity was imported from the Cape of Good Hope. The consequences of its sale may also have undermined the general belief in the more temperate habits of wine drinkers as, according to one account, '. . . a general intoxication prevailed for some time; but from the people having spent their money, and being pretty well glutted, a deal of wine [remained]. . . unsold.'

The plain fact was that the social character of the settlement itself − it was a penal colony − and the rather spartan nature of its early existence did not lend itself to either viticulture or wine production. These were the reasons George Suttor gave for abandoning his trials with oranges and grapevines on his land at Parramatta as early as 1801, although he was to take them up again later when circumstances permitted. Besides, the civilised drinking habits of the English upper classes − and the table and dessert wines they enjoyed − were not an extensive part of the social life of the colony. What little that was required was easily imported like most other luxury items. The prospects for viticulture and wine only started to improve as society began to assume a more settled character, and when more and more free immigrants began to arrive with new ideas and money. This happened in the years between 1810 and 1821 when Lachlan Macquarie was Governor, and in the following decade.

This engraving by J. Carmichael from James Maclehose's Picture of Sydney and Strangers' Guide in New South Wales *(1839) shows the Irrawang Vineyard & Pottery of James King, one of the pioneers of the Hunter River region. King was a Sydney merchant who sought to introduce civilised arts into the new land. An 1836 white wine of his was described by Maclehose as 'a sound, light, high flavoured, pure wine'. (National Library of Australia.)*

PIONEERS AND PROPHETS

One man who made a conscious effort to develop viticulture beyond a vine or two in one's kitchen garden, and to engage in wine production, was Gregory Blaxland who arrived in 1806 and settled on a 180-hectare property, Brush Farm, near Eastwood. Here he established a vineyard and made wine. In 1816 he contacted Macquarie, sending him some wine and detailing the work he had undertaken. His chief concern had been the search for a blight-resistant variety, and in the Constantia grape he thought he had found the answer. In time he was to settle on what he called the 'Claret' grape, but which historian W. P. Driscoll thinks may have been shiraz. If this is the case then Blaxland may have been responsible for the identification of what was to become Australia's leading quality red table wine grape.

Blaxland also made drinkable wine. In 1822 in response to the offer of a medal by the Society for the Encouragement of Arts, Manufacturers and Commerce he shipped a quarter of a pipe* of red wine to London, and was honoured with the award of a silver medal the following year. In 1828 additional samples received the even higher distinction of a gold medal from the same body. The judges considered these samples superior and free from the 'earthy flavour' which they considered was a characteristic of Cape wine. Blaxland also had a wider vision of his endeavours. In his correspondence with the authorities he urged the removal of restrictions on colonial wine-makers, especially as far as the production of brandy was concerned. This he regarded as an essential recourse in a wet year when the grapes did not properly mature, there having been two such years between 1812 and 1819. Blaxland, who fortified his own wine according to the conventions of the day, also saw brandy as a potential export.

A pipe was a wooden vessel used by the Portuguese to store and transport wine; it held 90 gallons (about 340 litres).

The Macarthur family of Camden are perhaps better known in Australia for their pioneering development of the wool trade, but in the second generation they were equally active as promoters of wine and viticulture. John Macarthur himself had observed early attempts at grape-growing with interest, and in 1815 and 1816 he toured France and Switzerland with the express intention of collecting vines and gathering information. He was accompanied by his two young sons, John and William, the latter of whom was to take up the cause over the course of a long life. Armed with cuttings, and fig and olive trees, the Macarthurs ventured to England, determined to return to Australia to introduce southern European agriculture into the new land, but they were forced to leave their plants in the hands of a nurseryman while they stayed a while in England. On the way back to Australia they stopped at Madeira, a British colony and another source of wine, and there obtained more cuttings.

Back in Australia the Macarthurs cultivated their vines and planted out about half a hectare of vineyard, firmly believing that it contained 'the best varieties grown in the Languedoc, at the Hermitage, Côte Rotie, in the Côte d'Or, etc., etc.'. They were fearfully disappointed to discover that in fact they had been betrayed, and had only been given one or

Gregory Blaxland (1778-1853), an Australian wine pioneer. Blaxland experimented with grapes and wine on his property near Eastwood, and in 1816 he sent Governor Macquarie some wine. Later he shipped his wine to London with a view to proving its export potential. (Mitchell Library, State Library of New South Wales.)

two varieties – 'our wine, too, did not arouse expectation' – and although the vines flourished, the enterprise seemed a failure, and all their efforts wasted.
Then in 1825 the Australian Agricultural Company
imported vines from the Horticultural Society's gardens at Chiswick. There could be no doubt about the
authenticity of these. Among them was 'the Ver-
deilho, one of the best sorts cultivated at Madeira'.
From this ('the first really good wine grape introduced [into Australia]') and two types of muscat they
gradually advanced to serious winemaking. But, by
his own account, William claimed they had lost ten
or twelve precious years in fruitless endeavour.

He was to make up for this in his determined
efforts to establish vineyards and wine production on
a commercial scale, and by popularising the arts of
viticulture and winemaking. He was active in over-
coming prejudice to allow the immigration of German vine dressers, and also in the dissemination of
cuttings to aspiring vignerons, many of them resident
in the other colonies. Under the pseudonym of 'Maro'
he contributed a series of articles to the *Australian* in
1842. These were later published as his *Letters on the
Culture of the Vine, Fermentation, and the Management of Wine in the Cellar* (1844) which became one
of the best known practical works of the day and one
of the few written with Australian conditions in
mind. It was Sir William – as he became – who was
mainly responsible for Camden becoming a viticultural area. He maintained his vineyards and cellars
throughout his long life, despite their uneconomic
return. This told heavily on them after his death in
1882. Even before the vines were discovered to be
phylloxerated in 1885 they were neglected, and the
discovery of the louse was merely the last straw that
caused them to be uprooted by authorities foolishly
inclined only to primitive methods of eradication and
quarantine as a defence against the pest.

An even more remarkable figure was James Busby
(1801-71), an educated Edinburgh-born son of a
good family. He emigrated to Australia in 1823 after
having spent several months in Bordeaux studying
French viticulture with a view to implanting it in his
adopted land. On the journey out he wrote his first

book, *A Treatise on the Culture of the Vine and the Art
of Making Wine,* which was published in 1825. A later
reviewer wrote, in 1833, that the colonists of the
period were 'wholly unprepared for such a work'.

Few persons had thought of the vine as anything
better than an ornament to their gardens, or an
addition to the dessert of their private tables. The
idea of its becoming a valuable mercantile staple
had never entered their heads.

Busby's book – the work of a complete stranger – was
of such a standard that it was likened to 'putting a
sum in compound interest before a child who had
never learnt the multiplication table'. What was
required was an 'elementary essay on the adaptation
of the soil and climate to the production of good wine
and raisins, and on the profits desirable to the products of the vinegrower; together with a few plain
directions for going about this novel sort of tillage'.
Instead Busby offered them 'a scientific disquisition
on all the mysteries of the manufacture of European
wines'! Busby himself later admitted that he was not

*Survivors of a bygone age of
wine – these underground
vats are among the few
remaining elements of one
of Australia's first working
wineries, that of Sir William
Macarthur at Camden.
(Photograph by David
Dunstan.)*

62

The most characteristic Marks for distinguishing and classing Varieties of the Vine, drawn from the Leaves and Fruit.

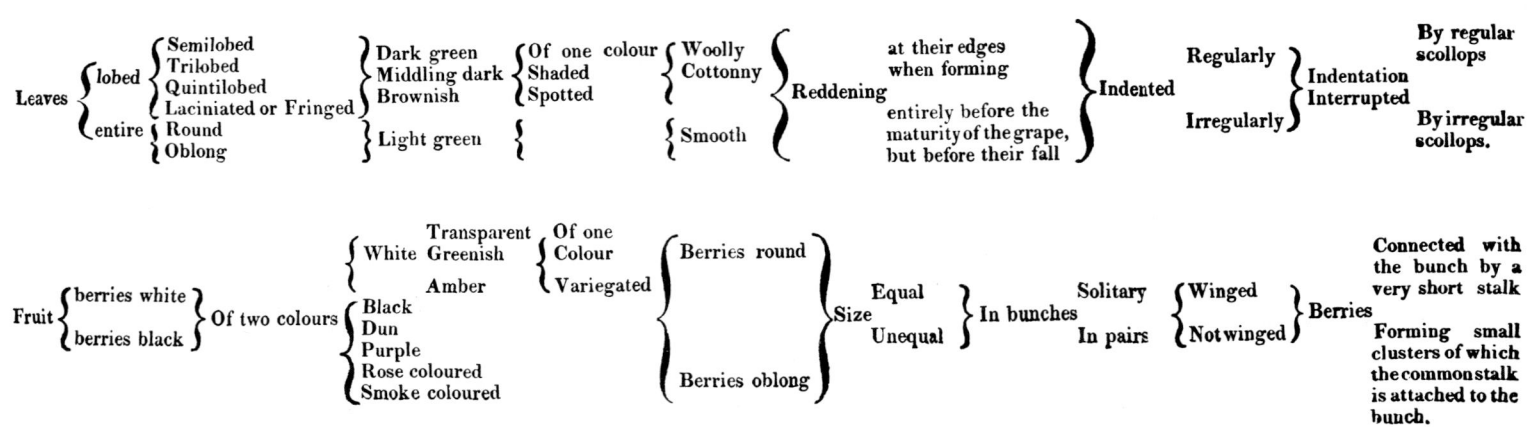

A page from James Busby's A Treatise on the Culture of the Vine and the Art of Making Wine *(1825) which, among other things, sought to explain the secrets of ampelography, or the science of identifying vines, to New South Wales farmers. His book was way in advance of what colonists were capable of absorbing, and in the words of a later commentator the book 'fell dead from the press'. (Mitchell Library, State Library of New South Wales.)*

aware of a single vineyard that had been inspired into existence by his treatise.

He was engaged to take charge of an orphan school at Bull's Head near Liverpool and to organise an agricultural institute on a 5000 hectare estate, one aspect of which would involve teaching the boys viticulture. In 1825 Busby planted half a hectare of vines, from which wine was made in 1829. But Busby lost his job in 1826 when the farm was closed down, and he started another career as a government official. Nevertheless, he retained his interest and became, along with Blaxland and Macarthur, one of the colony's wine enthusiasts. Given his undoubted technical knowledge and direct experience of European vineyards he was probably the colony's leading expert in the late 1820s and, as such, felt duty bound to pass on his knowledge. If, as was later said, his first book 'fell dead from the press' his second was more successful. This was the shorter and simpler *A Manual of Plain Directions for Planting and Cultivating Vineyards, and for Making Wine in New South Wales* (1830). A market had been created for this by new arrivals with open minds and money to spend, and a relative decline in the fortunes of wool which had

directed attention to other agricultural pursuits. Busby's new work was deliberately propagandist and geared to the needs and attitudes of small farmers in New South Wales.

In 1831 Busby returned to England to present his case for redress against the school authorities who had dismissed him, and, it seems, to win favour generally with the higher British authorities. Although he received little comfort on the former account he was rewarded with the post of British Resident in New Zealand and, as a result, was lost to Australia. But it was in conjunction with this journey that Busby again toured the vineyards of France and Spain collecting 678 varieties of vines – 433 of these came from the Botanic Gardens at Montpellier, 110 from the Luxemburg Gardens, 44 from Sion House near Kew Gardens in England and 91 from other parts of France and Spain collected over the course of four months. In a magnanimous gesture Busby presented this collection to the British authorities in order that they might be transported to Sydney to form an experimental garden there 'to prove their different qualities, and propagate, for general distribution, those which may appear most suitable to the climate'.

72

These vines were actually dealt with in the manner that Busby suggested and established at the Botanic Gardens in Sydney where at first they flourished. They were eventually neglected and in 1857 were rooted out.

Fortunately, extensive sections of the collection also found their way to Camden, to the Adelaide Botanic Gardens and to Busby's parent's property Kirkton, on the Hunter River, where Busby himself had previously planted 365 varieties. At Kirkton Busby's brother-in-law W. D. Kelman, who had arrived on the same boat with him in 1824, became an energetic and ambitious vigneron and winemaker. In 1911 about 20 of the original varieties still existed. The property was eventually to pass into the hands of the Lindeman family in 1914. Busby's biographer Eric Ramsden records that in 1924 the vineyard still bore a small crop and that this was bottled and presented at a celebration of the vineyard's centenary.

Busby also had an account of his tour published in Sydney in 1833, and one of the most interesting aspects is his listing of the varieties obtained and introduced into the new land, and his comments on them. We will most likely never know to what extent Busby's collection provided Australian vineyards with their rootstock but it seems that it was a considerable influence, especially as the fear of phylloxera was later to impose restrictions on the importation of vines for so many years. It is likely that Busby's collection was the source even of some of the more fashionable varieties of more recent years, such as the

chardonnay that was discovered at Mudgee and from which Murray Tyrrell from the Hunter and Bob Hollick from Mildura both took cuttings to establish vineyards. It is certainly recorded there in his book as 'Pineau Blanc, or Chaudeny' and described as the only variety of white grape cultivated in the best vineyards of Burgundy, Busby claimed he had distributed upwards of 20 000 cuttings, and claimed that the general plantation of vineyards dated from the appearance of his *Manual*. This was, in part, substantiated by the *Sydney Morning Herald* in March 1832 when it claimed that 'probably ten times as many vines were planted, as had been planted in any previous year'.

Busby remains of interest not just as an early disseminator of vine stocks but also as a proponent of wine as a desirable adjunct to colonial life, although in this he recognised that while the natural conditions favoured it the cultural climate did not. After a few years in the colony Busby became aware of the need to persuade people of the many blessings of the vine. He was aware that:

> ...the settlers of New South Wales, reared in a country where the vine does not flourish, and where the place of wine is supplied by malt liquors, and ardent spirits have brought with them to the Colony their prejudice in favour of these liquors, which they continue to use as at home, forgetting that even in cold countries they form but a poor substitute for wine...

He was not the first, or by any means the last, prophet of the vine to rely on temperance principles when he argued that the 'pernicious effects' of other alcoholic beverages are:

> ...increased ten-fold by the heat of such a climate as this, where few heads are able to withstand the stupifying effects of the *muddling ale,* and where the *liquid fire* burns more fiercely, and destroys more rapidly the health, and the happiness, and at length the life of those unhappy beings, who have become addicted to its use.

The Wynn wine cellars Coonawarra S.A. early 1900s

THE HUNTER VALLEY

After Busby's departure the Hunter Valley came to prominence as offering the best prospects for viticulture. This was the last of the major areas of the colony to be opened up to settlement and the scene of the first real, and enduring, triumph of the vine in the Australian colonies. To this day it remains metropolitan Sydney's own back garden of vines. It was the large landowners who first came to the district in the 1820s (and soon afterwards) that laid the basis for the district's enduring association with wine; although their vineyards were not in the Pokolbin–Rothbury area where wine has concentrated itself in modern times on the combination of sandy and volcanic soils of that district but on the alluvial flats adjoining the Hunter, William and Paterson rivers.

The most ambitious vigneron of this early period was probably Busby's brother-in-law William Kelman. By 1843 Kirkton had 6 hectares in bearing and

George Wyndham, the founder of the vineyards at Dalwood, which passed to Penfolds and more recently to the McGuigan family. The year 1835 was Wyndham's first vintage. (Courtesy of Mr Alward Wyndham.)

Kelman was claiming success with the white hermitage grape. But there were many others.

George Wyndham was a university educated Englishman who had given up an early ambition to be a clergyman for a life in distant parts. By the time he arrived in Sydney in 1827 he had already travelled the world, seen vineyards and agriculture in Europe and been married in Brussels. At Dalwood, near Branxton, he committed himself to experimental agriculture, and in 1830 planted maize, wheat, hemp, mustard, castor oil, tobacco, millet and Cape barley. He intended to plant vines but the ones he received from Busby 'were dead before I got them'.

Wyndham tried again the following season, and by January 1832 had 1400 vines, further increasing his plantings in 1833 and 1834. In his first vintage of 1835 he had fermentation troubles, observing that his Blackcluster 'should make good vinegar', but the next year he made 6246 litres of wine. The depression of the 1840s hit Wyndham hard. In 1845 he left Dalwood under a manager, crossed the New England plateau to the Richmond River where he took up another property, Keelgyrah. This he also left, crossing the Great Dividing Range to establish Bukkulla, near Inverell, where he planted another vineyard. By 1847 economic conditions had revived sufficiently for him to return to Dalwood.

Extensive new plantings were begun in 1854, and under Wyndham's heirs it became New South Wales' largest vineyard with its wines achieving distinction in exhibitions all over the world. Wyndham himself died in 1870 but the family only sold the property to Penfolds – the South Australian company who were then engaged in establishing themselves in the eastern States – in 1904, when it comprised about 32 hectares of bearing vines. In more recent times Penfolds sold it to the McGuigan family who trade their wines under the Wyndham Estate name. As recently as 1966 shiraz vines planted by the Wyndhams were still bearing. They were believed to be among the oldest vines in the world still doing so. They have now gone – along with the superb wines they made – to be replaced by fashionable new, high-yielding, aromatic white varieties under irrigation.

The National Trust has never, to my knowledge, classified a vineyard but they might have this one. Attention might equally be turned to the old Wyndham homestead which, when last seen by this writer, was in a state of neglect. More recently the historic character of a particular vineyard has been called to public attention by the battle fought to conserve another old Penfold property on the edge of suburban Adelaide at Magill.

Perhaps the most remarkable of all the early Hunter vignerons of this period was James King of Irrewang. He was born in 1800, the son of a Hertfordshire farmer who suffered as a result of the agricultural slump after the Napoleonic wars. Young King worked in various wool merchants' establishments in Leeds, and in 1827 arrived in Sydney and set himself up as a merchant. Soon afterwards he received a grant of 777 hectares near Raymond Terrace on the William River which he called Irrewang, but he continued to live in Sydney until about 1835.

King was a man of many parts: a successful merchant, a potter, and he was possessed of a keen scientific brain. He was aware of the importance of skilled labour and employed a German vine dresser in his vineyard. Although he first planted his vineyard in 1832 it comprised only 6 hectares in 1854, 2 of which were devoted to experimental varieties. And it is of some considerable interest that his experiments led him to persevere with one white grape only. This was the Shepherd's riesling, so-named after a nurseryman of Busby's time but which we know as semillon. King also experimented with pruning and viticultural techniques, and was interested in chemistry. He knew the work of the most celebrated chemist of the day, Baron von Liebig, and corresponded with him. It is also a matter of record that King made sparkling wines on a small scale, and was possibly the first Australian to do so.

Both King and Macarthur attended the Paris Exhibition of 1855 – the same one that saw the

Horsley, New South Wales. This vineyard is typical of the smaller operations of the period. (National Library of Australia.)

75

Large commercial vineyards throughout Australia last century frequently boasted some lookout or vantage point from which an overseer could assess the efforts of workers. This photograph taken from Samuel Mills, The Wine Story of Australia *(Sydney, 1908) is of the Dalwood Vineyard in the Hunter Valley. (National Library of Australia.)*

Valley. It might be argued Dr Henry Lindeman was his successor. Interestingly, Lindeman's success was as much the result of his activity as a wine merchant who popularised Hunter wines in Sydney as that of producer and the owner of Cawarra. But it was the little remembered King who gave an intellectual and scientific sense of direction to early Hunter wine-making, and he was also instrumental in the formation of the Hunter River Vineyard Association in 1847. This was a remarkable body of men – the first Hunter push in fact – who met regularly in a sympathetic environment for the purpose of fellowship and exchanging their knowledge on vines and wines. Interestingly, they held blind tastings of their own and the best French wines. They had the active support of a newspaper, the *Maitland Mercury,* which recorded their affairs in great detail and acted as their public relations arm. In all, they achieved a strong sense of purpose and high standards of skill which were reflected in the quality of their wines, that is if show success at an international level is any guide.

They also achieved an identity for a district's wines that was simply unprecedented, and still seems remarkable today. Hunter wines were known by the properties from which they originated as 'Dalwood', 'Irrewang', 'Kaludah', 'Porphyry', 'Cawarra', and the like, and not under broad generic titles like 'Australian burgundy' or 'hermitage'. There is an unfortunate irony in the fact that these old vineyard names – Dalwood, Cawarra and Porphyry, for example – are now themselves registered names emblazoned on unpretentious commercial products of no specific origin. In this instance, as in others, it seems as if time has passed the early Hunter winemakers by, washing over their efforts, principles and achievements as if they were of no consequence.

The story of winemaking in the Hunter Valley does not, of course, end here. Indeed, the history of modern family companies like Tyrrell and Drayton only begin at this point in the 1860s. But while after 1860 the Hunter was to maintain its own district identity as a wine-producing area, by this stage there were other exciting initiatives being taken in Victoria and South Australia.

châteaux of Bordeaux classified – where the judges commended the Australian wines they presented to them, likening them to the products of Madeira and Côtes du Rhône. King's own wines were successful and were among those served to Napoleon III at his table at the closing ceremony. While in Europe King visited von Liebig and toured the German vineyards. Sadly, he never returned to Australia. King's health broke down, and he died in London in 1857. In this same year his pamphlet, the title of which speaks for itself – *Australia May be an Extensive Wine Producing Country* – was published.

King was probably the leading personality of the first wave of winemaking enthusiasm in the Hunter

THE PROMISE OF VICTORIA

The great event in mid-nineteenth century Victorian history was not its separation in 1850 from the older colony of New South Wales, but the discovery of gold. This altered the face of Australian life, stimulated the already considerable growth of Melbourne and pushed settlement into the interior as swarming, gold-hungry diggers roamed the countryside in search of instant wealth. The gold generation, as historian Geoffrey Serle has called them, left their mark, arriving as young immigrants in the 1850s and staying to dominate Victorian affairs at least until the turn of the century. Victorians weren't the only ones who benefited. At least two South Australian wine pioneers got their start on the Victorian goldfields: John Riddoch, who established Coonawarra, and Samuel Hill Smith, of Yalumba fame.

Once the gold fever died down in the late 1850s the newcomers took breath and looked around for more settled activity. Agriculture in its various forms – and closely settled agriculture in particular – seemed full of promise in Victoria's comparatively well-watered and more temperate regions. Inevitably, this conjured up the image of viticulture in similar terms to those envisaged by men like Macarthur and Busby in earlier times in New South Wales, setting the scene for a burst of enthusiasm in the 1860s. As with gold fever, the fortunes of those who joined in the wine rush fluctuated dramatically. Wine production in Victoria reached an apparent peak in the 1890s, with the colony dominating Australian production, but Victoria's fall was to be dramatic. Federation in 1901 set the scene for South Australia's dominance of the national market which continues to this day.

In the past the vine louse *Phylloxera vastatrix* – which was first discovered in the Geelong district in the late 1870s – has been associated with Victoria's decline and South Australian supremacy, the latter remaining phylloxera free. But a single cause analysis does not stand up to scrutiny. It is likely that this was not even the major cause of Victoria's decline. It does not explain, for example, why districts like the Yarra Valley, which never saw phylloxera, went out of production. Phylloxera has undoubtedly obscured the Victorian story, which cannot be fully told here. But we might consider the economic fortunes of the gold generation themselves, the artificially boosted, State-supported nature of the industry, which collapsed when the market became glutted and props like protection were removed, and the over-enthusiastic ambitions of the vignerons themselves. The decline of wine-loving immigrant communities of German, Swiss and French settlers must be taken into account, and also the tastes of the predominantly Anglo-Saxon and Celtic population which leant towards strongly flavoured fortified wines, beer and spirits, and not the delicate table wines produced naturally and well in the southern, central and elevated areas of Victoria – something only now being rediscovered.

'DR BLAZES'

One man who clearly saw the promise of Victoria was John Ignatius Bleasdale, a Catholic clergyman who had been born in Lancashire in 1822 and who became, in Victoria in the 1860s and 1870s, the outstanding Catholic intellectual of his day. He was a

The Reverend Doctor J. I. Bleasdale (1822-1884), the outstanding Catholic intellectual of his day, a man of science and wine judge and analyst. Bleasdale devoted a large part of his very considerable energy and talent to promoting the cause of Australian wine. (State Library of Victoria.)

77

'Bonne Bouche' – *the jolly prelate imbibing. This image of Bleasdale remained familiar to generations of Australians long after his death, as an advertisement for Atkin's Quinine Wine. (State Library of Victoria.)*

man keenly concerned to advance the cause of wine and viticulture. Bleasdale's background was somewhat different to most of his co-religionists. For one thing he was an English Catholic and not an Irish one, and unlike most Catholic priests he had been trained in Europe, at the English College at Lisbon, Portugal, where he acquired a taste for wine and an interest in European agriculture. Later he was to become interested in chemistry – and was a trained analyst – as well as an expert in all manner of colonial affairs: technical education, mineralogy and public health. He justified his interest in wine along lines similar to those of Busby many years before in a famous anecdote which recalled his first experiences of the gold rush capital, Melbourne:

> As I walked up Elizabeth street in February, I think, 1851, I, naturally enough after a voyage of 100 days, bought a bunch of grapes, and then at once found myself again in a country that ought to grow good wine. Not many days afterwards, as I was passing down Elizabeth street before noon, I witnessed for the first but by no means the only time a dozen or so of bushmen, at the Bush Inn, near the corner of Great Bourke street, more or less drunk, who importuned me to have a drink, and one of them, having dipped a pannikin into a bucket lying on the footpath near the bar door, offered me the contents, say half a pint of rum and water, by the smell about half-and-half. From that time I turned my attention and all the knowledge I possessed then to forwarding wine growing and drinking as the one efficient cure for spirit-drinking and drunkenness.

Bleasdale's first appointment was to the country mission of Geelong and Colac from 1851 to 1853 when he returned to Melbourne and the seminary attached to St Francis' Church. In the Geelong district he visited the vineyards of Swiss settlers there and later observed that their slow and steady efforts towards wine production had been interrupted by the colossal demand for fresh fruit of all kinds which accompanied the gold rushes. He admitted that up until the

late 1850s, despite the enormous promise held by the new land, the taste for colonial wine could hardly be said to exist. The first successful promotion of native wines only occurred sometime late in 1859 or early in 1860.

Bleasdale, who was engaged in a scientific study on the subject, had already obtained samples of Macarthur's Camden wines from his Melbourne agent 'an excellent practical wine treater... [who]... could hardly get them off his hands, even at a sacrifice'. Into this indifference Mr J. Elliott Blake, formerly King's lessee at Irrewang in the Hunter and the Len Evans of his day, put something of a dint in sophisticated circles, as Bleasdale recalled, 'and in an incredibly short time made us thoroughly acquainted with Irrewang and Kaludah, white, red and rosy'.

> From this point the history of colonial wine in Victoria dates and starts. Till then no wine, the product of these colonies, was regarded as a beverage, which could be safely placed upon the table, save with great caution and an apology, and only in a few rare and exceptional instances; and it required considerable hardihood in anyone professing to know aught about wine to assert, in the company of gentlemen, that he could relish any of even our best colonial wines.

The vineyard and residence of James Goodall Francis at Sunbury, Victoria. Francis (1819-1884) was a prominent merchant politician and his vineyard, not far from Melbourne, was a favourite retreat. A wealthy man, Francis employed an Italian winemaker. The critic Dr Bleasdale regretted Francis' decision not to show his wines. (State Library of Victoria.)

Victorian wine labels of the nineteenth century. (The Troedel Collection of the State Library of Victoria.)

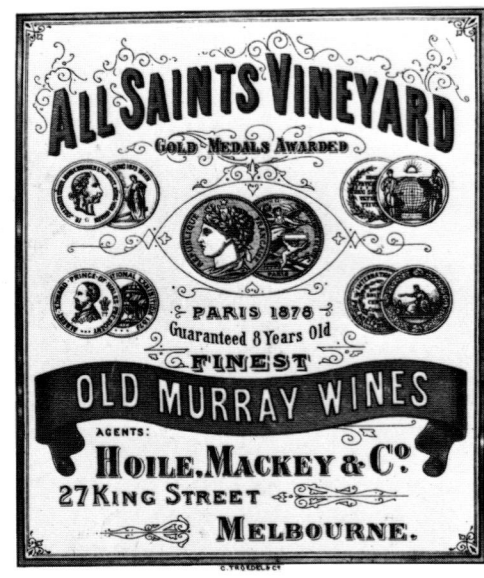

'The Vintage in Australia' — in the latter decades of the nineteenth century the great Yarra Valley estates owned by emigré Swiss aristocrats and noblemen came to the fore. (State Library of Victoria.)

Whether Blake was the catalyst or not, by 1861 there appeared a cult following for Australian wine that was not at all out of step with other preoccupations of the day, such as the zeal for exploring the interior of the continent or the acclimatisation of the birds, plants and animals of other countries to the new land. In that year the Acclimatisation Society sat down to a dinner at the Menzies Hotel in La Trobe Street that could not have occurred anywhere else in the world. Together with distinguished guests, including the French consul, they feasted on an all-Australian bill of fare, the delights of which included Cape Barren goose, porcupine (quills removed), wallaby, wombat, possum, black swan and wattle birds, together with locally grown fruits and, of course, colonial wines from New South Wales, Victoria and South Australia.

By this stage the vine was being promoted no less than it was planted. Earnest discussions on spacing, pruning and the like filled the columns of the daily papers. In 1862 the Duffy Land Act which offered colonists the long-awaited right to select small holdings also offered special benefits to intending viticulturists by virtue of its clause 47 – the so-called 'novel industries clause'. All across the country vineyards were inspired into existence, with or without the benefit of the Duffy Act: in the suburbs close to Melbourne, in areas like the Geelong district or the Yarra Valley where vines had already been planted, and in the new gold districts. In the Sunbury region close to Melbourne two politicians of the day – J. G. Francis and J. S. Johnston – quickly availed themselves of the legislation to secure land and establish vineyards. Two adventurers got up a speculation at a place called Tabilk in central Victoria; they were the poet and sometime associate of Charles Dickens, R. H. Horne, and a Burgundian with a passion for steam engines, Ludovic Marie. Desperate to begin they undertook the novel step of advertising in the press for cuttings,

Scenes from the cellars of St Hubert's Vineyard in the Yarra Valley: working a press (above right) and the centre of the cellars. In his book John Bull's Vineyard *(1886) Hubert de Castella wrote: 'To-day our gatherers are a curious assemblage of nationalities and characters. The pay is small, only two shillings* per diem, *with rations, but the work is light, the food plentiful and excellent; they get four times a day, a full tumbler of good wine each, and have all the while the luscious grapes to eat.'*

which they received and planted by the thousand. The venture deserved to fail, but it was rescued by the aforementioned J. Elliott Blake and sustained to the present day as Chateau Tahbilk by the efforts of two distinguished Victorian families, first the Bears and in this century the Purbricks.

Bleasdale revelled in this climate of enthusiasm. In 1865 he was appointed to a royal commission charged with the responsibility of staging an inter-colonial exhibition, and himself chaired the wine judging committee which reviewed the efforts of colonial winemakers. He was recognised as a disinterested authority as he neither owned vineyards nor made wine. A polymath capable of conversing with all manner of men, he regularly attended the meetings of the Medical Society of Victoria and – replete with samples – sought to convert them to the cause. In 1867 he delivered his paper 'On Colonial Wines' to the Royal Society, which he amplified for the first report of the newly formed Department of Agriculture in 1873. Some saw him as a figure of fun; *Melbourne Punch* dubbed him 'Dr Blazes' and a cartoonist depicted him florid-faced and glass in hand lolling atop a barrel.

He made some very astute observations which repay reading today. For example, he was well aware of the potential of the Geelong district, with its cool climate and limestone deposits, to produce wines of the hock and burgundy character. In his 1873 report he attempted to classify the wines of Victoria according to region, offering succinct observations as to style and quality. Ironically, Bleasdale was not to achieve lasting fame as either a critic, a man of science or of God, but as a crude commercial inducement which – to its credit – did at least further sales of Australian wine. Bleasdale's image was taken by one of his former parishoners, Charles Ager Atkin, as an advertisement for his quinine wine which became a great success. Bleasdale was represented as a jovial figure, serviette in hand, quaffing a glass of wine with the motto 'Bonne Bouche' attached. Of the hundreds of thousands of people for whom this image was to be part of their popular culture until quite recent times few knew anything of Father Bleasdale or his enthusiasm for good Australian table wine.

In the late 1870s he apparently became disillusioned with his lot in Victoria. A lull in the fortunes of the wine industry may have had something to do with this. Whatever the reason, he did not abandon his chosen beverage for he emigrated to another wine producing country of the New World, where he died, in San Francisco, in 1884. Unlike Busby's works, his have not been republished, and no memorial exists to him in the State of Victoria. In the neighbouring State of South Australia a winery at Langhorne Creek was named in his honour.

'The Vintage in Victoria: the Hon. J. S. Johnston's vineyard at Sunbury'. Like his neighbour, J. G. Francis, Johnston was a politician who took advantage of a special provision of the 1862 Victorian Land Act to establish his vineyard, 'Craiglee'. Johston built an impressive three-storey winery which still stands. A few years ago a cache of 1872 hermitage made by Johnston appeare on the Melbourne ımarket. Many bottles were still good even after a hundred years.

(State Library of Victoria.)

83

THE RISE OF SOUTH AUSTRALIA

The Saltram Winery in the Barossa Valley, South Australia, about 1890. William Salter (1804-1871) was an Englishman who emigrated to South Australia in 1839, moving to the Barossa Valley in 1844. In 1859 he and his son Edward (1837-1913) planted 4 hectares of shiraz vines. Edward later sold Saltram wine to Thomas Hardy, who encouraged it on to the London market. He died a prosperous man, survived by seven sons.

In 1895 an anonymous consumer wrote to the Melbourne *Age* commenting on the standing of the wines of the various colonies. About fifteen years previously, he claimed, those of New South Wales rated highly, but they had deteriorated of late. Twenty years previously Victorian wines were good, 'but now, I am sorry to say with one or two conspicious exceptions, our wines have gone completely to the rear'. Five years previously, this correspondent noted, South Australia 'scarcely produced a drinkable wine, but since that time winemaking has gone ahead by leaps and bounds, and it is now a difficult matter to get a bad glass of wine in that colony', and a bold prediction was made for the future:

There are a large number of competent growers in South Australia, and a still larger number of competent cellar managers, who between them produce palatable and agreeable wines, which bid fair to obtain the blue riband for Australian vintages in the European market.

Saltram Winery — circa 1890 — Barossa Valley

The reasons why South Australia came to dominate wine production in the twentieth century are complex, and not to be fully grasped here, but there is little doubt that when intercolonial tariff barriers on wine were removed after Federation in 1901 the South Australians were best placed to exploit the new national market. They had the capacity to produce the wines that were then attractive commercially – notably the full bodied dry reds then being sought for the British market – and to develop brandy and fortified wine production. Investors may also have seen a dimension of safety in South Australia as a result of the strenuous, and successful efforts made to quarantine it from phylloxera and its associated stigma, which may have been more damaging to Victoria than the vine louse itself.

There may be other reasons still. South Australia was fortunate to have a one-man brains trust in Arthur J. Perkins, Professor of Viticulture, Director of Roseworthy Agricultural College and ultimately South Australian Director of Agriculture. There were also the not inconsiderable skills of well-placed entrepreneurs, men like Benno Seppelt and Leslie Penfold-Hyland who were prepared to expand their empires. But there may be broader social reasons as well, like South Australia's free settler origins and its small-holding tradition. The German community may also have been a factor, although in the main they did not hail from the wine-producing regions of the Rhineland – as did those of the Albury region that so influenced developments in Victoria's north-east – but from Silesia which is not known for its wine. A close examination of the individuals involved in wine production suggests that determined, and in some cases idealistic, Englishmen may have been equally influential, if not more so. That says something about the Englishmen who came to South Australia.

VICTIM OF ECONOMIC CIRCUMSTANCES

Alexander Charles Kelly was not an Englishman. He was born in Scotland at Leith in 1811, but grew up in the sea port of Dunbar where his father worked in a bank. Young Kelly was educated in France and in Scotland, and studied medicine at Edinburgh, practising only briefly in his native country and then obtaining a post on an East India Company ship. Kelly's brother emigrated to South Australia in 1839 and this may have induced him to follow suit in 1840. At this stage the colony was not yet a decade old, but aspired to be something quite different from the penal settlements that had gone before. South Australia was modelled on the ideas of Edward Gibbon Wakefield and the notion that its sole asset should be land, and that by its sale other requisites, such as a labour force, might be obtained. The vision assumed a structured and primarily agricultural society with men of wealth and ability securing the large portions of land and a self-perpetuating structure resulting. Needless to say, the vision and the reality did not quite accord.

Kelly enrolled on the medical register and briefly practised in Port Adelaide, but he was evidently not all that keen on medicine. In 1842 he bought 32 hectares of land at Morphett Vale and began to cultivate his interest in 'agricultural chemistry'. By 1851 he had a vineyard of 3 hectares. Kelly's wine interests came to prominence in 1858 when the Geelong and Western District Agricultural and Horticultural Society offered prizes for two 'Concise and Practical Treatises on the Cultivation of the Vine in the Colony of Victoria'. Dr Kelly submitted an entry, but was unsuccessful, local entries winning the day. He was consoled by no less a figure than Sir William Macarthur – whom he visited in 1859 – that his was the better entry, and he encouraged him to publish. The result was Kelly's *The Vine in Australia* (1861).

This evidently inspired him to abandon his small holding and to persuade some of South Australia's wealthiest and most influential men to join in a partnership, and in 1862 the Tintara Vineyard Company was formed, intending to plant vineyards and make wine on 86 hectares of newly surveyed scrubland at Willunga. The responsibility was all Kelly's – clearing, planning, organising, architecture and building. He also had to obtain vineyard workers in times of short labour and high wages. By June 1866

he had 24 hectares under vine – 4 less than anticipated – and a further 8 ready for planting. In 1867 he published his second book, *Wine-Growing in Australia* which, together with his earlier work, was recognised as 'the best introduction to oenology available in the country', according to his biographers Dennis Hall and Valmai Hankel. 'They were critical

Alexander Charles Kelly (1811-1877), a Scottish doctor who saw a future for wine in the new land. (Library of South Australia.)

John Riddoch was a Scottish crofter who made his fortune as a provision merchant on the Victorian goldfields in the 1850s. Moving to South Australia, he acquired a vast tract of territory in the south-east. In his last years he served the cause of closer settlement by initiating the Coonawarra Fruit Colony. He died in 1901.

Peter Bond Burgoyne (1844-1929), the shrewd English merchant who found a market for Australian red wine in England. Burgoyne bought wine from Thomas Hardy, built a large winery Mt Ophir at Rutherglen and eventually turned his attention to South Africa.

works, examining theory and practice, and they gave access to the thinking of pre-Pasteur wine-growing in Europe and Australia.'

As the enterprise grew the problems became more those of selling wine than of making it, and in 1871 Kelly travelled to London. There he met a sharp young man named Peter Bond Burgoyne who was so impressed with Australian wine that he was to make a career as a merchant out of it and become a wealthy man. Unfortunately, he did very little for Kelly or Tintara at this stage, complaining that he could not sell his wines at a profit. Back at the cellars the wine began to accumulate. Hall and Hankel have claimed in their sympathetic treatment of Kelly that the subsequent purchase of Tintara by Thomas Hardy and the enormous growth of that concern has obscured Kelly's role as the real pioneer, and they defend him against real or implied charges of commercial incompetence, claiming instead that he and his wealthy backers were victims of economic circumstances.

There was, it seemed, little hope for South Australian wine in the 1860s and early 1870s. The local economy suffered from depression in the 1860s, and anticipated intercolonial sales did not eventuate as a result of tariff barriers erected by the two most populous colonies of Victoria and New South Wales. The English market had not yet become conditioned to Australian wines, as it later did. In any case British consumers were still enjoying Gladstone's 1861 relaxation of restrictions on the import of continental wines. Some time in the mid-1870s Tintara began a process of voluntary liquidation, and Kelly himself retired to the Adelaide suburb of Norwood, dying in 1877. The following year Thomas Hardy took possession of Tintara and, to his credit, was able to hold and make Tintara successful, the sale of wine in the cellars eventually paying for the whole property, the cellars, and the 32-hectare vineyard. P. B. Burgoyne was to become one of his best customers. The memory of Dr Kelly faded – although his son became active and successful in the wine trade – until 1977 when Christies of London offered for sale single bottles of 1864 and 1877 Tintara red wine, which attracted great interest, and in 1980 his books were reprinted.

Family and friends at Seppeltsfield, South Australia, about 1900. The founder of the Seppelt dynasty was Joseph Ernest Seppelt (1813-1868), but it was probably his son Oscar Benno Pedro Seppelt (1845-1931) who did most to carve out the Seppelt empire.

The view of Adelaide and suburbs from above Wood-ley's wine cellars. Market gardens, vineyards and wineries were among the hinterland agricultural concerns spawned by almost all major cities. Many of these have been swallowed up by suburbia as the cities have expanded. Despite the quality of the wine produced, many companies have sold their vineyards for real estate as the value of the land increased.

This surface here is only to be scratched. There were other notable late nineteenth-century figures like the Irish born Albury magnate J. T. Fallon, who for years tried to break down English trade barriers against the importation of high alcoholic Australian red wines which had been erected in the mistaken assumption that they were fortified, and the lengths he went to prove that they were not. Or, we might consider those who sought a very different style of wine, like the Italian Signor Bernacchi with his enterprise at Maria Island off the Tasmanian coast, or the great ventures run by emigrant Swiss noblemen and Melbourne businessmen in Victoria's Yarra Valley. And what of Coonawarra and the extraordinary development of the Riverland and other irrigation districts this century? What of Western Australia? And what of the spate of takeovers in recent times, and modern follies that made good like Rothbury and Mitchelton? Here surely is a rich field for a historian.

'Whiskers' Blake was employed last century at Hardy's McLaren Vale vineyards to scare birds away with his muzzle-loading eight-gauge shotgun. He's being told off by Tom Nottage, nephew of the company's founder Thomas Hardy.

A TRADITION
OF FAMILIES

Sir James Hardy

The Australian wine industry was founded by families, like the one begun by my great-grand-father, Thomas Hardy, who arrived in South Australia on Monday, 19 August 1850, from Devon, England.

He found his first job in Australia a few days later, with Mr John Reynell, who had also come from Devon, and who had established a mixed farm to the south of Adelaide. Reynell had arrived in South Australia just two years after its foundation and he gave his name – with an 'a' added – to the southern suburb that bears it to this day.

Thomas Hardy was paid seven shillings a week by Mr Reynell 'with the prospect of a rise in a short time', as he noted in his diary. He wrote:

This is splendid country indeed. Things seem very strange at first but one soon gets used to the ways of the country. Everything is looking prosperous. The wattle in the woods are in full flavour, some people have been barking them. The bark is used for tanning and it becomes an article of export. The fruit trees are finely in blossom. Master [Mr Reynell] has just finished pruning the vines... Peas are out in blossom fine. The man put in most of the seeds on Saturday. They have been filling up the vacant spaces between the vines with fresh cuttings. I hope to learn a little about vines and fruit trees this summer if I stay here... Tis rather a rough place for living at Reynells but I do not mind that much. He is a kind master and won't grumble if a person keeps moving.

Thomas Hardy (on the left) supervises vintage at his Tintara winery, McLaren Vale, some time around the turn of the century. The winery was set up so gravity fed the grapes, the juice and then the wine down through the winery, which was an old flour mill.

Thomas Hardy, founder of Hardy's Wines, with huge shiraz vines at Bankside, Adelaide, in the latter part of the nineteenth century. His great, great-grandson Bill Hardy, also a wine-maker looked at this photo nearly a century later and commented, 'Interestingly, the vine has two distinct fruiting levels, with an airspace in between. The ventilation, fruit exposure, crop-to-foliage ratio, and crop level appear to be excellent.'

They had to be enterprising people to survive. Reynell certainly was, and a portrait of him shows that character in his face. I believe the portraits of Thomas Hardy show that same determination and strength of character. It is that will to succeed that characterised many early settlers from England – and many settlers from elsewhere to Australia to this day.

So, late in 1850, Thomas Hardy left Mr Reynell and in the New Year he trekked east to try to find a fortune. He was a smart businessman, obviously, for he decided to drove cattle from Normanville, South Australia, to the booming Victorian goldfields, near Ballarat. In 1853 he returned to Adelaide to start his family wine company while Mr Reynell, gentleman farmer, continued to make wine in his Cellar Number One at Reynella.

The Hardys and the Reynells went their separate ways, though they must have met from time to time, as they were in the same business. From Thomas Hardy's vineyards and winery at Bankside on the River Torrens, to the southern district of Reynella was not so far, even for those horse drawn times. And at the time in 1876 Thomas Hardy bought what had once been a flour mill at McLaren Vale, and named it his Tintara Winery, Walter Reynell, son of John, was turning their family winery into a major force in the South Australian winemaking industry.

Like many other agricultural enterprises, wine-making *was* a family business, and remained so until well after World War II. That was perhaps the way of our society until quite recently, certainly in the lifetimes of many of us. I suppose it is also important

Unloading a wine vat at Chateau Reynella in the nineteenth century. This photo shows the problems faced by winery workers in loading and unloading equipment like this without mechanical aids. These jarrah vats were used for the storage and fermentation of wine in days before concrete and stainless steel were invented.

to remember that wine is basically a produce of the land, a primary product, and our nation has much to remain proud of, from the pioneering spirit in occupations including growing wool, wheat, cattle and making wine.

While my great-grandfather grew grapes in Adelaide and the McLaren Vale area, and the Reynells grew vines around Reynella, other families were doing the same thing elsewhere around Australia. The Penfolds established their dynasty in 1844 – marked later by billboards and railway ads that proclaimed '1844 to Evermore'. Christopher Rawson Penfold was a medico, like many who followed him in the Australian wine industry. He arrived in Australia to start making wine in that year, after training at St Bartholomew's Hospital in

London. He brought vine cuttings with him to New South Wales, and it is said that he dosed his anaemic patients with the wines he made, which seems very sensible medicine to me!

Another doctor, Henry John Lindeman, came from the same medical school in London, arriving in 1840, four years before Dr Penfold. He began his viticultural interests near the Hunter Valley in New South Wales. Today the companies that bear these two family names are no longer family owned, but they are among the biggest winemakers in the nation.

In 1849 Samuel Smith, a settler from Dorset, England, planted grapes around the charming hamlet of Angaston, in the Barossa ranges in South Australia. The Smiths and their descendants the Hill Smiths still call this area home. They called their beautiful

Waiting for a load of wine. The horse team is standing behind Hardy's old Currie Street premises in Adelaide, for many years the company's centre of distribution for South Australia.

The Reynells at their Homestead at Chateau Reynella around the turn of the century. Walter Reynell (in bowler hat) is with his children, Carew, Emily, Lenore and Gladys, plus a friend, on the verandah of the home. His father John Reynell began building the house in 1842. The restored house is now the head office of another family wine company, Hardy's.

winery Yalumba, which means 'All the country around', and that countryside is magnificent, with its cattle, horses and spreading vineyards with names such as Pewsey Vale and Heggies.

Below the Smiths, in the Barossa Valley itself, the English settlers' influence was balanced by immigrants more historically conversant with viticulture. Johann Gramp came from Bavaria and in 1847 he planted a vineyard at Jacob's Creek, said to be the first in the Valley. The first vintage was made in 1850 from young vines, and was a light white wine (perhaps the ancestor of Jacob's Creek Rhine Riesling?). Anyway, it filled only an 'octave', or one-eighth of a cask, and by 1887 Johann's son Gustav took over the vineyard and moved the winery to Rowland Flat nearby, where the giant Orlando operation is based today, with some Gramp family members still involved, though the company is now owned by Reckitt and Colman.

The Hardys lived at Seacliff, south of Adelaide, and most of us were passionate sailors. Before World War II I remember visiting the Hill Smiths at Yalumba when I was a young boy, and thinking

uncritically, 'If I was a horse, this would be a fine place to live.'

But the seas was the stuff of which Hardys were made, and I spent a lot of time near it and on it from a very early age. Yet I was also aware from then our family were winemakers, as were many other families whom we knew. This was something we all shared in our families' blood.

Wine was not just an enjoyable drink. In our household at Maitland Terrace, Seacliff, alcohol seemed to be the elixir of life. My mother used rectified spirit for the treatment of stubbed toes. If we children had a sore throat we had to gargle with brandy, lemon and honey. For football injuries it was olive oil with brandy. And if we had a stomach upset it was port and brandy – that works, I can assure you!

My mother Eileen – Aunty Eileen as she was just about universally known – was famous for opening a bottle of Hardy's champagne every morning at eleven, and it certainly didn't seem to do her much harm, as she lived to the age of eighty-seven.

The close family nature of winemaking was brought home to me with terrible force one afternoon when I was playing at home at Seacliff, overlooking the sparkling waters of the Gulf of St Vincent. I was five years old, almost six, and it was about half past three on 25 October 1938. I had just returned home from junior school and I was watching workmen paving an area of the garden with slabs of slate from old vats at the Tintara winery. My mum came out and asked me to come around to the front of the house, away from the men at work. 'James,' she said, 'you will have to come inside. Your father has just been killed in an air crash. We will all have to stick together as a family.'

My father, Tom Mayfield Hardy, was the managing director of our company, and he had been with Hugo Gramp, managing director of Orlando Wines, Sidney Hill Smith, managing director of Yalumba, and others on the 'Kyeema', a DC-2 which was taking them from Adelaide on their way to a wine industry conference with the Federal Government in Canberra. The aircraft was flying in cloud, trying to find Essendon Airport near Melbourne, when it flew into the slopes of the Dandenong Ranges, killing all on board.

It was a terrible tragedy for us, for the families of the others on board, and for our companies. Our industry was exporting a great deal of wine and was, unknowingly, about to face, with the rest of the world, a terrible war. For Thomas Hardy and Sons, it was one of a number of tragedies to afflict us that century. In 1905 our Bankside winery, established by Thomas Hardy himself, burnt down one Saturday afternoon. Many of us believe that accident meant

The Bankside fire put the Hardy company back many years. When Adelaide's horse-drawn fire pumps arrived on that Saturday afternoon in 1905 they could not get enough water pressure to control the fire, so in desperation they pumped port wine from the vats onto the fire. The result was disastrous.

Riding to hounds at Reynella. Carew Reynell, Walter's son, was an excellent horseman and at one stage earlier this century, leader of the Adelaide Hunt Club. He was also a popular manager of Chateau Reynella, and was killed at Gallipoli in 1915. The foxes, however, live on in the vineyards around his winery.

that our company did not fulfil its promise, to become the largest winemaker in Australia. The founder died in 1912, just two days short of his eighty-second birthday. In 1917 his grandson Robert Cyril Hardy died of wounds received at Bullecourt, in France.

Other family companies fared less well. Consider the tragic descendants of John Reynell. His grandson Carew Reynell, a handsome young man who was at one time leader of the Adelaide Hunt Club, also went to World War I, as a Lieutenant-Colonel. He was commanding officer of the Ninth Australian Light Horse (in which Tom Mayfield Hardy, my father, had also served as a lieutenant at one time), and was killed at Hill 60 at Gallipoli in 1915. The curse pursued his descendants: his son was killed in the air in Europe in World War II, with two other Reynells; his grandson was killed in Malaya in 1951. This was, perhaps, a grim portent for what lay in store for Australia's family wine companies.

As I was growing up I realised that all of the winemakers were family owned or controlled. The Penfold family, for instance, was the largest, with interests extending from their head office in Sydney to vineyards at Minchinbury (now a housing development to the west of Sydney), to the Hunter Valley, Griffith, and across to South Australia. If you didn't spot the '1844 to Evermore' signs on railway signs you might see on the stations, 'Tickets please – so do Penfolds wines.' (You might also have seen signs for Hardy's wines which boasted, ambiguously, 'Drink Tintara Wines – You'll never get better.')

Another family, the Seppelts, were big, with interests in Rutherglen and in Great Western in Victoria and a head office in Adelaide, plus a big winery at Seppeltsfield in the Barossa Valley, complete with palm-tree lined roads leading to the family mausoleum there.

Closer to home, our next door neighbour at Seacliff was one of the most brilliant winemakers of the century, Colin Haselgrove, a member of the famous family who owned Mildara wines. At that time Colin was technical director of Hardy's Wines and later to become managing director and manager of Walter Reynell and Sons. He was also, at one stage, technical director of the English wine producer the Emu Wine Company, established to supply sweet fortified wines to the United Kingdom. Colin was a master blender of wines, an art that many winemakers today seem to have either forgotten or discounted (not winemakers such as Wolf Blass or Lindemans, I hasten to add). Colin made regular pilgrimages to the Hunter Valley, writing home to my father in glowing terms of the wines being made there by people including Maurice O'Shea, the Tyrrell family and the Tullochs. In those days Hardy's Cabinet Claret (Haselgrove once quietly confided to me) was blended of a third portion each of grapes from the Hunter, the Clare Valley and the Barossa Valley. It's good today to see blended wines, with their complexity of flavours, coming back to popularity again.

Colin Haselgrove did much of the blending himself. He blended a pigeon pair of wines for the South Australian Centenary Year in 1936, Hardy's Cabinet Claret and Hardy's Old Castle Riesling. 'I blended the wines,' he told me years later, 'I chose the names and I selected the labels.' These days we have entire

At work in the Old Cave. Here in Reynella's Cellar Number One John Reynell started making wine, and Thomas Hardy got his first job in Australia. Jack Graves, Reynella's wine expert in the 1930s, checks his stocks in what has become Australia's oldest operating wine cellar.

marketing and winemaking departments to to those tasks!

The members of our family wine companies saw a lot of each other. I remember going to the Barossa Valley – we were mainly a McLaren Vale concern and most of the others were Barossa-based – and being awed by the size of the premises of Seppelt and Yalumba. When I went to school in Adelaide I was surrounded by or had contact with great names of the wine industry, people like H. M. Martin of Stoneyfell, the Hill Smiths, Norm Walker from the famous Romalo champagne cellars, Jeffrey Penfold-Hyland, Colin and Ron Haselgrove, the Angoves, the Seppelt family and later, after I moved to New South Wales, I was pleased to get to know the McWilliams. The extensive McWilliam family are still the largest family owned winemakers. Our families swapped young family members for work experience, beginning another enduring friendship between families. McWilliams have a number of big wineries in the Murrumbidgee Irrigation Area, and they bought Maurice O'Shea's Mount Pleasant winery. Our two firms have bought and sold wine to each other over the years.

Pressing at Houghton in Western Australia. Johnny Cox, who retired from the company in 1982, is operating a basket grape press by hand.

Then finally, years after the end of World War II, the long reign of the family wine businesses started to come to an end. When it started, the contagion spread like a bushfire. As the wine boom which began in the 1960s developed, family companies and family structures were put under immense pressure to either expand or sell out. Expansion was difficult because often, due to the family nature of the business and restrictive taxation and company laws, families could not generate the necessary capital to get bigger or more modern – or both.

Consider the takeovers, or some of them, that began in the 1960s and continue to this day. McWilliam's bought O'Shea. Lindemans bought Leo Buring. Tobacco giant Philip Morris bought Lindemans. Lindemans bought the Redman family's Rouge Homme winery (but the Redmans started afresh using their own name). Tooheys the brewers bought Samuel Wynn's wine company, who took over Ben Chaffey's Seaview wines; later the company acquired Tulloch's winery in the Hunter. Sydney brewer

Tooth and Co bought Penfolds Wines, which later bought the giant grapegrower-owned co-operative Kaiser Stuhl. Reckitt and Colman bought Orlando from the Gramp family. H. J. Heinz bought the Stanley Wine Company from the Knappstein family. Seppelt, after a takeover tussle with Adsteam (which also owned Penfold) gave in to the S.A. Brewing Company ... and so on. Doubtless there are more to come, and by the end of this century I have no doubt that 80 per cent of our wine will be produced by a handful of four or five big companies, primarily in the brewing, spirits or liquor distribution industries.

The company which bears my family name also recognised the need to get bigger – or get smaller. We chose the former course, and in 1976 we acquired the English Emu Wine Company, which included the Houghton Winery in Western Australia. Then in early 1982 we bought Rhine Castle Wines from the Walker family of Sydney and Melbourne, a distribution company. In late 1982 we bought another English owned company – John Reynell's Chateau Reynella (Walter Reynell and Sons Pty Ltd).

At last, many generations on, the wheel had turned a full circle. Perhaps I should say no more here than to express my belief that our company has treated this piece of living Australian wine history with the loving care which every Australian family winemaker, yesterday or today, would have expected.

What then of the place of the family winemaker in today's Australian wine industry? In the past few decades dozens of such companies have been sold to other, usually larger, companies. Often the buyers have had little involvement in winemaking, little commitment to the sense of history and little belief in maintaining the traditions of grape-growing or winemaking quality. Grape-growing itself is still largely a family business, with some 8000 grapegrowers scattered across Australia, but this industry is not without its problems either.

It is a tough marketplace, and even the toughest and fittest have to fight hard to survive in the cutthroat wine bazaar of the late 1980s. That is pretty obvious from a quick glimpse at the advertisements

in newspapers, magazines and on television, not to mention the stock market figures and the continuing takeover battles. Many of the best people in our business believe all this is going to get worse: more takeovers, more discounting of wine, more bloodletting, before making wine gets back to being a business operation which provides reasonable returns on investment.

Still, things were not easy for Samuel Wynn, Dr Lindeman, Dr Penfold, Johann Gramp, the Mc-Williams, John Reynell, or, indeed, for my own great-grandfather.

Some, I would like to think many, Australians believe that small and medium-sized wine companies offer wine-lovers what family companies have always tried to provide: fine, individual and distinctive quality wines. I include many families who remain in the business under this mantle. The magnificent Browns of Milawa, Victoria. The spendidly entrepreneurial Wolf Blass. The Redman family of Coonawarra. The Purbricks of Chateau Tahbilk. Newcomers such as Dr Peter Tisdall and David Hohnen of Margaret River in Western Australia, and Dr Andrew Pirie in Tasmania. Old timers like the source of the Hunter, the Tyrrells. And many others including, I would like to modestly suggest, all the members of my own family, the Hardys, descendants of Thomas Hardy, vigneron and vintner.

The team at Reynella was driven towards the end of the nineteenth and early in the twentieth century by Ben Sparrow. These magnificent horses hauled grapes around the vineyards and wine into Adelaide and its port. At the far left is Carew Reynell, whose grandfather gave his name to the winery and the suburb. The pigeon loft in the background was built in 1857 and still stands near the entrance to Chateau Reynella, south of Adelaide.

97

Robert Mayne

Camden Park Winery

*T*oday it is a run-down pile of stone, bricks and rotting timbers. But when the Australian colony was just thirty-two years old, it was the colony's first commercial winery.

The ruins of the Macarthur family's winery lie just 60 kilometres or so south-west of Sydney, inside the basin of hills which embrace Australia's largest city, surrounded by a patchwork of green fields and twisting reaches of the Nepean River near the town of Camden.

A few minutes' walk from the seldom-noticed ruins of the winery is another monument to the Macarthur family. Camden Park is a magnificent baronial residence, built outside Camden so it could overlook the spire of St John's Anglican Church, which dominates the township's rooftops.

Today the Camden Park property is occupied by Quentin Macarthur Stanham, the great, great-grandson of Captain John Macarthur. As he conducts visitors through the cavernous cellars beneath the house Quentin grouches good-naturedly about the restrictions placed on his family's occupation of the place by the National Trust. But the property is beautifully preserved, and the Macarthurs of Camden Park and nearby land, best known for their ancestors' introduction of Spanish merino sheep into Australia, are rightfully proud of their heritage.

It is not coincidence that there are large wine cellars under the house. The nearby ruins of the winery is today one of the sadly neglected reminders of our early colonial history. Lying

The old winemaking cellars.

near Camden Park estate, halfway down a hill, it is disguised by wild olives and fruit trees. The few visitors who stumble over the ruins appreciate that this was very probably, the beginning of Australia's commercial wine-making industry — and it was begun by one family, the Macarthurs.

In 1815 and 1816 the outspoken Captain John Macarthur and sons James and William spent eighteen months touring Europe to find suitable winegrape cuttings. They returned to

Australia and planted their first vineyard at Camden in 1820; then the winery was built on the side of a hill near Camden Park. Almost certainly on the Continent they picked up a few ideas about winery design in the days before electrical and mechanical pumps. Looking at the ruins today it is obvious that they appreciated the advantages of using the force of gravity to move the grapes from horse-drawn vehicles at the top through to the crusher, allowing the juice obtained to run downhill to the bottom, where they must have stored the wine in wooden vessels before bottling and despatch.

It must have been an impressive location for a winery. On 16 January 1824 (just before the vintage, no doubt) William Macarthur wrote, 'Our vineyard here is bearing a plentiful crop of fruit. It is the first vintage so the quantity will of course be trifling.'

Camden Park Estate; and its cellar.

Surviving photographs of the building used to make the wines, probably taken after 1860, show a brick structure with two pitched shingle roofs with a concrete walled pit – possibly for use as a primitive crusher – in front of a lean-to, bark-sheet-roofed verandah. Grapes grew all around. A visitor from England in the 1840s, Mr John Hood, described the 'winehouse':

Ten acres of the most beautiful vineyard imaginable, containing many different varieties of grapes, lay at a short distance from the house, and are managed by a colony *of vinedressers from the Rhine. This year ten thousand gallons of wine are expected from it, and next year a much larger quantity, which at four shillings per gallon would form a handsome item in the income of this wealthy colonist. The expense, however, is great, and a considerable outlay is incurred before any return. The winehouse itself cost twelve hundred pounds and is a most perfect construction.*

The Macarthurs were not the first people to grow grapes or make wine in Australia. But there is much to support the view that they were the real fathers of our wine industry today. Until his death in 1882 (after he had moved the Camden winery further down the Nepean to the Penrith area and was making some 75 000 litres annually) William contributed continually to the family viticultural and winemaking industries of New South Wales — and indeed Australia.

Vintage in Australia usually occurs in hot weather. Pickers in the Barossa Valley, South Australia, have lunch in the vineyard, and enjoy a chilled glass of flagon white wine.

WHITE WINES OF AUSTRALIA

James Halliday

A PERSPECTIVE

For most of the hundred and eighty years in which table wine has been made in Australia white wine has been the poor, and often forgotten, cousin. Not only was far less white wine made and sold than red, but all the critical attention was paid to the red wines. Not that there is anything peculiarly Australian about this: ask any expert to name the greatest wine he has ever tasted, and the overwhelming odds are that it will be a red. White wines slake the thirst at businessmen's lunches; in the evening they tune the palate for the serious matter of the reds to follow.

Yet in the last twenty years there has been a radical change: in 1962 sales of red wine were twice those of white, and total table wine consumption was a paltry 2 litres per capita. Today consumption is over 20 litres per capita per annum; more than 60 per cent of this is white wine, three-quarters of which is in turn sold in cardboard casks or glass flagons.

What has caused such a fundamental shift in so short a time? There is no single answer, but the most important factor has been the changing social context in which wine is consumed.

In 1962, 70 per cent of all wine sold was fortified, and much of this was sold in the wine bars which proliferated around the working class suburbs of the major cities. Table wine was the preserve of the

The crushed berries — in this case white grapes — are called must.

The leftovers. The unwanted stalks of grape bunches are separated from the grape berries.

upper middle class and was consumed with the evening meal. Since then wine has been taken to the heart of the ordinary (middle class, if you must) man and woman. And to an increasing extent, it has taken market share from both spirits and beer.

The cask has become a permanent fixture in the fridge and has almost replaced the six pack at the barbeque. Almost half (45 per cent) of all wine consumed in Australia today is cask or flagon white wine. Selling for as little as a dollar per litre retail – less than either Coke or beer – it has become the drink of the young. Equally, it has replaced the gin and tonic or scotch and water at the business lunch.

In both these extremes it is white wine rather than red which is consumed. Although it is of doubtful medical or chemical validity, the businessman has convinced himself that white wine does less damage to what remains of his afternoon's work than does red.

This open-hearted (or rather open-throated) acceptance of white wine has been tracked by equally far-reaching changes in its style. The origins of these

changes go back a few years earlier to the mid-Fifties, when Orlando introduced the German-developed stainless steel pressure fermenters. Pressure fermentation was soon replaced by controlled temperature fermentation, but the technology was essentially the same.

Prior to this Australian white wines were fermented in open, wax-lined concrete or old oak vats, and then matured in large old oak casks for twelve months or more. Some (notably Yalumba's Rudi Kronberger) had moved to early-bottled Rhine riesling, but masters such as Maurice O'Shea and Colin Preece continued to make white wine in the old way.

Whether a South Australian riesling, a Great Western chasselas or a Hunter semillon, you could be sure the wine had been fermented bone dry. It was equally certain that most of the aromatics of the grapes had been lost either in the inadequately controlled temperatures of fermentation or in the gently oxidative processes of the subsequent maturation. These full bodied, strong whites were not so different from reds, and were certainly constructed to be drunk with food. They also had an undoubted capacity to develop in bottle, with Hunter Valley semillons leading the way.

Nonetheless, to overseas palates they lacked both fragrance and fruit, exhibiting the same roasted uniformity which marked the reds. So, the *raison d'etre* of white winemaking since the mid-Fifties has been to capture as many of the aromatic fragrances of the smell and taste of the grape as is possible.

Success did not come overnight, and as late as 1969 the Australian Wine Board was encouraging the public to drink more white wine! But the winds of change were already blowing hard through the country's wineries.

By the mid-1960s stainless steel fermenters had to all intents and purposes replaced all others for white wine production, and temperature control of juice was generally available. This led to the development of techniques for the retention of a certain amount of unfermented sugar in varieties such as Rhine riesling, traminer and frontignan. Previously, massive sulphur additions had been necessary to stop fermentation

and keep sweet wines stable. Now, cold stabilisation and recently developed techniques of sterile filtration opened up new horizons.

Both at the quality end and at the bulk end of the market new styles appeared overnight. Ben Ean began the climb which took it from an insignificant brand (made in the Hunter Valley at Lindemans' Ben Ean Winery from pressings material sweetened by a little unfermented grape juice) to the largest selling brand in Australia, financing much of Lindemans' growth as it did so. The giant Karadoc winery (in the latter part of the Seventies crushing more grapes than any other winery) was specifically conceived and designed to produce white wine in the Ben Ean style (for both cask and flagon), while the equally large Padthaway vineyards of Lindemans were planted to satisfy the demand for the next wines up the ladder – Bin 23, Bin 77 and so on.

Ben Ean no longer occupies the number one spot as the largest selling brand in Australia, but the formula of perceptibly sweet, gently aromatic, slightly bland and distinctly soft white wine is still the basic prescription. Served well chilled, these wines are impossible to fault, so innocuously and pleasantly do

Full bins of white grapes are taken to the crusher (at left) of Lindemans' big Karadoc winery, near Mildura in Victoria. This is one of Australia's largest and most mechanised wineries, home of wines such as Ben Ean Moselle.

Technology makes fine wine, but manpower is still needed. Adam Wynn shovels grape stalks away from a destemmer at his family's Mountadam winery in South Australia.

they slide off the tongue and down the throat.

Australian white winemaking technology at this level is quite exemplary, and it is a constant source of amazement to me that people find it necessary to pay the extra for Blue Nun or Black Tower when there are numerous Australian equivalents for half the price. The fact that the Australian wines are technically better wines (made from better fruit) is apparently beside the point.

The next series of advances occurred in the late Seventies, some prompted by an unfortunate period in which the yeasts provided by the Australian Wine Research Institute turned out to be less than satisfactory. A number of the yeasts had mutated, giving the winemakers problems with both hydrogen sulphide and acetic volatility. Not surprisingly, this prompted considerable research activity by the private sector of the industry, and the introduction of a far wider range of yeasts than hitherto.

Reminiscent of *Star Wars*, 'R2', '316' and '729' are now standard parts of the wine writer's vocabulary, and discussion of the yeast character — its presence not always being regarded as desirable — of whites is very much part and parcel of the times. It is a debate, indeed, which becomes both overheated and confused thanks to other changes in technology of which the public (and, for that matter, many wine writers) are not aware.

These are directed to giving the utmost protection from oxidation to the grape juice and the resultant wine. Mechanical harvesting, initially seen as a pure economic expedient and inimical to white wine quality, has proved a great boon to winemaking in warm areas. Now a large part of each year's crop is harvested between midnight and 6.00 a.m., when the temperature of the grapes is up to 20°C below the daytime temperature.

In the old days hand-picked grapes would be picked into buckets, thence into 2- or 5-tonne tractor-drawn skips before being loaded onto trucks for the drive to the winery. Several handlings, and the sheer weight of the grapes in the skips, caused skin breakdown and juicing. More often than not, many hours would elapse between the time the bunch was picked and the time it was received at the winery – all of this in temperatures rising above 30°C. Such temperatures are ideal for oxidation, and no amount of sulphur dioxide will prevent its occurrence.

In an up-market modern-day alternative to mechanical harvesting, the grapes are picked into much smaller containers. In the boutique winery they may be picked direct into small, square, slatted plastic boxes and transported in these to a winery cool room where they will be stored for 24 hours before being crushed.

In either situation, the juice will be immediately chilled to below 10°C. It is either allowed to cold settle or is centrifuged before fermentation commences. An alternative is to allow the crushed grapes to remain in contact with their skins for up to 24 hours before they are pressed. This technique is used primarily with chardonnay, and to a lesser degree with semillon grapes.

The press will as often as not be of the air-bag type, in which a giant rubber bladder is inflated, gently squeezing the grapes against the slotted exterior. In turn, this may be contained within a stainless steel outer casing: these tank-presses are filled with nitrogen or carbon dioxide to absolutely exclude any possibility of oxidation.

In all circumstances, the amount of the preservative, sulphur dioxide, is kept to a minimum if not eliminated altogether. On the other side of the coin, enzymes are increasingly used to aid juice clarification; that juice may sit for several weeks before the winemaker decides to commence the fermentation. He does this by raising the temperature to around 14°C, and adding the yeast he has by now selected after carrying out extensive trial fermentations on small quantities.

It is at this point that the last of the new techniques and options makes its appearance: barrel fermentation. Since the mid-Seventies the use of new, small oak barrels for white wine maturation has grown at roughly the same pace as the use of chardonnay. It is now commonplace with semillon and sauvignon blanc, and virtually mandatory for chardonnay. But more recently, winemakers have been carrying out

the fermentation of part or all of their wine in new barrels. This is a sophisticated process, requiring a cool room (refrigerated) in which the barrels are placed so that the temperature of the wine in the barrel can be kept under 20°C. Along with malolactic fermentations for white wines, it is at the forefront of technology in Australia today, and more suitable for technical journals than a book such as this.

The maker of white wine in Australia today has a bewildering array of techniques to choose from. The great winemaker is the one who has the discipline and skill to select those techniques appropriate to the particular style he wishes to make, and to discard those which have no place. That may sound easy, but it's not. Take but one example: how few winemakers today are able to resist the temptation to leave just a few grams of sugar, regardless of whether they are making riesling (perfectly permissible) or chardonnay (an abomination)?

During and after the vintage, the winemaker has some hard decisions to make about his wines. Geoff Merrill is chief winemaker at Chateau Reynella in South Australia.

A middle-aged vine, at the height of its bearing capacity. This vineyard, near Renmark in South Australia, is flood irrigated from the River Murray, enabling it to yield an abundant crop of white grapes.

Grapes pour into the crusher at Arrowfield in the Hunter Valley, New South Wales. Some of the skins burst during harvesting or on the way to the winery, releasing some of the juice before crushing.

THE VARIETIES

There is only one variety entitled to pride of place, yet it is one which is in the course of falling from public esteem as quickly and as disastrously as shiraz fell fifteen years ago. Rhine riesling is, and long after the year 2000 will remain, Australia's most important quality grape. In 1983, 28 867 tonnes were crushed; only semillon, with 28 447 tonnes, came close. The boom grape chardonnay provided only 4627 tonnes, while the contribution of sauvignon blanc was too small to merit separate mention in the national statistics.

I suppose that I must accept a share of the blame for the decline in popularity of the grape. For some years I was critical of Australia's rieslings because they were all boringly similar. To make matters

worse, all were left with some residual sugar, and as the white wine boom really took hold, the quality deficiencies which occurred as quantities were stretched were masked by steadily increasing sugar levels. This period coincided with the yeast problems already mentioned, and I stand by the criticisms I made in the late Seventies and early Eighties.

Since 1982 there has been a remarkable turn-around. Chardonnay (and to a much lesser degree semillon) has assumed the stage, taking much of the pressure off Rhine riesling. Even brand lines, such as Hardy's Old Castle, Yalumba's Carte D'Or and Buring's Bin 33 are now virtually all Rhine riesling; five or so years ago such wines had liberal amounts of crouchen, muscat gordo blanco, sultana and/or pedro ximenez with some riesling thrown in for good luck.

Riesling, you see, means two quite different things in Australia: a wine style (which by no means necessarily contains the Rhine riesling grape) and the grape variety riesling, to which we have idiosyncratically added the word Rhine (perhaps to distinguish it from Hunter River riesling, which as any fool knows is semillon).

But I digress. Further up the quality ladder, riesling is enjoying a remarkable comeback, at least in my estimation. This is partly due to better material coming from the vineyards. It is also partly to the divergent styles now being made, with the advent of cool climate, botrytised material in addition to more traditional fruit.

The traditional Australian dry Rhine riesling is in a style quite unique to this country. It bears no resemblance at all to the wines of Germany, and little to Alsace. Riesling has a tenuous hold in South Africa and South America, and even New Zealand has paid relatively little attention to it to date. In Australia it has reached its greatest expression in the Eden Valley and Watervale (Clare Valley) rieslings of Leo Buring, made by John Vickery.

Those I have had the good luck to drink back to include the legendary Bin DWV12 of 1966, while I still have some bottles of the 1967 Bin DW83, 1972 DWB13, and the 1973 twins of DWC11 and DWC13. All are remarkable wines to drink in 1984,

with no hint of madeirisation nor the 'kerosene' character which develops with age. Orlando, too have made some marvellous riesling, by and large fuller and richer, from Barossa and Eden Valley fruit.

At the other end of the spectrum, and essentially a child of the Eighties, are the botrytised Rhine rieslings which have exploded like rockets in the night sky. Here the distinctive lime/passionfruit aromas and flavours are positively Germanic. As cool climate vineyards produce more and more fruit, and as Australian vignerons learn to control and harness naturally occurring botrytis mould in these cool vineyards, so will the taste become more common.

It lends itself naturally to the semi-sweet and fully sweet styles, those corresponding to the German gradation from spatlese to trockenbeerenauslese. The greatest naturally occurring trockenbeerenauslese so far made in Australia came from the tiny Seville Estate in the Yarra Valley in 1980; 190 litres were made in all. Spatlese and auslese styles are, however, common; they have come in recent years from Coonawarra and Padthaway through to the hills surrounding the Barossa (Yalumba's Heggies vineyard is a notable example), thence to Victoria.

Following in the footsteps of Californian winemakers, we have also proved ourselves adept at simulating natural botrytis. Closest to the real thing are the rack-innoculated botrytised grapes, placed on trays in cool rooms and sprayed with a culture of the mould. Tim Knappstein of Enterprise, Joe Grilli of Primo Estate and Tim Adams of Stanley Leasingham have been at the forefront of developing this technique, and have produced some startlingly luscious wines.

Another technique in vogue involves cutting (but not removing) the branches of the vine some weeks before harvest, and allowing the grapes to partly desiccate. This concentrates the sugar and acid as does the botrytis mould, but the wines lack the final complexity of the real thing.

The real question with botrytised Rhine, it seems to me, lies in the dry or near-dry style. Some magnificent wines have been made (such as the 1983 Hungerford Hill Coonawarra Rhine Riesling, winner

of four trophies in the first year of its life) but whether it will ever replace the traditional Clare Valley style as the nation's best remains to be seen.

Until recently semillon was synonymous with the Hunter Valley. Here it made a white wine which, with no assistance from new oak, special yeast, or cool fermentations, could develop in bottle for twenty years or more gaining in complexity and richness over the whole of that time.

Lindemans, its principal producers, were (and are) fond of describing it as either chablis, white burgundy or riesling (meaning, I assume, Hunter River riesling), descriptions which are of doubtful validity when the wines are young and which become quite meaningless as the wines age. When ten years old they all start acquiring a honeyed nut viscosity on the palate, and a voluminous burnt toast aroma – regardless of their baptism.

Of the newer vineyards, Rothbury has undoubtedly had most success. During the stewardship of Gerry Sissingh between 1972 and 1979 Rothbury provided a series of exhilarating young whites, none of which is yet past its best, and many of which are still developing. Upper Hunter vineyards have also made many excellent semillons, with unfashionable Saxonvale probably doing the most but receiving least credit.

While semillon flourished in the Hunter, it was the ugly duckling of the Barossa, so much so that Orlando were able to develop their late harvest styles at relatively little cost. Since no one wanted the grapes at normal maturity, Orlando were able to buy them on the vine for an agreed (and cheap) price, and let them hang until semi-raisined, at Orlando's risk. Initially released under a gaudy and shortlived label,

Goldberren, the wine has now graduated to half bottles of sauternes sporting a classy label with overtones of somebody's chateau in France.

This innovation sparked a revival of interest in the variety. de Bortoli in Griffith bought heavily botrytised material in 1982 to make the best sauternes seen in Australia for many years, and seem to be confident they will be able to repeat the exercise. (The 1983 was good, though not great.) But the interest also extended to its use for dry white, particularly wood matured. The Hunter's supremacy is now under constant challenge from many parts of Australia. Only the very cool areas do not have semillon planted, in seeming recognition of the fact that it is a late-ripening variety and therefore presumably more suited to the warmer areas.

Of the so-called 'new' varieties, one stands alone. Chardonnay was one of the 74 varieties brought in to the country by James Busby in 1832. He catalogues it thus: '48. Pineau Blanc, or Chaudenay – white. Produces indifferently; is the only type of white grape cultivated in the best vineyards' (of Burgundy). It is presumably descendants of those vines which struggled on in obscurity in Alf Kurts' Mudgee vineyards and at Penfolds' HVD vineyard in the Hunter.

The last of a batch of white grapes goes through the crusher at the Montrose winery, Mudgee, New South Wales.

In the vineyards at Rosemount Estate, upper Hunter Valley, New South Wales.

From the 1950s, and for all I know earlier still, Penfolds produced a wine blessed with the name Pinot Riesling (latterly Bin 365) which by some arcane logic might be divined as a blend of chardonnay and semillon. Chardonnay for long laboured in this country (and elsewhere) under the totally incorrect name of pinot chardonnay, which even the blessing of such an eminence as André Simon could not legitimate. So when Murray Tyrrell hopped across the fence in the dead of night in the late Sixties to help Penfolds prune their chardonnay, he too elected to call his first semillon chardonnay blend, 1970 Vat 63 Pinot Riesling, and his first straight chardonnay, 1971 Vat 47 Pinot Chardonnay.

It was a wine which fired the imagination of the public from the start. The 1971 vintage was deplorable in the Hunter, but the wine was (and is) remarkably good. Better things followed in 1972, and in 1973 and again in 1976 Tyrrell produced wines of such quality and character that the great lemming-rush to plant chardonnay was inevitable.

I cannot think of a significant winegrowing area in Australia, from Tasmania in the south to Mudgee in the north, from the Riverlands in the east to Margaret River in the west which does not produce chardonnay. Yet, from the late 1970s to the early 1980s significantly more chardonnay was sold than was made. As we move into the second half of the 1980s this problem, at least, will rapidly disappear. Supplies of the grape will equal (and I think exceed) demand; the rosy days (for winemakers and marketers) of high prices and empty shelves will become a thing of the past.

As the uncritical acceptance of any bottle labelled chardonnay diminishes, so will the debate about the areas most suited to chardonnay intensify. It is a debate already begun by winemakers, and one which will take a considerable time to resolve, if indeed it ever is. For at one level the debate misses the point we are trying to achieve with chardonnay. We are legitimately seeking to achieve a number of different things or, if you prefer, styles.

The most simple argument goes thus. Chardonnay is an early ripening variety, producing the

Late afternoon near McLaren Vale, South Australia. The vines, left, are about to leaf, and the almond trees, right, are in blossom.

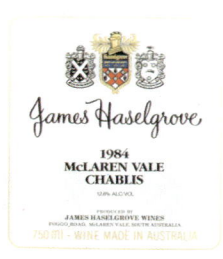

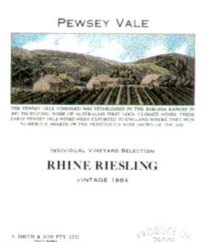

*Reg Drayton prepares
to taste one of his wood-
matured whites in his
Hunter Valley winery. The
milky colour will disappear
after filtration.*

greatest wines just south of Dijon (1115 heat degree days* or HDD) and around Reims (1065 HDD). It is a sheer historical accident that it was pioneered in Australia in the Hunter Valley (1874 HDD), a climate wildly unsuited to it, and it ought properly be grown in such areas as the Yarra Valley (1158 HDD), Coonwarra (1259 HDD) and certainly Tasmania (981 HDD).

This assumes, however, that we wish only to produce a fine, long lived wine which will probably take at least four years to start developing, and which will have distinct similarities to the wines of Burgundy. It leaves no room for the rich, buttery, 'peaches-and-cream' style, with a liberal topping of oak chips, which precociously blooms at twelve months, seducing all who take her to their lips. Such wines do not deserve the higher price tag customarily applied to them, but neither do they deserve to be thrown into the trash can like last year's pop ice-cream creation.

In every way chardonnay is a remarkably malleable grape, forgiving much mistreatment by winemakers and responding eagerly to a wide variety of making techniques and philosophies. It will steadily grow in stature, but it is necessary that both wine marketers and the public recognise the difference between medium and high quality wine; between that made for immediate release and that made for cellaring. Getting it all sorted out won't always be easy, but it should be fun. I say a little more on this subject later.

Sauvignon blanc remains an enigma. Until I visited New Zealand recently I felt that it had a significant part to play in the future of the Australian white wine industry. Now I am not so sure. Certainly I think it is worth persevering with only in areas as cool as or cooler than Coonawarra. In the warmer regions of Australia that pungent grassy gooseberry aroma and flavour which so sets this variety apart from others is altogether lacking. It normally makes a relatively bland wine, with much diminished varietal

This figure is derived from a viticulture formula to indicate the effect local climate has on speed of ripening, and hence the quality of resulting grapes. The lower the number the higher the fruit quality, as a rule.

character, and winemakers fall back on oak to fill in the holes, and call the wine fumé blanc.

This, admittedly, is a formula which has met with considerable success in the market place. But when the novelty of oak wears off (like residual sugar before it) drinkers are likely to require genuine varietal fruit flavour as a prerequisite to both wooded and unwooded styles. The sauvignon blancs of the Loire Valley and of New Zealand sell in Australia for less than the local product, and are, quite simply, better wines.

Nonetheless, Katnook at Coonawarra, Lindemans at Padthaway and Cullens in the Margaret River area have made some very good sauvignons, and better wines are probably on the way. Also in the future is the production of botrytised semillon/sauvignon blanc blends to make true sauternes-style wines. Here again the Coonawarra/Padthaway areas seem logical producers.

Next follow a tribe of varieties which enjoyed a brief vogue while the trend to varietal labelling was at its peak. Traminer has been around for a long while, as has crouchen (formerly known as Clare riesling), trebbiano (also called white hermitage or ugni blanc), chasselas (once called sweetwater), muscadelle (mis-named tokay) and a host of others. More recent additions include sylvaner, chenin blanc and colombard, the latter grown in increasing quantities in the River-lands of New South Wales, Victoria and South Australia.

These are ordinary varieties producing ordinary wines, which have tended to sell for a price not jus-tified by the wine in the bottle. Label buyers have always been, and will always be part of the wine scene, I suppose. But their fancies are fickle, and I cannot see these varieties playing a significant role at the top end of the market in the coming decades. All of which is not to deny that some nice wines can be made from these varieties from time to time. Wolf Blass shows what can be done with Riverland colom-bard in his Classic Dry White releases, while varietal specialists Brown Brothers and St Leonards have pro-duced some excellent wines from these and other even more obscure varieties (such as orange muscat)

over the years. Nor will I deny that some pleasant, softly fruity wines eminently suited to flagons and casks are made from a number of these varieties in the Riverlands, and there is no reason why they should not continue to do so in the future.

Mind you, the contribution of most of these var-ieties pales into insignificance compared to that of crouchen (14 000 tonnes), muscat gordo blanco (64 100 tonnes), trebbiano (24 500 tonnes) and sul-tana (51 000 tonnes). These are the true work-horses of the Australian table wine industry, accounting for 30 per cent of the total crush in 1982.

Crouchen is a declining, though still visible, force in the Clare Valley; while trebbiano bobs up all over Australia. In the Barossa Valley it is called ugni blanc, and in the Hunter Valley white hermitage. But by far the greatest proportion of these grapes are grown in the Riverlands of Victoria, New South Wales and South Australia along the Murrumbidgee and Mur-ray Rivers. Yields in excess of 30 tonnes a hectare are not uncommon, the principal factor in Australia's ability to produce cask wine at a price which (com-pared to the basic wage) is the lowest among all the developed countries of the Western World. What is

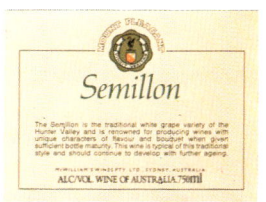

Getting the last drop. A cellarhand cleans out the residue from a centrifugal press at Tyrrells' Hunter winery.

Quality control on the run: Doug Bowen, right, at his makeshift laboratory at Coonawarra during vintage, talking with neighbour and fellow winemaker Richard Hamilton, from Leconfield across the road.

more, the technical perfection of this wine is virtually unchallenged in its price range; E. & J. Gallo of California would be the only serious contenders.

Over the past ten years Orlando have consistently produced some of the best – if not the best – casks and flagons under their Coolabah brand. Part of this excellence is due to their vast expertise in the filling of casks. They are acknowledged as world leaders: as the cask gains popularity in Europe the stream of technical visitors through Orlando's bottling line grows ever larger.

But usually there is not a great deal of difference in quality between Orlando and its major competitors, Lindemans, Penfolds, Wynn, Stanley and (most recently) McWilliam's. It is this very reliability which ensures that most casks sell on price and price alone: there is little brand loyalty. This has in turn caused the incessant price war which now sees the price of casks some 40 per cent lower in real terms than five years ago, or 15 per cent less on an unadjusted basis. It also renders any further discussion of style or quality somewhat irrelevant.

THE FUTURE

The past decade has seen the high-water mark in the unquestioned acceptance of two dogmas: varietal is beautiful and technology is all powerful. I believe that from now to the year 2000 (and beyond) we will see a more selective approach to all aspects of varietal selection and winemaking techniques.

This will represent the start of a far longer process, one which is likely to take the whole of the twenty-first century to run its course. This will see some resolution of the suitability of given varieties for specified areas. In France, riesling and traminer are grown in the Alsace; sauvignon blanc and chenin blanc in the Loire Valley; semillon and sauvignon blanc in Bordeaux; and chardonnay in Burgundy.

We will never see a neat division along these lines in Australia, if only because our climate is too permissive, allowing virtually any variety to ripen every year in all except the coolest regions. But hopefully there will be some consensus between winemakers and consumers on what styles we want, and where these can be best produced.

In the winery (and here I do not presume to look past the end of the decade) there will be increasing sophistication in the use of the battery of centrifuges, diatomaceous earth vacuum filters, ultra coolers, tank presses and the like, all of which have appeared over the past ten or fifteen years and are standard fixtures in the modern winery.

This sophistication will manifest itself as much in a decision not to use this or that machine as much as how or when to use it. Winemakers are going back out into the vineyard to taste the grapes; assessment of grape juice quality prior to fermentation is one of the most exciting developments of the past few years. (It is little short of extraordinary that winemakers should seemingly have paid so little attention to their raw ingredients.) In the same general vein, there is an increasing feeling that we may have become too clinical in our approach to white winemaking.

Whether to give chardonnay skin contact or not; whether to induce malolactic fermentations in white

Is this the future for the wine industry — more high technology? Spent grape matter, skins, stalks and seeds which have been pressed dry of their juice, are dumped from overhead at Lindemans' Karadoc winery.

wines or not; whether to ferment absolutely clean juice or juice with some solids; whether to pasteurise or not; which yeasts to use; how cold (and therefore long) should the fermentations be: these are all questions which the consumer is – rightly – not concerned with. You don't have a dog and bark yourself. But these are vital matters for winemakers, and the decisions they take will determine where our white wines are headed.

I believe we will see more attention paid to flavour and structure, to style. We have demonstrated we can produce wines showing exemplary varietal aroma and flavour, free from oxidation and taint. But maybe we have become a little too perfect, a little too similar. We need, and we will get, white wines with as much character and definition as red wines. Then the poor cousin status will disappear once and for all.

The way things were. Red grape juice and skins emerging from an old press still in use at McLaren Vale, South Australia.

RED WINES OF AUSTRALIA

James Halliday

A PERSPECTIVE

For the first half of the twentieth century Australia entered a viticultural and oenological dark age. The renaissance which has bloomed since the mid-1950s has been underpinned by the rediscovery of areas, varieties and even wine styles which our great-great-grandfathers knew well but which were then forgotten for three generations.

The typical Australian red wine of 1950 was red-brown in colour, verging on black, indicating its high pH. It had a distinctive roasted aroma; both its smell and the porty, jammy fruit flavours indicated it had been made from late picked shiraz and/or grenache grapes; and it was high in alcohol. The palate of the wine was packed with hard tannins which would take many years to soften. Oak aroma and flavour played no part in giving the wine its not inconsiderable character. Visitors from overseas stood in some awe of such wines, particularly as almost every one they tasted seemed identical to the last.

To be sure, master-winemakers Maurice O'Shea at McWilliam's Mt Pleasant, Colin Preece at Seppelt's

Great Western and Roger Warren at Thomas Hardy were all in their prime, making wines which by no means fitted this description. But their combined output was miniscule: the Hunter and Great Western were stagnant back waters, and the demand for quality table wine was almost non-existent.

Wherever one looked, the accent was on the production of fortified wine. Of all the great wine areas, only Coonawarra was exempt, but here most of the grapes were being used to produce (of all things) brandy. The Barossa Valley floor provided most of the red table wine; only the parochial Sydney-siders preferred the lighter bodied Hunter Valley wines to the jam of the Barossa.

And in the alcohol-starved post-war years, with a chronic beer shortage and several generations determined to forget the privations of wartime, the public was far from fussy about what it drank so long as it had the desired effect.

Yet the war had other longer-term consequences. It had introduced many Australian servicemen to other civilisations, other environments. Even if those who served in the Middle East did not become accustomed to Château Lafite, they returned with a far

119

One of Maurice O'Shea's famous Mount Pleasant Hunter wines.

more cosmopolitan approach to life. The war also caused the enormous influx of European migrants, for most of whom table wine was part and parcel of everyday life.

By 1960 it had become accepted behaviour for Australia's young to travel to Europe for a one- or two-year working holiday at the end of their schooling. By 1970 and with the advent of cheap air fares the overseas trip had become standard practice. The Australian steak and eggs had long since yielded pride of place to Coquilles St Jacques (my pride and joy as a bachelor-chef in the early Sixties) and ravioli (Sydney's Lorenzini's had been a home-away-from-home for impecunious university students since the mid-Fifties).

With all of these straws in the wind, it was not surprising that the style and character of Australian red

wine was about to radically change. But there was another entirely unpredictable stimulus. In 1949 a youthful Penfolds winemaker called Max Schubert went to France to study first-hand the winemaking techniques used in Bordeaux and to purchase the latest winemaking equipment to upgrade the then ancient Magill winery.

The experimental Grange Hermitage made by Schubert in 1952 was without question the most important single wine made in Australia this century. It proved to Schubert that the French techniques (as marginally adapted by him) would work in Australia to produce a red wine utterly different in style to anything previously produced. So different, indeed, that it was not until 1962 that the 1955 Grange swept all before it in the Sydney Show. In the meantime, Schubert had had to withstand the ridicule of wine experts (there were no writers as such at that time), and the censures and strictures of the Penfolds' board.

The vibrant deep purple-red colour, the clean rich fruit on both bouquet and palate, but above all else the added sweet spice flavours imparted by the new oak barrels in which the wine had finished its fermentation and then been matured were unprecedented. There was no other wine like it in Australia, and in fact there still is no wine quite like Grange.

But after that initial period of stunned disbelief, the practices adopted by Schubert were soon copied to a lesser or greater degree by every red winemaker in the country. The surge in the use of new oak barrels was accompanied by the rediscovery of the merits of cabernet sauvignon, one of the casualties of the dark ages. Schubert, indeed, would have preferred to make Grange from cabernet, but concluded that he simply wouldn't be able to get sufficient supplies, and so he opted for the readily available shiraz.

As late as 1958 only 230 tonnes of cabernet were crushed compared to 15 824 tonnes of shiraz and 32 228 tonnes of grenache in the same year. Max Lake braved the sneers and jeers of the old-timers to re-introduce cabernet in the Hunter Valley in 1963 (the last of the old plantings had been grubbed out in the 1930s); while until the early 1960s only a teaspoon of cabernet was produced in Coonawarra.

From the end of the 1960s, the Schubert principles were taken one step further (and modified) by Wolf Blass. Schubert made magnificently textured reds which needed fifteen or twenty years to approach their best; Blass makes equally complex though far lighter bodied reds which are designed to be at their peak when released four or five years after vintage.

Simply because he has been so successful, and partly too because he is very much *not* a part of the establishment, Blass has not been given the recognition he deserves. Certainly he has won more trophies than any other red winemaker in show history; certainly Wolf Blass reds are freaks in the market place, so seldom are they discounted. But there is a tendency to explain away his successes, to suggest his

A glass of red, straight from the tank, at a home bottling.

wines are manufactured by arcane methods and liable to become noxious if kept for more than a few months.

Although Penfolds do not like the comparison, Schubert and Blass also share a belief that a red wine blended from a number of different varieties grown in several different regions is likely to be superior to a single vineyard/single varietal wine. In this they have run counter to the other mainstream of development which has come with the establishment (or re-establishment) of new wine regions across the length and breadth of Australia.

The voluntary appellation control systems developed by the vignerons of Mudgee in New South Wales, the Margaret River and Mount Barker systems of Western Australia, and of Tasmania are tangible evidence of the belief in regional and varietal purity. The cynical observer might comment that there are substantial marketing advantages to be gained from such an approach and the more pragmatic winemaker might concede there are. But the far wider perception is that there is a special value in a wine made from grapes grown, nurtured, hand harvested by their owner/winemaker; made into wine by

The bright hue of a young red still in oak cask, here at Wolf Blass' winery.

his incessant care; and lovingly tended in the barrel, and bottled and sold by him (or occasionally her).

Sometimes there is, and sometimes there is not. The boutique winemaker produces some of the greatest red wines in this country, but also some of the worst. On the credit side, look what the doctors of the Margaret River in Western Australia (Pannell, Cullity and Cullen) have produced; glory in the reds of Doug Bowen at Coonawarra, Tom Lazar at Keynton, or Stuart Anderson at Bendigo; stand in awe at the best of the Yarra Valley (almost too numerous to mention, but doctors Carrodus, McMahon and Middleton are a worthy front row); and pay due homage to the skills of Lake, Robson and others in the temperamental climate of the Hunter Valley.

All of these makers concentrate on wines in which clarity of varietal character (as influenced by the climate and soil of their particular vineyard) is a primary aim. More often than not, these are wines which need both a catholic palate and a degree of patience to be fully appreciated. They are uncompromising wines made by dedicated but uncompromising winemakers; they are not made for the dilettante – or the poor of pocket.

In the middle range, as it were, are the good quality red wines made by the middle-sized companies. It is of enormous concern to me that the rationalisation at present going on in the industry may see the demise (through takeover) of many of these companies. Yalumba, Mildara, Seppelt, Tyrrell, Krondorf and Hardy have provided the red wine drinker with some marvellous wines at absurdly low prices over the past ten years. Indeed, no small part of the problem has been that the quality bottled reds have been far too cheap for most of this time.

This has been caused by the absolutely static performance of red wine. While white wine consumption has increased by more than 800 per cent in ten years, that of red wine has barely moved. In 1972/3 production was 26 018 hectolitres; in 1982/3 it was 31 856 hectolitres, having bottomed in 1979/80 at 27 667 hectolitres. But unlike white wine, there is as much red wine sold in bottles as there is in casks. It remains the preserve of the true wine drinker.

THE VARIETIES

Cabernet sauvignon is, I suppose, king. Certainly it is king of the top of the market. This is in no small part due to its ability to manifest its essential character wherever it is grown. Taste a cabernet grape in a vineyard in Bordeaux, Chile, California, South Africa, New Zealand or Australia and you will instantly recognise its assertive, pungent, grassy flavour.

Yet as I have already pointed out, it is a relative newcomer. Certainly small plantings had survived from the last century, but these were concentrated in the Barossa Valley and in McLaren Vale. A little was grown at Great Western and Tabilk in Victoria, at Coonawarra and Clare in South Australia, and in the Swan Valley of Western Australia. None was to be found in the Riverlands of the south-east, none in the Hunter Valley, next to none in Mudgee, and of course the new Victorian and Western Australian vineyards and Padthaway were not started until the latter part of the 1960s.

Today it is grown in virtually every district in Australia: in 1983, 4182 tonnes were harvested in New South Wales, 2048 tonnes in Victoria, 12 444

Ripe shiraz grapes in the high Barossa Ranges, South Australia.

tonnes in South Australia and 1168 tonnes in Western Australia. The total of 19 842 tonnes came from 3462 hectares of bearing vines (with an additional 302 hectares still to come into bearing), yielding 5.73 tonnes a hectare.

This low yield (accentuated by the drought conditions of 1983) is one of the principal reasons why cabernet all but disappeared from the wine map between 1900 and 1955. Under non-irrigated conditions in the Barossa Valley or the Hunter Valley it would seldom yield more than 3.5 tonnes per hectare; a totally unsatisfactory yield given that it would, more likely than not, end up in a fortified blend.

Since then improved grape clones and the widespread use of irrigation (or supplementary water, as it is euphemistically called) have seen yields improve greatly. Whether the quality of the fruit (and of the resultant wine) has similarly improved is a more debatable point which I touch on further when I discuss red wine styles.

Shiraz (often known as hermitage in New South Wales and Victoria) comes next, having been forced to abdicate because of the lack of any royalist forces to protect its undoubted claim to the throne. There are 6958 hectares in bearing, which in 1983 produced 45 787 tonnes, more than two-thirds of which came from South Australia.

For a hundred years or more it was the mainstay of the Australian industry. It has shown remarkable versatility in the widely differing climatic, geographic and soil conditions to be found in this country. It produces Australia's greatest red wine – Grange Hermitage – and was the only red grape of any importance

in Coonawarra and the Hunter Valley in the period 1900 to 1955.

Yet this very dominance has been one of the causes of its downfall. It was visited with the sins of its masters, the winemakers. When the brave new world of cabernet, small oak and cool climate viticulture unfolded, shiraz was unceremoniously consigned to the scrap heap. Those lucky enough to have any of the Woodley Coonawarra reds of the 1950s, Wynn 1955 Michael Hermitage, Lindemans 1959 Hunter River Burgundy Bin 1590, or 1955 Grange Hermitage in their cellar will know the magnificence of the variety. More recently Guill de Pury at the tiny Yeringberg winery in the Yarra Valley has produced superb shiraz, redolent of spice and the Rhône Valley. Yet there is no more: his customers wanted only cabernet or pinot, and resolutely refused to have anything to do with his shiraz – so out it came, to be replaced by chardonnay.

Shiraz has proved its worth in Australia for a century and a half. It is presently in critical eclipse, but future generations will come to realise it can produce wines of very different style but of equal quality to those of the cabernet family. It is salutory to

Bottles of red wine being taken out of stacks for labelling and packing at Henschke's winery at Keyneton, South Australia.

Red grapes ready for pressing. After initial crushing the skins, pulp and pips are pressed again in machines like this to maximise juice extraction.

Bringing in the red grapes at McLaren Flat, South Australia. The area is best known for reds and ports of flavour, but now white wines are making their mark.

John Brown Jr, winemaker at Brown Brothers of Milawa, Victoria. He makes an extraordinary number of varietal wines, red and white, each vintage.

remember that in the first half of the nineteenth century the shiraz-based wines of the Rhône were far more highly prized and expensive than the great wines of Bordeaux; and that the very best Chateau Margaux bottlings of the period proudly bore the word 'Hermitage' on this label to indicate the blending in of some Rhone shiraz.

Pinot noir, on the other hand, has been a consistent disappointment in almost all the regions it is grown in. If cabernet is the great traveller, pinot is the ultimate stay-at-home. Only in one tiny area of one country (France) does it produce great red wine, and even then only in one year in every three or four. I am reminded of the story of a French prince living near Paris in the seventeenth century who visited the fabled Romanee Conti vineyards in Burgundy to purchase vine cuttings so he could establish a vineyard on his own estate. He returned some years later to heatedly complain he had been sold inferior vines.

'Sire,' replied the vineyard manager, 'You purchased our vines, but you did not purchase our soil.'

Pinot has proved as difficult in California as it has in Australia. In both countries the majority of the wine produced lacks colour, body, flavour and, above all else, style. You have to be told it is pinot noir, and you then have to make excuses for it 'good colour for a pinot' and so on; a bit like 'some of my best friends are...'

The Americans have found that Oregon suits the variety. I think we are in the process of discovering that the Yarra Valley, Tasmania, Padthaway and the Margaret River can produce authentic (and occasionally great) pinot noir. It is perhaps some recognition of the lacklustre performance of the grape that in 1981 there were only 210 hectares in bearing (with a further 66 planted) producing a miniscule 1312 tonnes of fruit, less than 1 per cent of the red wine crush of that year.

Merlot is currently in vogue (on labels, at least), although so far plantings are so small that no individual statistics are provided. Along with cabernet franc and malbec, it usually finds itself as a blend mate with cabernet. All of these varieties threaten the position of shiraz for this function. Again I look further at this when discussing red wine styles.

Then there are the work horses: grenache (52 530 tonnes in 1982, almost all of which came from South Australia) and mataro (14 730 tonnes, again mainly from South Australia). Yet like the draught horses, they appear headed for oblivion, or at best for a vastly diminished role. While grenache is one of the most important quality grapes in Spain, with mataro also being important (and encouraged as a premium variety in Bandol in France), the two varieties in Australia have long been consigned to the anonymity of cask reds. With the surplus of better quality shiraz (and in the Riverlands even cabernet), demand for grenache and mataro has steadily declined.

Indeed, if the trends current in the early 1980s were to continue through to the year 2001, no grenache or mataro will be crushed in that year. An alternative and slightly less dramatic projection is for around 2000 tonnes of each variety to be harvested.

Harry Tulloch filling a wooden grape press with shiraz grapes at his Hunter Valley winery.

THE STYLES

Almost without exception, white wines are made from single varieties. The odd blends (semillon/chardonnay, semillon/sauvignon blanc, etc.) are as often the result of expediency as of any desire to improve the quality of the wine. It would be nice to say the opposite is true of red wines; in truth, it is only partly true, although I think the times are changing.

Historically, the classic Australian red wine was wrought from one variety – shiraz. In the Hunter Valley it made reds which were relatively low in extract and tannins, and which were not particularly deep in colour. This gave the impression that the wines would not age well, whereas nothing could be further from the truth. Between ten and twenty years (with the odd wine even longer, such as McWilliam's 1954 Richard Hermitage, still superb on its day), these wines acquired a velvety sheen, soft yet intense, delicate yet full of flavour. Rather like the French Burgundies with which they are so often compared, the vegetative/sulphide aromas and flavours, which could be distracting in the wines when young, integrated into the wine with age and contributed to its

Red grapes pouring into the hopper from a mechanical grape harvester at work in the Hunter Valley, New South Wales.

distinctive style. The 'sweaty saddle' or 'cowshed' characters of the old (and many of the current day) Hunter Valley reds are now part of folklore.

Although made in a totally different climate, the shiraz wines of Coonawarra produced between 1900 and 1960 had many things in common with those of the Hunter. First and most obviously was the capacity to age in bottle, for longer periods still. One of the most exhilarating tastings of Australian reds I ever participated in took place in the early Seventies at Len Evans Wines. We sat down to sixteen vintages of Woodley clarets spanning the years from 1956 to 1930. The 1930, 1943 and 1945 were my top wines, hotly pursued by the 1941, then the 1951, 1952, 1953 and 1956. I renewed my acquaintance with the 1953 only recently; it was no less startingly fresh than ten years ago.

This capacity to age apart, the Coonawarra shiraz reds were, if anything, even finer than the Hunters.

The tannin levels were (and are) extremely low, while the wines had none of the 'earthy cowshed' characters of the Hunter. Better acid and pH balances were no doubt crucial to the ability of these wines to age, and in the course of doing so, to scale the very heights.

But the birth place of Australian reds was the Barossa Valley, supplemented to a lesser degree by McLaren Vale to the south, and the Clare Valley to the north. Here over half the shiraz produced in Australia was grown on low bearing non-irrigated bush pruned vines, hugging the soil and rapidly reaching fourteen degrees of alcohol or more. These robust, ferruginous, tannic reds had found a ready market overseas between 1880 and 1930, often going to add stuffing (as an alternative to Algerian wine) to insipid French wines.

The first signs of change came with the increasing practice of adding a little cabernet to the shiraz: Orlando, Penfolds, Hardy and Yalumba were at the forefront of this move. Part of the change, indeed, lay not so much in the wine as in its labelling. Non-vintage brand names were replaced by vintage varietal blends, but in many instances there was no great change in the wine.

While the cabernet component was picked ripe (like that of the shiraz), it nonetheless ameliorated the jammy heaviness of the shiraz. The flood gates then opened; cabernet was planted at a furious rate; small oak added a totally new dimension. First Coonawarra and then Padthaway produced ever multiplying quantities of commercial wine of radically different style.

As I have said, the principal casualty in this time of rapid change was shiraz. Yet some of the new Hunter wine styles exemplified by Murray Robson and Brokenwood, are but one manifestation of a variety with enormous character and versatility. In the cool regions of Victoria some spectacularly spicy shiraz, outdoing the Rhône, come from vineyards such as Knight's Granite Hills, and from Seville Estate and Yeringberg in the Yarra Valley. The Barossa (and its surrounds) provides most of the material for Grange Hermitage, Australia's greatest red wine; while Coonawarra produces marvellous wood matured

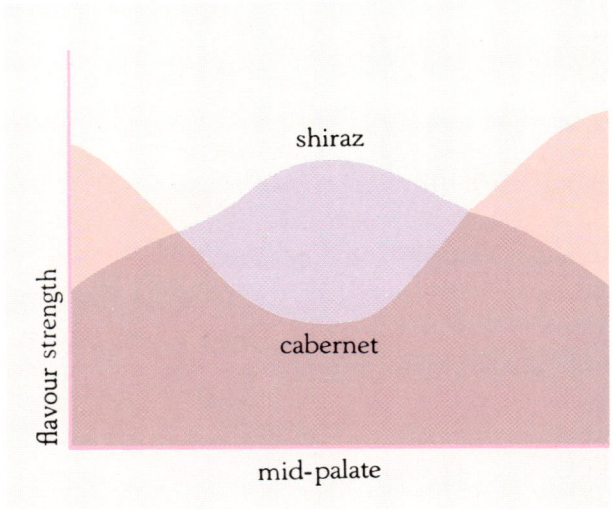

Winemaker Don Buchanan uses a steel pipette to check the progress of his red wine, maturing in wood in the Barossa Valley. The winemaker decides when a wine has picked up sufficient wood flavours.

shiraz with far greater complexity than even those great Woodley wines of yesteryear (look for example at the 1981 Hungerford Hill Shiraz). These are great wines, and time will prove their entitlement to the recognition they deserve.

But if there is a uniquely Australian red wine style, it is the cabernet/shiraz blend. Note I say cabernet/ shiraz, not shiraz/cabernet. The former means (under our labelling laws) that cabernet sauvignon is the dominant part of the blend, the latter that shiraz is the dominant part. It also follows that I believe it is cabernet which benefits more from the inclusion of some shiraz than vice versa.

More than fifteen years ago Len Evans devised some charts to show the flavour profile of shiraz and of cabernet; I adopted and slightly expanded the concept in an article I wrote for the *Bulletin*. These simple charts (opposite) show at a glance why shiraz is of such benefit in filling out the often hollow mid-palate of cabernet. In Bordeaux cabernet franc, merlot and occasionally a little malbec and/or petit verdot are used. The Californians, having gone through a virginal stage of varietal purity, have embraced merlot. Since Château Margaux gave up the practice a hundred and thirty years ago, Australia has been the only country to use shiraz.

In the brave new cool climate world – studded with boutiques – in which we live, it seems dogma that shiraz is inferior to the traditional French blending varieties. Once again, I am far from convinced that in

the year 2001 connoisseurs will view it this way. I think the answer may well lie in what style of wine one wishes to drink.

Penfolds Bin 389 Cabernet Shiraz has proved its class again and again over the past twenty years. It has its roots in the traditional style, yet it is very much a wine of the present and future. The emphasis is on the depth and richness of its flavour, the strength of its structure. Considerable fruit and wood tannins are balanced by fairly high alcohol (itself giving an illusion of sweetness) and ripe, lush, spicy, berry fruit flavours. American oak, especially seasoned by Penfolds before being made into casks, plays a vital role in creating the style.

It is a light-year removed from that of John Middleton's Mount Mary cabernets (a neat short-hand way of describing a wine which is a blend of cabernet sauvignon, cabernet franc, merlot and malbec). Here fineness, elegance and delicacy are taken to their logical conclusion. I would like to think there is room for each style in every serious cellar.

The Yarra Valley is as good a starting point as any to the new styles of red wines which have emerged over the past twenty years, and which centre on cabernet sauvignon. At the risk of repeating myself, straight cabernets were as rare as hens' teeth in the 1950s. Hardy made one (I well remember the 1955 Bin C9, a blend of McLaren Vale, Coonawarra and

Shiraz (or hermitage) grapes on their way to the crusher at Drayton's vineyards in the Hunter Valley. With mechanically harvested fruit some leaves, stalks and other unwanted material find their way into the crusher but not into the wine.

Eric Purbrick at his family's winery, Chateau Tahbilk in the Goulburn Valley, Victoria. The 120-year-old winery built its reputation on its reds.

Tahbilk cabernet); so did Eric Purbrick at Tahbilk and Colin Preece at Great Western. About the same time Ben Chaffey at Seaview started a line of wines destined to become famous, while Wynn and Rouge Homme produced small quantities of wines labelled cabernet sauvignon from Coonawarra.

The initial proliferation of cabernet took place in the Barossa, Eden and Clare Valleys and in McLaren Vale. Not surprisingly, the wines were ripe, chocolatey and warm, with occasional mint/cassis nuances. It was not until the latter part of the Seventies that grassy, herbaceous cabernets with real overtones of Bordeaux started making their appearance. Initially these new generation cabernets were greeted with unquestioning acceptance, not the least by myself. But already there is a recognition that green fruit flavours are not an end in themselves; that there is a happy medium between the extreme manifestations of cool climate viticulture and traditional 'Oz' burnt toffee reds.

This realisation has also involved a far closer look at optimum harvest times for red grapes, coupled with an increasing awareness of the contribution to wine quality made by acid and – above all else – pH levels. In warm to hot regions early picking may well be necessary to preserve any vestige of varietal character and to avoid the necessity of massive additions of tartaric acid. For a while some winemakers flirted with the same approach in cool climate regimes: many say Owen Redman fell into this trap in the 1970s.

In truth, ripeness and optimum flavours are an ever moving target. This cannot be determined on the laboratory bench (although some assistance may be gained there) and it varies from region to region and from year to year. The great cabernets of today (such as the 1982 Petaluma Cabernet) get this immensely complex equation right. The wine has suppleness, richness and backbone; it also has finesse, crispness and elegance. Most importantly, these characters are in harmony, and one is left in no doubt it will be a great wine in ten years' time. Whether it will be greater in twenty (or even thirty) years' time is one of the reasons I keep adding to my cellar.

THE FUTURE

In the short term much of the work will concentrate upon methods of maximising fruit flavour. This will turn in part upon vineyard techniques, and in part on winemaking improvements. In the winery some of the benefits of white wine technology will spill over into red winemaking. Other approaches, notably the Hickinbotham carbonic maceration process, hold much promise.

In the vineyard closer spacing of vines, new trellising techniques, and a wider selection of grape varieties will all contribute. Indeed, I think it true to say that it is in the vineyard that the next great step forward will occur. While viticultural practices are important for white wines, they are absolutely critical for red wine quality. Radical changes are taking place in vineyard management techniques and philosophies. Some are directed to maximising yield and minimising labour costs; others are directed purely and simply to improving grape quality by controlling yields to a predetermined level, lowering pH and enhancing grape flavour in so doing.

As ever, there is an element of rediscovery in all this. Close spacing of vines will be seen more and more in cool climates, coupled with canopy control techniques which are either copied or adapted from those in use in France for hundreds of years. Our first vineyards in this country were close spaced, and

those in France remain so. The advent of the tractor, and the realisation that it was possible to achieve the same yield per hectare with a quarter of the number of vines, pushed the rows apart and lengthened the distance between vines along the rows.

The return to higher density planting (from 1700 vines to the hectare to 5000) is not directed to increasing yield, but simply to quality. More, smaller bunches with less leaf cover is the aim. There are other sophisticated trellising techniques directed to the same end (not involving close spacing), but they fall outside the scope of a book such as this.

Nonetheless, the importance of the changes taking place in the vineyard cannot be over-emphasised. For too long we have been a nation of winemakers, not a nation of viticulturalists. We have got it pretty right in the winery; all we need now is better (not necessarily more) grapes.

After the vintage the grapevines' leaves turn yellow, then gold, then red, as they wait for the pruners. In the Hunter Valley.

Draining red wine from an oak barrel in the Hunter Valley, New South Wales.

133

People who love wine respect it, and what they respect they do not abuse.

ON WINE

Walter James

Wine, properly regarded, is a song without words. It is a gift of nature that wise men through long ages have loved by instinct without the needless prompting of speech and of books. But for all that most of us like to talk (and a few to write) about it because we want others to share our joy. No man likes to keep good wine to himself.

Why do we so love wine? Is there a reason for it? Few people get through life without a good many rough passages; fewer get through many days without some petty and pin-pricking irritation or annoyance. For these troubles wine is the great consoler, bestowing a soothing caress which never palls. This is due largely – let us disdain hypocrisy – to its alcohol, that precious emollient wholly beneficent in its use, malevolent only in its abuse, which helps us over the rubs of life and keeps us happily indifferent to the false allure of less innocuous consolations. True winelovers do not smoke reefers or dabble clean fingers in cocaine.

Alcohol is not an evil and never has been; only in excess (as with bread, potatoes, fat, sugar, salt and a dozen other things) does it invite trouble, but wine announces its own satiety and confirmed winelovers are seldom tempted to exceed overmuch. Men who love wine respect it, and what we respect we do not abuse.

Alcohol is integral to wine though some few people, I am told, find a strange pleasure in unfermented grape juice, which I myself once tasted. But alcohol, though important, by no means embraces the whole charm of wine. Alcohol is rather a catalyst – something that holds other factors together and acts as a stabiliser, for without the supporting arm of alcohol wine would soon fall by the wayside and decline into ditchwater.

The attractions of bouquet, of flavour and of aftertaste reveal themselves in succession but only when we drink slowly; wine, if we are to receive its full benison, may on no account be rushed. If worth drinking it should be sipped and relished, not just swallowed down with a distant mind while we bandy social fripperies. Wine took a lot of trouble in the winery; surely it is worthy of just a little trouble at the table.

But to drink fine wine every day is in my view a great mistake, altogether apart from the cost. Let wine be a daily companion but fine wine a less frequent visitor, for while choice vintages may not cloy

135

they can soon be taken for granted and so the impact of contrast will be lost. After savouring common weekday wines, how good that special weekend bottle will taste!

Contrast and change are what adorn the pathway to pleasure, as they do indeed spice certain of life's joys other than wine. One is reminded of the young French chatelaine who, sad at the waning affection of her husband, thought it would be an idea to enrol the help of the village priest. He had a most persuasive voice. One never knew.

'He is such a nice old man,' she told her errant husband, 'but so poor. It would be a kindness to have him at the chateau for a week or two to let him enjoy a spell of the larger life.'

The lord of the manor, who sensed what was in the wind, agreed at once and the abbé was installed.

'Tell me, my dear abbé,' asked the welcoming nobleman, 'what is your favourite dish and I shall see that you have it in plenty?'

'Ah, monsieur,' the old man replied, 'of all the worldly things permitted to my order I think partridge is the most delectable.'

The gamekeeper was instructed to provide partridges every day.

At their first dinner, with hot roast partridge, the abbé was suffused in ecstasy. Never had he tasted such a bird. The next day cold partridge at luncheon was delightful too. At dinner that night the partridge was still good, but had slightly less flavour than before. The same strange fault seemed to show itself in the cold bird at luncheon. After a week the abbé

plucked up courage enough to beg his host for a change of diet.

'But, Monsieur l'Abbé, you astonish me. You said partridge was your favourite dish and I have been at pains to provide it for you.'

'Ah, monsieur, I am not ungrateful, but here it is *perdrix, perdrix, toujours perdrix.* Could I not tonight have just a simple mutton chop for a change?'

The count looked at the old man with the faintest hint of a smile. 'I think, Monsieur l'Abbé, we understand one another.' The abbé blushed.

Whether the count developed a tolerance of mutton chops the story does not tell but its moral is plain. Do not yearn for partridge – or for Mouton – every night.

In Australia today there are any number of good sound wines for everyday consumption (dare one call them mutton-chop wines?) which are available for a modest outlay if you take the trouble to shop around. From observation, though not from experience, I know that there are also lots of wines even more moderately priced and put up in what appear to be discarded shoe boxes. These I have not tried, for there is a limit to those modern customs to which an old man can adjust himself.

This brings to mind a strange feature of drinking habits in Australia today. Putting wine into bottles and properly corking it is not a cheap process. Its purpose is to hold the wine until it has been given the chance to display itself adorned in the garments of maturity in place of the pinafores of childhood – let us say, just as rule of thumb, three years for a white wine and seven for red. Only then does well-made wine have a chance of showing its worth.

Wine must be given the opportunity to grow up; in spite of modern methods and inventions it cannot be made on Monday to be consumed on Tuesday; its inevitable rough edges and childish crudities may be smoothed only with time. The time increases with the weight of the wine – little for a light dry white; more, much more for a full bodied red. So when you draw the cork after it has had hardly time to moisten you throw away all the benefit of bottling. So-called 'freshness', lauded by winemakers who want to quit their vintages quickly, is a virtue in unfermented fruit juices but it is no virtue in wine, whose caress must be matronly rather than virginal.

With fortified wines maturity is not just important but essential to their development. Young sherries and young ports may pass young palates; they may be readily avoided by paying a modest premium. Sherry in this country is shrouded in something of a mystery. Why has it in recent years gone so out of fashion? For it has, with its sales quite stagnant, and this in spite of the fact that, at all events in my opinion, no other of our wines has shown so great an improvement over the past ten or twenty years. The best of our dry sherries, and there are many to choose from, are exceptionally good, yet for some reason – or maybe no reason, just fashion – they languish on the merchants' shelves while light dry whites are taken up overnight.

Our ports seem to retain their position, if not quite the position they occupied in the bad old days when the few Australians who condescended to drink wine at all took it for after-effect rather than present joy. Our ports may not be so good as the Portuguese but the best of them are for all that a delectable tipple, and here lurks a danger. Port is a most beguiling wine which it is so easy, so very easy, to drink a little too freely, as our English ancestors knew so well. With port we must be firm in restraint. Let the decanter go round the table twice and, unless you belong to the sturdy kangaroo-hunting farmer type, twice only. Muscat, that slightly out-of-fashion but excellent dessert wine, must like port be mature to be good. A friend once assured me that old muscat and ripe persimmons made the most piquant of gustatory nuptials.

Wine and civilisation have ever walked hand in hand. Which is the elder of the two I have no means of knowing but it is certain that practically all the worthwhile values in life have been developed in the great winegrowing lands. Palestine and Greece, Italy and Spain, France and the Rhineland – what a breed of world-weary morons we would be without them! What have the wineless lands bequeathed to us? The wandering nomads of the untilled steppes were reduced to fermenting their mares' milk into what they called koumiss (though I may not disparage a delight I have never known).

The savage British Druid-ruled islanders could do no better than rob beehives to make mead, emerging fearfully a step or two from their smoky caves only when they gained the wit to grow barley and make beer, but sadly they lacked the skill to plant vines. They left us nothing. The Scandinavians scratched frost-bitten fields for anything that might serve to make a coarse aqua vitae which after long centuries managed to inspire a few tormented playwrights and tremulous pianists. The desert-bred Saracens, perforce content with water, have left us only a few hints in architecture and the seductive charms of algebra. The Russians, when potatoes came over from Peru, could do no better than turn them into soul-destroying vodka to provoke novels of harrowing gloom. What a sad, arid record have these vineless people to boast! How little have they bequeathed to us to make the sentence of life more tolerable, let alone contributing to its fragile joy. What a pitiful contrast to the glory that was Greece and the grandeur that was Rome!

Wine is an intensely subjective, personal experience and one must curb any temptation to be opinionated and lay down laws about it. Having drunk wine, with nothing but good and gratitude, every day for sixty years I can feel only pity for those who have deprived themselves of one of the great consolations of life. But I repress any wish to rebuke, or to instruct, their folly. (Where I have failed please judge with charity.)

Wine, either heavy or light, makes the most constant of good companions. It eases the loneliness which, whether we hear it clearly or not, is the background music to most people's lives. Wine shapes and fits into our moods and talks with us, or at least whispers, but never quarrels, never rebukes our faults and errors. He was a wise man who once said there are four things really worth cherishing in life – old friends to talk with, old books to read, old wood to burn and old wine to drink. The rest, he said, were not worth the pursuit.

This might be the popular image of how grapes are made into wine, but not too much wine is made this way today. Here two enthusiastic revellers take part in a grape treading competition at the Easter Wine Festival in Clare, South Australia.

WINES AND WINERIES OF SOUTH AUSTRALIA

Paul Lloyd

ADELAIDE

To talk of the Adelaide wine region is largely to talk of history. Of course, the free settled colony that was to become the State of South Australia, with its advanced views of lifestyles, was quick to plant the vine, the South Australian Company having sent cuttings which struck and thrived in its nursery on the banks of the central Torrens River near Hackney. Some came from Hobart Town, others from the Busby collection in New South Wales. John Hack in Chichester Gardens (in what is now the fashionable suburb of North Adelaide), George Stevenson in his orchard to the north of the town, and Moor's garden down at the Reed Beds, had all shown that the vine would flourish. Its culture spread to the foothills, south to McLaren Vale, and later north to the Barossa.

George McEwin, a pioneer horticulturist, writing in an almanac of 1849, forecast that wine 'would become a source of great wealth to the colony, the climate and soil being ideal'. He believed wine 'rivalling the most famous growths of the old world will be produced in South Australia as soon as we gain the requisite knowledge and practical experience necessary to success'.

The winery that gave its name to one of Australia's most famous red wines, Penfolds Grange.

But the pioneers, mainly English and some of whom might have had some experience of the English vineyards which had by about that time gone into decline, were novices and their practices shocked those who came from continental Europe. The Silesians, and others from what is now Germany, were to make many great and distinctive contributions to the life of South Australia, but none as important as their introduction of Teutonically thorough winemaking practices. They were to head north to the Barossa, but they left Adelaide's viticulture the better for their passing.

In 1861 the *Advertiser* newspaper was able to report on 42 vineyards in and around Adelaide, and note at least another 18 still unreported. The peak came in 1925 with about 1570 hectares in the metropolitan region under vine, becoming through the century a lubricant to the economy, an export earner, a key to tourism, a source of pride and an essential part of the relaxed and civilised lifestyle of the populace, the vines being valuable as plants, as greenery, as spiritual refreshment, and as lungs to the growing city.

But this century, also, there has been a gradual whittling away, as vineyard owners succumbed to commercial pressures, allowing the real estate developers, and even supposedly enlightened governments, to join in a merry pack rape by replanting the greenery with tacky housing, tedious red roofs, rotary clothes hoists and Sunday motor mowers, cluttering the city at the expense of the potential of its satellites, and in direct contravention of Adelaide's original planning philosophies, which were for rings of green. The redevelopments have been ugly, they have eroded Adelaide's understanding of its proud wine heritage and, worst of all, they have tended to dehumanise, in that people's contact with nature becomes increasingly locked in the clammy maw of commerce. The vines that are ripped out are not an industrial inefficiency to be cast aside like spent chocolate wrappers; they are a reminder of the earth, which is our mother.

Still, up until the 1980s, Adelaide was able to boast the world's most significant suburban vineyards,

exceeded only by Vienna which has 760 hectares within its metropolitan boundaries.

Despite some intense passions, the bulldozers in 1984 moved in on the Grange at Magill which had been founded by Dr Christopher Rawson Penfold in 1844 and which must have been then, as much as through the succeeding 140 years, a sight of refreshing joy for all Adelaide residents who cast their eyes towards the foothills. All that remained were the winery buildings and a small surround of vines, giving once proud Adelaide fewer than 20 hectares in total of vineyards.

Penfolds, with its head office in Sydney and its muscle in the Barossa, thus kept some presence at its original home. It also continued as home, even in

semi-retirement, for Max Schubert, whose half a century with the company peaked with his invention of Australia's most noted wine, Grange Hermitage.

Rising from the traditional start as 'the boy', Schubert learnt diligently, he sparkled with personality, and he impressed with his innovative winemaking, abolishing wine-tainting copper and iron machinery, and introducing refrigeration and temperature control of fermentation. After a trip around European wine regions he introduced his bombshell: Grange Hermitage, named 'Grange', after the original Penfold cottage in the vineyards, and 'Hermitage', a synonym for shiraz. He had to battle for the style, which he developed in 1951. He made the first commercial quantity in 1952.

The man who made Grange Hermitage, Max Schubert, now retired from active winemaking but still a director of Penfolds Wines, dabbles with wines at his cottage at the company's Magill Winery. His first commercial quantity of Grange Hermitage was made in 1952.

Young vines growing on the slopes of the Mount Lofty Ranges, or Adelaide Hills, at Piccadilly, about 12 kilometres south-east of the city. Booth's wine tanker is carrying wine for the nearby Petaluma winery, operated by Brian Croser and Len Evans.

What remains of the vineyards established by Dr Penfold at the Grange in the 1840s. Houses have been creeping around the winery in suburban Adelaide for years, but in 1984 there was a storm of controversy when Penfolds bulldozed much of the remaining vines to make way for a housing development.

mate tribute to Max Schubert, for example, the Bin 60a, generally considered the greatest red wine ever made in Australia.

Like Penfolds, several other companies held on in Adelaide, although their operational centres moved out. Woodley — maker of the popular and beautifully labelled Queen Adelaide range which was named in 1961 after the consort of King William IV, as the city of Adelaide had been named 125 years earlier — nestles with rosemary and lavender hedges in the dress-circle suburb of Glen Osmond, and with maturation cellars in long mine drives into the hills behind. But the building of a new winery in the Barossa rendered this a purely cosmetic head office. Angove's at Tea Tree Gully was eclipsed by its Renmark headquarters. D. A. Tolley's vineyards at Hope Valley, although the Pedare winery continued, have been overtaken by the company's Barossa holdings. Other companies, including Hardy and Hamilton's Ewell, also moved out of Adelaide.

Almost next door to Penfolds is the historic stone building of the Seaview champagne cellars but sparkling wine production by the Allied Vintners company is moving to a vast modern centre at Reynella.

Adelaide also boasts Patritti, a grand-looking brick place with a range of unashamedly commercial wines from its McLaren Vale vineyards, and several other blending companies, notable wine merchants such as the Caons, and some wine company head offices, including Seppelt.

There is only one winery left which can claim to be nearly totally Adelaide and that is Norman's in suburban Underdale, with its vineyards on the market-garden Adelaide Plains. It owes its origins to Jesse Norman who arrived in Adelaide from the ship *Epaminondas* in 1851 and bought a few hectares in the region that came to be called Thebarton. The family wine business expanded with vineyards at Sturt (also replaced by housing) and on the Plains. For 131 years the wine was made by members of the Norman family, until it was sold to another family. But the name continues.

Sadly, little else of Adelaide wine does.

'It was controversial,' the craggy faced maestro admits. 'It had an overwhelming power of flavour and character. It wasn't until it mellowed with years of cellaring that people could accept it.'

He modestly maintains that making Grange was simply a matter of 'getting the right grapes from the right area and getting the most out of them. I saw it in the Medoc, where it was all laid out like an open book.' But Schubert was the one man with the courage to read that book and to take radical departures from conventional winemaking practices by translating it and applying it to the Australian condition.

Technically the main 'secret' of Grange Hermitage is a high level of volatility, a combination of acids developed by bacterial action which has the effect of seeming to force the fruitiness up from the glass to seize the drinker's nose. But it must be in harmony with the wine if it is not to be a fault and Grange is made matchingly powerful in all respects, so that after some 15 years of maturing in the bottle it becomes subtle and gentle. Indeed, most other Penfolds reds have similar characteristics as a spin-off from the Grange techniques. But perhaps it is other wines, lesser known than Grange, that are the ulti-

ADELAIDE PLAINS

The fertile alluvial plains to the north of the city are Adelaide's breadbasket. But market gardeners also grow grapes and a small industry of some 40 growers developed here, mostly supplying grapes to nearby Barossa wineries. Climatically it is similar to the floor of the Barossa Valley, perhaps a bit hotter in summer with north winds, but also frequently tempered by sea breezes. Indeed, there is always some doubt about whether the Adelaide Plains should be classified as a sub-region of the Barossa or of Adelaide. (And how does one classify the lone adventurous wine producer, Eastern Cove Wine, on nearby Kangaroo Island?)

Several Adelaide Plains growers have at various times set up as winemakers but few have survived long. One who has found the secret is Joe Grilli at Primo Estates.

Like a comet foretelling good things, Grilli burst upon the wine scene in 1979 as the right person at the right time for dramatic changes in the mood of Australian wine. In his twentieth year he graduated dux of his oenology course at Roseworthy Agricultural College and won wine show medals with his first wine. As probably the youngest person to run an Australian winery, he was soon noticed also for his innocent enthusiasm, total dedication and serious pursuit of character in wines through radical experimenting.

His father, Primo, was a market gardener turned vigneron with, as his sunshine smile and gnarled hands show, a touch for the soil. He built a winery, a neat and efficient Mediterranean looking building, 'to supply work for the boys Joe and Peter when they grew up. It's the Italian way.'

Joe Grilli is unconcerned about his being in a warm region. 'Areas such as this have a lot to offer when winemakers understand their fruit. And winemaking is about understanding your situation.' His understanding has included double pruning techniques, which consist of hacking off the cabernet sauvignon

crop in early summer so it will grow again, ripening in the cool late autumn.

Of his winemaking he says, 'To feel good about yourself, you've got to please yourself. I'd feel depressed if I made only standard wines. I could have got a job somewhere else doing that. There is so much ordinary wine being made. It is a privilege having a free rein and I want to exploit that.

'My winemaking is fairly straightforward. It's all geared to preserving flavour of fruit. The Australian emphasis had been on trying to get clean wines. But it became time to move on, to look for ways of converting clean fruit to something more complex. Making clean sound wines is kiddy stuff.'

He blames the wine industry in general for failing to get flavour in riesling, the popular white wine style of the 1970s. And hence a lot of winemakers were caught when consumers suddenly turned around and made fashionable such full flavoured styles as chardonnay.

Another of his experiments in the quest for flavour and complexity is the use of cultured botrytis ('noble rot') in making rich, luscious dessert wines, after the cellar style commercially pioneered by Tim Knappstein of Enterprise in Clare. His half bottles of beerenauslese Rhine riesling, first made in 1981, became rivals to fashionable French sauternes with the dinner party set. Grilli, believing botrytis a 'magic mould' that gives wines characteristics after a few years cellaring that were never even hinted at when bottled, devotes half his time and energy at vintage to making these dessert wines which account for less than 10 per cent of the company's output.

'This wine is for the future,' he says, 'for a flagship, not for direct monetary gain. I want to be known for them, the way Max Schubert started out with Grange Hermitage, defying the sceptics to build a classic style of which to be proud.

'It's the duty of a small winery to get away from the mass styles and give people something different.'

BAROSSA VALLEY

In 1847 Johann Gramp planted grapes at Jacobs Creek, near what his succeeding family was to build into the giant Orlando winery. In the same year Samuel Hoffmann arrived, and his name survives in a winery. Joseph Seppelt was to follow. These were the major early Silesian pioneers who were to lay the foundations of the great tradition of winemaking excellence that is the Barossa Valley, Australian wine's foremost centre of industrial and technological expertise and extent.

Joseph Ernst Seppelt's story is typical. He was born in the small Silesian town of Wustewaltersdorf in 1813, liberally educated in music and the arts, widely travelled in Europe, and trained in the family business of tobaccos and snuff and the distilling and blending of liqueurs. But his homeland was troubled. It had been ravaged by the Thirty Years War, the wars of the Austrian Succession, the contesting of the Empress Marie Therese and the Napoleonic wars. Even in peace, as a Prussian possession, Silesia was to become a battleground for religious wars. In 1822 Frederick III of Prussia had imposed a new liturgy which violated the Lutheran conscience and evoked fierce resistance. This in turn was answered with persecution, fines and imprisonment.

If the shedding of blood could not drive the hard farming stock of Silesia from their home, persecution of their religion would. And by a long series of

Harvesting grapes by machine is not only much cheaper than hand picking; it also offers winemakers a chance to get their fruit at night, when it is cooler than during the day and the quality is better. Many major companies, like Tollana Wines here at High Eden, above the Barossa Valley, harvest all night.

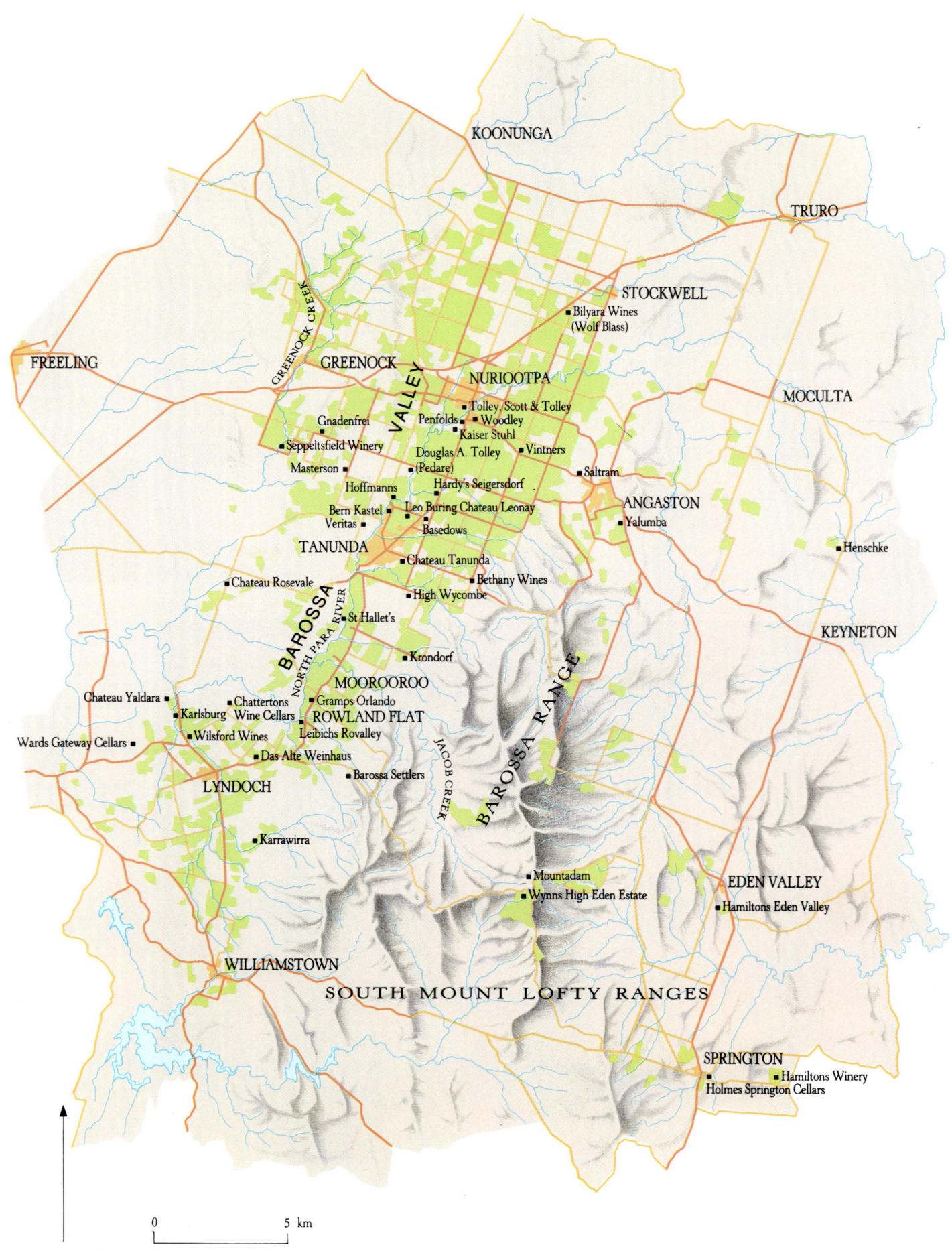

KOONUNGA

TRURO

STOCKWELL

■ Bilyara Wines
(Wolf Blass)

FREELING

GREENOCK VALLEY

NURIOOTPA

MOCULTA

■ Tolley, Scott & Tolley
Penfolds ■ ■ Woodley
■ Gnadenfrei   ■ Kaiser Stuhl
■ Seppeltsfield Winery   Douglas A. Tolley   ■ Vintners
Masterson ■   (Pedare) ■
■ Hoffmanns   ■ Hardy's Seigersdorf   ■ Saltram
Bern Kastel ■   ■ Leo Buring Chateau Leonay
Veritas ■   ■ Basedows

ANGASTON

■ Yalumba

GREENOCK CREEK

NORTH PARA RIVER

BAROSSA

TANUNDA

■ Chateau Tanunda

Henschke ■

■ Chateau Rosevale   ■ Bethany Wines
■ High Wycombe

■ St Hallet's

KEYNETON

■ Krondorf

MOOROOROO

BAROSSA RANGE

Chateau Yaldara ■   ■ Gramps Orlando
■ Chattertons
Karlsburg ■ Wine Cellars   ROWLAND FLAT
Wards Gateway Cellars ■   ■ Wilsford Wines   Leibichs Rovalley
■ Das Alte Weinhaus

JACOB CREEK

■ Barossa Settlers

LYNDOCH

■ Karrawirra

EDEN VALLEY

■ Mountadam
■ Wynns High Eden Estate

■ Hamiltons Eden Valley

WILLIAMSTOWN

SOUTH MOUNT LOFTY RANGES

SPRINGTON

■   ■ Hamiltons Winery
Holmes Springton Cellars

0   5 km

chances, Joseph Seppelt and many others were lured to the new free settlement of South Australia. In patriarchal fashion, he took his family, 13 families of his neighbourhood and a group of young men from his factory, proposing to set up a tobacco and snuff manufactory in the Antipodes.

And in 1851 he settled in the Barossa, which had been named by surveyor Colonel William Light for a part of Spain, and established as a farming area by George Angas. But tobacco did not flourish, or rather it flourished too prolifically and when it came to curing it was found that the leaf was too rank. Seppelt, apparently a man of vision, confidence and energy, soon realised that his capital and technical knowledge could be turned to correcting the abuses of the vine which were then prevalent in South Australia. And by resisting the lure of the Victorian goldfields in the 1850s, he prospered in wine.

It was a primitive life, of course, carting the wine by bullock dray to Adelaide, then later to the rail terminus at Gawler. One story of the early days in this virgin bush concerns the remnants of Aboriginal tribes who were strung along the Murray River and who every year trekked to Adelaide for the free Queen's Birthday issue of blankets and flour, passing through Greenock Creek and Seppelt's little settlement. Each year they demanded wine and Seppelt, fearful for his family, gave it them, until one year he gave them vinegar instead of wine. The Seppelt reputation among the tribes was suddenly lost and he was never again troubled. The Seppelts, incidentally, set up a major commercial vinegar plant as part of the winery complex, which grew into Seppeltsfield, its own little town of supporting workers, having even its own postcode. And the pioneering spirit of the Seppelt family was to continue, taking over operations elsewhere in Australia and charting new vineyard areas such as Keppoch, Drumborg and the Adelaide Hills.

Back in the Barossa, within two decades of its settlement, people such as Seppelt, Gramp and Hoffman in this self-reliant community had established a wine industry and a tradition of unique 'Barossa Deutsch' subculture in Australia.

The German influence in South Australia's Barossa Valley is readily apparent. This sign points to the Krondorf winery, not far from Rowland Flat at the southern end of the valley.

While most of the English settlers, especially those of a wine bent, tended to move south to the McLaren Vale region, some were also attracted to the Barossa, which offered attractive climates and a hardworking people, while still being near Adelaide. Two who had early on moved to higher elevations within the Barossa were Samuel Smith who in 1849 founded a profound exercise in dynastic faith by starting what has become the Yalumba winery, and William Salter who in 1859 began the Saltram winery, both near Angaston.

Many early settlers had made wine as an adjunct to their farming life, but from the 1890s they were to experience a common boom, an enlightened South Australian Government attitude to viticultural development, the devastation by the phylloxera louse of competing Victorian vineyards, and Federation's freeing of interstate trade which the State Government used to push Barossa wines into the eastern States and then England. When the chances presented themselves, the Barossa took them. And the next chance was the table wine boom of the 1960s.

The Barossa was able to capitalise again, thanks to Colin Gramp, descendant at Orlando of Johann

Gramp, who in 1953 had introduced the chilled, pressured fermentation techniques which had recently been developed in Germany. This gave the nation Barossa Pearl, a best-selling introduction for many Australians to wine drinking. Other companies followed these new techniques, which made possible great delicacy in white wine flavour, and thus paved the way for the white wine fashions of the 1970s. It was no coincidence that the South Australian Government had, in the 1880s, chosen proximity to the Barossa as the site for setting up Roseworthy Agricultural College, which was to become the nation's foremost viticultural and oenological (winemaking) school.

The Barossa Valley wine region, considered to be virtually at the back door of Adelaide and certainly a comfortable distance for a day's outing visiting the cellar doors, has its highest points in the Mount Lofty Ranges at the towns of Angaston and Kyneton, where the North Para River rises at the northern tip of the Barossa Range. It follows this river – which is, in truth, a creek unless in flood and then, as so tragically shown in 1983, it swells to a lethal lake – down to Nuriootpa, while vineyards fan out across the plains to north, from Moculta and Truro to Koonunga which, at latitude 34°23'S is the northernmost part of the region. The fairly narrow, central Barossa Valley heads south from Nuriootpa to its physical and cultural heart, the town of Tanunda, then down through Rowland Flat and Lyndoch, under the shelter of the Barossa Range. The North Para River runs its course through Gawler onto the Adelaide Plains, departing from the vineyards which spear back into the western foothills of the Mount Lofty Ranges at Williamstown.

Climatically it is an ideal region for growing grapes for fortified wines and, this, indeed was how it developed a major industry. But the fortified market dried up and the concentration of expertise turned to table wines, mostly using grapes from either the Murray River or Eden Valley vineyards, the former for mass-market commercial wines, the latter for premium styles. However, there are good patches of grapes for table wines in the valley, notably shiraz, as

A grapepicker near Tanunda, South Australia, shows the heavy load of red grapes on the vines.

Present at the creation: winemaker Stephen Henschke tastes at the onset of fermentation which is about to convert crushed shiraz grapes into Henschke's 1984 Hill of Grace red wine. Some Australian winemakers still use the traditional open concrete fermentation tanks like these, believing they enable the extraction of more fruit flavours, colours and tannins, though most now use stainless steel enclosed tanks for the same job. Henschke's Hill of Grace, one of the family's best known wines, is named after the nearby Hill of Grace vineyard, not far from Keyneton, east of Angaston in the high Barossa Ranges.

well as some cabernet sauvignon and pinot noir, and semillon grows as a rival to the Hunter, to be made into broader flavoured white burgundy styles and, especially, dessert wines.

But if the Barossa is not viticulturally the country's best area for a cool climate to grow the great wines, nor a hot climate for mass-market irrigated wine-growing, it has collectively developed the attitude that grapes should be grown where they grow best and should be processed where they are processed best – which is the Barossa. While the vineyards of the valley and the adjoining Adelaide Hills region grow about 45 000 tonnes of a fruit a year, the major wineries of the Barossa crush more than 100 000 tonnes annually, much of the fruit coming from the Riverland.

The expertise of the region can be demonstrated by wine show statistics of a typical year (1980): Barossa-based wineries represented 12.4 per cent of exhibitors in the shows throughout Australia's State

capitals and took 51 per cent of the trophies. When the valley is on the march it is like a blitzkrieg.

Industrially, the Barossa is usually seen as a collection of wine 'factories', being headquarters or at least principal production centres for most of the biggest names in Australian wine – Penfolds/Kaiser Stuhl, Orlando, Seppelt, Tollana, Yalumba, Tolleys, Masterson, Wolf Blass, Woodley and Saltram, plus such aspirants as Krondorf and Basedows. It also has its eccentricities, such as the Disneyland castle appearance of Karlsberg and the magnificent artwork collection of Chateau Yaldara. And it has its pocket handkerchief wineries such as Chattertons and High Wycombe. In all, there are about 34 companies and families processing grapes into Barossa wine.

If the Gramps, the Seppelts and the Hoffmans were the early symbolic masons of the valley's Teutonic thoroughness, the modern symbol is Wolf Blass, whose entry to Australia in January 1960 was quietly noted by a filler item in Adelaide's morning newspaper, the *Advertiser,* headlined 'German wine expert here'. It was the last quiet thing about Blass, who was soon shouting about the Pineapple Pearl he

Winemaking is a business involving moving things from one place to another: a worker at Yalumba's winery near Angaston, above the Barossa Valley, operates a pump to move wine from tank to tank for blending.

Australia's favoured quaffing wine. Here an automated cask-filling machine puts 4 litres of Orlando Coolabah Moselle into a silver-lined plastic sac, which is then placed inside the cardboard box from which it will later be dispensed.

Wolf Blass toasts his remarkable success in his office at the Bilyara winery, outside Nuriootpa, at the north-eastern end of the Barossa Valley. Blass came to Australia in 1960 to make sparkling wine for Kaiser Stuhl. He began making his own wine in 1966 and has since made some remarkably good wines.

Adam Wynn pumping the juice of freshly crushed pinot noir grapes over their skins at the Mountadam winery, operated by Adam and his father David Wynn on High Eden Range, on top of the Barossa Valley. In 1972 the Wynn family relinquished control of the wine company which bore their name to Allied Vinters (which includes Toohey's Brewery, among other holdings).

was making for Kaiser Stuhl. 'The best bloomin' Pineapple Pearl ever made,' he cried, brandishing the hand-grenade shaped bottle which was to become a star exhibit in any later collection of Australian kitsch. He promoted the sparkling wines which he had been hired to make, and on which he had trained in Champagne, France, by serving them to the press through a petrol bowser. He became a major horse-racing identity, with bow tie, jangling jewellery and a yellow Mercedes-Benz. He jumped on tables with mock Nazi salutes and led outbursts of the Barossa anthem, *'Ein prosit'*. And Blass, when he set up his own winery, was to capture headlines with a pheno-menal run of gold medals at Australian wine shows.

For Wolfgang Blass is not just a promoter. Born in 1934 in what was to become East Germany he grew up in a nation torn apart by war. This gave him a strong emotional survival kit and also deep sen-sitivities and human warmth. He has a genius for

understanding vines and palates and all that goes bet-ween. 'I had tasted Australian wines when working in the wine industry in England,' he recalls, 'and I thought, "Oh yes, I can do something out there." These wines were shocking. I can make a landmark in Australia.'

He might have been long dismissed as an arrogant upstart by many in an insecure wine industry but he made that landmark, precisely by understanding that wine is for drinking, and he made wines that Austra-lians found a pleasure to drink, notably his reds with their silken warmth. Indeed through the 1970s nobody so influenced the dramatic changes in Australian wines, their consumption and their enjoy-ment.

The Barossa is home to another of the great names in the modern Australian wine industry – Peter Lehmann, who might well be called the human face of the valley. Son of a local Lutheran pastor, he set

Making wine at Orlando's Rowland Flat winery in the Barossa: pressure and temperature controlled tanks like these gave Orlando — and later the rest of the Australian wine industry — the ability to make white wines and sparkling wines which retained original fruit flavours.

new standards of hospitality and happiness for all who passed by Saltram, where he was winemaker in the 1960s and 1970s. He is something of a bishop to the flock of the valley's three hundred private grape-growers, although his chasuble is likely to be a holey old jumper, somewhat stretched around the middle regions to indicate his love of living, his chalice a decanter of fine red wine, his anthem a Mozart piano concerto and his texts the writings of Damon Runyon. As an act of faith with the growers, when times got tough, he set up his own winery, Master-son, which he named after a gambler in the musical *Guys and Dolls,* and he took the gambler's card, the Queen of Clubs, as his symbol.

'If ever anything was a bloody gamble, this was,' he says. The idea was to buy all the grapes, including the unwanted varieties which were still grown because tastes in the wine market change more rapidly than

vines can be replanted and come to bear again. Thus he frequently took in some 7000 tonnes of fruit which would otherwise have been left to rot on the vines. And from it all, he made wines to be sold in bulk to other companies, mainly for blending into cask and flagon ranges but sometimes premium wines which won show medals under their new names. By looking after the growers, they made sure he got their best fruit, and thus he was also able to make the Peter Lehmann range of wines, some of which play with glory.

Not only the wine but the culture of valley, epitomised in combination by the pomp of the winemaking fraternity of the Barons of the Barossa, has made this area an important tourist asset to the State of South Australia, whether it be individual travellers seeking the distinctive foods and beauties of the area or coachloads of tourists getting smashed

Maturing red wines at Wolf Blass' Bilyara winery in the Barossa Valley. Oak barrels like these usually hold 300-500 litres of wine and cost when newly imported between $350 and $450 each.

Harry Mahlo, master cooper. The art of fitting wooden staves together to make oak barrels is an ancient one, and a dying trade. Harry makes the oak casks for Yalumba near Angaston, above the Barossa Valley.

in the numerous cellar door tasting areas. Tourism peaks at the Barossa Valley Vintage Festival, a week-long frolic held every two years at Easter time. The 13 000 residents of the valley grit their teeth for an invasion by some 200 000 visitors for this festival which mixes hard-nosed commerce and a measure of irrelevant Tyrolean kitsch with the profound and earthy culture that is the valley's heritage, and which is characterised by the performances of the internationally acclaimed Tanunda Town Band, the Tanunda Liedertafel choral group, the street fairs and markets, massive carnivals and dinners, art

shows, quiet functions in the many Lutheran churches and the almost constant feeding on mettwurst, dill cucumbers and wine. It adds a strange extra dimension to the lush pasture country, the distant blue hills, vineyards rolling across the plains, and everywhere the great gums and stunning light that are the classic beauty of Australia. Visitors are rarely left untouched by the complexity and depth of the region and will unselfconsciously learn to sing the toast to 'good health and happiness' that is the anthem of the Barossa: *Ein prosit, ein prosit, der gemütlichkeit.*

CLARE

It must be the touch of Irish that gives the Clare Valley of South Australia that extra charm. It shows in the names of towns (Auburn, Clare and its suburb of Armagh), of such properties as Inchiquin and Donnybrook, and of pioneer Gleeson, winemakers Barry, and grapegrower Hanlin... It shows in the misty green mornings when fat cattle graze, and lush grow the vines. It shows in that gentle ratbag blarney into which so many of the valley's settlers slip.

It is not all Irish, of course. Sevenhill was named by a Jesuit priest from Austria because Rome was built on seven hills (an association which may not be obvious to the casual visitor), as was the local creek named the River Tiber. A touch of Germany comes with a major winery name, Quelltaler, which was originally

A grape treading contest during the Clare wine festival.

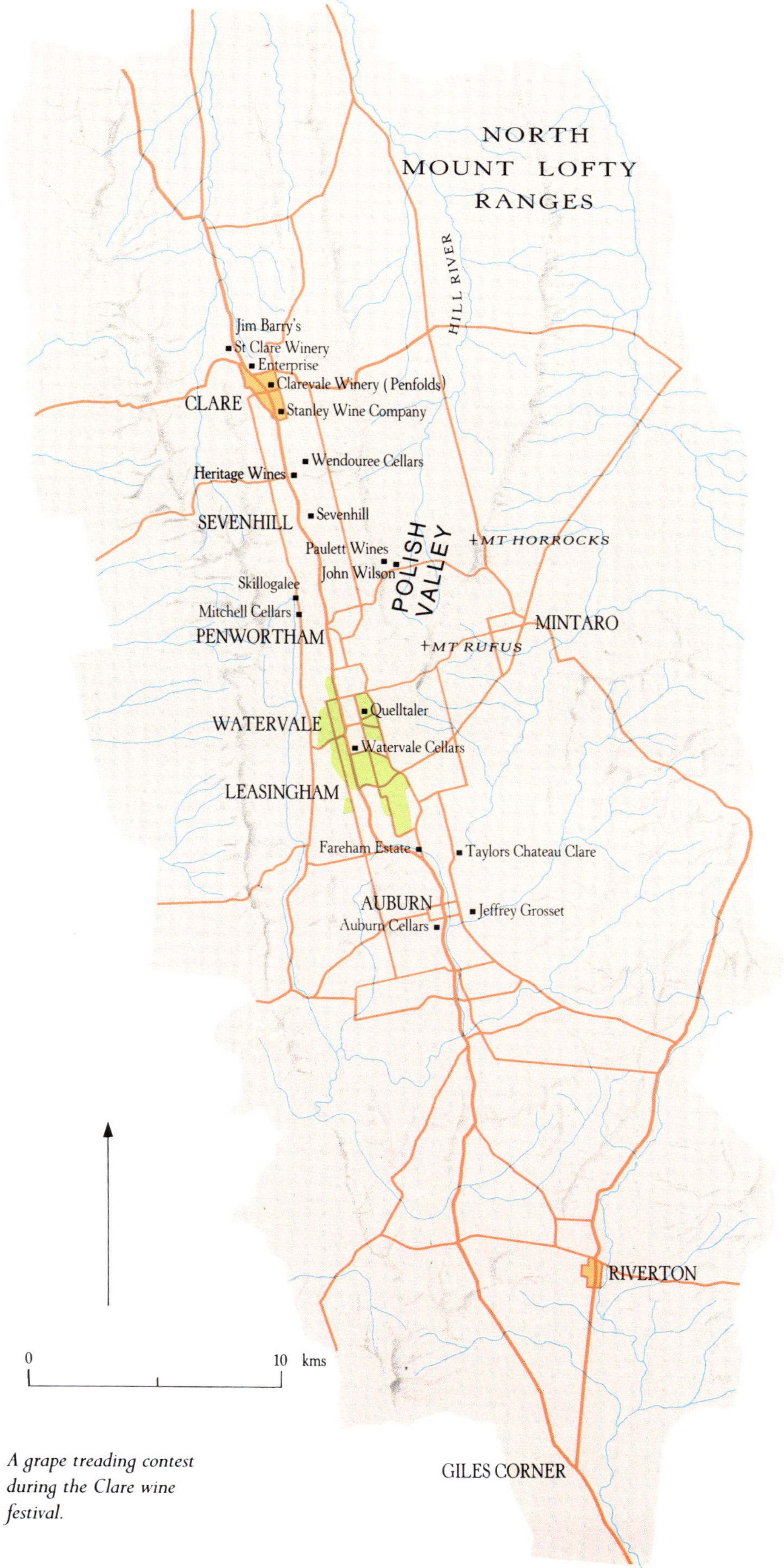

NORTH MOUNT LOFTY RANGES

HILL RIVER

Jim Barry's
St Clare Winery
Enterprise
Clarevale Winery (Penfolds)
CLARE
Stanley Wine Company

Wendouree Cellars

Heritage Wines

SEVENHILL
Sevenhill

POLISH VALLEY

+MT HORROCKS

Paulett Wines
John Wilson

Skillogalee

Mitchell Cellars

PENWORTHAM
+MT RUFUS

MINTARO

Quelltaler

WATERVALE
Watervale Cellars

LEASINGHAM

Fareham Estate
Taylors Chateau Clare

AUBURN
Auburn Cellars
Jeffrey Grosset

RIVERTON

0   10 kms

GILES CORNER

The scars of the 1983 bushfires still show behind vines near Clare.

spelled Quellthaler, a literal translation of the nearby town of Watervale, and coined by its English founder. Polish River derives from the settlement of that region by Poles. Names of nearby towns Mintaro and Burra show, respectively, Spanish and Hindustani origins. Penwortham is a Lancashire name – although it was the early home of the parents of Ned Kelly, and they were certainly Irish.

Culturally and historically the Clare Valley is a mixed bag, but overriding it all is the unique Australianness of its beautiful gum trees. And there is something uniquely Australian about the wine it produces, a uniqueness that comes from its history of settlement and its particular climate.

The valley extends some 30 kilometres north from the town of Auburn, birthplace of the poet C. J. Dennis, to just past the town of Clare, on latitude 33°50'S. Viticulturally, which must be the basis of all wine, it is classified as a warm to moderately cool winegrowing region, with a heat summation range of 1550 to 1700 heat degree days and annual rainfall of 559-610 millimetres.

As for soil characteristics, the valley is part of that almost continuous low range stretching across former seabed for about 1000 kilometres north from Kangaroo Island. It is called the Mount Lofty Ranges across the Fleurieu Peninsula and through the Adelaide Hills, petering out by Angaston. Some 65 kilometres north it surfaces again at Auburn for the Clare Valley, dipping again until near Port Pirie, where Mt Remarkable signals the start of its being called the Flinders Ranges, which rises to St Mary Peak and peters out into the desert past Leigh Creek. The highest point in the Clare region is 615 metres near Watervale, and major town elevations are Auburn 303 metres, Watervale 414 metres, Sevenhill 464 metres, and Clare 398 metres.

The skeletal characters of the Mount Lofty Ranges are not so strongly exhibited at Clare, where the hills seem older, more worn down, like uniform mounds of old rubble. Old soil it may be, but good, and there are excellent aspects for grapes, generally to the east of the highway running up the centre of the valley and again over the hills to the east before the land flattens out to the wheat belt; similarly there are poor patches. And, indeed, vignerons who have been active in the region for nearly a century and a half are still engaged in the process of sorting them out as they doubtless will be for another century and a half.

John Horrocks was the first settler in the region. He was a pastoralist who first entered the area while heading north from Adelaide to find fresh country. He encouraged his servant, James Green, to plant vines at Penwortham and they were established in 1842. Close behind were George Hawker, who planted vines at his property, Bungaree (Aboriginal for 'my country'), and Edward Gleeson, the Irishman who founded the town of Clare and the Inchiquin vineyards.

It was, of course, farming which brought people to the Clare Valley, that and the bedevilled politics of land settlement in the new free colony of South Australia, plus a touch of the mining boom. Farmers had to be self-sufficient which meant vineyards developed as extensions of kitchen orchards and gardens. The 1840s saw significant intensive agricultural development, and paid labour came to the area, as well as townspeople to service the farms. This meant

an extra demand for wine, frequently as a form of payment, and thus developed the concept of each season's 'harvest wine', which is said to have varied in quality from obnoxious to delightful.

Then came the wine boom. The rush to tame the difficult land of South Australia meant many poor farming practices, including ignorance of the need to give nourishment back to the soil. The 1880s saw economic depression with widespread declines in wheat yields; but wine flourished and had its golden decade across the State in the 1890s, especially 'helped' by the devastation of so many Victorian

vineyards by the phylloxera louse. This decade saw the vineyards of Clare increase from 94 to 600 hectares. The valley, described in 1892 by the *Observer* newspaper of Adelaide as 'the garden of the north', was on the wine map, and its quality wines were in good demand in London, which was then the export market to which most of the State's winegrowing aspired.

That market was eventually to crash and Clare staggered along, the number of wine producers dropping to five by the 1960s, when the next boom, with Australia's interest in table wines, started. Clare was

Drip irrigation lines provide much needed supplementary water between rains. Temperatures are high around Clare as the vintage approaches each summer.

159

Brother John May, winemaker at the Sevenhill winery in the Clare Valley, South Australia. The Jesuit Fathers had their first vintage here in 1854, making it the oldest winery in the valley. One of the winery's main activities is to produce altar wines, some of which are exported to a number of countries.

target for a dramatic influx of winemakers, not weekend farmers or tax dodgers so much as young people who loved the feel of Clare and saw it as a good place to make wine, and to live. Within a decade 12 wineries started operations, and by the 1980s the number became 18. These producers own just less than half the 2500 hectares of the Clare Valley under vines, the rest being owned by private growers or outside interests, such as the Barossa company, Leo Buring.

The oldest surviving winery, and a place of great fascination, is the Sevenhill winery attached to St Aloysius College and the beautiful little stone church set in the vineyards. Jesuits from Europe, led by Father Aloysius Kranewitter, settled here in 1851 and developed a mission centre for the region's Irish, German and Polish Roman Catholics who were seeking religious and other freedoms in South Australia. It also became a training centre for priests for the Society of Jesus. By 1856 the Jesuits had a vineyard bearing to make sacramental wine. The first cellarmaster (1851-84) was Brother John Schreiner from Austria, his successors being from Ireland, Switzerland and Australia. The latest, and only the seventh, winemaker is Brother John May who is acutely aware

God and the grape: part of the vineyards at the Sevenhill winery, run by the Jesuits, south of Clare in South Australia. Their church (which has a crypt) is in the centre and the winery building at the right rear.

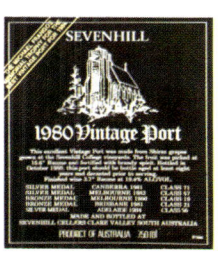

of the heritage, including fermentation tanks made from Mintaro slate, the diesel-driven crusher, the vaulted underground cellars carved into a hillside of solid slate and even the museum of mousetraps in the cellar door sales area. But behind the old winery, there is a modern operation, for the Sevenhill brothers also make a considerable amount of excellent wine for public sale. Brother John says, with typical Jesuit pragmatism, 'The winery makes money for Jesuit education. It is more honest, working with the hands, than begging for charity.'

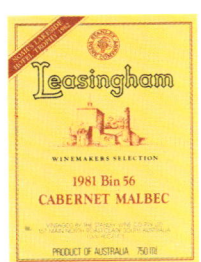

Quelltaler Wines at Watervale, founded 1865, is a noble place with a chequered history, now in the hands of the French Remy Martin multinational, a company with enough commitment to quality to place Alsace winemaker Michel Dietrich in charge. He is selling off in bulk all the vineyard produce he doesn't like while keeping only the best for his Quelltaler Estate label, expensive wines but of an extraordinary new dimension of flavours in Australia. Dietrich – offering the perspective of a newcomer from a traditional European wine region – is thrilled with the Clare Valley, saying it offers room for experiment, and soil compositions the equal of those in Alsace and Burgundy in France and the Rheingau in Germany. 'But it has a wide range of quality,' he says, pointing to variations in pH of 7 to 8.5 as one rises to the top of a hill.

Next oldest of the valley's wineries is Wendouree Cellars, founded in 1892. It sometimes seems as though time has never moved on here and the wines, overseen by Roly Birks, son of the founder, still have an enormous tannic depth, a quality that gives them longevity and a totally devoted band of followers.

The dominant presence in the valley is the Stanley Wine Company which was set up in 1893 when a consortium of pioneers – merchant Joseph Knappstein, medico Dr V. Wein-Smith, lawyer Magnus Badger and brewer John Christison – formed a company to process local grapes and capitalise on the wine boom. From 1912 it was controlled by the Knappstein family, who had ensured Stanley's export trade to Britain thrived until 1938, when imperial preference duties for wine imports were abolished.

The Knappstein family then were to find new local markets. In 1976 the company was taken over by the H. J. Heinz corporation which set about conquering new markets, especially with spectacular growth in cask wines. Stanley has its own vineyards, not notably at Leasingham, but buys a considerable amount from private growers, so much that they say in the valley that if Stanley sneezes, everybody catches cold.

At one time another large name was the Clarevale Co-operative Winery at Clare, which was founded in 1928 and re-formed in 1930 by local growers finding difficulty in selling their fruit. Its big market was Britain. But as it was born with the upswing of the nation's co-operative movement so was its demise inevitable and by the 1980s it had become largely a blending cellar in the hands of the Penfolds/Kaiser Stuhl combine.

The table wine boom of the 1960s led to a rash of new wineries, the frontrunner being St Clare Cellars, which Clarevale winemaker Jim Barry set up in 1959, eventually to be run by his sons. Within a decade the Sydney wine merchant family of the Taylors had twigged to Clare and established Taylors Chateau Clare at Auburn, a stylish looking place which has also employed some of the region's great characters, such as winemakers Morgan Yeatman and his successor Andrew Tolley (formerly at Clarevale).

Smaller newcomers include Skillogalee, set up by grape-grower Spencer George in 1970, and Mitchell Cellars, where youthful partners Andrew and Jane Mitchell are traditional in many ways, but have an uncompromising attitude to quality and a correct belief that the rieslings from their two vineyards, at Watervale and at Sevenhill, like most from the region, need several years bottle age.

At Fareham Estate, Peter Rumball occasionally produces a fine wine but basically he opted to be a bottler, setting up a sophisticated quality operation which attracts many large names from elsewhere to use his equipment.

One of the ironies of Clare, apart from the way that the dynastic Knappstein family seems to be involved in everything, is that Stanley's son and heir, so to speak, winemaker Tim Knappstein, moved out

with the 1976 Heinz takeover, set up his own winery, appropriately named Enterprise, in the building of what was once a brewery run by John Christison, who had started Stanley. Tim Knappstein, who while Stanley winemaker had won 499 show medals for table wines (plus one for a fortified), became a leading light among Australian winemakers for his uncompromisingly meticulous attitude to both grapes and their processing and for his openness to new ideas, such as establishing a supplementary vineyard in the Adelaide Hills.

Meanwhile there was Richard Robertson who settled just south of the town of Clare at Donnybrook in what he called 'more ravishingly beautiful country even than Tuscany in autumn'. He may not have made many great wines. But he, more than anybody in the wine business, moved to make life great in Clare. He attracted hordes of a new generation of enthusiasts not only for cellar door sales throughout the valley but for the tourism industry which the region came to see as increasingly important. Robertson believed in fun, and the need to feed wine tourists not

Young vines establishing themselves in the Clare Valley.

163

Eucalypts add a typically Australian touch to vine-yards in the Clare Valley.

only with barbecue steaks and convivial drinks, but with drive-free train excursions, warming winter log fires, folk and rock music concerts, and the attraction of his own personality at Robertson Wines.

It was the entrepreneurial Robertson who set up Watervale Cellars down the road apiece, perhaps as a way of showing that he was also interested in more traditional concepts of fine wine, perhaps as a way of appealing to yet a different market. Its running was taken over by the equally eccentric Robert Crabtree, who shows in the little old cottage a pretty taste for Bloomsbury paintings.

Another venture of Robertson's was Auburn Cellars, an old stone building in the main street of the town of Auburn. It would come as no surprise to his devotees to learn that this was formerly a temperance hall. He set it up as a cellar for blending and selling fortified wines and it went into the worthy hands of one Kevin John Casmir Jacob Donovan Symonds.

Nearby, in a former ice-cream factory, is one of the valley's most serious winemakers, Jeffrey Grosset of Auburn, a young man disciplined by work in large companies, but not so much that his personal sense of artistry has been dulled. His range of hand-crafted wines is small, but of extraordinary beauty.

Beautiful wines also result from noted show judge Brian Barry, whose Jud's Hill vineyards are just to the east of Clare and who makes the wines wherever he can, usually at the St Clare winery of his brother Jim or at Petaluma in the Adelaide Hills. This last company, under oenology guru Brian Croser, also has its own vineyard at Clare, supplying mostly riesling grapes, and in the late 1970s Petaluma Rhine riesling, made from Clare fruit, set new standards in Australian white wines.

Across the hills to the east of the Clare Valley is a pocket between Mount Horrocks and Mount Rufus called Polish Valley, settled last century by Poles who had progressed a little further north than their Silesian cousins who stopped at the Barossa. They came mainly as stonemasons, having built, among other places, the Sevenhill college and church, and the St Stanislaus church around which they settled, and they turned their hand to the vine. With what local vignerons today call excellent conditions (clay-loam soil over slate, acid, well drained, 711-762 millimetres rainfall, and 439 metres altitude) it is still successful grape country.

The large Barossa companies of Wolf Blass and Penfolds have established extensive vineyards at Polish Valley to feed their demand for Clare fruit, especially riesling and chardonnay. Local growers John Wilson, an Adelaide doctor of medicine, and Neil Paulett, formerly a winemaker for large companies, began making their own wines. They consider themselves as a district sub-region of Clare and give their wines a regional certification. Jeffrey Grosset also buys fruit from Polish Valley and makes one of his finest wines of it.

Near Clare is a rather isolated winegrower, Wakefield River Estates to the west at Balaklava, and, to the south, almost half way to the Barossa, is the district of Riverton, where there are only the ruins of a few open fermentation tanks to speak quietly of a flourishing wine industry there in the 1890s.

It is not only wineries and winemakers but growers who make Clare; such growers as John Eaton, whose vineyards at the southern end of the town of Clare show meticulous care in their unique and attractive loop trellising; and the progressive atttitudes and green fingers of Bernie Hanlin, who manages the Jud's Hill and Petaluma vineyards as well as his own Guilford Farm.

Like the winemakers, the growers have great love for the region, its wines and its lifestyle, and while many are prepared to experiment with new directions, they still hold most faith in riesling as the great grape on which the district made, and continues to hold, its reputation. This reputation is enhanced, especially since Stanley moved its cask operations to the Sunraysia region, by the fact that Clare is a remarkably 'pure' area compared with most other wine regions, with virtually no bulk wine being trucked into the valley. The wines of Clare and especially those from the small makers who constitute most of the valley are unquestionable.

There are precious few fortified wines produced in the Clare Valley and not many red table wines. The

red grape here tends to be heavily tannic and the wines – both cabernet sauvignon and shiraz and blends – tend to be of the solid, extractive style, the classic being those of Wendouree. On the other hand, Jeffrey Grosset has made red wines of ethereal poise and elegance. In the white wines, there has been a realisation in the 1980s that semillon grows to rival that of the Hunter Valley, and that some fine chardonnays, of a full and fruity style, can be made.

But it seems always to come back to Rhine riesling, which produces an uncompromising, aromatic, firmly spined white wine. It's not the German style riesling, nor the rather pedestrian quaffing white wine which the grape produces in so many Australian areas, but one of Australia's great unique wine styles; a wine which, from such makers as Enterprise, Mitchell, Grosset and the top of the Stanley range – and outside companies such as Lindemans, Petaluma and Leo Buring – will, after several years maturing in the bottle, reveal the glories of Clare.

Rhine riesling vineyards around Clare produce some of the best fruit in Australia.

165

COONAWARRA

A family business: Malcolm Redman (left) and his older brother Bruce have recently taken over the operation of the Redman winery at Coonawarra, South Australia, from their father, Owen Redman, who is still involved in the family winemaking concern but who lives in Adelaide.

Most winemakers in Australia, and most wine regions, consider themselves obliged by the traditional demands of their customers to produce a wide range of wine styles. There are few which engage in the specialisation that is the key to excellence. One region which does specialise is Coonawarra, near the centre of the Green Triangle of the south-east of South Australia. A rare beast is the port made here;

and there are no sherries or spumantes or champagnes or moselles or pop wines. Only late in the twentieth century has there been marked interest in the growing of white wine grapes in Coonawarra, and then without spectacular success.

Coonawarra is the home of red wine. Indeed, by virtue of its climate and soils, it is reputed to grow the greatest red wines of Australia. There is, of course,

argument about whether the best grape is shiraz or cabernet sauvignon, many producers opting for a blend of the two. While other varieties for blending purposes are being developed (such as cabernet franc and merlot), it is possible that the definitive Coonawarra wine has yet to be made.

It is a small settlement of twelve winemaking operations, a few local growers, and vineyards owned by outside companies such as Penfolds and Petaluma. Such are the inconsequentialities of distance in Australia that Coonawarra is often also said to embrace the Keppoch winegrowing district, some 90 kilometres north-north-west. And as vineyards are planted anywhere across the vast, flat and fertile plains of the Green Triangle – which is, for fat sheep and cattle, for cheese, fruit, vegetables and sunflowers, the most important breadbasket of South Australia as well as a major source of timber in its whispering pine forests – they too will doubtless also attach to Coonawarra's famous name.

But Coonawarra proper has virtually defined itself as a patch of dirt, of red earth running in a strip 15 kilometres long and varying from 200 metres to 1.5 kilometres wide, the red soil ranging from a few centimetres to half a metre deep below which are a layer of hard limestone and calcareous clay over vast underground reserves of pure water. Surrounding this strip is rendzina soil, a grey to black clay which is typical of the south-east, on which the vine grows but not so easily because of this soil's inferior drainage properties. There has been much viticultural thinking that such soils, since the Government drainage scheme for the Green Triangle came into effect, can be suitable for white grapes. Winters under Coonawarra's leaden skies are soggily wet and bone-chillingly cold, with frosts a problem under earlier viticultural techniques. The ripening period is long and slow, which makes for fine fruit quality. It is one of Australia's few true cool climates for an established viticultural region, with a heat summation figure of 1285 heat degree days, which is the same as Bordeaux in France. Coonawarra lies low across the districts of Penola, Comaum and Joanna, the vineyard elevations ranging from 56 to 60 metres above the level of the

Coonawarra vineyard in autumn. Many wine-lovers believe that this flat area, some 350 kilometres south-east of Adelaide, produces Australia's finest red wines.

sea, which is 65 kilometres to the west-south-west. Its latitudes centre on 37°17'S, while Keppoch, similarly 65 kilometres from the coast, lies below 36°37'S.

The vineyards of Coonawarra, otherwise distinguished from the surrounding countryside by a general store at a crossroads and a Telecom communications tower, are a day trip from nowhere for urbanised Australians, lying half way between Melbourne and Adelaide, although not on any of the established highways. That they came to be important was an accident of history, and that winegrowing survived through its motley history, a narrow accident.

The region was settled as grazing land in the 1830s. The extensive holding of Yallum Park came into the hands of John Riddoch, father of Coonawarra, who in 1890 subdivided much land into blocks as the Penola Fruit Colony, the name later changed to the Coonawarra Fruit Colony. It was set back by the bank crash of 1893 but the soil worked its magic with fruit and vines. By 1899 Riddoch and his 'blockers', as those who had bought his blocks and who supplied their grapes to him were known, had some 140 hectares under vines, mostly shiraz and cabernet sauvignon. Other varieties included pinot noir, which was disappointing, as indeed it continued to be in subsequent attempts. Early on, nature was pointing to Coonawarra's vinous future.

In 1891 work had started on Riddoch's cellars, later to be called Chateau Comaum. Today this is the centre of the Wynn company's Coonawarra operations, as depicted by woodcut on the labels of that company's wines. Indeed, the stone cellars are, with the poplars planted around Mildara's vineyards, the visual symbols of a region whose landscape attractions are usually revealed to only the sensitive afficionado of the south-east.

Riddoch died in 1901, just as Federation was to give a new trade freedom to the larger wine regions which were more accessible to markets, and just as demand for such wines as his Coonawarra Vineyards Claret was to fade in the face of the boom for fortified wines, especially for export markets. That first chapter of Coonawarra was glorious in its vision, but brief in its span.

One person, Bill Redman, who as a fourteen-year-old had arrived in the region in 1901 with his family seeking work, was to see Coonawarra grapes fed to pigs and Coonawarra Claret distilled into brandy. But he was also to buy part of the Riddoch estate being auctioned off and was to stand by the region — as the once-enlightened South Australian Government paid growers a bounty to rip out vines – with a faith that his family continued. The Redmans made

Padthaway Estate, a magnificent stone building at Padthaway, about 300 kilometres south-east of Adelaide. The vineyards around the old homestead are planted to the grape varieties pinot noir and chardonnay, for the production of quality champagnes.

At work during vintage time at Coonawarra. The mechanical harvester has been along these vine rows, shown by the leaves and canes lying on the ground.

Serried rows of vines march along the rich, red/black soils of Keppoch (also known as Padthaway). These vines, including the varieties shiraz, cabernet sauvignon, malbec, pinot noir, Rhine riesling, chardonnay and sauvignon blanc, were planted here by Hardy in the late 1960s.

wines which they sold to companies in Adelaide, for eventual release under other labels. It was Colonel David Fulton of Woodley's in Adelaide, who turned around the fortunes of the Redmans and indeed the long-term fortunes of Coonawarra. He asked that the wine being made for him should not be the ripe burgundy styles but a less ripe, lighter-bodied 'claret' style. The Redmans succeeded and a succession of winemakers was to beat a path to their door first seeking their wine, then wanting help in buying or establishing vineyards.

Meanwhile David Wynn, son of the founder of the Wynn company, bought the Chateau Comaum property in 1951. In this magnificent building the visitor finds not only a major wine company but a wonderful warmth of atmosphere.

In rapid succession came Mildara from Mildura with vineyards and winery, Penfolds with vineyards, the Brands family, Lindemans which bought out Redman's Rouge Homme winery, leaving the family to start again, and such smaller operations as Bowen Estate, Leconfield, and Zema Estate. Rivalling Wynn as the biggest holder of vineyards in the region is the Coonawarra Machine Company, which makes small amounts of premium wine under both the Riddoch and Katnook labels, selling the remainder to outside companies.

Meanwhile the pioneering Seppelt company from the Barossa established a vineyard at Keppoch in 1963, which some companies, confusingly but with some validity, call Padthaway. A string of red soil some 16 kilometres long here, and again floating on a water table, was considered ideal for grapes. Seppelt was followed by Lindemans, Hardy and Wynn, all with broad-acre vineyards. While these plantings were set up to produce high-yielding quality fruit for commercial blends, a surprising number of good individual wines were to come from this sub-region in what the Aborigines called Tatiara, the 'Good Country'.

With the boom of Coonawarra in mid-twentieth century came sophisticated viticultural and winemaking techniques, the spreading of the great name of Coonawarra, and inevitable problems. Heavy traffic

170

Vintage time discussion at Bowen Estate in Coonawarra. Richard Hamilton, left, from his family's Leconfield winery across the road, compares notes with winemaker Doug Bowen.

arriving from Victoria to collect bulk wines, and the interchange of the mechanical harvesters which are so widely used in Coonawarra, carry the constant threat of phylloxera, from which Coonawarra has been spared. The attitudes of various companies – Petaluma and Wynn being the extremes – raise a question of whether Coonawarra's ideal red wine style is low-yield, rich, full and long-lived or high-yield, light, elegant and short-lived.

There are fears that coal mining on the coast would, in the long term, deplete the underground water reserves. And there are the constant threats of

complacency or greed. Indeed, the vignerons of Coonawarra lament that this could well be outside their control since some 40 per cent of the Green Triangle's grapes are processed outside the area. More than half of Coonawarra's wine appears under the name of outside companies, often blended with their own produce to add the distinctive Coonawarra finesse, elegance and flavours. But at least that which is labelled Coonawarra, especially from reputable companies, can be assumed the genuine article. At its best it is a red wine to which many French clarets from Medoc have been compared.

McLAREN VALE

No other area in the country has so many wine producers. There are usually about fifty, although it is difficult to be specific when they spring up like mushrooms with each new wine fashion, some of them seeming to have little longer a lifespan than a mushroom's. Although, industrially, McLaren Vale does have some large companies present, and there are numerous private grape-growers, it is here that the small-scale winemaker is king. It is here, in the most accessible wine region of the country, that the tourist visiting the cellar door invariably finds that the person pouring the tasting samples and dispensing the wisdom of the grape is the same person who made the wine.

McLaren Vale, the region being named after the central town, has a long wine history, having been founded as a supplier to the cultivated thirsts of Adelaide citizens and the local farmers themselves. It prospered because tempering sea breezes from the Gulf of St Vincent offer many excellent microclimates for viticulture and, despite occasional disease problems in wet summers, a general consistency of quality from one vintage to the next. It endures because its beauty continues to attract those who, for whatever dreams, want to make their own wine amid long tranquillity, amid undulating slopes crossed with serried vines, orchards and pastures, and punctuated by massive old blue gums.

Almond blossom time — and also time to prune the grapevines at McLaren Vale, 40 kilometres south of Adelaide. Pruning is hard work and these two pruners have stopped for a cup of tea.

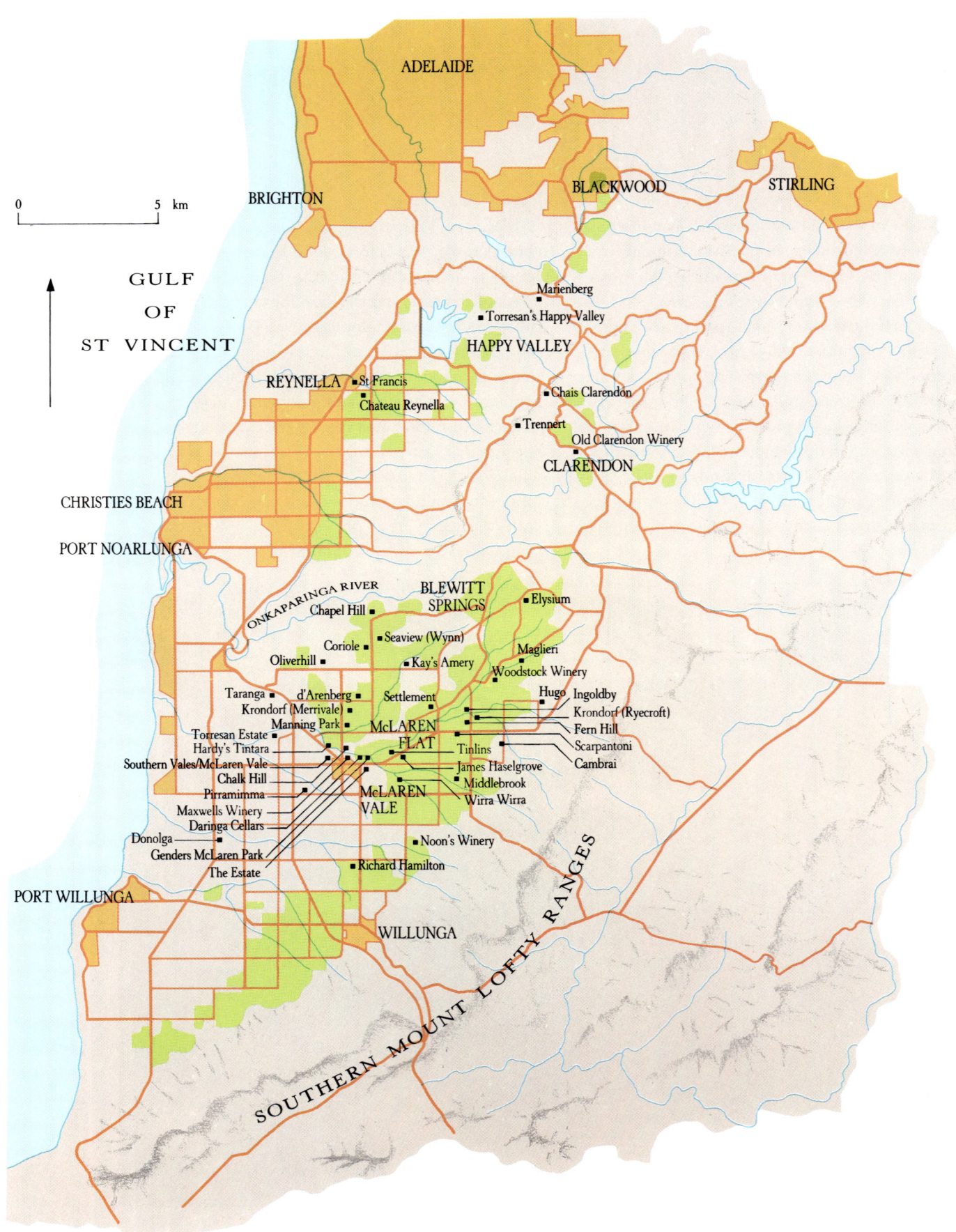

ADELAIDE

BRIGHTON

BLACKWOOD

STIRLING

0   5 km

GULF
OF
ST VINCENT

Marienberg

Torresan's Happy Valley

HAPPY VALLEY

REYNELLA   St Francis

Chateau Reynella

Chais Clarendon

Trennert

Old Clarendon Winery

CLARENDON

CHRISTIES BEACH

PORT NOARLUNGA

ONKAPARINGA RIVER

BLEWITT
SPRINGS

Elysium

Chapel Hill

Coriole   Seaview (Wynn)

Oliverhill   Kay's Amery   Maglieri

Woodstock Winery

Taranga   d'Arenberg   Settlement   Hugo   Ingoldby

Krondorf (Merrivale)   Krondorf (Ryecroft)

Manning Park   Fern Hill

Torresan Estate   McLAREN   Scarpantoni

Hardy's Tintara   FLAT   Tinlins   Cambrai

Southern Vales/McLaren Vale   James Haselgrove

Chalk Hill   Middlebrook

Pirramimma   Wirra Wirra

Maxwells Winery   McLAREN

Daringa Cellars   VALE

Donolga   Noon's Winery

Genders McLaren Park

The Estate   Richard Hamilton

PORT WILLUNGA

WILLUNGA

SOUTHERN MOUNT LOFTY RANGES

One of the eccentric gentlemen of the region, winemaker Greg Trott, holds court behind the tasting room bar in his old stone winery, Wirra Wirra. He speaks with the air of an ecclesiastical pronouncement of his coming to the region, 'I couldn't possibly work in a place I didn't like. I want to have fun doing what I like, which is making wine. I'm a great believer in the good things of life, good food, good music, good conversation, and they are all stimulated by the grape.'

Physically the region extends from the creeping suburbia of southern Adelaide, which has inexorably replaced many vineyards with the accoutrements of a city's over-rapid expansion, up to the foot of the southern Mount Lofty Ranges (so close that in some cases it is difficult to determine which vineyards should be classified as McLaren Vale and which as Adelaide Hills), through the wide and undulating valley of the McLaren Vale and McLaren Flat

townships, west to the expansive beaches, and over to the Willunga Hills running across the Fleurieu Peninsula, which is a holiday playground for the city of Adelaide with its sea resorts, beaches, forests, hobby farming and almond groves. A separate region across these hills – Langhorne Creek – is sometimes considered part of McLaren Vale, extending south from the Bremer River near the shores of the vast, shallow, salty and frequently treacherous Lake Alexandrina which is the Murray River's last gulp at freedom before dribbling its dregs into the ocean at Goolwa.

The McLaren Vale region lies between latitudes 35°30'S and 35°05'S and is generally classified as a warm region, with a heat summation of about 1600 heat degree days, although there is a wide range of microclimates among the undulating slopes. Like the Hunter and the Barossa, it is not a region that would be chosen in the 1980s for the highest levels of viticulture; in the 1840s, however, it was seen as ideal, and, most important, it was close to the city.

Here is the oldest continuing winery in Australia, Reynella, which was founded in 1838 by an English migrant from Devon, John Reynell, who added

Greg Trott outside his Wirra Wirra winery, near McLaren Vale, South Australia. The winery's rustic front and cavernous interior belie the modern equipment at the rear. The wines are among the best from the district.

Fermentation tanks at Woodstock winery, near Blewitt Springs, in the McLaren Vale district of South Australia. Winemakers Scott Collett and his father Doug are skilled producers of quality wines, especially reds.

Winemaker David Noon compares wines in Noon's winery at McLaren Vale. He and his wife Nerida established the small property and had their first vintage in 1971.

squabbles with European wine producers were frequent and because the new colonies of Australia were seen as ideally sunny for horticulture, the English looked to Australia to provide their wine. And thus the first winemakers were English (interestingly, from the West Country, and therefore possibly with some experience of winemaking in England, which had about that time been going into decline). The English connection endured and a century after the first landing, Hubert de Castella wrote a book on Australian wine, called *John Bull's Vineyard*. And the wines which could be produced in such regions as McLaren Vale, especially heavy clarets and fortified ports and sherries, were in demand 'back home'. An example of English tastes of the time could be found in the cellar of Beau Brummell. When he fled his creditors in 1816, his cellar was found to contain '10 dozen of capital Old Port, 16 dozen of Claret (Beauvais), Burgundy, Claret and Still Champagne – the whole of which have been nine years in bottle in the Cellar of the Proprietor'. Queen Victoria's reign saw the growth of sherry, and the accession of

grapes to his mixed farm and had his first harvest in about 1843. He discovered early an answer to Australia's heat problems – temperature control, by excavating a cave, his Cellar No. 1. Another West Country migrant, Thomas Hardy, obtained his first job in Australia working Reynell's cave before leaving to start his own company, Thomas Hardy and Sons, in 1853. By a nice irony, the thrusting modern Hardy organisation 130 years later took over the Reynella company, adopting Chateau Reynella as company headquarters and centre of white wine production, while continuing its red wine production 20 kilometres south at the Tintara winery in the town of McLaren Vale. It also has wineries in the Barossa Valley and the Riverland, and vineyard holdings at Keppoch in the State's Green Triangle to the south-east of the State.

McLaren Vale historically demonstrates that England was a wine-drinking country and, because

Bringing in the grapes at McLaren Flat. Although mechanical harvesting is gaining popularity for its economy and technical advantages, most winemakers still acknowledge that hand-picking, particularly for some varieties of grapes, is best for quality and best for quantity.

Steering the family company: the Board of Thomas Hardy and Sons Pty Ltd at a regular Board meeting. From left around the table at Hardy's Reynella winery are managing director Wayne Jackson, directors Bill Hay, Ken Price, David Hardy, Sir James Hardy (Chairman), Robert Hardy (Deputy Chairman), Ian Gray, Bryan Dolan and company secretary Brian Edwards. (Director Ray Drew is absent.)

Edward, as a result of his Prince of Wales lifestyle, saw a sudden unfashionability of claret and sherry in favour of champagne and port.

Through all the changing tastes of England, McLaren Vale was to follow, for, while much of the wine produced in other Australian regions was to find ready local markets in a land starved for entertainment and stress-relievers, this area concentrated on exports. The two predominant styles were the none-too-dry red table wines, which were sold by such companies as Emu and Stephen Smith as 'Australian burgundy', and fortified wines, ports and sherries which, because of the added dose of brandy spirit, were able to travel well. And they travelled, even though advances in transport in the 1920s and 1930s, especially for meat, meant table wines should have travelled as well as the ports.

However, it was not an ideal market. A noted gastronome André Simon had this to say as late as this century:

There are winemakers in Australia and Africa who make good wine, what I call 'hand-made' wines, which are made with loving and intelligent care from one or another species of grapes, whichever is the most suitable for the type of wine made; wines the fermentation of which is not unduly interfered with; wines which have an individuality of their own; wines with character and charm. But there are other Empire wines which I call 'machine-made' wines; wines made from every kind of grapes grown by any of the many known tea addicts, members of syndicates or associations of winegrowers who never drink wine. They are wines which are handled in huge quantities, scientifically and economically, but not lovingly; wines which are blended, loaded, brought up to a certain standard of colour, strength and sweetness; wines which are neither better nor worse than similar wines made in a similar manner elsewhere; above all, wines which serve a purpose and give to an increasingly large number of people all they need and all they know in the way of wine. But wines also, that damn the other and better wines bearing the names they themselves bear.

At work in the vineyards during the harvest. Mechanical equipment has lightened the workload and reduced costs in Australian vineyards.

David Hardy enjoys a glass of champagne made from grapes grown in vineyards just outside the stone walls of Padthaway Estate. In 1980 David and two partners restored the splendid old home, built in 1882, and it is now an imposing country guest house.

The rolling vineyards of the area south of Adelaide often described as the Southern Vales, looking south towards the foothills of the Mount Lofty Ranges (on the left) and the Gulf of St Vincent (to the right). At bottom left is Wynn's Seaview winery. In the middle background is the township of McLaren Vale. The white puffs across the middle and along the slopes of the ranges in the background are almond trees in blossom.

181

Cud Kay, whose family has been making wine at their Amery winery since 1895, crushes red grapes. Cud and his son Colin, who now makes the wines at Kays, still operate the property near McLaren Vale, South Australia.

Making champagne the real way — the méthode champenoise — is a laborious and labour-intensive process. Steve Kennedy, chief champagne cellar hand for Hardy's Wines, examines maturing Grand Reserve champagne at Hardy's Reynella cellars.

the 1925 import duties, 'colonial wines' were not highly regarded, for all that they had a market. Still, for more than a century, McLaren Vale was to provide wine in anonymous bulk for Britain, especially the red wines, many of which were big, overripe and jammy, rubbery with hydrogen sulphide (long believed to be the typical 'cowyard' characteristic of the region, but in fact a result of general winemaking faults which by the 1980s had become rare), high in alcohol and said to have a high iron content, and prescribed by English doctors to restore the vitality of anaemic patients in the winter cold.

The name McLaren Vale on a label in Australia was extremely rare until the late 1950s, when Ben Chaffey started making a new, more elegant style of wine in the early cabernet sauvignons at Seaview, and the early 1960s, when Jim Ingoldby and Eg Dennis formed the McLaren Vale Wine Company, to sell

McLaren Vale, like most regions of Australia, has produced both. And how it kindles memories of the writing of Adelaide journalist and politician, Ebenezer Ward, who last century had written, certainly, that South Australia would become one of the most important wine countries of the world, but with the rider that standards needed to be upgraded and winemakers needed to hold their wines longer for release with more maturity, rather than the then prevailing position that 'strong, raw liquors are readily purchased at low rates, and retailed at a larger profit than would perhaps accrue immediately from the sale of a better article, and many persons having tasted such stuff become ever afterwards abominators of Colonial Wine.'

Even though in 1917 England introduced wine import licences which favoured the colonies, a treatment that was to become actively preferential with

the region's produce through the Sydney merchant company, H. G. Brown. Seaview winery was to become part of the Allied Vintners organisation and, indeed, Allied Vintners and Hardy are the only large names of Australian wine operating in the region, although the Barossa company Krondorf can almost be counted for its involvement. Generally it remains an area of cottage industry, dominated by Anglo-Saxon stock, with most wineries being family concerns.

The boom came during the decade from 1966 to 1976, through which time Australian wine consumption doubled. At the start of this period, there were

about fifteen wineries operating in the McLaren Vale region; ten years later there were more than forty. By about 1978, as the red boom gave way to the white boom, there was a general realisation of the need for new viticultural practices as much as for processing technology. The major modern influence on the region came from the Oenotech partnership of Tony Jordan and Brian Croser from the Adelaide Hills, consulting first to Wirra Wirra then to some other wineries in the region.

Nearly every grape variety known in Australia is planted somewhere here, as befits such a collection of individuals, but the concentration is on table wines,

Maturing red wine in wood puncheons and hogsheads at Hardy's winery, McLaren Vale. Hogsheads (330 litres) made from French oak cost about $350 each and puncheons (500 litres) around $450.

183

Kay's Amery winery, north-east of McLaren Vale, occupies one of the most commanding spots in the Southern Vales, sitting on top of a hill with views to the Gulf of St Vincent.

both red and white, with the principal styles being firm reds from shiraz and cabernet sauvignon, and heavily flavoured Rhine rieslings (a style pioneered by Cud Kay) and large bodied chardonnays and sauvignon blancs. There are, of course, ports and pop wines too, and several winemakers of other than Anglo-Saxon origins joyously expanding the stylistic possibilities. The region is also an attractive source of fruit for Barossa companies.

But one does not talk so much of the grapes in McLaren Vale, where it is the winemaker who is king. This shows most in the annual Bushing Festival, held every October since 1972 to mark the release of the

vintage's wines. Its origin lies in the Elizabethan custom of English inns hanging out ivy bushes to advertise the arrival of each new season's wines. In contrast to the mass entertainment of the Teutonic Big Brother Barossa's biennial vintage festival, Bushing is more of a country fair, with the emphasis on dinners, small cellar parties and sampling wines rather than swilling them. The winemaker judged to have made the best wine of the year is declared Bushing King and that is an excuse for a bit of pomp, for more fascinating Oz culture in the making, and for symbolising the importance placed in this region on the people who make the wine.

LANGHORNE CREEK

While sometimes considered with McLaren Vale, Langhorne Creek, although small, should stand apart. This, one of the least sung wine-producing regions of Australia, is surprisingly cool for its geographic position, having a summer heat summation of about 1450 heat degree days. Its low profile results from some 80 per cent of its grapes being trucked to the Barossa, plus a little to McLaren Vale, for blending into other brand wines. Wolf Blass is one of the notable advocates of the fruit from this region.

This oasis of tall gums, some 70 kilometres from Adelaide, was named after its first settler, Alfred Langhorne, who had been driving a mob of cattle overland from New South Wales in 1841. Vines were planted in the early 1860s by Frank Potts, who set up a winery named after his friend, the Reverend J. I. Bleasdale. The Bleasdale winery, with its proud air of rustic pioneering, its massive red-gum constructions, is still run by the Potts family, while just down the road is Bill Davidson's little Bremer, founded in 1975. Around them are some 25 private grape-growers, mostly of Anglo-Saxon stock.

The tempering of the ripening of the grapes comes from the climatic influence of Lake Alexandrina, but grape quality is also enhanced by the deep, rich alluvial soil washed down from Callington and Mount Barker almost every winter when the Bremer River

floods. A system of flood banks and sluices controls water which is flooded onto the vineyards. There are also occasional flash floods. One historic photograph on the walls of Bleasdale winery shows a rowboat being used for harvesting the grapes during an unseasonal summer flood. The king grape here is cabernet sauvignon, which in Langhorne Creek develops a rich, sweet taste and can make wonderfully full flavoured wines.

More small vineyards and wineries have been developed south along the shores of Lake Alexandrina, including Temple Bruer and Santa Rosa, and they enjoy similar climatic conditions. Some of the best sauvignon blanc in the country is said to be grown at Currency Creek.

Shiraz grapes ripening near McLaren Vale, South Australia. The vintage here occurs in February and March, but later in some of the cooler parts of South Australia and elsewhere.

MURRAY MASSIVE

More than half of Australia's wine – 57 per cent – is totally dependent on one river, the Murray. Vast holdings of vineyards irrigated solely by the Murray developed early this century a strength in producing brandy and fortified wines; and even though changes in taxation structures and society's drinking habits saw a massive swing to table wines in the 1970s, the Murray remained important for its ability to produce mass market wines cheaply and efficiently. Plus a few of its own rare vinous styles. This River is – for its produce, its symbolism and its beauty – Australia's most important inland feature.

The Murray rises in the high country of the Great Dividing Range, the peak of its watershed being the 2231-metre Mount Kosciusko. And it flows, often sluggishly, always majestically, for 2560 kilometres to the sea, almost halfway across the continent. As it descends from the high country and the high rainfall areas, the River laboriously seeks the easiest course across the vast, flat land, almost barren and saltily dry

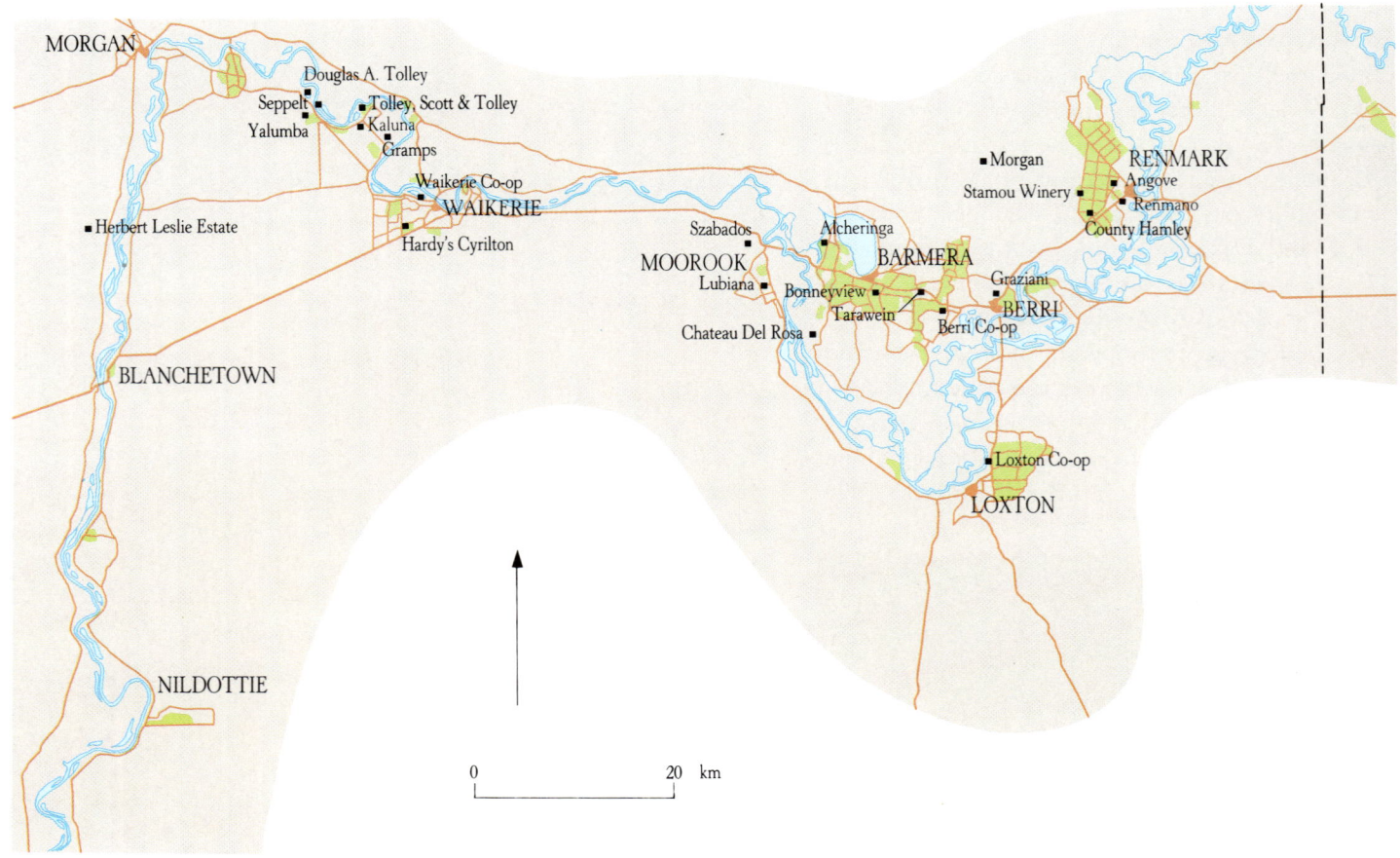

since the ocean rolled back millions of years ago. So flat is the land that at Swan Hill the River is only the height of a large city office block above sea level, and it still has another 1400 kilometres to flow. The Murray commands its respect not by being the longest of the world's great rivers, nor the widest, but the slowest.

Much of its course is inhospitable mallee scrub, stunted eucalypt and sandy desert where, if it's possible to run sheep at all, the farmers talk not of how many they can run to the hectare but of how many hectares it takes to support one animal. But nature has given the River sometimes cliffs, red, white and gold, sometimes prolific wildlife, and always the giant red river gums by its banks. Along the Murray Valley, as the slender ribbons of trees flanking the River are called, views of the winding khaki, silver, blue and mud-brown waters at every turn constantly surprise the visitor just by their being there. Man has added to the views, with towns and with irrigation, making it possible at distances of up to 15 kilometres from the water for vineyards to grow, and also citrus groves and stone-fruit orchards, frequently hedged with feral growth of brilliant sunflowers and aromatic fennel. Part of the wilderness has been tamed, if with a verdancy that seems alien to Australia's natural colours. The Murray has become a sort of market garden to that village, clinging precariously to the seaboard, which is urbanised Australia.

There are vineyards in the higher, wetter country around Rutherglen, but for climatic reasons these

must be considered separately. After Tisdall's vineyards at Echuca, the irrigated regions proper begin at about Swan Hill and cover three States and several sub-regions: Kerang/Swan Hill with an annual rainfall of 340 millimetres, the Victorian and New South Wales Sunraysia with about 250 millimetres of rain and the even drier South Australian Riverland. The differences between Sunraysia in New South Wales and Victoria, respectively north and south of the Murray, are for viticultural and even social purposes minimal, although traffic across the bridges late in the evenings attests that residents are keenly aware that the pubs on the New South Wales side stay open an hour later.

Water is the stuff of life in the Riverland districts of New South Wales, Victoria and South Australia. Here water is pumped from the Murray River near Mildura, in north-western Victoria.

There is even an increasing co-ordination of both State Departments of Agriculture in horticultural matters along the River. After the Murray runs a particularly barren 260 kilometres from Wentworth into South Australia it meets greater political and organisational differences, although the vine again flourishes blithely oblivious to man-made lines on maps. The irrigated areas peter out at Morgan where

Without irrigation there would be no grapes from the hotter, drier parts of Australia. Grapes from vines like this one near Karadoc, not far from Mildura in Victoria, are watered by sprinklers fed from the Murray.

the Murray takes a sudden turn southward, after which the broad brown leftovers from more than 1000 kilometres of irrigation are to become the notorious turgid tapwater of Adelaide or a dribble into the sea at its mouth, Goolwa.

Once the Murray's main use to the white man was for transporting the wool clip from the vast stations of western New South Wales on the Darling and Murrumbidgee rivers, each a vital tributary of the Murray, to the sea. Railways and irrigation have changed this watery commerce, and the sounds of the hooting paddlesteamers have been replaced with the clunking of waterside pumps. Grape-growing ranks with citrus fruit as a major industry now, and 62 per cent of each vintage's grapes from the estimated 49 million vines along the Murray are dried or supplied fresh for eating. The remaining 286 000 tonnes become wine or brandy.

This accounts for more than half of Australia's wine, making the River the backbone of the nation's industry, if the least known name in wine. It is also, of the major winegrowing regions, the newest.

While the Barossa, Hunter, Swan, McLaren Vale and numerous vinous pockets of Victoria were significant in the nineteenth century, the Murray was yet to be tamed. This took the vision of a politician, Alfred Deakin, and the enterprise of two Canadians, George and William Chaffey, who in 1887 started transforming a drought-ridden sheep station into the Mildura Irrigation Colony that water might be pumped from the Murray on to the surrounding land and that food might flourish. In fact, politicking drove the Chaffey brothers from Victoria to South Australia and they started work on developing an irrigation colony at Renmark. But they soon were lured back to Victoria and to Mildura, a town which was to take pride of place on the River with the 1903 opening of a rail link to Melbourne.

The towns along the River tell the history: Swan Hill, a racy rural centre which can stand back enough to make a lucrative tourist magnet from the riverboat

Vintage is a family affair in many grape areas of the country. Andrew Sarunic, aged two and a half, eats grapes on the tractor driven by his father Tony Sarunic in the Victorian Riverland.

Giant tanks in a 'tank farm' at Lindemans' Karadoc winery, near Mildura, provide winemakers with the ability to make delicate, fruity wines like Ben Ean Moselle and Leo Buring Leibfrauwine in quantity and yet retain quality.

189

A patchwork of vineyards stretches across the landscape near Mildura, on the Victorian side of the River Murray. Yields are high in vineyards like this, where water from the river is plentiful.

Tony Sarunic stands in an irrigation trench on his 17-hectare vineyard in the Riverland. Vines are irrigated by flood irrigation — like this — or by sprinklers or, in areas where water is scarcer, by drip irrigation from plastic pipes.

Vineyards sprawl along the mighty Murray, the source of their existence. These vineyards, near Berri, South Australia, are typical of the areas that produce some of the fine quaffing wines of Australia.

days; Robinvale, a tight little community with its soldier settlers, now nearing retiring age *en masse*, worrying about the future of their fruit blocks as the kids have been seduced away by the materialism of the cities; Mildura, queen of the River, well served and extraordinarily lush, and keeping itself handsomely facelifted; Renmark, conceived as a twin to Mildura, but now looking like an ageing socialite, clinging to its traditions and smiling wryly at these modern times; Berri, the thrusting, progressive young commercial centre; Loxton, hiding its dour Germanic heritage and its considerable bulk mostly in the mallee farms to the south; Barmera, set not on the River so much as on one of its lakes and consequently seeming expansive and relaxed (and even sporting a croquet lawn); Waikerie, solid and honest and covering any feelings of downstream inferiority by casting its thoughts more towards the city of Adelaide; and Morgan, almost buried in the detritus of its past.

The Chaffey brothers take the honour of founding the first (legal) winery on the River, when Chateau Mildura (later to become Mildara Wines) gathered its first grapes in 1891. But this is more a region of growers than processors. In the South Australian section of the River there are some 2400 grape-growers, and a similar number upstream. Some are descendants of original blockers; more, however, came after World Wars I and II, when governments offered small plots of land to those who had served their country.

It can be a good life on the River. Consider Jack Murphy of Trentham Cliffs. His father took up a

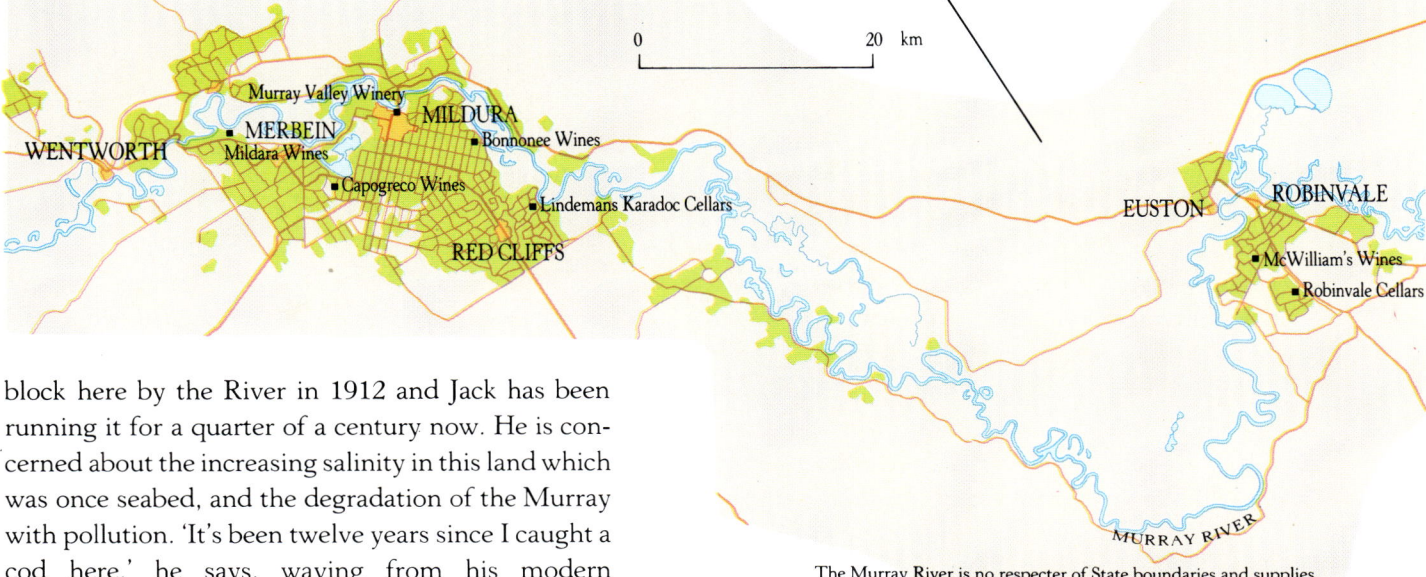

The Murray River is no respecter of State boundaries and supplies vital water to vineyards in three States: New South Wales, Victoria and South Australia. For ease of reference we have included this region in the chapter on South Australia.

block here by the River in 1912 and Jack has been running it for a quarter of a century now. He is concerned about the increasing salinity in this land which was once seabed, and the degradation of the Murray with pollution. 'It's been twelve years since I caught a cod here,' he says, waving from his modern loungeroom to the water at the bottom of his backyard. And as president of the local grape-growers' association he has a constant fight against increasing costs of power and irrigation water and against winery pressures for cheaper grapes. 'It's got its ups and downs,' he says, 'but I am my own boss and I'm happy.'

Like almost all other growers his main grape varieties are sultana and gordo. These are not trendy varieties, not the way cabernet sauvignon, Rhine riesling and chardonnay are known, but they are the nation's most numerous wine grapes. Gordo (also known as muscat of Alexandria, and more properly as muscat gordo blanco), and the ubiquitous sultana, which many Australians grow in the back yard as a table grape, are the basis of most white cask wines, most popular champagnes, indeed most mass-market white wines. Oenologically, they are simple

grapes, not highly flavoured but cheap and flexible, and modern technology in winemaking has given a new boost to their usefulness. Brian Bergin, the progressive manager of one medium-sized winery, Woorinen Estates, asks rhetorically: 'What's wrong with sultana? It's time we pulled our fingers out and became honest with labelling.' Thus his company puts out a cask riesling clearly stating grape varieties, including sultana and gordo, and the region of origin, Swan Hill.

For the growers such varieties retain their popularity by being flexibly suitable for three purposes: winemaking, drying and table fruit. When one market is in the doldrums – for example, dried fruit in the face of heavily subsidised exports from Europe – the grower swings his crop to another purpose. This happens more in Victoria and New South Wales than in South Australia, where there is a greater reliance on exclusively wine varieties of grapes, leading to the politically sensitive issue of surpluses of grapes left hanging on the vines most seasons because they are not wanted by the wineries.

As Renmark grape-grower Roly Telfer, grandson of a Mildura blocker and son of a soldier-settler, explains it: 'Fashions in wines change very rapidly; but it

Sunrise at Lindemans' Karadoc winery in north-western Victoria. During and after the vintage each year most wineries work around the clock, harvesting and crushing the grapes, then processing them through fermentation and beyond to the finished package.

Jo Graziani, owner and winemaker of his self-named winery near Berri, in the South Australian Riverland, tastes his 1983 port, fresh from the barrel where it will mature for a year or two before being offered for sale.

can take a grower several years of non-productive land to rip out vines and wait for the new varieties to grow. Who can say that even then they will still be wanted?' But the progressive growers, the wineries and government departments are putting considerable effort into attempting to match produce and markets. Much progress is being made with top-grafting techniques for more rapid changeovers, while the better growers are looking to mechanical pruning to match the almost universal mechanical harvesting that enables them to produce grapes more efficiently.

The wineries are under considerable pressure in the marketplace to keep costs down while making better wines, and for them, too, technology has been the tool. But the grapes are still the essence and winemaker Stuart Auld of Renmano in Renmark puts it this way: 'The next frontier in viticulture is persuading growers to meet the challenge of such

Students at Roseworthy Agricultural College in South Australia are taught how to operate a pressure centrifuge at the College's winery. Oenology is the science of winemaking, and the course normally takes three years.

The lasting appeal of small winemaking concerns is the individual attention given to wines from grapevine to bottle. Here Tom Bodroghy fills bottles of wines by hand at his County Hamley winery at Renmark, South Australia.

new broadacre regions as Padthaway/Keppoch in planting premium varieties, if only so we can keep upgrading the quality of cask wines.' Of course, there is still disagreement about what are the desirable varieties although it seems that pinot noir, sylvaner and traminer are three which do not do well, while considerable hopes are held for chardonnay, ruby cabernet and merlot.

Along the River more than two dozen wineries process these local grapes. Several of the wineries are small, run by battling blockers who want to make wine of their own grapes. They crush perhaps 20 tonnes, perhaps 100, largely to serve local markets or small pockets in the big cities. Some concentrate on such ethnic specialities as retsina, a white wine flavoured with pine resin which, although it can taste like turpentine strained through a bishop's socks, is indispensable for cutting through the fattiness of much Greek-style cooking.

They battle on, growers such as Jo Graziani at Renmark who, for all that he rants about governments and bureaucrats making life miserable with taxes and regulations, is happy – and it shows in the vitality of his red wines. But his wines are rarely seen in the cities: it's all local, cellar door sales to tourists, and mail order. Which is also the case with Bruno Capogreco of Mildura, who like so many growers has discovered along the Murray the New Calabria. He loves the soil, and it delivers its best for him. He joins

his family in saying that fresh zucchini and homemade salami are more important than video recorders or swimming pools, and says of his life-style: 'It's purity, and quality in quantity, a hobby, an art. But we work for it.' As with Graziani the essential joys of his life are reflected in his wines, made in trad-itional, natural Italian ways. There are attempts, too, at wines in more mainstream Australian traditions, for example from Bonneyview at Barmera where a charming young Englishman named Robert Minns, who somehow found himself on the River, is dedi-cated to experimenting with radical viticultural techniques that better wines may be made.

But the River is essentially the home of the big wineries. The nation's largest processors are here, including the Berri Co-operative, Lindemans at Karadoc, the Loxton Co-operative, Stanley at Buronga in New South Wales, Renmano at Renmark (which is now amalgamated with the Berri Co-op under the name of Consolidated Co-operative Wineries Ltd), Angove at Renmark, Mildara at Mer-bein, Penfolds/Kaiser Stuhl at Waikerie, McWil-liam's at Robinvale and Hardy's Cyrilton winery at Waikerie.

Some of these names are surprising. Lindemans, Stanley, Penfolds/Kaiser Stuhl, McWilliam's and Hardy are thought of as wine companies based elsewhere. This they are, but they also have wineries on the Murray to buy the cheap and plentiful fruit to make into the mainstay of their mass-market blends, especially cask and flagon wines, and for distillation as brandy or fortifying spirit.

And some of these names are unfamiliar. Loxton, for example, although the nation's third-largest win-ery, puts out less than 2 per cent of its produce under its own name, the remainder being bulk wine for other large companies elsewhere to buy and blend.

Angove is better known for its subsidiary lines, such as St Agnes brandy, Stones Green Ginger wine and Marko vermouth, than for its own branded wines. Even Berri and Renmano are hardly trendy names in wine circles because they have concentrated on the bag-in-box cask market. And with extraordi-nary success. Berri Fruity Gordo Moselle, at more than 6 million litres a year (in casks), is considered Australia's largest-selling wine.

It is estimated that of the 228 million litres of wine (including equivalents in brandy and fortified) made along the Murray River, less than 7 per cent comes

threats of diseases at the wrong time of the year, high yields of fair average quality grapes are possible. And at some of the cheapest prices in the nation.

As discounting in the marketplace puts increasing pressures on the wineries they must seek more economical means of processing and the River wineries tend to be Australia's most efficient and modern. Lindemans at Karadoc – an 8-hectare compound of 140 stainless steel tanks, the several largest holding 1.5 million litres of wine each – exemplifies the new mythology of wine in Australia: that the beverage for drinking comes from places gleaming like petrochemical refineries rather than from wise and wizened men with stained feet and a few oak casks.

Part of the Berri Co-operative winery in the South Australian Riverland. Berri merged with Renmano Co-operative at nearby Renmark several years ago and is probably the biggest winemaker in the nation, crushing over 60 000 tonnes of grapes each year.

onto the market labelled by its origins. Some 59 per cent is manufactured and sold by the Riverland wineries, although nothing is said on labels about its origins (e.g., cask wines). The balance – some 77 million litres – is taken by road tankers from these wineries, and from the several medium-sized River wineries which exist largely or solely on contract crushing for outside companies, to be blended in cellars elsewhere, principally in the Hunter and the Barossa. In addition, the equivalent of 40 million litres of wine is trucked out of the River areas in the form of grapes, almost entirely to the Barossa, for processing.

These figures vary from year to year, but not significantly. For the very attraction of the River to Australia's wine companies is that it is consistent. With abundant sunshine, with water supply controlled through irrigation, and virtually no rain to bring

The Murray River has flowed a long way from the days when it produced some of the nation's best brandies and fortifieds (as indeed it still does, for the few who want them). And it will continue flowing, with new viticultural techniques and winemaking technology, by producing fresh, light, fruity wines for early drinking. Most Australians are already drinking its produce, if unwittingly. For the Murray fuels the nation vinously.

Wines are constantly moved around big modern wineries, such as Lindemans' huge plant at Karadoc, in Victoria, for blending, fermentation, fortification and finally to be packaged.

197

*A master maker of varietal wines. John Brown Jr, the third to bear that name, outside
Brown Brothers' winery at Milawa, Victoria. Each vintage John Brown makes more than three
dozen distinct varietal table wines, an extraordinary winemaking feat.*

THE TASTE OF WINE

Max Lake

SMELLING AND TASTING

There are a handful of tastes, but thousands of smells. We are born with a flavour computer in good working order, and over a lifetime we increase its memory bank. You can and should learn more of the variability of your own senses of smell and taste (which amount to flavour) so that the enjoyment of the rest of your life will be enhanced by increased perception, and a bigger and better flavour library.

For wine tasters, one of the most important variations is threshold, and the concept of liking or disliking the same substance depending on its level. There are positive or negative responses to the same flavour.

Consider one example, methoxy isobutyl pyrazine, conveniently called M.I.P. It is a very powerful odorant, a few drops in a swimming pool will be picked up by some people. Others might not detect a bottle full. One subject quite liked it above his threshold of 3, and up to 8 parts per billion, but

started to dislike it over that figure and gave it the full negative blast (hated it!) over 20 parts per billion.

M.I.P. is the dominant capsicum or bell pepper-like character in the red cabernet and white sauvignon grapes grown in cold areas. Not everyone likes their wine to taste like Hungarian goulash. The French and Californian winegrowers strive, by careful control of vine growth, to lessen the M.I.P. of their cabernets. There is currently a fad for Australian cool climate cabernets; people forget the great reputation of Coonawarra reds was based on shiraz, not cabernet.

Blackcurrant is the ideal varietal fruit flavour in young cabernet. That is the one that oxidises (matures) to the superb cedar bouquet of the aged wine. M.I.P. changes to mint, of which a little goes a long way.

The alcohol threshold, where sensitive mucous surfaces in the mouth may start to feel a burning sensation, occurs at more than 11 per cent alcohol by volume.

People have different thresholds to the perception of sugar. It is difficult to be sure of its presence below 4 grams a litre, and may only be perceived as actual

Tasting wine at the cellar door, especially with the winemaker or his family, is one of the pleasures of visiting wine areas — here at Henschke's, Keyneton, in the Barossa, South Australia.

sweetness at double this level, before which it may taste like fruit flavours. Sometimes, apart from the lingering aftertaste of sugar, and glycerine, the only way to be certain is testing in the laboratory. Much of the middle flavour 'sweetness' of good wine gives a negative test for sugar, e.g., the true varietal 'sweetness' of cabernet sauvignon.

If sweetness is balanced, the flavour is always attractive. The perception of sweetness in wine is deceptive. There are numerous interactions which modify its taste. Acidity and cold lessen it. Dry is the opposite of sweet, on the palate. It can mean all grape sugar is totally used by the yeast fermentation, as in Champagne *natur,* which may be almost shocking in its dryness, till it is slightly liqueured to 'brut', when it then paradoxically tastes 'natural'! Dry vermouth on the other hand can contain up to 4 per cent sugar, but still tastes dry because bitterness lessens sweetness. So there is a reciprocality between sweetness and acidity, and also between sweetness and bitterness.

Sweetness increases the perception of fragrance. Cold lessens smells, e.g., bouquet and off flavours.

Flavour preferences may be ethnic, and regional. How appropriate is the resiny coarse wine of the Greek hills, with roasted fat lamb, under the azure Mediterranean sky, with the aroma of wild herbs floating on the breeze. And perhaps there only!

A cellar palate is getting used to, and finally preferring above all, a certain flavour or style, sometimes even a wine which a wine judge or winemaker would consider 'off'. This is to be avoided at all costs by the wine judge and winemaker.

There are also people who are label drinkers. Who ever heard of anyone criticising a bad Chateau Lafite? But such bottles can occur. The same people also fail to praise the rare top wine in a carafe. Even judges slip occasionally.

Many find it helpful to keep notes of their favourite wines and how they change. One of the simplest and best is this pleasure (hedonistic) profile.

1. Like it very much
2. Like
3. Okay
4. Dislike
5. Dislike very much.

Try this on your twelve-year-old; that is when you get the real evaluation of fruit flavour.

PALATE LENGTH

What you clearly experience is the liveliness of flavour due to acid, and the fullness from alcohol and sugars when the wine is in the mouth. In fact the body of a wine can be actually subjected to precise measurement, if you wish – alcohol plus extract. But your palate does it just as well. Later, during swallowing comes the hardness of certain acids and the bitterness/astringency of tannin – the 'finish'. Then comes the aftertaste, of variable length, depending on the amount of fruit flavours and sugars. Great length here is like a carillon played by the younger Scarlatti.

But go and taste. Don't talk about it. Do it!

The perfect partners. The civilising habit of drinking wine around meal times has developed quickly in Australia in the past decade — here over an outdoor lunch at the Yalumba winery, Angaston, South Australia.

TASTING WINE

The beginner might care to remember these in threes.

THREE 'GOODS'

Good Air No perfume, tobacco*, furniture polish, cooking smells, etc. Get your priorities right!

Good Light Daylight or white light, to see through the wine and check its colour – ordinary fluorescent light enhances yellows and browning.

Good Glass Clear, clean and colourless, rim narrower than waist to concentrate the bouquet.

THREE SENSES

Sight Inspect the colour and clarity. Very bright red colour indicates high acidity, for starters.

Smell Smell with concentration, repeating till you know what the wine smells like. Swirl the glass, even shake the wine up, to release the aromas.

Taste Firstly a general feel of the wine, and then suck air in with your mouth slightly open to swirl the mouthful. (You only choke the first few times.) This method gets the wine fragrance to the top of the back of the nose, where it counts. Finally, spit it out, if you don't want to intoxicate yourself with a series of wines. It is quite acceptable to spit carefully into waste vessels at tastings.

You should keep on reviewing wines tasted, particularly reds as they change character fairly rapidly in the open glass.

TWO QUICK TESTS

★ *For Quality* How long does the bouquet haunt the empty glass? Ordinary wines don't.

★ *For Longevity* Assessing its future. Keep trying the quality for as long as twenty-four hours if necessary. The longer the wine stays good in the glass, the longer will its life be in the bottle.

* *Writing as a former smoker and current international wine judge, I believe smoking only seriously affects the judgement of nearby non-smokers.*

WHERE THE FLAVOURS COME FROM

SEASONS AND REGIONS

The seasons flavour the wines that follow. From its winter sleep, half a year passes and the vine promises wine from the harvest of ripe fruit. We hope. Actually nature intends making vinegar. The winemaker interrupts the cycle.

During the growth period, much of the sour acid of the summer fruit is slowly converted to sugars. Quite marvellous that grapes are among the sweetest *and* most acid fruits eaten by man. And without the unique and strong flavours of the various varieties, wine would be about as interesting as beer. Without the high level of natural acids in the ripe fruit, wine would taste flat.

The most extraordinary single moment of the season, to the grapegrower and winemaker, is to smell the perfume of the grape flowers in spring. Few

Lunch between the almond grove and the vineyard. As the almond trees blossom near McLaren Vale, South Australia, the vines are being pruned ready for the next season.

When water is available in abundance, the simplest way to give the vines a drink is flood irrigation. Many vineyards along the Murray River, like this one near Mildura, are irrigated in this way.

scents are more heady, more ravishing, and they are very close to the fragrance of the mature wine to follow later. How unbelievable to enjoy this at the moment of conception, years before it is to be poured into your glass. Wine voyeur!

Autumn in several latitudes is sufficiently cool for grapes with skin damaged by ice or rot, to lose water without losing fruit flavour. From these come the finest and most intensely flavoured sweet wines. Other regions consistently produce flavour profiles in certain varieties of grape that encourage easy identification of their wines. With sufficient distinction, they greet the wine-lover with every glass.

The influence of drainage, orientation, and slope are obvious to anyone who has grown anything. The grape is not an all-or-nothing flavour factory. Where and how it grows may be paramount in most varieties. The flavour balance of a particular season is the

optimum mix of ripening sugar and falling acid. In warm climates this can occur in a day; in cold areas it may take a fortnight. The best flavour is achieved by limiting the time or area of picking, one of the advantages of making wine in small quantities.

The generous chardonnay is an excellent example of regional response to a wide spectrum of climate and region. Consider the wines from the north of France to a few hundred kilometres south. The still white wine of Champagne, Chablis, Corton, Meursault, the Montrachets, and Macon. With some friends, you may be able to line up wines representing each region to impressively show just what changes occur in quality and size in the wine of one grape variety with graded change in microclimate.

Riesling on the other hand is very localised. It will grow in a lot of places, but to achieve the definitive flavours, its climatic needs are rather

The fruit of vintage in the Hunter Valley, New South Wales. Hermitage (or shiraz) grapes come in by the bucket at Drayton's property.

localised. The wine of this variety is one of the best demonstrations of the truth that wherever great wines are made, they are only *just* made. Where wine is easy to make it is rarely great.

Some seasons, the climate frowns. Rain, hail, frost, wind; wrong time, too much, not enough; whatever. In the classic areas, something like three years in ten, on an average, see everything just right. From these vintages come some of the most exciting flavours we taste, the great wines. Paradoxically, occasionally a great wine emerges in poor years.

THE GRAPE AND ITS PROCESSING

There are over 500 chemical components in wine, principally acids, sugars, alcohols, fruit flavours, colours and tannin. Skin, pips and stalks contribute the latter. Skin 'colour' dominates flavour in both red and white wines. Except in one or two curios, white grapes are pressed and the skins discarded after pressing and only the juice is fermented, which helps avoid coarseness of flavour. Red grapes ferment on their skins, with extraction of colour and flavour increasing as the alcohol rises during the ferment.

The flavour structure reflects this, particularly in cabernet sauvignon wines where there is an increase in texture and body towards the actual wine finish. This is the flavour of the sauvignon polyphenols, and may be so marked as to suggest a hole in flavour in the middle palate, what once amused the author to call 'the doughnut'.

Pinot noir on the other hand has none of this accentuation. If pressed hard, such a wine may finish astringently but the flavour body is absolutely uniform from start to finish. Without pressing or wood astringency, wines of pinot noir finish fairly softly, which is one of their main attractions, and at the opposite end of the pole to the firmness of cabernet sauvignon.

The insides of a grape has similarities to the insides of a human, with one or two interesting differences. Returning to the grape, the juice that keeps the

The winemaker may be the conductor, but he has to get the other members of the orchestra to play in tune, especially at vintage time. Making wine at Krondorf's winery near Tanunda, South Australia.

yeast spinning happily by the hearth at home, is loaded with sugar, acids and salts; these make the 'body' of the wine.

The astringency of any wine is increased by the time on skins, or the addition of hard pressings, at the decision of the winemaker. Some marvellously soft, deep coloured, and aromatic wines are made without any pressings, particularly those left to first 'compost' in a closed fermenter for a few weeks' carbonic maceration.

SPECIAL GRAPE VARIETIES

Of the hundreds of grapes from which wine is made around the world, a few of the principal European fine varieties have been selected to discuss here, because that is where it all began.

The great Michael Leunig has a cartoon in the *Wine and Spirit Monthly* (Australia) which ranks with

Making wine is hard work and it involves transferring grapes, juice, wine and, finally, packaged wine around the winery. Stephen Henschke draws a sample of wine from a concrete underground storage tank at his Keyneton winery, South Australia.

James Thurber's New Yorker cartoon, 'A naive little domestic burgundy, I think you'll be amused by its presumption.' Leunig's has a nose in a glass, 'mintiness with peaches and strawberries… a chocolate smokeyness with leathery insinuations… hessian… apes and peacocks… and a faint, elusive yet startling aroma of wine…'

Jargon and garbage switch joy off. No doubt. However it is possible to devise a code of access to your own memory bank, and even perhaps communicate to someone else just what you mean. All professionals use memory hooks. Here is one set for the commoner varieties which I have used over the past twenty-five years.

...mintiness with peaches and strawberries … a chocolate smokeyness with leathery insinuations. … hessian… apes and peacocks …. and a faint, elusive yet startling aroma of wine …

UNIQUE GRAPE FLAVOURS

WHITE GRAPES	AROMA *smell of the grape*[1]	BOUQUET *wine fragrance*[1]
Muscat	complex, typical, strong	spicy, floral (rose, geranium, etc.)
Traminer	carnation, clove	spicy
Riesling	tropical fruits	tropical fruits
Semillon	greenskinned ripe fruits	fruity, fresh straw
Sauvignon blanc	capsicum, bell pepper	spicy, strong
Chardonnay	fig, melons, limes, other citrus	stone fruits, quince, hazelnuts, butter, cinnamon

RED GRAPES

Cabernet sauvignon and relatives[2]	Dusty, musty, blackcurrant, capsicum, bell pepper, peppermint	cedar oil, fragrant flowers, small ripe berries, truffles
Pinot noir	ripe fruit	strawberry, beetroot, field flowers
Gamay	raspberry	raspberry
Shiraz (hermitage)	blackberry	ripe fruit

[1] *These are memory hooks only. You may perceive them differently. Not all occur at one time.*
[2] *Cabernet franc, malbec, petit verdot, merlot.*

Most grapes are more or less the same colour inside. The colour of red wine is extracted from the skins — the longer time the juice lies with the skins after crushing and pressing, the more intense the colour of the final product.

YEASTS

Yeasts flavour wine. They create alcohol which is sweet, and has a texture and body of its own. Alcohol also has an attractive, sweetish fruity aroma. But the range of odours of the yeasts themselves is vast, from tropical fruit to bready. Some stink or make vinegary notes, especially the wild ones of which twenty or more varieties may co-exist in the seething broth in the fermenter. One usually dominates.

Those with the most attractive and strong characters are eagerly sought and cultivated by master technologists in an attempt to get complete control of the wine. In fact some are given names, ostensibly from their breeding place, like 'Montrachet', 'Champagne' and the like. The trouble is that the yeasts are so involved in their trade of reproduction, they miss their stroke at times and mutate, behaving like the new baby brought out for the visitors, only to relieve itself on the carpet.

Anyhow, many of the yeast characters, both cultivated, and uninvited, have integrated into wine flavour by the end of the first year. All that is really asked is: did the dominant yeast of a particular vintage do a reasonably efficient job in terms of rate of ferment, tidy alcohol production from all sugar in the must, and not make more off-odour than can be swept under the carpet of wine maturation?

Champagne is one of the best examples of persisting yeast flavour. Broken down cells from the second fermentation may impart a fresh cheesy smell to the bouquet of a great champagne, not unpleasant in small amounts. They certainly do not taste like a health food. In fact there are marked sexual overtones, attractive to all sexes, which is not an uncommon finding. Some of the great Champagne houses leave special Champagnes on their yeast lees for a decade or more to enhance this character.

A carpet of flor yeast is deliberately encouraged on

*Storing wine in oak at
Mildara, Merbein, Victoria.
As the barrels get older,
they impart less oak flavour
to the wine or brandy.*

the surface of part-filled sherry casks. The smell of bean sprouts and olives gets close to the nutty flavour of good fino sherries. Add a hint of old dry straw and you have the 'rancio' of the great old white fortified sweet wines of Madeira and muscat.

WOOD

Wooden barrels make two separate contributions to wine. Oak is one of those timbers which permit air in, and wine out, through its pores. Up to 15 per cent of the volume of the contained wine is lost in a given year. This controlled oxidation matures the wine, a process continuing in bottle, at least for table wine. Chestnut is a beautifully flavoured timber, but hopeless for wine, because its loss is perhaps twice that of oak. A 200- to 230-litre hogshead is the biggest empty cask one man can reasonably handle. It also happens to be the size which produces the best rate of maturation of the great wine varieties. Serendipity!

All new oak fermentation and storage gives several flavours to the wine therein. They are: vanilla, resin, 'toasty' (if you are looking for 'buttery', it sometimes follows secondary fermentation in wine), sweetness, acidity, colour, and tannins. One of the principal odour peaks in the gas liquid chromatographic tracing of oak is the 'whisky' lactone, from an eight-carbon acid, which smells like much of the bouquet of mature cabernet sauvignon. The great single variety wines would be little more than shadows without the Lautrec silhouette of their fruit, by this oak lactone. And I mean the pinot noirs of Burgundy, merlot of Petrus, even several of the Medocs in odd years. Remarkably, cabernet sauvignon has little need of this magic because it is already present in the wine of that grape. On one occasion at a masked tasting, the 'oak balance' of a steel tank fermented and stored cabernet was preferred to those fermented in new oak, or steel tank fermented and stored in new oak.

Early in my winemaking, the barrels of twelve different woods were put on trial. Different forests and species of oak have different flavours. The side of the tree facing the sun is different to the dark side! You never stop learning.

OTHER

Uncontrolled oxidation of fruit flavour flattens, coarsens and finally destroys it.

You might find it amusing to read some of the vivid, even coarse, but accurate descriptive words heard during a quarter of a century of wine judging. Some are barely fit to be mentioned here, and some are definitely not. You could cause a sensation if you whip a few out at the appropriate occasions.

Closed, dumb, short, lifted, faded, are okay, and clear statements of flavours. Odd, 'off' characters are due principally to moulds and bacteria, e.g. corky, bilgy, swampy, wet baggy, mousey.

One change actually encouraged in many high acid wines is the second fermentation of new wine's malic acid by bacteria, to the softer lactic acid. Esters of both acids enhance complexity of flavour in clean wines.

Rotten egg gas, H_2S, is a common and contentious problem in winemaking. It can come from vineyard

mismanagement, wild yeasts and so on. When conjugated with other wine compounds, the range of off-odours is amazing; cabbage, rubber, iodine, wet leather, bad onion or garlic, and, of course, bad eggs. What has to be faced is that combined sulphur is a basic building block of so many of the great natural flavours. You can see it in paw paw, and great traminer wine also has a mercaptan note, among its spicy aromatics. So many of the great wines preferred at masked tastings have a touch of combined sulphur, that it is obviously one of the threshold substances with the positive and negative levels for each individual already described. The average threshold is 0.1-0.2 micrograms per litre.

A little acetic acid is produced by the yeast in fermentation. It also results from the basic degradation of wine by acetic bacteria. Most wines have less than 0.5 gram per litre, at which level it lifts flavour, increases complexity, and improves the finish of the wine. Double that amount is acceptable, and is seen in several great wines. Once you can smell and taste vinegar, however, the wine is at the beginning of the end; 'volatile' as we say, or 'pricked' on the palate.

Time is the secret ingredient that often produces fine wines. Wine maturing at the Sevenhill Cellars in the Clare Valley, South Australia.

Using a hydrometer to check alcohol levels in wine at Drayton's Hunter Valley winery, New South Wales.

209

WINE FUTURES

DEVELOPMENT

Moving wine around the winery for blending is one of the necessary skills for modern winemakers. Blending may be done for improving quality, changing the flavour or attaining consistency. Lindemans' Karadoc winery in Victoria.

One often hears the word complexity used as a favourable character in wine flavour. Here is the mathematics of it. Consider only four of the alcohols in wine (ethyl alcohol or just 'alcohol', is the main one). With age in bottle they slowly oxidise to form aldehydes. In turn these yield four acids. These would combine, esterify with some of the initial alcohols, resulting in sixteen different esters. With

the remaining alcohols and acids, the grand total of twenty-eight different flavoured substances have sprung from the first four. And there are over 400 separate compounds already identified in wine.

White wines live and last on their acid. If they lack it, they die. Generally a white wine has to smell and taste pretty good at the time of bottling, because so much less development occurs in bottle. However, white wines from new oak barrels mature and develop more like a red wine.

Red wines are preserved by their colour and tannins, but they also need acid to develop. They do so

beautifully in bottle. But age is no guarantee of improvement. Look at the people around you. It used to be thought that to go the distance, and improve during the journey, a young red wine had to be huge in size, and hard as the hobs of hell. Not so; many top wines are exciting in their youth.

One of the most fascinating discussions that can take place over a good bottle, is whether a wine attractive in its youth is *absolutely* better or not, than another of virtually equal attraction for which we have had to wait so many years. Or whether it is worthwhile waiting for more development in the younger ones. Spend time talking about such wines. Don't waffle about ordinary wines, just enjoy them.

GREAT WINE

The secret of all good table wine is *balance:* harmony between alcohol, acid and tannin and oak flavour, if present. A balanced young wine will last, and develop more flavour.

The stamp of greatness is *fruit.* You can smell it. You can feel it in your mouth, and it lingers later, gift of the sun and rain from that grape's season.

Elegance and finesse are words frequently used in connection with great wines.

★ *Elegance* is maximum fruit flavour, with the minimum of alcohol. A high alcohol, big fruit wine may be balanced, but it is not elegant. Low alcohol, meagre fruit flavour may also have a certain balance, but neither is it elegant.

★ *Finesse* is, simply, infinite complexity, understated. There is an implied restraint in all aspects of the flavour of such wines.

So, finally, what is a great wine?

A wine that reeks of fruit, before, during and after you drink it.
A wine that has improved and lasted.
A wine that is balanced, and not overstated.
A wine that delights you.

If it smells and tastes great, it *is* great. Train and trust your palate. Enjoy yourselves!

Old basket press and barrel outside Wirra Wirra winery, McLaren Vale, South Australia.

READING

Amerine, Maynard & Roessler, Edward, Wines, Their Sensory Evaluation, *Freeman, San Francisco, 1976.*

Broadbent, Michael, Pocket Guide to Wine Tasting, *Christie's Wine Publications, Mitchell Beazley, London, 1982.*

Lake, Max, The Flavour of Wine, *Jacaranda Press, Brisbane, 1969.*

Lake, Max, Start to Taste, *Published by the author, Sydney, 1984.*

Peynaud, Emile, Le gout du Vin, *Dunod, Paris, 1980.*

Floating over a sea of cloud in the early morning, balloonists from the Balloon Aloft company get an overview of one of the Hunter Valley's promises. The two balloons are drifting over the top of Tulloch's winery with the Brokenback Range in the background.

WINES AND WINERIES OF NEW SOUTH WALES

James Halliday

The viticultural map of New South Wales has changed little during the course of the twentieth century. Certainly there are some new vineyards, and even some aspiring new regional associations, but their hold is as yet tenuous and their lasting worth yet to be proved. There have been far greater changes in each of the other wine producing States: and these days this means every State and mainland territory of the Commonwealth. It will be interesting to see whether the trend changes over the next few decades.

Yet for all that, wine is produced commercially in an extraordinary number of areas: not less than seventeen on my count, and there are quite probably more. Listed alphabetically they include Camden/Cobbity, Canberra/Queanbeyan/Murrumbateman, Corowa, Cowra, Forbes, Hunter Valley, Inverell, Mildura/Sunraysia, Mudgee, Murrumbidgee Irrigation Area, Nowra, Orange, Richmond (near Sydney), Upper Hunter, Young, Wee Waa, and Wellington.

Three of these regions, the Hunter (Upper and Lower), the Murrumbidgee Irrigation Area, and Mildura/Sunraysia, account for 90 per cent of the area under vines (a little over 14 000 hectares in total in 1981), and for over 95 per cent of the grapes used for

Vintage in the Hunter is often a race against rain — or a fight with it. Rains not only make the picking difficult because of mud, but promote grape diseases.

winemaking (a figure which fluctuates around 110 000 tonnes). Mudgee and Corowa (the latter an area of declining importance) in turn account for the major portion of the balance, leaving a teaspoonful from the other areas.

Drayton's vineyards on the slopes of the Brokenback Range. At their best, Hunter wines can be superb, with many decades of cellaring potential.

THE HUNTER VALLEY

A picturesque scene on the banks of the Hunter River.

Sunrise near the Brokenback Range at the western side of the Hunter Valley. The slopes of the range are covered with layers of volcanic soil which are ideal for growing high quality red grapes — but most of the good land was taken early by wise vignerons.

The distance from Cessnock (the main town in the Lower Hunter) to Scone (that of the Upper Hunter) is 120 kilometres. For much of that distance there are no vineyards to be found. This alone seems to me to put beyond argument the proposition that the two regions (Upper and Lower) are quite separate and should be recognised as such. More importantly still, however, the viticultural practices, the wine styles and even the climates of the two areas are distinctly different. So although the vignerons of the Upper Hunter would like to be regarded as part of the same region, I beg to differ. However, for the moment I am

forced to treat the two regions as one, because the statistical records of both State and Federal bodies do not differentiate between the two.

The importance of the Hunter cannot be gauged from its size. It has been, and always will be, a relatively small producer of grapes and of wine. After the golden years of the 1870s and 1880s, the region went

into a period of more or less continuous decline from its peak of between 1600 and 2000 hectares. By 1915 the vineyards were down to 840 hectares; after a brief increase to 1000 hectares in 1925, they diminished steadily until 1956 when only 466 hectares remained. Many of these were in poor condition, with missing vines, virus infections and general neglect all contributing to an overall derisory yield of 2.5 tonnes per hectare.

As the table wine boom of the 1960s got underway, the Hunter was one of the first regions to feel its impact (along with Coonawarra and Padthaway in South Australia). Curiously, in the Lower Hunter, it was not the long established companies such as Lindemans, McWilliam's or Tulloch who made the

Mechanical harvester at work during the vintage period. Most work by slapping or shaking the vines to make the ripe grape bunches fall onto a moving platform, which carries them to the overhead transfer arm into the tractor-drawn bin in the next row.

first moves. Sydney's Dr Max Lake planted a cabernet sauvignon vineyard in 1963, to be followed a few years later by Cessnock's Dr Lance Allen. Penfolds had made the ill-fated (for them, at least) move to the Upper Hunter when they established Wybong Park even earlier, in 1960.

The trickle turned into a flood overnight: between 1 July 1969 and 30 December 1969 420 hectares of hermitage (shiraz) grapes were planted, more than doubling the total of the then existing hermitage plantings. Indeed, as at 1 July there were only 250 hectares of hermitage in bearing, the balance of 146

hectares being young vines less than three years old.

In both the Lower and Upper Hunter there was a mad scramble for land. Within ten years much of it had proved totally unsuited to viticulture, and the high water mark of the mid-1970s (4137 hectares as at 31 December 1976) had already receded to 3479 hectares by 31 December 1981. In the intervening years Penfolds had come and gone; Arrowfield in the Upper Hunter and Hungerford Hill in the Lower Hunter had slashed their vineyard area by over half; Saxonvale had been sold by the Gollin Group liquidators; Tulloch had been reduced to a mere shadow of its former self; Lindemans had sold off most of their Lower Hunter vineyards; and Hermitage Estate had gone into liquidation.

On the other hand, Tyrrell went from strength to strength in the Lower Hunter; Rosemount bloomed in the Upper Hunter; while Brian McGuigan welded the Wyndham group into a colossus straddling both regions.

The vineyards, too, were seeing massive changes. At the end of 1969 there were only 27 hectares of cabernet sauvignon in bearing, with another 33 hectares planted. Seven years later there were 457 hectares in bearing, and (ominously) only 19.7 hectares coming into production. The plantings have indeed shrunk since, but at 336 hectares seem fairly stable. Certainly, there is a steady demand for the 1500 tonnes they produce in an average year.

Shiraz (hermitage) remains the dominant red grape, with 892 hectares producing 2446 tonnes in

1983 – a sure sign that significant quantities of the variety were left unharvested. 1983 was a very low yielding year, to be sure, but this is a long way short of the 6157 tonnes harvest in 1977. It is hard to see anything other than a continuing decline for shiraz in the years ahead; 1984 was a watershed vintage, with more grapes left on the vines than ever before.

The white variety, semillon, partners shiraz; slightly fewer hectares (817) produce between 3800 and 5700 tonnes, depending on the season. Chardonnay (fast rising with 276 bearing hectares and 54 coming into bearing in 1983), traminer (204 hectares), and Rhine riesling (183 hectares) are the only other white varieties propagated in any quantity. Demand for chardonnay continues unabated (for the time being at least), but in 1984 winemakers could buy semillon for a song. The Hunter Valley is undergoing a hard time, and the surgical knife for economic reality has yet to finish its bloody work.

The mechanical harvester straddles the trellised vines, slapping or pulsating them to make them drop their ripe fruit. The fruit falls onto a tray and is carried up the escalating carrier which transfers it to a bin being pulled by the tractor.

THE LOWER HUNTER

The Lower Hunter (which I shall henceforth call the Hunter) remains an enigma. One of its great characters and supporters Dr Max Lake, once said, 'The only thing wrong with Coonawarra is that it is not 100 miles from Sydney.' To paraphrase Dr Lake, it would not be hard to say 'The only thing right with the Hunter Valley is that it is only 100 miles from Sydney.'

What, you might cry, possesses anyone to say such a thing about an area which for long has been regarded as one of Australia's great wine regions? Well, for a start the grape yields which are apparent

from the statistics are little short of appalling. For thirteen years I tended the vines at Brokenwood (of which I was a part-owner), and over that period the vineyard averaged significantly less than 2.5 tonnes per hectare (or less than one ton to the acre). The much higher yields from the irrigated vineyards of the Upper Hunter swell the average yields for the region as a whole, but the Lower Hunter would average no more than 3.7 tonnes per hectare over the years.

These low yields are due to a combination of low to moderate fertility soils (by no means a bad thing in

An old sulphur duster used last century to suppress disease in ripening grapes, now on display at Lindemans' Hunter museum.

SINGLETON

HUNTER RIVER

BULGA

BRANXTON

Wyndham Estate

Saxonvale

Belbourie

Hermitage Hunter Estate ■   ■ Marsh Estate   ■ Sutherlands Wines   ■ Millstone
■ Terrace Vale

BROKE

Littles Wines ■   ■ Kindred Lochleven
Elliotts ■   ■ Wollundry
Hungerford Hill   ■ The Rothbury Estate
Tyrrells ■   Lake's Folly
Brokenwood ■   ■ Verona   ■ Allandale
■ Tamburlaine   ■ Dawsons
Chateau Francois ■   ■ McDougalls
Audrey Wilkinson   ■ Tullochs
Lindemans Hunter Valley Winery

BROKENBACK RANGE

W. Drayton ■   ■ Happy Valley

McWilliam's Mt Pleasant ■

KURRI KURRI

Mount View
Petersons ■   ■ Robsons

CESSNOCK

WOLLOMBI

0   10   km

Disused vineyard in the Hunter Valley. Plantings come and go with fads and fickleness, booms and bust. In the 1870s and 1880s there were grape plantings here of between 1600 and 2000 hectares; by 1915 the figure was down to 840. In 1956 there were 466 hectares, and plantings now stand at around 3000 hectares.

Making wine means transferring things from one place to another — grapes from vineyard to winery; juice, and then wine, around the winery (here at Lindemans' Hunter Valley winery); and then into bottles and out to consumers.

itself), frequently poorly drained (a significant disadvantage), supporting vines in an extremely warm climate with a relatively low rainfall. To add insult to injury, much of the rain falls when it is needed least: from January to March.

High humidity reduces water transpiration stress in the vines and compensates for the gap which would otherwise be caused by the extreme heat and the modest annual rainfall (675 millimetres). But it also creates the ideal environment for downy mildew disease on the vine leaves. Spraying is a never-ending part of the life of the Hunter vigneron, and adds to the formidably high cost of growing grapes in the region.

Yet despite all these problems, and that massive heat load (1874 heat degree days compared with 1517 for the Barossa Valley and 1259 for Coonawarra), the Hunter consistently produces great white wines from semillon and chardonnay, and less consistently (but still frequently) great reds from hermitage and cabernet. Certainly they are wines of a style; certainly they can be said to be an acquired taste; certainly some of the reds can be regarded as old-fashioned. But they all have one of the sure indicators of wine quality: an extraordinary capacity to age in the bottle, and no company has demonstrated this more effectively and frequently than Lindemans.

LINDEMANS WINES

The Lindemans of today is a very different operation to that of twenty, or even ten, years ago. Most obvious is that the lovely old whitewashed Ben Ean winery (much of it unchanged for one hundred years) is no longer called Ben Ean. Rather it is called Lindemans Hunter River Winery, so that the bureaucratic guardians of the public welfare cannot accuse Lindemans of deceiving the public with their Ben Ean moselle (which of course does not come from the Hunter).

But quietly Lindemans have also largely forsaken their traditional vineyards and sources of supply. In recent years they have planted a large vineyard on fertile river flat soils at Fordwich, north-west of

Cessnock. Here yields are much higher than in the Hunter, and the economics of grape-growing an altogether different proposition. Whether the quality and style of the wines will remain the same remains to be seen, but Lindemans have surprised me so often in the past I am sure they will do it again.

Their wizardry reaches its peak with their semillons. Hans Mollenhauer in the 1950s, followed by Karl Stockhausen in the Sixties and Seventies, produced an endless stream of magnificent whites released under the Hunter River Riesling, White

Burgundy and Chablis Reserve Bin labels, with a constantly changing four-figure bin number just to add to the confusion.

When first released at around twelve to eighteen months of age, these wines are mere shadows of what they will become if cellared in good conditions. To this day, Karl Stockhausen feels (particularly if given time) that semillon does not need the flavour of new oak to bolster it. Certainly the stream of great wines from the Sixties and early Seventies had no oak in their makeup.

Karl Stockhausen, born in Germany, learned to make wine at Lindemans' Ben Ean winery (now called their Hunter Valley winery), and has produced some of the company's, and the valley's, classic dry white and dry red wines.

221

Looking across some of the vineyards of the Hunter Valley. In the centre background is Lindemans' Hunter River winery.

Old bottle rack at Lindemans' Hunter Valley winery.

Making wine is hard work. A cellar hand cleans a centrifuge used to press juice from grapes, at Lindemans' Hunter Valley winery.

At around five to seven years they begin the transformation from ugly duckling to swan. Like so many adolescents, they can go through a difficult period while the transformation takes place. Once the transformation is complete, the wines are glowing buttercup yellow (with a green tinge lingering here and there); the aroma is a unique combination of fresh toast, nuts and honey; while the wine rolls off the tongue and down the throat as if it were liquid velvet, buttery and lingering.

The reds, all made from hermitage, are by no means as consistent. But they, too, can reach rare heights of perfection. Bin 1590 of 1959 is one of the all-time greats, while bins 3300 and 3310 from 1965 are equally magnificent wines which will see out the turn of the century with ease. Bin 3565 of 1967, released for the first time in 1983, is another superb red. Rich in fruit and deep in flavour, it retains that silky velvety smoothness which is so much part of Hunter burgundy style.

I suspect, though, that Lindemans' red wines of the future will go down a slightly different track. The older reds were made without any attention to their acid or pH balance, and also with relatively little concern for mercaptan. The vegetative/earthy/tobacco flavours which emerged were accepted as part and parcel of Hunter Valley character, and so in part they may be. But that so-called 'sweaty saddle' character is far from attractive in young reds; and there is an unquestioned swing to fresher, brighter, fruitier wines. Bacterial infection, too, made its appearance from time to time in those older wines.

Lindemans accept and recognise much of this, and their future red releases will show it. For a time these wines will look much like any other well-made young Australian shiraz. The fascinating question is whether, at the end of the day, the Hunter will have its way and re-exert its authority. It is my guess that it will.

McWILLIAM'S WINES

For much of the twentieth century, the reputation of the Hunter rested on just two companies, Lindemans and McWilliam's. McWilliam's, indeed, was the dominant force for much of this time due to the eccentric genius of its master-winemaker Maurice O'Shea. O'Shea reigned supreme at Mount Pleasant from 1925 until his death in 1956.

Both Lindemans and McWilliam's have always purchased a substantial proportion of their annual grape intake from independent growers – growers, incidentally, who act as a safety valve in balancing the vagaries of fluctuating supply and demand, and who in 1984 found themselves with unexpectedly unwanted grapes.

Semillon grapes growing in the Lower Hunter Valley. The area made a name for itself with high quality whites made from semillon (sometimes called Hunter River riesling) and shiraz (also called Hermitage).

Hoops like these are used to hold oak casks together.

Under O'Shea, McWilliam's took this process one step further, buying parcels of wine made by others, notably Dan Tyrrell, Hector Tulloch and Doug Elliott. It was O'Shea's ability to recognise the quality of wines just out of the primary fermentation, and also to engage in judicious blending, which so set him apart from his fellow winemakers.

These wines were often bottled separately; the Mount Pleasant label of the time would have such cryptic names as 'Richard', 'TY', 'HT', 'Charles',

'Mountain A', 'Mountain C' to differentiate them. The most famous wine of the Fifties was 1954 Richard, a wine made by Dan Tyrrell and bought in its infancy by O'Shea; for the next fifteen years this wine disputed the honours with Lindemans 1959 Vintage Bin 1590. Like the Lindemans wine it won countless gold medals; while there is considerable bottle variation, on its day the wine is still perfection.

I regret to say it, but the label is now but a shadow of its former self. McWilliam's Mount Pleasant Philip Hermitage, in particular, lacks fruit flavour and vinosity in most years. Its distinctive tarry character – an extreme manifestation of district style – is something I personally dislike, although obviously it has its supporters in the marketplace.

Mount Pleasant Elizabeth Riesling is one of the top selling brands in Australia (a massive 75 000 cases a year, according to the *Financial Review*, 27 May 1983). If this is all made at Mount Pleasant,

The front of the Hunter Valley Wine Society, on the road to Wollombi.

it would account for upwards of two-thirds of the reported total crush of 1500 tonnes. I think it is generally accepted McWilliam's buy in bulk white wine from other Hunter Valley winemakers (particularly Upper Hunter) to supplement their own production: given the quantity of production, Elizabeth Riesling is a reliable, if unexciting, wine.

The third basic Mount Pleasant wine is the sauternes, which can be very good indeed. The 1975 was on release not so long ago, and given that botrytis played no part at all in its production, it is a wine of considerable character and structure.

In a way it comes as no surprise that McWilliam's launched a new range of wines in mid-1984; while bearing a Mount Pleasant badge, the label is entirely new and gives prominence only to the variety. The initial release comprised a 1980 chardonnay, 1981 semillon, 1977 traminer riesling, 1979 cabernet

sauvignon and 1978 pinot noir/hermitage. Interestingly, only the 1979 cabernet specifically claims to be made from grapes 'grown in the Lower Hunter River Valley'. Although the format of the other labels is similar, they are silent on the grape source.

The semillon is typical of McWilliam's style: these wines seem to have the ability to age almost indefinitely, yet they seldom if ever develop the honeyed/nut/vanilla flavour and texture of those Lindemans' whites. It is not a bad wine, but I thought that the cabernet sauvignon was by far the best of the five wines (notwithstanding the two gold medals won by the traminer riesling in its youth). While light bodied, it was devoid of the tar character which I so object to, had good balance and fair varietal flavour. But I cannot see the wines restoring McWilliam's lost glory, nor can I see the 1984 recommended retail of $8.65 being sustained in real life.

225

J. Y. TULLOCH & SONS

Now under the fourth owners in the past fifteen years (from the Tulloch family to Reed International to Gilbeys to Allied Vintners), Tulloch is but a shadow of its former self. Successive owners have sold off vineyards and land to the point where virtually none of the grapes are estate grown.

Stock rationalisations, label changes, marketing turnarounds and the ensuing lack of morale have not

helped, although Jay Tulloch remains faithfully at the helm in the Hunter as general manager, and Patrick Auld tries hard to produce the best wine possible.

Some magnificently powerful wines have come out under the Tulloch Private Bin Dry Red label over the years. In the first half of 1982 I was privileged to taste a line up of Tulloch reds from 1931, 1944, 1947, and 1952 to 1982 inclusive (with the exception of 1956, 1970 and 1971, especially troubled years). The forty or so wines included some magnificent bottles, with the 1947, 1952, 1954, 1955, 1961, 1963, 1965,

Early morning fog over Tulloch's vineyards in the Hunter Valley.

1967, 1973 and 1975 leading the way in their respective decades.

It is no secret that since 1958 the standard (as opposed to Private Bin) Tulloch Dry Red has contained a significant percentage of McLaren Vale material, while the Private Bin was a blend of material from the old vines around the winery and from Tulloch's Fordwich vineyards. The Tulloch style, therefore, has always remained a little apart from the mainstream of Hunter Valley reds, and I cannot say I object to that in the least.

Until 1974 Tulloch made two white wines (a standard and a Private Bin) which were not memorable, always well behind the quality of the reds. In that year, the then winemaker Ian Scarborough, made three magnificent whites: a straight semillon (which is still regularly winning gold medals at shows), a semillon/chardonnay and a semillon/verdelho. It marked a turnaround, as many of the whites in subsequent years proved the 1974s were no fluke. The semillon/chardonnay in particular (augmented more recently by a top quality straight chardonnay) are consistently impressive. The semillon/verdelho has been made with residual sugar in some years, a trap for those not in the know.

Where Tulloch will head in the years to come, I do not know. It has made some excellent cabernets and chardonnays, varieties which are far easier to market than the traditional styles. But some stability and a sense of direction are badly needed.

TYRRELLS VINEYARDS

Lack of direction and commitment is not something one can accuse Murray Tyrrell of. Under his energetic guidance and stentorian voice, Tyrrells has grown at an astonishing rate over the past twenty years. Where others have been decreasing vineyards and reducing their crush, Murray Tyrrell has been expanding his.

First Tyrrells took a long-term operating lease of Chateau Douglas in the Upper Hunter, increasing

Fermenting grape juice at Tyrrells' winery in the Hunter Valley. Some winemakers still use open fermenters believing they can extract more flavour, but most now use enclosed stainless steel tanks.

production enormously. Then in early 1983, Penfolds finally severed all association with the Hunter, and it was Tyrrells who were the successful tenderers for Penfolds' historic HVD Vineyard.

In 1984, when a number of the other companies in the district reduced their intake and left growers unprepared, Tyrrells filled much of the gap. The companies concerned are somewhat sensitive about their figures, but it would not surprise if Tyrrells produced more wine in 1984 than any other Hunter Valley company with the exception of the Wyndham Group.

This impressive output is marketed under three series of labels. First are the Vat Wines, white and red, which are basically sold cellar door and through Tyrrells' extensive and very well controlled mailing list. One great aid to sales is an 'If you don't cancel, we'll send you the wine,' approach. Once you have

Murray Tyrrell, winemaker, cattleman and horseman, is never afraid to express his opinions on wine or anything else.

Murray Tyrrell and his son Bruce still run their family company from their property overlooking the Hunter Valley.

ordered a wine in a particular year, the wine automatically arrives (followed by the invoice) in subsequent years.

The most prestigious of these wines is Vat 47 Chardonnay. While one may say it was only a question of time before someone did something with chardonnay, the fact remains that person was Murray Tyrrell. The fact also remains that while pretenders to the throne abound left, right and centre, over the past ten years Tyrrell has made more great chardonnay than the rest put together.

He has also made some magnificent semillons, principally Vat 1 and (occasionally) Vat 16. The 1973

Vat 1 remains one of my favourite Hunter Valley whites, matched only by 1973 Vat 47.

His success with chardonnay is emulated, on the face of it, by his pinot noir. His 1976 brought fame to Australia, winning a major competition in Paris, and from there finding its way onto the cover of *Time* as one of the twelve great wines of the world. This notwithstanding, I do not think the early ripening pinot noir is the least bit suited to the warm Hunter Valley climate, and that in most years it is exceedingly difficult to invest the wine with sufficient colour and body, yet retain identifiable varietal character.

The Vats of hermitage – 5, 7, 8, 9 and 11 leading

The Tyrrell family have made wines of quality since 1858. Much of the winery has a distinctive earthen floor.

Red grapes fermenting in an open tank at Tyrrells' Hunter winery. The wooden poles are used to push the 'cap' of skins down into the juice while the fermentation proceeds, giving more extraction of colour, flavour and tannin.

the way in most years – are full bodied, robust reds made in a traditional style. Only in recent years has new oak played any part at all, and even here its role is obvious only in the cabernet (Vat 70) and cabernet shiraz (Vat 12A) blend. All of these wines benefit from at least ten years bottle age, and are representative of the Hunter Valley as it has always been.

The next series of wines are the 'Old Winery' releases for retailers, offering the top end of the Tyrrells' range after the Vat wines. These comprise a semillon, semillon/chardonnay, fumé blanc, pinot chardonnay, hermitage, cabernet/merlot, cabernet sauvignon and pinot noir.

Finally there are Tyrrells Vineyard varietal releases, including the ubiquitous Long Flat Red (despite the controversy about its name and origin, often representing outstanding value for money) and Hunter River Riesling, that outmoded name for semillon.

Murray Tyrrell sets high standards for himself and all of those who work for him. It shows in his wines, and I believe the Hunter owes a considerable debt of gratitude to him.

THE ROTHBURY ESTATE

Early morning along the rows of vines at the Rothbury Estate. More wineries today are trying to pick grapes in the evening, at night and in the early morning when the grapes are cool and quality is high.

Born in the baby boom of the late 1960s, and sired by the one and only Len Evans, Rothbury has seen it all in fifteen short years. Its first vintage (1971) was the wettest ever, with mould rampant throughout the Valley; after a couple of reasonable years the Hunter entered an unparalleled eight-year drought; the red wine boom disappeared in a puff of smoke to be replaced by a white wine boom, for which Rothbury was no more prepared than anyone else; and then the discounting war took hold in earnest.

Despite this, and the continuous losses which have dogged every step Rothbury has taken, it is still there. It is there in part because of a series of marvellous semillons made by Gerry Sissingh between 1972 and 1979; and in part because of the tenacity and courage of its founder and chairman, Len Evans.

After a few troubled years in the wake of Gerry Sissingh's departure, compounded by errant yeasts beyond the control of anyone, Rothbury seems

David Lowe,
winemaker at Rothbury,
watches hermitage grapes
being dumped into the
crusher. For the winemaker
the vintage is a race against
time and weather, and
other outside enemies.

A laboratory assistant
checks juice quality at
Rothbury as the grapes are
processed through the
crusher not far away.

largely back on course. Its red wine quality has shown steady improvement, with the 1982 reds the best yet. (Evans refuses to admit the earlier reds had any problems, claiming they are misunderstood, but that is no more than one would expect from any loyal father.) Interesting carbonic maceration reds, flavourful pinot noir, and some good cabernet add both depth and variety to the output.

But the long term viability of Rothbury – like, I suspect, the Hunter as a whole – must rest with its semillons. Since 1972 these have equalled, if not bettered, any from the Valley. They seem to be setting their own style, somewhere in between the crisp, bony wines of Murray Tyrrell and the rich, developed, honeyed wines of Lindemans. With the exception of some of the Black Label 1974s, the Rothbury wines have remained lighter and fresher than most of Lindemans. The 1972 is a veritable Peter Pan, showing a little toasty development in its aroma, but otherwise utterly belying its age.

As winemaker David Lowe gains in experience and feel, I see every reason why Rothbury's whites should again scale the heights. And with Hunter Valley, Fordwich and Cowra chardonnay to draw on, Rothbury may also become one of the pretenders to that throne of Tyrrells'.

HUNGERFORD HILL WINES

Hungerford Hill is another company to recently undergo a change of ownership, with the Yunghanns family of Melbourne now in the driver's seat. Like Rothbury, Hungerford Hill was conceived in the late Sixties; like Rothbury, it went through troubled times in the Seventies, resulting in radical surgery which saw its vineyards reduced from 235 hectares to 116 hectares.

For reasons which are difficult to pinpoint, Hungerford Hill has never been a trendy product. Yet right from the word go, it has produced some excellent wines. Indeed, since the advent of Ralph Fowler some quite brilliant examples have emerged. Perversely, the greatest have come from Coonawarra Rhine riesling (the 1983 most of all), which are outside the scope of this chapter. But Fowler learnt his trade well in his years with Tyrrells, and has produced some lovely wooded semillons and chardonnays, with impressive oaked cabernet and cabernet/malbec blends, and good hermitage.

Few cellar door sales operations are as big or as busy as Hungerford Hill's village in the centre of the Hunter Valley. A visit to the sprawling winery, with its excellent restaurant, craft shop, riding centre and pottery shop is a must during a Hunter trip.

W. DRAYTON & SONS

An intensely conservative and traditional company, little is seen or heard of Drayton these days outside of its traditional markets: cellar door and Newcastle. When Drayton changed distributors a few years ago, there was a brief flurry of excitement, a press lunch and a few press releases. Now life goes on much as it ever did; Drayton has always offered value for money. I well remember buying trips to Hunter in the mid-Sixties with Drayton whites selling for 75 cents a bottle.

In 1979 Drayton produced an outstanding chardonnay from its Mangerton vineyard and in 1983 a quite brilliant carbonic maceration hermitage, bottled in pints and aimed at the restaurant market. These high points to one side, the Drayton whites (tending to be very tart and apple-like in flavour) and reds (smooth but lacking complexity) have changed little over the past twenty years. Unfortunately, I think the wine market as a whole has changed, and Drayton is in some danger of losing its place in it.

Bringing in the hermitage grapes during a Hunter vintage at Drayton. These grapes, also known as shiraz, are the backbone of Hunter Valley reds.

Reg Drayton is one of the best known identities of the Hunter. The Tyrrells and the Draytons alone, among family wine companies, have survived the past century in the valley. Reg and his son Stephen, who helps market the family's wines, compare notes on one of their shiraz (hermitage) reds.

235

WYNDHAM ESTATE

Wyndham Estate, by contrast, is in absolutely no danger of losing its place in the market or in sensing changes in public taste. Indeed, it has been at the forefront of creating that taste. In the early Seventies, Brian McGuigan formulated the traminer/Rhine riesling, a residual sugar blend, which yielded its place in the top twenty-five selling brands in Australia only to the Wyndham Traminer.

The Wyndham group of companies spreads from Wyndham Estate at Branxton to Hermitage Estate in Polkolbin to the Hollydene Winery in the Upper Hunter, taking in the Richmond Grove vineyard (and label) along the way.

Managing director Brian McGuigan is a tireless publicist for the group's products, but Mark Cashmore (who joined the group several years ago as general manager) makes McGuigan look like a small boy in short pants. Many – myself included – do not agree with many of Cashmore's methods, nor many of his labels, but as the old adage has it, you can't argue with success.

There isn't a great deal of point in talking too much about the style of the wines. They are well made; many show little or no regional character, but ample fruit and colour (the reds are made in an unusual horizontal rotofermenter); and the whites rely heavily on residual sugar. Output is prodigious, and significant quantities are exported, particularly to the American market. The best wines are released under the Hunter Estate label.

Brian McGuigan, winemaker and managing director of the Wyndham Estate at the Dalwood property, near Branxton in the Hunter Valley. McGuigan's apparently boundless energy has made the winery and its subsidiaries one of the fastest growing and most successful in the valley.

Wyndham Estate, founded in 1828, is the oldest continuously operating winery in Australia. Its cellar door sales operations attract vast numbers of tourists in cars, buses and even by helicopter. Its owners unashamedly promote good wines for ordinary drinkers.

*Jim Roberts of
Belbourie winery where he
is owner and winemaker.
His distinctive wines are
among the most unusual in
the Hunter Valley, with
their brand of devoted
followers who can buy them
at his cellar door.*

THE BOUTIQUES

From the largest to the smallest; from the world of towering stainless steel tank farms; from national brand advertising and discounting to the Lilliputian and often struggling world of the small winemaker. Here bleary-eyed doctors, lawyers, academics and businessmen think there has to be a better way to spend their holidays, as they work around the clock in the searing heat of a Hunter vintage. Or if not heat, knee-deep in mud, as they struggle to haul bins to the end of the rows. I know; I've done it all, more times than I care to remember.

Max Lake started it all with Lake's Folly; by dint of digging holes all over the Valley, he ended up with one of the best vineyards in the district, sharing the first hill to rise out of the river flats with McWilliam's celebrated Rosehill Vineyard. It was Max Lake who introduced cabernet to the Hunter; it was Max Lake who was the first weekend vigneron in Australia; it was Max Lake who promoted the Hunter and his

*It was Dr Max Lake's 'folly'
that started Lake's Folly
winery in the Hunter
Valley. Son Stephen now
makes the wines.*

wines so effectively in Australia and overseas that he became a legend before he was fifty.

These days he has handed over the day-to-day winemaking responsibilities to son, Stephen; but having finally given up his busy practice as a hand-surgeon, he is never far from the thick of things at vintage time. Lake has elected not to exhibit his wines in wine shows, so objective yardsticks are hard to come by — separating fact from the aura of mysticism which surrounds Lake is not easy. He is in no doubt he has made first the greatest cabernets, and then the greatest chardonnays, in Australia. Like the Bishop, he will rest easy in his grave, certain of the life hereafter (for his wines at least). Others, myself included, have seen signs of human weaknesses, of human failings in those wines.

But let no one doubt that Lake has made some good wines, and even more, let no one denigrate the massive contribution he has made to the Hunter Valley in particular and Australian wine in general.

Another highly innovative, if not controversial, winemaker followed Lake a year later. Jim Roberts at Belbourie has always done things his way, with flair and with scant regard for accepted standards. From his vivid impressionist labels, often saying little in words, to his highly unconventional whites made on a semi-solera process, the personality is there for all to see. I have been told his operation is on a much diminished scale these days.

Dr Lance Allen followed next when he set up Tamburlaine in 1966. Sadly, as at mid-1984, he too was endeavouring to sell, his vineyard and winery having become too much for him, and his hopes for his family to take it over having failed to materialise. Nonetheless, if he does so, it will be on a high note, having won a trophy at the 1983 Hunter Valley Show for one of his young reds.

Oakdale (still only a vineyard consortium with its wines made for it by Reg Drayton), Chateau Francois and Brokenwood came next. I was one of the three founding partners of Brokenwood; between the winter of 1971 when we planted our first vines and mid-1983, when I moved to Melbourne (and severed my relationship with Brokenwood in consequence)

A lunchtime drink at Brokenwood winery during vintage. The winery was established in 1971 by a syndicate which included wine writer and lawyer James Halliday. Today it employs a full-time winemaker. Brokenwood wines, notably the reds, are generally excellent Hunter styles.

most of my weekends and holidays were spent in the Hunter in a love affair which has faded but which will never die.

The Brokenwood of 1984 bears no relationship to that of 1973, the year it made its first wine with equipment temporarily housed in Rothbury. First a tractor shed (1974), then a full scale winery (1975) and finally a brand new winery (1983) have transformed Brokenwood into a lavishly equipped winery making more white than red wine, winning both gold medals and praise for its semillons and chardonnays. Yet until 1982, we had never made a white wine. The advent of the first full-time (and qualified) winemaker, Iain Riggs, and the new winery, changed all that.

I have always thought that the Brokenwood reds had more in common with those of Murray Robson at Robson's Vineyard, tucked away in the folds at Mount View, than any of the other Hunter makers, large or small. Both wineries seem to produce reds with greater freshness and deeper colour than the others, although it is perfectly true that both release their wines very young. Small new oak barrels also figure large in the armoury of each, and in shows and

masked line-ups in which it was reasonable for each to be included, I often had no idea which was which.

Murray Robson is a perfectionist, and in recent years has taken over from Max Lake as defender of the Hunter faith. Always as immaculately groomed as his winery, I envy Robson his *savoir faire,* and commend his reds (though not so much his whites) to any yet to encounter them.

Allandale Winery, commenced by Ed Jouault in 1978, is unique in that of all the small wineries, it alone has no vineyards. Perhaps Jouault's training as an accountant, coupled with the time spent working in the Hunter Valley industry, told him that what little money there is to be made is in making wine, not growing grapes.

The Allandale wines have been, in a word, erratic in quality. Quite why this should be, I don't know, but they are. At their best they are superb, as witness the Farmer Brothers Trophy won in 1982 for the best two-year-old chardonnay at the Canberra National Show. Jouault also evidently profited by winning a trip to Champagne one year, as he has produced some glorious sparkling wine, albeit in small quantities.

Talking of small quantities leads me to Chateau Francois, where the New South Wales Director of Fisheries, Dr Don Francois, planted grapes in the very foot of the Brokenback range in 1970. Entirely self taught (his initial forays into winemaking were with materials such as rhubarb and rose petals in the

240

basement of his Chatswood home), and relying on his own labour to the virtual exclusion of outsiders except for picking, Francois has made many fine wines over the years. I doubt that he (or anyone else) has tallied up the medals won by each of the small makers in the Hunter, but I fancy Chateau Francois would come out on top.

This success has been gained by his semillons, his shiraz and his pinot noirs. The latter are, in my view, the best to come out of the Valley, although they are almost invariably blended with his hermitage (to its great benefit, I might add).

Elliotts, Kindred's Loch Leven, Marsh Estate, Millstone, Mount View, Oakdale, Petersons, Tamalee, Terrace Vale and Wollundry complete the list of vineyards marketing wines. Petersons have recently swept all before them in local shows; though some of their wines are better than others, like those of Terrace Vale. Petersons will be worth following in the years to come. All of these wineries sell cellar door and by mailing list; they make a weekend excursion to the Hunter crammed full of interest and activity (not to mention wine) from the moment you arrive until the moment you leave.

Murray Robson, former Sydney businessman, on the verandah of his Robson's Vineyard winery at the southern end of the Hunter Valley. From rose-decorated vineyards to lavishly equipped winery, it invites the description 'boutique', but produces some fine wines.

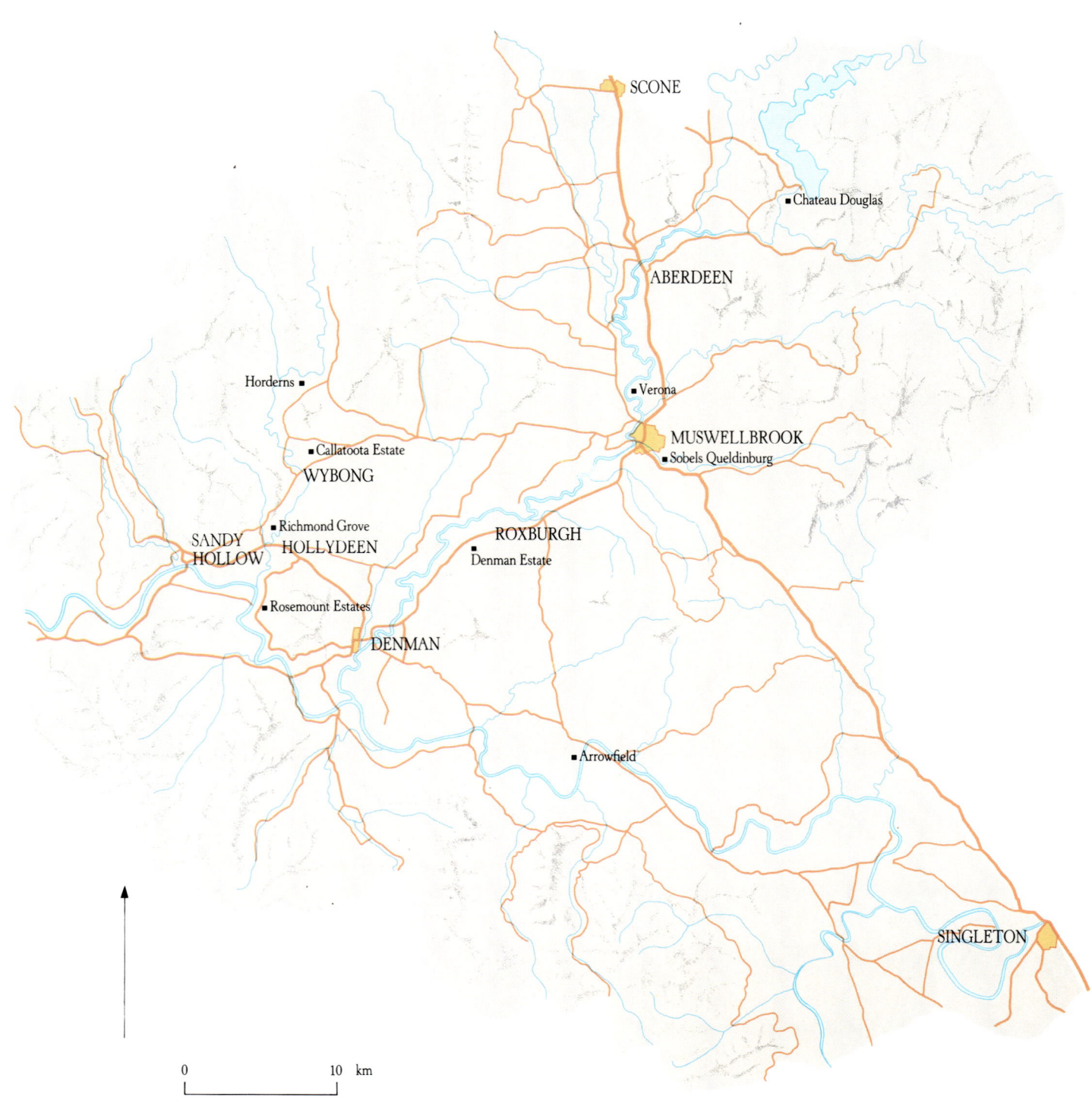

THE UPPER HUNTER

Spread out over a distance of 40 or more kilometres, from west of Denman to south-east of Scone, the vineyards of the Upper Hunter all came into being in the wake of Penfolds Wybong (1960), most in the boom days of the late 1960s. If the Lower Hunter has had its problems, they are nothing compared to those of the Upper Hunter.

Yet, as elsewhere, it is not an unrelieved picture of gloom. The region has proved its ability to produce large crops (15 tonnes to the hectare and more) of white grapes from vines growing in fertile alluvial soil, usually with the aid of irrigation. And apart from Wyndham, one company has been successful in capitalising on what the region has to offer.

ROSEMOUNT ESTATES

Founded by New Guinea plantation owner Bob Oatley in 1969, Rosemount has turned to gold all it has touched. John Ellis, now of Tisdall, made his mark at Rosemount, producing its first vintage in 1975. In the ensuing few years Ellis' undoubted skills as a winemaker, coupled with a very effective (and no doubt expensive) marketing campaign, saw Rosemount move from an unknown to a national brand.

For a brief period around the time John Ellis left to join Tisdall, Rosemount appeared to falter, at least so far as wine quality was concerned. But it was

Keeping weeds under control in a vineyard belonging to Rosemount Estates. The Upper Hunter is about an hour's drive from the better known Lower Hunter, but the wines are quite different, with more emphasis on white wines such as Rhine riesling.

243

Rosemount Estates produce some top white wines, including oak-treated chardonnays. The winery overlooks the upper reaches of the Hunter River, near Denman, in picturesque horse and cattle country.

Tools of trade of the modern winemaker: refrigeration pipes and plumbing at the Rosemount Estates, owned by coffee millionaire Bob Oatley.

nonetheless a period of spectacular expansion in terms of output. In 1977 Rosemount purchased the Penfolds Wybong Estate Winery and vineyards from Penfolds. Since then it has purchased the Roxburgh Vineyard from Denman Estates, Mount Dangar from Adelaide Steamships (in 1983), and established several new vineyards of its own — one in Coonawarra, on the outskirts of the township of Penola at the southern end of the Terra Rosa bank.

Philip Shaw (ex-Lindemans) is now firmly in control as chief winemaker; he and general manager, Chris Hancock, make a formidable team. Shaw, indeed, must rank as one of the best winemakers in Australia; he picked up Rosemount where Ellis left off, and lifted its wines up another dimension again.

Most startlingly successful are its wooded chardonnays; I simply don't know how so much colour, flavour and richness of texture can find its way into a one-year-old wine. These chardonnays are at the far extreme of the 'peaches and cream' Australian style, made to fill the mouth from the moment they are released. The show wines at six to nine months are positively dazzling, although judges are becoming increasingly wary of too much precocity.

The oaked semillons are very nearly as good; throughout 1983 I thought the 1982 show semillon had few challengers for sheer sensual flavour and pleasure. Once again, while these wines will live on for a few years, I think they are basically drink-now propositions. Indeed, I am starting to think the same may even be true of one of the most extraordinary wines ever made in the Hunter Valley, Rosemount's 1982 Trockenbeerenauslese Rhine Riesling. Without going into detail, it is rare for botrytis to do its work in the Hunter without destroying the grape altogether. In the wet finish to the 1982 vintage, Rosemount's remaining Rhine riesling somehow clung on, to produce one of the most luscious and intense sweet dessert wines I have ever tasted.

The wooded chardonnays and semillons have stolen the limelight from the traminers and Rhine rieslings on which Rosemount first made its name. They also sidetrack attention from some interesting reds, particularly cabernet and cabernet malbec/shiraz blends made by Shaw. Contrary to experience elsewhere in the Upper Hunter, these can be every bit as rich as their Lower Hunter brothers; Rosemount is a very successful wine company. For my money it deserves every bit of that success.

ARROWFIELD

Success is a commodity which for most of its years Arrowfield neither knew nor tasted. If Rothbury was the vision splendid at Pokolbin, so was Arrowfield in the Upper Hunter. The higher they rise, the harder they fall, and great indeed was the fall of Arrowfield. Had it been owned by virtually any company other than W. R. Carpenter, with all its financial strength and corporate pride, Arrowfield must surely have been sold.

It was caught in part by the collapse of the red wine market, but also by the sheer lack of quality of the vast amount of red wine which came off its large irrigated vineyards. Thin and lacking, they were really not marketable. This led to marketing practices born of desperation, and Arrowfield lost all credibility with retailers and consumers alike.

That it has pulled itself so far back up the ladder is in no small measure due to the dedication of its youthful winemaking and marketing teams, led by Gary Baldwin (until late 1984) and David Haviland respectively. It is also due to some tough decisions to

Arrowfield winery, near Jerry's Plains. One of the Hunter Valley's problems was big plantings of red grapes which came into full bearing just as the public was turning to whites.

Vineyards at Arrowfield.

pour a lot of indifferent wine down the drain, and to drastically reduce the size of its vineyards.

In the course of each year I undertake up to ten major 'blind' tastings of currently available wines; usually these encompass more than 100 wines at each tasting, sometimes 400. It is quite remarkable how consistently Arrowfield's white wines have performed in the past two to three years. Even more remarkable is their price, usually 25 per cent or more under wines of comparable style and quality.

They typify the Upper Hunter style. Made with less technical sophistication than those of Rosemount, they are soft, fleshy wines with good overall flavour and which reach their peak in two or three years after vintage. Semillon, chardonnay and a blend of the two are the main strength, though from time to time Arrowfield produces a lovely, soft forward Rhine riesling or Rhine riesling/traminer blend.

246

THE OTHERS

The others have had a tough time of it. Labels which from time to time have appeared on the market include Denman Estate, Hollydene, Horderns' Wybong Estate, Mount Dangar Vineyards, Queldinburg, Richmond Grove, Segenhoe (also known as Chateau Douglas) and Verona.

Hollydene and Richmond Grove fall under the Wyndham group umbrella; while Segenhoe/Chateau Douglas is part of the growing Tyrrells' empire under a management lease. Hordens' Wybong Estate and Cruikshank are the two small wineries in the district,

the latter a recent addition. Hordens' Wybong is a partnership between Sydney orthopaedic surgeon Bob Smith and local grazier David Horden. Established in 1965, winemaking started in the 1970s, and a superb semillon in 1974 won many medals and trophies. Quality since has been decidedly uneven.

Verona has suffered even more from lack of consistency; many of its wines show marked winemaking faults, while there was no consistency in the occasional forays of Denman Estates and Mount Dangar onto the market. Admittedly, these forays account for only a small percentage of their production, most of which is sold in bulk. Finally, Queldinberg continues in a quiet way, selling most of its production cellar door.

Cedric Bayliss ready for vintage at Denman Estate, near Muswellbrook in the Upper Hunter Valley of New South Wales. The winery makes good dry whites and Rhine rieslings.

Carlo Corino, winemaker at Montrose, Mudgee. Today his winery, owned by the Transfield Group, is the biggest in the area, and makes — under the Montrose label and the more recently acquired Craigmoor brand — many of the best wines coming from this relatively new wine area.

MUDGEE

Mudgee follows the historical pattern of so many other regions of Australia. Grapes were first planted in 1858 by Adam Roth at Rothview, later renamed Craigmoor. By 1893 there were fifty-five grape-growers in the region, the same number as today. At that time almost all the wine produced was fortified, although one Frederick Bucholtz made table wines of outstanding quality in the 1880s.

In the first sixty years of this century production steadily declined until the only winery in production was that of Ferde (Jack) Roth, Craigmoor. Mudgee Wines joined Craigmoor in 1964; the other fourteen wineries are all creatures of the 1970s and 1980s.

In any discussion of Mudgee these days, the first and most vexed question is how its climate should be classified. On the one hand its vineyards are at an average height of 500 metres, and the whole grow-ing-ripening cycle is at least one month later than the Hunter Valley, which is at the same latitude.

But by no stretch of the imagination can it be cal-led a cool climate area. It is classified by Richard Smart and Peter Dry as 'hot, moderately continental, very sunny, moderately arid, humid'. With 1821 heat degree days, it is only marginally below the Hunter Valley and significantly warmer than, for example, Rutherglen with 1620 heat degree days. But like Rutherglen, its cool nights slow down the ripening cycle which continues unabated in the Hunter; while by the time vintage gets into full swing in March, the worst of the summer heat has passed.

The soils are derived from shale, siltstone, lime-stone, alluvial deposits of all kinds, and sandstone. They vary from yellow-brown to red in colour, and in texture from sandy clay loams to clay loams. The clay subsoil allows for good water retention, essential given the low rainfall of between 600 and 670 milli-metres a year.

The drought which gripped the Hunter in the 1970s also affected Mudgee, but in 1983 it intensified to the point where many vineyards were not even picked, so scanty was the fruit.

*Birds are one of the
enemies of ripe grape
berries, and this is the oldest
— and cheapest — method
of scaring them away. In
the background, Amberton
winery, Mudgee.*

About 440 hectares were under vine in 1982, with a strong preponderance of red grapes. The principal white grape is chardonnay (56 hectares but increasing rapidly), which was first planted by Bill Roth at his Westcourt vineyard in 1930. The cuttings came from Col Laraghy's Kaluna Winery at Smithfield on the outskirts of Sydney. The clone was a particularly good one and the nematode-free soils of Mudgee ensured that the chardonnay remained virus-free. Mudgee became one of the most important sources of root stock for the chardonnay explosion of the 1970s. Some superb, full bodied chardonnays have been made in the district, none better than those of Miramar.

Not surprisingly given the proximity of the Hunter, the next most important grape is semillon (47 hectares) although it was unknown in the region until the early Seventies. One of its principal producers is Huntington Estate, which makes both a dry and slightly sweet style. At Montrose it is used (along with a little sauvignon blanc) to make great sauternes.

Rhine riesling (14 hectares) is another late arrival, and shows very considerable promise from a winemaking viewpoint. Viticulturally it has problems with low yield and 'die-back' disease, a little understood viral infection. Plantings are nonetheless on the increase. Paradoxically, traminer (6 hectares) grows vigorously and produces well, which is not always the case in other regions.

The most widely propagated grape is shiraz, 158 hectares but declining. As elsewhere in Australia, it

GULGONG

■ Beaulieu

■ Platt's

■ Hill of Gold

■ Miramar

■ Amberton Wines   ■ Bramhall

■ Montrose

■ Botobolar Vineyard

Pieter van Gent ■   ■ Huntington Estate

Craigmoor ■   ■ Mansfield

Mudgee Wines ■   ■ Augustine

Burnbrae

■ Erudgere Wines

Thistle Hill

MUDGEE

■ Mt Vincent Meadery

0   10 km

249

grows and produces well. But in some vineyards in Mudgee it also produces wines with a distinctive and seemingly impossible-to-remove earthy 'sweaty saddle' character. This apart, the shiraz reds of Mudgee are smooth, well structured, medium to full bodied (distinctly fuller than those of the Hunter Valley) wines with good ageing capacity.

Cabernet sauvignon vines (97 hectares) were planted in 1961 by Alf Kurtz, and the first wine made from them in 1964. The initial quarter-hectare planting came from an experimental half-hectare vineyard established at Molong by Jack Pride. One of Jack Roth's award winning wines of the early Sixties is said to have contained wine made from the Molong cabernet grapes.

Cabernet performs with its customary vigour and flair in Mudgee. Its wines show distinctive varietal character, usually with warmer minty/sweet berry/ chocolate flavours than the cool climate herbaceous

characters – which, after all, is what one should expect. The particular style then depends on the maker; virtually every winery in Mudgee produces cabernet, though none better than Bob Roberts at Huntington Estate.

Pinot noir (14 hectares) is grown and produced by Craigmoor, Huntington Estate and Hill of Gold wineries; one or two others may have small patches, but I do not recollect tasting the wines. Pinot noir is as difficult a proposition in Mudgee as in any other warm to hot region of Australia, all too frequently producing wines lacking in colour, body and flavour.

Other varieties grown include crouchen (10 hectares), frontignan (4.6), muscat gordo blanco (10), sauvignon blanc (2.5), traminer (5.87), trebbiano (5.87), merlot (2), aleatico – an old established Italian variety going back to the days of Dr Fiaschi, and new plantings at Montrose of the Italian grapes, barbera, sangiovese, and nebbiolo.

The rows of vines at Huntington Estate, Mudgee. From these vines and his nearby winery Bob Roberts produces some of the best white and red wines of the area.

THE SOCIETY FOR THE APPELLATION OF THE WINES OF MUDGEE

Since 1978 Mudgee has had in operation the most effective and strictly controlled appellation control system in Australia. It is a voluntary system, although all the commercial wineries participate, and it is they who fund its operation.

It is administered by a firm of independent chartered accountants, which acts as the Controller. Vineyard plantings, grapes harvested, and litres of wine produced are declared to and registered with the Controller. He has the absolute right to make random checks of records and wine stocks.

The aim of the Society in awarding its official certificate is to guarantee three things. First, the wine is of Mudgee origin: in other words that it is made and bottled in Mudgee from grapes grown in Mudgee.

Second, that the label faithfully describes the wine in the bottle. Not only does this mean the grape variety must be stated exactly (if one variety is stipulated, it means 100 per cent, and not 80 per cent, as is the case under Pure Foods Act regulations which govern normal wine labelling in Australia) but that if any subjective description of the wine appears on the label, it must be that of the winemaker, signed by

him, and considered by the Wine Assessment Committee to be fair. If the wine is said to have been 'aged in Limousin oak', that fact will have to be verified by the Controller before the wine is bottled and labelled.

Third, the wine must be free of objectionable faults. All wines for which appellation is sought are subjected to a blind tasting by the Wine Assessment Committee. The maker provides a sworn declaration which deposes to all of the facts necessary to qualify the wine for examination; the Controller then visits the winery, checks the records, and selects random bottles for assessment. An important feature of the system is that the wine must all have been bottled at the time the certificate is given.

The rejection rate is around 10 per cent; the seal does not guarantee the wine is of gold medal standard, but rather its authenticity and that it is (at the least) of commercial quality. I have grave reservations about the applicability of such schemes for Australian wine in general, but for areas such as Mudgee it has great advantages.

From their hands to yours: Vincie Wahlquist and helper label and package Botobolar wines at the winery. The bird on the carton is their symbol of the natural, organic way the vineyards and winery are operated by Vincie and Gil.

Checking the water supply at Craigmoor's vineyards, Mudgee. This drip irrigator provides what is known as supplementary water, usually pumped from bores or dams, to each grapevine during hot or dry spells.

251

AMBERTON WINES

Amberton is one of the most recent arrivals in the region, with plantings commenced in 1975 and the first vintage made in 1979. The original concept saw an annual crush of over 200 tonnes, but I suspect it may be held around the 100 tonnes mark with the slow down in the growth of the wine market.

Particularly in the period after John Rozentals took over winemaking responsibilities, Amberton has produced some excellent wines. Mudgee has relatively few trained winemakers, and could do with more. A graduate of Wagga, Rozentals accepts without reservation the Brian Croser view of a winemaker as a quality control officer, whose primary task is to protect what nature has given him. That protection is in turn chiefly concerned with retaining fruit flavour by preventing oxidation.

This approach manifests itself in the brilliantly clear and clean semillon, chardonnay, shiraz and cabernet based wines which are the principal labels. Lesser quantities of Rhine riesling, sauvignon blanc (for sauternes) and traminer are also made. Rozentals has since left Amberton, and as at mid-1984 was helping with the revitalisation of the run-down Augustine Winery.

David Thompson making wine during the 1984 vintage at Amberton Wines, Mudgee. The day's vinicultural events are listed on the board on his right, and the juice of the day's grapes is still on his hands.

Inside the winery: red wines being matured in oak barrels at Amberton. The bungs on top of each are carefully sealed to avoid too much air harming the contents.

Moonrise over vintage.

*Gil Wahlquist,
former journalist, now
turned winemaker at his
Botobolar Winery, outside
Mudgee, New South Wales.
Gil and his wife Vincie
produce distinctive area
wines of guaranteed origin
from organically operated
vineyards.*

BOTOBOLAR VINEYARD

I once likened Gil Wahlquist to a latter-day Viking chief: wild and woolly flaxen hair, blue eyed and broad shouldered, staring nature in the eye and meeting it on its own terms. Gil and Vincie Wahlquist are tireless ambassadors for the district in general, and for the virtues of natural grape-growing and winemaking in particular.

Gil is an ex-journalist and produces a newsletter 'Botobolar Bugle', which features a spectacular colour photograph on its first page, and which gives continuing insights into his highly original philosophies and approach to winemaking.

All pesticides and weedicides are banned from the vineyard. Fungicides such as Bordeaux mixture (but not systemic sprays) are applied if absolutely necessary. A natural food chain extending from weeds and plants, such as hyssop and penny royal, extends all the way up to peregrine falcons. All live in harmony, and nature keeps vine predators in check.

Wahlquist is strongly opposed to stereotype wines: this reflects his personality and the impact of the vintage to the full.

CRAIGMOOR

This is by far the oldest winery in Mudgee, and of great historic interest. For over one hundred years it remained in the hands of the Roth family, before passing on the death of Jack Roth to interests associated with Cyrille and Jocelyn van Heyst. A number of changes in winemakers has seen some variation in style (and quality) of the wines, but some of Craigmoor's wines are among the better wines of the district.

In 1984 Craigmoor was purchased by Montrose, and all of the bulk and bottled stock was disposed of. I understand Montrose will keep the vineyard identity alive, but inevitably the style and quality of the wine will change, hopefully for the better. It will appear under the Craigmoor label which will be maintained separately. The winery is being restored as a museum, restaurant and barbecue area.

HUNTINGTON ESTATE

In my view Bob Roberts of Huntington produces the region's greatest red wines. Montrose may conceivably throw out a challenge in the future, but for the past ten vintages Huntington has stood head and shoulders above the rest of the field.

Bob Roberts is a remarkable man of even more remarkable modesty. He decided to quit his New Guinea plantation in the late 1960s and – with no winemaking experience – set about establishing Huntington in 1969. With the aid of his manager, he designed and built his winery with his own hands.

He taught himself how to make wine, and with miraculous ease started to produce wines of gold medal quality. His 1974 Cabernet Sauvignon won numerous gold medals, narrowly missing one of the major red wine trophies at the 1980 Royal Sydney Show.

Laying drip irrigation through the vineyard. Judicious use of extra water improves yields without dropping grape quality in hot areas such as Mudgee.

Montrose winery, largest in the Mudgee area, uses modern winemaking technology to make good white and red wines, including unusual red wines from Italian varieties such as nebbiolo and barbera.

His greatest strength undoubtedly is in his cabernets and cabernet/merlot blends. Aided by the sensitive use of American oak, these wines have consistency, flair and style. They have marvellous colour, intense yet refined flavour, and handsomely repay six to ten years cellaring.

In recent years Roberts has made some startlingly good semillons and attractive chardonnays. By and large he refuses to oak-mature the latter, arguing that the flavour of chardonnay is so complete and attractive on its own it does not need oak. I don't agree, but *chacun à son goût.* The pinot noir and shiraz wines are not of the same quality as the cabernets, but are at least distinctive wines. Bob stoutly defends his shiraz, and more power to him for so doing.

MIRAMAR

Miramar is a joint venture between winemaker-manager Ian McRae (who is a Roseworthy graduate) and a group of investors. Since 1977 it has produced wines of the highest quality. Its Rhine rieslings are very good, its chardonnays quite magnificent.

The best chardonnay so far released at the time of writing has been the 1982, an enormous, complex, rich and generous wine. A large part of the wine was barrel-fermented, I understand, adding emphasis to the particular grapefruit-like flavours of Mudgee chardonnay. Ian McRae has also made some spectacular rosés in his time, one a major trophy winner on the national show circuit.

MONTROSE

Italian-owned, and with the urbane Carlo Corino as winemaker, Montrose may yet surprise us all. The appointment of Oenotech as consultants prior to the outstanding 1984 vintage certainly makes Montrose a winery to watch.

Carlo Corino has brought a distinctly Italian touch to his winemaking. One of his first acts on arrival was to rid the winery of as much as possible of its near-new small oak barrels.

Until very recently, most Italian winemakers believed that new oak flavour was an unwelcome distraction in the make-up of a red wine. So Carlo aimed at a red which was relatively light bodied, soft and fresh – and walked off with a major trophy at the Hunter Valley Show with one of his first reds made this way.

In recent times, he has been much engrossed with his crops of nebbiolo, barbera and sangiovese, but the wines which have most caught the public eye have been his chardonnays, Rhine rieslings and – perhaps above all – his Bemosa sauternes. The 1980 release, a blend of 70 per cent semillon and 30 per cent sauvignon blanc, was (and is) one of the best Australian sauternes seen for many years, and deservedly won numerous gold medals.

THE OTHERS

The other wineries in the region include Augustine (recently undergoing a revival), Burnbrae (with some excellent reds made by Paul Tuminello), de Windmolen (where district veteran Pieter van Gent now presides), Hill of Gold, Mansfield, Mudgee Wines and Mt Vincent Meadery. The most recent arrivals are Bramhall, Beaulieu and Erudgeree Wines.

One of the great attractions of Mudgee is the proximity of all the wineries, and the camaraderie and co-operation between virtually all the wineries. It is a friendly and relaxing place to visit; you won't be disappointed if you make the effort.

Pieter van Gent's small winery at Mudgee. The former Dutch winemaker started making wine at Craigmoor in Mudgee, then launched his own winery under the de Windmolen name, but finally adopted his own name for his hand-crafted products.

Crushing white grapes at Montrose winery. Winemaker Carlo Corino, at left, watches the fruit of the harvest.

257

THE MURRUMBIDGEE IRRIGATION AREA

The M.I.A., as it is known, is centred around the town of Griffith, with Leeton (45 kilometres to the south-east) of much lesser importance. On any view of the matter, the M.I.A.'s role is a major one. In 1981 it produced almost 75 per cent of the total New South Wales crush, and near to 20 per cent of the Australian total.

It is a highly significant producer of medium quality white table wine, and from time to time provides wines of real class. Its basic strength lies in the

Irrigation channels, vines, rice fields and citrus in the M.I.A.

economies of production: its 1981 crush of 85 000 tonnes came from 4877 hectares of grapes, an average of 17.42 tonnes per hectare. The average for the rest of the State was 3.65 tonnes per hectare.

This is due principally to the benefits of irrigation, but also to the intuitive skills of the Italian grapegrowers and winemakers who so dominate the industry, if one excludes the biggest winery of all – McWilliam's. These unlikely strands – Scottish and Italian – have woven the fabric of the industry in the area since its foundation in 1912.

J. J. McWilliam was, so far as I know, the first to plant grapevines in the region, putting in 35 000 cuttings at Hanwood in 1912. It is a little known part of history that McWilliam's base was then in Junee; and that the first Hanwood vintage was crushed there. Even less well known is the fact that McWilliam's continued to make red wine from Junee grapes until 1952: I have shared in several bottles of that wine (and also a Junee white) from the cellars of the New South Wales Wine and Food Society. The last I tasted, in the mid-1970s, was in excellent condition.

The McWilliam family stayed, multiplied and prospered. The might of the company, once at the very forefront of all private companies in Australia in terms of assets and earnings, was built on the M.I.A.

The district has treated the two waves of Italians (one in the Twenties, the second in the aftermath of World War II) no less kindly. Yet the average Italian has suffered greatly from the stigma arising from the murder of local anti-drug crusader Donald MacKay. Most of the Italian families are now second and third generation Australians, with an accent as broad as any bushie.

Griffith is a vital town, and the wine industry is in far better shape financially than most in Australia. There is a great spirit of optimism: the winemakers

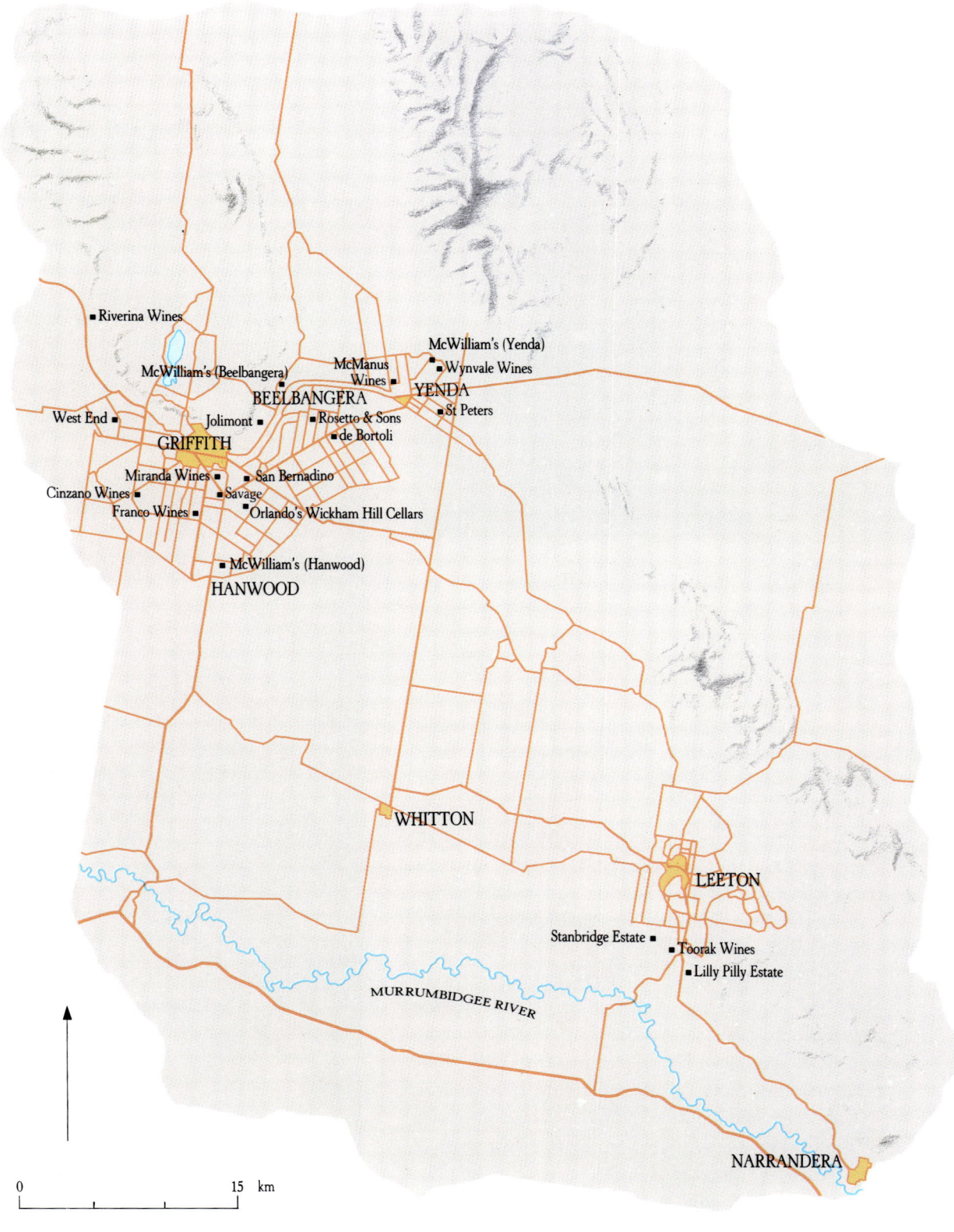

Riverina Wines

McWilliam's (Yenda)

McManus
Wines

Wynvale Wines

McWilliam's (Beelbangera)

BEELBANGERA

YENDA

St Peters

West End

Jolimont

Rosetto & Sons
de Bortoli

GRIFFITH

Miranda Wines

San Bernadino

Cinzano Wines

Savage

Franco Wines

Orlando's Wickham Hill Cellars

McWilliam's (Hanwood)

HANWOOD

WHITTON

LEETON

Stanbridge Estate

Toorak Wines

Lilly Pilly Estate

MURRUMBIDGEE RIVER

NARRANDERA

0   15   km

Bigger than all their tribe . . . the Big Bottle is one of the tourist stars at McWilliam's Hanwood winery, south of Griffith. Inside the concrete bottle, a huge replica of a McWilliam's Traminer Riesling bottle, is a wine bottle museum.

The flat but incredibly generous vineyards of the Murrumbidgee Irrigation Area. In the foreground is McWilliam's Hanwood winery, the largest in the area. The Big Barrel and the Big Bottle, major tourist attractions for the company, are in front of the winery.

honestly believe they can do better than simply be the cow which fills endless bags-in-boxes with cheap white wine.

As long as the region continues to accept that this – cask wine – is its basic product, it will continue to prosper, even though the price of casks is ludicrously low, less per litre than either Coca-Cola or beer. Acceptance of this role does not prevent makers from skimming the cream off the top, as it were, to make five or ten per cent of superior quality bottled wine. Every now and then, as with the de Bortoli sauternes, these wines will be quite superb; and equally, wines such as the 1983 Jolimont Cabernet/Merlot can provide unequalled bargains.

Virtually all the major varieties are grown, with the accent on white grapes. Shiraz utterly dominates the reds with 802 hectares, followed by cabernet sauvignon (233), grenache (115), and mataro (118), while other varieties make up the remaining 166 hectares.

Cabernet sauvignon remains a disappointment. Introduced by McWilliam's in the first few years of the Sixties, it showed enormous early promise. The 1963, an experimental wine, which I most recently tasted in 1983, was nothing less than magnificent. It

Griffith, capital of the Riverina district of New South Wales and its wine-producing areas. The homes of the town abut the ordered vineyards which spread for kilometres around, making it an oasis of green in a brown and dry landscape in central to southern New South Wales.

had held its colour, flavour and body as one might expect a Coonawarra red to do; yet more recent vintages have shown little or none of the same ability.

Indeed, looking at those awaiting release, I am convinced McWilliam's have gone up the wrong path. Instead of holding them back in bottle for four or five years, they should bottle and market them as quickly as possible. That 1983 Jolimont Cabernet/Merlot I mentioned earlier was on the market within eight months of vintage. At around $3 a bottle retail in Sydney one could ask for nothing better in a fresh light summer red at the end of 1983.

Shiraz, grenache and mataro (along with cabernet) find their way into cask reds. Not much attempt is made to elevate these wines to bottle status; where this occurs, there has usually been some special attention paid to the vines (and the grapes) in the vineyard prior to harvest.

A technique of double pruning developed by the local Viticultural Research Station has been carried through to small-scale production by Orlando and one or two others. This involves pruning the vines for a second time after flowering, forcing secondary buds to shoot and produce what is called a second crop. This is much reduced in quantity (as little as a quarter of a normal crop), and ripens later. Colour, pH and acid are all improved. Orlando has made some most attractive shiraz utilising this process.

Because red wine quality is much more sensitive to (and adversely affected by) high yields than white quality, the region is dominated by white grapevines. Of the 4439 hectares in bearing, 3005 hectares are planted to white varieties. These include semillon (995 hectares), trebbiano (840), palomino and pedro ximinez (188), doradillo (155), Rhine riesling (86), traminer (62), chardonnay (44), colombard (81) and sauvignon blanc (25).

If cabernet sauvignon is a disappointment, the performance of Rhine riesling is even more so. For some reason it totally fails to show any varietal character or real flavour once made into wine. This variety to one side, there is increasing interest in and use of the other classic varieties. Statistics for 1990 and 2000 will show substantial increases in the area of sauvignon blanc and colombard, while there will have been a veritable explosion in the amount of chardonnay.

Obviously enough, trebbiano and semillon are the work horses. Semillon yields 20.25 tonnes per hectare; trebbiano 18.18 tonnes. Both are used extensively in the production of cask wines, but along with chardonnay, colombard and sauvignon blanc, significant quantities find their way into bottles. The use of new oak barrels (and no doubt oak chips) fills out both chardonnay and semillon; while the latter has also been employed in the use of spectacular botrytised sauternes.

de BORTOLI

de Bortoli is one of the longest established (1923) and largest wineries in the district. Like so many of the older operations, for much of its time it produced only fortified wine. Since the Sixties, the percentage of table wine has increased as that of fortified wine has decreased. de Bortoli's production is roughly 40 per cent table and 60 per cent fortified wine.

Vittorio Spumante, selling at $1.80 a bottle cellar door in 1983, is its biggest selling bottled brand. The success with this is said to have caused de Bortoli to turn its attention to methode champenoise sparkling wines with a chardonnay/riesling/trebbiano base. 'Jean-Pierre Traditional Champagne' was an 'exciting release' at $6.50 per bottle, again in 1983.

While one may have reservations about the labelling, de Bortoli are approaching their methode champenoise production seriously, installing extensive cool rooms for wine maturation and undertaking considerable research and development work. With the base wine costing them 40 cents a litre, it is not hard to see why they sense a market opportunity.

Along the vineyards of the Murrumbidgee Irrigation Area, an Australian grapegrower of Italian descent checks his vines and irrigation channels. Two large migrations of Italians came to the area, the first after World War I, and the second after World War II. They brought with them expertise and an interest in viticulture and viniculture.

263

De Bortolis make their contribution to the biennial wine festival held at Griffith.

Robert Fiumara's small Lilly Pilly winery in the Murrumbidgee Irrigation Area stirred plenty of interest with his first vintages in the 1980s with the high quality of his white wines, notably a blend of semillon and traminer grapes which he dubbed 'Tramillon'.

The other outstanding initiative has been their partly accidental making of a magnificent sauternes in 1982. Excess grape production is deeply embedded in the Australian industry at the present time, and no area is entirely free from its effects. In 1982 substantial quantities of semillon remained unsold well into the harvest period and then the rain came. Infection spread rapidly, and de Bortoli's were able to buy the 'rotten' (in the eyes of the growers) grapes for almost nothing. To be fair, de Bortoli's had asked one grower to leave some semillon unpicked with this very use in mind, but instead of a trial quantity they had a very large parcel indeed.

The grapes reached 23 baumé, and the resulting wine won seven gold medals in the first five shows at which it was exhibited. Along with an even richer pedro ximinez wine made the same year, it has set a benchmark, selling for up to $16 a bottle retail. Much of it, in half-bottles, has been exported to the United States.

A massive and bewildering list of products from chocmint nip to cabernet port in 'a wood-chip bottle' (whatever that may mean) to traminer/riesling to casks and flagons complete the range of a winery which has shown considerable innovation and flair in the past ten years.

LILLY PILLY

Robert Fiumara runs a winery as different from that of de Bortoli as one could possibly imagine. It burst into prominence in 1983 when Fiumara won the inaugural State Bank Trophy for the best small-maker white wine at that year's Sydney Show. A blend of semillon and traminer, it was cleverly made and equally cleverly called 'Tramillon'.

Fiumara, the son of a local grower and merchant, trained as a winemaker at the Riverina College of Advanced Education. He designed and built a small winery designed to take grapes from an 11-hectare vineyard owned by the family, the maximum crush of which will be 200 tonnes. All wine made will be sold in bottles; no casks, spumante or chocmint nip here, thank you very much.

McWILLIAM'S WINES

McWilliam's dominates the M.I.A. Its three wineries at Hanwood, Yenda and Beelbangera crush over 30 000 tonnes of grapes a year. The debt the M.I.A. owes to the McWilliam's family is immense. Not only did they start the industry, but they have been instrumental in reshaping it to meet the needs of the Eighties and beyond.

A family of remarkable engineers, they developed both winery and fermentation tank designs well in advance of contemporary thought, and introduced the principles of successful white table winemaking to the region. Even more importantly still, they introduced the first high quality varieties to the region (cabernet sauvignon and Rhine riesling) in about 1960, and have been at the forefront of experimentation with, and introduction of, numerous other varieties.

Their varietal table wines need no introduction. Both the numerous white varietals (chardonnay, Rhine riesling, sauvignon blanc, traminer and traminer/riesling) and the two reds (cabernet and

At work in the tank farm. Stainless steel is the common denominator of most big wineries today, enabling winemakers to control fermentation and storage temperatures. The tanks are cheap to build, easy to maintain and sterile in operation.

The Big Barrel, a huge tasting room in front of the Hanwood winery, which crushes around 14 000 tonnes of grapes each vintage, making some varietal and generic wines which are widely thought to be excellent value, and which are usually ready to drink when sold.

Keith McWilliam stands inside a 75 000-litre stainless steel tank at McWilliam's Beelbangera winery, outside Griffith. The technology employed inside and outside tanks like this allows winemakers to keep flavours fresh in the journey from vineyard to bottle.

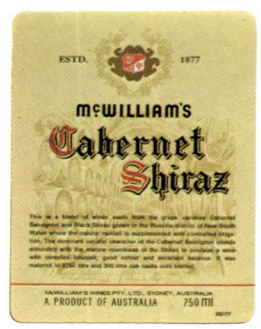

cabernet/shiraz) offer both reliability and remarkable value for money. My only criticism is that both the whites and – more particularly – the reds should be marketed (and consumed) earlier than has been the pattern so far.

The group has recently entered the cask market with the battle cry 'we will not be undersold', which some would say is not quite what the industry needs. It has experimented with all sorts of packaging from foil sachets to the ill-fated styrene coated 'Big Mac', looking exactly like a large bottle of soft drink. And of course it continues to produce prodigious quantities of cream sherry, tawny port (Hanwood) and other fortified wines. Its Tartan Vintage Port is a very good aged wine.

MIRANDA

The third generation of the Miranda family is about to become actively involved in the running of an enterprise which produces over one million casks, one million flagons and three to four million bottles of sparkling wine each year from its 8000 tonne crush. Miranda's Golden Gate Spumante, of unimpeachable technical quality and consistency, comes off a quarter million dollar bottling line at the rate of 6000 bottles per hour. Miranda are not bulk resellers: 98 per cent of annual production leaves Miranda in a packaged form. Indeed, just to reverse the normal flow, Miranda buy both Hunter semillon and Clare shiraz, which they make, bottle and sell in the upper sector of the market.

An ultra-modern laboratory permits bacterial plating procedures once or twice every day to ensure total sterility in the bottling line; two fully qualified winemakers preside over the winemaking; and the family devotes its considerable energy and talent to marketing the products. The Mirandas believe they have the formula for survival; I am sure they are right.

SAN BERNADINO

Stan Aliprandi of San Bernadino certainly seemed to have got the formula right. A local Griffith chemist, he was instrumental in the growth of San Bernadino from 35 000 cases of wine a year in 1973 to 800 000 cases six years later. The growth continued at breakneck speed, with a major marketing offensive in the United States. The product range was immense: over 100 different table, fortified and flavoured wines were available.

One of these – a variant of Irish Cream called O'Malley's Emerald Cream – contributed to the collapse of the dream when it encountered major technical problems in the United States. For several years, San Bernadino was in receivership, and for a while it seemed liquidation would follow. But Aliprandi is a tough warrior who doesn't know when to quit, and at the time of writing San Bernadino has just come out of receivership.

It will be a leaner and less flamboyant San Bernadino in the years ahead, but it will still be a very important part of the local scene.

Champagne being made and matured in McWilliam's Griffith cellars. The fungus growth on the bottles does not affect the wine as it ages and improves.

Among the largest wineries in the Murrumbidgee Irrigation Area is de Bortoli's, founded in 1923 and still owned by the de Bortoli family. They make a wide range of good quality table, fortified and sparkling wines.

THE OTHERS

I have somewhat arbitrarily selected six of the eighteen wineries in the region to give a more detailed picture of the people whose drive and ambition make the M.I.A. what it is. But visit any of the others, and you will find similar stories. At the bottom end of the size scale is the unconventional McManus Wines, and the extremely dedicated and intelligent approach of Roger Hoare at Stanbridge Estate. Dr McManus is a local doctor who is a dedicated individualist; Roger Hoare is president of the local grape-growers' association, who makes between 1000 and 1200 cases a year of varietal white wines from relatively low yielding vines in a tiny insulated corrugated winery he calls Chateau Lysaght.

Rosetto and Sons, Franco's and West End are medium-sized wineries owned and run by Italian

families; while Calamia, renamed Jolimont, has passed into ownership of the makers of Uncle Toby's Oats and been revitalised, under the winemaking skills of the youthful John Swanson. Jolimont takes its fruit from the lower yielding Cal Cal Vineyard, some distance away from the main Griffith area.

Then there are the major processing wineries of Wynvale (Wynn) and Orlando's Wickham Hill Cellars. Both these wineries play a major part in the production of each company's casks and flagons. Orlando's Coolabah range has long been recognised as Australia's best, while Wynn is making a determined effort to regain the pre-eminent position once held.

Finally, there are the special purpose wineries of Cinzano (for making vermouth) and St Peters (brandy), although the latter has just had a major change of direction following its acquisition by the Saxonvale group.

Laid down and all but forgotten . . . these barrels of sweet white fortified wine can improve for many years, aided by oak storage in warm conditions inside a Griffith winery.

Filling oak barrels using a pump and hoses is one of the chores of post-vintage winemaking. These stacked barrels are used for maturation of fortified wines and brandy as they are too old to impart much wood flavour to table wines.

*Michael Hill Smith in his family company's wine museum – seen here examining
one of Yalumba's own wines.*

ME AND MY CELLAR

Michael Hill Smith

André Simon, the founder of the International Wine and Food Society, had a great cellar. Rather than leave any of his previous bottles to posterity, or anyone else for that matter, he swore he wouldn't die until his cellar was empty. After his death, it was revealed that his cellar contained one bottle of wine, but Simon's greatness did not diminish – after all – it was a magnum.

My family legacy is totally different, as the Yalumba Wine Museum is one of the finest collections of old wines in Australia, and a product of generations of ancestors who didn't drink their cellars dry.

The cellar began in the 1920s as a disorganised collection of old show samples, reference wines, bottles swapped with other wineries, and winemakers' favourites that lay around the tasting room known as 'the Den'. These wines became the nucleus of the current collection which is still housed in the Den, although three adjacent wax-lined underground tanks have been requisitioned for the expanding cellar, now estimated to hold over 24 000 bottles.

The Museum is not made up of Yalumba and Hill Smith Estate Wines only. The collection is 'non-

Yalumba's cooper, Harry Mahlo, puts an oaken wine barrel together from imported wood.

denominational', as many wines come from other makers, areas and countries. In addition to pre-1900 Yalumba Ports and dry reds, many famous wines made by famous men are represented. Early Mt Pleasants made by Maurice O'Shea, old Hardy's wines by Roger Warren, those of Colin Preece from Seppelt and Max Schubert, who pioneered Grange Hermitage. These names are to wine what Bradman, Larwood and Richardson are to cricket.

A great cellar should have variation and balance – after all – who wants to drink 1955 Grange Hermitage for the rest of their lives!

As a young child, my sole interest in the Museum was that in it was stored a large, stuffed brown bear, who, in a previous career in advertising had extolled people to 'Bear in Mind Yalumba Wines'. The bear under my direction, was used to scare my friends. Scene 1: Unsuspecting eight-year-old is led into the Museum. Scene 2: 'Action' as Bear spot lit by torch. Scene 3: 'Exit' as terrified youth runs shrieking into the cellar!

Later, during school holidays, we young Hill Smiths were given the job of checking for ullaged bottles and topping these up, first sparging with carbon dioxide and finally re-corking and wax sealing the dusty old relics. The most complicated job was deciphering cryptic bin cards that made the *Sunday*

Times crossword look easy. Over the years, using logic Sherlock Holmes would envy, I deduced the 1933 Sweetwater was not an old-fashioned lemonade, but a wine made from neutral white grapes without muscat character; and that the 1942 Mt Pleasant T.Y. Hermitage was made from grapes bought from Tyrrells, as their winery was blown down by storms in both 1942 and 1943 (I assume these were unusually ferocious winds or that Tyrrells changed builders as this phenomenon has not been repeated since); and that Bin C120 contained the same old 4 Crown Port blend that Sir Douglas Mawson's Expedition took to the Antarctic in 1929/30 and prompted them to sing:

'Lay me down on the first piece of pack ice
With Yalumba uncorked near my mouth
And leave me to die unmolested
For I see now we'll never get South.'

Recently I remembered a wine labelled 1926 Tokay/ White Bordeaux, which sadly creates some precedent for Richmond Groves' use of this unfortunate generic term.

The Museum had become the classroom for my narrow but highly specialised education!

In recent years, many wines have been added to the collection, including some early Penfolds reds, Orlando Rhine rieslings, Petaluma chardonnay, Tyrrells pinot noir and some early Rothbury semillon. Aged, international styles include pre-Lautrec absinthe, old Bordeaux and a range of nineteenth-

At the Yalumba winery, late in the nineteenth century.

century Madeiras bought from John Avery in Bristol.

Wines are also bought at auction at Christies, as was the 1921 Château d'Yquem, which is generally considered the greatest d'Yquem vintage of the century. This wine was the feature of the 1983 Museum Tasting, a biennial event held on the first Monday after the Barossa Valley Vintage Festival. The 1983 tasting nearly became a national wine tragedy. The day before, helped by Len Evans and others, we prepared 40 litres of cassoulet – that great French provincial dish of beans, sausage, pork and duck – to serve at the post-tasting luncheon. Due to lack of energy, lethargy or an oversight, we elected not to refrigerate the cassoulet overnight. Next morning I discovered our lunch fermenting merrily away. White-coated microbiologists were summoned from the laboratory who assured me the contents of the pot were non-toxic. The cassoulet was heated to arrest fermentation, but the beams were discarded due to a strange 'fizzy' lactic character and an unfortunate blue mould.

To serve or not to serve…? The loaves and the fishes…? Or to be immortalised as the Reverend Jim Jones of the Barossa Valley by successfully poisoning the wine industry elite!

Nervously I served the dubious dish. People came back for seconds and thirds and although I didn't eat any myself, Gai Bilson from Berowra Waters Inn assured me it was marvellous!

Building a good cellar is like playing poker; you have to discard to improve your hand. The wines are regularly tasted to assess their quality, development and future in the Museum. Lesser wines are discarded and all bins are checked annually for leaking bottles or cork deterioration and appropriate action taken.

I have always loved getting presents, so I am overjoyed that people in the wine industry have begun donating great bottles to the Museum, which are then featured at the Museum Tasting. Recently James Halliday has contributed an 1834 Roriz Vintage Port, Andrew Simon an 1825 Hungarian Tokay Essence and Len Evans an 1865 Apsley House Sherry, to mention a few. Long may this trend continue.

The Museum has been likened to the catacombs in Rome, or Hitler's bunker, although I doubt if Adolf or the early Christians drank quite so well! I have no intention of drinking the Museum dry, but in the event of a nuclear strike, you will find me secure in the Museum – corkscrew in hand – conducting the final Museum Tasting.

I'm sure André Simon would approve.

One way to keep warm in the frozen Antarctic. Sir Douglas Mawson and his men took Yalumba's 4 Crown Port blend with them on their 1929/30 Expedition to the Antarctic.

The clocktower at Yalumba still watches barrels of wine leave on their way to the markets of Australia and the world.

11.45 a.m.

A DAY
IN THE LIFE
OF A
WINEMAKER

Paul Lloyd

16 MARCH 1984

6.02 a.m.: With a lusty yell, Nicholas Knappstein six months old, is awake. Within minutes his sister Emily and mother Anne are yawning themselves into an autumn Clare morning. Meanwhile father Tim sleeps on for another hour ('Just pretending to be asleep,' says Anne as she changes another nappy). Tim had been working in his winery overseeing the day's vintage until nearly midnight last night, and when he does rise it is a matter of wonder that he still has a Peter Pan complexion and eyes as crisp as the morning air in the vineyards surrounding the house, some 4 kilometres east of Clare, South Australia. The dishwasher hums, somewhere a tap runs, and bare feet plop on the tiled floors. Here the winemaker is no dream hero of the public relations industry, but just another human being, breakfasting on muesli, cleaning teeth, dressing Emily in a pretty pink pinafore. Anne is scolding Nicholas for playing with his mashed Weet-Bix rather than eating it. But nobody speaks much, no radio blares and it could be any rural household. However, so early in the day, there are strong undercurrents, which Anne touches on by saying: 'If a marriage can survive a couple of months of this [vintage time] it can survive anything.'

7.05 a.m.

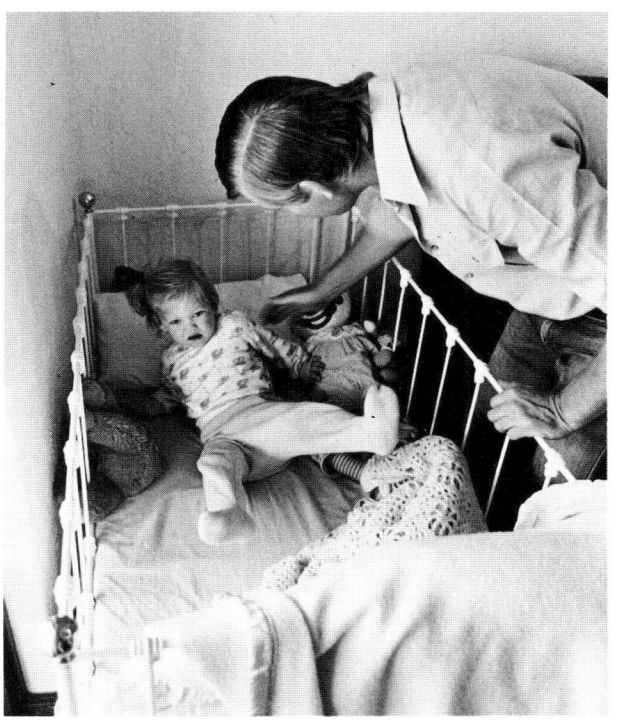

275

7.30 a.m.

7.55 a.m.: Tim is ready to leave, but the household water softener is playing up. Out with the tools. A winemaker is also a handyman just as he will prove to be, as any day of vintage progresses, viticulturist, oenologist, microbiologist, inventor, improviser, mechanic, carpenter, plumber, cooper, businessman, administrator, salesman, bon vivant, athlete, visionary, artist, dreamer and dedicated toiler.

8.15 a.m.: 'A late start,' he says, pulling gumboots over his jeans and stretching up into the Toyota Hilux four-wheel-drive ute. (The Porsche stays locked up in the garage for the duration of vintage.) First call is down to the bottom of his riesling vineyard by the whirring pines, where there's a little patch of perfect riesling fruit being left for late picking. Tim checks it every day, for he is shooting for a botrytis auslese style with the 7 or 8 tonnes he will harvest from this patch. It is one of his special babies and now, as the end of vintage nears, he is more concerned than ever. He looks cursorily across the rest of the 18.5 hectares of vines surrounding the house, for a last minute check on what will be picked today. 'It'll be a great vintage — if we don't stuff it up in the winery,' he laughs.

8.45 a.m.

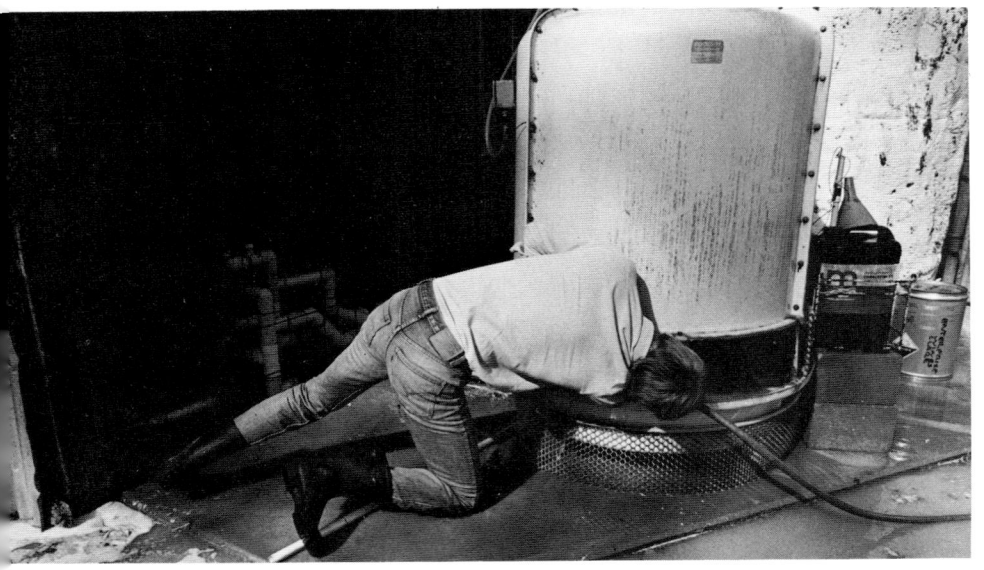

9.22 a.m.

startling: 'titizip' as insects hit the electric bug-zapper; 'ssss' of gas cylinders; 'plonk' of gumboots; and always almost out of earshot the crinkling old cold sound of running water. Tim strides in to greet his assistant winemaker and his cellarhand, every bit the captain of the ship, but his authority communicated not so much by gold braid as by enthusiasm and the conviction in his eyes. He starts the day by preparing to check the fermentation tanks.

9.22 a.m.: But there is a problem in the refrigeration plant, the least glamorous aspect of winemaking but one of the most essential in Australia's warm autumns. Again he is out there wielding the spanner himself, for a smallish operation such as this, crushing about 275 tonnes of grapes, is not a great deal more than a one-person operation.

9.13 a.m.: Into the winery on the northern outskirts of the town of Clare, a historic looking building which has spent all its one hundred years serving thirsts, first as a brewery, then as a soft drink factory and now as the Enterprise Winery. Morning sunlight probes a grotto of stainless steel stalagmites inside the thick stone walls. It is so quiet that noises are

9.35 a.m.: Vineyard manager Bob Hammond, his face etched with the wit of the soil, comes by to discuss the day's delivery requirement. He reckons a bloke down the road has an additional tonne of riesling he can't handle. 'I know the vines,' says Tim. 'Yes, it will be worth $350. We'll fit it in somehow.'

10.12 a.m.

9.53 a.m.

There will be one load after lunch and another in the evening. Only a two-load day. 'Well that's a bit of relief after the pressure for the last month.'

9.51 a.m.: Back to the refrigeration plant. Tim, in a most ungainly position, is stumbled upon by a group of executives from a large wine company, 'just having a look around the Clare region'. Tim figures they're not here to try and buy him out and he makes time to explain his operation, and does it with pride, showing them how the crusher is physically separated from the winery for cleanliness, how the white wine juice is pumped through a chiller, to help overcome oxidation problems, straight into the press, made by Josef Wilmes GmbH of Germany. He has his own system of computerised temperature control for all the stainless steel tanks. 'Looks like a duck's guts, but it works,' he says of this embryonic high technology. His greatest pride is for the cellar downstairs with new barrels of French oak in which a chardonnay is fermenting.

10.12 a.m.: A phone call. Some highly technical trade talk with a counterpart down at Tim's former winery, Stanley. It is the first of fourteen times he is on the phone today.

10.40 a.m.: The heavies depart, after the ritual exchange of a few bottles of wine. Tim is back to the refrigeration plant, fixes the problem and devises a scale inhibitor so it won't happen again. So soon.

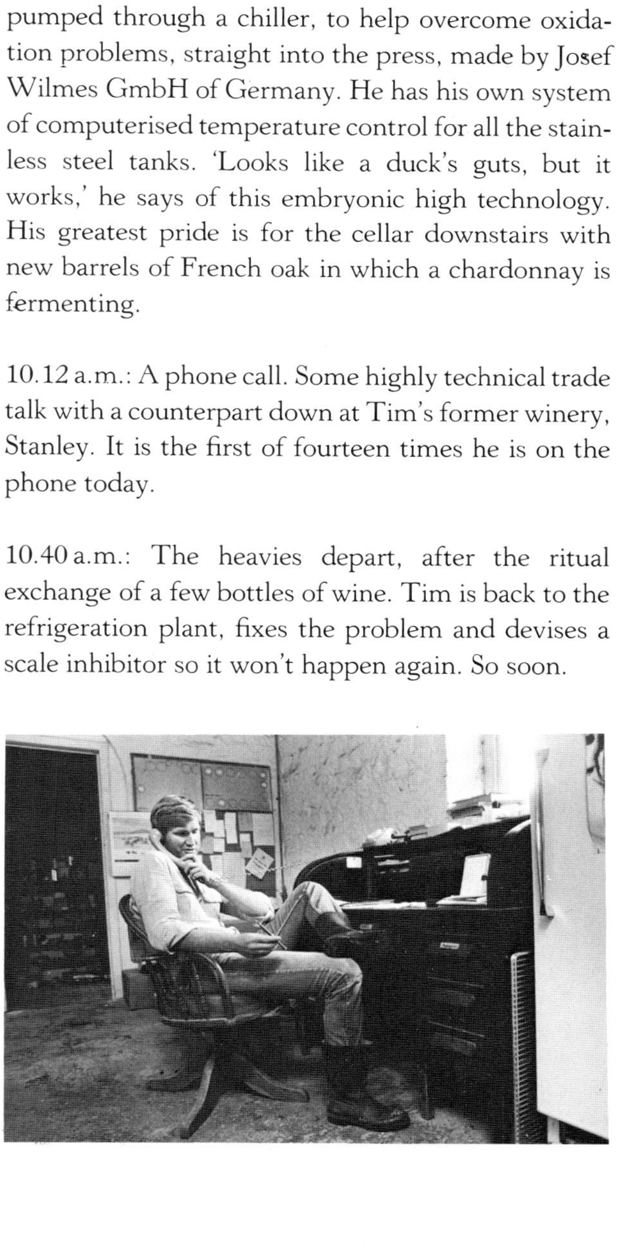

10.46 a.m.: We still haven't seen any actual wine-making by Tim. But his assistant, Andrew Phillips, fresh from oenology college, and his cellarhand, Ian Lomman, a local who's worked with Tim for near on four years, are busy inside, pumping things about, seeding fermentations, checking, checking, cleaning, cleaning. Tim reads the mail, pausing over a mass-circulation offer: 'Hey, here's a French champagne at $10.50 a bottle if you buy in bulk.' But then he drifts off looking perplexed about some tax problem. Not only is he a winemaker, but a businessman overseeing a million-dollar operation.

11.10 a.m.: Andrew reports a fault developing in the brine system. A quick look convinces Tim that the electrician must be summoned for this one. 'At least it has got us through most of vintage.'

11.25 a.m.: The daily ritual of checking the tanks is resumed, testing with thermometer, hydrometer and palate. Now we are seeing the more conventional image of the winemaker. Taste, spit. 'Tank 16 is going to have a magic palate.' Taste, spit. 'Tank 15 looks like being a bit skinny and grassy...'

10.40 a.m.

11.20 a.m.

11.42 a.m.

12.20 p.m.: Everybody walks off for lunch, a stroll down the main street of Clare for mortadella and salad rolls. Back in the winery restroom, Tim sprawls over the *Bulletin,* discussing politics, interspersed with interruptions from Anne who, with the kids left for the day at her friend's place, is now in the front office and wanting various commercial decisions. A snooze. Everybody rests. It feels like the calm before the storm.

1.46 p.m.: A thunderstorm indeed suddenly breaks. Consternation. 'How long till the pickers [10 kilometres south at Auburn] cop it? I hope we're ready.' Tim doesn't actually give orders. The others know pretty well what to do. More, he makes observations, with just a hint of a reminder. Preparing for the crush means connecting all hoses and pumps from crusher through chiller through press to the storage tank. The lines must be sparged with carbon dioxide to rid them of air, the oxygen in which can cause oxidation.

2.20 p.m.: There's a total of about 15 tonnes coming in today. The tank space may not be enough. What about yesterday's juice in tank 12 which probably won't make the grade for the Enterprise label? Tim is on the phone to another winery: 'Say, how would you like 3000 litres of Rhine juice? I'm holding it at 13° baumé. Lovely stuff. OK?'

3.09 p.m.

3.35 p.m.

2.55 p.m.: A minor crisis from out the front, the public tasting room, where Tim rarely ventures. Sales assistant Margaret reports that the cold spell has meant a run on the tawny port and she's sold out. Enterprise wines are normally bottled at Stanley but, for the port, he takes a few empties down into the cellar and siphons them full from a cask of ten-year-old tawny port.

3.06 p.m.: A delivery truck arrives with a treasure. Eight new oak casks from France, worth some $300 each, for maturation of the red wines. The winemaker turns cooper and shows Ian how to drive the hoops so he can carry on with the others.

3.29 p.m.: 'My sixth sense tells me grapes are coming,' says Tim. And within less than two minutes, Bob chugs up in the old red Austin 7-tonne truck (about 1955, he says, 'but still does a bloody good job'). And there's the day's first couple of tonnes of grapes.

3.34 p.m.: Les' white truck weighs in with an additional 3.86 tonnes, enough to fill the crusher. These are the moments the whole year in the winery has been geared to, and this is the moment for which the day has waited. The load of grapes slowly subsides into the crusher which, with hums (pitched in the key of G) and whirrs and rattles and spits, blows off the stalks and leaves into a pile to be collected later for vineyard mulch. Into the juice tray at the bottom dribbles the 'must', that vile sticky mass of skins, seeds and juice which, with a constant drip of sodium metabisulphite to prevent oxidation, is pumped into the winery. The cellarhand mans the crusher, and woe betide him should he let the pump run too fast or too slow. The trucks are hosed down, as everything is hosed down. It is a sobering thought that in this winery, which produces about 1.2 million litres of wine annually, some 2.5 million litres of water a year is used for cleaning. Obviously cleanliness comes before even godliness here. As the must flows through the chiller its temperature drops from about 25 to 3.7°C. Tim is overseeing the air bag press which, with a whistle pitched in the key of E, squeezes the juice free from the mass of skins.

3.36 p.m.

3.38 p.m.

283

4.25 p.m.

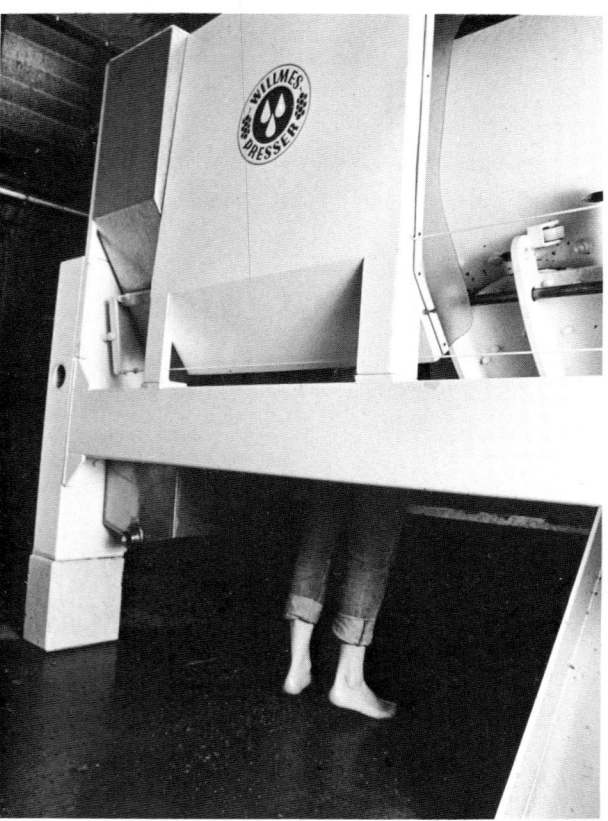

6.10 p.m.

4.00 p.m.: Andrew, who has been spending most of the time doing tests in the laboratory, takes over the press controls because a solenoid in the cooling system is stuck. Tim removes it and replaces it with a solenoid from an old washing machine. 'It will do until the electrician can return tomorrow.' By now the press goes onto automatic with the juice flowing into tank 5 to be left to settle there for a few days before being racked off gross lees, filtered through a *superfiltro autopolente* by Velo of Italy, fined with bentonite and seeded with yeast for the magic of fermentation. Meanwhile everybody is pitching in to clean up.

4.22 p.m.: Tim is in the ute again to pop down to Stanley. The telephone is not adequate for the complexity of this technical discussion. He says: 'At vintage time I live on the phone or in the ute. Last week I reckon I drove 500 kilometres and never got further than 10 kilometres away from the winery.'

5.23 p.m.: Tank 7, containing fermenting cabernet, has to be pumped over for 25 minutes. This is a twice-daily job since the header boards in the tank have broken. 'A real nuisance,' says Tim. 'It means sterilising the lines and gassing them every time. But it's got to be done.' He sets the pumping in operation and leaves it to Ian.

5.50 p.m.: The tanker has come and the contents of tank 12 pumped into it. Now the tank must be cleaned out to receive the next batch of juice. Tim crawls inside with the scrubbing brush, the caustic soda and the hose. Again he simply says: 'Somebody's got to do it.'

6.23 p.m.: The sun sets. Darkness closes and a full moon rises through the tall gums by the creek. Inside, the wet winery floor glistens under the fluorescent lighting and the stainless steel tanks shimmer eerily. The press is empty and cleaned up and the only sounds are the dull hiss of gas sparging a tank with carbon dioxide. The hoses are cheesed down with a precision to which very few yachtsmen would aspire.

285

10.40 p.m.

7.10 p.m.: Under the harsh glare of floodlights outside, swarming with insects, the red truck and the white truck return with fresh loads of grapes. And the whole crushing, pumping, pressing, cleaning ritual starts again.

11.00 p.m.: The juice is secure. The winery is clean. All tanks are wished goodnight and the temperature controls checked. And in the cobwebbed laboratory, with Bunsen burners, glass tubings, rolltop desk, pitted concrete floors and a crumbling Gothic stairway leading to the disused tower, Tim checks the 'hot fridge', a yeast propagation plant made from a converted 400-litre refrigerator. Tim and Andrew and Ian stand around as though receiving communion from the hot fridge. They fold their arms and stare blankly, not wanting to speak. Eventually Tim suggests that 'Adrenalin is what keeps you going. Right throughout vintage, you're teetering on the brink of exhaustion. Time to call this one a day.'

11.36 p.m.: Back home, Anne has the children asleep and dinner on the table: grilled chicken breast with

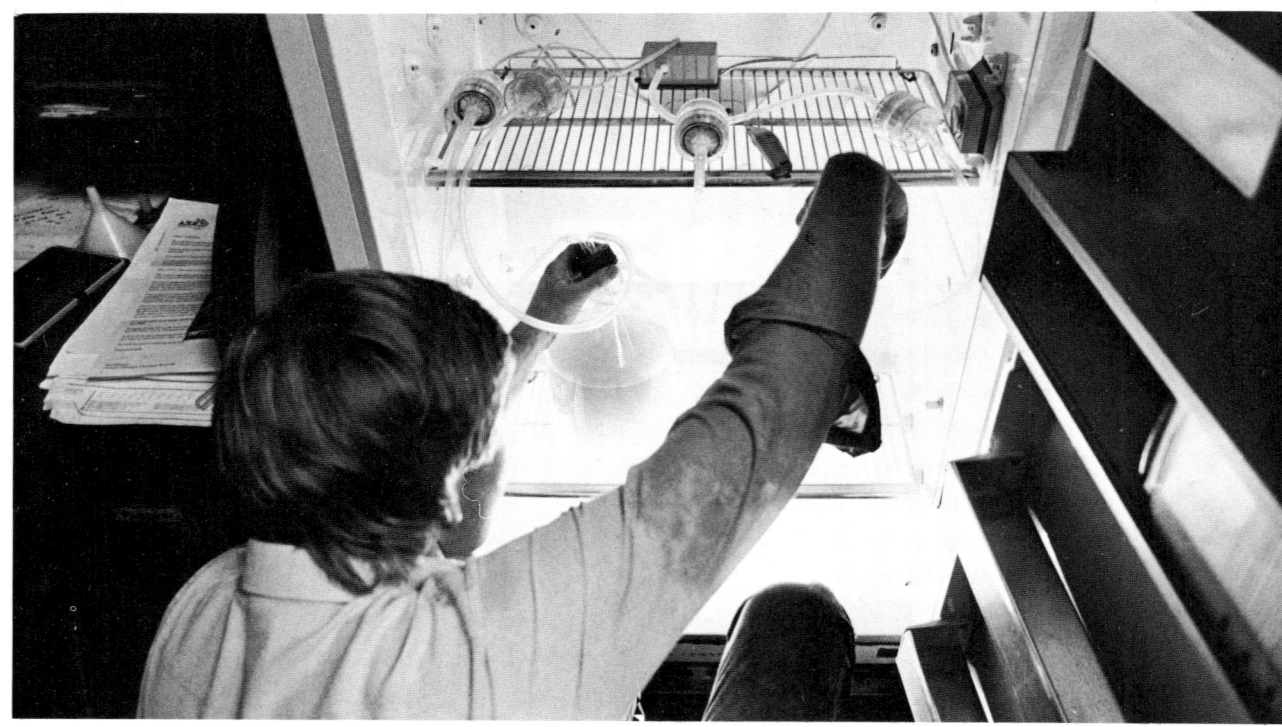

11.04 p.m.

ginger, real vegetables and rockmelon and local ice-cream. Tim had been philosophising on the way home: 'Winemaking is more than turning fruit juice into an alcoholic beverage; it is also maximising the quality and appeal of the wine, expressing imagination, sensitivity, knowledge. Personally, I make wine to keep the wolf from the door, to make the best possible from my vineyards in Clare and (when they come into bearing) the Adelaide Hills, constantly to upgrade, and to sell it to the lower end of the top wine market.' But now, over dinner, he would rather talk of political and social issues, and treat wine not as the mucky baby whose nappy he's been changing all day, figuratively speaking, but as the great broad piece of life it is. He opens a Wehlener Sonnenuhr 1970, but rapidly replaces that with a Hugel Tradition Riesling 1976, then a Lanson non-vintage champagne for the dessert. It makes a change from dealing with his own wines all day. 'Oh, they're mucky when they're new,' he says, 'but like babies, they grow up, and you love them.' He starts rambling a bit, making jokes about the ubiquitous winery worker's gumboots, and how they need a company emblem and GT stripes.

11.42 p.m.

17 March, 1.03 a.m.: The murmuring snores attest that Tim is asleep. Anne is asleep. Emily is asleep. Only the nocturnal stirrings of Master Nicholas are a reminder that, for the Knappstein household, another day of vintage is coming. And another. And another.

11.55 p.m.

ROBERT MAYNE

Me and My Cellar

I never thought I would be the master of a cellar. I had believed that drinking the stuff was more fun than collecting it, but getting a job in the wine industry changed all that.

Now I own some 2 tonnes of wine. I know it's 2 tonnes because I had to work it out recently when we moved from Sydney to Adelaide. That translates to around 120 cases or about 1440 bottles. It ranges from the abominable through the F.A.Q. (fair average quality to the wheat boys, but fair average quaffing to imbibers!), to the excellent.

If you plan to keep wine for a few years, don't buy much until you have some idea of firstly what is good and, secondly, of what you feel you will eventually like drinking yourself. I made plenty of mistakes at the beginning, spurred on by some proud vignerons and overconfident wine colleagues.

The distilled wisdom I think I got from the first three years or so is this. Be very careful buying wine from winemakers you do not know or whose wines do not come highly recommended by people who really do know their wines. Buy small parcels to begin with, because big parcels can mean big and expensive mistakes. Don't buy strange or exotic grape varieties (such as zinfandel, blends of cinsaut and oueillade . . . that sort of thing) and never buy from people selling wines, particularly imported wines, door-to-door.

Above all other things, regularly try some of the wines you are storing. The process is educational and can prevent doubling up on poor buys. No amount of written or spoken words beats actually tasting the stuff before committing yourself, and also when you have it stashed away under the house.

It is also important to make some estimate of your future needs. Buying wine for profit is difficult (though certainly not impossible). Most people prefer to buy for their own enjoyment, and this means working out how many bottles you wish to use a week. You may well be buying cheap commercial wine (in bottles, flagons or casks) for quaffing, but good things still come in 750-millilitre glass bottles, and you may decide you eventually want to drink three or four good bottles a week. That's 156 to 208 bottles a year (or 13 to 17 cases), which obviously enough means you will have to build up to that level and then buy enough wines to keep the cellar full.

Depending on what you buy, a good working cellar could run on a stock level of about 40-50 cases which could be (again depending on your tastes) about two-thirds red to one-third white. Cellaring most other types of wine, with the noble exception of vintage port, is hardly worth your time and trouble as you can readily obtain good mature sherries, tawny ports, muscats and even older champagnes in major retail outlets around Australia, or by mail order through reputable wine clubs and societies.

Cellaring good vintage ports is worthwhile if you like the stuff, and is not a bad way to leave your descendants a valuable liquid asset. Good vintage ports from reputable makers will improve for ten, twenty, even thirty years or longer. Among reputable makers I include Yalumba, Lindemans, Hardy, Reynella and some of the north-east Victorian makers.

One of the great problems with cellars (if you have solved the problems of actually having one) is finding ways of storing the wine. I wanted single bottle access without the

often considerable cost of prefabricated modular storage racks. After all, if you have to add a dollar or more to the cost of each bottle just for storage, a cellar starts becoming an expensive indulgence. My answer was to find some old metal soft drink (or beer) crates and stack them one atop the other, wiring some together for vertical stability. When I ran out of crates, I bought some Masonite assemble-yourself boxes which I have found excellent. They hold 24 separate bottles each, and when I bought them a year or two ago cost about $9 each (which is 37 cents a bottle).

As I had no suitable storage area in my Sydney home, I used the sandstone basement of my mother's North Shore house, which was almost ideal: cool, dark, secure and almost free of damp. It had the additional advantage of being ten minutes' drive from my house, which tended to discourage the midnight raider syndrome, a habit I usually regretted the next morning!

The trouble with cellars, as James Halliday points out elsewhere, is that they are seldom easily transportable. Moving 2 tonnes of wine the 1300 kilometres to Adelaide in mid-summer presented some problems.

We spent some days packing the bottles tightly in their individual slots, using newspaper and rags. The more valuable bottles were removed, wrapped in paper and jammed back firmly in place, then extra paper was stuffed around them in an attempt to insulate and protect them. The crates were loaded aboard Mr Amos' pantechnicon, packed tightly, on their backs with the bottle necks up, and then despatched to South Australia. And they arrived without the loss of a single bottle or drop!

As I write this (sipping a nice glass of Victorian cabernet sauvignon which survived the trip) I am trying to work out how to store it in my new Adelaide home. One option was to burrow into the cliff at the rear of my house and either build a new cellar in there, or drive into the cliff one of those concrete caissons used in bridge building, and which are occasionally available in mildly damaged condition. While practical, this would have been too expensive, so I decided to use a large back garden lock-up tin shed, which has a concrete floor. I will paint the top, front and back white to reflect heat, then spray insulate the inside walls with the styrene foam used in winery buildings. The doors and window will be temperature sealed with heavy duty tinfoil flaps and then, I hope, I will have what every good cellar needs, whether it be for 2 cases of wine or 2 tonnes: temperature stability, absence of direct sunlight, no vibration and absence of moisture.

MARK SHIELD

Cellaring... Been There, Done That!

I don't own or maintain a cellar. Why? Because, like the rest of me, my palate is in a state of decay. Perhaps 'decay' is too strong a term for my palate; that should read 'change', the rest is decidedly in decay.

In the early Seventies I was bitten by the cellar bug. It was trendy to fill every nook and cranny of the house with bottles. Wine under the bed, in the linen closet, beneath the stairs. Using a box of vintage port as a foot stool in front of the television. It was all the rage, and pretty soon, like a miser with his hoard of gold, I was gloating over five hundred bottles. I assumed that my drinking comfort during my dotage was assured.

Not so! In those days I harboured a penchant for gutsy reds and sticky ports. If a wine didn't have hairy armpits and muscles upon muscles, I wasn't interested. Naturally the north-east of Victoria was my happy hunting ground.

The other mistake that I made was to pay attention to the wine snobs and salt away any bottle that was labelled cabernet sauvignon. In those days it was well known that all cabernets keep. The wheel fell off, as the saying goes, when I started to open my booty. In the five years that had elapsed, my palate had matured somewhat. It was like having developed a liking for Mozart after spending your life listening to brass bands.

Elegance and subtlety had crept up on my palate and did the heroic reds a mortal blow. I simply no longer liked what I was drinking. There was nothing wrong with many of the wines, they were simply big, fat and dumb. They were never going to be memorable, nor would they launch a thousand ships. Perhaps they would have gone well across the bows of a dinghy?

There was nothing left to do but to drink the stuff. After all, it is vulgar to sell your cellar for a profit. Surprising how fast five hundred bottles can be made to disappear. Also surprising how many bottles were either past it or senile. It didn't matter if the label extolled the virtues of its cellar life, many wines were decidedly tired. I had cellared them carefully, so my only conclusion was that some wine labels speak with forked tongues.

So that was that. I resolved I'd never start a cellar again. This flirtation with elegance might be a fleeting affair, instead I've made the wine shops of Melbourne my cellar. It is surprising what wine you can buy, admittedly at a price. I'd rather pay the extra and know that I'm going to enjoy the wine.

There is also the theory that you should have your last bottle from your cellar on your deathbed. I'm afraid that I'm not that organised. Besides, everyone tells me that I'm going to come to a very sticky end. I can't see any advantage in having the best cellar in the cemetery and the thought of my freeloading friends mixing it with lemonade at the wake almost hastens my demise.

My advice is to forget about hoarding wines and don't be troubled about the great bottles that you might miss out on as a consequence. Good wines are like the trams and trains should be; there's another one along every ten minutes.

Chateau Hornsby's vineyards. Certainly the sunniest vineyard in Australia, according to its owner. Sometimes vintage is so early he has trouble working out which vintage year to put on the label.

A NICE LITTLE DESERT WINE

Paul Lloyd

The grapevine, *Vitis vinifera,* in its multitude of varieties, travels only with humankind. And although it flourishes in certain areas, between certain latitudes and then only under certain conditions of climate and civilisation, it has been taken to some of the most unlikely places. Such as the Red Centre of Australia.

This is one of the remotest parts of the world, thousands of kilometres from the seashore to which the Australian population tends to cling. Once seabed itself, it is now an elevated arid zone, where occasional small mountain ranges shift colours, dramatically pink and blue and red and purple with the day's changing light, and conceal even rarer lush canyons. Mostly, however, it is flat, seemingly eternally flat, thatched together with low scrub and spinifex grass. There's precious little exotic intrusion here, such as the grapevine.

Central Australia conceals 390 species of native flora, 22 native mammals, 151 native birds and a race of people who in their natural state live by laws laid down in the Dreaming and by a civilisation so subtle and mystically profound that it is largely beyond the comprehension of the Western mind. Most of this

Denis Hornsby, Outback vigneron, at his Chateau Hornsby winery outside Alice Springs, in the Northern Territory. He says, 'We had a bit of trouble with early plantings. They used to get eaten by the bloody 'roos.'

Denis Hornsby makes his Northern Territory wines in the figurative shadow of Ayers Rock, though it is 450 kilometres away; such is the scale of distances in the Territory.

The best known — the only — winery in the Northern Territory, Chateau Hornsby is some 15 kilometres south-east of Alice Springs. Winemaker Denis Hornsby had his first commercial vintage here in 1979, and though the vineyard is about 650 metres above sea level, it can hardly be described as being one of Australia's cool climate wine areas.

will not be seen by the casual visitor.

Figuratively in the shadow of the monolithic Uluru (Ayers Rock) – in fact 450 kilometres away, although the tyrannies of distance have come to count for little in the Australian Outback, where a person might drive for half a day just to call on a neighbour for a cup of tea and a chat – the pioneer of the wine grape, and indeed still its only real husband in the Northern Territory, is Denis Hornsby.

He planted the vine not as a joke as some locals like to believe, nor as a tourist gimmick as many visitors imagine, nor even as a high-minded expansion of scientific frontiers, as the romantics would like to have it, but for the very simple reason – and the reason why people first made wine anyway – that he wanted to drink the stuff.

And although he has a background of scientific training, Hornsby's attitude is simply one of wanting to make wine. When asked why, in his vineyards, he adopted low T-trellising with 45-centimetre wires, he just shrugs, swigs from the can of beer which is never far from a man's hand in the Territory, and says, 'It's just an arbitrary figure.' Why does he spur-prune the

vines? Another swig. 'Again, nobody seems to know. And it's the easiest way. There are so many theories about tonsilectomies and circumcision, and they seem to change every year – it's the same with viticulture.' And what is the heat summation figure for the region? 'I think I've forgotten. But it is certainly the sunniest vineyard in Australia.'

It is indeed refreshing, in one of the last outposts of human civilisation, to find a bloke who just gets out there and does it. But if Hornsby exhibits the casual facade and the orchestrated appearance of an ocker ratbag (those endearing and enduring characteristics of the Territorian personality) one can with a little scratching find some serious sensitivity about wine.

Once Denis Hornsby was a sane southerner. He was born in Deniliquin (N.S.W.), and studied pharmacy in Melbourne. He visited the irrigated oasis of Alice Springs, which must serve as capital of Central Australia, while on his honeymoon, got bitten by the Centralian bug, and soon returned as a pharmacist. But like most university students he had acquired an interest in wine, an interest that was a little out of place in the town of Alice Springs, where the frigid can of beer is king.

'People grew table grapes in Alice Springs, so I thought, why not wine?' And if anybody says it is an impossible dream in the Red Centre where the temperature on almost every summer's day will exceed 37.8°C (the Fahrenheit century), Hornsby was all the more resolved to give it a go. While continuing at the

The winemaker (wearing white T-shirt) enjoys a beer at his winery while friends and tourist guests try a white wine.

pharmacy he bought a wine textbook and set to work, part-time, learning as he went. He had the ubiquitous Territory T-shirts made up, his bearing the legend 'Grape and pillage' (which he explained as 'Grapes in the winery: pills in the pharmacy. Not that there's much association – but the wine's better for you.')

The first wine was in 1973, made in rubbish bins from an acre of grapes planted at the Hornsby home on the Emily Gap Road, a cottage of such humility that Territorian wit had to dub it 'Chateau Hornsby'. Nobody minds much that none of those early wines

is still available, although the bizarre purple labels might be sought by kitsch collectors.

Undaunted, he bought new land at the Ooraminna Ridge, a 120-hectare block about 15 kilometres south-east of Alice Springs, on gently undulating scrub over very deep, coarse red sandy soil. It was most recently a failed orange orchard and the two bores are kept flat out keeping the thirsty *terra rosa* sand supplied with essential drip-irrigation moisture for the vines. In 1979 Hornsby made his first commercial vintage from two and a half planted hectares

Drip-irrigated vine growing at Chateau Hornsby. Denis Hornsby saw table grapes being grown at Alice Springs, so he decided to try to grow wine grapes. Water is the deciding factor, and he gets it from two bores.

of shiraz, cabernet sauvignon, semillon and Rhine riesling grapes grown to the south of the shifting hues of the MacDonnell Ranges and under the scorching blue of a Centralian sky.

Surprisingly for its being on the plains of the Centre, the low scrub is elevated 610 metres above sea level. For all that the days are fiercely hot, the climate is desert rather than tropical, with the nights often being bitterly cold. Thus picking the grapes can start as early as 4.00 a.m. and they can come into the winery as cool as in most other regions. Picking is done by local friends and volunteers, and Denis and his wife Miranda (whose culinary talents and hospitality flourish in her restaurant, above the winery and overlooking the vineyards and the ranges) ensure that picking finishes with a great party each day before everybody goes off to their normal jobs at 9.00 a.m.

Harvest at Chateau Hornsby is the nation's earliest, starting in December and usually before Christmas. 'Thank God the vintage continues into January, or we'd have problems knowing what year to put on the label.' As a dig at 'trendy late-picked wines', he claims his are 'early picked'.

The venture, still dubbed Chateau Hornsby although more properly called Hornsby Estate, has not been without its problems. 'We had a bit of trouble with early plantings,' Hornsby says laconically. 'They used to get eaten by the bloody 'roos.' Feral rabbits also nibbled, but the area has of late become more settled and the birds, which delight in the exotica of grapes, are now the only faunal pests. He's got pretty handy with the shotgun and says he's eliminated the crows. Next will be the black-faced cuckoo shrike, which doesn't just eat the grapes but destroys the vines. The iridescently verdant Port Lincoln parrots and the red-capped robins are 'so pretty that I haven't got the heart to shoot the bastards'. And that means 5 per cent of the crop is lost.

Then there are the excesses of heat and sunshine. The wind curls into vicious willy-willies. There's a danger of powdery mildew. The underground winery, although boasting a couple of stainless steel tanks and even a digital pH meter, is no model of scientific studiousness. And the second-hand maturation casks which Hornsby buys 'don't seem to last the distance'.

Eventually he gave up the pharmacy to run the winery full time and still the all-pervasive red Centralian dust doesn't have much time to settle on his battered viticultural and oenology textbooks, usually kept on the cabin floor of his gaudily emblazoned truck. Even so, he has for some vintages been helped by consultant Gordon Cook, winegrower, winemaker and a lecturer at the Regency Park School of Food and Catering in South Australia. When ferment and maturation are complete the wines are shipped to Adelaide for bottling and distribution and Cook has occasionally, discreetly, blended in a little of something else, 'just to make up the volume,' he explains. Chateau Hornsby also does a line in other wines, especially ports, which are bought from other manufacturers. But Denis Hornsby is proudest of those which depict on the label the windmill behind the winery – 'my own wines, and especially the ones that are 100 per cent mine'.

The wines themselves – a semillon/riesling blend, a dryish white which is light and fresh and meant for early consumption, and a shiraz/cabernet sauvignon blend, which can be quite solidly flavoured but again no great cellaring proposition – sometimes amaze even Denis Hornsby, certainly they delight him. Over the years they have varied somewhat in quality, but they have generally been getting better.

The main thing is that they are there, thanks to the Outback spirit of enterprise of Denis Hornsby.

The Central Australian sun shines on vines growing near the MacDonnell Ranges. The area is surrounded by sacred sites of ancient Aboriginal tribes.

BRENTON BAKER

I Am Vine

All is quiet and I, one of man's oldest cultivated plants, enjoy the new-felt warmth of spring. I am a grapevine, a warm temperate zone plant belonging to the genus Vitis. I am one of many hundreds of varieties used for wine production which form the most commonly grown species of grapes in the world, Vitis vinifera. These words are of Latin origin, vitis meaning to bind or twist and vinifera, the combination of two words vinum and ferens, meaning wine bearing.

Below ground I have been growing new roots for some two or three weeks now with no sign of growth above the ground. As the average daily temperature reaches 10°C, buds on my fruiting canes or spurs (last year's matured annual shoots left for fruit production this season) begin to swell. This is the commencement of shoot growth and the sign to my master, the vigneron (and any other casual observers) that I am beginning to rouse.

My annual cycle of growth has commenced. I am slow at first but, after three or four weeks as the temperatures rise, I commence my grand period of growth when I make maximum shoot growth per day. This continues for about a month when at about flowering my rapid shoot growth begins to slow down. Although I continue to make growth until the end of the

season, given good growing conditions, my rate of growth per day slackens.

You may be wondering where my fruit is born. As my new shoots appear and are quite small, not only are leaves and tendrils formed, but also between one and four ever-so-small bunches which are so prized by my grower. The mature dormant buds left at pruning contain virtually a fully formed shoot including rudimentary leaves and flower clusters for the next season. These flower clusters are defined in the new buds about three to six weeks after blooming and the degree of fruitfulness depends on temperature, light intensity and other factors during this period. Blooming normally occurs at about the end of spring, some six to eight weeks after budburst.

Most experts argue about how pollination is achieved — wind, insects, self-pollination? Self-pollination seems to be the most favoured in most varieties.

Ancestors of mine have been recorded as single vines covering several hectares. As a cultivated plant I am grown at densities of 1100 to 10000 vines per hectare. The higher the density the more I suffer from competition and the more my total growth is restricted. For wine, these days in Australia I am generally grown at a density of 1250 to 2500 vines per hectare. In very dry conditions I may yield only one bottle of wine per vine, but when irrigated as many as four or five bottles. Scientists who have studied me have found I produce poorer quality grapes for wine when I grow very vigorously, producing a dense, very shady canopy of leaves.

Talking about ease of management, I must say I take offence at the amount of mechanisation I am subjected to. First of all there was mechanical harvesting, which is good for my grower but gives me a rough time at harvest. I guess I was spoilt by the gentle hands of

humans at harvest however, costs and difficulties in obtaining suitable labour stimulated the development of mechanisation. Mind you, it was not without cost because special trellises had to be built by my grower and the machine harvesters were also complex and expensive.

I guess mechanisation would have been easier to take if only my grower had stopped at harvest. But he found he had a form of harvest which could pick large or small bunches for a similar cost. So he started looking at mechanical pruning, which left many more buds per vine and resulted in many more but smaller bunches. He found crops could be increased to some degree, that the extra bud numbers reduced the strength or vigour of my shoots and at the same time gave a greater total yield per vine. The reduced shoot vigour, which makes me feel like a weakling, delighted my grower because research had shown how

reduced bunch shading and better balanced vines resulted in better fruit for quality wine production.

Of course, other factors such as soil, fertiliser and irrigation affect how strongly I grow and these are carefully limited where quality grapes are the aim of my grower.

I am a very adaptable, hardy plant and grow best between 34° and 50° latitude north and south of the equator. I am grown in climates varying from hot, arid areas to cool areas with relatively dry summers. The cool areas are again favoured for quality grapes where maturity takes longer, giving time for the development of delicate flavour components and better sugar and acid levels.

I have an extensive and deep root system under good growing conditions but the majority of my roots are in the top 1.5 metres of soil. If need be, my tap root can go as deep as 10 metres searching for moisture; in shallow soils my roots are much shallower. I absorb water and mineral nutrients dissolved in that water from the soil through very fine root hairs attached to my smallest roots. The nutrients I obtain from the soil include hydrogen, oxygen (from water), nitrogen, phosphorus, potassium, calcium, magnesium, iron, zinc, boron, manganese, copper and molybdenum.

I also obtain carbon from carbon dioxide in the atmosphere. You've all heard of photo-synthesis — how we plants purify air by using carbon dioxide from the air and hydrogen from water to produce plant food or carbohydrates. I'm no exception, with photosynthesis taking place in my leaves utilising light energy, and in the process releasing oxygen to the atmosphere. Some of these carbohydrates are used by me for immediate growth and development but I also transform and store some of these carbo-hydrates as glucose and fructose in my fruit and as starch, my principal growth food, in my canes, trunk and roots.

I am a long-lived plant, commencing fruiting at about three years old, but my economic life is generally regarded as about thirty-five years when, because of my system of culture, I begin to decline. I can grow from seeds but like many fruiting plants I do not breed true to type. So commercially I am reproduced from mature cuttings which ensures I breed true to my parent. In fact these days researchers select superior plants of my type (which they call clones) and from which they propagate to produce vineyards with superior performance.

I enjoy being a vine and producing wine grapes. I get enjoyment from the pleasure I bring. I hope my story helps you understand my complexity and further improves your enjoyment of my end products — fruit and wine.

Grafting a vine over to a different variety or onto hardier rootstock is a skilled business.

An old and gnarled vine at Redman's Coonawarra vineyards. Grapevines can bear commercial quantities of grapes for well over a hundred years.

'You are what you eat', the Greeks advised a thousand years ago.

THE GOOD COMPANIONS

Tony Hitchin

Setting aside for the moment such arguable qualities as the ability to communicate with one another through language, and possession of a jointed thumb opposing our fingers which allows us a firm grasp, what sets the human race apart from the many other species that inhabit this planet is that we are the only group which has raised the basic acts of sexual intercourse and eating to a level where we are able to obtain intense pleasure from them. Indeed, you could fill a large library with the many thousands of books which have been devoted to the two subjects over the years – and if it should occur to you to query why the number of books on food so greatly outweigh those on the other seemingly much more compelling topic, I ask you to ponder the simple truth that even the most ordinary dinner party can be made to last four hours...

We are, as far as I know, the only species that actually cooks its food. And we are, of course, the only species that accompanies its meals with wine.

We have been doing this in many countries over many hundreds of years, to the point where it is an integral part of the fabric of life for people of all ages of many nations.

Why then do we make such hard going of it in Australia?

For it is my observation that we do. I never cease to marvel at our still-too-widespread ability to turn good food into bad with a mere flick of the cooktop ignition button, and we have surrounded that most natural of products, wine (which can fairly be described as pure uncooked fruit juice, containing no artificial colouring, preservatives or flavours, and merely enough alcohol to hold it together), with a mystique which would be laughable if it didn't make *us* so laughable.

True, things are getting better. The huge surge of interest in cooking, in cooking classes and cookery books over the past five to ten years, has seen us entertaining more in our own homes and taking those skills into the preparation of our daily meals. Our well-deserved reputation as a nation of travellers has had the commendable side-effect of making us more adventurous with what we will eat and more importantly what we will attempt to cook in our own kitchens. Our infatuation with gadgetry and the regularity with which it appears in the shops has helped to take the drudgery out of much kitchen preparatory work

A glass of the product smoothes the arguments about making wine.

Hermitage winery in the lower Hunter Valley has had a chequered history since it was established. The Wyndham Estate group is now involved in its operation. It has an excellent motel in the adjacent vineyards.

(a homemade mayonnaise at the push of a button in four minutes rather than after 20 wearying minutes with a handbeater) and has also simplified the clearing away. The quite remarkable growth of knowledge about our diet, the need for it to be balanced, and commonsense presentation of readily understood facts about the make-up and merits of individual foods, have at last added real meaning to that insidiously deceptive little phrase, 'You are what you eat' – a mere couple of thousand years or so after the Greeks first used it. And the quite dynamic growth of our wine industry, with its seemingly infinite variety of products of all styles, standards and prices, in bottles and in boxes, has given us greater familiarity with wine on a basis that has become daily for many of us. But we have a long way to go before we achieve the same natural ease with food and wine that you will find, say, among the French and the Italians. And I do not accept the excuse that they have been at it for a lot longer than we have – I think we have just wasted too much time.

Still, we've made a start. And given the richness and excellence of our produce – I've heard it said so often in recent times that no other country on earth

is so abundantly blessed, and I only hope that the frequency of the saying doesn't make us become blasé – and the comparative cheapness of our consistently good and sound wine, things can only go on improving.

Just as long as we don't follow our British heritage along the path of food and wine elitism and/or snobbery; though I'd like to think that our increasingly multicultural nature will guarantee us against that.

Enjoying food and wine is something that is within the daily reach of almost every Australian – certainly within the reach of anybody interested enough to buy a book like this. You don't have to be rich, nor do you have to be highly skilled with a skillet, and I am heartened by the number of people who ask us at *Epicurean* for advice on this or that facet of wining and dining and cooking and entertaining. I find it quite a thought that on a leisure day like a Saturday, quite apart from those frequenting our many restaurants, tens of thousands of people are doing that most civilised of things, sharing their table with each other, in homes all around Australia.

Perhaps you'd allow me a few thoughts on some favoured topics.

MATCHING FOOD WITH WINE

If you took all the drivel that has ever been written on this topic and laid it end to end, I wouldn't be at all surprised...

Generally it comes down to the utterly meaningless cliché that you should do what you like but that basically red wines go with red meats and white wines go with white meats and seafoods. My own advice is that you should ignore that completely and do what you like, remembering that basically red wines go with red meats and white wines go with white meats and seafoods... After that I suggest you look for better advice.

I am not being facetious. There are so many different red and white wine styles that even the experts have difficulty picking a dish to go with some of them; and indeed some were never intended to be married with food and should be drunk for their own sake – say late on a sunny weekend autumn afternoon, between two or three talkative friends. Or on a cool late spring morning, ditto.

At that so-important dinner party when, not being too sure of your wine knowledge, you want something that will suit the dish and will be respected without costing an arm and a leg, there is no disgrace at all in playing safe; indeed it is essential commonsense, given the total cost of having a dinner party these days. Stick with familiar wines like the white varieties, Rhine riesling or semillon, at the start of the meal (light entree, seafood, fish) and with our two best red varieties, shiraz and cabernet sauvignon, for the main courses (chicken, veal, lamb, steak, and the cheese). After *that* have some fun learning, or make a friend of the guy in the local wine shop who clearly knows what he is talking about and who can see that you are anxious to learn.

Shoot anyone who carries the 'Drink what you like' philosophy to the point of saying you can drink shiraz with crayfish – you'll simply end up ruining a good wine and an expensive piece of seaflesh, and end up

The bottles above the fireplace are empties, which is just as well as this would otherwise be the quickest way to ruin stored wines.

with a taste like a mouthful of iron filings. Still, doing what you truly like remains a good rule; then you can always do what everybody else has had to do and learn as you go along (the more arrogant of them forget their days of ignorance).

And should you still have moments when you feel insecure in your choice, give yourself a treat and line up this nation's undisputed twenty best wine palates and ask them what wine they would serve with that centuries-old international favourite, roast pork and crackling.

Heh-heh. You will get twenty different answers, ranging from champagne and spicy gewurtztraminer, to crisply acid white and soft butter-wood chardonnays, through rosé and beaujolais to light or full blooded reds. And more self-justifying waffle than you will hear in the average election campaign.

If nothing else, it will make you feel a lot better as you pour your ice-cold beer.

WINE ENJOYMENT AND WINE SNOBBERY

Many years ago, having been bidden, I lived and worked in Paris for a couple of years. I would like to say I was a classic example of impecunious youth and lived half-starving in a garret but in truth although I was stoney broke for most of the time, comfortable accommodation and meals were provided, the meals including wine – a bottle at lunch and a bottle at dinner. And I could hardly let it go to waste, could I? (Well, I *was* young). Thus began a lifelong relationship that has given me a great deal of pleasure over the years, and if along the way it has occasioned in me a complexion with the same rich gleam you find on the well-worn leather upholstery of a vintage Rolls-Royce – well, one wears life's honours as best one can.

A cultured people, the French. They taught me a number of very important things about wine: that it should be your pleasure and not your drug, that it is always to be shared and often to be talked about, and that it rewards the generosity of anyone who has the advantage of a good bottle (or a cellarful) and who shares it with a less fortunate enthusiast. They taught me to glance appreciatively at its colour, to test its soundness with a swirl of the glass and a quick sniff, to assess its quality with a lingering first mouthful. And then to chug-a-lug . . . often.

They also taught me to abhor wine snobs.

This country seems to be full of them these days. I read them in the newspapers and have had the satisfaction of barring them from my magazine. I hear them at the table and at tastings. I can't avoid them at the cellar door, and they bash my ear at parties, proudly parading their extra knowledge of this winegrowing area or that baumé, this hint of residual sugar or H_2S, or that varietal's characteristics – all valid and interesting wine topics in themselves but not when they are used to try to browbeat the listener into agreement. It never happened to me in France.

And then I look at them and wonder where they came from. You see, when I first came to this country in the mid-Sixties, one or two States still had early closing and its accompanying 6 o'clock swill, a restaurant meal was often a steak and three veg (tomardasors optional), and hardly one person in a thousand drank table wine. Recently, *voilà*, ten thousand experts. They will forgive me my knowing smile when I say that with too few exceptions they are johnny-come-lately in their expertise.

Now, ask one of those wine snobs what's the best bottle of wine he has ever had and watch him flounder. Yet the wisest wine man I ever met, elderly, experienced, cultured and travelled, had no hesitation in naming a retsina. You are not familiar with retsina? Well, at the risk of offending the Greek community at large, it is a wine which rates only about three notches above Brasso on my list of desirable alcoholic beverages (which in turn is just below any wine labelled 'Bottled under the influence in our own laundry'), and to be fair there is even the occasional drop of Brasso which isn't too bad as long as you take the trouble to filter it through a doubly folded nylon stocking, or a piece of bread, to remove most of the chalky bits.

Ah, he said, but he had been in his early twenties when he had this bottle of retsina, seated on the sunny terrace of a tiny restaurant perched halfway up a hill on a small island overlooking the distinctive hazy blue and white beauty of the Aegean, lunching with a girl who had smitten him with the thunderbolt and with whom he was madly and desperately anxious to make love.

Varied indeed are the things that make wine taste sweet.

SETTING THE MOOD

Restaurateur friends tell me that it is not unknown to have to kiss goodbye to half a million dollars setting up a top-class licensed restaurant, and that is a lot of schnitzels. Yet how many restaurants really make you feel welcome with their ambience?

For those of us entertaining at home, I believe the

mood we create with our setting and decor is perhaps the single most important factor in being successful (which is to say good) hosts. And I confirm *that* with a quick mental picture-show of my most memorable meals – a country kitchen in the north of France, a family setting in an English farmhouse, a sunny harbour view through wide glass in Sydney, among others, and no detailed recollection of what I actually ate.

I think that 'welcoming' is probably the single most important ingredient. I have one friend who is always at the door to meet arriving guests; they never need to knock. I have another who entertains only in winter (but then does so often) because her modest home takes on a whole new character through the beautiful, wide log fire in her lounge-dining room. And another whose invitations to summer Sunday lunches under a sprawling vine canopy over a brick courtyard are among my most highly prized. I think you will agree that starkness or lack of warmth (physical and emotional) are to be avoided. Laughter is a great help. Being ready with the welcoming drinks instead of having to disappear for twenty minutes while you mix this or that will help get the smiles going. And if you haven't got a natural joker in your pack of guests, make the pace yourself. People can always argue themselves puce about politics, sex and religion later...

Chef Cheong Liew runs one of Australia's best and most interesting restaurants, Neddy's in Adelaide. He has applied Chinese culinary excellence to French cuisine in an Australian setting, and the results are outstanding. Here he is relaxing over a glass of champagne with Krondorf winemakers, Grant Burge (centre) and Ian Wilson.

PRESENTING YOUR TABLE

Choose your guests and their number with care. I have friends who find they entertain best giving buffet meals for twenty or more, others with elegant long tables (in elegant long homes) just perfect for twelve or fourteen, others whose tables are just right for eight, and people like me who find that when I'm in a group of six everyone is in the conversation, it never flags and never splits infuriatingly into groups.

Obviously you will set it as attractively as possible, but don't believe that expensive dinnerware is all you need. I believe a table should make your dinner statement for you before the guests have even sat down, that without being ostentatious it should make them aware of the care you have taken to create a special occasion for them, and that it should be full without being cluttered, because fullness to me suggests variety and interest. It is no good me talking colour schemes and table arrangements with you, since these are matters of individual taste and circumstances, but I think we can all learn something

every time we go into a good restaurant or open the appropriate pages of homemaker or entertainer magazines.

However, your glassware is more than important, it is critical. There is an old saying that even the most ordinary wine tastes better out of beautiful glassware, and that does not mean you have to spend $50 a glass to get the right effect.

First, though, let us make it clear that we are talking about glasses made of *glass;* metal has no place in wine drinking, and though those goblets be solid silver, chuck them out. Glasses should be clear, plain and generously sized. The best single meal ever put before me in a private home (my wife paid the hostess the compliment of going home and attempting every one of the dishes over the next few days) was accompanied by wine served in thick, green, heavy cut-glass goblets. I couldn't believe it! I'd never realised how *bad* red wine looks in bilious green glass.

The need to have wine glasses of a reasonable size cannot be sufficiently emphasised, and the company that has put those piddling 120-150 millilitre things on the tables of every other cheap and nasty cafe and pizza house in the land deserves to have a bomb put under it. If you are going to err, do so on the large side. Large glasses, with 210 millilitres the minimum size and preferably softly curved in the style of a tulip, filled perhaps one-third to halfway, allow the drinker to give the wine a gentle swirl now and then to release its fragrances. They are more comfortable to hold, more comfortable to drink from, and seem altogether more generous. Good glassware need not cost the earth, and even top brands crop up in sales in the big department stores from time to time. A tip is to buy glassware that is dishwasher-proof – it sparkles that much more when you set it out, and wine in a sparkling glass speaks its own special language.

If using a dishwasher, beware of putting in the very finest of glassware or crystal; it is the high degree of lead content that makes this kind of glassware what it is, but given the extraordinarily high water temperatures of modern dishwashers the lead can melt within the glass, ruining its looks with a 'milky' tinge.

Candles are a personal choice, though it's hard to argue against them. But if you are going to use them, make sure they do not sit too low on the table – even a softly fluttering light like that does nothing at all for anyone's looks when thrown from below. Either way, soft light is better than harsh light – it improves the look of the food as well as people! It's not a bad idea to consider having a dimmer device on lights in your dining room; that way you can experiment to get the best effect.

Make sure your chairs are comfortable to sit in for a long time; the trend of recent years has been not to disrupt the flow of a dinner evening by moving away for coffee and after-dinner drinks but to stay, restaurant style, at the table. And please, no benches – guests who have to crouch forward for lengthy periods will end up with bellyache, which in turn will do nothing for their impression of your cooking.

And finally, having presented your table at its best, *stay there* and enjoy yourself as much as your guests. For one thing you've earned it, and for another it is embarrassing for the hostess to be continually in the kitchen. This merely entails planning and preparing at least one course, possibly two, in advance – for immediate presentation or for a quick warm-through at the last moment. It's worth it. For all concerned.

BACKGROUND MUSIC

Homes are not restaurants and therefore are not normally so large that they have to be filled with some kind of sound in order not to seem cheerless, cavernous or that most commercially disastrous of things, empty. My recommendations begin with the kind of music you should not play, which is to say almost all of it, and come down to specifics...

Some years ago, newly arrived in the city in which I now live, I often shared dinner evenings with a dear friend (I call him dear because he was so expensive) who had moved there at the same time, whose habit it was to regale his guests with the resounding marches of John Philip Sousa, played at full belt. His wife always cooked lasagne and I can assure you that to this day I still eat that dish with quite military precision. (Dining to the brisk *baroom-pah-pah* of Sousa is not easy but at least it has the advantage that if you begin dinner at, say, 8 o'clock, you are through all courses by about twenty past, leaving everyone free for the serious business of the evening which in the case of this host was drinking; later he changed his lifestyle when his doctor told him he was on a certain winner if he entered his liver in the national Charleston championships.)

No, music for wining and dining should be leisurely and relaxing, and these days even the most modestly situated of us can have our own private

Wining and dining in restaurants is an increasingly popular habit in a more affluent Australia.

307

orchestras, players and singers waiting to entertain us at the touch of a stereophonic button. Easy does it though; whatever your choice of music (and I won't weary you with that old one about always finishing dinner with a slight Liszt to port) it should never by played at a volume that will intrude upon the sound that is the sweetest of all music to absolutely everyone – the sound of their own voice.

COOKING WITH WINE

Use only the best. I am not by nature a vindictive person but whoever perpetuated the myth about inferior wine being suitable as 'cooking' wine should be dangled by piano wires attached to his eyelids over a boiling cauldron of the stuff, and gently lowered in.

Should you not be aware of what happens to wine during the cooking process, the alcohol is cooked off, leaving only the *taste* of the wine. So obviously your flavouring agent should taste good, not bad.

Should the dish call for only a glassful or so of wine, you can often use some from the wine that will accompany the meal. Recorked, the wine should not deteriorate in quality, and if you have any misgivings on that subject you can store it in the refrigerator until an hour before dinner.

LATE ARRIVALS

Start without 'em. Anybody can have the misfortune to be delayed when going out to dinner but nobody with any manners would want a meal to spoil, or their hosts or their fellow dinner guests to be inconvenienced, because of their lateness. And how late can one be – all they are likely to miss is the pre-dinner drinks and possibly the first course.

And anyone who hasn't yet heard of that dinky little invention that someone named Alexander Graham Bell came up with in Boston, Massachussets, in 1876, doesn't deserve a place at your table anyway.

BEING A GOOD GUEST

This goes much further than turning up sober, clean and punctually, leaving your domestic bickering in the car, and carrying the obligatory bottle for the host. For a start you have already failed to consider the single most important person present at the gathering – your hostess.

This lady – we are in Australia in the 1980s and the gender remains female in 99.9 per cent of all instances – will have spent a minimum of one full day on the subject of pleasuring you. And if you think that's exaggerating, she has had to think of the event, think whom to invite, think of the balance, of the seating arrangements, think of the menu (again that word 'balance'), do the shopping, the cooking, set the table and then present herself poised, groomed, dressed and smiling. Yet *he* gets the bottle. *She* gets nothing.

The first person I ever invited to dinner in this country (I am now an Australian but arrived here English) brought a bottle of white, two excellent clarets and half a dozen Tooths KB lager, which both impressed me and prepared me for many years of Australian generosity. I said I assumed this was a natural progression from those Colonial country days when calling on neighbours could well mean a lengthy trip and one didn't like to go empty-handed. 'Nope,' he said. 'Din wanna runya outa grog.' (For a lawyer he was a laconic sod; still is, come to that.)

These days we are all more circumspect about our gifts, but still too few of us think of our hostess. May that change – but meanwhile please remember the effort she has put in your behalf and have a good evening. For her sake.

She has paid you a supreme compliment with her effort on your behalf and it takes very little effort on yours to arrive even-tempered or better still good-humoured, on time, courteous and as pleasant company, maintaining what we shall politely call a healthy appetite. You don't have to actually sing for your supper. But you should at least earn your invitation.

BARBECUES

Dining *al fresco* is rightly considered part of gracious living in the Old World, especially in those countries where the weather allows the privilege all too seldom, and why we should have relegated the barbecue to a national joke and a boozy rort is beyond me.

Chuck some chops on the barbie as a no-fuss family weekend meal by all means, but if you are entertaining for heaven's sake do the thing as thoroughly as you would an indoor dinner – good wines, good meats, good accompaniments, good setting, and a fire of long-glowing charcoal that won't give up blackened burnt-offerings with which to crisp the stomach lining of your already smoked-out guests.

ON REFLECTION...

To entertain and to be entertained is as old as time itself and makes humanity unique. The scope of the event, and your place on the social scale (if such things concern you) is of no relevance compared with your ability to be at ease, as host or guest.

Chronological history assures us that the Jewish mothers of New York were not the first people on earth to crystallise a philosophy summing up the merits of the pleasures of table, but the several I have met are sure way in front with that brief instruction of theirs: 'Eat. Enjoy.'

The perfect command. It's one you enjoy obeying. And you can take it in any sequence you like.

Checking champagne bottles at Reynella, South Australia.

SPARKLING WINES

Frank Doherty

Today's Australians, as polyglot a community as is to be found anywhere in the English-speaking world, are not overly conscious of the presence of their respective State Governors or of the Governor-General. As far as most of the country is concerned, these eminent gentlemen are there to perform such functions as opening Parliament or similar gatherings, laying foundation stones and attending some of the better-known sporting events such as the Melbourne Cup where they are seen making presentations to leading lights. For the rest of the time, they spend their gubernatorial days in comparative obscurity.

But the Earl of Hopetoun was not like that. Not for him the role of a shy violet. He was a gregarious soul in his days as the Governor of Victoria around the turn of the nineteenth and into the twentieth century. He cut a dashing figure, was immensely popular, and loved nothing more than to entertain rather lavishly at Government House. Indeed, so much did he love company around him and enjoy plying it with champagne that he used to find his annual stipend of £10 000 somewhat inadequate. So he turned to the then owner of the winery at Great Western, Mr Hans

Irvine, with a suggestion which he thought might help him out of his predicament.

If Mr Irvine could provide him, His Excellency said, with a champagne which would 'satisfy the most exacting connoisseurs' he, in turn, would serve it at Government House dinner parties and receptions. In other words, a viceregal nod to an ambitious winemaker. This, in turn, would mean Lord Hopetoun would have no need to buy the expensive imported champagne.

Irvine, one may be assured, jumped at the chance to improve both his wine and his status in viceregal circles and eventually provided Lord Hopetoun – by this time it was 1901 and Federation year and Lord Hopetoun was the Marquis of Linlithgow and the new Commonwealth's first Governor-General – with a *cuvée* that not only satisfied the 'most exacting connoisseurs' at his table but others of a similar disposition in faraway England to whom Irvine exported it.

In due course an imposing statue of the Marquis of Linlithgow was commissioned and erected just off Melbourne's then gracious St Kilda Road, not far from his former residence. One would like to think it was the brainchild of some enthusiastic wine-minded

One of the new ways of making champagne: remuaging by machine. The shaking and turning of bottles has traditionally been done by hand, a labour-intensive business. Here machines shake and rotate these wire bins full of bottles slowly over a number of weeks to bring the sediment, or dead yeast cells from the second fermentation, to the top of the neck, ready for disgorging.

individual or group but there is no evidence to support such thinking. Nevertheless, it would do no harm for all of us who love good wine to make some acknowledgement (a wave? a smile? a doffing of the hat?) when passing his statue of the part he played in this country.

It should not be thought that Hans Irvine's was the first sparkling wine to be made in Britain's antipodean colonies. There were earlier attempts, but he deserves much credit for refining the quality of it. After his death in 1918, the vineyards and winery at Great Western — a sleepy little hamlet on the road and railway from Melbourne to Adelaide — passed to his friend, Benno Seppelt. His descendants, and the shareholders of their company, still own it. They have seen the two words Great Western become synonymous, in many people's eyes, with Australian champagne.

Many Australians blithely but inaccurately have a tendency to call almost any wine with effervescence champagne, a custom which purists both within the wine industry and the community dispute. To them, only the sparkling wine which emanates from the Champagne district of France should be entitled to be called Champagne but they are in the minority. It is a safe bet that Australia will continue to use the

word widely.

The accepted father of champagne-making by the méthode champenoise — that is, of there being a second fermentation allowed to take place within the bottle which one eventually buys — is Dom Pierre Pérignon, a Benedictine monk who was winemaker and cellar master at the abbey of Hautvillers in France in the latter part of the seventeenth century. The story of how this new style of wine with its own gas in it sprang from his hands onto the world is romantic, probably apocryphal, but worth telling.

Those who subscribe to it say that one summer's evening about 1675 Dom Pérignon went to the abbey's cellar to get some wine for the monks' dinner. When handling one bottle, it exploded and wine came gushing out. Quickly, Dom Pérignon brought out a glass and captured some which he drank while it was bubbling. His reaction, the romantics say, was to rush upstairs to the refectory, proclaiming to his fellow monks, 'Come quickly, I'm drinking stars!' A pretty phrase, but possibly borrowed from a fairy tale.

If it were true — and let us concede for a moment that it was — what happened would have been something like this.

In the previous autumn around September and October, Dom Pérignon would have made his annual batch of wine, cleaned it and filtered it as best he could after the fermentation process was complete and then bottled it. It would have lain dormant through the ensuing summer and spring and then, with the approach of warmer weather, a phenomenon would have occurred. Unknown to him, a little yeast and some sugar would have escaped Dom Pérignon's filtering of the wine and, as they came to life again, would have set up a *second* fermentation, this time within the bottle. It was the carbon dioxide gas created by this fermentation which caused the wine to burst forth from the bottle as it was touched by Dom Pérignon.

The people of France, in appreciation of the joy and happiness Dom Pérignon's discovery has brought into their lives — or perhaps in gratitude for the mountainous pile of francs that has accrued to

their national coffers from it – have done what the more phlegmatic Australians have done for a representative of Queen Victoria. There is a statue of the priestly winemaker at Hautvillers but there is a marked difference between the attitudes towards the two. People come with bouquets of flowers to place at Dom Pérignon's feet; the Marquis of Linlithgow's replica goes largely unnoticed.

Today in Australia, as in Champagne itself and elsewhere in the winemaking world, the happy result that Dom Pérignon came upon by accident is achieved with deliberate intent; in other words, a second fermentation is brought about scientifically.

A still white wine, fairly neutral in character, is poured into a punted bottle – that is, one with a dent in its base – and topped up with carefully calculated amounts of cane sugar (the only time in Australia when it is legally allowed anywhere near wine) and yeast. The bottle is then sealed with a Crown seal and placed in 'riddling' tables made in the shape of inverted Vs with holes in them. They are left there for periods ranging from six months to several years. The sugar and yeast act upon each other as in the primary fermentation, creating a fraction more alcohol and some carbon dioxide gas. After a time, the bottles are expertly shaken to bring the dead yeast cells down the neck of the bottle, and twisted slightly every day. Then comes the disgorging of the sediment, which is done by freezing the pellet of unwanted yeast matter and carefully removing the cork after which the wine's own gas will force the dead yeast cells out of the bottle. The wine is then topped up with some champagne from the same batch and a new cork put in place and wired down. Champagne made by this traditional method is entitled to be labelled 'Fermented in this bottle', the operative word being 'this'. It is usually the most expensive to come to the market because its production is so labour-intensive.

Wine produced this way is *brut* (dry) but, if a slightly sweeter wine is required, a small amount of sugar mixed with some previously made champagne and a little brandy is added. Obviously, the sweetness of the final product will depend upon the amount of sugar, known as the expedition liqueur, included in the mix. Sparkling burgundy, which has begun a noticeable return to popularity after some years of public indifference, is made by the méthode champenoise, using a base red wine (usually shiraz) in place of a white. Pink champagne, that romantic drink of the Edwardian era in England, is properly made by the same procedure with the exception that a tiny quantity of cabernet sauvignon or malbec still wine is included before the second fermentation takes place.

There are many wine companies in Australia which market champagnes bearing the words 'Fermented in this bottle' but, in a number of instances, they do not themselves have the facilities for such a process, preferring to send their own wine, made from grapes of their own choice, to a company which does have the necessary equipment. Wynn Winegrowers use their secondary fermentation process at their Seaview Champagne Cellars at Magill, a suburb of Adelaide, on behalf of a number of other companies as well as for themselves. In fact, their staff there is occupied almost the full year round making wine by the secondary fermentation in bottle method. Penfolds make for others, as do Kaiser Stuhl in the Barossa Valley, Hardy at Reynella in South Australia and the fairly new Yellowglen, near Ballarat in Victoria.

But the majority of sparkling wine drunk in this country is made by methods other than the classic champenoise, including the *transfer* method and the *charmat* process, named after the French wine scientist who invented it in 1910.

With the *transfer* process the procedure is the same as for the champenoise wines, except that the second fermentation is carried out in a beer bottle, which is then emptied into a tank with the contents of several thousand similar bottles. The wine can then be pumped through filters, thereby obviating the need for labour-intensive hand shaking and disgorging to remove the expired yeast cells. Only then is it transferred to the traditional champagne bottle, corked, wired and dressed.

This is the wine style which, more than any other, has been responsible for the extraordinary rise in

Cellarhand Steve Kennedy checks a bottle of Hardy's Grand Reserve Champagne.

315

public acclaim for sparkling wine in Australia since the mid-1970s. It is less expensive than the wine made by the authentic 'this bottle' champenoise method because, filtered in bulk, it eliminates the long and tedious man-handling that is an essential part and parcel of the 'Fermented in this bottle' wine. It is in this field that competition between sparkling wine marketers, such as Penfolds' Minchinbury, Seppelt's Great Western and Wynn's Seaview, is so intense and that the practice of discounting is so rife.

For charmat wines, the same process is adopted with a similar base wine as used in the initial stage for champagne except that, in this instance, the secondary fermentation (when the sugar and yeast culture are added and mixed in) is carried out in large pressure tanks. When the required pressure has been reached the tank is chilled almost to freezing point and the wine is filtered under counter-pressure to another tank. Here it is allowed to warm to bottling temperature and is filled at pressure into champagne-style punted bottles.

The so-called 'pearl' (correctly 'perle') wines which came onto the Australian scene in the mid-1950s are also made by bulk fermentation using a base wine of slightly lower quality. They can be made by either the charmat method or by carbonation and they are less delicate than the champagne or other charmat styles. They are presented in white and rosé styles which usually are for those of the wine-drinking public who are young and/or who are sweet toothed. They are often flavoured with fruit essences or cordials.

These wines are not as popular as they once were. Carbonation produces a sparkling wine by the addition of man-made carbon dioxide gas, as with the production of aerated waters (soft drinks). In the days of inadequate laws governing the labelling of Australian wines one of the very few stipulated that any wine made by carbonation should carry the word on the label.

The story is told of one winemaker, despondent at the unsatisfactory response to his carbonated wine, who decided to emphasise the one word required by law. Accordingly, he amended his label to include the words 'Guaranteed Genuinely Carbonated'. It was not long before he had difficulty in coping with the extra demand for his product.

Nevertheless, in spite of the admirable fillip given by Lord Hopetoun and his viceregal circle (who could buy Hans Irvine's champagne for 45 shillings a case in those days) sparkling wine remained, quantitatively, in the doldrums for close to seventy-five years. It remained the province of the wealthy and was used by those outside that class only for toasting newly-weds, greeting Christmas, honouring birthdays and launching ships. Few drank it regularly and those who did drank it from unhygienic, saucer-shaped glasses with hollow stems which, though they allowed the drinker to see the bubbles rising from the very base of his glass, could not always be cleaned thoroughly.

Then, in the mid-1970s, sparkling wine of all kinds really became the vogue wine throughout the country. Thousands of people, most of whom had not previously been able to afford sparkling wine in any quantity in the home let alone when dining out, discovered a new taste sensation and, more importantly, liked it and stayed with it. As the 1980s began, sales of sparkling wine were more than double the figure prevailing at the beginning of the 1970s. During the 1970s it became the fastest growing of all wine styles and, midway through the decade, it achieved an enormous increase of approximately 16 per cent in one year.

This was the time when, right through the country, people began making sparkling wine the fashionable and favourite drink during the Christmas-New Year holiday period. Even now during the months of November and December they buy more than four times as much as they do during January and February.

Though the spectacular growth rate of the 1970s and early 1980s has steadied and settled down, much more sparkling wine is drunk than ever before – about as much as dry red wine.

Observers of the social and financial scene put the impressive success story of sparkling wine down to several factors. It has been promoted by the makers and merchants alike as more than a wine for special occasions – but rather as one to make an ordinary

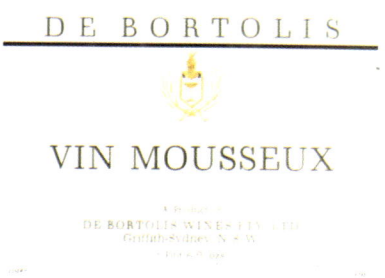

Disgorging champagne. It is a natural method of removing the dead yeast cells of the second fermentation.

occasion (say a home-cooked meal) slightly special with a glass or two of sparkling wine either as a prelude to it or a conclusion. The widespread practice of discounting, though frowned upon by some sections of the wine industry, has undoubtedly played a significant part in the bringing of sparkling wine within reach of most sections of the general community.

One aspect of the story of sparkling wine in Australia which may have escaped the notice of many – though not of the practised and consistent drinker of it – is the subtle though discernible change for the better in the quality of many of our top-ranking wines in the sparkling class. For many years, makers of even the best of the type were if not uncaring then inconsistent in the style of the base wine which would be converted to sparkling wine. The grape variety ondenc, even when it was known as Irvine's white, was widely used, as was crouchen, chenin blanc, tokay and even sultana.

But with the increased popularity of (one might even say craze for) chardonnay winemakers began using it for their best champagne-style wines, as some of them also did pinot noir and even small lots of pinot meunier. These are the classic grapes of Champagne in France. The use of them, plus a willingness to leave their wines ageing longer on lees than had been the custom, means that, in some areas anyway, Australia is now able to produce excellent champagne-style wines closely approximating the established French Champagnes.

Any treatise on the impact of sparkling wine on the lifestyle of this country's inhabitants must take some account of the amazing growth in the consumption of true (French, that is) Champagne. Australia imports almost one million bottles annually, a rise which has made it ninth among the countries to whom France exports sparkling wine from Champagne. This is a tenfold upsurge over the past decade. When one takes into account the fact that most French Champagne costs $20 to $30 a bottle (in one instance, more than $50) this is quite remarkable. Australia is a very important market to the Champagne houses of Rheims, Ay and Epernay, so much so that not only are their products distributed here by various Australian wine companies but many of them send their top executives out here to promote their wine and to assess the prevailing situation in relation to it. Several leading Champagne houses now have their own permanent representatives here charged with the duty of covering the Pacific area.

Sparkling wine – which should be stored in the horizontal position and later served chilled but not excessively so – is divided broadly into two categories, dry and semi-sweet. The first style is usually light in colour and delicate in texture and is intended to be drunk before luncheon or dinner. There are some who consider it the finest aperitif in the world. The second style is best when taken to accompany fresh fruit or a dessert dish. Occasionally one will come across a champagne or champagne-style which, though dry, has more body than the light aperitif type. This may quite satisfactorily and enjoyably be drunk while one eats a dish such as bacon and eggs, a quiche or an omelette.

The appearance of the tall, flute-shaped glass has largely done away with the saucer-shaped glass. The flute-shaped glass is considered more suitable for the drinking of sparkling wine as it exposes a smaller area of wine to the air, thus retaining the bead (bubbles) longer.

When opening a bottle of good sparkling wine, the cork should be allowed to emerge gently, not let

rocket across the room to the accompaniment of a stream of wasted champagne. The noise made by its withdrawal should be something like a gentle hic-cough rather than the crack of a pistol shot.

It seems appropriate here to quote from an earlier writing by a contributor to this book – Len Evans – if only because what he had to say about a particular sparkling wine in his *Complete Book of Australian Wine* was, and is, so true. At the chosen point, he reflected on Orlando's Barossa Pearl which he called 'a wine of natural effervescence, with some delicacy, a crisp finish and a rather pleasant, sort of softly sweet middle palate'.

Mr Evans then went on to say that this 'resulted in its being widely accepted by all sorts of palates, espe-cially young, uneducated palates and people who had normally loaded their tables with bottles of beer ... I believe the significant thing about the wine was that it launched thousands of people into drinking wine ... there is no question that Barossa Pearl was the great educator ... the wine industry should be immensely thankful for it.'

Certainly, the world of sparkling wine – indeed, the world of wine – has never been quite the same since that day in 1956 when Barossa Pearl made her bow to the Australian public.

Champagne has showed the strongest sales growth in the Australian wine industry in recent years. Many new producers, like Yellowglen, have emerged to challenge the traditional makers.

319

Chateau Tahbilk, perhaps Victoria's most famous winery, began life in 1860. The Purbrick family continue to make fine wines here — but they have plenty of competition from wineries springing up all over the State.

WINES AND WINERIES OF VICTORIA

Mark Shield

Old German wine barrel at Chambers' Rosewood winery, Rutherglen.

It is unromantic to start this chapter with a quote from a computer, but in this case the all-pervasive computer cannot be denied. Roseworthy Agricultural College in South Australia built a computer model of the most desirable soils and climate for viticulture. The model was made from data collated from the famous premium wine areas in the world. Australian conditions were then fed into the computer and the results showed that 70 per cent of the best areas were located in the tight confines of Victoria.

Even more interesting was the fact that of the desirable locations, only 30 per cent were under vine.

If there is a feeling that pervades the Victorian wine industry it is of optimism and a belief in the future. Cool climate viticulture is the cry in Victoria.

Another Victorian wine landmark, the tower at Mitchelton winery.

Chateau Remy's vineyards near Avoca in central Victoria as the leaves turn in autumn. The company is now controlled by Remy Martin of France.

Grapes grown in cooler climates develop more acid, flavour and complexity. Wines of elegance and finesse with great longevity should be the reward for planting vines in such climates. 'Wines of world class' is the dream. To emulate or better the wines of Bordeaux, Burgundy and Champagne is the lofty ideal of many Victorian winemakers. So, will it ever come to pass? If that question implies the production of carbon copies of the world's great wines, the answer is 'no'.

Victoria is a small State. A few hours drive in any direction will find a State border. Yet Victoria is providing a quality component to the wine industry, and its proliferation of small- to medium-sized vineyards adds individuality to the already complex wine scene.

The rebirth of the Victorian industry would make a fine plot for a B-grade science fiction movie – 'Alien force field zaps Australia while people sleep, they awake with the compulsion to plant a vineyard.' It would seem that people from all walks of life were infected with the romance of owning a vineyard: veterinarians, lawyers, dairy farmers, doctors, plumbers, pharmacists, artists. There was no real common denominator, save the drive to plant vines and make wine.

The majority of vineyards in Victoria are less than fifteen years old. In terms of quality, the early promise of many vineyards is only the beginning. When these new vineyards have mature vines, the quality should undergo a quantum leap.

322

THE VIGNERONS

There is no one person who typifies the Victorian vigneron; the spectrum of personality, experience and philosophy is very broad indeed. If one wished to chart the limits of this spectrum, the acme would possibly be Stephen Hickinbotham.

Stephen is a controversy in his own right. He moves ahead of the pack and constantly breaks new ground. Some winemakers view some of his ideas as 'crackpot', and he views *them* as 'insular'. This rewriting of the record books has resulted in some spectacular wines.

His theory about the desirability of *Botrytis cinerea* (noble rot) in red grapes causes an uproar with the traditional winemaker. Stephen dismisses such outcry as the ramblings of 'armchair' winemakers. 'You can tell a good winemaker by his hands; by the

second day of vintage they should have at least six screwdriver gouges.'

Not that he is a dirt farmer, he is possibly the most qualified winemaker in this country, having done post-graduate studies in Bordeaux. Armed with these degrees and a lot of determination he set about rewriting the rules. His directness may ruffle feathers, but this directness cannot be construed as arrogance or brashness. There is a sensitivity and modesty in his make-up that people find endearing. His scientific mind and artistic sensibilities set him apart from the norm. A cheap description such as a 'star' can only be applied in so much as he is outside the normal wine solar system.

If the anatomy of a great winemaker is ever blueprinted, it will probably read as follows. A person with a high level of training, dedication and skill; an appreciation of the finer things of life as well as a lively sense of humour are also prerequisites; a pinch of stoicism also helps.

Roy Dempsey is the viticulturist at Buller's winery, based in north-east Victoria. He has worked in and around the area for forty years.

Stephen Hickinbotham, winemaker at his family's winery, which they bought in 1981. He and his father Ian are both skilled and innovative winemakers.

Tradition in
winemaking lives on at the
All Saints winery at
Wahgunyah, in north-east
Victoria. Max Cofield
racks wine after the
1984 vintage.

Pat Carmody picks
the grapes at the Craiglee
winery, Sunbury, Victoria.
His son Pat Jr makes the
wines at the business they
bought in 1976.

Hickinbotham has all of these qualities. He is not just a technocrat, he is a nuts-and-bolts winemaker right down to his habitual wearing of a checkered flannel shirt.

His inventiveness is already a legend; his full impact on the industry will not be measured until his wines are fully mature. There is one thing that is apparent – there is a solid stamp of individuality and quality about the wines produced thus far. This individuality is a consequence of not being afraid to take a chance. 'The rewards go to the daring' could well be his motto.

The others who are pushing back the barriers (the new breed, if such a term applies) are also a blend of scientist and artist. People like Dominique Portet at Taltarni, John Ellis at Tisdall, and Don Lewis at Mitchelton are perhaps less radical than Hickinbotham, yet they are not afraid to break new ground.

Any such list of the new breed is dangerous because more than likely many will be wrongly omitted. Names like Warren Randall, Christian Morles, Trevor Mast, John Middleton, Dominique Landragin and Ric Burge should be on this ever-growing list.

Perhaps it will clarify the situation to note that there are two types of vigneron in Victoria. There is the formally trained and the enthusiastic amateur. The latter populate the small cottage industry segment, and they add character and variety to the wine spectrum. Some of these vineyards are making the

very best, others however are fielding some expensive mistakes in the market place.

Not that mistakes are exclusively the property of small vineyards. Wine is a variable science at best, that is where the art comes in, as well as luck. It is possible to programme drought into a computer, but it is a different matter when standing on site in the middle of a three-year one.

Add frost, rain during vintage, high winds, storms, fungal diseases and an army of parasites and pests to the list of things sent to try a winemaker. Even if all these are countered, simple things like mechanical failure of a pump or forgetting to switch off a drainage cock can spell disaster.

If Hickinbotham is the *enfant terrible* of the Victorian wine industry the doyen must be John Brown senior. He is a man of great dignity and gentle charm; the perfect father figure. Although he says that he is retired and takes no active role in the winemaking at Brown Brothers, his influence is still felt. It would seem that old winemakers never retire, they turn into elder statesmen.

One of the nicest things in the Victorian industry is the almost universal feeling of camaraderie. It is an industry with a healthy tradition of helping your neighbour and no one has done more to foster this co-operation between companies than John Brown. It is quite remarkable that companies can be fighting tooth and nail in the market place, yet back at the farm they will be co-operating to solve each other's problems.

Do not assume that the Victorian vineyards are a picture of tranquillity. Winemakers are individualists at heart; form a committee and that becomes very apparent. (It took one district committee three meetings to decide on its name.) Many of the squabbles revolve around the climate. 'My vineyard is cooler than his vineyard.' 'I don't irrigate and he does.' 'My district is better than your district.' The only real accord comes when foreign wines (wines from any other State) are the subject for discussion.

It is not only the winemaker who is displaying this strong State chauvinism. It has also affected the consumer and the retailer. Melbourne has wine lists

Stephen Hickinbotham at the family's Anakie vineyards. He trained in Alsace, Champagne and the Rothschilds in France.

which feature only Victorian wines. An annual exhibition of Victorian wines is held in Melbourne. The Victorian Wine Centre exclusively stocks the produce of the Garden State. It is cold comfort for the companies across the border, but many Victorians seem to be drinking Victorian wines first.

The cry that 'the best wines in Australia are made in Victoria' is oft repeated. Coonawarra is regarded as a slip of the pen made by some errant surveyor. The light-hearted banter goes, 'If only we could annex Coonawarra...'

Other States have their 'wild man' personalities, the two-fisted drinker and tearaway who is described as a 'character' or 'hard case'. But Victorian winemakers are conservative.

They seem to take a serious view of themselves.

Although they don't make the 'hard case' category, there are some delightful characters, entertainers in their own right. One is Carlo Monochino who has a vineyard and winery at Katunga. Carlo could be described as unbridled Latin enthusiasm looking for someone to convert to his way of thinking. He is passionate about the wines that he makes. Another is Peter Fergusson who has a style and flamboyance all of his own.

As for the rest of the winemaking fraternity, they are universally nice people. That may sound like a rash generalisation, but this is a hospitality industry which attracts the type of person who enjoys meeting plenty of people.

Eric Purbrick at Chateau Tahbilk. The family epitomises the family wine business, with Eric's son John marketing their wines, and grandson Alister making them.

MACEDON DISTRICT

This area is not a new one but, as with many others, it is undergoing a rebirth. There is a diverse range of personalities among the men involved in the revival. Gordon Knight, for example, bears the nickname Silent Knight, because he ties up the telephone for hours. Pat Carmody from Craiglee is almost shy and introverted. Mark Shepherd is droll and reserved, while the team at Flynn and Williams give the feeling that they are honest artisans and sons of the soil.

The wineries also show a sharp contrast. Craiglee is like a picture postcard or movie set. The original bluestone buildings from the first Craiglee winery are preserved in good condition. Brooks babble, Moreton Bay figs spread majestically, and the whole place speaks of history. So attractive is the property that it finds its way into movies and television series. Its proximity to Melbourne (80 kilometres from the G.P.O.) makes it an ideal location.

In contrast, Knights at Granite Hills is a modern winery perched on the crest of a ridge. The vista of rolling plains and grazing land is quite spectacular, and the winds that funnel up the slopes are equally cutting.

Flynn and Williams have a compact and neat winery set in an incredible garden, complete with peacocks, ponds and fountains and a model railway of people-carrying proportions. The home-built steam engine features the use of the bell of a euphonium for a funnel. The Flynn house almost defies description. It is peanut shaped and designed so that each room makes the maximum use of the sun. The Flynn and Williams wines are crafted to exacting standards. One would expect no less from this dedicated duo.

Virgin Hills is yet another stark contrast. It is set in splendid isolation in the middle of a forest. It was the brainchild of the delightfully eccentric Melbourne restaurateur, Tom Lazar. Tom decided that he was going to make the best red wine in Australia. Whatever he does, be it flying a Tiger Moth, cooking or

First come the leaves, then the grapes.

making wine, Tom tackles the exercise with verve.

The wines of the district are full of promise and individuality. Knights make spicy shiraz, steely Rhine rieslings and elegant cabernet sauvignons. Craiglee is in the process of rewriting the chardonnay record books and contributing a stylish red which is a blend of shiraz and cabernet sauvignon. The wines from Flynn and Williams are works of art.

Perhaps the best feature of the wines from this area is their realistic price structure. They are in the upper bracket, but only modestly so. This area contributes an elegant plank in the platform for the cool climate side of the viticultural debate.

BALLARAT/ BENDIGO

It is one of the Australian wine industry's minor quirks that some of the great names of the wine industry got their starts in life during the gold rush around the middle of the nineteenth century: Samuel Hill Smith, founder of the Yalumba winery; John Riddoch (to establish Coonawarra) and Thomas Hardy (founder of his family wine company). Having made money in this area, all went to South Australia.

Approaching a century and a half later a new form of liquid gold is coming from the areas centred on Ballarat and Bendigo, some 150 kilometres to the north-west of Melbourne. Areas such as these are among the hard core of the higher, cooler vineyard areas which are so much discussed and sought after by winelovers in the 1980s.

BALGOWNIE VINEYARDS

Stuart Anderson, a Bendigo pharmacist whose passion for wine became all-consuming, has developed a reputation for fine red wines, particularly the cabernet sauvignons.

Stuart is a complex man and he cuts a pukka figure in his ageing yet immaculate Maserati. He is an oboist of considerable reputation and he occasionally plays with symphony orchestras. His passion for French wine takes him to Bordeaux during vintage, where he offers his services free in return for knowledge gained.

This knowledge is translated into his wines, which have a very evident French stamp about them. Cabernet sauvignon is his forte, but his experiments with pinot noir and chardonnay are very encouraging. The neglected (by the consumer) wine of his

flock is the hermitage. The cabernet is always snapped up; it usually takes longer for the buyer to discover that the hermitage is also a fine wine. The cabernet seems to be trendy and the consumer has yet to discover the glories of shiraz, particularly when it comes from the cooler regions of Victoria.

Balgownie was acquired by Mildara early in 1985.

MT IDA VINEYARDS

This is the brainchild of artist Leonard French, who says, tongue firmly in cheek, 'I'm the only bloke who claims that he is making French wines in Australia.' These 'French' wines are just finding their way onto the market and while it is too early to comment on the wines from Mt Ida, hopefully they may be as entertaining and complex as the owner.

CHATEAU LE AMON

The word 'chateau' is something of a misnomer, yet up-market industrial shed is perhaps too hard. The quality is not in the buildings, but the wines and the personality of the family that makes them. Phil and Alma Leamon are delightful people with down-to-earth views. Phil's accent is the model of Australian country drawl, his ideas are simple and solid. He likes to make wines that he enjoys to drink, and Phil likes the great wines of the world.

His son, Ian, has joined him as winemaker. A graduate in oenology, he worked in several wine districts to gain experience. He and his father make a good team and, as it so often is with father and son combinations, there is a certain air of creative friction. Winemaking is a one chance per year affair, unlike brewing where a tap can be turned on. Vintage

time is a time of tension, and father and son are naturally less inhibited in expressing their frustrations.

The wines that result are stylish and reflect none of the tensions. In their short history these wines have distinguished themselves in national shows. They are elegant wines that drink well from the beginning.

Phil is determined to keep up the high standard, and has established an enviable reputation for consistency. Ian is no less dedicated. The squabbles are just part of the process – perhaps the last word on the Leamons should be the observation that they are both redheaded!

YELLOWGLEN VINEYARD

Yellowglen started as the ambitious project of Ballarat businessman, Ian Home, and the initial vintages were made by Neil Robb (Redbank). This vineyard had set its sights on the premium end of the sparkling wine market; to this end Dominique Landragin (who was then working at Seppelt's Great Western) was offered a partnership in Yellowglen.

Yellowglen also had the facilities to handle the tiraging, maturation on lees, rummaging and disgorging for other companies. In a short time the company had picked up quite a portfolio of customers who wanted to enter the premium sparkling wine market. One of their customers was Mildara, who had placed them in charge of the production of their chardonnay champagne.

Then Mildara purchased Yellowglen in mid-1984. Ian Home was offered a position on Mildara's board, and Dominique Landragin was retained as manager/winemaker. Mildara runs Yellowglen as a separate entity, which is encouraging, as the early promise shown by this vineyards is exciting.

The sparkling wines have been of good to excellent quality. Their Tradition (a premium fizzy) has been a winemaking and packaging example for others to follow. ly awaited.

If there is anything negative about the company, it is the extreme cold of the area. This has taken cool climate viticulture to its outer limits.

In years with mild summers there may be difficulty in ripening the grapes.

A partnership of commercial experience and winemaking skill: Ian Home (left) built a successful supermarket business and became interested in wine and food; Dominique Landragin, a French winemaker from Champagne, became Home's partner in a new sparkling winemaking business near Ballarat in Victoria. Yellowglen winery was bought by another Victorian winemaker, Mildara, in 1984.

Philip Leamon turned his name to advantage when he retired and started Chateau Le Amon, just south of Bendigo, in 1973.

CENTRAL
VICTORIA

Passing Clo
Viney
KINGO

Blanche Barkley ■
Wines

DUNOL

MOONAMBEL
Taltarni Vineyards ■   ■ Redbank Vineyards
                        ■ Summerfield
                    ■
                Warrenmang Vineyard

PYRENEE

                        ■ Chateau Remy

        Mount Avoca Vineyard ■   ■ AVOCA

RANGE

MARYBORO

LAKE
BURRUMBEET

0   20 km

Yellowglen Vineyards
■

BRIDGEWATER
■ Water Wheel Vineyards

LODDON RIVER

Balgownie Vineyard ■   BENDIGO

■ Chateau Dore

■ Chateau Le Amon

■ Huntleigh Vineyards
■ Jasper Hill

LAKE EPPALOCK

Mt Ida Vineyards ■   HEATHCOTE
The Heathcote Winery ■
■ Zuber Estate

Romany Rye Vineyards ■

■ Harcourt Valley Vineyard

CASTLEMAINE

BAYNTON
■ Knight's Granite Hills
Vineyard

■ The Mill Winery

■ Flynn and Williams

Virgin Hills Vineyard ■   KYNETON

DAYLESFORD

WOODEND

CRESWICK

MACEDON

GREAT   DIVIDING   RANGE

Mt Aitken Winery ■

GISBORNE

BALLARAT

UNES

Craiglee ■

■ St Annes Vineyard

SUNBURY

THE GEELONG AREA

This historic area has been revived by a dedicated band of enthusiasts. Its extreme southerly location lends itself to cool climate viticulture, and the table wines produced from this area exhibit all the attributes of fruit grown in such locations.

Small vineyards typify this area. These operations are all under 20 hectares and in the case of Prince Albert Vineyard, the vineyard is only 2 hectares. Is size important, if the quality is there? Prince Albert has only pinot noir planted and thus it represents the Australian equivalent of a small domain in Burgundy.

What the area lacks in volume it makes up for with high quality. There are several new ventures that have not yet come into production, which will bolster the wines from the district.

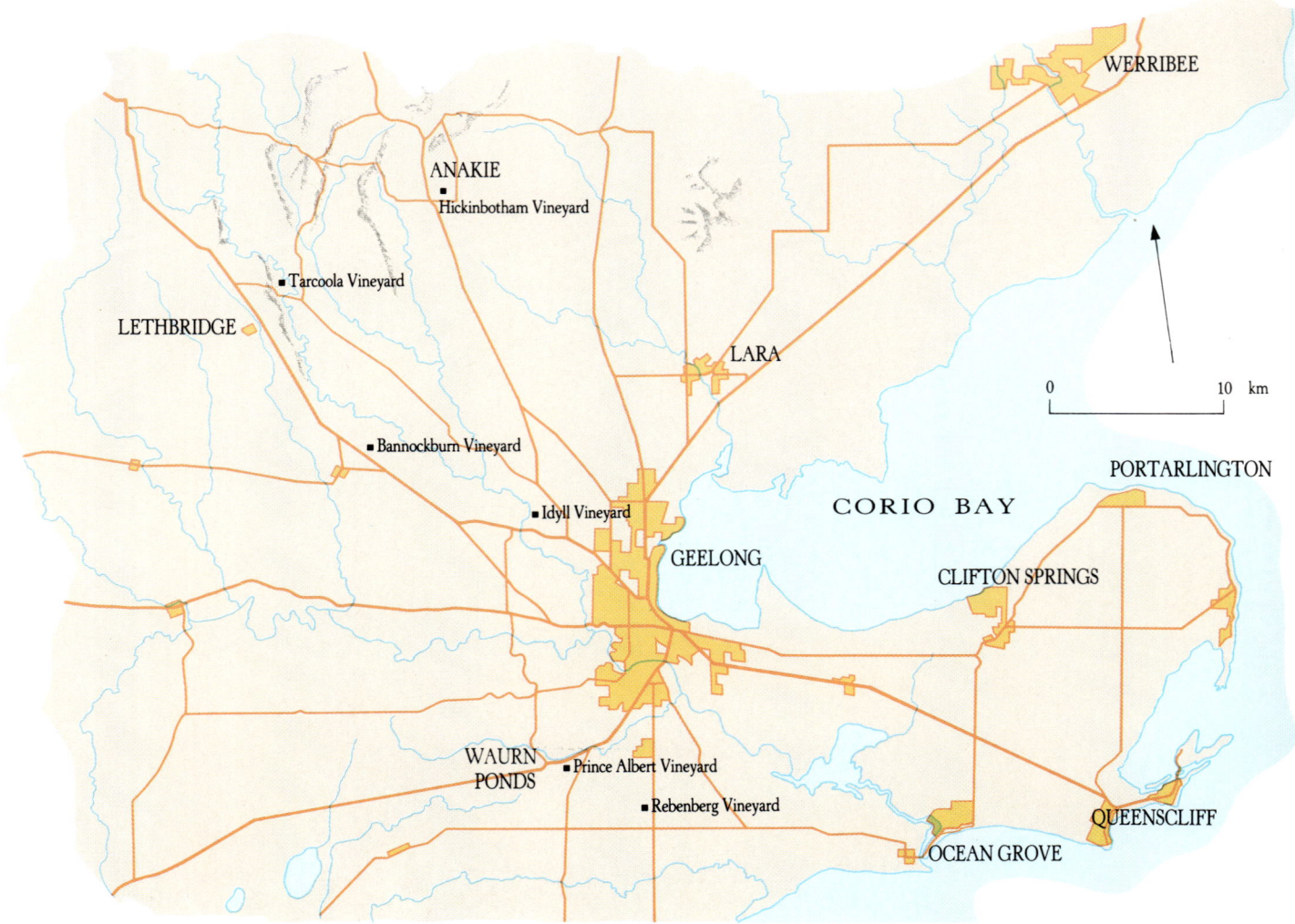

HICKINBOTHAM VINEYARDS

Stephen Hickinbotham and his father, Ian, lease the vineyard which was planted by Tom Maltby on the slopes of Mount Anakie, the pressure dome of an extinct volcano. This is a very cool location; in the winter the Hickinbothams christened it 'Pleurisy Plains'. The wines from this vineyard are very fine indeed, but they are only the beginning of the Hickinbotham saga. They have invented their own process for making the wine and taken out a patent which they have then sold to other companies. The resultant wine from this process is called Cab Mac, a delightfully fresh early drinking style.

They also buy fruit from other areas. Tasmania supplies cabernet sauvignon and sauvignon blanc is on the drawing board from New Zealand, where Stephen believes there is some fine fruit to be had. The wines from Hickinbotham are usually of the highest quality and have an individual stamp.

Stephen's sister, Jenny, a graduate from the viticulture course at Wagga (N.S.W.), is in charge of viticulture, while Ian, with his long experience in winemaking in Coonawarra and the Barossa Valley, supplies a broad overview. They make a dedicated, albeit intense, family team.

Another family member, Andrew, is following in Stephen's footsteps and studying in France. His particular area of interest is the Bordeaux region.

The vineyards of the Hickinbotham family, from Mount Anakie.

333

Daryl Sefton is a veterinary surgeon turned winemaker. He and his wife Nini, an artist, run Idyll Vineyards near Geelong.

Idyll's vineyards were re-established in 1966. But in the mid-1860s there were more than 50 vineyards around Geelong.

IDYLL VINEYARDS

This vineyard was one of the pioneering ventures that re-opened the Geelong district to viticulture. The location on the banks of the Mooroobool River certainly lives up to its name. Although the surroundings are charming, owning and managing a vineyard is not for the faint-hearted. Idyll has been subject to frosts that have decimated the yield on a couple of occasions.

Daryl Sefton attacked the frost problem as he attacks most things: head on. He built a sophisticated frost alarm that allows him to react in time to save the grapes. Daryl is forever building something. The winery, press and mechanical harvesters are all his own creations. The harvester was one of two that were torched by vandals and written off by the insurance company. This enterprising vet rebuilt the two and sold one at a profit.

Daryl and Nini Sefton make wines under the chateau concept. They release one red (a blend of cabernet sauvignon and shiraz), a gewurztraminer, and a rose style that they have called Blush. Nini Sefton is in charge of the marketing. She also attacks the problem head on, using her charm and eloquence to win through.

In the early Eighties Daryl finally settled on the style that he considers to be the best for his vineyard. The wines are elegant and exhibit considerable staying power in the cellar. They also have the advantage of being reasonably priced.

GREAT WESTERN

Everyone who has any interest in wine will at some time or another have tasted Great Western Champagne. This ubiquitous beverage finds its way into every type of celebration or sporting event. The fact that at least 50 per cent of the base material is made from sultana grapes that are not grown in the district does nothing to diminish its popularity. Great Western Champagne is an institution and the consumer doesn't equate the wine with an area. It is simply Great Western.

The district has much more to offer than mass produced bubbly. Some of the greatest Australian table wines have been made there. It was the cradle of cool climate viticulture in this State. The climate is fickle and it sorely tries the patience of even the most saintly vigneron. Frost, drought and storms seem to work in rotation to make the winemaker's lot a difficult one.

Why not opt for an area with a more equitable climate? The answer lies in the rewards that come from a benevolent year. The resultant wines can be spectacular. Some of them are the stuff of legend.

Among the area's most notable wines are the vintage sparkling burgundies from Seppelt. These remarkable wines are snapped up when they are periodically released with Seppelt's customary modesty. (They don't tell anyone and the wine simply appears.)

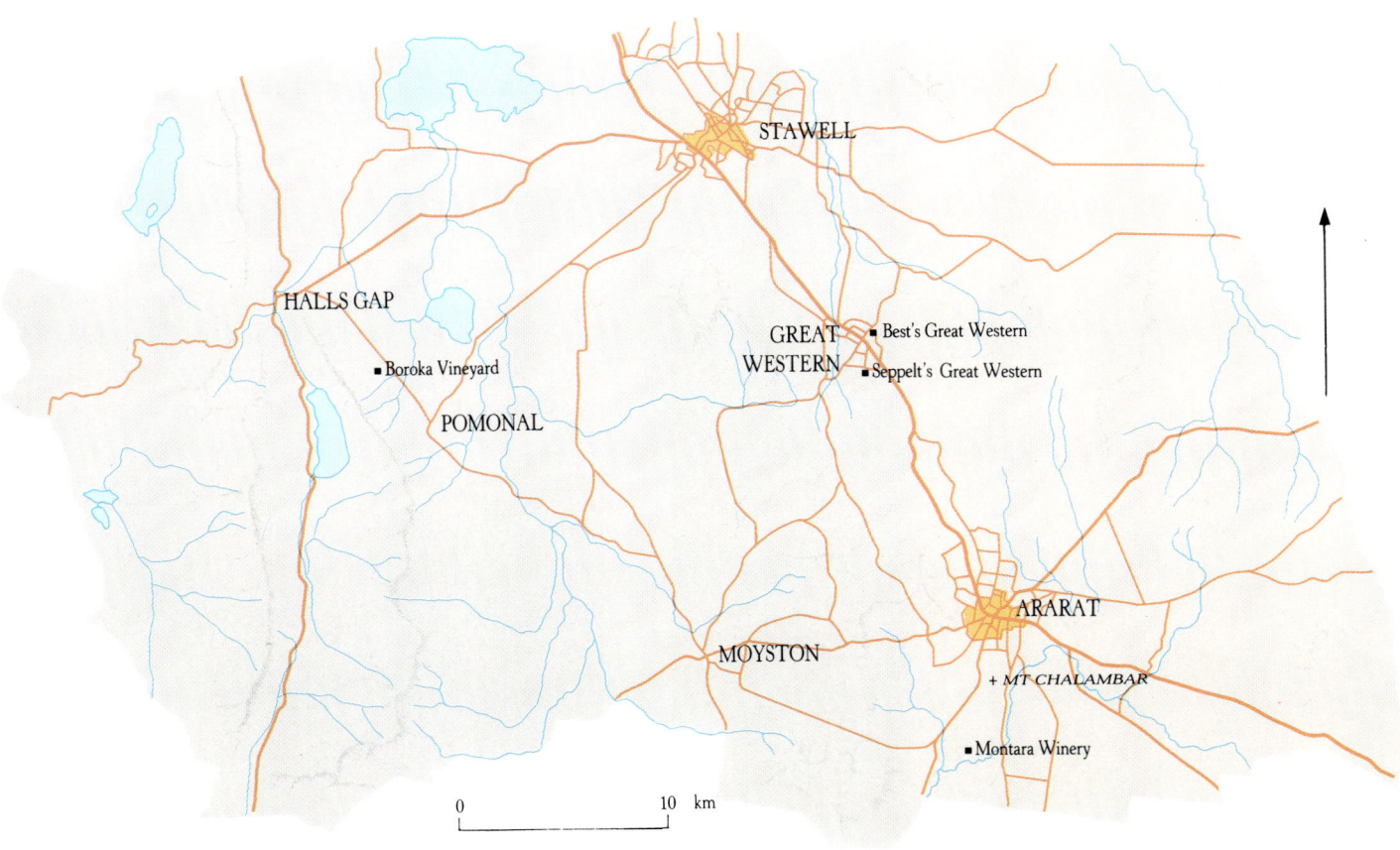

*Detail from an old
oak cask at Best's Great
Western winery.*

*Tasting, the old-fashioned
way, at Best's winery.*

BEST'S GREAT WESTERN

This historic vineyard is owned by the compact and dapper Viv Thompson. He bears the climatic capriciousness with stoicism. He and his winemaker, Trevor Mast, have managed to come to grips with the conditions and they usually manage to make wines of good to outstanding quality. The red wines have proven longevity, the whites have that steely power and intense flavour that are the benefits of a cold climate.

One of the most recent developments is the making of a sparkling style that is marketed without reference to champagne on the label. This wine is much sought after. There is never enough of it because the production is limited to the amount of cellar space that is allocated for the wine to rest on lees. Trevor Mast – one of the most talented winemakers in the country – admits that sparkling wine is an obsession with him. He was trained at Geisenheim in Germany and this fostered his belief that Australia could produce wines equal to the great beverages of Champagne.

He has his own small vineyard at Mt Chalambar and there is a system of contract growers providing chardonnay from cool areas like Macedon and Ballarat. The results of this will be worth waiting for. There is every reason to believe that the Mt Chalambar vineyard will be one of the stars of the future.

*Bottling Great
Western Champagne: the
wine that has launched
a thousand ships.*

*Vines today, champagne
tomorrow, from Seppelt's
Great Western vineyards.*

SEPPELT'S GREAT WESTERN

Great Western Champagne has launched a thousand ships, toasted millions of births, weddings and divorces. It is mandatory at race meetings. It is more than a fizzy drink; it is an institution.

The commercial wine is made by the transfer process – it would take an army to disgorge such volume by hand. This process is said to oxidise the wine less than the traditional method.

However, there is more to Seppelt's operation at Great Western than bubbles. They make some very fine table wines and they process the fruit from the Drumborg vineyard. These wines are consistent performers on the show circuit and they make a significant contribution to Seppelt's success in being awarded the trophy as the most successful exhibitor at many national wine shows.

The winemakers at Seppelt are a dedicated bunch and as is the way with large companies, they are less visible to the public. The champagne maker is Warren D. Randall, a personable young man who doesn't seem the least bit fazed by being responsible for the production of a large proportion of Australia's quality sparkling wine. The quality control factors here are enormous. Nothing in life stands still, so Warren feels that it is important to continually upgrade the product. Remember that Great Western Champagne cannot afford the luxury of variation of

Warren Randall (left) is in charge of Seppelt's champagne making operations and is also a leading wine judge. With him is Seppelt's winemaker Brian Fletcher, at Great Western.

vintage. It must remain consistent – rain, hail or shine.

There is also considerable research being conducted on the traditional champagne grape varieties, chardonnay, pinot noir and pinot meunier, and the results are encouraging. These champagnes already entered in wine shows usually reach the buying public at very reasonable prices when released for sale.

Ian McKenzie is in charge of the red wine production and these wines are the cornerstone of many a fine cellar. Brian Fletcher looks after Rhine riesling and all the other white wines.

No discussion of this winery would be complete without the mention of another institution, Great Western Sparkling Burgundy, a wine which fell from grace in the Seventies. The management were within an inch of delivering the *coup de grâce* in the form of a stop-production order. A bump in the sales graph saved this wine. It was decided to promote it 'just once more', and suddenly the marketing executives were embarrassed by running out of the standard line.

From time to time the vintage sparkling burgundies are released at sensible prices and they are usually magnificent, timeless old wines of indescribable velvety richness. These unique wines are now being

appreciated by the consumer. They will never be plentiful. They were made in small batches, there is a high attrition rate caused by failing crown seals, and some of them are blended into the standard wine.

MONTARA VINEYARDS

Montara is the labour of love of the McRae family. It is sited in a picturesque location at Ararat that offers spectacular views from the cellar door. There have been some wines of high quality produced from this vineyard; however there has also been a certain hesitancy about evolving a distinctive style.

The pinot noir is promising and Michael McRae has used some of this wine as a base for an experimental sparkling wine. Although the wine is only for family consumption, the results are encouraging. To date there has been no firm decision to enter into full production. That segment of the market, particularly in Victoria, is becoming a crowded battlefield. The option is to continue as before and keep producing a burgundy style from the pinot noir.

Another interesting wine that is produced at Montara is a vintage port. Being from a cool area it is an interesting specimen.

The McRaes are determined to succeed and the indications are that they will. As the vines mature, particularly the pinot noir, there should be some spectacular wines in the offing, be they red table wine or premium sparkling.

Great Western Champagne sits in these riddling tables to bring the sediment of secondary fermentation down to the necks before disgorging. Note the chalk marks on the base of the bottles to help cellarhands rotate the bottles accurately each day.

AVOCA

This is rugged and beautiful country some 55 kilometres to the east of the Great Western area, with the Pyrenees Ranges sprawling into the distance. It is not perhaps an area usually associated with wine-growing. Certainly the area is cool climate, and it is fascinating to see a strong French/Italian influence in the district.

CHATEAU REMY

The Remy Martin Company of France planted this vineyard at Avoca with white hermitage grapes for the production of brandy. The quality of the fruit was a pleasant surprise. It was almost too good for brandy

Pressing red grapes in a Rotapress at Chateau Remy.

Vineyards at Chateau Remy, one of a number controlled by the company. Chateau Remy also makes quality sparkling wines at their Victorian winery. Some 10 000 bottles are on the tables here.

and lent itself to the production of sparkling wine. The famous Champagne house Krug was part of the Remy empire, so bubbly was a logical point of departure.

The fruit quality also encouraged the management to plant varieties like cabernet sauvignon and shiraz for the production of table wines and chardonnay to upgrade the quality of their sparkling wine.

Winemaker Christian Morles is a quiet, unassuming young Frenchman with a dedication to the quality of his products. Chateau Remy is undergoing a transformation. Remy are constructing a lavish cellar door area, and the label changes, as well as an improvement in the quality, mean that this vineyard is a strong performer. With Krug expertise at work, the enthusiast can look forward to some exciting wines. As the chardonnay proportion increases in the sparkling wine, we will be treated to a drink that is similar to that of the Champagne district.

The red wines from this vineyard had some false starts in the Seventies. The wines of the mid-Eighties will be worth waiting for, as this is a great district for red wine.

The Remy Martin Company has demonstrated its dedication by sinking large amounts of capital into this project. It also has access to great winemaking talent, so the long-term results should be excellent.

REDBANK VINEYARDS

For the owners, Neil and Sally Robb, this venture has been one of toil and struggle. The Robbs buy grapes from surrounding districts as well as using those produced in their own Sally's Paddock.

The wines from Sally's Paddock are the standard bearer for this company and they are very good indeed. There will be wines from merlot and pinot noir coming on stream soon, and if they are up to the usual Robb quality, they will be in demand in the market place.

*Dominique Portet
makes wines of character
at Taltarni in central
Victoria. His brother
Bernard runs another high
quality winery in
California's Napa Valley,
and their father worked
at Château Lafite
in France.*

TALTARNI

Allow me to write in the first person about this vineyard near Avoca, at Moonambel. The reason for this key change is that I spent two years before the mast at Taltarni.

It might not sound like it, but Taltarni is an Aboriginal word for red clay and this red clay was a part of the reason that the manager/winemaker chose the place in the first place. The vineyard is owned by John Goolet, a wealthy overseas businessman with an acute appreciation for the arts. Taltarni strives to be a work of art under the management of Dominique Portet. Dominique is the son of the former Régisseur of Château Lafite in France. His brother Bernard fulfils the same function at Clos du Val in the Napa Valley in California. This vineyard is also owned by John Goolet.

During my time at Taltarni I was constantly amazed by the orgy of spending on equipment. Nothing but the best would do, with the result that Taltarni was one of the best equipped wineries in Australia. It is also one of the cleanest, Dominique being fanatical about hygiene. This cleanliness is the cornerstone to making disease-free and consistent wines.

Dominique is a complex character; he can be full of Gallic charm, not to mention stubborness. He is the master of the Gallic shrug when he doesn't want to answer a question. His time in Australia has softened his accent to a curious blend of 'francostrine'. He delights in picking up Australian slang and misusing it to jangle the ears of the listener.

Above all he is determined to make Taltarni one of the best labels in the country. He is also promoting Taltarni wines on the international market. Clos du Val made it relatively easy to penetrate the United States market and Taltarni wines are highly regarded in the States. The 1979 Cabernet Sauvignon was named as wine of the year by the *Los Angeles Times*.

The red and sparkling wines are the stuff that has founded Taltarni's solid reputation. With the exception of the sauvignon blanc, the white wines have not been memorable. Taltarni was the first on the market with a high quality sparkling that was not labelled champagne.

The Pyrenees Ranges form a natural cradle for the vineyard. It is very cold in winter and snow is common. The vines are a spectacular sight, viewed through double glazing from in front of a roaring log fire. Pruning in the snow is not a pleasant task!

One of the early problems with the vineyard was that the consumer expected carbon copies of Bordeaux wines from a French winemaker. The first wines that were marketed were as Australian as meat pies. They were monsters, huge in tannin and acid. Since then the style has lightened off and settled down on the side of elegance. As grape varieties like cabernet franc and merlot come on stream there will be echoes of Bordeaux, but Taltarni wines will always be Australian and proud of it!

There has been wide acceptance of the wines and they are consistently improving. The weather is the joker in the pack, and since money is no object, efforts have been made to control the forces of nature. Drought is the major problem in the area. Taltarni, with its network of six dams and nearly 500 hectares of catchment, can survive up to four years without rain.

It all adds up to a recipe for excellent wines. My feeling is that the best is yet to come as the vines are not yet fully mature.

MOUNT AVOCA VINEYARDS

This 18-hectare property is the labour of love for John and Arda Barry who planted the first vines in 1970. John Barry is a stockbroker whose interest in wine led him to establish a vineyard centred around the red varieties of shiraz and cabernet sauvignon.

The Barrys have taken a purist approach to winemaking and they use only estate grown fruit to make wine. Sauvignon blanc and chardonnay have recently been planted for white production. It will be interesting to see the styles when produced; sauvignon blanc seems particularly suited to this district.

Mount Avoca is well established in the local market, however due to the crippling drought of 1982/83, there is a shortage of wine. The wines produced to date have shown promise.

As a non-commercial sideline the property produces some marvellous olives and the Barry children have a thriving mini-craft market at cellar door.

WARRENMANG VINEYARDS

The proprietors are interesting people. Luigi Bazzani runs 'La Scala', a successful restaurant in Ballarat, and Russel Branton owns and runs Seabrooks, a historic wine wholesale business in Melbourne. Between these activities they find time to maintain and make wine at the vineyard.

The picturesque vineyard nestles in the Pyrenees Ranges. The winery/cellar door leads to an ingenious tunnel through a hill, taking care of the temperature control.

The wines of Warrenmang have a distinctive minty character about them, particularly the cabernet sauvignons. One theory is that the mint comes from the stands of peppermint gums that abound in the area. Whatever the cause, the character is quite appealing. Warrenmang wines are good cellaring propositions, as are most of the reds from this district.

SWAN HILL/ECHUCA

Swan Hill is riverboat country, the lazy middle reach of the Murray halfway on its winding way to the Southern Ocean. And like a number of other stretches of the great river system, it also provides the lifeblood of a wine industry here along the border of Victoria and New South Wales. Because of its comparative remoteness it is one of the less known and less understood wine-producing areas of Australia. There are some excellent wines made from Beverford, not far to the west along the Murray Valley Highway from Swan Hill, all the way back along the river to Echuca, where the Campaspe and Goulburn Rivers meet the Murray.

WOORINEN WINE ESTATES

With over 2000 hectares under vine, this co-operative winery is the biggest in Victoria. It fields wines under the Woorinen label, as well as supplying wine and grapes to other producers.

The Swan Hill district is becoming a popular tourist resort and Woorinen is one of the attractions. Woorinen features a wide range of wines, the most notable being a sweet dessert wine that bears the

The Tisdall winery gets grapes from a number of regions, and makes some excellent dry red and dry white wines.

name Melifera. This wine, affected by noble rot, has distinct ageing potential. The name was coined to avoid terms like trockenbeerenauslese.

The bulk side of the operation provides wines for other companies. The Hickinbothams made their Cab Mac on site from Woorinen shiraz.

In the minds of the consumers, co-operatives and large wineries lack the romance and attractiveness of the small maker. In many ways this is a pity, as co-operatives have no less soul because there are 240 shareholders.

BULLER'S WINERY

Richard Buller Jr operates this winery and distillery at Beverford. Its main function was to provide fortifying spirit for the larger brandy producers as well as spirit for the renowned Buller's fortifieds.

The production of table wines is thriving because of increasing demand for Buller's table wines. (*See also* Buller's Winery, Rutherglen.)

BEST'S ST ANDREWS

Best's take grapes for their economy range as well as material for fortified wines from this vineyard at Lake Boga. The climatic differences between here and Great Western mean that the same winemaking team can service both vineyards.

The varieties like cabernet sauvignon and Rhine riesling make decent wine that, although not memorable, represents better than average drinking at affordable prices. (*See also* Best's Great Western.)

TISDALL

To understand Tisdall, the creation of Dr Peter Tisdall, it is necessary to realise that the vineyards are in two locations: Mt Helen in the Strathbogie Ranges,

and at Rosbercon on the Murray River, near Picola. The winery is situated at Echuca in a converted cheese factory. This means that Tisdall have a foot in both the premium and the commercial camps, sometimes confusing to the consumer because of the price difference between the two groups.

The Mt Helen wines aspire to the heights of cool climate viticulture, whilst the Rosbercon wines represent good commercial wines at reasonable prices. The first winemaker was John Ellis who now works on the political side of the industry for the Victorian Vignerons' Association. He was replaced in late 1984 by a promising young winemaker, Jeff Clarke. Jeff worked for two vintages under John so the transition has been very smooth. Both makers have been influential in setting a style for the grape variety chardonnay and the product from the Mt Helen vineyard is highly regarded. Another area of their expertise is in thermovinification, which results in wines of brilliant colour and low tannin extraction. These red wines are designed for immediate consumption and, although they will last quite well in the bottle for a few years, the ageing potential is limited.

If there was a word to sum up this company, it would have to be innovative. Tisdall are always willing to break new ground. They were among the first in Australia to market a fumé blanc wine.

Tisdall have invested heavily in modern equipment and temperature controlled wood storage. The cellar door is quite commodious, but the absence of vineyards subtracts from the atmosphere.

GOULBURN VALLEY

The Goulburn Valley directly to the north of Melbourne is another river valley with historic links going back to the early explorers. Major Thomas Mitchell explored the area when he was Surveyor-General of New South Wales, giving his name to Mitchellstown and from that to the impressive Mitchelton winery. His 1836 travels led to the establishment of grazing properties and then to vineyards, one of which was the Tahbilk Vineyard Proprietary Company, incorporated in 1860, not far from the township of Tabilk (how the 'h' came to be in the Chateau's name no one can explain).

There are a number of vineyards in this area supplying fruit to other areas; for example, the Mt Helen vineyard (one of the key premium fruit sources for Tisdall Wines at Echuca) is in the Strathbogie Ranges part of the Great Dividing Range, to the south-east of Tabilk.

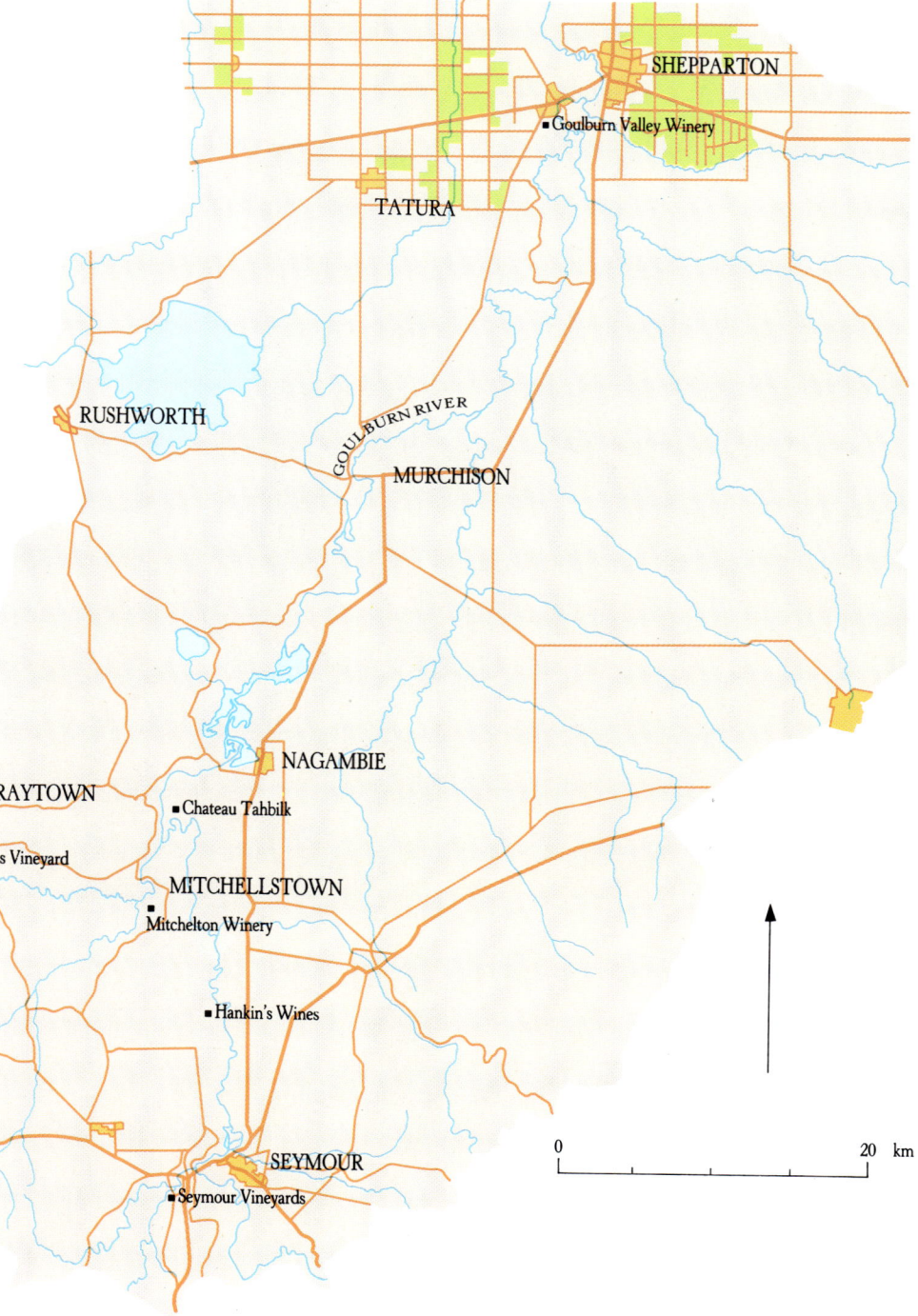

The grounds of the old winery at Chateau Tahbilk; for reasons no one can fathom, the district is spelt 'Tabilk'.

CHATEAU TAHBILK

A charming place to visit – the seduction of the wooden tower and the underground cellars is very difficult to resist. But history is not enough. To make fine wine, technology must play a part. Realising this, Tahbilk built a discreet modern winery that tastefully blends in with the old buildings.

The winemaker is Alister Purbrick. Since he took over the winemaking chores in the early Eighties there has been a steady elevation of the quality of the products. The familiar Tahbilk label has a timelessness about it and when the company tried to change it in the mid-Seventies there was a blood curdling protest from the consumer. The startled Purbrick family quickly reverted to the old label and order was restored.

The label will remain constant, but there has been a concerted effort to improve the content. The reds of Tahbilk have great depth of flavour and are a medium- to long-term cellaring proposition. The most notable white wine in Tahbilk's arsenal is the Marsanne which enjoys a spell in the cellar. As a young wine it is a typical chablis style, but with cellaring it develops an attractive honeyed character.

Tahbilk fell victim to the scourge of phylloxera and eighty years later it is still in evidence in the district. Some recently planted chardonnay (cuttings and not root stock with American roots) fell victim to the louse – 25 hectares of vineyard were lost. The patient Purbricks are stoically replanting with American root stock.

The future looks bright for Tahbilk; in the few years that he has been at the helm, Alister has demonstrated an ability to come to grips with the local conditions. When the new varieties like chardonnay and sauvignon blanc come to maturity it will be interesting to see how he copes with them.

MITCHELTON WINERY

Mitchelton at Nagambie is a brave venture that had a couple of stumbles before it found its stride. An element of controversy dogged its early days – after all it is a tourist complex. Many purists were quick to condemn. The folly, a 60-metre tower, was like a beacon to the critics, contrasting starkly with the historic Chateau Tahbilk across the river.

The most recent management has concentrated on developing a consistent style in the wines, believing that the key to Mitchelton's salvation was consistent quality. This belief proved correct and the sun now shines on the project.

The spire at Mitchelton.
The winery has restaurants,
and a lookout atop
the tower.

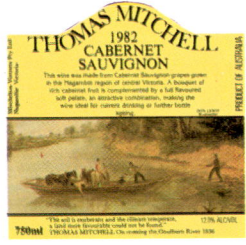

Sunrise in the vineyards of the Goulburn Valley, Victoria.

Winemaker Paul Osicka.

The styles of wines at Mitchelton are distinctive. The Rhine riesling is the model for the modern Australian style with the emphasis on well-defined fruit and complementary acid. The wood-aged marsanne is a pioneering style and some would say that it was an essay in oak treatment. This wine has a devoted following.

The cabernet sauvignons are fine wines that have the capacity to be drinkable when young, yet they can be cellared for an intermediate period, say about five years. That statement gives some indication of consistency of this wine. The makers, a tight-lipped duo of Don Lewis and David Tregear, seem to be able to rise above the variations of vintages and produce a wine of high quality that is a consistent medal winner in the shows. If Tregear and Lewis exchange more than thirty words in a day they would tell you that they'd 'talked up a storm'. They have converted the art of communication by silence to an enviable art form.

Also in their range is the Thomas Mitchell label, a value for money line in which consistency is the hallmark. Yet a third label, the Winemakers' Selection, is utilised when the company buys fruit from another district, namely Coonawarra. There is one more label that sports the company banner, the Print Exhibition label.

The winery, on the banks of the Goulburn River, is probably the best equipped in Victoria to cater for tourists. There are three restaurants and the tower can be used as a conference centre.

OSICKA'S VINEYARD

The geographical centre of Victoria is not the easiest place to find, and Graytown is hardly a metropolis. The Osicka vineyard is off the beaten track some 20 kilometres west of Tabilk and often only the lost stumble across it by accident.

Osicka's at Graytown has a unique microclimate, and the owner, Paul Osicka Jr, makes some exciting reds from the cabernet sauvignon grown on the property. Only in the last decade have Osicka's wines been marketed under their own label. Prior to this they were sold to other companies or merchants for blending or bottling.

Paul's wines are not of gigantic proportions, but they have a certain firmness about them.

Paul is a charming, modest man, and seclusion seems to suit him. His mother ably looks after the cellar door sales area because, in spite of the remoteness, there is usually a steady flow of Osicka devotees in search of some cellaring reds.

GLENROWAN/ MILAWA

Visitors to this part of Victoria will be forcefully reminded that Ned Kelly once roamed the hills. There are statues of that helmeted gun-pointing out-law beside the road, there are Kelly cafes, and it would not be surprising if there were Kellyburgers for the asking. As Ned once said, 'Such is life.'

Viticulturally this area has a different climate to Rutherglen. Although there is a tendency to group the Glenrowan area into the Rutherglen district, it produces distinctive wines and really stands by itself. The red wines from Baileys and Booths are meaty, tannic brutes. They start life with their knuckles dragging on the ground, but a decade or two in the bottle turns them into very civilised beverages.

The wines of Milawa are yet another story. They tend not to be as heroic as those of Glenrowan. Both Browns and Ric Morris (Markwood) produce more elegant wines that still live for years in the bottle. The

reason for the difference in styles is partly due to the subtle difference in microclimate. Baileys and Booths are subjected to cooling evening breezes from the Warby Ranges whereas the vineyards around Milawa are on the plains and subject to different climatic influences.

It is possible to accuse the wines from Glenrowan of being out of step with the modern developments of the new lighter styles, but for those who like wines of character they are a real delight. The other style that does well in this area is fortified wine. Baileys make a superb muscat; to many it is the definitive example of these famous wines. Brown Brothers contribute some fine ports; Ric Morris produces his own fortifying spirit for some excellent sherries.

BROWN BROTHERS OF MILAWA

'Dynamic' is the word that springs to mind when discussing this company. It is managed by four brothers, each being in charge of a particular discipline. The wines are made by John Brown Jr, the marketing is the province of Ross Brown, Roger Brown is in charge of graft and corruption (i.e. propagation of cuttings and graftings), and Peter Brown is vineyard manager.

The dynamism is clearly fostered by John Brown senior. Now retired, he was a canny almost statesman-like figure in the Victorian wine industry for decades. It was his vision that launched Brown Brothers into making and marketing varietal wines. By the late Seventies Brown Brothers' range was so prodigious that they could almost fill a small licensed outlet. Recently there has been some rationalisation of that range.

Perhaps the most puzzling aspect of this company is a certain hesitancy in the area of label design; it seems that approximately every two years Brown

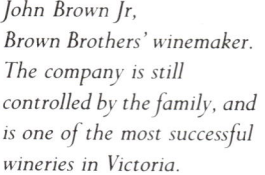

John Brown Jr,
Brown Brothers' winemaker.
The company is still
controlled by the family, and
is one of the most successful
wineries in Victoria.

Brothers redesign their labels. It seems strange that such a go-ahead company can't seem to get the label to their satisfaction.

As personalities, the brothers are quite diverse. Roger is ebullient, Peter retiring, John is laconic, and Ross, although of comparatively tender years, is developing some of the statesman-like qualities of his father. They have one thing in common – that country slowness in replying to a question. But be assured that when the answer returns it has been carefully considered with each word meticulously weighed.

The family has been adroit in keeping a homespun

image. This personal profile leads people to the conclusion that they are a small family business. In fact this vineyard is one of the largest in the State, supplying healthy international and national markets. In the trade, the Browns are often referred to as 'the ubiquitous Brown Brothers'.

Part of the success of this company is the quality of the wines. It is their policy to buy grapes from other districts, including the cool, high plains areas, and turn them into outstanding wines. The cabernets from the Koombahla vineyard have been consistently excellent. Another star in the Browns range is the Noble Riesling, which is made when late picked Rhine riesling grapes are affected by noble rot.

As well as the stars, the bread and butter for Browns is a burgeoning bulk wine market, where they sell large quantities of 10- and 20-litre casks. Another consistent seller is a fruity spatlese lexia. The wines from the Milawa vineyard are respected by consumers for their consistency.

The cellar door is ideally placed to do thriving business. It is on one of the major routes to the snow fields. When it is not snowing, the skiers flock to the cellar door for consolation.

Since Browns are innovators, it is certain that they will continue to pioneer new areas, varieties and styles. They are not afraid to take a chance and their impeccable public relations usually make trail blazing less difficult.

Export is high on the priorities and Ross Brown has had some success in developing an export market in the United States. It is early days yet, but the fine wines from Milawa make worthy ambassadors for Australian wine.

The most important export market is presently the United Kingdom and this success is the result of hard work. Ross Brown had no illusions that it would be easy, or that the development would happen overnight.

Another priority is the development of a high altitude vineyard in the King Valley. Browns see this as the next logical step in Australian viticulture. They feel that this is where the quality wines of this country will come from.

Mt Prior and its surrounding vineyards, near Rutherglen.

RUTHERGLEN

The mighty River Murray has become a holiday playground. The towns on its banks are blessed with a great climate. They offer superb golf courses, a host of water sports, fishing and general relaxation. The wineries of Rutherglen play their part as an attraction, but perhaps the major attraction for Victorians is the sinful poker machines. Victorians show an inordinate fondness for giving their money to these machines. It is all part of a delicious wickedness that can only really be understood by a fellow Victorian.

It is also important to note that mother nature is also a powerful attraction. The scenery along the river banks is superb. The stately river gums have delighted generations of artists and photographers. Even on hot days the cool shade on the river banks makes the ideal picnic spot.

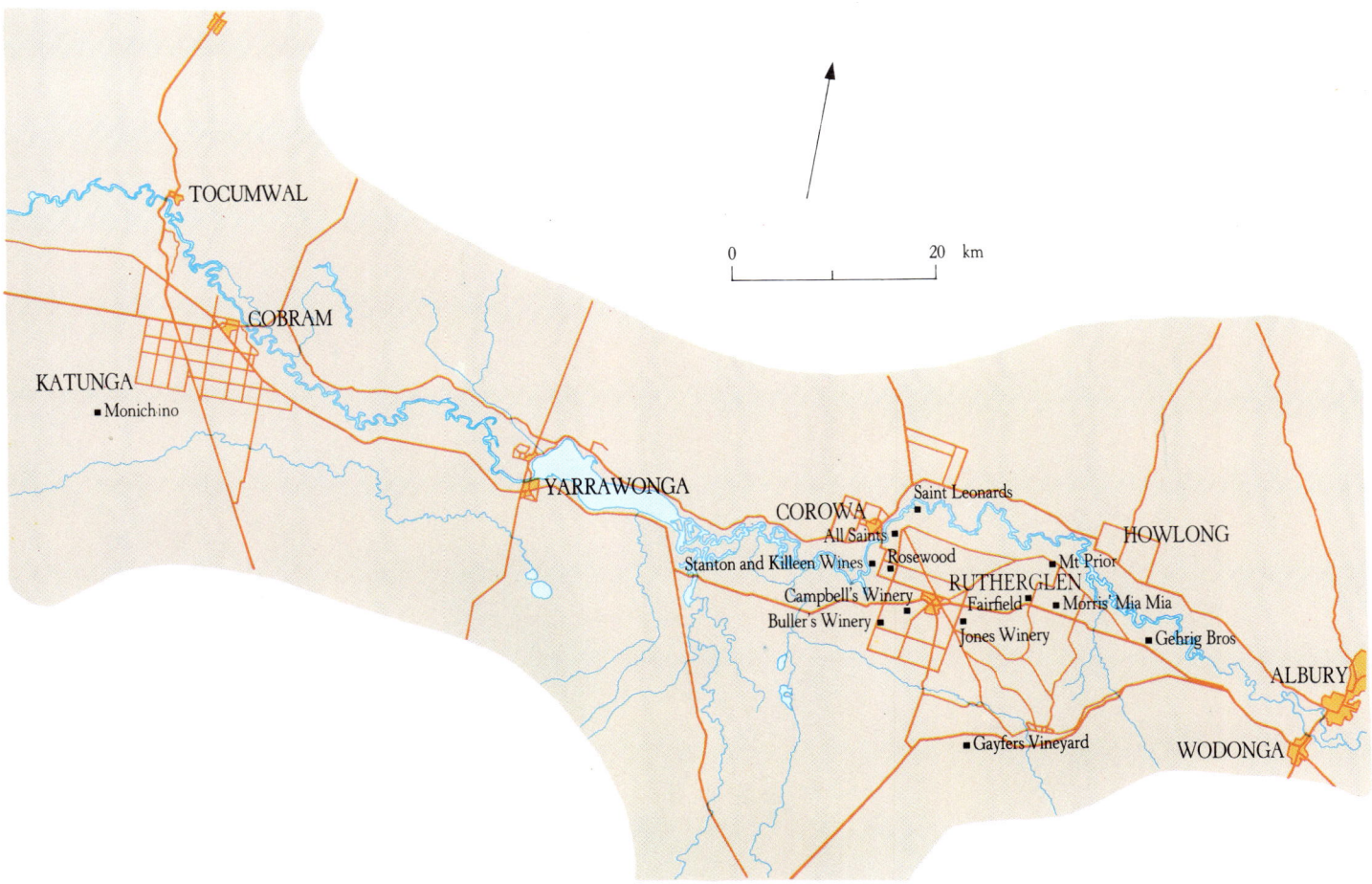

BULLER'S

This vineyard and its buildings would not win the award for the most picturesque location. But handsome is as handsome does and some of the wines produced here are exceedingly handsome, particularly the black label fortifieds. If Buller's were to win an award it would be the Nicest People Award; Dick and Val Buller are gun-barrel straight and generous to a fault. They make honest wines to the best of their ability and the prices that they charge for their products are exceedingly fair.

To counterbalance the rather drab winery, they have spent time, effort and money in the surrounding gardens. This area is for the use of the public for picnics and barbecues. The main attraction is a comprehensive bird park which is a labour of love for Val Buller. She has many rare species of birds and watching them makes an entertaining diversion from tasting wine.

The Bullers have another winery at Swan Hill which is run by Richard, the eldest of the three brothers. Richard is a chip off the old block and has also inherited the family characteristic of being generous to a fault.

Andrew Buller has spent time in Portugal making vintage ports, and the knowledge gained is being applied at Rutherglen. He too has the family characteristics as well as a tendency to shoot from the lip. The youngest, Graham, has completed his winemaking course at Roseworthy and the family is toying with the idea of establishing yet another vineyard in a cool location.

Dick Buller at his Calliope winery. He and his family make some excellent vintage ports.

International recognition for the All Saints winery in 1895.

ALL SAINTS

No industry is complete without a feud and although this feud doesn't rival the famed spats in the Ozarks, it can be entertaining. The protagonists are George and Ian Sutherland Smith. Never make the mistake of calling them brothers, they are cousins. This agreement to disagree adds an air of creative friction to the operation.

George is the winemaker and Ian handles the marketing of the wide range of company products. Recent improvements in the packaging of their wines and a vast improvement in the quality of the table wines (their fortifieds have always been strong) mean that the All Saints star has risen high of late.

Here too we find some of that hot climate miracle working. All Saints make a fine chardonnay and lovely wood-aged marsanne. The cabernet sauvignons are consistent medal winners at national shows. Of the fortifieds the sleeper of the range and perhaps the most outstanding is the madeira.

The winery is styled after a Scottish castle and George is usually on hand and he is an entertaining and generous host. This genuine atmosphere of friendliness typifies the spirit in the district and is one of the main reasons for the popularity of the area with tourists.

Cooper Kevin St John repairing oak barrels at All Saints.

355

Pruning the vines at Morris' Mia Mia vineyards, near Rutherglen. Winemaker Mick Morris makes some of Australia's most renowned fortified wines, notably a sweet dessert wine described as Liqueur Muscat, plus some admirable red and white table wines.

MORRIS' MIA MIA

The winemakers in Rutherglen tend to look south in bemused bewilderment – according to their southern winemaking cousins, they should be making only fortified wines because of the hot climate. According to the cool brigade it is impossible to make white table wines in this area, yet Mick Morris seems to achieve the impossible year after year. His chardonnays have disgraced many wines from the theoretically right areas. This wine usually reaches the marketplace with a price tag that is half that of its competitors and a quality that is sometimes twice as good.

No mention of Morris would be complete without a salute to his famous fortifieds; they have earned this company wide acclaim, and deservedly so. When Mick Morris sold his winery to Orlando some said, 'That's the end of Morris wines.' That prediction did not prove correct. The injection of capital and a non-interfering management has seen Morris go from strength to strength. They have allowed this maker to develop some distinctive styles. There is no wine that bears the signature of Mick Morris that could be accused of wanting flavour.

STANTON AND KILLEEN

This small winery contributes some stylish wines to the district. Norm Killeen is a charming man and in years past he was a noted crooner. Norm's son Chris is now the winemaker and this enterprising young man has set his sights on developing an export market. They see a future for the famed Rutherglen Muscat as a standard carrier for Australian wines.

The muscats from this property would indeed be good ambassadors for Australia. They are luscious and have the flavour of recently picked berries. The other wines of note from this vineyard are the shiraz/cabernets which display a fine elegance and a good depth of flavour.

CHAMBERS

Bill Chambers makes some superb fortified wines at his Rosewood winery, just west of Rutherglen. He is also a skilful maker of premium red wines and some unusual white wines.

Bill Chambers is a quiet, thoughtful man. Shy is too strong a term for he is given to public speaking on occasion, but one gets the feeling that he would be happy with his own company.

His quest has been to make an elegant cabernet sauvignon, and on many occasions he has succeeded.

His fortified wines are legend, and rightly so. Customers spend an inordinate amount of time trying to wheedle that 'extra' bottle of very old tokay out of Bill, and damn the price, it is worth it!

CAMPBELLS

This important vineyard jostles with St Leonards for the title of the jewel in Rutherglen's crown. The winemaker is the personable Colin Campbell. He has a direct gaze, firm handshake, and dresses in the mode of a country squire, but there is nothing squirish about his demeanour. He is always friendly and approachable.

Campbells have been doing well of late and this success is in large part due to some spectacular white wines. Again we find some super whites made in this so-called impossible climate.

From time to time Campbells release some spectacular fortified wines which, although not cheap, give an indication of some of the best wines produced in the district. A Rutherglen fortified in full bloom is an awesome thing.

ST LEONARDS

This vineyard is owned by Brown Brothers of Milawa. The winemaker, Rick Burge, is a young man who could be described as one of the new breed. His efforts at St Leonards have been spectacular and some of the white wines have upstaged those of his boss, John Brown Jr.

These wines surely put to rest any speculation that the area doesn't make fine table wines. These wines are first class and the vineyard has the policy of selling them at cellar door only.

The picturesque vineyard is worth a visit and a conversation with the winemaker can be rewarding. Rick Burge has a head on his shoulders and while he might appear to be a young man in a hurry, his winemaking is carefully controlled.

YARRA VALLEY

Although land is expensive in the Yarra Valley, vineyards continue to mushroom in this area to the east of the city and up to 70 kilometres away. Many of the vineyards are new, having only marketed a few vintages to date, and none is large. Restaurants have mushroomed along with the vineyards. The wines from this area rank among Australia's best table wines. They are expensive, but many consumers think that they are more than worth the money.

No mention of the area would be complete without noting the champagne cider made at Kelly Brook. This unique product is made in the traditional méthode champenoise manner from cider apples.

There are well-kept historical buildings in the area; Dame Nellie Melba's residence is faithfully preserved and the winery at Yeringberg is the original building from the first vineyard. The medals won by Baron de Pury adorn the walls. This vineyard is not open to the public, but the property can be inspected by appointment.

The newer vineyards, Yarra Burn, Prigorje and Warramate, are adding some interesting wines to the collection. They are in the process of establishing a style. The older vineyards – the oldest was established in 1966 – are well established and a distinctive style has evolved. This style could be described as elegance and finesse.

There is one problem in the area and that comes from the birds. They gorge themselves on very expensive grapes each year and in some cases the loss is above 50 per cent.

WANTIRNA ESTATE

Wantirna is a south-eastern suburb of Melbourne and so it seems strange to find a small plot of vines nestling at the end of a suburban street. The estate is owned by Reg Egan, who is a lawyer by profession, and he insists that winemaking is a hobby. The standard of the wines produced is well beyond that which would be expected from a hobby farmer. They are wines of great complexity and finesse. His 'hobby' has taken the dry humoured Egan to France on numerous occasions to study viticultural techniques.

The wines of Wantirna are seldom in plentiful supply. They are snapped up by the consumer when they are released on a biannual basis. They include an attractive blend of cabernet and merlot and some distinctive white wines.

CHATEAU YARRINYA

There was great jubilation when this vineyard won the Jimmy Watson Trophy in 1978. That event seemed to confirm that this was *the* area to make Australia's premium wines. No matter that the feat has not been emulated by another Victorian vineyard since.

The man who made the wine is Graeme Miller, a dairy farmer who became interested in viticulture in the early Seventies. Situated at Dixons Creek, the company specialises in table wines and a vintage port has also been made. This port is quite surprising considering its cool origins. It is very fine and dry and it indicates what can be done in the Yarra Valley.

LILYDALE

A partnership between Alex White and Martin Grinsberg, previously chemists at Carlton and United Breweries, is responsible for this fine vineyard that specialises in white wines. The releases to date have left little room for disappointment. They are very clean and elegant.

The vineyard is not open to the public, but can be visited by appointment.

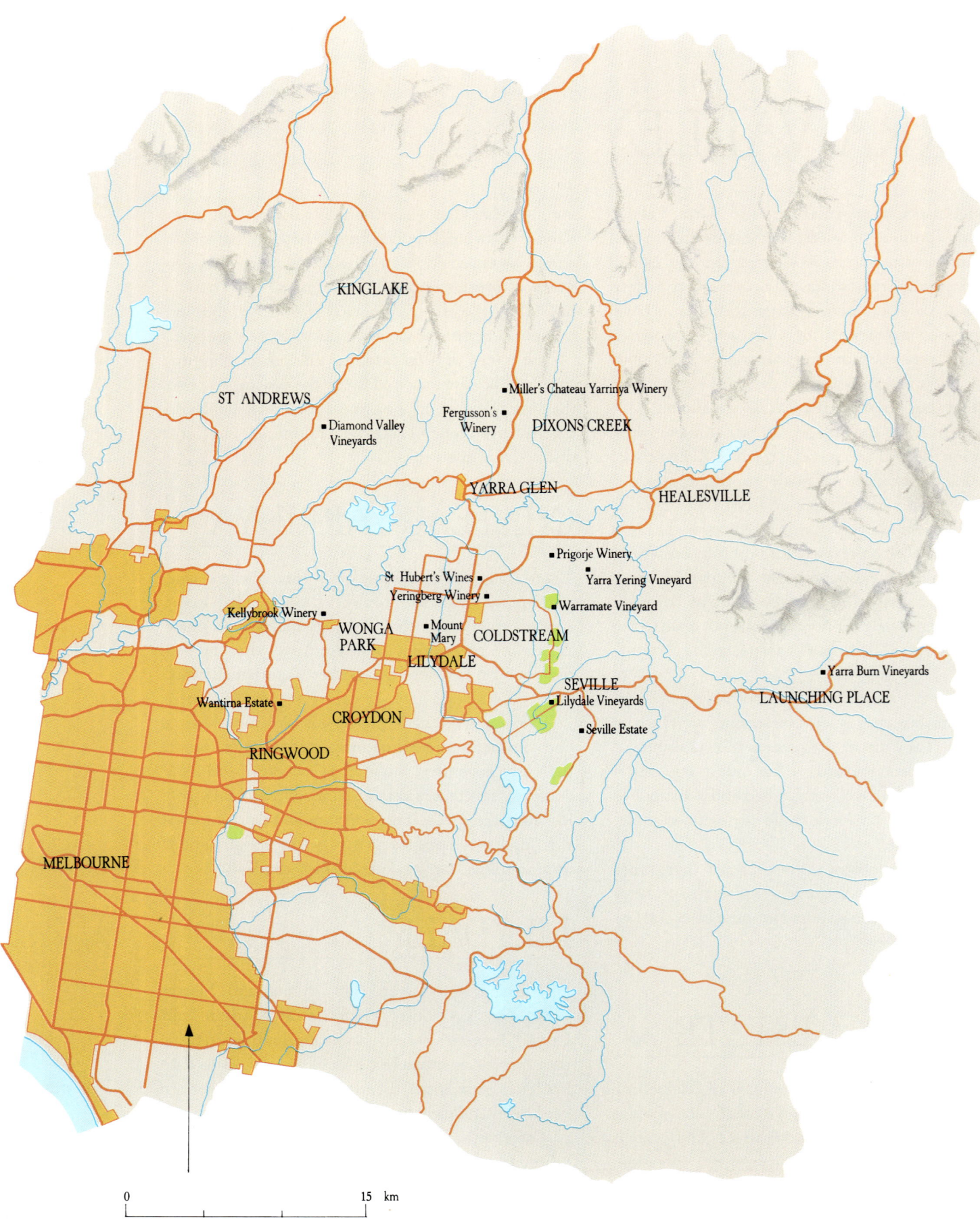

KINGLAKE

ST ANDREWS

■ Miller's Chateau Yarrinya Winery

Fergusson's ■
Winery

DIXONS CREEK

■ Diamond Valley
Vineyards

YARRA GLEN

HEALESVILLE

■ Prigorje Winery

St Hubert's Wines ■
■ Yarra Yering Vineyard

Yeringberg Winery ■

Kellybrook Winery ■
■ Warramate Vineyard

WONGA
PARK

■ Mount
Mary

COLDSTREAM

LILYDALE

SEVILLE

■ Yarra Burn Vineyards

Wantirna Estate ■
■ Lilydale Vineyards

LAUNCHING PLACE

CROYDON

■ Seville Estate

RINGWOOD

MELBOURNE

0   15   km

YARRA YERING

Dr B. B. Carrodus is a dapper man, and it is not inconceivable that he makes wines while dressed in a three-piece suit and trilby. The wines of Yarra Yering (at Coldstream) are simply marketed as Yarra Yering Dry Red Numbers One and Two and Yarra Yering Dry White.

The adoption of this French nomenclature is typical of Bailey Carrodus. He is a microbiologist who was bitten by the winemaking bug in the late Sixties. His wines have great character and when nature is kind these wines demand long-term cellaring to achieve their potential.

DELATITE VINEYARDS

This modern winery at Mansfield looks out on to a dramatic vista that is framed by Mt Buller and Mt Stirling.

The vineyard is the property of the Ritchie family and initially the grapes were sold to Brown Brothers of Milawa, who marketed them under an individual vineyard label.

Then daughter Rosalind, newly graduated in oenology and eager to work, came back to the vineyard. In the short time that Delatite wines have been marketed under their own label they have won great critical acclaim. The strong suit at the moment would

The distinctive, low-key labels on the wines made by Dr Bailey Carrodus. At their best his reds, particularly, are excellent — look for his pinot noir.

seem to be Rhine riesling, however varieties like char-donnay are on the way.

The winery is compact, modern and beautifully equipped; it was designed by Dr Tony Jordan of Oenotech. The vineyard is also immaculate.

The feeling about Delatite Vineyards is one of untapped potential. These are early days and it is sure that the best is yet to come.

DIAMOND VALLEY VINEYARDS

The personable David Lance is responsible for the fine reds that emanate from the diminutive 2.4 hec-tare vineyard. Lance is part of the winemaking team at St Hubert's, so although his vineyard is relatively new, he has amassed considerable experience in the valley.

The wines have a very Bordeaux character. David has planted the classic varieties, cabernet sauvignon, cabernet franc, merlot and malbec, and the result is complex wines. The vineyard may be visited by appointment only.

HENKE VINEYARDS

This vineyard is situated in a rugged location in the hills behind the blink-and-miss-it village of Yarck. Access is by four-wheel-drive only.

Tim and Caroline Miller (Caroline being the daughter of Herb Henke, the founder) make mainly red wines and the vineyard has had some hard times due to drought. The Millers have been working hard to overcome the difficulties and the wines that are coming on stream show that they are succeeding. One of the most remarkable things about these wines is that they appear on the market at reasonable prices, even more remarkable because this is one of the low-est yielding vineyards in Victoria.

ST HUBERT'S

Chateau chicken shed could be an apt title, because up to a short time ago the wines were indeed made in a chicken shed and they seemed not to suffer as a con-sequence. St Hubert's at Coldstream was founded by the Cesta family and is now distributed by Elders IXL.

In the formative years the winemakers were chemists with Carlton and United Breweries, and consequently were clandestine about their wine-making activities. After leaving Carlton and estab-lishing their own vineyards, their identity could be revealed. Ironically Elders now owns Carlton, so the trio are back working with the brewery again!

The trio who came in from the cold are David Lance, Martin Grinsberg and Alex White. From the beginning they set St Hubert's up as a premium pro-ducer and the wine community was staggered by the high prices being asked for the wine.

St Hubert's makes brilliant reds and whites and sets the standard for others to follow.

THE YARRA VALLEY DOCTORS

There are two doctors, John Middleton and Peter McMahon, who have vineyards in the Yarra Valley, and it seems appropriate to discuss them in tandem because their approaches to winemaking and the vineyards have striking similarities. They are both perfectionists and their respective labels, Mount Mary (Middleton) and Seville Estate (McMahon), have become synonymous with the highest quality. They are masters at making red wine, their cabernets attain lofty heights and they are proving a point about pinot noir.

The vineyards are not open to the public and the wine is sold by thriving mailing lists. The wines are in the upper price bracket, but frantic buyers would seem to confirm that they are worth every penny.

FERGUSSON'S VINEYARD

In an industry that is rich with characters and personality, Peter Fergusson stands out as one of the most flamboyant. He founded this enterprise at Yarra Glen on a restaurant that caters to large groups. The fare is simple, he specialises in spit roast beef, and the atmosphere is hearty, baronial and sometimes bawdy. It is a great place to visit and a difficult place to leave. The prudent hire a bus to beat the .05 problem on the return trip.

The restaurant tends to overshadow the winery which is making a significant contribution to the wines of the district. These wines are in short supply and the range is supplemented by wines from other districts within Victoria. This second label does not bear the appellation 'Yarra Valley'. Great Western is one of the districts that Peter draws on for suitable material.

The wines from the vineyard are elegant and a lengthy term in the cellar is usually required. They tend to be in the upper price bracket and although they are not as expensive as some of the neighbours' products, they are not in the everyday drinking league.

Peter Fergusson is an energetic promoter, ebullient host and a man about town. The bottom line in all this is the wines that he produces. They have a firm stamp of quality and the unmistakeable Fergusson zest for living.

A tiny cluster of grape berries waits for the vine to pump water and nutrients in and the sun to help them ripen.

THE NEW AREAS

MORNINGTON PENINSULA

Mornington is a bayside suburb of Melbourne that boasts a number of small vineyards that have yet to market their wines. This area has an extremely cool climate; when summers are mild there could be problems in ripening the grapes.

Some of the early wines, particularly from Main Ridge vineyard and Elgie Park (made by Hickinbotham) show considerable promise, and lend credence to the belief that this could be a significant premium area.

One of the vineyards to watch on the Mornington Peninsula is that of horticulturalist Garry Crittenden (no relation to the wine merchant Crittenden family). The layout of this vineyard is impeccable and the viticultural practices are advanced. Hopefully the fruit will be superb and the first step to a great wine.

CENTRAL WESTERN DISTRICT

This district takes in the area around Ararat, Stawell and Halls Gap. Great Western could also be regarded as being in this area, however it couldn't be classified as new, so it has been omitted from this segment.

This is a high plains area and altitude plays a part in the moderation of the temperatures. The producing vineyards have recorded early vintages of promise. Boroka, Cathcart Ridge, Mt Langi Geran, Mt Chalambar, Crawford River and Montara Vineyards have all made handsome wines.

If my crystal-ball gazing is in any way accurate, this should be an area of significance, particularly because the winemaking talent of Trevor Mast will be playing a part. Trevor is the proprietor of Mt Chalambar and consultant to a number of vineyards in the area.

EAST GIPPSLAND

This is another area that is opening up to the vine. There are vineyards at Lakes Entrance and Lindenow that are producing wines under the Lulgra and Golvinda labels respectively. There are other plantings in the district that have not yet produced fruit. It is again too early to pass judgement on the significance of this area. The temperate climate augurs well for the vigneron.

Vignerons often have problems establishing which grape varieties and clones are best suited to new winegrowing areas.

MELBOURNE

TALAVERA WINE COMPANY

This is not a vineyard but rather part of an old Melbourne tradition that is being preserved. The name of Seabrook is still renowned in wine circles. The Seabrook family were the most respected wine merchants in Melbourne; their shop in Lonsdale Street was a mecca for wine enthusiasts intent on buying quality.

One line always in demand was the house fortifieds which were blended in the cellar and marketed under the Talavera label. When Doug Seabrook retired, he sold the business and the retail licence went in one direction, the wholesale in another, and the Talavera label and the stocks of the old fortifieds became the property of an enterprising young gent, Hugh Cuthbertson.

Hugh is maintaining the tradition in marketing this fine range of fortifieds. In spite of fortified wine's waning star, he believes that there will always be a market for quality wines. His conviction is proving correct. Talavera wines derive their quality from being carefully aged in wood and, if the sales are too brisk, there is a danger of running out of old base material.

A good rosé should have intense pink or salmon colour, sometimes with a hint of purple showing through the wine. The wine should be served slightly chilled.

ROSÉ

Helen Guy

Rosé, as a wine style, has been around for some time. In Australia Kaiser Stuhl have been producing their popular Gold Medal Rosé since the 1960s and Leo Buring were making a vin rosé in the 1950s. Other makers had similar products available around that time.

Overseas, it is produced and enjoyed in France, America, Portugal and Italy. Portugal's Mateus is the top selling rosé around the world, while outstanding styles are produced in the Rhône, the home of the famous Tavel, and the Loire regions of France. Rarely are these wines seen at their best outside their country of origin, for they are designed as early drinking wines to be enjoyed in their youth. Travel and additional shelf life does nothing for the wine.

Rosé has always been an underrated wine in Australia. For too long it has not been accepted as a serious wine. Perhaps it has been regarded as being a woman's wine or as a fun wine and not the real thing, or perhaps it has suffered from lack of definition.

Whatever the reason, both the wine and we, the consumers, have suffered. The wines have suffered from being slow to move off the retail shelves and therefore gaining unnecessary and often detrimental bottle age. We have suffered by not using this versatile wine as an alternative to red wine and white wine.

Rosé is not, as some people think, made from vintage leftovers. Nor is it made from blending red and white wines together to obtain the necessary colour and flavour. Rosé is a separate wine style and its making requires a much winemaking attention as does that of its red and white cousins.

At its worst it can suffer similar problems which beset red and white wines; it can be oxidised, it can lack fruit definition and it can be tainted by off, non-vinous characters. At its best it is a wine with plenty of character, flavour and interest. It does not taste like red wine, nor like white. It has its own individual flavour.

Rosé is produced from red grape varieties, such as cabernet sauvignon, shiraz or grenache, and in that respect it is closer to red wine than white. However, it is here its similarity to red wine ends, for it does not have the body, the depth of colour or the tannin-acid structure of a red wine, nor is it produced with cellaring potential in mind.

The ideal colour of a rosé is a bright light pink to

a pink-red. Sometimes it can display purple tints. The pink or pink-purple colour of the delicate fuchsia flower is a good guideline to the colour of rosé.

The colour is most important and a knowing eye can almost determine how the wine is going to taste from its colour. If its colour is fresh and alive, the chances are its flavours are going to be lively and attractive. If its colour is beginning to lose life and is showing hints of orange or brown, the possibility of the wine lacking the necessary life and flavour on the palate is high. If the colour is dull and lifeless, the wine will probably also taste dull and uninteresting.

Production methods vary from maker to maker, depending on the style of rosé the maker wishes to achieve – be it dry or semi-sweet; softly coloured or tinted with purple; delicate in flavour or medium bodied.

Normally one grape variety is selected by the winemaker, with the winemaker's choice being determined by two things: the availability of a particular variety and the style of rosé to be made. His choice could be cabernet, grenache or shiraz.

When the grapes have reached the required degree of ripeness they are crushed and the free-run juice is then given a short period of contact with the skins to pick up the necessary rosé colour. This time can vary, but it is normally around twelve to twenty-four hours. Fermentation is controlled. Again here the winemaker's determined style dictates the method of production – whether it is fermented out dry or whether the fermentation is arrested to leave the wine with a touch of natural residual sugar. Both wine styles are currently made in Australia and both have a place.

The end result – irrespective of whether a dry or semi-sweet style has been made – should be fresh, light flavoursome wine, showing signs of the varietal fruit from which it was made. That is, if it was made from cabernet sauvignon, it should display some berry fruit character; if made from shiraz, it should display some spicy characters; and if made from grenache, it should exhibit light fruity flavours. A hint of natural gas from the fermentation may also be found in the wine. This is known as spritzig and it gives the

wine a lift and a slight prickle to the palate.

Rosé is made to be enjoyed in its vintage year. It is not a wine for cellaring, although it does deserve a permanent place amongst our drinking stocks.

It is ideally suited to our lifestyle and our climate. It is a great picnic wine, an outdoors wine, and a wonderful barbecue wine, especially if chicken, veal or lamb are on the menu. It is equally at home accompanying an entree at a dinner party – try serving it with a seafood ragout or a warm duck salad or perhaps with brains wrapped in filo pastry. It also teams perfectly with spicy oriental cuisine.

It's the ideal wine to serve on warm days and balmy evenings, for it is at its best served slightly chilled. It can also make a welcome change from white wine, no matter how comprehensive and varied your white wine selections may be.

Kaiser Stuhl, Houghton, Tollana, Hardy and Chateau Reynella are all companies currently producing top Australian rosés. You may find them hard to locate on retail shelves for until now you did not demand them, but a visit to a reputable wine merchant or a special request at your local liquor store should see you quickly armed with an assortment.

So, join me on my bandwagon. Try rosé and share it with your friends. Make it the drink of the Eighties. After all, the world looks so much better after a glass or two of rose-coloured wine!

Me and My Cellar

*M*e and my cellar; me and my carapace, more like it. In the past few years, I have moved four times, the last from Sydney to Melbourne. And if, like me, you have a large cellar, this can only be described as a traumatic experience.

In the outcome, the cellar is spread over 900 kilometres in warehouses and other storage places, few of which ever seem to be accessible when I want that bottle. It all harks back to my bachelor days in the Sixties when my cellar started to grow; having filled the space under my bed, the linen cupboard and the spare room, it flowed under friends' and relatives' houses.

By the time I built the first house I owned, my wines were secreted in different locations between Sydney and Moss Vale. Then for thirteen years I was in heaven: the cellar was excavated out of solid rock, roofed with a concrete slab (and a two-storey house on top of that) with internal access from the lounge room.

It really was a resplendent place, yet totally functional. Thanks to a happy mistake by the builder who excavated the length of the house instead of half of it, it was able to hold all the eight thousand bottles I then owned. Tooths' beer crates gaves me single bottle storage for most of the bottles, and I knew exactly where every bottle I owned was.

It has grown somewhat in the meantime. I think some of the bottles get carried away in the dark, and multiply themselves. Certainly my attempt to keep my computer stock list up to date is a running sore, and the odd bottle I drink has done nothing at all for my short-term memory recall. Shortly put, I no longer know where every bottle is. Indeed I don't know where half of them are.

Yet it would be churlish of me not to admit that I get by. One of the advantges of a large cellar spanning all of the major wine-producing countries and one hundred and fifty years (in vintages) is that I can organise theme dinners or tastings with relative ease. Over the years I have explored the conventional themes many times: all the wines from a single vintage; young/old comparisons; or matched pairs of wines from the same vintage but different countries, more often than not France and Australia.

The real challenge comes when you have a special guest of honour. Last year I returned the hospitality Gerard Jaboulet, from the leading Rhône Valley house of Paul Jaboulet. Because this is the home of hermitage, I decided to build a dinner around only two grape varieties, semillon and hermitage.

We started with 1946, 1953 and 1964 Seppelt Great Western Sparkling Burgundy (with spiced Chinese pancakes as hors d'œuvres); with the first course of smoked Tasmanian trout and eel went Lindemans Hunter River White Burgundies of 1965, 1966 and 1967; Penfolds Grange Hermitage of 1955, 1962, 1971 and 1976 matched the barbequed whole fillet of beef and snow peas, and continued onto the Brillat Savarin cheese; while a brace of 1962 sauternes – Penfolds Bin 414 and Lindemans Porphyry – rounded off the meal with the fresh fruits and homemade sorbets.

More recently, I had a dinner for some special guests which took the young/old game to its logical conclusion: Moët et Chandon of 1976 and 1911 started proceedings; then Erbacher Marcobrunner of 1971 and 1886;

followed by Puligny Montrachet of 1959 and 1923; Grands Echezaux (of the Domaine de la Romanée Conti) of 1976 and 1970 and of 1937 (from Leroy); Château Lafite 1958 and 1919; while Château Coutet of 1961 and 1918 finished the meal (and its attendees) off.

Collecting these wines has taken time, obviously enough. Particularly with Australian wines, I have made mistakes. Both my palate and the style of wine being made have changed markedly over the past twenty years. For a while I also had a stamp collector's mentality: I had to keep the set going.

My buying patterns these days are much more eclectic. While I would seldom if ever buy less than a case of a wine I like, and usually two, my pace has slowed somewhat. Like the old bull, I look increasingly for quality rather than quantity. I also do not hesitate to dispose of my mistakes, and in theory try to watch the development of the wines by tasting at least one bottle each year. And I most certainly drink my share of the golden oldies I have garnered over the years!

People stare at me and say, 'But how can you drink such a valuable old wine?' Simple; you won't live forever and neither will the wine. I collect wine to drink, not to fondle and put on the trophy shelf. True, I probably won't get around to drinking all the bottles I own today, let alone those I will buy in the future. But, I have no desire to emulate André Simon, who when he died had only one bottle of wine in his cellar. Surely that fact would be cause for an autopsy to rule out the possibility of suicide.

So when I go, there will be more than enough for the wake to end all wakes, and I have commanded my executors to see to it.

Dr Andrew Pirie at his Pipers Brook winery. He is one of Australia's most talented small winemakers.

IN PRAISE OF SMALL WINEMAKERS

Robin Bradley

Odd, isn't it, how the wine scene has changed? When you and the world were twenty years younger, a tight little club of big producers controlled every aspect of Australian wine: from the high volume, low quality end of the market right up to the pinnacles. Of course there were smaller makers, but their customers were mostly local, and in horribly many cases the winemakers were beer-drinking farmers who regarded their product as mere agricultural produce. (It was intriguing to observe how these same people were transformed into instant experts, groaning under the weight of arcane knowledge, as they became confronted with increasing adulation from a new wave of neophyte wine enthusiasts. Oh, well.)

Then something happened. A Sydney surgeon planted some vines in the Hunter Valley ('Cabernet sauvignon, the fool!') under the amused eyes of the established makers, and a revolution was under way.

Just have a look around now. Wineries have proliferated like Melbourne massage parlours. New areas have been developed – areas much more suitable for the production of quality wine than are the traditional Australian vignobles; grape varieties previously

ignored have become up-market staples; the gamut of vinous complexity and depth has been unimaginably extended. Oh, and yes: the Sydney surgeon's folly has created one of the world's great wineries. In short, the wine-lover has been well served.

Lake's Folly, the small winery begun in the Hunter Valley in 1963 by Sydney doctor Max Lake. Above the winery is their house.

The tasting bench at Harry Tulloch's Mount View winery in the Hunter Valley.

It's not that small is necessarily beautiful. It can be ugly, unhealthy, half-hearted or downright incompetent, and the big company sneer at 'L-plate winemakers' is frequently justified. But, warts and all, it is never cynical, bored or creatively inhibited by marketing expediences. It is not my brief in appreciating the small maker movement to disparage the big boys, but there are dramatic philosophical differences between the two. These are neatly exemplified in considering two newly established areas: Keppoch and Margaret River.

Keppoch is a big company development on a band of red soil superficially similar to Coonawarra. Yields have been embarrassingly high, to the delight of boardroom accountants, but quality is too often sadly mediocre: many wines being noteworthily vacuous and apologetic. Margaret River, as I am sure you don't need to be told, is a very different story. Yet the risk inherent in the latter's establishment and development was entirely assumed by small makers.

And it's not just Margaret River for which we have to thank the intelligent, dedicated amateurs. Reading from left to right, one could exhaustively tour Frankland, Mount Barker, the Mount Lofty area (South Australia's only genuine cool climate vignoble), Central Victoria, the Goulburn Valley, Mount Macedon, Geelong, the Yarra Valley, the Mornington Peninsula, Gippsland, Mudgee and the entire island of Tasmania and never encounter a label of one of the top ten companies. Yet in making such a tour the wine-lover could taste and buy all but a meagre handful of Australia's greatest wines. In grudging fairness, and at the risk of lessening the impact of a splendid argument, Drumborg (Seppelt) and the high Barossa Ranges (Yalumba) are both significant recently developed areas of extreme potential not to be lumped together with the Keppoch venture.

So much for areas, but our debt to small makers is greater than this. Until the advent of these good people our very best wines were created almost as the hobbyist endeavours of some big companies' winemakers – and full credit to their employers, whether or not the latter's indulgence was whole-hearted. Thus were born Grange Hermitage, Steingarten, the great Colin Preece wines and the marvelous four-figure bin wines of Lindemans, to name but a few (the only few I can think of offhand; a rather different situation existed with Maurice O'Shea's Mount Pleasant wines as he had established the wines prior to the vineyard's acquisition by McWilliam's). But with the best will in the world it was still perilous to diverge too far from the stylistic mainstream.

Not so for the little guys. The small winemaker's eye, in a fine frenzy rolling, can confront the most idiosyncratic of visions. Not for him the three months' market research, the long look at past trends and future extrapolations, the corporate agonising over product names, label colour and design and so

Redgate Winery at Margaret River, Western Australia, one of the smallest wineries of this relatively new area.

John Brocksop, manager of the Leeuwin Estate winery at Margaret River, tastes a cabernet sauvignon from the 1981 vintage with winemaker Bob Cartwright (on the right).

I am not sure what, if anything, this proves, except that it might serve to highlight the unwisdom of confusing size with significance. (If you are interested in the other end of the spectrum, McWilliam's are current leaders in a somewhat fluctuating production ladder with 2.2 million cases. And just to put even that in perspective, the Gallo Brothers winery at Modesta in California belches forth 250 000 cases a day.)

What then for the future?

It seems inevitable. The massive investment of the major companies demands their domination and control of the volume end of the market. Wine in Australia is now a staple, entrenched and enduring, and it appears most unlikely that there will be any diminution of that broad-based market sector – indeed, the reverse seems probable. The small maker, on the other hand, is not only uninterested in this area but is actually financially incompetent, or at least under-capitalised, to make any inroads in this direction even if he were interested. In short, his place is the top end; the big producers – the bottom end.

But nothing is unassailably secure, and particularly not complacency. There could well be said to be a minimum size less than which a winery is a hobbyist venture dependent upon one man's enthusiasm and ability to survive even the next vintage. And there is a limit to the number of people who will be prepared indefinitely to pay homage and coin of the realm to someone making faulted wines simply because those wines are from a tiny production. So as long as the one talented man is in the chair, all is well. But any unlooked-for drop in quality will erode public faith – not just in that particular label, but in small makers generally.

The risk is very much less with the 20 000-case winery. There is too much to lose for there to be much danger of capricious quality variation, as long as the winery is aiming at the high priced end of the market.

After all, it is expensive to establish and develop a vineyard and winery. Far more lucrative investments or fields of endeavour exist, from plantations of

on before the ultimate heroic launching of another concrete submarine. Master of his own destiny, he can plunge, however ill-advisedly, into the most self-indulgent course of action and see what happens. Yet, remarkably, it is not he who labours and brings forth a loathsome sparkling port or a slosh-pack of drench. His contribution can afford to be unaffordable.

How else could there still exist a few half-bottles of Seville Estate's improbably opulent 1980 Trockenbeerenauslese Rhine Riesling, or a case or two of Moss Wood's 1980 Chardonnay with its flavour component cast of thousands, or the memory of the coconut bouquet of the 1973 Balgownie Cabernet Sauvignon, or the Montrachet stature of Lake's Folly 1974 Chardonnay, or the arrant magnificence of Bailey's 1953 Old Matured Hermitage still developing after a generation and a half?

macadamia nuts, through chains of unofficial 'private hospitals', to the odd hundred hectares of *Cannabis sativa* hidden in the bush somewhere (this last being as risky as a vineyard and winery, but significantly more remunerative). Stuart Anderson (of Balgownie fame) once gave a talk on starting a small winery in which he stated 'You don't have to be mad, but it helps.' I am sure he could have added that a bottomless purse would also be an advantage.

Yet, wealth and mental instability apart, these good people prefer to strive in vinous areas – why? Clearly, it can only be because they find it personally fulfilling to try to make the best wines they can, without obsequious obeisance to the marketplace. Failure to achieve a pretty high standard means ruin, because you can't economically make small lots of wine unless they are of a quality to fetch very good prices.

The net result is that we have a unique situation wherein the big producers follow the market and the market follows the small producers. Different ends of the market, admittedly, but nevertheless true.

But by now, one or more of you must be musing 'This is all very well, if true, but what's "small"?' Good question. Awfully good, in fact, because I don't know.

Let's forget about areas under vine, crush tonnages, gallonage (litreage?), and some of the other industry jargon measurements and speak of cases of wine. The range in Australia is from 800 (cases per year) – indisputably small – to some millions. To help us all generate some perspective, cast an eye over the following comparisons.

Cases	Australia	France
800	Yeringburg	Romanée-Conti
2 000	Mount Mary	La Tache
3 000	Moss Wood	Grands Echezeaux
4 000	Pipers Brook Vineyard	Château Petrus
5 000	Balgownie	Château d'Yquem
6 000	St Hubert's	Château Haut-Batailley
7 000	Idyll Vineyard	Château Boyd-Cantenac
8 000	Lake's Folly	Château Coutet
9 000	Peel Estate	Château Olivier
10 000	Katnook	Château Cheval Blanc
15 000	Petaluma	Château Haut-Brion
20 000	Leeuwin Estate	Château Latour
25 000	Redmans	Château Lafite

Consider the small winemaker. He is a purist for a start, perhaps even a pedantic purist. He has theories – passionately held – but puts his money (or at least his wine) where his mouth is. His bank manager thinks him a lunatic. He strives to make each vintage a little better than the last, and is optimistic enough to believe that he is succeeding in doing so. He is wary of praise, bitterly resentful of criticism. He is a hard-headed, practical, painstaking worker who claims to have no illusions, but looks suspiciously like a romantic dreamer when his guard drops.

We owe him.

Peter Robertson, one of Australia's small winemakers, at his Barwang winery, near Young, New South Wales.

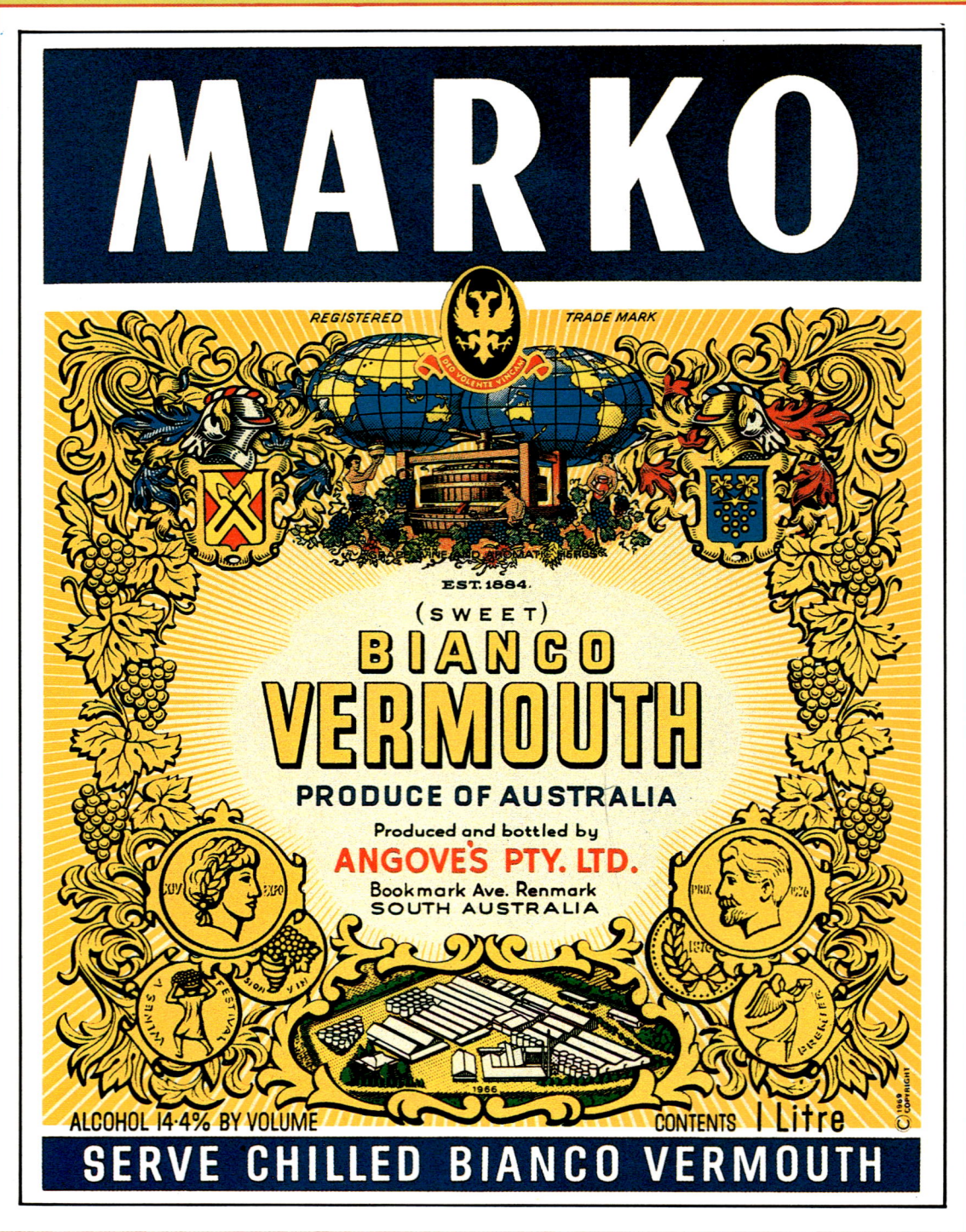

Marko is the trade name used by Angove's for their big-selling vermouth range, made at their South Australian Riverland winery.

VERMOUTH AND MIXERS

Samuel Cook

Vermouth – or *ver-mooth,* as our American acquaintances so poetically pronounce it. Without it the world would not have the martini cocktail, wherever that might have left us.

In fact, without vermouth the continuing interest of civilised mankind in wine itself may have been in doubt. As one convivial winemaker of my acquaintance puts it so splendidly and accurately, 'Let's face it, making vermouth was just a way to stop the wine going crook.' The wine purists among us sometimes argue that vermouth itself tastes 'crook', though I'm not so sure.

Remember that vermouth is made from wine of various types. It is said to be almost as old as wine itself. In Roman times certain herbs and spices were believed to have had restorative and tonic effects, and the herbalists of the day infused these in wine to make them more palatable to patients. Herbalism and its associated activities have a strong advocacy and following today, so maybe the Roman method of making the medicine acceptable is worth another try. In the fifth century the Romans called wine infused with cinnamon and sweetened with honey *vinum Hippocratum.*

The popularity of spiced and aromatised wines continued through the intervening centuries. It seems certain that the use of herbs, flowers, barks and other natural spices also served to help preserve wine before science and technology provided winemakers with the means to prevent oxidation in wine. In any case, if the wine wasn't preserved, as my winemaking friend observed, at least it didn't taste as 'crook' as it would otherwise have done. I've always believed that a similar logic has led Australians to bathe meat pies in tomato sauce.

In the sixteenth century an infusion of the flowers of the wormwood* shrub made its way into Rhine wine. These 'wermut' flowers were adapted by the French to 'vermout' which was anglicised to 'vermouth'.

These wines obviously tasted different to those we now know. Today vermouth is the generic word we use for a blend of wines, usually but by no means always white and flavoured with a variety of herbs,

---

* *Wormwood* (Artemisia absinthium) *is no longer allowed to be used because of its toxic properties. In this case, absinth didn't really make the heart grow fonder!*

377

barks, roots, seeds and spices. The drink is usually fortified at some stage with alcohol and – if necessary – sweetened with either sugar syrup or with mistelle. Mistelle is grape juice in which further fermentation has been prevented by the addition of spirit; it therefore retains the natural sugar.

Vermouth is an even more complex beverage than wine itself, which makes it a complex taste sensation indeed. Because it is a wine-based product, unlike grain-based alcohols, it makes a good aperitif. And its considerable complexity turns the simple-sounding martini – essentially vermouth and gin in variable proportions – into a cocktail of much discussed finesse.

Vermouth is made in a number of countries, but it is best known from France and Italy. It is often assumed that French vermouth is dry and Italian sweet; in fact both countries make both styles, though generally in different ways.

The methods of vermouth production vary considerably, but include the main flavouring techniques of infusion, maceration and distillation. Essentially, ways of getting the flavours of the other materials into the wine itself.

With *maceration* the aromatic ingredients are steeped in a vat of wine for several weeks, the exact time depending on the rate of extraction (which in turn is affected by temperature). The wine is then drawn off and solid matter remaining is pressed to give a highly aromatised liquid which is portioned out into casks filled from the vat.

Infusion is similar to maceration, but the wine, or sometimes the alcohol that is involved, is continually passed through the herbs instead of lying on them.

Distillation involves using a still (as with brandy spirit) to obtain an aromatic liqueur which is added to and blended with the base wine. Sometimes a combination of two of the methods is used in vermouth production.

The aromatic ingredients may come from a long list. They include camomile flowers, elder flowers, gentian, marjoram, coriander seed, cinnamon, sage, thyme, vanilla, juniper, rosemary, cloves, orange and/or lemon peel, Chinese rhubarb, lemon balm

and even rose petals. I am told frogs' legs are a No-No. While the recipe for the basic mix is a well-kept secret (though some say as many as 59 herbs and other essences are used in various types), the base wines are simpler.

The different styles – which we will consider shortly – have the appropriate flavouring materials applied as per the particular maker's recipe. The exact formulas of the major makers (such as Cinzano and Martini) are as secret as the recipe for Coca-Cola. As with major brands of soft drink, biscuits, baked beans and wines, consistency is important with commercial vermouths.

If all these herbs and spices sound highly romantic, my winemaker mate (who used to make vermouth in Australia for a major maker) quickly disillusions one. 'When we were making the stuff,' he says, 'we used to buy from Italy bags of stuff labelled "Bianco herbs".' So much for gathering the flowers, bark and herbs in the fields. This stresses that there is not a tremendous market for vermouth wines in Australia, though it is certainly strong enough to make it profitable for several major foreign-owned makers and a few local winemakers. Though vermouth is made in many countries, including the United States, South America, Spain and Australia, clearly France and Italy are the key producers.

Several major foreign makers, notably Martini, Cinzano and Noilly Prat, operate and sell their products here. As times have become tougher in the domestic wine market place and rationalisations of one type and another (both by takeover and of product list) have taken place, the number of major makers making their own vermouth has declined. It is usually cheaper and simpler to buy the product from somebody else. Of the Australian makers, two stand out today: Yalumba in the high Barossa Valley, who until recently made their own brand most capably and who now make it under licence for Martini and Rossi; and the large Angove winery in the South Australian Riverland, whose excellent Marko brand is perhaps the leader in the small vermouth market.

Cinzano, who make their local product near Griffith in the New South Wales Riverina, make four

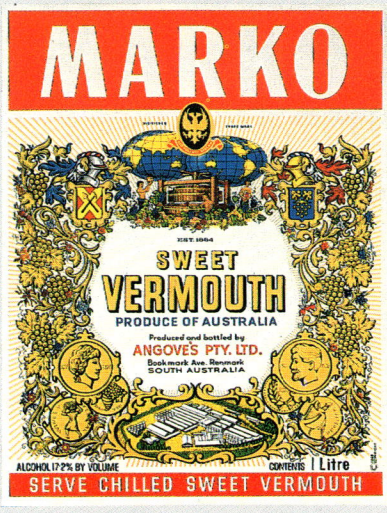

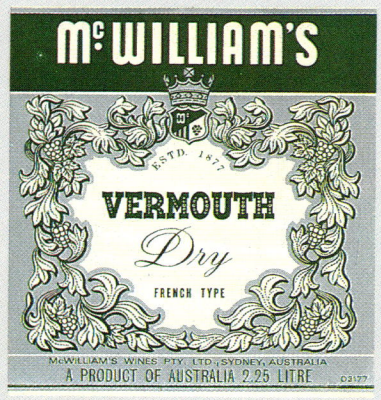

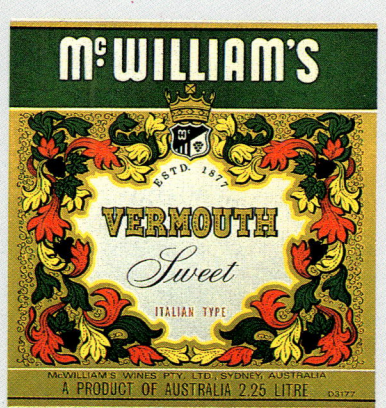

Neutral flavoured white wines from vineyards like these are used as the basis for the production of vermouth.

basic types: Rosso, which is red, and tastes tangy sweet; Extra Dry, almost colourless, and described as 'crisp dry'; Bianco, clear or pale yellow, and tasting sweet-soft and smooth; and Amaro, brown, and tasting creamy, bitter-sweet. The bitterness that comes from some herbs and flavourings is usefully offset in some of the vermouths by their sweetness, which comes from the addition of unfermented grape juice. Dr Max Lake discusses this elsewhere in 'The Taste of Wine'.

Most marketers of vermouth in Australia sell a range of products very similar to the Cinzano range. Cinzano, an aggressive marketer of vermouth and other alcoholic beverages, are market leaders, with some 60 per cent of vermouth sales.

How do you drink it? The aficionados of vermouth prefer it straight or with ice. After all, it *is* a complex palate sensation, especially as a pre-food appetiser. But most Australians prefer to mix it with something, either short (for example, as a martini), or long (with lemonade, soda, fruit juices or cordials). It really is a refreshing drink on a warm day.

But, you ask as a wine and food connoisseur, what do you eat with it? I would suggest better not to eat *with* vermouth, but later. I am, though, amused by the story of one English acquaintance, the managing director of a large City of London wine firm, who searched for years for a suitable drink to match asparagus. He eventually discovered what he claimed to be the perfect match: a dry vermouth from Chambery, one of the homes of French vermouth. He may be right, but with Australian asparagus I would suggest a Marko Dry vermouth.

VERMOUTH POSERS

HOW LONG WILL VERMOUTH KEEP?

Vermouth is fortified, usually to an alcohol level by volume of about 14-16 per cent; that is, it is somewhat stronger than most table wines and slightly lighter than most fortified wines. Therefore when opened, a bottle will keep some weeks but will eventually deteriorate, though slowly. Unopened, the wine will keep for some years and, while changing in character, will not improve.

WHAT BASE WINE IS USED TO MAKE VERMOUTH IN AUSTRALIA?

A number of bases are used. For example Cinzano use gordo dry white, a relatively bland white grape which crops vigorously in the irrigated areas. Others have used a similar dry sherry base wine or even a port wine base.

CAN IT BE MIXED WITH SPIRITS?

Certainly. Vermouth is the basis for some classic cocktails. With white rum in equal parts, Rosso vermouth makes 'El Presidente' (add crushed ice and stir well; garnish with a cherry). With Scotch whisky it makes the 'Rob Roy' (equal parts of Rosso vermouth and Scotch, dash Angostura bitters and stir well, garnish with a cherry). With Bourbon it makes the 'Manhattan' (Rosso vermouth plus two parts of Bourbon, add a dash of bitters, stir with ice and add a cherry). With vodka the 'Vodka Cooler' (one part dry vermouth plus two parts vodka, add juice of an orange, a big squeeze of lemon, stir and pour into a tall glass, serve with a dash of soda water and a slice of orange).

HOW DO I MAKE THE PERFECT MARTINI?

A fitting challenge with which to finish, as easy as answering 'Is there a God?' and 'Why do jam sandwiches always land on the carpet wrong way up?'

The classic *Savoy Cocktail Book* (Constable, London, 1930) gives these recipes.

★ Dry Martini: One-third French (dry) vermouth, two-thirds dry gin, shake well and strain into cocktail glass.

★ Medium Dry Martini: One-quarter French (dry) vermouth, one-quarter Italian (bianco) vermouth, one-half dry gin, shake well and stir into cocktail glass.

★ Martini Sweet: One-third Italian (bianco) vermouth, one-third London (not-so-dry) gin, shake well and strain into cocktail glass.

★ Martini Special Cocktail: Four glasses of gin, 1½ glasses of Italian (bianco) vermouth, one-third of a glass of orange cordial or juice, shake and add a couple of dashes of bitters. (Serves six.)

The winery at Robinson's Family Vineyards has some of the best equipment in the Granite Belt.

WINES AND WINERIES OF QUEENSLAND

David Bray

Years ago a senior government official told me that no acceptable wine was likely to be made in Queensland until new varieties of grapes were bred and people became used to the idea that wine could be made from these grapes. That thinking is no longer valid.

Grapes are grown and wine is made in Queensland centres as far apart as are Melbourne and Brisbane, but most of the State's wine comes from the Granite Belt, high on Great Dividing Range around the town of Stanthorpe. Just how much wine is actually made in Queensland from Queensland-grown grapes has never been established. Certainly it is a tiny proportion of the wine consumed in the State.

Statistical returns from makers do not provide exact answers, partly because of some interesting provisions of the law. Under the terms of Queensland's Wine Industry Act, there are three kinds of winemaker – restricted vignerons (who make wine for sale on land of which no less than 1 hectare is used for cultivation of grapes or other fruits or honey), vignerons (who make at least 20 000 litres of wine a year for sale from honey or grapes or other fruits grown within the Commonwealth); and vigneron-vinters

(who own premises for making wine situated on land having under cultivation not less than 10 hectares of grapevines or other fruits for winemaking and have an annual production of at least 50 000 litres). They

Vintage time on the Granite Belt has the touch of the old style about it. The whole family pitches in.

John Robinson is a lawyer at Toowoomba. He has put a good deal of money into the vineyard and winery at Lyra, most southerly of the Granite Belt wineries. This is the view from the terrace outside the tasting room.

must also comply with all sorts of health, local authority and other requirements.

There is more! Vignerons and vigneron-vinters 'may use for the purposes of blending wine that is not made by them to the extent of 30 per cent of the total quantity produced' and 'may bring onto their premises for use in the production of wine raw products to the extent of 50 per cent of the total raw product produced on the premises'.

Robinson's Family Vineyards moved the industry a step forward in April 1984, when they opened a retail cellar beneath their home in Margaret Street, Toowoomba. This was, obviously, their second licensed outlet and they achieved it by obtaining a vigneron-vintner's licence, then winning approval from the licensing and appropriate local authorities. The licence allows them to sell their own wine and Australian wine in single-bottle quantities, but the

amount of other people's wine they can sell is prescribed by an order-in-council.

A co-operative of Granite Belt wineries had gone through the same process several years earlier, opened a retail outlet in a Brisbane suburban shopping centre and, through a combination of circumstances, not all of them under their control, folded quite quickly. The Grays of Rumbalara tried a similar move, but ran up against the might of the Queensland hotel industry in suburban Brisbane and could not win the required licence. So the Robinson move is being closely watched by both their fellow winemakers and the whole liquor business.

In mid-1984 just nine wineries held Queensland vigneron's licences (allowing them to sell single bottles seven days a week at the winery). One of them was at the time in receivership and two others concerned themselves with wine made from fruit other than grapes. Another sixteen held restricted licences, which allowed them to sell a minimum of nine litres. These were either traditional old-style winemakers or newcomers to the industry, still building up their quality, quantities and facilities to meet licensing requirements.

The bulk trade is where it all started. The first grapes sent to the Brisbane market from the Stanthorpe area were grown by Thomas Fletcher, who arrived in the Ballandean district in 1872. It is recorded that Fletcher made some wine, but there was no great enthusiasm for either the grapes or wine until Father Jerome Davadi planted out a vineyard at his presbytery in 1878 and made some wine in his cellars. The remains of those cellars can still be seen.

Enthusiasm waned after a few years and there is no record of winemaking activity in the district until 1928, when Messrs Constanza and Musumeci put in table grapes where Joe Ricca and Dick de Luca now have their vineyards. Within a few years there were other vineyards around Ballandean and a little to the north, around Pozieres.

Two generations and more ago the grape-growers, many of them of Italian parentage, found a demand from the cane and tobacco growing areas along the

coast for both their grapes and their wine. They were more than happy to send off 44-gallon drums of their highly individual wines. Some of them still do just that. Others have converted (or are still doing so) their vineyards and wineries to produce and use grapes that are these days believed to produce better wine.

Around the southern Darling Downs and the southern Granite Belt there are probably twenty enthusiasts of varying degrees of skill, knowledge and financial weight. Not all of them are licensed to sell their product. There is good wine being made in small quantities at Jandowae, at Chinchilla, and at Severnlea. And well into the tropics there is a very promising enterprise – Sunshine Wines of Mackay, run by an expatriate Canadian electronics entrepreneur, L. H. Bakken. Peter Love, who had the small Elsinore vineyard and winery on the outskirts of Brisbane, has re-established at Glen Aplin. We should hear more about these people in the next few years.

Old Caves is the only Granite Belt winery with its cellar door right on the main road. David Zanatta built it here, just on the northern outskirts of Stanthorpe, and here he made the best red of the 1985 Stanthorpe Show, from grapes grown by Preben Jacobsen.

The Grays of Rumbalara have their standards . . .

*The fruits of his labours . . .
John Robinson in the
tasting room of Robinson's
Family Vineyards. He made
the lot.*

turning out quality wines. It is doing just that – some of the time. It can be argued that the Granite Belt is at the same stage as the Hunter Valley one generation ago.

The argument applies at several levels. There are five, perhaps six, serious winemaking operations; technical expertise is just beginning to influence the instinctive skills of the enthusiastic winemakers; tourist facilities in the district are improving (there are plenty of motel beds, but nowhere near enough good eating places), and public acceptance is less than whole-hearted.

Already there are moves to make two wine districts of the Granite Belt. From the New South Wales border north to Fletcher would be known as Ballandean, anything north of Fletcher would be Stanthorpe.

Whether or not this technical division should be made, or made public, is a matter for argument. What is fact is that the southern part of the Granite Belt has by all accepted standards an eminently suitable climate for growing wine grapes. It is, for example, significantly cooler than the Hunter and has a lower summer rainfall than that part of the world. Although January and February are wet months (sometimes very wet indeed), the rainfall figures drop dramatically after that, and April, when many grapes are picked, is the driest month.

A good deal of statistical work in this area is being done by Peter Scudamore-Smith, a scientist with the Queensland Department of Primary Industries, who is also a wine judge at major shows. He is Queensland's second Riverina College (N.S.W.) wine science graduate and probably the most knowledgeable authority on Queensland wines. In brief, the figures seem to show that the climate of the southern part of the Granite Belt is very much like that of the area around Avoca, Victoria.

If the grapes are good, it is then up to the winemakers to acquire the technical skill to make the best possible use of their material. The technical training of Queensland winemakers tends, for geographical reasons, to come from the Riverina College of Advanced Education at Wagga Wagga, rather

But, to return to the established names. Far, far to the north, at Herberton on the Atherton Tableland, the Foster family have for some years been improving their wines – and incidentally the palates of the local drinkers who (like many north Queenslanders who bother with wine) tend to prefer the grappa style. Out west, 500 kilometres from Brisbane, David Wall has been working for years to bring Bassett's of Romavilla up to date with wine technology. Sometimes he must wonder why he bothers, such is the devotion of so many people west of the Divide to the old style of Bassett's sauternes and port (Romavilla Vineyards have been winemakers since 1863). It is with the fortified styles, madeira, sherry, muscat and port, that Romavilla's immediate future seems to lie. They are winning recognition from show judges and drinkers, while the dry table styles seem generally to have some way to go.

Which brings us back to the Granite Belt, which many people, particularly Queenslanders, think also has a way to go but is in fact very nearly there.

This is one of Australia's great table grape areas and there is no real reason why it should not also be

than South Australia's Roseworthy College. Bob Gray, of Granite Belt Vignerons, was Queensland's first graduate of the Wagga wine science course. His son Chris will be the third. John Robinson of Robinson's Family Vineyards also studied there under Brian Croser. Angelo Puglisi, who for practical purposes pioneered the making of quality wines in the Granite Belt, however, spent four months in Europe in 1977 on a Churchill Fellowship studying winemaking, viticulture and marketing. He has recently appointed a Roseworthy graduate to his winery staff.

Queensland wine is at present no business for beginners who want to make money. The technical expertise is there, but like wine anywhere else, it is a business requiring canny marketing. The business is not big enough to justify buying professional marketing advice – but without that advice its future is limited.

One of the more important tools of wine marketing is the wine show, with its public awarding of

medals by experienced judges. The Stanthorpe Agricultural Society has some hard thinking to do if it wants its wine section to be, as it could be, the principal show for Queensland wines. There are two other contenders for that title – the Royal National Association Brisbane Exhibition, and the Redlands Show at Cleveland, an area that has no apparent connection with winemaking other than enthusiasm for the product. Brisbane has the advantage of having senior interstate judges and professionally organised publicity. But it is held too soon after vintage for many winemakers (the Granite Belt vintage is for the reasons already explained later than many) and the Queensland element tends to be overwhelmed by the numbers of the open, national competition.

Redlands also uses at least one interstate judge and generally has the enthusiastic support of Granite Belt and Roma winemakers. But it is held even earlier than Brisbane, in June, while many wines are still bubbling away in their fermenters.

The Stanthorpe wine show is held in February, and should be favoured by the winemakers, but in 1984 its committee stepped backwards by appointing only two judges, both of them Queenslanders. The

Insulated fermenting tanks in the cool room at the well-equipped Robinson's Family Winery.

Angelo Puglisi's Sundown Valley has some of the oldest big wood in Queensland. Cleaning it up was a problem, now well in hand.

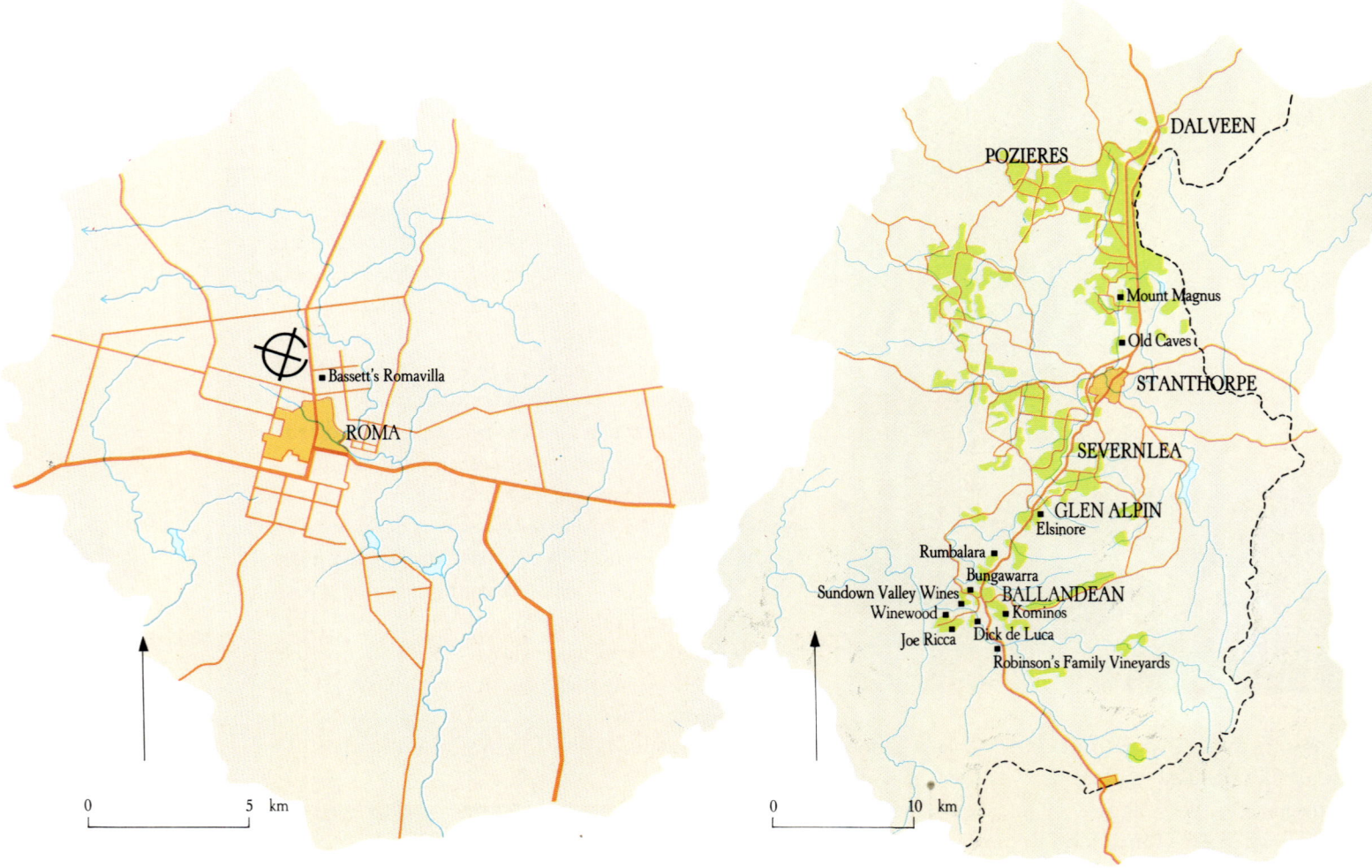

men concerned were very well qualified and highly experienced, but there was some feeling that a panel of two was too small. It was not a matter of the workload on judging day (entries in 1984 were disappointingly low), but of the statistical chances of avoiding palate preferences. Not having an interstate judge simply compounded the problems of perceived parochialism. That said, it must also be recorded that judges were far from impressed and found it necessary to record that 'the quality of the white table wines, both dry and sweet, tended to show that close attention is required to retain varietal character'. They awarded only four bronze medals to current

vintage wines – to Granite Belt Vignerons for its semillon and its chardonnay, and to Robinson's Family Vineyards for its chardonnay and sweet traminer. They were much more impressed by the 1983 reds, giving golds to both Robinson's and Bungawarra for their cabernets, silvers to Sundown Valley for cabernet and for shiraz, a silver to Bungawarra's shiraz and a silver and a bronze to Robinson's pinot noirs.

Here, then, starting from the south (just north of the New South Wales border) are the Granite Belt wineries that hold vignerons' licences.

ROBINSON'S FAMILY VINEYARDS

John Robinson is a lawyer at Toowoomba and was a wine enthusiast even before he married his wife Heather, formerly Salter, of Saltram's, Angaston. They began work on their vineyard at Lyra in 1969. They now have 9 hectares there and another 6 hectares a little further north. They specialise in classic white and red varietal wines and have had their share of show awards in both areas. The wines made are Family Chardonnay (with Limousin oak), Family Traminer (clean, aromatic, with some residual sugar), Family Cabernet Sauvignon (elegant, with Nevers oak; a gold medal winner), Family Pinot Noir (soft, flavoursome with unusually good colour), Family Shiraz/Cabernet (90/10, well-balanced, gold medallist), and Lyra White (a fruity blend with some chardonnay and some residual sugar).

John Robinson is well qualified in the art of winemaking, as well as being president of the Queensland Winemakers' Association.

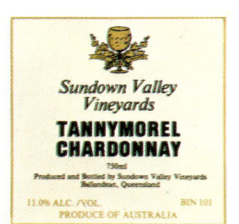

Angelo and Mary Puglisi are among the real pioneers of the newlook Granite Belt wine industry. This is their Sundown Valley shopfront.

Churchill Fellow winemaker Angelo Puglisi, of Sundown Valley, appraises his handiwork.

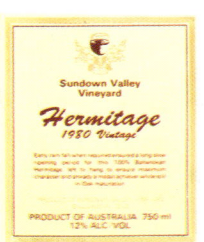

SUNDOWN VALLEY WINES

Angelo and Mary Puglisi moved this older vineyard (established by Angelo's grandfather Salvatore in 1930) into wine grapes in 1969. In 1974 they won the first medals ever awarded to Queensland wines at a major show with two bronzes at Brisbane with cabernet and a shiraz/cabernet. They have had their good and hard times since then, but in 1984 Sundown was the most successful exhibitor at the Stanthorpe Show. They offer eighteen different wines at cellar door, and a smaller number in 25-litre, 60-litre and 204-litre drums. Among the bottled lines available in 1984 were: 1981 Cabernet Sauvignon, 1980 Hermitage (a well-balanced wine that is a house wine at Brisbane's Crest International Hotel), 1980 Claret (light,

fruity shiraz), 1983 Rhine Riesling, 1982 Semillon (with new oak and a medal winner), 1980 Port (Angelo's first, and one with which he is delighted) and Goldminers Liqueur White Muscat (luscious, full bodied and fortified).

BUNGAWARRA VINEYARDS

Bungawarra is run by a thundering herd of partners who give every appearance of enjoying life while making some interesting, and often enough good, wines. The vineyard was established in the late 1920s by an Italian farmer who, like more than a few of his compatriots in the district, made wine (from the table grapes) for Italian communities from south of the border to Cairns. An English couple owned it briefly, then Alan Dorr and Philip Christensen bought the place and produced their first vintage in 1979. They surprised most people by winning a gold medal at the Redland show with the first Bungawarra shiraz. There are now seven partners, all professional types

and all but one from the Darling Downs. As well as Dorr and Christensen, they are Ian Mathieson, Jon Davies, Allan Edwards, Henry Eastment and Greg Lamerton. Bungawarra has just over a hectare of chardonnay, almost one of cabernet sauvignon, and half each of traminer and pinot noir and a little bit of malbec. They are looking at another hectare or so and then at extending storage and bottling plant.

Their 1982 Hermitage won the trophy for the best entry in the Dry Red, Soft Finish (Burgundy style) 1982 vintage Small Vineyard class at the 1982 National Wine Show, Canberra. It is still available. The 1982 Cabernet won a similar trophy in its class at the same show, and three local Queensland trophies. It has sold out. On the current list are: 1982 Hermitage (light and soft), 1982 Hermitage/Cabernet (complex, 12 months American oak), 1983 Semillon (clean, with some sugar), 1983 Wood Matured Semillon (five weeks in new American oak), a moselle style blend using some wine from northern Victoria, a dry red ordinaire blend of hermitage and muscat, and a liqueur muscat.

Not so long ago, Bungawarra had not much more than the most basic equipment. Here's the new setup.

The Granite Belt lies high on the border between Queensland and New South Wales. The rock mass in the background behind the Bungawarra vines is typical of the area.

391

GRANITE BELT VIGNERONS

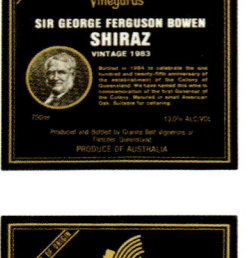

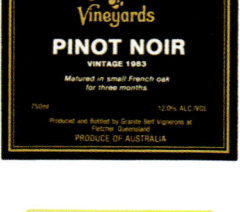

This is a partnership (Bob Gray, Doug Hall and Doug Custance) producing limited quantities of quality table wines under the labels Rumbalara and Girrawheen. They have a total of 24 hectares planted, and the significant varieties are chardonnay, Rhine riesling and semillon, cabernet sauvignon, shiraz and pinot noir. The wine is made at Rumbalara, a property bought by Bob and Una Gray from the Verri family in 1974. Bob is an engineer by profession and made the partnership wines until the last few years, when son Chris took over. As previously stated, Bob was Queensland's first graduate from the Riverina College wine science course and Chris will be the

third. Bob still makes the fortified wines and ciders (among which have been award winners in interstate shows). GBV has sold white wine to Germany, is on the wine list of several of Brisbane's top restaurants and has won its share of trophies, including Best Dry White Queensland Classes at Brisbane 1983. Wines on the general list are: Girrawheen Dry White, Girrawheen Weisswei, Girrawheen Granitegold, Rumbalara Gluewein, Rumbalara Shiraz, the 1983 Vintage Port, dry and sweet vermouth, liqueur muscat, and two ciders.

On limited release are 1983 Rhine Riesling, 1983 Semillon (the trophy winner), 1983 Chardonnay (full, soft palate and a Brisbane silver medallist), 1983 Cabernet Sauvignon (with 5 per cent cabernet franc and 10 per cent mataro, a gold and a silver medal), and 1983 Sir George Ferguson Bowen Shiraz named to celebrate separation from New South Wales.

Winemaker Chris Gray at home with his vines.

OLD CAVES WINERY

David and John Zanatta are still buying in most of their grapes, but this newest winery on the Granite Belt is the best situated in the district – right on the highway just outside Stanthorpe. The list includes riesling, moselle, spumante, mead, rosé, claret, sweet sherry, tawny port, rummy port, blackberry nip and coffee marsala.

MT MAGNUS

Formerly Biltmore Cellars, this was set up by the Zanatta family in 1933 and stayed with them until November 1980, when it was sold to a Brisbane family. John Matthews bought the property late in 1984 and installed Kevin McCarthy as winemaker. He inherited thirteen different lines, including moselle, riesling, 1982 Cervant, 1980 and 1982 Rosé, 1981 Shiraz Cabernet (80/20), 1982 Shiraz, muscat, and apricot nip.

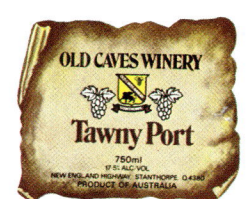

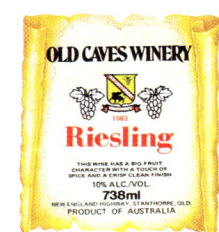

Old Caves is strongly salesorientated, as this setup suggests.

Rumbalara is where Bob, Una and Chris Gray have their home and make some of the district's best whites.

393

The imposing entrance to Leeuwin Estate, near Margaret River, about 250 kilometres south of Perth. The winery, owned by millionaire Perth businessman Denis Horgan, is the jewel in the region's wine crown.

WINES AND WINERIES OF WESTERN AUSTRALIA

David Foster

As with most other parts of Australia which were settled after 1800, the Swan Colony shared the experience of vines being planted almost within minutes of the British flag being planted. New arrivals to Western Australia, like their fettered brothers and sisters who misguidedly headed for the eastern seaboard of *Terra Australis,* came mainly by the Cape of Good Hope, where vine cuttings were as much a part of bills of lading as fresh water and foodstuffs for the final leg of the trek.

The evolution of Western Australia's wine industry, taking a retrospective look, can be seen as occurring in four distinct phases.

★ Post-1800 settlement of the Swan Valley, near Perth.

★ The arrival of central and southern European immigrants which started with the gold rush of the 1890s and accelerated at the end of World War I.

★ The singular efforts of Jack Mann, who put in more than fifty vintages at Valencia-Houghton in the Swan Valley from 1922 onwards.

★ The mid-1960s research which paved the way for latter-day development of new viticultural areas in the south-west of Western Australia.

Winemakers also have to be labourers when vintage is underway. Evans & Tate's Bill Crappsley lends a hand.

Jon Reynolds, chief winemaker at Houghton, based in the Swan Valley. He was born in the Hunter Valley, New South Wales, and worked as a winemaker in South Australia before going to Perth. His best known product is Houghton White Burgundy.

Among the first colonists to attempt winemaking seriously was a botanist, Thomas Waters, who was commissioned by the Viticultural Society to spread the word among would-be vignerons through an almanac. Waters set up a vineyard and winery on the banks of the Swan River at South Guildford, close to what is now Perth Airport, making his first wine sometime in the early 1830s. Waters, who had had some practical winemaking and viticultural experience in South Africa, dug a cellar at his winery, which is still used today by the Yurisich family, proprietors of Olive Farm Wines.

The first surveyor-general of the colony, John Septimus Roe, took up a land grant on the Swan at Caversham, upstream from Waters' property, and planted vines in 1840. Grape-growing has continued virtually uninterrupted since and the Roe family still has a direct interest in the company now known as Sandalford Wines.

Possibly the most significant nineteenth century step on the road to a wine industry being established in Western Australia occurred in 1856 when the Ferguson family took over the Houghton property in Middle Swan and commenced commercial wine pro-

duction in 1859. This was the first step in the establishment of Houghton Wines, today the top volume producer in the State.

It has been remarked on many times that the medical profession has had a profound influence on various phases of Western Australia's wine industry. It was Dr John Ferguson, Western Australian colonial surgeon, who made the first wine at Houghton and, to a large extent, it was Ferguson's latter-day colleagues who led the way in pioneering the Margaret River region in the 1960s. Whatever science or art Waters introduced to winemakers during his time as the leading authority was taken a step further in the 1890s when Mauritian-born Adrian Despeissis, a viticultural authority, seconded to the Western Australian Bureau of Agriculture from an equivalent body in New South Wales.

Despeissis, who eventually opted to join the Western Australian department at the end of his term of secondment, had studied at the Royal Agricultural College in London and worked in the French wine industry. In addition to writing his comprehensive *Handbook of Horticulture and Viticulture of Western Australia,* published in 1895, Despeissis was the first man to introduce local winemakers to fermentation temperature control, cultured yeasts and sterile bottling.

The period between Federation and World War I saw the Swan Valley become entrenched as the heart of Western Australia's winegrowing industry while

occasional small-scale producers battled to make wines at various locations in the south-west corner of the State. Yugoslavian migrants, mostly from Dalmatia, who had settled in the Swan during the gold-rush days, were joined by their countryfolk in the post-war years, making a distinct impression on the region – not only because of their labour and diligence, but also due to the types of wines they made, primarily for home consumption. The region became known for its fortified styles, made from any grapes ranging from grenache and shiraz to pedro ximinez, muscat, and doradillo.

It's not putting too fine a point on it to say the Western Australian wine industry grew in virtual isolation until the 1950s, largely oblivious to happenings in the winemaking regions of South Australia, New South Wales and Victoria. An occasional ripple ran through the infant Western Australian industry with events such as Jack Mann's oloroso sherries winning awards in the Eastern States in and around the 1930s, with the occasional liqueur frontignac or other sweet whites thrown in for good measure in the trophy stakes. Some sort of Australian record must

Dusting the vines behind a tractor at Houghton's Frankland River vineyards, some 300 kilometres south-east of Perth. The spraying keeps pests and vine diseases under control.

Checking wine quality at Houghton's quality control centre in the Swan Valley.

1936 or 1937 when Jack Mann convinced the Ferguson family to purchase a Seitz germ-proof filter – the first to be imported into Australia – giving him newfound access to sterile filtration. One of the first wines which went through the filter was a chenin blanc which found immediate success at the Melbourne Show. It was a white wine such as judges of the day had not seen before and they were taken by its full flavour, softness and a touch of honeyed character.

Prophetically, as it transpired, one judge, W. W. Senior, likened Mann's chenin blanc to the white Burgundies of France. *Voilà* . . . the birth of Houghton's legendary Blue Stripe White Burgundy in 1937 – the first Western Australian table wine to capture any sort of attention in the Eastern States.

Houghton White Burgundy (HWB) became the flagship of Western Australian table wine from the 1940s onward, with a great deal of visible and vocal

Jack Mann – his white burgundy changed the face of Western Australian wine.

Harvesting the grapes at Redgate's vineyard. Getting ripe fruit in before the birds eat the grapes is sometimes a problem in the Margaret River area.

have been set by Jack Mann when he won the Australian champion award for his oloroso thirteen years in succession.

It was Jack Mann, in fact, who battled the odds for years in carving out any sort of reputation at all for the Western Australian wine industry east of the Nullarbor Plain. He succeeded his father, George, as winemaker at Houghton in 1930 after starting his apprenticeship at the age of sixteen in 1922. George Mann had been enticed to Houghton by Charles William Ferguson in 1910 from Chateau Tanunda, South Australia, which he had joined in 1890, shortly after its formation, working alongside a French winemaker.

The mainstay of Houghton at the beginning of the Jack Mann era was fortified wines – products uniquely suited to the warm climate of the Swan Valley and matched only for quality in Australia by sweet wines from the north-east of Victoria. Stories are legend of the high grape-sugar levels Jack used to get from his Middle Swan vineyards.

Although the event has since paled into the mists of Western Australian winemaking history, a major turning point in table wine production occurred in

support from a Sydney restaurateur and wine man, Johnnie Walker, who had also done much to help Maurice O'Shea's Hunter wines gain the recognition they so deserved. HWB went on to become one of the top Australian table wines in sales.

It was largely due to the demand for HWB that Houghton, then owned by the English-based Emu Wine Co., started looking for viticultural land out-side the Swan Valley. The company's search eventu-ally led it to Gingin, some 40 kilometres north of what is generally considered the northern boundary of the valley, where 1000 hectares of land were bought in 1968.

With more than 100 hectares under vine, Houghton's Moondah Brook Estate at Gingin is planted to the two white varieties which constitute HWB, chenin blanc and tokay. The first major expansionary phase of the Western Australian wine industry had begun.

At around the same time that Houghton was look-ing to spread its vines, there were the first signs of what were to become significant new regions in the south-west corner of the State. The establishment of the Gingin, Margaret River and Mt Barker-Frank-land regions can be fairly said to have had its origins in several directly connected circumstances in the post-World War II period.

The first was the appointment of Bill Jamieson in 1950 as government viticulturist. Jamieson, a returned serviceman who completed a Roseworthy College Agricultural course, was to have a profound influence on the Western Australian wine industry before he retired in 1978.

The second circumstance which was to have far-reaching effects was the arrival in Western Australia in 1955 of Professor Harold Olmo, a world-renowned viticulturist from the Davis campus of the University of California. Olmo spent nearly a year in Western Australia under a government-sponsored research trust fund studying the State's winegrowing and vit-icultural industry. Olmo, in his comprehensive study of the Swan Valley, drew attention to the viticultural possibilities in the cooler climes of Western Australia's south-west corner (vindicating, by the

way, similar prophecies made earlier by Jack Mann and Maurice O'Shea; the latter is reported to have said that if he had his time again in the Australian wine industry he would have headed for those areas).

Olmo's report, among other things, included two recommendations which, in retrospect, completely changed the nature and complexion of the State's winemaking industry.

The first was the appointment of an extension oenologist to assist small winemakers in the Swan Valley. The appointee was Dorham Mann, son of Jack, who graduated from Roseworthy College in 1963 after completing an agricultural science degree at the University of Western Australia. The second was the establishment of a grape industry committee in 1963 which was given the specific assignment of investigating potential regions south of Perth. The committee comprised Bill Jamieson, Jack Mann and David Roe, then winemaker at Sandalford.

Dorham Mann spent the years 1963 to 1973 mainly in the Swan Valley, quietly going about persuading small winemakers to reassess their winemaking practices and procedures. There is little doubt that in the cases of many producers there was a strong need for reassessment. Swan Valley table wines, particularly reds, had gained the unenviable reputation of being clumsy and coarse with an inherited 'Swan Valley stink'.

It was largely due to Mann's influence that the region's producers gradually upgraded their plantings, installed new equipment, and took a more pragmatic approach to the marketplace for both table and fortified wines. The change in attitudes and winemaking procedures was timely as the great flagon and cask war was about to be unleashed by major Australian producers against whom Swan Valley winemakers could not hope to compete.

The real metamorphosis of the Western Australian wine industry occurred between 1965 and 1967, with a chain of events which resulted in the establishment of two of the most potentially exciting winegrowing regions in Australia. In 1965, Dr John Gladstones, a winelover and then an agronomist with the University of Western Australia's Institute of

Vineyards near Margaret River, about 250 kilometres south of Perth. Some of the most exciting young red wines in Australia are coming from this area.

Picking ripe black grapes for Plantagenet Wines, near Mt Barker. Here, about 380 kilometres south-east of Perth, is one of the most isolated wine areas of Australia.

Agriculture, published a report. 'The Climate and Soils of South-Western Australia in Relation to Vine Growing', in the *Journal of the Australian Institute of Agricultural Science*. Gladstones' paper was the first scientific look at the viticultural potential for areas south of Perth and he drew particular attention to the opportunities offered around Margaret River, with its Mediterranean-type climate.

In 1967 the Department of Agriculture's viticulture section, following the advice of the government-appointed grape industry committee to establish an experimental vineyard in the Great Southern area, leased 3 hectares of land on the Forest Hill property of Tony and Betty Pearse, planting it to roughly half Rhine riesling and half cabernet sauvignon. The first vines in the Margaret River region were planted in 1967 by a Perth physician, Thomas Brendan Cullitty, at Vasse Felix. He was shortly followed by another doctor, Bill Pannell, at Moss Wood.

The first major planting programme in the Mt Barker-Frankland region was inspired by the Department of Agriculture in 1969 within an 8000-hectare grazing property at Frankland River owned by a former Lord Mayor of Adelaide, John Roche.

In 1972 Sandalford Wines, which had sought the advice of Dorham Mann, selected a large tract of land over the road from Moss Wood and set about planting a 140-hectare vineyard at Margaret River. It was no coincidence that Mann joined Sandalford from the Department of Agriculture the following year.

The early wines from Pearse's Forest Hill vineyard at Mt Barker and Roche's Frankland River Grazing Co. property were made at Sandalford by Mann. Neither he nor the industry could have wished for a more auspicious introduction than a 1975 Rhine riesling from Forest Hill which appeared under a Sandalford label. The wine won five gold medals and several trophies in Perth, Melbourne and Adelaide. The first cabernet sauvignons did not achieve the same acclaim, but at least served the purpose of establishing that the region had the potential for red varieties and eventually led newcomers to consider alternatives such as shiraz.

Although the future of the industry is surely linked

to areas south of Perth, with possible room for expansion within tracts of land such as Gingin to the north and Bindoon to the north-north-east, there are several big question marks hanging over the Swan Valley. The industry's two major companies — Houghton (controlled by Thomas Hardy & Sons) and Sandalford (controlled by Calbeck Macgregor Australia Ltd) — have established production bases in the valley, accounting for something like 80 per cent of Western Australia's total production. But the real future of the region will be decided by government attitudes.

The local authority, the Shire of Swan, faces the problem of rating equity for a primary industry within an otherwise urbanised area. The Metropolitan Regional Planning Authority is a strong proponent of vineyards being retained as green belt and the Tourist Development Authority is pushing retention of the wine industry, appreciating the opportunities on Perth's doorstep. However, it remains an open-ended question as to how long second- and third-generation winemakers of Yugoslav and Italian stock can resist the temptation of escalating land values, and selling out to developers.

Boxes of late picked, hence very ripe, fruit arriving at Mike Goundrey's winery near Denmark, in the south-western corner of Western Australia.

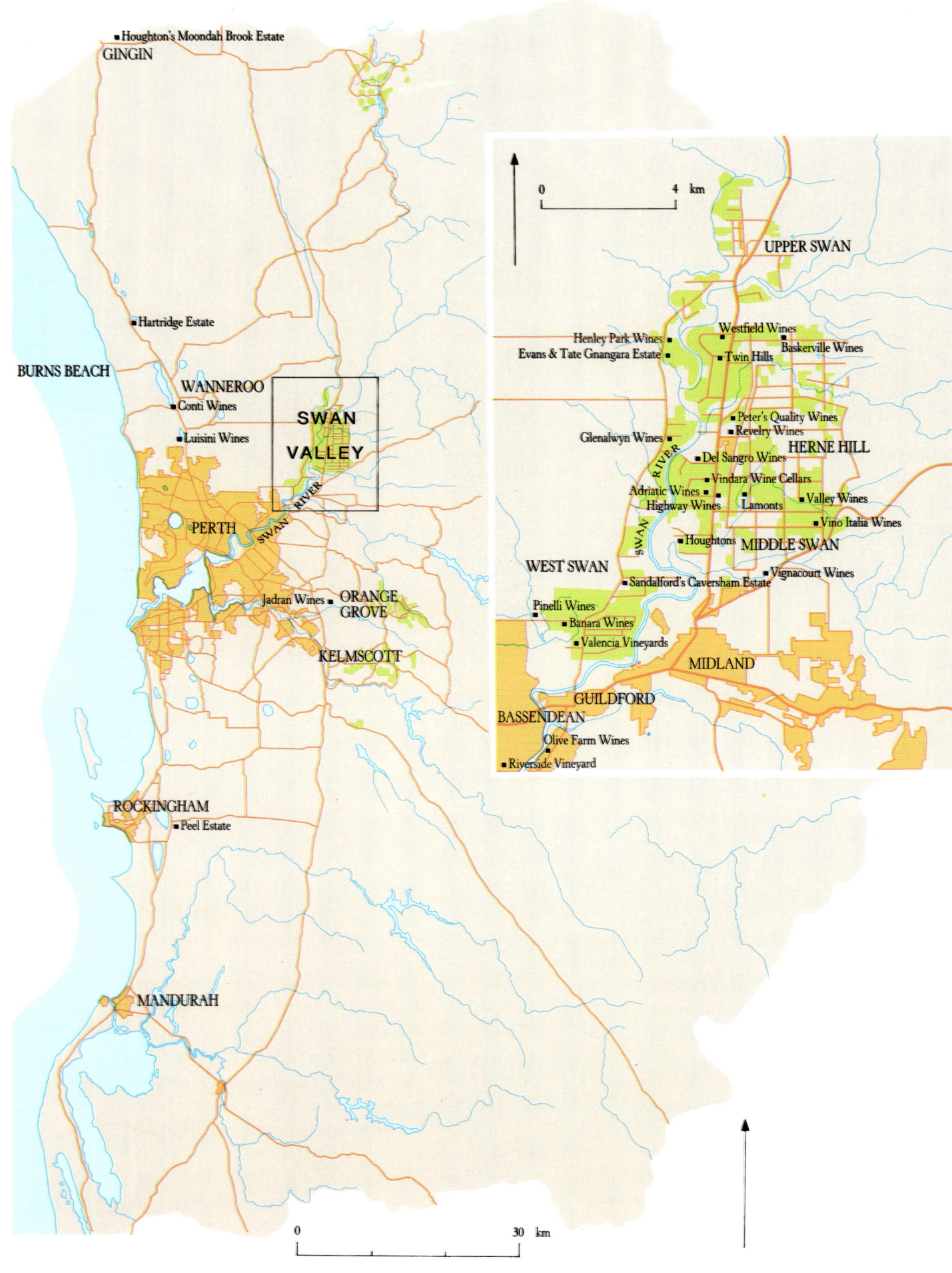

■ Houghton's Moondah Brook Estate

GINGIN

■ Hartridge Estate

BURNS BEACH

WANNEROO

SWAN
VALLEY

■ Conti Wines

■ Luisini Wines

PERTH

Jadran Wines ■

ORANGE
GROVE

KELMSCOTT

ROCKINGHAM

■ Peel Estate

MANDURAH

UPPER SWAN

0   4 km

Henley Park Wines ■   Westfield Wines ■
Evans & Tate Gnangara Estate ■   ■ Baskerville Wines
                        ■ Twin Hills

Glenalwyn Wines ■   ■ Peter's Quality Wines
                ■ Revelry Wines
                        HERNE HILL
                ■ Del Sangro Wines
                ■ Vindara Wine Cellars
Adriatic Wines ■   ■   ■ Valley Wines
Highway Wines ■   Lamonts
                        ■ Vino Italia Wines
                ■ Houghtons
                        MIDDLE SWAN
WEST SWAN   ■ Vignacourt Wines
        ■ Sandalford's Caversham Estate
Pinelli Wines ■
        ■ Banara Wines
        ■ Valencia Vineyards
                        MIDLAND

GUILDFORD
BASSENDEAN
        ■ Olive Farm Wines
■ Riverside Vineyard

0   30 km

SWAN VALLEY

The region's vineyards and wineries, contained within its 104 square kilometres, are a diverse lot, to say the least. In any appraisal of the State's and the valley's wine industry, one keeps coming back to the fact that the big two, Houghton and Sandalford, dominate the scene like a pair of benign, older brothers.

Production levels in the valley fall away dramatically from those of Houghton (200 000 cases of wine) and Sandalford (85 000 cases) to the remainder which are mainly small, family controlled operations.

A combination of factors (including the Dorham Mann influence, the emergence of a new breed of graduate and work-experience winemakers, reassess-ment of varieties and plantings, installation of new equipment, and gradually increasing sophistication of the marketplace) have given rise to some remarkably good wines from the Swan Valley since the late 1960s. By and large the new breed of winemakers has overcome the problems associated with hot ferments and come to accept the desirability of using high technology. Apart from its unique fortified and dessert styles, the valley is perfectly capable nowadays of coming up with eminently drinkable table wines with reds made from cabernet sauvignon, shiraz and zinfandel, and whites made from chenin blanc, verdelho and semillon, all of which would hold their own at blind tastings.

Grapeskins being taken out of a press at Evans & Tate's Swan Valley winery, renowned for its Gnangara reds.

Immature grape berries are shielded from the sun by their canopy of leaves.

The valley's very climate and concentrated ripening season defy the likelihood of grapes achieving natural acid levels to give its wines the staying power of counterparts from lower latitudes. However, whenever I hear Jack Mann's comment that 'a good wine should be glowing with life, adorned with flavour and blessed with refinement', I'm tempted to reach for an easy drinking Swan Valley cabernet or a luscious helping of verdelho; and, dare I say it, remind those around me that there's not a lot of difference in latitude between the Swan and Hunter Valleys. Every region, it seems, has its cross to bear and glories to offer.

I have written about only eleven of the valley's thirty-plus wineries. If there are such things as sins of omission, I would prefer to think of the sins that have been perpetrated by those producers who have yet to witness the dawn of twentieth-century winemaking in Australia or those whose inexorable libations are delivered to the back doors of second-rate eateries under the cloak of night.

COORINJA

By some sleight of geographic hand, Coorinja Vineyard is generally classified as a Swan Valley producer, despite the fact it is located at Toodyay, 50 kilometres north-east of Perth, and at least 40 kilometres away from its nearest Swan 'neighbour'. Brothers Hector and Doug Wood can fairly lay claim to being their own people when it comes to making wine, dismissing (in the nicest possible way) many of the fripperies of modern-day wineries. Not a great deal has changed at Coorinja since the Wood family took over the property in 1919, 49 years after vines were first planted, with the exception of a new 8-hectare vineyard planted in 1970.

The 85-tonne crush from the 25-hectare Coorinja vineyard comprises mainly shiraz, pedro ximinez, grenache and muscat from which a limited range of red and white table wines and port styles are made – essentially in the 'traditional' way with open concrete fermenting vats and large, old wood and storage. Coorinja has developed a small, devoted following over many years and the people least concerned about comparison are the Wood brothers. Given the demand for their wines, albeit assisted by what can only be described as giveaway prices, they know they are doing something right. The company's main claim to fame is its ports, distinguished by their fruitiness, body, and sound, clean spirit.

EVANS & TATE

Perhaps no other small producer has done more for the Swan Valley's growing reputation for premium quality tables wines than Evans & Tate, a partnership which started as a long-time interest in wine shared by business associates John Tate and John Evans.

John Tate is a respected wine judge who shared a

After the wine has been made, the winemaker must decide whether blending is needed, perhaps with wines from other varieties or other areas, to get the desired result. Bill Crappsley, right, discusses a young Evans & Tate red with John Tate.

Winemaker Bill Crappsley drawing a young red from wood storage to monitor its progress.

Co-owner of Gnangara Estate John Tate and his wife Tony relax with a bottle of their wine.

long-standing love of French reds with his partner.

In 1971 the two established a vineyard on John Evans' property at Baker's Hill, 60 kilometres east of Perth. The following year Evans & Tate purchased Gnangara Estate on the western margin of the Swan Valley, replanting the vineyard to selected shiraz and cabernet sauvignon. Evans & Tate expanded their vineyard interests to Margaret River and the first wines from the company's 25-hectare Redbrook vineyard at Willyabrup were made in 1979. The plantings included sauvignon, shiraz, merlot, semillon, chardonnay, sauvignon blanc and gewurtztraminer.

Gnangara Estate crushes 44 tonnes of cabernet sauvignon and shiraz from West Swan and 100 tonnes from Margaret River, which will rise to 150 tonnes when Redbrook is in full bearing. The company's maiden wine, a 1974 Gnangara shiraz, won medals in Perth, Melbourne and Canberra, blazing the trail for what was to become one of the most decorated reds produced from the Swan, the 1977 Gnangara Shiraz, which won 14 medals and 2 trophies at capital city wine shows. In 1978 a talented winemaker, Bill Crappsley, joined them after 17 vintages with producers such as Basedow, Redman, d'Arenberg and Houghton. Ownership of Evans & Tate passed to John Tate and his wife, Tony, in July 1983. The combined talents and dedication of John Tate and Bill Crappsley will continue to see Evans & Tate among the leaders in Australia's quality wine stakes.

GLENALWYN

If one was looking for a model of the effect Yugoslav migrants had (and continue to have) on the Swan Valley wine industry, it would be hard to go past the 9-hectare vineyard and winery established by George Pasalich shortly after his arrival in Australia in 1933 and now run by his son, Len, one of the industry's most affable characters.

Most of Glenalwyn's crush of around 50 tonnes is destined for flagons, the backbone of its sales for many years. Len has continued his father's tradition of making excellent vintage ports and has given increasing attention since taking over the reins to developing sales for table wines from estate-grown chenin blanc, verdelho, shiraz and cabernet sauvignon.

One attribute of Glenalwyn wines which never fails to impress me, be they fortifieds or table wines, is the true-to-variety character which Len manages to obtain. His verdelho and cabernet sauvignon, for example, are tributes to the progression of winemaking practice in the Swan Valley.

HOUGHTON

The start of the latter-day Houghton story was 1976, the year Thomas Hardy & Sons won a protracted battle to wrest control of the long-established producer from the Emu Wine Co. of the United Kingdom.

In the process, Hardys acquired 20 hectares of potentially valuable real estate around the old Valencia vineyards winery in Caversham (taken over by Emu in 1945), the Houghton winery and 90-hectare home vineyard in Middle Swan, the 1000-hectare Moondah Brook Estate at Gingin, and the real jewel of the empire, Houghton White Burgundy, an established national brand.

Within what seemed to some an indecently short period, the Hardy hierarchy quickly set about rationalising its newfound possession, at the same time treading the fine line between absolute control and ostensible autonomy. The rationalisation included tidying up more than ninety combined Valencia–Houghton product lines, effectively bury-

Houghton winemakers Jon Reynolds, left, and Peter Dawson contemplating the merits of one of their reds outside The Homestead at the Houghton winery.

Part of the Houghton coat of arms in stained glass at the winery, established 1859.

had taken most of the fruit from Frankland River for processing in the Swan Valley. Part of the lease arrangement entailed Houghton providing the capital for an extensive supplementary irrigation system to be installed at Frankland River.

In 1983 Houghton embarked on a $3.5 million expansion and modernisation prorgramme at its Middle Swan headquarters, installing modern crushing and juice processing equipment and building a large insulated, air-conditioned fermentation building designed to handle a crush in excess of 4000 tonnes. A new cask hall was also added with a 1600-barrel capacity for reds and whites. Houghton has its future production geared to 80 per cent whites (of which more than half will be Houghton White Burgundy), 15 per cent reds, and the remainder to be fortified.

The 90 hectares of the Houghton home vineyard is given mainly to chenin blanc with smaller plantings which include tokay, Rhine riesling, verdelho, cabernet sauvignon, pedro ximinez, shiraz, semillon, malbec, muscat, madeleine and frontignac. The company intends extending the area under vine to 120 hectares, at which time the total production will amount to around 1350 tonnes.

Moondah Brook Estate vineyard had its first commercial vintage in 1972, and will be extended from its original 107 hectares of plantings to 120 hectares, the major varieties being chenin blanc, cabernet sauvignon, tokay, verdelho, chardonnay and sauvignon blanc to give an anticipated total production of around 1250 tonnes.

The real future of the Frankland River vineyard will be determined by whether Houghton decides to exercise its option to purchase the property. Meantime, the 90-hectare vineyard supplies about 600 tonnes of fruit, comprised mainly of Rhine riesling, cabernet sauvignon and shiraz with small quantities of other varieties available including malbec, pinot noir, chardonnay, zinfandel, gewurtztraminer and sauvignon blanc.

The man responsible for putting it all together as wine is the diminutive Jon Reynolds, Houghton's senior winemaker, a Roseworthy graduate whose

ing the old Valencia label, transferring winemaking operations to Houghton, upgrading and modernising the Houghton winery and related facilities, revising plantings at Moondah Brook Estate, and introducing some supplementary irrigation.

Hardys then negotiated a five-year lease, commencing in 1981 (with an option to purchase), the 90-hectare vineyard of the Frankland River Grazing Company. The arrangement formalised a situation which had existed for four years whereby Houghton

path to Middle Swan included stints at Rothbury Estate in the Hunter Valley and Reynella in South Australia. When he first arrived at Houghton for the 1977 vintage at the age of twenty-eight, many people (myself included) were deceived by the self-effacing Reynolds and his apparently laissez-faire approach to winemaking ('Ah, we just chuck a bit of fruit in the crusher, make a few adjustments along the way and hope it turns out all right at the other end').

With some help from Bill Hardy, who was primarily responsible for reds between 1977 and 1980, and assistant winemaker Peter Dawson, Reynolds has quietly gone about transforming and revolutionising Houghton's output. In 1981, for example, Houghton wines won 7 trophies, 13 gold, 16 silver and 37 bronze medals around Australia.

Most successful of the entries that year was the 1981 Moondah Brook Estate Cabernet Sauvignon Rosé which collected 5 trophies, 6 golds and a silver in a trail of glory which saw Houghton making immediate plans to double output of the line. Reynolds also matured the chenin blanc component of the fabled HWB in wood, giving it an added touch of complexity, possibly upgrading its claims to be considered as a white burgundy style.

Other Houghton lines which have experienced the Reynolds 'magic' include a chablis made from Moondah Brook Estate chenin blanc, an autumn-harvest semillon from Swan-grown fruit which has all the potential in the world to develop into a truly luscious sauternes, chardonnays from Moondah Brook Estate and Frankland River, Frankland River Rhine riesling which has all the regional aromatic attributes and remarkable length of finish (in most years), and a Moondah Brook Estate verdelho which is a benchmark wine for anybody seriously interested in what this variety is capable of under Australian conditions.

For reds, the 1982 vintage stands out like a neon-lit indicator of Houghton's future direction from all three of its regions. The freshness, elegance and lack of extractive heaviness in the 1982 Frankland River Shiraz, not to mention 'drinkability' at a comparatively early age, summarises Houghton's reading of the marketplace.

LAMONTS

One of the first clues to the origins of this small Swan Valley producer appears on the labels of several of its wines – the familiar profile of Jack Mann, nosing a tulip glass. Lamonts, on the eastern perimeter of the valley, is owned by Neil and Corin Lamont, son-in-law and daughter of Jack Mann. Apart from a paternal interest, Jack is still involved in production of the 14 000 litres or so made each year.

The vineyard is being doubled in size from the initial 3 hectares and varieties planted are verdelho, cabernet sauvignon, semillon and muscadelle, supplemented by shiraz bought in from Bindoon for dry red and vintage port production. The eventual crush will be around 12 tonnes from the home vineyard, plus whatever else is purchased.

The range is being deliberately limited to white burgundy, cabernet sauvignon rosé, cabernet sauvignon, shiraz and vintage port with occasional small quantities of special fortified styles. The first cabernet sauvignon was made in 1978 and the other lines followed the year after.

OLIVE FARM

Among the greatest defenders of the Swan Valley faith are Vince Yurisich and his son, Ian, a Roseworthy graduate who took over as winemaker at the family-owned Olive Farm Wines in 1978, relieving his father who had successfully masterminded the previous fifteen vintages.

Ian is the third generation Yurisich at Olive Farm. In 1933 his late grandfather, Ivan, purchased the property established by colonial botanist-winemaker, Thomas Waters, who is reported to have sold wine in 1842 made on the original vineyard fronting the Swan River at South Guildford, present-day site of the winery and scaled-down home vineyard.

Ivan Yurisich was born in Yugoslavia in 1894 and migrated to Western Australia in 1912, spending the next 21 years mainly in the Kalgoorlie goldfields before heading back to Perth and investing 900 of his hard-earned pounds to buy Olive Farm. The patriarch of the Yurisich family spent many years toiling behind a horse-drawn plough, resurrecting a vineyard which once occupied pride of place in the colony. His first vintage of 900 litres of claret was made using basic equipment and skills picked up during his adolescent years in Yugoslavia.

Under Vince's reign from 1963 to 1978 Olive Farm firmly established itself as one of the valley's leading producers, consistently winning trophies for the most successful Western Australian producer under 135 000 litres at the Perth Royal Show.

Since Ian's return from Roseworthy, Olive Farm has been progressively placing more emphasis on fruit grown in the Bindoon area, some 20 kilometres due east of Gingin, on the eastern face of the Darling Range escarpment. The majority of Olive Farm's 100 tonne-plus crush is from Bindoon with selected parcels of fruit being supplied by various growers in the Swan Valley.

Dry white styles for which Ian is gaining a reputation include chardonnay, semillon, chablis, hock and a fruitier style made from muscat of Alexandria and a late-harvest chenin blanc which line up with several straight varietal reds and a cabernet shiraz blend.

Olive Farm enjoys the distinction of being the only Western Australian producer of a methode champenoise wine in commercial quantities – a first-class champagne made from early-picked madeleine grown in the Swan Valley, and much sought after by hometown devotees.

PETER'S QUALITY WINES

Based on the north-east fringe of the Swan Valley, Peter's Quality Wines, established in 1955 by Peter Talijancich, incorporates a 5-hectare vineyard and a small, efficient winery.

For years, this small producer slumbered contendedly off the beaten tourist track, quietly supplying the odd table wine and fortified to establish clients, but dependent mostly for survival on the flagon and bulk trade. Around the late 1970s and early 1980s, the word started spreading that Peter's Quality Wines produced some pretty nifty vintage and tawny ports. By happy coincidence, Peter's son, Jim, joined his father in the winery at this time.

The Rip van Winkle analogy is hard to resist. Before he knew it, Peter was witnessing a rapid transformation of the family business: Jim had set up a mini-lab, changed the labels, revised the pricing structure (particularly in the ports), and set about adding verdelho and semillon to the shiraz and muscat grown on the home vineyard. Jim makes a nicely rounded shiraz in a soft burgundy style and some of his early whites, which include a chablis and a late picked chenin blanc, are reasonably encouraging indicators of what is to come.

The real story of Peter's Quality Wines for the time being, however, is the truly superb fortifieds, made mainly from muscat, accompanied by excellent shiraz-based vintage port. One of the most memorable Swan 'stickies' I've come across was a wine made by Peter from muscat in 1960 and released some twenty years later. Despite its age, the wine has a haunting complexity derived of time spent in a dark corner mingled with a devastating freshness and vitality.

RIVERSIDE VINEYARD

One of the enigmas of the Swan Valley is Laurie Nicoletto, proprietor-winemaker at Riverside (also known as Basendean Estate). He is the Scarlet Pimpernel of the valley who, when not off driving trucks, finds time to make outstanding burgundies which have built up a steady following in the Eastern States.

The home vineyard consists of several hectares of grenache, but by far the greater proportion of the 50-tonne crush comprises shiraz bought in from other

Swan Valley growers. Laurie also makes a full bodied chenin blanc from other vineyards within the valley.

Riverside Vineyard's burgundies have carved out for themselves a special place of honour among the valley's wines, made all the more remarkable when the basic winery equipment is taken into account – the same open concrete fermenting vats installed by Laurie's father are still in use and the only wood to be seen in the entire winery is the rafters holding the asbestos roof in place.

SANDALFORD

Despite an association with the Swan Valley dating back to 1840 when John Septimus Roe took up his land grant at Caversham, nobody connected with Sandalford denies the company's future is very much allied to the Margaret River region.

Sandalford's Caversham Estate vineyard, covering 37 hectares, has cabernet sauvignon, chenin blanc,

Dorham Mann in his company's Swan Valley vineyards near their Sandalford winery. His father Jack Mann developed Houghton White Burgundy in 1936. Now Dorham works for Houghton's major opposition, in the Swan Valley.

Sandalford Wines, like a number of other Western Australian wine producers, draw grapes from a number of areas. Margaret River supplies fruit for some of Sandalford's finest reds.

semillon, pedro ximinez, shiraz, verdelho, zinfandel and muscadelle planted from which some 230 tonnes is crushed each year.

The company's Margaret River Estate vineyard, the largest in the region and one of the biggest in Western Australia, covers 138 hectares and the plantings (in order of scale) range from Rhine riesling (63 hectares), cabernet sauvignon (28), verdelho (15), chardonnay and shiraz (10), sauvignon blanc (4), semillon (3), and chenin blanc and gewurtztraminer (2). With all varieties in full bearing, Margaret River Estate will produce over 600 tonnes of grapes which will be crushed on site and shipped to Caversham.

Between 1973 and 1978 Sandalford started carving out for itself a reputation as Western Australia's premium wine producer, overshadowing its rival Houghton most years in general recognition and show results. While the majority of Sandalford's award-winning wines were produced from either Mt Barker-Frankland or Margaret River fruit, winemaker Dorham Mann consistently made the few 'surprise packets' from Caversham Estate, notably some full bodied whites from chenin blanc and ver-

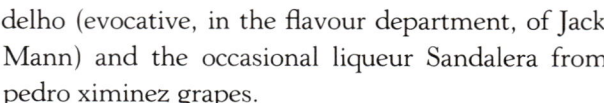

delho (evocative, in the flavour department, of Jack Mann) and the occasional liqueur Sandalera from pedro ximinez grapes.

The giant Inchape Group obtained the Westralian International (later known as Tricontinental) 60 per cent interest in Sandalford in 1979, effectively tying the company's Eastern States marketing efforts to the group's Taylor Ferguson division of Inchape's Caldbeck Macgregor Australia Ltd.

The race between the two majors of the Western Australian wine industry for market supremacy was under way, with Houghton embarked on a major overhaul of its vineyards, management, winemaking equipment and marketing. It was a battle of capital expenditure and winemaking skills to see who would come out on top in the post-1979 years.

Houghton outspent Sandalford and outpointed its

Mann describes cabernet sauvignon as being 'outstandingly suited to the region's soils and climate and, compared with some of the white varieties, it has worked out magnificently from the outset'. He is so enamoured of the variety that he sees less and less wood being used by Sandalford, giving it every chance to display its distinctive regional herbaceous charms.

It would be a mistake to assess Sandalford on its Margaret River wines alone. Its Caversham Estate vineyard is full of potential to produce some beautifully drinkable cabernet sauvignon and shiraz, along with an estimable zinfandel, and the full bodied chenin blanc and verdelho wines – steeped in the best tradition of the Mann family. Not forgetting one of the best-kept 'secrets' from the Swan – the Liqueur Sandelera made from pedro ximinez, a truly luscious dessert wine, made in a dry Portuguese style.

A lineup of Sandalford white wines made from the verdelho grape. The variety is widely grown in the West but is little known in other States.

Winemaker Dorham Mann tries one of his verdelho dry whites. The variety helps make some of the famous sweet wines of Madeira.

main competitor in the show ring most years – through no particular fault of the Roe family or Dorham Mann. Dorham Mann claims that it wasn't until the 1982 vintage that Sandalford got what he called the 'first orthodox crop of Rhine riesling'... from Margaret River Estate and what a crop that turned out to be, the 1982 Sandalford Auslese Rhine Riesling won a trophy at that year's Perth Royal Show for the best Western Australian sweet white table wine, repeating the performance later in the year at the Mt Barker Wine Show.

Sandalford's great strength and asset is Mann's determination to apply a free mind to making the company's wines, particularly those of Margaret River, which will continue to tax winemaker's skills for many years to come as regional styles and differences evolve.

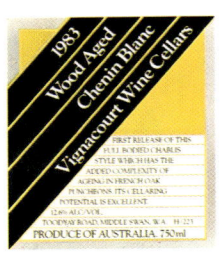

VIGNACOURT

David Atkinson forsook the relative security of a job with an oil company marketing division in 1972 to embark on the entirely new and foreign field of winemaking. He and his wife Beverley bought a run-down winery located on 6 hectares first planted in 1921 at Jane Brook, on the south-east fringe of the Swan Valley. The second bold decision was in 1984 when they bought an adjoining 4-hectare property and set about completely revising their plantings.

In the twelve vintages to 1984 David progressively carved out for himself a reputation as a winemaking tyro unafraid to challenge the conventional wisdoms which dictated many of the valley's credos. The Vignacourt label won increasing recognition in the show ring, particularly in the small producers' classes at the Perth Royal Show. His full bodied dry whites, made mainly from locally grown chenin blanc, and moselle styles, made from chenin and frontignan, developed a strong local following.

Having come to terms with Swan Valley fruit David then led the way in the small-producer stakes by buying in grapes from outside the region – mainly Rhine riesling and cabernet sauvignon from the Mt Barker-Frankland area. His second phase of experimenting won similar acclaim to his original efforts. Along the way he wasn't afraid to break new ground such as giving his 1983 Mt Barker Rhine Riesling a brief spell in French oak before bottling. The Atkinsons have also carved out a consistent track record for vintage and tawny ports and liqueur styles made from muscat, tokay and verdelho, which account for a substantial portion of the 60 000-plus litres produced annually at Vignacourt.

WESTFIELD

One of the Swan Valley's most respected 'quiet achievers' is John Kosovich, a veteran of twenty-five vintages, who set about making wine soon after leaving school on the property established by his father at Baskerville in the early 1920s.

Westfield has impressed me for years for the soundness and lack of faults in the wines. John devotes himself to virtually every aspect from budburst to crushing and for whatever period thereafter in an immaculate winery which has been progressively updated and modernised. Westfield has won more than its fair share of trophies for being the most successful local exhibitor at the Perth Royal Show.

The 7-hectare home vineyard is planted mainly to cabernet sauvignon, chenin blanc, verdelho, shiraz and semillon with patches of Rhine riesling, merlot and chardonnay, giving John an annual production of around 40 000 litres.

Westfield verdelho is one of the valley's most outstanding white wines, notable for its charming delicacy and delightful build-up of smell and flavour, especially given a year or so in the bottle. Kosovich has two fellow admirers of his verdelho in Jack and Dorham Mann, whose shared familiarity with the Portuguese variety spans some sixty years!

John also makes a consistently fine semillon which, like its chenin blanc cellar mate, has none of the coarseness or overripe traits which occasionally still show up in the wines of the valley made from these two varieties. John also makes a limited quantity of methode champenoise wine from (of all things) cabernet sauvignon, a diversion shared with his long-time friend, Dorham Mann, who makes the odd bottle or two of similar wine in his spare time. This delicate pink bubbly is meted out to friends and esteemed customers through the cellar door.

SOUTH-WEST COASTAL REGION

The south-west coastal region can probably make claim to being one of the world's biggest winegrowing areas populated by the least number of vignerons for any tract of land which professes to be a region. The region is contained within a narrow strip of plain country which extends down the Western Australian coast from Yanchep, 40 kilometres north of Perth, to Capel, some 230 kilometres south. Much of the region is distinguishable by its light, sandy loam overlying porous limestone. Only the southernmost winemaking inhabitant of the region, Capel Vale Wines, enjoys a dramatically different soil type on the fertile banks of the Capel River, some 30 kilometres from the township of Busselton, which is the northern limit of the neighbouring Margaret River region.

The total land area within the south-west coastal region is about 2700 square kilometres, making all the more remarkable the fact that it boasts eight wine producers. Despite their geographic distribution, there are more similarities than differences in the region's wines, with both whites and reds showing lightness and elegance with generous helpings of varietal flavour.

CAPEL VALE WINES

Bunbury doctor Peter Pratten, and his wife Elizabeth, planted vines on the banks of the Capel River in 1975. Their 10-hectare vineyard now has cabernet sauvignon, shiraz, Rhine riesling, chardonnay and gewurtztraminer from which around 40 000 litres are made each vintage.

The quality of Capel Vale's products are a tribute to Peter's willingness to experiment and cajole the best out of his fruit in the quest for distinctive styles. Not being totally dependent on the winery for income was an undeniable advantage in its formative years. Margaret River doctor-winemaker, Mike Peterkin of Pierro Wines assisted at Capel Vale in the formative years and Oenotec were called in for the 1983 and 1984 vintages.

Few small wineries in Australia could have had a more lauded introduction than Capel Vale: its 1980 and 1981 reds were warmly reviewed in James Halliday's annual assessment of wines in the *National Times*, being rated among the best cabernet sauvignon and shiraz.

With the 1982 shiraz Peter set out to make a 'Grange style' wine, destining one batch of the crush to American oak and another to Nevers oak. The American oak-matured wine was released as Bin 1 and the other as Bin 2. Looking at the two side by side, it was hard to imagine they came from the same vineyard.

In 1983 Capel Vale made a chardonnay which won a gold medal in Melbourne and the trophy for the best dry white at the 1983 Mt Barker Wine Show. The 1983 Rhine Riesling also picked up a gold medal in Melbourne.

Peter claims Capel Vale, located on the southernmost limits of the south-west coastal region, shares more similarities than differences with the nearby Margaret River. In climatic terms that may be true, but I question whether the similarities are more than climatic as Capel Vale reds especially have distinctive nuances which set them apart from the neighbouring region.

PAUL CONTI WINES

Modesty is Paul Conti's middle name. In his unassuming way he has made some giant contributions to the local industry since taking over the reins in 1968 at the Wanneroo winery founded by his father, Carmelo, in 1925.

BUNBURY

■ Thomas Wines
■ Leschenault

BOYANUP

■ Capel Vale Wines

CAPEL

DONNYBROOK

DUNSBOROUGH

YALLINGUP

BUSSELTON

■ Happ's

Moss Wood
Pierro   Cape Clairault
Ribbonvale   ■ Redbrook Vineyard
Graylyn Wines   Sandalford Wines
Cullens' Willyabrup Wines   WILLYABRUP

■ Albert Vinci

KIRUP

Willespie Wines   ■ Sussex Vale
Vasse Felix   Ashbrook Estate
Wright's

COWARAMUP

Chateau Xanadu
Cape Mentelle ■   MARGARET RIVER

BRIDGETOWN

Redgate ■   Leeuwin Estate ■

WITCHCLIFF

Gillespie

FLINDERS BAY

0   20 km

The home vineyard, Woodvale, has been reduced over the years to 2 hectares of cabernet sauvignon. Several kilometres north of Woodvale is the Mariginiup vineyard, covering 10 hectares of shiraz and frontignac, and several kilometres further north of Mariginiup is another vineyard planted to chardonnay and sauvignon blanc with a small patch of merlot within 5 hectares.

Paul had enormous influence on the developing reputation of the Mt Barker-Frankland region in the 1976-83 period. During that time he took practically all the Rhine riesling and cabernet sauvignon fruit from Tony and Betty Pearse's Forest Hill vineyard which sold under a joint Conti-Forest Hill label. It was an unusual winemaking-marketing venture, playing a great role in determining the future of Mt Barker-Frankland. Paul manages to extract occasional great heights of flavour from grapes grown at Wanneroo. His Woodvale cabernet sauvignon and Mariginiup shiraz are consistently among the most drinkable reds produced in Western Australia, with generous varietal flavours quite unlike any other wines produced in the Swan Valley or in the southwest.

The Paul Conti frontignac, or 'Conti's fronti' as it has been known for years, is a classic example of how to tame the excesses of muscat grapes to produce a table wine of distinction. Loaded to the hilt with grapey muscat flavour, but nevertheless beautifully balanced with acid, it is an antipodean moselle of some note.

The first Paul Conti chardonnay from Wanneroo made in 1983 was seen by many industry observers as being an indicator of other great things to come from this modest man. The wine showed none of the buttery or fruit-salad character some may have expected from a warm climate such as Wanneroo's. Rather it was more of an austere chablis style of real promise.

LESCHENAULT

Dr Barry Killerby, the proprietor of Leschenault, changed from being a doctor-winemaker to winemaker-doctor as his vineyard, planted in 1973, became more mature. The 18-hectare property is planted with cabernet sauvignon, shiraz, gewurtztraminer, semillon, pinot noir and chardonnay which will yield a total crush of around 100 tonnes when in full production.

The Killerby vineyard is a kilometre from the Indian Ocean, separated only by dunes and a stand of trees on the western front. Barry makes no secret of his quest to achieve maximum varietal character and flavour in his wines. A classic case in point is the Leschenault pinot noir which has been known to bemuse judges because of its deep colour.

Other notable wines produced by Leschenault have included a 1980 traminer, which was full of spice and elegance with none of the oiliness often associated with the variety, and two 1982 reds – a cabernet sauvignon and a shiraz – which both showed outstanding depth of flavour and refinement.

One of the regular sellers made by Barry is Leschenault April Red, a shiraz/cabernet blend which varies slightly from year to year but is always delightfully refreshing. It is marvellously light, easy drinking with lashings of flavour.

LUISINI WINES

The Wanneroo vineyard of Luisini was established in 1929 by the father of present owner, Ernie Mondello. It developed into one of the larger holdings in Western Australia as demand grew for bulk fortified wines. The Luisini sherries, particularly, had a huge following.

The home vineyard has been reduced to 4 hectares, all planted to shiraz, and the majority of the 100 tonnes or so crushed by Luisini is bought in from the Swan and Bindoon. Commencing with the 1981 vintage, winemaker David Cooper, who joined Luisini Wines in 1980 after five vintages in Mildura, had to convert the balance of production from fortified to table wines. David is also developing his own Morangup Estate vineyard at Gidgegannup, 80 kilometres north-east of Perth, the fruit from which will go to Luisini. Initial plantings at Gidgegannup include

chardonnay and sauvignon blanc.

Table wines bearing the Luisini label include a claret style shiraz, a cabernet sauvignon/shiraz blend, a chablis style blend of semillon and chenin blanc, a chenin blanc/chardonnay blend, straight chenin blanc and late-picked chenin blanc. In the phasing out of quaint lines such as blackberry nip and other 'fruit salad' oddities, Luisini has thankfully retained some excellent stocks of fortified material. David has been setting up a solero system with ten-year-old base wine for truly luscious liqueur styles.

PEEL ESTATE

The affable Will Nairn, owner of Peel Estate, had a dream debut to the world of winemaking. His first wine, a 1980 shiraz, won a gold medal and a trophy for the best locally produced red from a small maker at the 1980 Perth Show. Not a bad start for a bloke who, before planting grapes in 1974, was a farmer, tending 80 hectares of cattle country and 40 hectares of lucerne.

Located at Baldivis, between Perth and the popular seaside resort of Mandurah, the rustic-style winery and tasting area has become a stopping off place for wine-lovers.

Today Peel Estate has 13 hectares, the main varieties being shiraz, chenin blanc and chardonnay, with smaller patches of cabernet sauvignon blanc, semillon, verdelho and zinfandel. When in full bearing Peel Estate will produce around 10 000 cases.

A shiraz continues to win acclaim from critics with its brilliant colour, medium body and intense varietal characteristics. In most years Will releases a private bin line and a slightly down-market version, the difference being a variation in oak treatment.

Peel Estate has elevated chenin blanc beyond the 'workhorse' classification with some superbly generous and voluptuous wines over the years. The variety's versatility has enabled Will to produce variations, ranging from a bone-dry product to a fascinating wood-matured wine which is often bottled with a touch of residual sugar. The latter wine, given

a year or so in the bottle, rounds out into a gutsy, white burgundy style. Peel Estate's small planting of zinfandel has given the company the flexibility to market a straight varietal or a shiraz/zinfandel blend, both of which are given a few months in French oak. The two wines are easy drinking at an early age, but a few years' cellaring can produce rewarding results.

THOMAS WINES

There have been times, says Bunbury pharmacist-winemaker, Gill Thomas, when he wondered whether any sort of involvement in winemaking was worthwhile. His vineyard at Gelorup, 10 kilometres south of Bunbury and 180 kilometres south of Perth, had a black frost in 1981 so severe that many vine trunks burst. A lot of the vines never recovered and this led to one of several replanting programmes which have taken place over the years.

The Briar Holme property has 2 hectares of pinot noir and almost half a hectare of chardonnay. 'I'm quite happy to have the smallest vineyard in Western Australia,' Gill says.

The first commercial release of Thomas Wines was the 1978 Cabernet Sauvignon grown at Moss Wood and made there while Gill was building his own winery at Briar Holme. The wine was released in 1984. The depth of fruit flavour and fruit-wood complexity were sensational. Judges at the 1981 Perth Royal Show gave it the trophy for the Best Western Australian dry red in open classes. To prove his debut in the winemaking stakes was no fluke, Gill again picked up the Best Western Australian dry red trophy at the 1982 Perth Royal Show for his 1980 Cabernet Sauvignon.

The Thomas family was given a donkey when they purchased Briar Holme in 1969 and now have the original animal plus one of her progeny – hence the donkey on their label. Asked about the significance of the donkey on his label, Thomas jokingly responds, 'It's a picture of the proprietor.' True or false, Thomas Wines is a label to mark down in the cellar book for the future.

MARGARET RIVER

A Perth heart specialist, Dr Tom Cullitty, planted the first vines at Vasse Felix in 1967, and since its first wines were produced in the mid-1970s, Margaret River has probably received as much attention as any new winegrowing area. Fortunately, both for the region and its producers, 'Maggie R' (as a British wine scribe once quaintly called it) has experienced more highs than lows.

The early wines from Vasse Felix, Dr Bill Pannell's Moss Wood and Dr Kevin Cullen's Willyabrup Wines set a cracking pace for those who joined the throng of doctors, engineers, investors, accountants, farmers, teachers, and even the occasional winemaker. Within fifteen years of Vasse Felix's planting, the region had over twenty producers, ranging from Sandalford and Leeuwin Estate down to the majority

The Margaret River region has experienced more highs than lows since its first wines were produced in the mid-1970s.

ASHBROOK ESTATE

Tony Devitt is senior Western Australian government viticulturist and member of the Devitt family which runs this enterprise. Happily, Tony is big enough (in more ways than one) and objective enough to do justice to both his regular employer (the Department of Agriculture) and the family winery/vineyard complex managed by his brother, Brian, a Bachelor of Science and former school teacher.

The Devitts began an 8-hectare planting programme in 1976 which includes cabernet sauvignon, semillon, verdelho, chardonnay, sauvignon blanc, merlot and cabernet franc. The crush at Ashbrook Estate varies between 30 and 60 tonnes, depending on the amount of fruit bought in — a policy the company will continue to pursue when it believes fruit from neighbouring growers or from other regions meets its needs.

In the 1980-84 period Ashbrook released estate-grown semillon and verdelho and wines made from

The azure blue skies and green vines are typical scenes at Margaret River, a relatively new but exciting wine area of Australia.

Ripe shiraz grapes await the pickers.

of holdings of 5 to 15 hectares.

The pace quickened when Sandalford endorsed the region with its 160-hectare purchase in 1972. Californian winemaker Robert Mondavi encouraged a Perth businessman, Denis Horgan, to establish a vine nursery in 1974 on his cattle property, which developed into Leeuwin Estate – the second largest producer in the region.

The pre-1984 period in Margaret River was a sorting-out progress, not untypical of any emerging region. The wine world is now entitled to expect a generally high standard of reds made from cabernet sauvignon and pinot noir and, occasionally, shiraz. White varieties which have gone part of the way to proving their potential are chardonnay, sauvignon blanc, verdelho and semillon while legitimate questions can be posed about Rhine riesling and gewurtztraminer.

Many of the wineries in the region bear witness to the individual natures of the inhabitants, being built from local timber, stone and rammed earth or mud bricks to keep them in harmony with their surroundings.

bought-in local Rhine riesling and chenin blanc. The only reds released to 1984 were two 1980 wines made from malbec grown at Frankland River – one a straight varietal and the other with a small proportion of Ashbrook cabernet sauvignon added to the blend.

The Devitts obviously intend giving their estate-grown reds every chance to be at their peak when released onto the market. Soon after the 1984 vintage, the company still had its bottled cabernet sauvignon from 1980-1982 in the cellar and the 1983 in wood casks.

CAPE MENTELLE

To understand the wines of Cape Mentelle, one must first attempt to understand the winemaker, David Hohnen, winemaker graduate of Fresno State University, California. After graduating he returned to Australia to help a friend, Dominique Portet, establish Taltarni Wines in Victoria, and not surprisingly there are many similarities in the styles of Taltarni and Cape Mentelle reds.

Cape Mentelle. The success of the cabernet sauvignons from here is doing much to enhance the region's reputation for red wine.

David Hohnen, winemaker at Cape Mentelle. He amazed the wine world by winning the Jimmy Watson Trophy for his young cabernet sauvignons two years running.

Vines were first planted at Cape Mentelle in 1970 on a cattle and sheep property owned by David's brother, Mark, chairman of Oceanic Equity Ltd which has an 80 per cent interest in Cape Mentelle. The remainder belongs to David who is managing director and winemaker.

The 17-hectare vineyard is planted to cabernet sauvignon, shiraz, zinfandel, semillon, chenin blanc, sauvignon blanc and chardonnay. The 1984 crush comprised 91 tonnes of estate-grown fruit and around 30 tonnes of bought-in grapes, mainly sauvignon blanc and semillon from local growers.

The Cape Mentelle vineyard in full bearing will yield some 100 tonnes with the crush being equally distributed between reds and whites. Apart from bought-in fruit, additional supplies will be available from a nearby 8-hectare vineyard in which David has an interest, planted mainly to chardonnay, sauvignon blanc and merlot.

The two Cape Mentelle cabernet sauvignons either side of the 1982 wine, which won the Jimmy Watson Trophy in 1983 are proof that Cape Mentelle's success in 1983 was no fluke. The 1981 version is almost the equal of the 1982, perhaps missing out by a whisker in the ripeness of typical minty, herbaceous fruit, but containing, nevertheless, all the power and elegance now associated with Hohnen's reds. The 1983 wine only fails in comparison with its aromatics being slightly down on the 1982, but still exhibiting incredible length of flavour and stunning fruit-oak complexity. Eastern States judges obviously rated the 1983 wine highly, awarding it the Jimmy Watson Memorial Trophy in 1984, thus completing a 'quinella' for Cape Mentelle which did much to enhance the region's reputation for cabernet sauvignon.

Both Cape Mentelle cabernet sauvignon and shiraz are made to keep and go on improving for at least eight years although the soft tannins of the region make them eminently approachable within a year or so of bottling. Zinfandel is the 'sleeper' in the Cape Mentelle pack, usually brimful of immense, berry-like flavour and rich, almost plum jam, bouquet.

The Cape Mentelle winery,
near Margaret River.
Winemaker David Hohnen
trained in California.

Hohnen has also developed a wood-fermented semillon/chenin blanc blend as a standard line which has developed a firm position in the marketplace. It is big, bold and brassy needing a few years' bottle age for its fruit-wood components to strike up a degree of compatibility.

Bearing in mind what Hohnen has done with his big reds and occasional robust white blend or straight verdelho, his followers await the chardonnays and sauvignon blancs to come.

CHATEAU XANADU

Chateau Xanadu wines became available in reasonable quantities from the 1984 vintage. The winery was founded by Dr John Lagan and his wife, Dr Eithne Sheridan. The property was named Chateau Xanadu for a variety of reasons, including the fact that it was the original name of the Lagan residence in Ireland. In 1968 the family arrived in Margaret River from Ireland for a twelve-month stay and so enjoyed the beauty of the south-west of Australia that they decided to stay.

Around 100 tonnes of cabernet sauvignon, semillon, chardonnay, cabernet franc and sauvignon blanc were crushed in 1984 and Dr Lagan anticipates the vineyard will produce around 200 tonnes in full bearing.

CULLENS' WILLYABRUP WINES

The Cullen family set about planting a 20-hectare vineyard in 1971 on their Willyabrup farm, completing the third leg of a medical trifecta (doctors Tom Cullity and Bill Pannell being the first Margaret River medico-winemakers in 1967 and 1969 respectively).

The early wines were made by Kevin Cullen and his medical colleague, Roseworthy-trained Dr Mike

Willyabrup is one of the most attractive wineries in the Margaret River region.

Wines are taken from wooden bins for cleaning and labelling at Willyabrup winery, run by Kevin and Di Cullen.

Peterkin, with Di Cullen assigned to general navvying duties in the vineyard and winery Kevin managed to run a medical practice, oversee the farm, introduce and mastermind a revolutionary twenty-year community health assessment program in Busselton — and then take a super active part in the winery. Having served her apprenticeship over six or so vintages, Di took over winemaking in 1981 — and what an introduction she had! Practically every wine she made that year went on to win an award at shows around Australia. The Cullens' 1981 Cabernet Sauvignon won a gold medal at the Melbourne Royal Show and gained top points in a strong class of 180 entries.

The 1982 wines set the benchmark by which Cullens' wines might be judged in future. Di decided to let the chardonnay and sauvignon blanc ferment right out in wood, resulting in bone dry wines with hardly a trace of residual sugar but which, at the same time, are brimful of enticing varietal flavour.

The 1982 Cullens' reds, released in late 1984, are collectors' items, particularly the cabernet sauvignon with 5 per cent merlot – an incredibly full and complex wine.

The vineyard has now pretty well reached maturity, yielding 120-140 tonnes and their biggest problem is a perpetual shortage of wines. Annual production is somewhere around 7000-7500 cases with Rhine riesling accounting for 900 or so, sauvignon blanc the same, chardonnay about 700, and cabernet sauvignon/merlot about 800. The balance of production comprises pinot noir, usually a late-picked Rhine riesling, a cabernet sauvignon rosé, a semillon/sauvignon blanc blend, not to mention a 'hobby' wine of Di's – a blanc de noir made from cabernet sauvignon, the 300 cases or so of which are always in demand through the cellar door.

LEEUWIN ESTATE

The Leeuwin Estate vineyard-winery-function complex of Perth merchant banker, Denis Horgan, is the jewel in the crown of Margaret River. No expense has been spared in the winery and by the end of 1983, when a grand new tasting-function building was officially opened, something like $5 million had been spent over nine years.

Leeuwin Estate came into being when Robert Mondavi, probably the doyen of American winemakers, was asked to act on behalf of an investment syndicate. Mondavi's brief was to determine the best winegrowing region in Australia and to find a suitable property. His investigations led him to Margaret River and the property he settled on was a 1000-hec-

Bob Cartwright (on the right) demonstrates the quality of one of his wines at the Leeuwin Estate winery.

Leeuwin Estate, built in a green hollow amid trees in the Margaret River area, is one of the most spectacular sights in the Australian wine industry.

Visitors taste wines in the winery's tasting area.

tare cattle farm which just happened to be owned by Denis Horgan. Mondavi made an offer, which was refused, but resulted in the Mondavi syndicate entering into a joint venture agreement with the Horgan family.

A nursery was started in 1974 and the first plantings took place the following year over 34 hectares. The 90-hectare Leeuwin Estate vineyard now comprises Rhine riesling (31 hectares), cabernet sauvignon (27), chardonnay (18), pinot noir (5), sauvignon blanc (4), gewurztraminer (3) and malbec (2).

The first vintage at Leeuwin Estate was 1978 when 16 tonnes of Rhine riesling and three tonnes of cabernet sauvignon were picked. By the 1981 vintage the crop had risen to 185 tonnes and later levelled out to its optimum cropping rate – 400 tonnes – around which the winery is designed.

Under the terms of the joint venture with Mondavi and his fellow syndicate members, Mondavi provided Leeuwin Estate with technical expertise and Leeuwin Estate had the option of selling up to 50 per cent of its production to the United States, an option rarely exercised as there has never been any shortage of local demand for the company's wines. During the duration of the agreement, which terminated in 1981

when Denis Horgan and his family took up total ownership, two container loads of Leeuwin Estate wines were sold to America. Between 1978-81 either Robert Mondavi or one of his two sons, Tim and Michael, attended each vintage at Margaret River and the association continued occasionally after the joint venture ended.

The Mondavi connection was important to the development of Leeuwin Estate in more ways than one. It is still freely acknowledged that Mondavi's understanding of chardonnay and pinot noir provided the base on which Leeuwin Estate quickly established its reputation, especially with chardonnay.

A lot of eyebrows were raised around Australia when the first Leeuwin Estate chardonnay (1980) hit the market with a recommended retail price of around $18. But the wine sold – as did its successors, the 1981 and 1982 which sold at around $23.50. One of the sidelights to the Leeuwin Estate chardonnay story revolves around the first crop in 1979. The wine was not considered fit to release as a varietal and became the base for a méthode champenoise blanc de blanc – a wine which led Robert Mondavi to declare, 'I didn't believe a champagne of this quality could be made in Australia.'

Standard wines now offered by Leeuwin Estate, apart from its trail-blazing chardonnay and pinot noir, are Rhine riesling, gewurztraminer and cabernet sauvignon, the latter usually having around a 5 per cent merlot component.

MOSS WOOD

The first cabernet sauvignon made by Dr Bill Pannell at Moss Wood in 1973 was described by him later as 'an interesting foretaste of what was to come, but without a great deal of depth'. Bill was certainly right about the wine's indicator value, but absolutely wrong about its lack of depth. Over ten years later it was holding together remarkably well – hardly the sign of a wine lacking depth.

Bill and his wife Sandra started Moss Wood, a venture which progressed from being a weekend hobby to a time-consuming winery. Any doubts they may have had about the wines have been displaced by the majestic cabernet sauvignons from the small Margaret River holding from the 1975 vintage onwards. The 1975 'impressed a few people', as Bill modestly said, and the wine picked up a string of gold medals around Australia in very quick time.

After an exhaustive search for suitable viticultural land, Bill and Sandra started with some of the best cabernet sauvignon Australia had to offer, planting Moss Wood in 1969 with two hectares of cabernet sauvignon.

The comparatively small size of Moss Wood today (10 hectares), belies the reputation and acclaim which has built up around the wines of the company since the first small parcels of cabernet sauvignon trickled through to the marketplace. The 1980 Moss Wood chardonnay was soon to join Bill's cabernet sauvignon and pinot noir well up on the list of Western Australia's most sought-after wines. The 1980 vintage also produced one of the finest Moss Wood cabernet sauvignons, a wine which, among other honours, won the Montgomery Trophy for best dry red at the Adelaide Wine Show.

Quite rightly, Bill considers his 1981 pinot noir, the original version of which was made in 1979, to be the best wine made by Moss Wood in its first fourteen years. The wine was widely regaled as one of the greatest Australian pinot noirs made since the variety was first planted in the country.

PIERRO

The proprietor of Pierro, Dr Mike Peterkin, is in a fairly unique position to comment on the past and future of the Margaret River region. He graduated as a doctor in 1973 and later decided to become a qualified winemaker, graduating from Roseworthy in 1977, having worked during the 1976 vintage at Sandalford's Caversham winery alongside Dorham Mann to gain practical experience. In between practising as a doctor, he worked at Enterprise Wines in 1978, and for the following two vintages with Kevin and Di Cullen at Cullens' Willyabrup Wines. During the 1980 vintage he also made the white wines for Merv Lange at Alkoomi in the Frankland River region, an association he continued on a consulting basis for the 1982 and 1983 vintages. When he moved to Margaret River in 1979, Mike was one of the few qualified winemakers in the region, the others being David Hohnen at Cape Mentelle and Bob Cartwright at Leeuwin Estate.

He started planting his own property in 1980 and by the 1984 vintage crushed 15 tonnes of fruit from the 3 main varieties growing on 4 hectares – chardonnay, pinot noir and sauvignon blanc – plus 5 tonnes of local cabernet sauvignon which he bought. The 1984 vintage marked a turning point in the frenetic life of Dr Peterkin, the decision being made to concentrate exclusively on Pierro and gear the annual throughput of the winery to around 50 tonnes from a 10-hectare vineyard.

REDBROOK (EVANS & TATE)

I have already referred (in the section on the Swan Valley) to the early wines from this picturesque vineyard. Redbrook, where vines were first planted in 1975, is located on the western boundary of Sandalford's property and just over the road from Moss Wood, so the Margaret River address placed it in

VASSE FELIX

Vasse Felix winemaker David Gregg joined the winery's creator, Dr Tom Cullity, in 1972, having arrived in Australia from the United Kingdom several years earlier and commenced work as an agricultural contractor in Busselton. Part of his service was crop spraying and it was in that context that he first came across Vasse Felix. Tom offered David, a qualified dairy technologist, an assistant's role in 1972 and his first vintage was 1973. The association, at least from an outsider's viewpoint, was a rare example of compatible human chemistry.

Vasse Felix's first plantings in 1967 covered 4 hectares of Rhine riesling, cabernet sauvignon, verdelho and malbec – all supplied from the Swan Valley vineyards of Houghton and Valencia. As the vineyard got to its ultimate size of 10 hectares, the verdelho was replaced by more Rhine riesling and a small patch of gewurtztraminer. The current balance of planting at Vasse Felix is 60 per cent cabernet sauvignon, 25 per cent Rhine riesling, 10 per cent malbec and 5 per cent shiraz.

David and his wife, Anne, have leased from Tom Cullitty since 1979 and looking back on the achievements of Vasse Felix, David makes no secret of his belief that it has evolved as a red-oriented producer. By 1979-80, David says, Vasse Felix has progressively developed confidence, both in viticulture and winemaking, to the extent where the realisation struck home 'that we were really on to something, with our reds in particular'.

The producer was not the only person sharing that view. Around then inquiries were received about the wine from overseas. Sales were made to a merchant in New York State and Vasse Felix now sells 25 per cent of its wine in North America.

'Flavour must bounce out of the wine. Our business depends on making eyes roll – not just producing wine,' says David. With red production under control at Vasse Felix, the company will devote more attention to whites such as sauvignon blanc and chardonnay.

The entrance to the Margaret River vineyards of Evans & Tate.

good company. An impeccable neighbourhood, one might say.

Varieties planted by area at Redbrook are cabernet sauvignon (8.2 hectares), shiraz (1.7), merlot (1.8), semillon (3.6), chardonnay (3.6), sauvignon blanc (1.0) and gewurtztraminer (1.0). The first commercial vintages were cabernet sauvignon and shiraz (1979), semillon (1980), merlot, sauvignon blanc and gewurtztraminer (1983), and chardonnay (1984).

A total of 100 tonnes of fruit was picked during the 1984 vintage and it is anticipated that the optimum cropping level at the Margaret River vineyard will round out at about 150 tonnes. The company intends to continue trucking Redbrook fruit to its Swan Valley winery.

The 1981 Redbrook Cabernet Sauvignon and the 1981 Shiraz, both of which picked up a fair share of gold medals when they were shown, share the Evans & Tate trait of elegance as well as depth of varietal flavour. The cabernet sauvignon, particularly captured the distinctive regional berry and mint characters, while the shiraz (to which a dash of cabernet sauvignon was added), had one of the most attractively long finishes anyone could expect of a wine from such young vines.

WRIGHTS WINES

Margaret River winemaker Henry Wright is a hard man to keep up with; in his fiftieth year he was still playing competitive soccer and teaching opponents half his age a thing or two about fitness on the local squash courts.

Henry makes no bones about being a self-taught winemaker. He and his wife, Maureen, planted 10 hectares of vines in 1974; their first commercial vintage was 1979. The vineyard was subsequently extended to 12 hectares, incorporating cabernet sauvignon, shiraz, Rhine riesling, semillon and chardonnay from which around 50 000 litres are now produced each year.

The Wrights deserve credit for developing a shiraz style from 1979 onwards in the face of the Margaret River cabernet sauvignon boom which was erupting all around them. Their faith in the variety has been well placed, with Wrights shiraz (or hermitage, as they call it) continuing to win a small army of admirers. The wine has glorious colour, rich varietal flavour and enticingly soft, tannin, coming together as a red which, with a year or two of bottle age, is easy drinking.

The Wrights have also produced an occasional Rhine riesling which typifies the robustly floral regional character; a shiraz/cabernet sauvignon blend which is worth tracking down for its medium body, elegance and depth of finish; and some excellent vintage ports.

MT BARKER-FRANKLAND REGION

While doctors led the wine rush to Margaret River, Mt Barker-Frankland was kicked off by farmers who became increasingly aware of the area's viticultural potential from 1975 onwards when Sandalford's 1975 Rhine riesling made from fruit grown at the Forest Hill experimental vineyard at Mt Barker hit the wine world.

Known as the Great Southern Region until 1982 when local winemakers and vignerons got together to effect the change, one of the most important clues to the region's identity is the hyphen between Mt Barker-Frankland. In many ways, they are regions

within a region, the Frankland part of the zone (80 kilometres west of Mt Barker) generally experiencing a lower rainfall. Supplementary irrigation has been installed at the two largest Frankland vineyards, Alkoomi and the Westfield property leased by Houghton.

Mt Barker-Frankland is undoubtedly the coolest winegrowing region in Western Australia. The 'cool climate' classification fits Mt Barker-Frankland far more accurately than Margaret River. It is not unknown for Mt Barker-Frankland producers to be picking in late May and there have been isolated

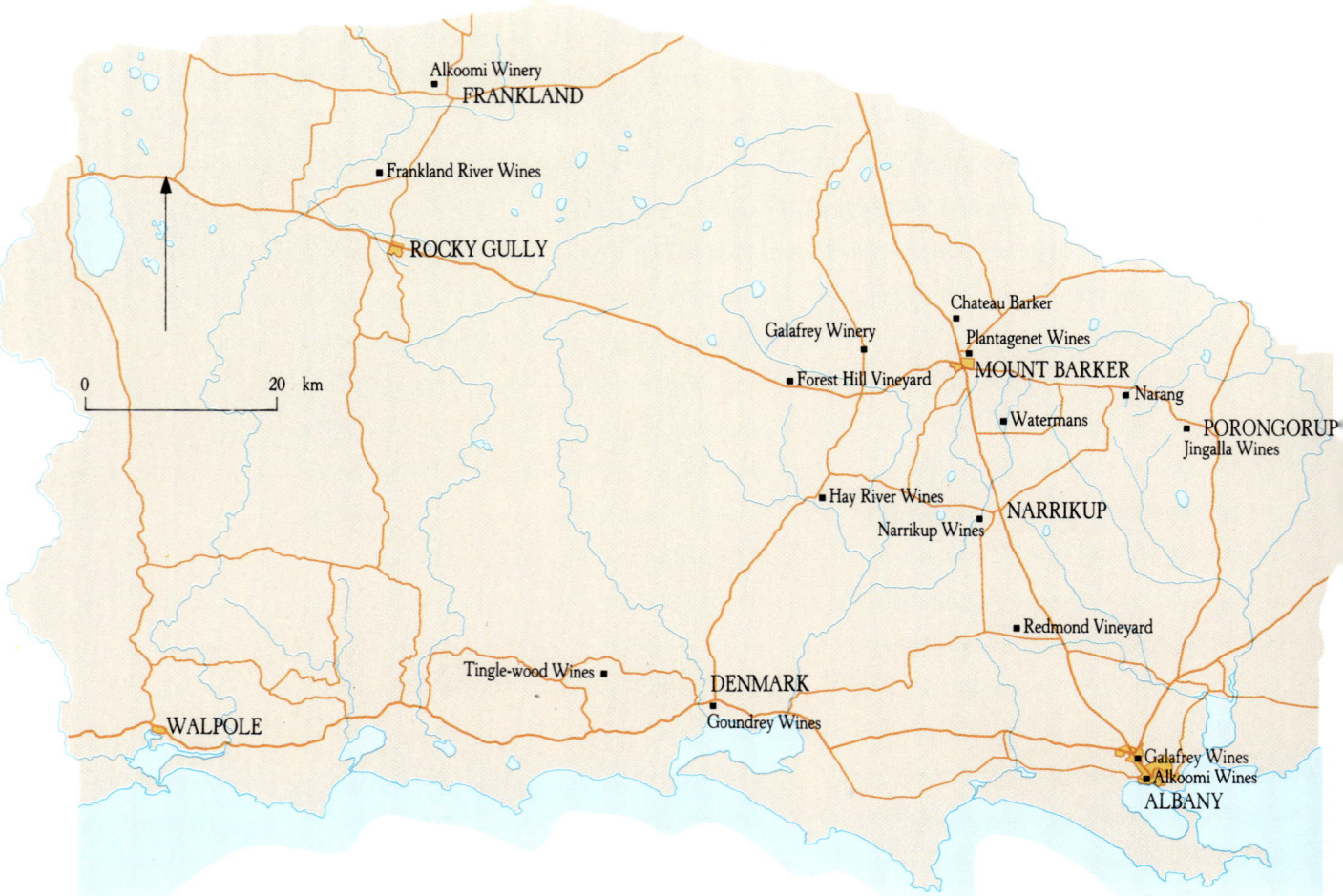

instances of fruit still being on vines in early June.

Further proof, if it were needed, has been provided by occasional crippling spring frosts and the region's few winemakers have been known to resort to wrapping electric blankets around tanks to keep fermentation ticking along. Snow fell on Tony and Betty Pearse's Forest Hill property in November 1976.

While there are some climatic similarities between Mt Barker-Frankland and Margaret River, one of the more notable differences is the former's annual rainfall, 700-1000 millimetres, which includes occasional light summer rains as a result of cloudbanks moving northwards off the Southern Ocean. Margaret River receives an annual average of 1200 millimetres, mostly between May and September, and has dry, mild summers. The predictions of Professor Olmo in 1956 about the potential of the region have been borne out by some brilliant wines, but by comparison with the Margaret River region (200 kilometres west), there is still much to be done.

The Department of Agriculture's 2-hectare experimental vineyard at Forest Hill reverted to the Pearse family in 1975 and at that time there were only a few other vignerons of any scale in the Mt Barker-Frankland region: Tony Smith at Plantagenet Wines; the Roche family of Adelaide whose Westfield property was the site of another Department of Agriculture experimental vineyard planted in the late 1960s; Merve Lange at Alkoomi Wines and Mike Goundrey of Goundrey's, both of whom first planted in 1971; the Cooper family at Chateau Barker; Nigel Levinson at Genesta Estate whose first vines went in during 1973; and Ron Waterman of Waterman's Wines who planted a small patch of Rhine riesling in 1975.

While the early Margaret River wines from Moss Wood, Vasse Felix and Cullens were beginning to make their presence felt at wine shows in the mid-1970s, Mt Barker-Frankland was still in a formative stage. The only vines with sufficient maturity to produce wines of any quantity or quality were from the Forest Hill and Westfield experimental vineyards. Significantly, it was two Perth-based winemakers who made the wines from both locations – Dorham Mann at Sandalford and Paul Conti at Conteville.

The first recognised winemaker to work permanently in the Mt Barker-Frankland region was David McNamara who left the Swan Valley to join Tony Smith, a farmer, at Plantagenet Wines for the 1974 vintage. By the 1984 vintage there were only four wineries that could be described as commercial in the Mt Barker-Frankland area: Alkoomi, Chateau Barker, Goundrey's and Plantagenet.

The region in 1984 had a number of small 'vignerons-in-the-making' and one or two established vineyards which were either in the process of changing hands or being left to run down.

The grapes come in at Plantagenet. The winery was the first to release wines under its own label in the Mt Barker area.

The formative years of the region substantiated Olmo's predictions to the extent that shiraz was to become an established variety, cabernet sauvignon outstanding in the better growing years, Rhine riesling a consistently good producer, and gewurtztraminer occasionally good. Legitimate question marks were raised over the other varieties planted in small quantities such as chardonnay, semillon, merlot and pinot noir.

ALKOOMI WINES

Proprietor-winemaker Merv Lange is typical of much of the region's early development – he is a farmer who planted a few vines in 1971 and who now spends most of his time making wine.

Merv and his wife Judy found a corner of their 1200-hectare farm at Frankland which they thought might be suitable for vines and started off with 1 hectare of cabernet sauvignon. That has since grown to 13 hectares made up of cabernet sauvignon, Rhine riesling, and shiraz, with smaller plantings of malbec semillon, sauvignon blanc and merlot, from which around 100 tonnes is crushed each year.

Frost has been an enemy at Alkoomi. During the spring of 1981 the Langes lost two-thirds of the total crop, with Rhine riesling being hardest hit. The following year saw a similar disaster which led Merv to buying in a wetting agent with which to spray vines prior to frosts.

By the 1980 vintage, Merv had started getting to grips with Alkoomi reds. His cabernet sauvignon from that year went on to win a gold medal and a trophy at the 1981 Mt Barker Wine Show. The 1982 and 1983 Alkoomi Cabernet Sauvignons were equally impressive.

A variety with which Merv has developed an affinity and respect is malbec, and Alkoomi is one of the few Mt Barker-Frankland producers to market a straight varietal. Alkoomi Malbec has become a regular medal winner since the 1979 wine showed the world what the Frankland area was capable of, picking up a medal at the Royal Perth Show the first time it was judged. The quality of the malbec is such that very little is left each year for blending with other red varieties.

The first reasonable quantities of semillon and sauvignon blanc were obtained from the 1983 vintage and blended to a bone-dry, medium-bodied white which picked up silver medals at the Perth and Mt Barker shows.

Merv's progress as a winemaker since the late 1970s has been undeniable and the three-year stint

(1981-83) when Dr Mike Peterkin acted as a consultant did wonders for Alkoomi wines. There was a distinct Peterkin influence on the 1983 Alkoomi Rhine Riesling which I saw as one of the most exciting wines of the variety to be produced in Mt Barker-Frankland to that date.

Wine has become so much a part of the Langes' life that they obtained a 'vigneron's licence and opened a wine shop in Albany in August 1984.

The intensity of colour and varietal flavour that Merv gets in his reds make them great ambassadors for the Mt Barker-Frankland region and his Rhine riesling is notable for its depth of flavour and remarkably long finish.

FOREST HILL

Tony and Betty Pearse have yet to install a winery on their property, but back in 1965 the Department of Agriculture planted the first 2 hectares of vines in the region. The first vines didn't take, incidentally, but were re-established successfully the following year.

In 1975, when the land on which the experimental vineyard was located passed back to the Pearses, Tony and Betty set about adding a further 18 hectares – mainly sauvignon and Rhine riesling which was later supplemented by small patches of gewurtztraminer, chardonnay and merlot.

From 1976 to the 1983 vintage, the Pearses had an arrangement with Paul Conti at Wanneroo whereby Paul took all the fruit from Forest Hill and made wine under a Conti-Forest Hill label. The arrangement was a happy marriage of mostly superb fruit being sympathetically handled by a master winemaker. The reputation of Mt Barker-Frankland's capacity to produce Rhine riesling with a long palate and cabernet sauvignon of generous dimensions was greatly enhanced in the process.

The Pearses started looking for alternative buyers for their fruit from the 1983 vintage. A Victorian producer, Mitchelton, was quick to seize the opportunity, buying 20 tonnes of Rhine riesling for its upmarket 'Winemakers' Selection' label. Mitchelton

Mike and Alison Goundrey taste one of their cabernet sauvignon wines at their Denmark winery.

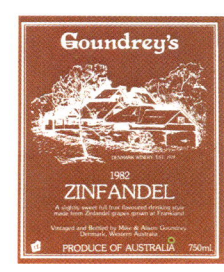

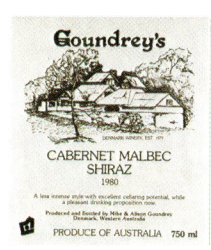

returned to Forest Hill during the 1984 vintage, taking 10 tonnes of Rhine riesling and a similar amount of cabernet sauvignon. The rest of the Pearses' fruit that year went to Plantagenet to be made under the Forest Hill label.

GOUNDREY'S WINES

When I first met farmer-shearer Mike Goundrey in the mid-1970s he was busily plunging the cap on a vat of shiraz at the Bassendean winery of the owner of Sveta Maria Wines, Ted Grassi. Having planted his first vines in 1971 on a section of an 80-hectare Mt Barker property inherited from his parents, Mike set about learning the winemaker's trade in his spare moments.

His choice of mentor was fortuitous, Ted Grassi being a winemaker who extracted sheer magic from

red grapes. Grassi's Swan Valley shiraz and cabernet sauvignon were wonders of their time, bursting with varietal character and elegance. His vintage ports were also masterpieces.

Between 1975 and 1978 when the first crops came off his vines, Mike moved between Plantagenet and Grassi's wineries, processing his own fruit while waiting to get a winery together. In 1978 Mike and his wife, Alison, bought a rundown butter factory at Denmark on the south coast, which they lovingly restored and converted into a winery in time for the 1979 vintage.

Goundrey's first planting was 2 hectares of cabernet sauvignon, followed by 3 hectares of Rhine riesling in 1973, and 1 hectare each of sauvignon blanc, chardonnay and gewurtztraminer in 1983. The first commercial crop of cabernet sauvignon was picked in 1975 and the Rhine riesling four years later. By the 1984 vintage, Mike was processing 50 tonnes of his

435

Visitors taste Goundrey's wines at the cellar door. The winery was once a butter factory.

own fruit and small parcels bought in from other growers in the region. The first wines from his chardonnay, sauvignon blanc and gewurtztraminer were expected in 1986.

Wines exhibited by Goundrey's in 1976 soon established Mike as a winemaker of excellence and led to his continuing success, one pinnacle of which was reached with his 1981 Cabernet Sauvignon – one of the most incredibly vibrant wines of the region it had been my pleasure to drink when I first came across it late in 1983.

The 1981 Goundrey's Cabernet Sauvignon bordered on greatness, attaining 19 points at Mt Barker and carrying off the trophy for the Best Open Dry Red. Nose of the wine was an enticing minty cabernet at its best with traces of camphor and mulberries. On the palate there was a marvellous combination of fruit-wood complexity and the wine had a finish with more farewells than Melba.

Goundrey's is a must for any discerning wine buyer wanting to follow the progress of Mt Barker-Frankland.

The wooded areas around
Margaret River have been
partly cleared for vineyards,
and are among the most
scenic in Western Australia.

Rob Bowen, winemaker at Plantagenet, has won many medals at Australian wine shows. His rosés are among the best of these wines in Australia.

PLANTAGENET WINES

Following the arrival of winemaker Rob Bowen on New Year's Day, 1979, the reputation of the Mt Barker-Frankland region burgeoned. Rob succeeded David McNamara at Plantagenet. A wine science graduate of the Riverina College of Advanced Education, Rob had worked for Lindemans and had a vintage or two with Brian Croser and Tony Jordan at the College before heading toward Mt Barker.

The winery he walked into at Plantagenet, in Mt Barker township, was a disused apple-packing shed purchased in 1974 and converted into a winery in time for the 1975 vintage.

Tony Smith and his partners in Plantagenet, Michael Meridith-Hardy and Perth accountant Rob Devenish, planted the first 2 hectares of shiraz and cabernet sauvignon vines at the Bouverie vineyard, west of Mt Barker, in 1968. Three years later, Plantagenet added a further 5 hectares of Rhine riesling and malbec at its Wyjup vineyard, south of Bouverie. There are now 23 hectares planted at both locations, comprising 3 hectares of cabernet sauvignon and shiraz at Bouverie and the remainder at Wyjup comprising one-third cabernet sauvignon, one-third shiraz and one-third Rhine riesling and chardonnay.

Future vineyard development will be concentrated at Bouverie and Plantagenet has access to some excellent Bindoon chenin blanc and frontignan from the Graystone vineyard of Rob Devenish's family.

There's little doubt that the star of the Plantagenet line-up most years will be shiraz, a variety with which Bowen started making some outstanding wines soon after his arrival. The consistently outstanding feature of Plantagenet shiraz (or hermitage, as the company prefers to call it) is its 'black pepper' nose and rich, almost perfumed, fruit. The 1980 Plantagenet Cabernet Sauvignon was almost as stunning. The wine was also a benchmark for Plantagenet, its refinement and elegance being understated, largely due to the Bowen philosophy of not over-wooding his reds. The release of both 1980 reds in 1982 was accompanied by three excellent whites.

In between evolving distinctive red and white styles, Bowen has turned his hand to making some excellent cabernet sauvignon rosé and giving a whole new direction to Plantagenet's vintage ports, the latter generally made from shiraz. Plantagenet vintage ports, not surprisingly, are given the names of Plantagenet kings if they pick up medals in shows. Bowen's first crack at making a local vintage port in 1979 was nominated as the best of its class at the 1980 Perth Royal Show; the 1980 somehow managed to pick both gold and silver at the 1981 Sheraton-Perth Wine Awards; and the 1981 was again judged to be the best of its class at the 1981 Perth Royal Show.

Plantagenet Wines has travelled a long way since becoming the first producer in the Mt Barker-Frankland region to release wines under its own label. Through the activities of its partners and the skills of Bowen, the company has earnt its rightful recognition as the pacesetter among the small producers in the region.

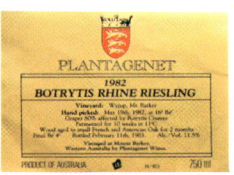

Smoko for grape pickers during vintage at Mt Barker.

CHATEAU BARKER

Winemaking has become very much a family affair since Don and Margaret Cooper settled in Mt Barker in 1973 with three sons, James and David, and immediately set about planting the whole of their 16-hectare property to vines.

James went on to attend Roseworthy, returning to Chateau Barker for the 1981 vintage. David has since become one of Western Australia's few qualified coopers with his own business which also takes in work from as far afield as the Hunter Valley, Mudgee and Rutherglen.

Add the sons' qualifications to Margaret's botanical training and Don's practical experience as a wheat and sheep farmer and the Coopers of Chateau Barker become a force to be reckoned with in the region. Chateau Barker's non-irrigated vineyard contains cabernet sauvignon, shiraz, malbec, merlot, Rhine riesling, semillon and gewurtztraminer.

The continuing lines of Chateau Barker are Quondyp Rhine Riesling, Pyramup Cabernet-Shiraz-Malbec, Tiger's Eye Pinot Noir, gewurtztraminer, semillon and cabernet sauvignon.

If a viable market is to be found for Mt Barker-Frankland gewurtztraminer, wines such as Chateau Barker's 1983 will lead the way. It was a sound, clean wine with a spicy-appley nose, a touch of residual sweetness and good firm acid backbone.

Tony Smith and winemaker Rob Bowen examine fruit coming in from the vineyard during vintage at Plantagenet winery.

GREET
YOUR MAN
WITH A
McWILLIAM'S
Cream
SHERRY

When he comes home have a Cream Sherry waiting for a pleasant moment of relaxation. McWilliam's Cream Sherry, of course . . . McWilliam's is the specially selected sweet sherry with the smooth creamy body that everyone enjoys. Serve McWilliam's Cream Sherry chilled—more and more people are liking it that way.

Always buy
McWILLIAM'S

SHERRY ON THE ROCKS
Simply place two ice cubes in a glass and pour over 2 or 3 ozs. of McWilliam's Cream Sherry.

McWILLIAM'S
Cream **SHERRY**

THE   CREAM   OF   CREAM   SHERRIES

An old Women's Weekly advertisement for one of Australia's most enduring fortified wines. McWilliam's Cream Sherry. The ads may have changed, but McWilliam's still sell plenty of sherry.

BRANDY AND FORTIFIED WINES

John Stanford

BRANDY

Brandy is the distillate of grape wine, as whisky is of malt beer, and rum is of fermented molasses and sugar residues. Brandy flavours derive from the sweet pure alcohol of fermentation, spiced with very small amounts of selected volatile elements distilled over with it.

These volatile elements include grape oils and aromas of the base wine and traces of related aromas formed during fermentation, together called the 'congenerics'. They vary with grape type and ripeness, but also with the speed of distillation, the type of still, and the skill of the operator in separating the best fractions of the distillate from the rest.

Brandy spirit is given further complexity by flavours extracted from the oak casks in which it is matured. Australian brandies are subject to strict laws. They can only be made from fresh grape wine and must be aged for at least two years in oak casks before blending and selling. They relate broadly in flavour style to the French Armagnacs, rather than their more spiced and flowery Cognacs.

South African, American and German brandies have similar flavours. Spanish are traditionally highly liqueured and must be drunk neat. Portuguese have pungent aromatics similar to French marc or Italian grappa brandies which are distilled from a base containing all the grape solids – skins, seeds, and some stalks – adding heavier congeneric oils to the distillate.

Brandy is distilled and consumed in all the world's wine countries. It is the natural and adjustable economic safety valve of each wine industry, balancing fluctuations in grape production. In years of plenty, more reserves of brandy spirit are made to balance out years of grape shortages.

In Australia, Captain John Macarthur imported the first brandy stills in 1807. Governor Bligh petulantly confiscated them and sent them back to England before they could be used.

After his resignation as Governor and over the next sixty years, distilleries were established in all the vineyard regions. The majority of spirit production was for sweet fortified wine using higher strength spirits, but consumption of locally produced beverage brandy had grown to 100 000 litres of alcohol by

Most of Australia's brandy comes from stills such as this one, in the Riverina area of New South Wales.

1900. During World War I and the prohibition rallies of that period and the 1920s it fell by almost half, but by 1930 had recovered, and trebled.

By 1970 Australians consumed a steady 4 million litres of alcohol (lal) a year as their own brandies. This increased to 4.8 million lal in 1975. It was slashed to the present 2-2.5 million lal a year after the Federal Government condoned the dumping of subsidised French brandy surpluses on the Australian market in 1975, and raised additional excise tax from Australian brandy.

Australian distillers use two types of brandy still: the copper pot still and the continuous still. The batch-type copper pot still ranges in capacity between 2000 and 20 000 litres. These stills are steam-heated rather than direct-fired, as in French Cognac distilleries or the whisky distilleries of Scotland. (Only one or two small Cognac-style Charentais stills are installed in Australia.)

A large volume of Australia's bulk blending brandy is processed in continous stills – multi-column fractionating stills. They produce clean, but

442

less distinctive and more 'heady' brandies. Against sales of 2-2.5 million lal Australian distillers carry over 10 million lal of ageing reserves.

Most of Australia's brandies are produced in South Australia, at the large Riverland distilleries. Here, in roughly descending order of volume, the makers are Berri/Renmano, Loxton, Angove's and Hardy's Cyrilton. They distill the brandy from base wines made from grapes such as sultana, doradillo, Waltham cross (rosaki), grenache and so on, grown under irrigation. They each use a combination of multi-column continuous stills and pot stills. The latter produce their best spirits because they can separate more precise fractions of the vapours.

The big co-operative wineries/distilleries age and supply stock brandies to a number of large-selling company brands in the major Sydney and Melbourne markets. The Angove's St Agnes Five and Seven Star old brandies, the Renmano Old Show Brandy and Berri Estate Old Barrell Brandy are superior marques from the region under the producers' names.

In the Barossa, Tollana (Tolleys/T.S.T. marque), Orlando, Seppelt, Yalumba and, to a lesser degree, Penfolds, are the major distillers and holders of aged reserves. They each employ some continuous and some pot stills. Tollana has the most sophisticated computer-controlled multi-column still in this region. In addition to the standard three star brandies bottled by all those houses as the majority of their output, Seppelt's VSOP Liqueur, Yalumba Galway Five Star, Penfolds VSOP and Orlando Barossa Liqueur are superior aged styles, among others.

In the Southern Vales, south of Adelaide, the Hardy group dominates brandy production. They double pot distill the brandy at Waikerie in the Riverland and then transport it to McLaren Vale for ageing in oak casks. The Reynella Creme de Fine Brandy – which is sweetened in the Spanish liqueur brandy style – and Hardy's excellent old Armagnac-style VSOP and standard grade Hardy's Black Bottle are all superior brandies. Like the Barossa distillers, they use a balance of locally grown base wines and those from the Murray Valley vineyards which have proved very suitable for brandy production.

In Victoria there is a small pot still in operation in the north-east and another at Chateau Remy at Avoca in the south-west. Most of Victorian brandy is made at Merbein in the Sunraysia irrigation area. Mildara at Merbein is the largest, oldest and most famous distiller in Victoria. They use a combination of a sophisticated multi-column still and a series of copper pot stills. The Mildara brandies, especially the superior Extra Reserve marque, are light and spiced, tending to the flowery Cognac style more than most Australian brandies.

In the Riverina region, McWilliam's are the major winemakers and also the major distillers of brandy. Their MAX brandy, produced at the Yenda distillery, is a consistent, full flavoured, smooth and aromatic style. As a three star rating for Australian brandy it is a superior style.

The Australian brandy industry supplies an essential balance against over-production of grapes as well as a pure, high quality product. It has perfected distillation techniques, accumulated reserves of aged blending brandies and acquired sophisticated distilling equipment. To its credit it has achieved this status with no help from a central government to the degree accorded its overseas competitors.

Angove's winery, in the South Australian Riverland, near Renmark, makes some of Australia's best known brandies.

Bottling fortified wines is somewhat less of a problem than bottling table wines, due to the higher degree of protection from bacteria provided by the higher alcohol levels.

FORTIFIED WINES

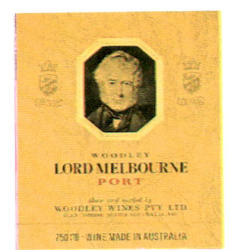

Since vines were first planted in the Hawkesbury region and Captain Macarthur made ports at Camden in the early 1800s, ports, sherries, muscats, tokays and madeiras have been a significant proportion of all Australian wines. To a lesser degree they still are today.

The nineteenth-century founding settlers came from a country where Portuguese and Spanish fortified wines were established and popular. They found the Australian climate warm and temperate compared with northern Europe and very suitable for these styles. They had aspirations to produce the high quality, light table wines that dominate Australia's production today, but found it easier to preserve and export them by adding brandy or neutral spirit.

Along with the colony of South Africa, they became John Bull's antipodean vineyards, making wines patterned on the sweet ports, Madeiras and Setubal muscats of Portugal and the sherries and Malagas of Spain.

Especially in the periods 1860-1900 and 1920-50, they were the principal wine styles of Australia, representing 80 per cent of all production as late as 1960. Since 1960, with improved winemaking technology, Australian tastes have swung dramatically to table wines, which now represent over 83 per cent of all production.

Some 16.5 per cent of Australian wine is still made as fortified wine – 49 million litres per year in a total of almost 300 million litres. This is made up of 4 million litres of dry sherry, 5 million litres of medium dry, 14 million litres of sweet sherry, 16 million litres of port types, 3.5 million litres of muscat and madeira styles, 2.5 million litres of fortified wines using berry-fruit and other flavourings, and 4 million litres in the form of dry and sweet vermouths.

Many of Australia's older vineyards are still planted principally with grape varieties selected for making these fortified styles and brandy. A majority of those same grapes have now been adapted to make

light table wines instead – mainly in the ordinary bulk white wine category. They are being replaced by grafting and replanting, with the world's superior fine table wine varieties.

The dry fortified styles like dry sherry or dry vermouth require a neutral-flavoured white wine base. In Australia these are generally made from the Spanish pedro ximinez and palomino varieties, semillon, or the plainer and more prolific sultana doradillo and Waltham cross dual-purpose wine and distillation, or drying grape types.

The sweet white fortified wines use pedro, several strains of muscat, muscadelle (called tokay) and a few Spanish or Portuguese grapes like verdelho. The sweet reds use grenache, shiraz, mataro and cabernet and small amounts of touriga.

The normal fully fermented strength potential of the grape juices – 11 to 13 per cent alcohol, as in table wines – is raised to 17-20 per cent alcohol by the addition and mixing of distilled brandy or neutral grape spirit. Ripe grapes contain 20-30 per cent grape sugar according to the degree of ripeness. Some are even higher.

At that higher level of alcohol yeast is unable to re-ferment retained grape sugar sweetness and the wines are stable. They are generally aged in oak casks for upwards of two to three years to marry the wine and spirit harmoniously, and accumulate oak flavour complexity. Dry sherries and vermouths have up to 2 per cent retained grape sugar, medium dry 2-5 per cent, the average port or sweet white 6-8 per cent, and rich liqueur muscats and tokays 10-18 per cent.

Older fortified wines of the tawny port, madeira or tokay and sherry styles are oak-matured for up to fifty years for blending with younger wines.

As production and consumption has fallen, and a Federal tax on spirit went on, then was removed, the volume made and average age of these wines has fallen off.

Next to Portugal, Australia makes the most distinctive and consistent sweet reds of the port style and sweet whites of the madeira style. They are generally more full bodied, richer and sweeter than the Portuguese styles. The full bodied, intensely aromatic, aged liqueur muscats – especially those of the Rutherglen region in north-east Victoria – are superior to any other muscat styles in the world. For a century, our fino and amontillado sherries, along with those of South Africa, have rated next to those of the best bodegas of Spain for quality, and classical style.

Production of fortified wines today is concentrated in only a few regions – the Murray Valley, the Riverina, the Barossa and Clare region, the Southern Vales south of Adelaide, north east Victoria around Rutherglen and the Swan Valley near Perth in Western Australia. The major volume is made in the hot, dry inland regions under irrigation – the Riverina in New South Wales and the Murray Valley. The central Murray regions are divided between Mildura

and Swan Hill on the Victorian side – the Sunraysia district – and Renmark, Berri, Loxton and Waikerie down-river on the South Australian side – the Riverland districts.

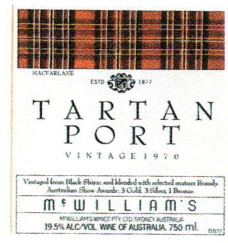

The Riverland contains some of Australia's largest processing wineries, mostly grape-grower co-operatives. Between them they crush around 25 per cent of Australia's total grape crop in most years. The Berri and Renmark co-operatives are the largest. They market their wines jointly under the title of Consolidated Co-operatives today. They also produce the major proportion of Australia's brandy.

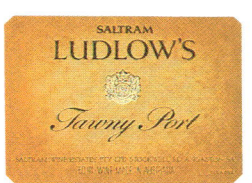

Their wines are mainly light bodied young bulk table wines, young fortified sweet whites and a smaller proportion of young sweet reds. Loxton is the third largest of these co-operative wineries and distilleries.

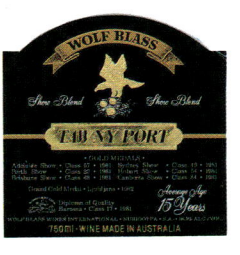

The majority of this wine is sold in bulk to large private wine companies who control the retail markets in the major cities where most of Australia's wine is consumed. They blend it with more costly full bodied styles from their dry-farmed vineyards in places such as the Barossa, Southern Vales, Rutherglen, etc.

Under their own labels the co-operative wineries sell selected blends of more mature sherries, muscats and sweet reds in smaller volumes.

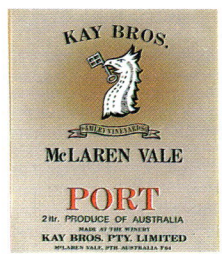

The largest private winemaker in the Riverland is the family company, Angove's at Renmark. It has extensive vineyards of its own. Apart from its St Agnes and Angove's brandies, it produces a variety of fresh young sweet whites, muscats and ports, and a large range of light table wines.

The Loxton Co-operative produces large volumes of brandy spirit and bulk fortified wines as well as non-alcoholic grape juice.

The Hardy group owns a large vineyard, winery and distillery at Cyrilton, near Waikerie. It produces blending wines, brandy and spirits for their lower priced, fast turnover brands.

Yalumba, Tollana, Orlando and other large Barossa winemakers maintain extensive private vineyards in the Murray Valley. They transfer the fresh grapes from these and from other contracted grape-growers directly to their Barossa wineries 260-300 kilometres south for crushing and processing for the same purposes.

Up-river, the Sunraysia district is dominated by two major private companies – Mildara Wines at Mildura and Lindemans at Karadoc. Mildara also own the Hamilton's Ewell marque and wineries and the marketing company, Haselgroves. They are the oldest traditional winemakers in the region, with cool

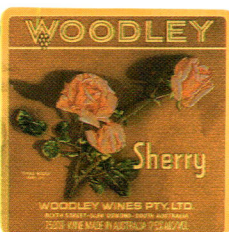

region vineyards at Coonawarra and Eden Valley in South Australia.

Their brandies are among Australia's best. Apart from table wines and sparkling wines they make some of the Murray Valley's best fortified tawny ports and sherries. These include Mildara Special Reserve Tawny and the 'George' and 'Supreme Dry' fino sherries, amontillado sherries, and 'Chestnut Teal' oloroso style sweet sherry along with lower priced muscats, sweet whites and sweet reds.

Lindemans' Karadoc winery in Victoria is one of Australia's biggest modern private wineries. They make large volumes of white wine there for the country's principal white table wine brand Ben Ean Moselle, and smaller volumes of cabernet dry red as well as base wines for their fortified wine brands.

The non-irrigated regions around Australia produce its most distinctive and intensely flavoured fortified wines, but in smaller volumes.

The Barossa Valley and Clare regions, 80-100 kilometres north of Adelaide are headquarters for a number of Australia's oldest large private wine companies. They maintain a high proportion of the country's aged blending reserves of sweet and dry fortified wine in oak storage in century-old stone cellars.

The principal Barossa companies still marketing these superior types are Seppelt (Para Liqueur Ports,

Special Bin and Show reserve tawny ports and sherries, etc.), Penfolds/Kaiser Stuhl (Grandfather and Magill tawny ports, vintage ports, tokay and old sherries), Yalumba (Galway Pipe and Directors Special tawnies, wood-aged sherries and madeiras), Orlando (old tawny ports, madeiras, brown muscats and sherries from extensive blending reserves), and Saltram (Mr Pickwick tawny and some distinctive old sweet whites and sherries).

Other companies in this category with smaller reserves are Tollana, Krondorf, Leo Buring, Wolf Blass, Basedow, St Halletts, Yaldara, Rovalley and Karrawirra.

South of Adelaide, the Hardy group dominates the Southern Vales fortified wine field with fine old tawny and full bodied vintage ports, a distinctive madeira style using sauvignon blanc and a range of sweet whites and sherries. Wynn have a large winery there but it produces mainly table and sparkling wines. Their fortified wine operations are centred at Nunawading, near Melbourne.

In the Swan Valley near Perth in Western Australia a number of small winemakers produce soft sweet reds and sweet whites. The oldest and largest is Houghton Wines, famous for liqueur muscats, rich sweet whites and old tawny ports. Sandalford is the only other large company making fortified wine in that region, notably their distinctive Sandalera liqueur.

In north-east Victoria, around the towns of Rutherglen, Glenrowan, Corowa and Milawa are made some of Australia's richest, full bodied liqueur muscats using the red frontignac grape variety, luscious sweet whites from muscadelle grapes (often described as tokay) and distinctive sweet tawny ports. This historic region became famous for sweet wines in the nineteenth century when it was the centre of gold-mining and the Eureka Stockade rebellion.

It was almost wiped out by the phylloxera plague at the turn of the century, at which time it was Australia's largest wine-producing region. It is only now recovering some of its former prominence. By the 1920s South Australia had taken over most of its markets.

In the Hunter Valley fortified wines are only a small proportion of production today. Tyrrells, Rosemount, and to a lesser degree, Wyndham Estate and Tulloch maintain aged blending reserves in oak storage for port and madeira production. Several small makers, including Murray Robson, produce a distinctive locally grown red muscat style.

The largest fortified wine centre in New South Wales is in the rich and productive Riverina wine region around Griffith and Yenda, 700 kilometres south-west of Sydney. It grows its grapes under irrigation, but its soils are heavier and its wines more full bodied than those of the Murray Valley.

One of Australia's major family wine companies, McWilliam's, dominates the area and produce most of the fortified, table and sparkling wine there. McWilliam's have maintained large reserves of sherry and sweet white blending wines for more than half a century. They are Australia's largest marketers of medium priced standard sweet and dry sherries.

Most of the 18 wineries in the Riverina make some soft and attractive sweet white and sweet red fortified wine, although most concentrate on light table wines. It is a hot, dry climate and grapes can reach high sugar levels at full ripeness.

Wynn's major winery at Yenda supplies their main blending cellars in Melbourne. Other, smaller, winemakers with distinctive sweet reds and sweet whites of this region are de Bortoli, Rosetto, Miranda and San Bernadino.

The northernmost commercial vineyards and winery in Australia are at Roma, in southern central Queensland. The climate is warm and subtropical. Bassett's Romaville winery there makes distinctive sweet white madeira styles from muscats and rare grape varieties like solverino.

The actual volume of production and consumption of fortified wines in Australia has shown a small increase over the last thirty years. As a percentage of all wine now being consumed however, it has fallen from 80 per cent to 16-17 per cent of the total due to the dramatic increases in overall Australian wine drinking, mainly in the form of light table wine, over that period.

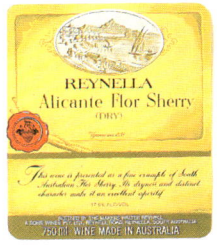

447

Two older vintages of top-selling South Australian wines: Wolf Blass 1969 Rhine Riesling, and Australia's biggest selling bottled red wine, Orlando Jacob's Creek Claret, here from 1970.

A TOP DOZEN

John Parkinson

The important wine consumer is not the person who drinks only first growth French claret. It's the person who keeps a cask in the fridge, enjoys a bottle of sparkling wine every now and then and, in table wines, likes whites with perhaps a touch of sweetness and reds which are smooth and fruity and don't bite as they go down.

So my selection is of twelve wine styles which are not only popular with consumers but which have also played a significant role in shaping the development both of the public palate and the industry itself. I have limited myself to selecting wines which still have significant influence on consumers today. That means leaving out wines like Barossa Pearl and Cawarra Claret, both of which have played an extremely important role in the Australian wine scene in years past, but whose place has been taken by new market leaders.

I also hope that this will help to recognise the tremendous contribution made by the winemakers responsible both for creating and maintaining these styles. To evolve a new style and then maintain a consistent level of quality as the volume grows to massive proportions is every bit an example of consummate winemaking skill as producing the one spectacular small parcel of a wine which embodies all the classic characteristics of the style and/or variety. In fact I believe the former may even be the greater achievement.

Here then is my 'top dozen'. The names are undoubtedly familiar but perhaps they are so familiar that you haven't even bothered to consider what goes into making that particular wine what it is. Next time you buy one of these wines you can feel a touch of pride in the Australian wine industry's achievement in raising the quality not only of our 'classic' wines, but of the wines you regard as everyday drinking styles.

SUMMERWINE
(KAISER STUHL)

Nancy Sinatra and Lee Hazelwood could never have foreseen the effect that their popular standard of the 1970s was to have on the Australian wine market. Their song 'Summer Wine' was to provide the inspiration for the most successful new product of the

decade, which is today the biggest selling table wine in Australia.

It came about because of a request by Kaiser Stuhl to their advertising agency at the time, McCann Erickson, for a new 'lifestyle' concept in wine – something which embodied the joys of life outdoors and the Australian approach to entertaining. Summerwine was one of the two concepts the agency came up with. The wine itself – a light refreshing sparkling white which was a cross between a spumante and a sparkling moselle, without quite the same sweetness – was the creation of George Kolaravich and his winemakers.

The 'rightness' both of the concept and the product is perhaps best illustrated by the fact that neither have been changed since the product was first released in Newcastle in 1976. In a distinctive silver, yellow and black label and selling for under $1.50 a bottle it quickly became the hottest product on the market. A large measure of its success was that it didn't conform to the accepted criteria for wine. It didn't talk about vintages or regions or varieties; it just typified the Australian way of life for many consumers who enjoyed drinking wine, rather than talking about it. Perhaps one of the best examples of that is the way it sells in Queensland. There it is not unusual to see 20-30 dozen stacked in a coolroom alongside the beer, because that's how it sells – as a drink rather than as something to be sipped and savoured.

Today it still sells for around $2 a bottle and is Australia's top-selling wine in bottle, at some 400 000 cases a year. It seems that Summerwine is destined to remain a 'wine for all seasons' for many years.

BEN EAN MOSELLE

(LINDEMANS)

Who can honestly say they have never drunk a bottle of the wine that for more than a decade was Australia's national white wine beverage and remains today one of the biggest selling still table wines across the country?

Ben Ean Moselle was the brainchild of Ray Kidd, now Managing Director of Lindemans Wines. In 1956 he was the Cellar and Vineyards Manager. He saw then that the current popularity of the sweet, 'sparkling pearl' styles would lead to a demand for a still table wine offering the same basic qualities of soft easy-to-drink flavour with a touch of sweetness. So Ben Ean was created, taking its name from one of Lindemans vineyards in the Hunter Valley (as did all the other Lindemans' generic styles such as Cawarra Claret and Kirkton Chablis). The first Ben Eans were true to label too, being blends of Hunter semillon with a little verdelho.

The Ben Ean era really began with the wine boom in the late Sixties and continued through an astonishing growth period to a peak in 1979. During that time Ben Ean ceased to be a regional wine and became a true cellar style blended to a consistent standard of quality, flavour and sweetness that struck a strong responsive chord with Australian consumers. In recent years the moselle market has been steadily declining, and with it Ben Ean's pre-eminent position as Australia's national white. The nominated heir apparent and now the biggest selling still white table wine is another Lindemans' house brand, Leo Buring's Leibfrauwine.

Paradoxically, Ben Ean is probably a better wine today than it has ever been, benefiting in freshness and fruit flavour from improved winemaking technology and a better varietal base. It is still a wine that delights in blind tastings in embarrassing those of us who thought we had outgrown the product.

KAISER STUHL ROSÉ

Kaiser Stuhl Rosé was the first to capitalise on the success of the Portuguese rosés in Australia in the early Sixties and it remains today easily the biggest selling rosé style on the market, comfortably ahead of the wine that started it all – Mateus.

One of the reasons for that success is that Kaiser Stuhl did not fall into the trap of making a 'me too' style. Instead they developed a style of their own –

softer, fresher and with an attractive touch of sweetness. The first blend was released in 1962, but the wine as we know it today, with its distinctive clear glass bottle modelled on the German crock, first appeared in 1965. In those days it was labelled Gold Medal Rosé and lived up to that label too, being a consistent medal winner both here and overseas. (The 'Gold Medal' tag was dropped in 1983 because by then its Show appearances had become far less frequent.)

The product itself has changed slightly over the period, dropping its level of alcohol from 12 to 10 per cent which is more in keeping with the easy drinking nature of rosé. At the same time it has become a little less sweet and a touch more petillant, or spritzig, to keep it in touch with current trends.

While Kaiser Stuhl Rosé has been a real success story the market in general for rosé has steadily declined since those boom years in the Sixties. A pity, since rosé as a style would seem a natural for our climate and lifestyle.

Victoria remains the 'rosé State' although Kaiser Stuhl Rosé sells strongly right across Australia. Perhaps the next decade will see a new generation of wine drinkers who will rediscover the joys of drinking rosé, as their parents did two decades ago.

SEAVIEW CABERNET SAUVIGNON

Seaview Cabernet Sauvignon is a style that for many wine drinkers still is the benchmark for reliability and quality in reds. Its reputation was undoubtedly helped by the fact that in those exciting early years of wine discovery in the Sixties Seaview was one of the few cabernets readily available on the market.

Seaview was then owned by the Chaffey Brothers. Ben Chaffey had first produced a cabernet from the Seaview vineyard at McLaren Vale in the mid-1950s. Unfortunately in those days Seaview was truly a boutique winery. Even the famous 1962 vintage was only 1200 cases. So when people started clamouring

for the wine Chaffey started to stretch the blend to satisfy demand. As a result, when Tooheys purchased Seaview in late 1971 they found they had to rebuild the brand.

It was 1976 before they could return to the original concept of using mainly Southern Vales fruit. The mix was and still is the pick of the cabernet from Seaview itself plus grapes bought in from Southern Vales and the Adelaide Hills district. The result has been a genuine revival of the qualities that made the original Seaview cabernets so attractive – soft, round, flavoursome fruit without excessive tannin.

Today 80-85 per cent of the wine sees wood, the oak being a mixture of new American oak puncheons and 300- and 500-litre casks ranging in age from one to seven years. The wine is definitely a straight cabernet and is released at about three years' bottle age.

Today it is the biggest selling cabernet in Australia. Wine writer and judge, James Halliday, reviewing the 1980 Seaview Cabernet, said that it was a return to the old standard. That standard is a tribute both to the skill of the winemaking team and the consistency of the Southern Vales area from which the fruit comes.

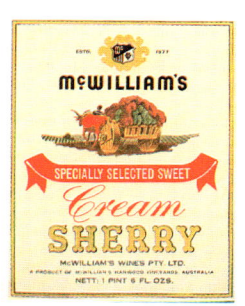

McWILLIAM'S CREAM SHERRY

It might seem strange to see this wine included in a modern line-up of currently popular wines. Yet McWilliam's Cream Sherry is still a dominant force in the market nearly thirty years after it was released.

The real boom days of the sherry market may have gone and cream sherry might seem an anachronism in a wine world that only seems interested in chardonnay and chablis. Yet McWilliam's Cream Sherry still sells the equivalent of four million bottles a year; and there are a lot of people who still have a glass or two every day, something even the top selling brands cannot claim.

It started in 1956. One of the most popular wines of the day was a Lindemans sherry called Montillo

Sweet, basically a young sweet gordo style that was rather like an overstrength moselle. McWilliam's at that time had a range of minimum price sherries under their Royal Reserve label. They felt there was a market for a premium sweet sherry in the same style as the Lindemans but fresher and more luscious. They took the name from Harvey's famous Bristol Cream in the United Kingdom, and made the wine out of fortified gordo bottled within six months of being made. McWilliam's then attacked the market with full page wine ads, unheard of at the time, under the slogan 'the smoothest of them all'.

The wine was an instant success, so much so that McWilliam's had to rapidly expand their production to meet the demand. They even had to build a new winery at Robinvale (N.S.W.) to process the fruit they needed.

At its peak in the 1960s it was the biggest selling wine in Australia. Even today the production of McWilliam's Cream Sherry is still not far off its best-ever sales year, an amazing tribute to the staying power of this style.

Spraying the vines at Frankland River, one of Houghton's major sources of grapes.

HOUGHTON WHITE BURGUNDY

The distinctive label with its blue stripe (designed incidentally by Sydney restaurateur and wine merchant Johnnie Walker) has long been the consumers' way of recognising Australia's best known white burgundy.

Houghton White Burgundy, the wine that put the Western Australian wine industry on the map, has been around since 1936 when that great character, Jack Mann, decided to make a big, full flavoured white wine from chenin blanc. The grapes were picked ripe and squeezed until every last bit of flavour had been extracted. No wonder it needed two years in bottle before you could drink it!

But it was definitely a wine of character, and when it was introduced into the Eastern States of Australia twenty-five years ago it was an instant success. The then Prime Minister Bob Menzies was among the early converts. So popular was the wine that it was only available on quota – a situation that remained until 1981 when increased production meant that the quotas could be lifted.

During that time a lot of changes took place. The blend had been stretched in the early Seventies to cater for demand. When Hardy took over Houghton in 1976 the brand was languishing.

The new management, under winemakers Jon Reynolds and Bill Hardy, set about revitalising the brand, bringing it more into keeping with the needs of the new consumer who was looking for greater freshness and less of the big 'gutsy' flavour of the old style.

Modern winemaking techniques have seen the traditional blend of 80 per cent chenin blanc and 20 per cent tokay and verdelho become fresher and lighter in body. It's a long way from the old Houghton White Burgundy in character, but the changes obviously appealed to consumers because sales doubled in recent years and the demand is still growing strongly.

Further changes are planned, including the gradual introduction of chardonnay and sauvignon blanc to replace the tokay in the blend. However Houghton will continue to be what it always was – a distinctive cellar style offering consistently good quality and value to the consumer.

GREAT WESTERN CHAMPAGNE
(SEPPELT)

To most Australians the name Great Western is synonymous with champagne, at least Australian champagne. Whether it be Imperial Reserve, Brut Reserve, N.V. Brut or Vintage Brut, it has been the catalyst at millions of parties and celebrations since it was released back in 1892.

It was not, however, always the biggest selling Australian champagne. That position was held for many years by Penfolds Minchinbury. The rise to the leading position in the market place was largely due to the efforts of one of Australia's greatest winemakers, Colin Preece. When he took over in 1932, Minchinbury was outselling Great Western three to one. By the early 1960s when he retired that position had reversed, due to the public's recognition of the superiority of Great Western over its competitors.

By the early 1970s Seppelt's dominance of the market was such that nearly 60 per cent of all Australian champagne sold was Great Western. Since then the sparkling wine market has continued to boom, but with that boom has come greatly increased competition, so that today Great Western's share is only 40 per cent, although their total sales are higher than ever.

What has made Great Western so popular with consumers? Undoubtedly consistency, a light, easy drinking style and a constant process of improving the brand. In recent years Seppelt have spared no effort to maintain Great Western's position as the market leader. They have used overseas winemakers to get more expertise in their production. They have significantly improved their base wines and they have spent $5 million on vast maturation storage cellars so that they can guarantee that their products get at least 12 months on lees – that vital period when the natural effervescence is added and the all important flavour build-up starts to occur.

Today champagne has ceased to be regarded as just a celebration drink; it is being used as an aperitif and as the automatic party starter. It is increasingly the wine everyone chooses to put life into any occasion. That means continued growth in the market, and for Great Western an increasingly important role in the future of the Australian wine industry.

PARA LIQUEUR PORT
(SEPPELT)

Para Liqueur may not be the biggest selling port in Australia (the honour belongs to Penfolds Club), but there is no doubt it is the best known. Although an 1878 port was released onto the market with a Para Liqueur label just a few years ago, the Para brand (named after the Para River in South Australia) itself only came into being in the early 1950s.

The distinctive dump bottle was originally of Portuguese origin and the word 'Liqueur' was added to give the product additional status. The material itself was an old blend of shiraz, grenache and mataro from the Barossa Valley of South Australia. The bottle carried a vintage date – 1922 – which led to the somewhat erroneous belief that Para Liqueur was in fact a vintage wine. It wasn't. Para Liqueur has always been a blend of years, the vintage really indicating the age of the base wine in the blend.

It was not until the early 1970s that Para Liqueur really jumped into the limelight. The story goes that the phenomenon known as Paramania was begun by someone paying $400 for a bottle of 1927 Para Liqueur at a charity auction. Immediately everyone thought that every bottle of 1927 Para was worth $400 and so it began. For five years the wine auction

scene went crazy and Paras of all ages fetched ridiculous prices. It is interesting to look back and note that you could buy the 1933 Para in 1971 for $3 a bottle and even today the current blend which has an average age of over twenty years sells for just over $16 a bottle.

One other factor which tended to accentuate the rarity of the so-called Vintage Paras was the fact that in 1976 Seppelt dropped the vintage dating for legal reasons and introduced the blend numbers. The first 101 was a good wine but lacked the venerable image of its predecessor, the 1947.

Nevertheless Para Liqueur remains one of the benchmark styles for Australian premium tawny ports. It is still very much in the classic old style, rich in aged rancio character and still quite sweet and heavy on the palate; yet it retains that marvellous complexity which can only come with prolonged wood ageing.

JACOB'S CREEK CLARET
(ORLANDO)

Jacob's Creek is Australia's most popular dry red – and New Zealand's too for that matter. The most remarkable thing about Jacob's Creek is that it was born at a time of great decline in the dry red market, yet, by the end of the decade, it was firmly established as one of the real marketing success stories of the 1970s.

It was released quietly onto the market in 1976 as part of a new 'Orlando vineyard' range, the other wines being Lyndale Riesling and Moorooroo White Burgundy.

The idea of the range was to promote the concept of blending to a style. The marketing slogan was 'one grape brings out the best in another'. Each was named after an Orlando vineyard holding in the Barossa, Jacob's Creek being just up the road from Orlando's main winery at Rowland Flat.

The first Jacob's Creek was the 1973 vintage; a blend of shiraz, cabernet and malbec, the fruit

coming from Keppoch, Coonawarra, Barossa and the Southern Vales. It had more pronounced wood character and less cool climate fruit than the later wines which have a higher percentage of Keppoch and Coonawarra fruit in the blend.

Jacob's Creek wasn't an overnight success. Lyndale Riesling was initially the most popular wine in the range. But in 1977 Jacob's Creek won several significant show medals, including a gold in Canberra. That success sparked consumer interest to such an extent that four years later it had become Australia's top selling dry red.

Jacob's Creek as a wine is very much in the modern Australian dry red mould – soft, clean flavour, still fresh and fruity, but without excessive sweetness or tannin. It set a new standard for red wine in Australia and has been largely instrumental in the swing back to reds by Australian consumers in the past ten years – a trend for which the industry must be very grateful.

COOLABAH CASKS
(ORLANDO)

'Where do you hide your Coolabah?' was the jingle which helped launch Orlando into the cask market in 1973. They were not the first to market cask wines. Wynn must take the credit for introducing the wine cask, as we know it, in 1971.

Orlando's entry was to have far-reaching effects both for the consumer and the industry as a whole. It was Orlando who really 'legitimised' the cask, who gave it that extra touch of class both in the product and the pack, and who helped to convince the Australian consumer that here was a really exciting new way to buy and enjoy wine. The cask has never looked back.

Neither has Coolabah, which is still the biggest selling brand in the cask market today.

Orlando decided that for casks to really be successful they had to be seen as part of the Australian way of life and that they had to be a little trendy as well – not just cheap *vin ordinaire*. Hence the slick packaging, with wistful outdoor period scenes. And the television ads emphasising that you only hid you Coolabah cask because otherwise everyone would want some – not because it was cheap.

The first Coolabah casks were launched in July 1973. There were five styles in all – riesling, moselle, rosé, claret and white burgundy. Although there are now nine products in the range, riesling and moselle remain the best sellers.

The name was not new. Orlando had used Coolabah on flagons and a range of 750 ml bottles. However it was as a cask that Coolabah has passed into the Australian idiom, alongside such household names as Vegemite and Fosters.

The wines themselves have always been a cut above the standard cask in flavour. Orlando took the position of being the price leader in the market and only reduced their prices when the discount pressures got too great in the late Seventies. It was also Orlando who revolutionised the pack design with the squat fridge pack, for greater consumer convenience.

The result is Coolabah is one of the few casks to retain any brand loyalty – a fitting reward for Orlando's efforts in helping to take wine to the people in style.

WOLF BLASS RHINE RIESLING

In 1960 a young German winemaker came out to advise Kaiser Stuhl on sparkling wine production. A quarter of a century later he had set himself up as one of the most successful and profitable wine producers in Australia.

Wolf's only real experience with red wine was handling it at Harvey's (the English wine merchants) cellars in Bristol, just prior to coming to Australia. Yet his extraordinary record for winning trophies with red wines in wine shows in the 1970s will probably never be equalled. This man, having firmly established his reputation as a master blender of reds,

turned around and produced Australia's biggest selling premium Rhine riesling, only five years after he seriously entered the market. Wolf Blass' success with whites is all the more remarkable because he came into the market so late. Also it was a market which was probably the most hotly contested in the industry.

Wolf had been making Rhine riesling since 1969. It was not until he returned from an overseas trip in 1976 that he knew exactly what he wanted to do with the style. Characteristically he told everyone he had found the answer to producing the sort of riesling style best suited to Australia and Australian consumers. Just as characteristically he has been proved right.

The 1977 vintage saw a totally new Wolf Blass style – crisp, fresh, fruity and with a definite touch of sweetness. Others had been there before Wolf, but none has managed to capture the public's imagination as he has. Over the next five years Wolf Blass Rhine Riesling sales went through the roof and are still climbing at an astonishing rate. The style is undoubtedly 'commercial', but as Wolf has said, if 'commercial' means providing what people want to drink then he takes that as a compliment.

The real secret of Wolf's success is that his belief in his own product is so strong that consumers find it easy to believe in it too. He backs that with an astute ability to assess what the consumer really wants in a wine, rather than what they or the industry think they want.

GRANGE HERMITAGE
(PENFOLDS)

Grange Hermitage is Australia's most famous red wine.

It is now over thirty years since Max Schubert returned from France with the idea of making an Australian equivalent of the classic French Chateau bottled dry red, a wine made by selecting only the best fruit, giving it extended maturation in the best new oak, then letting it have a reasonable period of maturation in bottle prior to release.

Those early judges, who rejected the early Granges because they thought the style too fruity and over-oaked, have had plenty of time to ponder on those judgements. Even Penfolds themselves, who were nervous after the early criticisms and ordered Max to stop wasting money on new oak to produce such an unpopular style, have had time to thank Bacchus that recognition came before the style was lost forever.

And after some early doubts about the style Grange has been unchallenged as Australia's premier dry red for the past 25 years. It is the ultimate cellar style. Experience has taught Penfolds winemakers how to select the best fruit from Kalimna, Magill and Coonawarra vineyards, the sources from which Grange is made. They even know which rows in their own vineyards produce the fruit most suitable for the Grange style. And, despite rumours to the contrary, Grange is very much a shiraz wine. The amount of cabernet is sometimes as low as 2 per cent and usually no more than 5 per cent.

It is the oak treatment that really helps to give Grange much of its distinctive character. Only new American oak is used and the wine remains in the wood until the chief winemaker says it is ready. Grange is truly a winemaker's wine – not a wine marketer's creation.

Penfolds have also been fortunate in having Max Schubert and more recently Don Ditter to oversee the production of Grange. There is no substitute for experience. Over the thirty-odd years that Grange has been made it has managed to remain remarkably true to style – which is in itself a remarkable achievement when one considers the dramatic changes that have occurred in the industry during that time.

That Grange holds a fascination for Australians is obvious. Despite a price well over $20 a bottle on release, each vintage still sells out in a week. Penfolds could obviously sell a lot more if they wanted to. It is also becoming an increasingly important ambassador for the Australian wine industry overseas. Around 20 per cent of the current vintage has been exported.

In the light of the tremendous value that Grange represents to Penfolds, why haven't there been more imitators trying to cash in on the extraordinary profile of the product? Perhaps the answer is that Grange is in a category of its own. Even if someone were to be able to access the same fruit, afford the same new oak, exactly copy the winemaking techques used and then afford the enormous cost of keeping the wine for six years before releasing it, the wine would at best be regarded as a Grange copy – not the real thing. There is only one Grange.

If you are fortunate enough to have some it is worth remembering that Grange takes more than a decade to begin to reach its peak.

It is a wine that demands respect, but the rewards are worth waiting for.

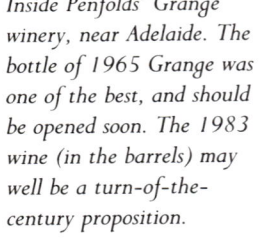

Inside Penfolds' Grange winery, near Adelaide. The bottle of 1965 Grange was one of the best, and should be opened soon. The 1983 wine (in the barrels) may well be a turn-of-the-century proposition.

Frank Doherty

Geoff Donaldson's Cellar

*I*n April 1972, a group of thirty dinner-jacketed and bow-tied Victorian wine-lovers sat down to a dinner which had been convened for one specific purpose – to drink a 100-year-old wine. It had all been Geoff Donaldson's idea. In his cellar had been the last three of a two-case lot of the 1872 Hermitage from the Craiglee vineyard at Sunbury, 40 kilometres north of Melbourne. He had been willing to donate them to then Wine and Brandy Producers' Association of Victoria in the cause of promoting Victorian wine which at that stage was only beginning the remarkable renaissance it has since seen.

The 1872 wine had been discovered at Craiglee early in the 1950s after having lain undetected behind some casks for the better part of 80 years. Dr William Johnson, grandson of the founder of Craiglee, offered them to the late Tom Seabrook, Melbourne's foremost wine merchant at the time who, in turn offered them to his friends and customers for 10 shillings a bottle 'all faults found'. If one got an ullaged bottle or one that had oxidised, it was part of the bargain. Geoff Donaldson bought two dozen and, fortuitously, all had been sound.

The three opened that night in 1972 by Tom Seabrook's son, Doug – now also deceased – with a surgeon's tenderness and care amid hushed expectation, were in prime condition though, once poured, the wine lasted no more than twenty or twenty-five minutes in the glass before pleading tiredness after a century's confinement in bottle.

In its way, it was appropriate that Geoff Donaldson (now seventy-two and recently retired as chairman of the Woodside Petroleum company and having been made an Officer of the Order of Australia for his services to the industry) should have presented a wine that night which had come through Tom Seabrook's hands, for it was the eminent judge and merchant who had been responsible for his introduction to wine.

Like most servicemen of World War II, he had been a beer drinker but Seabrook, a neighbour of the Donaldson family, had encouraged him to cultivate a taste for wine. Seabrook must have taught well and quickly for it was not long before the apostle was not only buying wine from his master but also accompanying him on some of his forays to interstate vignerons.

Under Tom Seabrook's influence, the young Donaldson soon became a member of the Viticulture Society of Victoria and remains so. Indeed, he is one of its more generous members, having been known on more than one occasion to say to the winemaster, Clifford Heard: 'Here's the key to my cellar. Take what you want, up to five dozen or so, preferably in three-bottle lots.' He joined the august wine body in 1947, a year of some significance in his wine-drinking career.

'In the early 1950s,' he recalls, 'a Melbourne wine merchant – not Seabrook – had to get rid quickly of some top quality wines it had and which were stored on the third floor of a William Street building under a galvanised iron roof. There were 1947 and 1949 Châteaux Margaux, Latours and Lafites and I picked up about ten or twelve cases for prices ranging from 17 and 19 bob a bottle to about 25 bob. I still have a few and it was those wines which formed the basis of the cellar I have today.'

Although he's a wealthy man, Donaldson has virtually stopped buying first growth Bordeaux and Burgundy wines, claiming they are 'far too expensive these days'. As it is, his cellar holds about 1500 bottles – 'enough for a man my age. What will I leave? We can only wait and see.'

Geoff Donaldson, a widower, lives in a charming 100-year-old terrace house which his grandfather built and which he acquired in 1959 after some years residence in Heidelberg (in a home with its own below-ground cellar). His cellar today occupies what used to be a maid's room, a few metres to the rear of the house itself.

His wines – about 50 per cent imported and 50 per cent Australian ('still with a great fondness for the wines of John Brown of Milawa; John senior and I were at school together and slept in the same dormitory') – are housed in neat rows of wine racks made of wood and tin, the type much favoured by collectors a few years ago. Donaldson stands 203 centimetres (6 feet 8 inches) and, with that height, has no trouble reaching, without the aid of a small stepladder, wines in the top rows. The cellar also has a small refrigerator in which are kept whites and sparkling wines intended for immediate use.

Red wine maturing in large wood casks. Wines can spend from several months to several years in wood.

GREAT AUSTRALIAN WINES

Robin Bradley

Some decades ago, when the allure of wine had only recently seduced me from the stony paths of temperance, I acquired a bottle of red of which I was inordinately proud, and which became the centrepiece of my modest collection. I forget the maker now (I think it was from the Rutherglen area) but well remember that the vintage was 1943 – then nearly twenty years past.

Anyway, after several years of boastful possession of this jewel in Australia's vinous crown, I organised a bibulous occasion worthy of such nectar, decanted it amidst a fog of religious awe and hushed reverence, and served it.

Not to put too fine a point on it, the wine was loathsome: a brutal slurry with a foetid stench bordering on the homicidal, a swamp palate and a finish like steel wool. My wine education had begun with a harsh lesson – old and rare does not necessarily mean good.

Now it gets interesting. Good, on the other hand (or at least very, very good), can frequently mean both old and rare. Old, because time can work a miracle upon wines with the potential for greatness, and rare because by the time such a miracle is wrought there is not too much of the wine left undrunk, and everyone wants what little remains.

All of which explains and partly justifies why wine writers, when encouraged to bore people with their experiences in encountering great wines, are wont to embark upon nostalgic reminiscences into the distant mists of the past.

I shall attack this syndrome later, but first let me commit the same offence myself, recalling a few of my favourite wines.

It seems particularly appropriate to begin with homage to the 1953 Baileys Old Matured Hermitage. This was released in what seemed unlimited quantities in about 1961 at a very reasonable four shillings a bottle, which price included the specially designed label of unusually horrific aspect, the black and red *trompe-d'oeil* truculence of which still affronts the sensitive soul today. More eloquent tongues than mine have struggled to verbalise the unique characteristics of this wine, the most memorable efforts being 'liquid steak and eggs', and 'this isn't wine: it's wine, food and a good cigar'. When young (in other words for the first twenty years) it smelt like a handful of the soil in which the vines grew, or, as the less imaginative would have it, like compost. Now that it has reached its long awaited maturity, its elegance and sleek power are such that a visiting wine luminary with an unimpeachable palate mistook it for a 1955 Romanée-Conti only a couple of years ago. If this seems incomprehensible for this most Australian of all wines, I can only suggest that you unearth a bottle of it (it still turns up at the occasional auction) and see for yourself. Probably my favourite Australian wine.

Then there is the 1973 Balgownie Cabernet Sauvignon. I first saw this wine in a half bottle drawn from the wood, together with its hermitage sibling. Its impact made me speechless (a rare condition for me). It seemed for all the world like a young Latour except for a unique desiccated coconut character in the bouquet: a new star had swum into my ken. I've drunk many a bottle of this wine since then, all of them supreme, but none quite as impressive as a magnum I shared with the winemaker and a group of wine-lovers who were winners in a newspaper wine competition. I was delighted to find on that occasion that the wine had not lost its extraordinary knack of rendering conversation unnecessary.

And what of the Maurice O'Sheas (Mount Pleasant, up to and including the 1956 vintage)? So much has been said of these legendary wines that there is almost an unconscious backlash of attempted debunking occasionally discernible. Make no mistake about it, these are among the best wines ever made in this country, however short the shortlist. There were so many superb wines that to single out one is unfair to the others, but certainly one can point to the 1947s as impeccable exemplars of the series – wines of uncanny grace and beauty from a winemaking genius.

Talking of virtuoso winemaking suggests another man whose single-mindedness and imagination created a wine of greatness: Max Schubert, the father of Grange Hermitage. Undoubtedly Grange is Australia's most famous wine, and deservedly so. But the year which to me towers over the others and dwarfs the much vaunted 1955, 1962 and even the fabled 1953 is 1956. Three times I've seen this wine, once when it was eight years old and twice (in one day!) when it was twenty-four, and can only say that it would be a very great first growth Medoc indeed which wouldn't be forced to lower its colours to the 1956 Grange. Rich, dark hue, sumptuous blackberry nose, satin-smooth palate – what a wine!

Another master who made improbably good wine in a virtual vacuum of indifference was Colin Preece

The small Cape Mentelle winery has won many awards for its cabernet sauvignons.

of Seppelt's Great Western. His main task was to maintain the high standard of the champagne which he had created, but – almost as a hobby – he made a series of Private Bin reds unlike anything made before or since. These were given odd names comprising a letter, indicating the year (starting with 'A' in 1944), and a number, indicating cask number. Hence the 'J34' of 1953, the 'Q97' of 1960 and, believe it or not, the 'T114-115' of 1963. 1964 ('U') was the last in the series, being the year of Colin's retirement. The wines were aged in old, 'big' wood and rarely contained any cabernet sauvignon, yet the fruit quality and softness of the tannin were beyond anything I have ever seen from the Rhône Valley. Fabulous wines, and a whole string of them without any low spots.

There are more, many more, which come readily to mind (and those evocations come delightfully to the palate), but you will surely tire of my serving you an unrelieved diet of superlatives, so I will try to use a lighter and briefer touch. Lindemans have produced a laudable series of four-figure bin number burgundies, some of which, while markedly unBurgundian, are very fine indeed. The best by a longish chalk was the 1959 release: bin 1590 – now beginning to fade, but still gracious and beguiling. Lake's Folly scales the pinnacles with unlikely regularity, and no list of this country's great wines could omit that Colossus, the 1974 Chardonnay, or the 1972 Cabernet Sauvignon, still a sleeping giant. And then there's Leo Buring, who have been producing some of the world's most beautiful rieslings under their Reserve Bin labels for more than a quarter of a century highlighted by the 1971 'DWA' wines, and the 1973 'DWC'.

'Where in this list,' I hear the fortunate experienced among you mutter, 'are the 1938 Reynella, the 1872 Craiglee, the Penfolds Trameahs, the Burgoynes Mount Ophirs?' Where indeed? Let's make an end to misty-eyed nostalgia and answer frankly – they are in the past where they belong.

And harking back to the beginning of this chapter, investigating Australia's greatest achievements in winemaking is not necessarily an exercise in ancient history. Great wines can be, and indeed are being, made today.

To test this statement, arm yourself with a chequebook and a persuasive tongue, waylay a cooperative winemerchant and try to seek out the following.

Brown Brothers Noble Riesling 1978 – arguably the best sweet white ever made in this country.

Cape Mentelle Cabernet Sauvignon 1982 – a giant of a wine with the world at its feet.

Moorilla Estate Chardonnay 1982 – an amazing wine: intense, breathtakingly beautiful and, unfortunately, as rare as hen's teeth.

Moss Wood Pinot Noir 1981 – an entirely convincing pinot of impeccably Burgundian style and depth.

Mount Mary Pinot Noir 1980 – another supple, seductive pinot from one of the Southern Hemisphere's best makers.

Pipers Brook Vineyard Cabernet Sauvignon 1981 – a multi-faceted wine of great beauty and Bordelaise elegance.

Pipers Brook Vineyard Chardonnay 1983 – a glorious, complex creature with a nose like smoked peaches, if that's possible.

Wantirna Estate Pinot Noir 1978 – lissom and graceful, a unique collector's wine.

And while we are on the subject of great Australian wines, what about the muscats of north-east Victoria, particularly those of Bailey and Morris? Not a style for the faint-hearted, nor for those who expect all after-dinner wines to have the velvet power of Portuguese vintage ports, but for flavour in the megaton range there is nothing in the world to match these sumptuous beauties once they have slept for some decades in big old casks. Lovely things, they are.

We live amidst wine, here in Australia, and while it would be paltering with the truth to claim the magic fluid as our heritage or even as our birthright (one would need a short memory to do that – remember the six o'clock swill?), it is most certainly a staple and, at its increasingly encountered best, of extreme quality.

The idyllic setting at Tamar Vineyards, in Tasmania's north-east. Run by Mark and Marion Semmens, the vines at Tamar were only planted here in 1980 but have shown remarkable growth.

WINES AND WINERIES OF TASMANIA

Mark Shield

Tasmania has a grim history. Deportation to its shores meant the ultimate punishment. Today many people wish that it was possible to be deported to this beautiful island. Tasmania boasts many scenic attractions as well as a leisurely lifestyle. It is traditionally famous for the production of apples and their alcoholic byproduct, cider. Hops are also an important part of its agriculture, and Tasmanians are justly proud of their beer. Recently there is another reason for pride; this island is developing a healthy wine industry.

The industry is still in its infancy. At the time of writing there are only 65 hectares planted on the entire island. Seppelt or any other large company would consider such a planting to be a fair-sized paddock. But small can be beautiful and these plantings are yielding some excellent fruit. This bawling infant is making some of the finest wines in Australia, and its cries are being paid heed to.

The island is not without its fair share of controversy. One noted winemaker stated that he had inspected Tasmania with a view to starting a large vineyard. He rejected it because in his opinion, 'It was too windy, too wet, and the soil was too rich.' It might

sound paradoxical to declare that soil can be too rich, but there is a widely held adage that for the wine to be good, the vine must suffer! Another reason for his rejection of Tasmania was its large bird population.

New vineyards, new wineries. In Tasmania, it's early days for the winemakers, but results look promising.

463

Tasting a Rhine riesling wine from the cool vineyards of the Tamar Valley, in northern Tasmania, about 41 degrees south of the Equator. It's the cool ripening season which helps enhance grape flavours.

The early results would seem to prove his opinions rather incorrect. He *was* right about the birds; they have been a major problem. Some vineyards lose over 50 per cent of their crop. Birds can be infuriating; they have the canny knack of harvesting the grapes just before man. While the winemaker may be delaying his picking until the grapes reach 12.5 baumé ripeness his feathered foe will settle for 12 baumé and the vigneron can see his beloved cabernet disappear in a day.

Tasmania is also not immune to drought, flood or bushfires, so the vigneron faces much the same struggle as do his mainland counterparts. Still, growing grapes between latitude 41°S and 43°S has its compensations. It is the epitome of a cool climate location, and indeed these are the most southerly vineyards in the world. It should be an ideal location for the production of fine table wines and champagne styles.

However this is not a new industry to Tasmania. The first vines were planted by Bartholomew Broughton in 1823. The first vintage of 1200 litres earned this enterprising winemaker a pretty penny. In its heyday the vineyard was producing 6000 litres annually. Tasmania also provided cuttings for the mainland, with John Reynell using cuttings from Port Arthur. The demise of this industry was not the dreaded phylloxera louse, but rather a downturn in the demand for table wines and an unsympathetic government that forbad the making of the then more popular brandy or fortified wines.

MOORILLA ESTATE

The revival of the wine industry in modern days – the dawn of a new age – was led by prominent Hobart businessman, Claudio Alcorso, who established his Moorilla Estate on the banks of the Derwent. The property was originally acquired as an orchard and the first grapes were planted to 'see if they would grow'.

The results were encouraging and Claudio planted his vineyard in 1960.

The first problem was the birds. In the early days they destroyed much of the crop. The only solution, guns and scarecrows proving ineffective, was to place nets over the entire vineyard.

Alcorso also experimented with the trellising and pruning of the vines. In such southerly climes (43°S) sun is at a premium. For proper growth and ripening, the buds and the fruit must be exposed. Great care was exercised in clonal selection of the vines to suit the microclimate.

The early wines from Moorilla showed promise if not polish. They were individual right down to their

The colourful tanks at Moorilla Estate owe something to modern art.

Claudio Alcorso, opera buff, businessman and winemaker.

cloth labels. (Claudio was a textile manufacturer.) It was the dimensions and intensity of the fruit in his wines that gave notice that Tasmania was an area to be watched.

Moorilla is not a large vineyard (2.4 hectares) and it claims one of the lowest yields in Australia, so the early production was not widely distributed. The few bottles that did find their way onto the mainland whet the appetite of wine-lovers.

Claudio's nearest neighbouring vineyard was on the mainland, so he could not lean over the fence and say: 'What should I do now?' Problems had to be solved in the best way possible for a one-man operation, and Claudio coped well.

These days his son Julian is the winemaker, with guidance from the ubiquitous Brian Croser and Dr Tony Jordan at the consulting firm of Oenotech. The Alcorsos also pay homage to the research of the eminent viticulturalist Dr Richard Smart. With such

On the other side of the Derwent River, upstream from Hobart, the Alcorso house stands on a promontory in the river. Behind the house is the winery and covered vineyards.

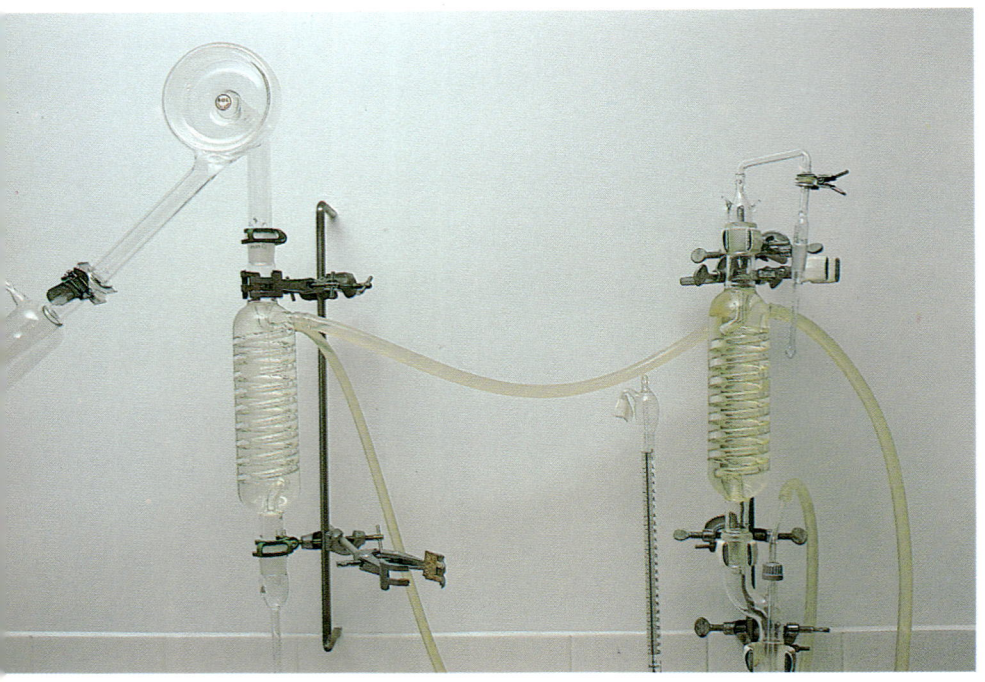

In the laboratory, checking grape juice and wine quality.

Julian Alcorso makes the wine at Moorilla, near Hobart.

Tasmanian red wine maturing in oak.

advice and guidance the Alcorsos are vying for the crown of the best producers on the island.

The family has major interest in a vineyard at Bream Creek, on the east coast, which covers 6 hectares. This vineyard is the work of a syndicate. After the typical Alcorso research, they have opted for the varieties cabernet sauvignon, Rhine riesling, chardonnay and pinot noir. All these varieties, particularly the latter, should be ideally suited to the microclimate of the area.

Pinot noir is a grape which enjoys a cool climate. If you look at where it is planted on the mainland (in most cases warm to hot climates) it is easy to see why it hasn't reached its full potential in Australia. Tasmania is the land of high hopes for pinot noir and the early experimental wines from Moorilla show these hopes to be well founded.

The same applies to chardonnay. The only unfortunate thing about the exercise is that the wine will never be in plentiful supply due to the low yields.

Bream Creek has not been bird-proofed and the birds cause substantial losses. These cause the wines to be expensive but this has not deterred the consumer who appreciates quality. Moorilla wines can be

found as far afield as Germany. The proof with any export is repeat business – the Alcorsos have dispatched several shipments.

Another aspect of the vineyard is the irregular occurrence of noble rot. In 1982 they made a remarkable botrytised Rhine riesling which sent sauternes fans scrambling for more. Many of the experts were lavish in their praise for this wine and some went as far as giving it the accolade of 'the best sweet wine made in Australia'.

Visitors to Moorilla estate are struck by the Mondrian murals painted on the fermenters. They are a nice touch, typical of the Alcorsos' flair.

The Tasmanian industry owes a debt of gratitude to its modern founder, Claudio Alcorso, who proved that quality table wine could come from the Apple Isle. His vision and perseverance set a path for others to follow and the consumer will be grateful they did.

HEEMSKERK VINEYARD

This vineyard, at 20 hectares, is the largest on the island. It is located at Pipers Brook, about 35 kilometres north of Launceston. Graham Wiltshire, the owner, was also a pioneer. He is an eloquent man with a distinguished air. He is absolute where his beliefs about wine are concerned. He is a difficult man to catch, so contact with the vineyard is best established through one of his partners, Mark Fesq, who distributes the wines in Sydney. Wiltshire

Graham Wiltshire is winemaker at Heemskerk, north of Launceston.

The deep south: vines are thriving in the cool latitudes of Tasmania, as this beautifully laid out vineyard at Heemskerk shows.

planted a small vineyard in 1966 at Legana (west of Launceston) and the results were encouraging enough for him to form a consortium and plant the Heemskerk vineyard at Pipers Brook. The site was chosen after considerable research into climatic conditions.

But life is not all that easy at Heemskerk. The location is superb, although wind and excessive moisture problems are wont to assert themselves occasionally. This is nature's way of keeping the viticulturalist on his toes, and the impeccable husbandry practised at Heemskerk usually overcomes these problems.

The first wines from Legana showed promise. In 1979 a blend of cabernet sauvignon from Legana and

Heemskerk – the location is superb, but wind and moisture problems keep the viticulturalist on his toes.

Heemskerk won a gold medal at Hobart in the open class – a strong class including many mainland wines.

The plantings at Heemskerk embrace the classic cool climate varieties, gewurztraminer, chardonnay and cabernet sauvignon. There are also small stands of pinot noir, Rhine riesling and sylvaner. The chardonnay is an exciting prospect; the climate is right for wines similar to classic white Burgundies to be produced. Similar could be said of pinot noir grapes, and this area may produce wines similar to those of France.

All wines from the two vineyards are made in a compact winery at Legana where they are given a maturation period in small French oak.

*Vineyards in the T
Valley of Tasmani*

PIPERS BROOK

This is perhaps the jewel in the Tasmanian crown. It is difficult to avoid superlatives when describing Dr Andrew Pirie's project. One glance at the elegant label sets the theme. To me, this label is one of the most attractive in Australia. It epitomises what Pipers Brook is all about – classic elegance.

The owner-winemaker holds a Master's degree in Agricultural Science and a Ph.D. in vine physiology from Sydney University. He carefully maintains the vines' leaf canopy during the growing season and the vineyard layout closely resembles the French system. This is paying dividends and yields have been high in quality and encouraging with regard to quantity. As with Heemskerk, the wind can be a nuisance and reduce the yields. Another welcome reducer of yields, noble rot, occurs when conditions permit.

This venture started in 1974 when 7.5 hectares were planted. Further plantings brought the total to

Dr Andrew Pirie, the owner-winemaker at Pipers Brook.

472

10 hectares. The varieties include cabernet sauvignon, pinot noir, riesling, chardonnay and traminer. The traminer should be singled out for special mention because aficionados of this spicy white from Alsace had all but given up hope that it could be duplicated locally. Most of the Australian efforts fall well short of the mark because they fail to capture the crisp elegance of the original and tend to be oily and coarse. Andrew Pirie's traminer has no such vices. If it were to be included in a line-up of Alsace traminers it could be singled out for its exceptional quality.

The other wines all need bottle age but it seems that these will be well worth waiting for, particularly the cabernet sauvignons.

Andrew Pirie is a polished man, an erudite speaker

who also conducts well-supported wine education classes.

The wines from this estate are full of vitality and character. Now that the original vineyard is approaching full maturity, Andrew has set his sights on modest expansion. Varieties like cabernet franc and merlot will be planted for blending with the existing promise to warrant further expansion, as has a small trial batch of sauvignon blanc.

It is easy to fall for the trap of isolating Tasmania from the rest of Australia. Pipers Brook wines should be considered in the context of wines from the premium cool climate regions around Australia. They are up with, perhaps ahead of, the best which gives further indication that in spite of the problems, Tasmania is a great place to grow grapes.

MEADOW BANK

This 2.5 hectare vineyard on the banks of the Derwent is a little removed from its winery, which is located on the Victorian mainland at Anakie near Geelong. Gerald Ellis, the viticulturalist, presides over plantings of cabernet sauvignon and Rhine riesling, not to mention waging a constant battle with birds.

The grapes are harvested in a single day, straight into refrigerated sea containers. These are dispatched post haste all the way across Bass Strait to the dynamic Stephen Hickinbotham.

When they arrive the next day at Anakie, all hell breaks loose. There is a mad scramble to process the grapes and start fermentation. There seems to be no detectable deleterious effect from this, save the wear and tear on the nerves of the participants. It is quite an adrenal experience; but it is really little different to trucking fruit from, say, Coonawarra to Mildura for processing. It is the crossing of Bass Strait that lends the excitement.

The wines have won acclaim with their consumers. It is also nice to see that there is a real connection between the Tasmanian industry and the industry on the mainland.

TAMAR VINEYARDS

This enterprise is run by Mark and Marion Semmens, at Deviot, West Tamar, in north-eastern Tasmania. The vines, established only in 1980, have a remarkable record of growth, with five and a half tonnes crushed in 1983. Mark Semmens believes that plenty of water is essential in establishing a young vineyard. Heavy black plastic, for heat absorption and retention, has been used between the rows to help growth.

At this stage the wines can only be regarded as experimental. The varieties planted are pinot noir, cabernet sauvignon, chardonnay and muller thurgau.

Establishing new vineyards and a winery is a bit like building a new house: hard work. But at the end of the day there's a drink for a couple of thirsty Tasmanians.

There is plenty of land in Tasmania suitable for viticulture, however it is already closely farmed with other crops. It is said that the future will establish Tasmania as the quality area in Australia.

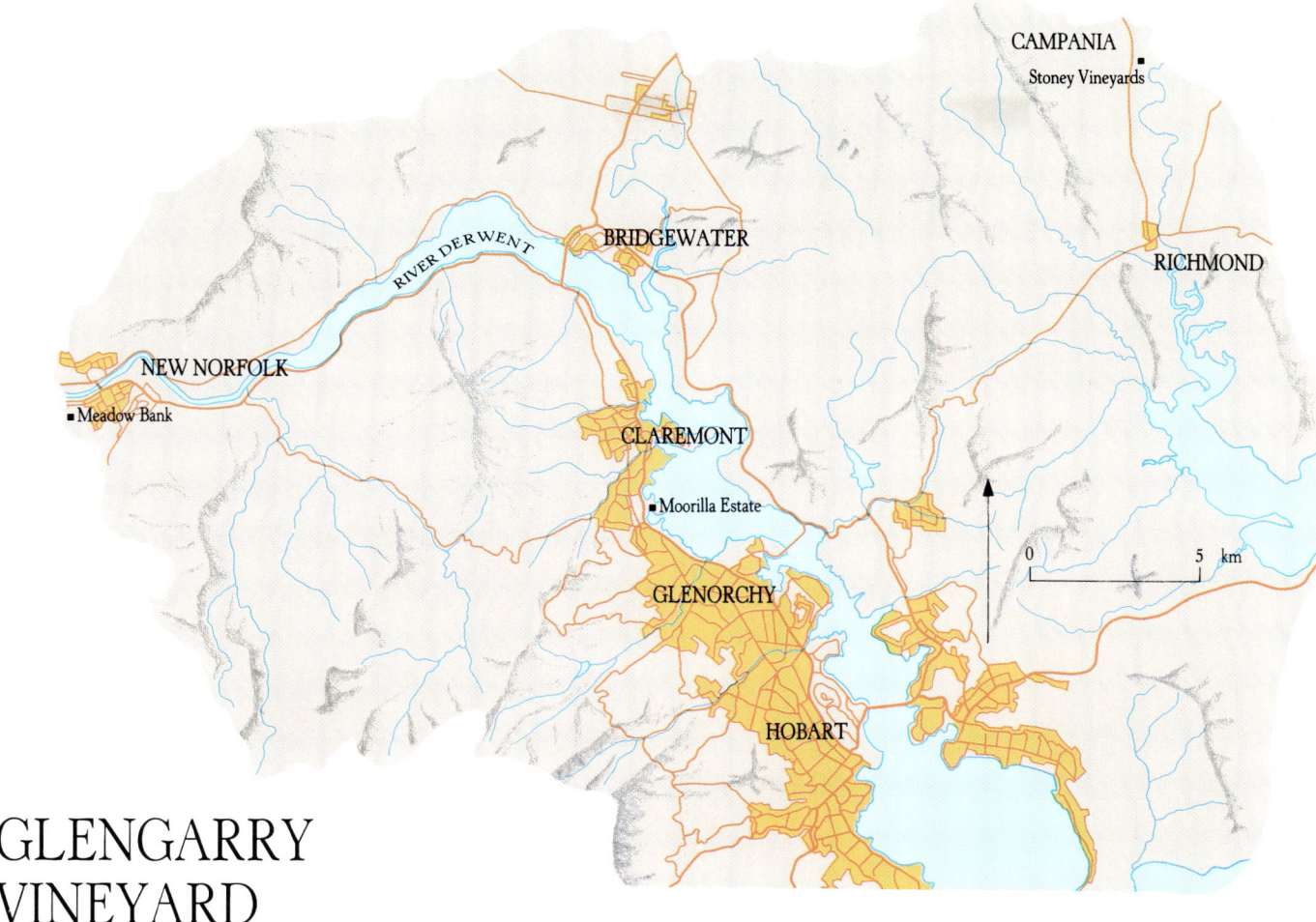

GLENGARRY VINEYARD

Gavin Scott has 3 hectares near Exeter in the Tamar Valley. These were planted in 1980, coinciding with the start of a severe drought. Until the drought broke in 1983 it was a bitter struggle for vines and owner. The plantings are of pinot noir and cabernet sauvignon. To date only tiny volumes of wines have been made on an experimental basis.

STONEY VINEYARDS

George Park established this tiny 0.5 hectare vineyard in 1973 at Campania, north of Hobart. Obviously, there is not a lot of wine from this vineyard on the market. The vineyard also suffered from the drought which reduced yields by up to 50 per cent.

The varieties are shiraz, cabernet sauvignon, pinot noir, riesling and traminer.

OTHER PLANTINGS

There are several scattered small plantings across the island. They are mostly hobby farms rather than commercial vineyards. This is not to denigrate them

in any way. Many of these small plantings will expand because indications of quality are sound. Some of the fruit will find its way into larger blends; perhaps more mainland wineries will become interested in this fruit in the future.

THE FUTURE

One man with a good overview of Tasmania sees a rosy future. Graham Lynch owns and runs Aberfeldy Cellars in Hobart and displays particular interest in the projects going on around him. He believes the future will establish Tasmania as *the* quality area of Australia.

There is plenty of land in Tasmania suitable for viticulture, however it is already closely farmed with other crops. There have been several sightings of representatives from large mainland companies who have inspected properties. It can be assumed that they were attracted by the quality of the wines which have reached the mainland.

Just as it became important (if not trendy) to establish a vineyard in Victoria, or for large companies to gain access to Victorian fruit, it could be that Tasmania will undergo the same transformation.

Murray Tyrrell signs his Official Little Red Wine Bluffer's Guide.

AT THE CELLAR DOOR

Don Hogg

Around Australia each year tens of thousands of Australians pay millions of dollars for wine at the cellar door – in other words at the winery at which it was made. Most wineries offer their cellar door visitors free tastings of their range and more often than not buyers will pay less for the wine than they would at the local pub or wine and spirit merchant.

The price advantage, where it applies, is not the only advantage to buying at cellar door. At many of the smaller wineries the tasting and sales area is manned by the winemaker or one of his family, giving interested visitors the opportunity of discussing the wine with someone who has had a hand in its production.

But the big advantage is, of course, that you get to try before you buy, if buy you do. What's more, wineries are very pleasant places often decorated tastefully and displaying industry artefacts, and the welcome is invariably warm and friendly. There is no compulsion on the visitor, having tasted the range of wines, to buy, but the winemaker does not appreciate the visitor who, having spent an hour tasting his range, and some wines three or four times, telling him as he stumbles from the premises, 'Shorry bud

theresh nudding to shuit my palled.'

The winemaker does not expect his wines to suit everyone. That's why he offers tastings free. Neither does he wish to be seen as someone who is simply offering an inexpensive day out to anybody who wanders by.

Most winemakers will tell you (except, perhaps, some in the Hunter and the Barossa) that the incidence of 'free-loading' is agreeably low. Indeed most people visiting wineries intend to buy if they find a wine or wines they really like. In short, never enter a winery to taste in the belief the winemaker regards you as a freeloader until you have shown him otherwise. That simply isn't the way it is. Here is what one winemaker, Gil Wahlquist of Botobolar Winery, Mudgee, says:

It is a worldwide custom for wineries to offer a taste of wine to intending purchasers. This pleasant ritual removes the uncertainty from wine-buying and makes winery visits an enjoyable way to purchase.

The success of the tasting ritual depends on two things. On the one hand the winemaker needs a

A group tasting wine at Tyrrells' winery in the Hunter Valley, New South Wales. A bark hut, earthen floors, wood casks and gruff-voiced winemaker Murray Tyrrell draw visitors from around the world.

Gil and Vincie Wahlquist welcome visitors at their Botobolar winery, near Mudgee, New South Wales, and on request will send customers their regular winery newsletter.

This is due to the advent of the big liquor retailing chains with their enormous purchasing, and therefore, bargaining power. These companies buy in huge quantities at prices to make the average winelover's mouth water. They then retail at minimal profit margins – margins *below* those the manufacturer himself could afford. After all, the manufacturer is not involved in city retailing, his overheads per bottle sold may be as much as ten times that of the discounting liquor chains. Hence you can sometimes find the price of wine at cellar door to be anything but a bargain. There is a certain chief winemaker I know who buys his own company's champagne from a big Adelaide liquor merchant because even with the discount his company offers him, he can buy the bubbly more cheaply at the shop.

Then there's the question of how some wine distributors and merchants treat the question of lower

generous attitude, being prepared to provide a suitable glass for nosing and contemplation of the wine, together with a bucket to receive the remains of the wine once it has been sampled. It is not necessary to swallow the contents of the tasting glass.

On the other hand, the taster plays his or her part by treating the experience strictly as a tasting. The taster is the guest of the winemaker. The winemaker hopes to make a sale following the tasting. If the wine is thought not suitable, the taster may say so and thank the winemaker for his or her consideration in providing the wine for examination. A wine tasting at the vineyard is not an obligation to buy, nor is it a free drinking session.

In recent years the price advantage offered by most wineries at cellar door over the recommended price of their wines at retail outlets has tended to diminish. In fact, in the case of some of the bigger wineries it has disappeared altogether. There are instances, and plenty of them, where a wine will be more expensive at cellar door than it is at liquor discount outlets.

Many Australian wineries run lovingly prepared formal dinners during the year. Here 150 people sat down to a $100 a plate dinner prepared by some of Australia's finest chefs at Chateau Reynella, South Australia, and washed their food down with some old wines from Australia and overseas.

cellar door prices. Many of them take the view that if the wine is going to be cheaper at cellar door it's going to be harder to sell at retail outlets, therefore why should they bother to handle it? This situation applies quite frequently to the medium-sized wine-producing companies. Clearly the distributor/merchant argument often prevails. It must not be forgotten that with most companies only a small percentage of their production is sold at cellar door. A good distribution system is vital to their survival; they are anxious not to upset the system.

It is at the cellar door of the smaller producer that the buyer will find the best value, as well as the best service. But even here the modern marketing procedures have had their effect. Even ten years ago you would find most lines in smaller wineries 15-20 per

cent cheaper than retail. Today 7½-10 per cent is more the rule. Nevertheless, that's a significant saving. And remember, you've tried the wine first.

Most of the smaller wineries will give discounts when a significant sale is made at cellar door, but each winemaker has his own view of what 'significant' might mean. One might regard it as the sale of a dozen bottles; another may see it as two dozen. Yet a third could have a bigger sale in mind before he would agree to a discount. My experience suggests there's nothing to be lost by asking. An important point to remember whenever discounts are discussed is that if you intend paying by cash or cheque you should say so early in the piece. The winemaker will agree much more readily to a discount if he realises you are not going to present a credit card. With credit

*Casual dining out has
become very much a part of
entertainment in Australia.
Visitors to Hungerford
Hill's winery, restaurant,
tasting area and the crafts
and produce village at
Pokolbin, in the Hunter
Valley, New South Wales,
can relax and eat over
a bottle or two of
local wine.*

card payment he has to wait for his money as well as being charged a percentage of the sale, sometimes as much as 6 per cent.

Cheques are readily acceptable to all the wine-makers of my acquaintance, and most are happy to freight your wine on to you at your home address and bill you for it if you wish. The cellar door part of the wine industry does not, I'm happy to report, suffer the bad debt syndrome to any significant degree – which says something, I'm sure, for the integrity of cellar door buyers.

Once at cellar door you will be confronted with a list of the winery's products. How do you go about this business of tasting all these things?

The best advice I can give is to say you should be guided by the person attending you. Often you will be asked what kind of wine you are looking for. The

questioner will simply be seeking to ascertain what style of wine you like so he or she may take you directly to that style. By style I mean dry or sweet, table wine or fortified – that kind of thing.

If you are not sure of what you want, or are not quite sure how to best describe it, don't hesitate to say so. Every winemaker I know says he'd rather deal with people who approached him on that basis than on any other. Uncertainty about wine is no offence – although there are those pompous poltroons who would have it so. Indeed it is refreshing to meet folk who have recently come to drink the stuff and who profess their uncertainties as readily as they charm you with their enthusiasm.

Very many people at cellar door will press the winemaker for his opinion as to when he believes this wine or that that he is selling will be at its best. This is a very difficult question for him to answer because

he almost certainly cannot give you, with any confidence, an answer that time will prove to be accurate. All he can do is draw on his experience of previous vintages of the same wine and how they behaved to make an intelligent and honest guess. Further, he will not know how you will cellar the wine once you have it home, and that's going to have more than a small bearing on the wine's behaviour. All winemakers will give you an opinion in reply to your question, but that's all it can be – an opinion.

The other question that's often asked is, how long will the wine live? Again, all the winemaker can offer is an informed estimate. Every vintage varies and so too does the handling of the fruit of each vintage.

We are all looking for old wines at the right price, and we may all be excused for believing that a winery would be the right place to find them. After all, they were made there, and there just might be some tucked away in some dark corner. Nothing could be further from the truth! Perhaps the occasional large producer may have some old wine at cellar door, but if it's to be found there then you can guarantee there's more of it in the bottle shops.

The smaller wineries rarely have reds older than three or four years and whites older than twelve to eighteen months. They don't want to have old wines in stock – that would mean they haven't been able to sell them. You might hear a winemaker say he has a six- or seven-year-old red that you're enquiring for in his museum, but not for sale. That means he tucked

some away up the back of the winery somewhere before it all sold out because he wishes to taste it from time to time to guide him in his treatment of subsequent vintages.

If you don't find what you want at one winery, ask the winemaker there where you might find it. Most won't hesitate to direct you to a colleague if they think he might have just what you want.

The cellar door buyer should not be afraid to travel from winery to winery taking notes of the wines on offer and their prices before making a purchase. Winemakers are very used to seeing people armed with clipboards enter their premises and go about the business of making comprehensive notes. From the winemaker's standpoint, it's an indication the people are serious and discriminating buyers.

Many cellar door visitors, when confronted with a number of wines from a number of sources, each of them equally appealing to their palates, will make their decision on price. And there's absolutely no fault to be found with that approach. Too often I have met people who have spent their wine-buying budgets early in their stay in a wine-producing region

Tasting and buying at Brown Brothers' big and well-run cellar door tasting area at the winery at Milawa, near Wangaratta, Victoria. Tasting is a privilege, not an excuse to swill.

and then gone on to the next winery to find a wine they've immediately fallen in love with. Alas, there's no money left to buy!

In some wine regions, the Hunter Valley, Mc-Laren Vale and the Barossa Valley, for instance, there are thirty or more wineries to visit. All of us suffer constraints on our time, and most of us will be tempted to rush through as many wineries as we're able each day. The most experienced of cellar door buyers will tell you that five wineries – six at the most – in a single day is the most they can deal with and still make unhurried, intelligent decisions. It is a good practice to plan your sortie the evening before. Find a map of the district and plan your morning's activity devising an itinerary that minimises travelling time between destinations. In other words, from the map, select a compact knot of wineries and deal with them. Treat the afternoon in the same way.

Some people choose to spend their mornings looking at wines of a similar style – dry whites, for instance – and their afternoons looking at something else, perhaps dry reds. The rationale for this approach is that the taster is in a better position to make comparative judgements, while hopping from whites to reds in each winery may dull the palate for any given style.

Getting the wine home, if you've been on a wine-buying binge a long way from home, is a matter that may well exercise your mind. It's worth knowing that a carton of one dozen 750-millilitre bottles weighs in at 17-18 kilograms. Four cartons approximate the weight of another passenger in your car, and five cartons the weight of a Rugby front row forward. This many or more cartons may readily fit in your boot, but don't be surprised when your petrol stops become much more frequent.

I well remember a Sydney friend travelling back from his wine-buying spree in South Australia with the family sedan stacked with eleven cartons. He wrote describing the journey and expressed disappointment with his vehicle's fuel performance. It had, he said, given 26 m.p.g. on the way over. On the way back, he said his consumption of petrol increased

The tasting room at the Macdougall's premises on the way into Pokolbin, in the heart of the Hunter Valley, is one of the many charming places to stop for a sip in the area.

by about 25 per cent. Certainly he had 'a bit' of booze in the boot, 'but I'll have to have the car looked at'. I wrote back and told him he'd taken the equivalent of two 104-kilogram passengers with him. Then it dawned on him.

My friend could have had the wine road-freighted back and delivered safely to his door for only a handful of dollars more than what the additional petrol cost him. What's more, he wouldn't have had to suffer the poor handling and sluggish performance his dear old family car turned in on the way home. The wine may have arrived at his address a day or two after his arrival, but he would have enjoyed a much more comfortable ride, and so would the wine.

I have heard many stories of bottles of wine, particularly ports and dry reds, popping their corks in the boots of their proud owners' cars. In summer this is almost certain to happen if the wine is left in the boot for more than a day or so in hot conditions.

The other trap is putting cartons of wine on roof racks. It may be a cloudless day when you set out, but there's always the likelihood of rain. Cardboard doesn't like being wet, and glass breaks when it hits the road!

The most sensible way to transport wine in any quantity is to use the road transport companies. While their charges have escalated over the past few years, they are reasonable compared with what it will cost you in actual dollars and discomfort to get the stuff home in your own car. Any winemaker will arrange the transport for you – not only for the wine you bought from him – but for the wine you have bought all round the district.

If you insist on carrying cartons in your car, do what you can to place them inside the vehicle. Carrying them in the boot will affect the safety and performance of the car, and the wine will get a good deal hotter there in summer.

Something to taste at the Leconfield winery in Coonawarra. The Hamilton family run this winery and the Richard Hamilton winery near McLaren Vale, South Australia. (The big bottle is an Imperial, which holds 6 litres or 8 normal bottles of wine.)

Sometimes the winemakers come to the customers; here at the Expovin wine show in Sydney's Centrepoint.

You will discover as you move around wineries, and from State to State, that in one place the law may require you to buy but a single bottle while there (and that's just down the road) you may have to buy three bottles, or even a dozen. In all but rare instances it is the law that makes these conditions, not the winemaker. Different wineries hold different licences and different States have different laws. In South Australia the minimum purchase you could make at a winery in 1984 was two litres – three 750-millilitre bottles or one 2-litre flagon. In other States the law differed and the nature of the licences also varied. It is well worth enquiring when you enter a winery just what the minimum purchase is. Many wineries display the conditions under which they may sell.

Very often on stepping through the door of a tasting room you'll find yourself surrounded by certificates proclaiming the medals the winery has won at this show or that. Many winemakers are in the habit of plastering their walls with these, which to my eye are singularly unattractive.

A great number of winemakers believe that medals sell their wines, hence the long-established ritual of hanging the certificates up where you can't help but see them. If you take notice of show performances you may be impressed, but the only medals and certificates that you should allow to influence your choice are those that apply to wines currently on sale. The others, you'll find, go back to the year dot. Granted they say something about the winery's desire and ability to produce quality wines, but then there are also heaps of wineries about the place who have won major awards with the produce of one winemaker or another who has now gone to work somewhere else. It's worth pointing out that there are plenty of winemakers with stunning wine to offer who simply don't ride the wine-show roundabout.

You will do better to take notice of your own likes and dislikes and what your wallet tells you, than to be blinded by awards.

Overall, buying at the cellar door is not difficult. All that's needed is a little commonsense, a few simple guidelines and, above all, a sense of adventure. There's a lot of wonderful wine out there just waiting to be experienced, and the men and women who make the wine are an experience in themselves. They are ordinary men and women hoping for a decent living by turning the humble grape into an agreeable drink. Your opinion of it is all their bank managers want to know about. If they carry on a bit about the merit of their own wares just remember that they made it, and that it wasn't always the fun it is often imagined to be. And they're proud of their wine!

At the cellar door. You are likely to meet the winemaker, especially at smaller wineries like this one.

Efficient and careful storage, plus modern transport techniques, are an essential part of winery operations.

JUST
THE
FACTS

Chris Quirk

The forces which shape the destiny of the Australian wine industry – and so what we drink – began long ago and still influence the character of Australian wine. An appreciation of the ancestry of the industry may help you understand what you might drink tonight.

A historical overview is provided by the illustrations, showing total vintage crush, wine production and trade. The reliability of the figures is more suspect the further back in time we go – indeed, the really early figures can only be taken as a rough indication of the quantities involved. But nevertheless they tell a story.

Initially production was limited and somewhat experimental, the output being almost entirely for local consumption. Significant export trade developed in fortified wine for Britain between the two world wars and in fact during the 1930s more wine was exported from Australia than was sold in Australia. It appears much of the wine came from the many vineyards in and around Adelaide, the nearby districts, and the Barossa Valley. But increasingly, it came from the newly settled irrigated areas along the River Murray and its tributaries. The export trade

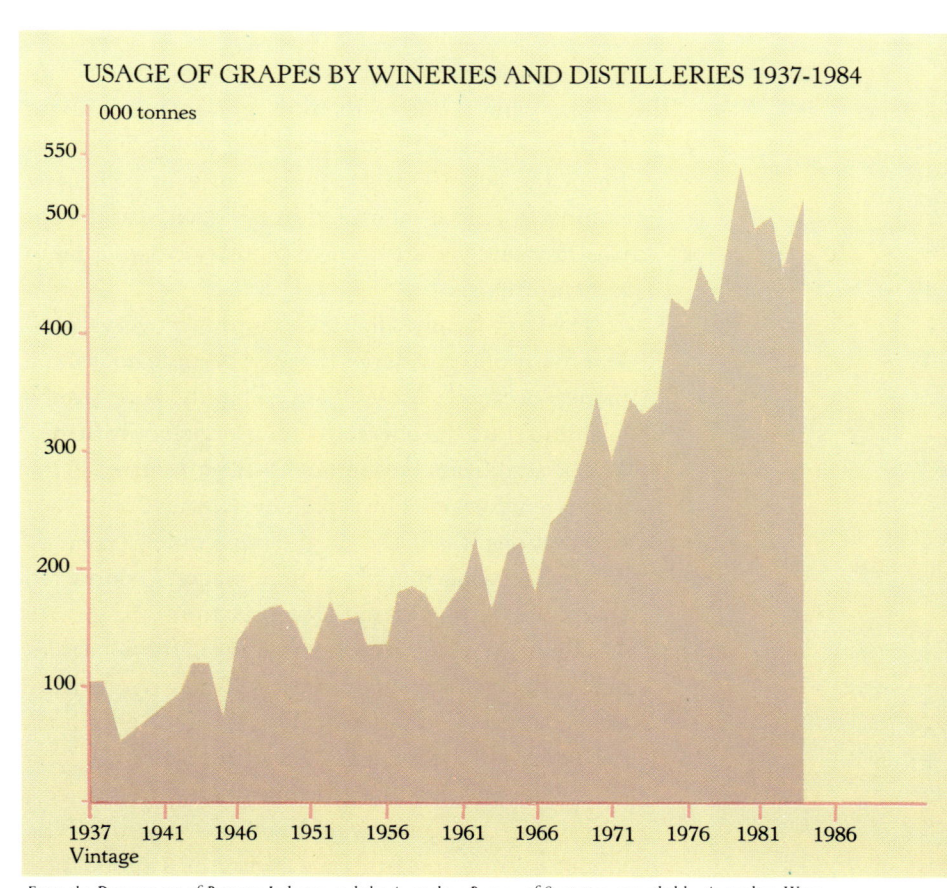

USAGE OF GRAPES BY WINERIES AND DISTILLERIES 1937-1984

From the Department of Primary Industry and the Australian Bureau of Statistics; compiled by Australian Wine and Brandy Producers' Association

489

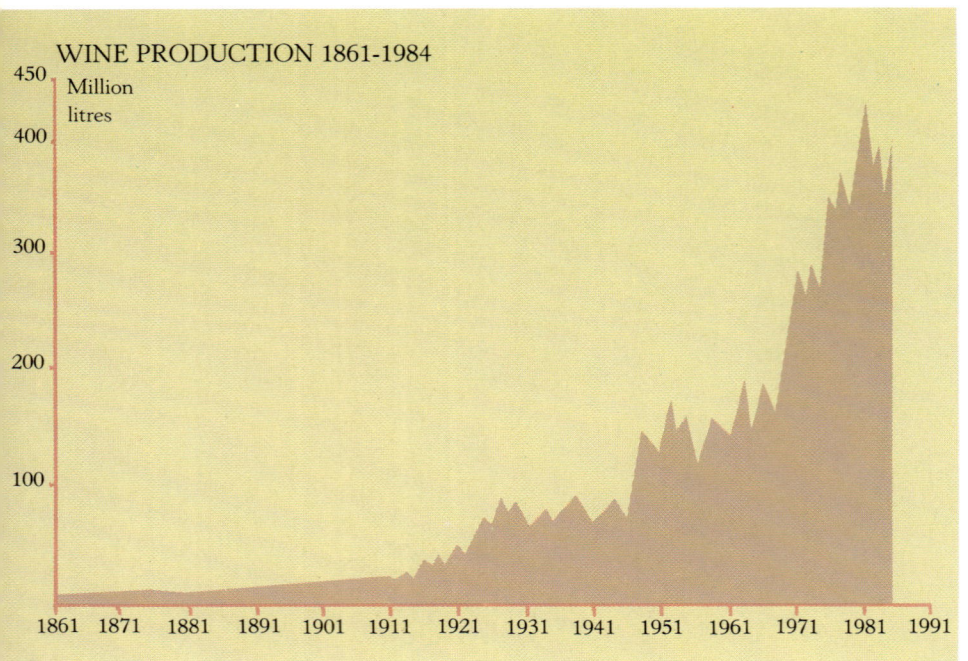

WINE PRODUCTION 1861-1984

From the Australian Bureau of Statistics; compiled by the Australian Wine & Brandy Producers' Association

USAGE OF GRAPES BY WINERIES & DISTILLERIES		
Year	Fresh Grapes (tonnes)	Dried Grapes
1937	104 270	3 075
1938	104 871	2 301
1939	59 931	435
1940	70 883	610
1941	86 046	50
1942	96 112	52
1943	116 376	73
1944	115 973	567
1945	77 378	1 556
1946	146 369	887
1947	168 159	3 337
1948	180 492	4 082
1949	187 500	3 348
1950	174 033	4 637
1951	134 644	5 969
1952	187 984	1 933
1953	165 988	1 296
1954	170 774	1 892
1955	130 406	191
1956	129 250	269
1957	170 707	–
1958	186 584	1 710
1959	177 158	1 029
1960	152 103	1 501
1961	187 641	827
1962	234 493	1 132
1963	169 300	–
1964	214 330	–
1965	225 426	–
1966	186 741	–
1967	241 468	–
1968	253 381	1 059
1969	299 553	1 545
1970	357 701	2 253
1971	293 629	1 345
1972	345 368	–
1973	330 475	–
1974	344 009	1 511
1975	432 526	1 973
1976	413 069	671
1977	458 309	504
1978	423 732	–
1979	488 056	–
1980	538 394	–
1981	489 421	–
1982	499 338	–
1983	440 392	–
1984	518 929	–

was severely affected by World War II and never fully recovered.

The wine industry today is not so much about fortified wine as table and sparkling wine production. From the late 1950s Australians in ever increasing numbers became interested in table wine, and what was in many ways a cottage industry began a rapid metamorphosis.

The large family wineries became takeover targets. Not many of the wineries that had become household names escaped. McWilliam's, Hardy and Smiths (Yalumba) are the only remaining large family firms.

The significant developments have occurred in the past twenty years. The rapid development of the last two decades was based on the burgeoning domestic Australian wine market; export markets contracted sharply. Contrary to initial expectations the growth was found in white wine, not red. From the wine sales graph, one gains an appreciation of how wrong were these early expectations. This caused enormous problems for the wine industry because of the long lead times involved in growing grapes (four to five years) and producing wine (one to two years). The industry, suffering from the legacy of a production base geared to fortified wine production, compounded the problem by gearing up for red wine consumption which never eventuated. By the mid-Seventies it became obvious that white wine was the future; the turning point was mid-1975. And white wine consumption continues to exceed most expectations.

The rapidity of this change in consumer demand caused much indigestion in the grape-growing and winemaking industries, and the re-adjustment con-

tinues. In absolute terms New South Wales is a clear market leader for wine consumption, with Victoria next. Per capita consumption of red wine is significantly higher in New South Wales, and white wine consumption is highest in Victoria.

PER CAPITA CONSUMPTION OF BEER, WINE AND SPIRITS
Litres of Product

YEAR	BEER	WINE	SPIRITS[1]
1950-51	89.8	7.3	2.6
1951-52	96.5	8.2	2.2
1952-53	99.3	6.2	1.4
1953-54	104.8	6.3	1.7
1954-55	110.3	5.5	2.0
1955-56	109.9	5.3	2.1
1956-57	104.0	5.2	1.9
1957-58	104.6	5.2	1.7
1958-59	100.8	5.2	2.0
1959-60	102.9	5.3	2.1
1960-61	102.6	5.1	2.2
1961-62	101.8	5.1	2.2
1962-63	103.1	5.3	2.1
1963-64	106.4	5.5	2.3
1964-65	109.9	5.5	2.5
1965-66	110.1	6.1	2.2
1966-67	113.1	6.8	2.2
1967-68	116.9	7.6	2.4
1968-69	120.4	8.2	2.4
1969-70	123.5	8.9	2.7
1970-71	126.5	8.8	2.7
1971-72	125.6	8.8	2.9
1972-73	129.5	9.8	3.2
1973-74	139.0	11.0	3.3
1974-75	140.3	12.3	3.1
1975-76	137.4	13.0	3.0
1976-77	136.7	13.5	3.3
1977-78	138.8	14.2	3.5
1978-79	134.6	16.4	3.0
1979-80	131.2	17.3	2.6
1980-81	132.2	18.2	2.9
1981-82	128.9	18.5	3.1
1982-83	121.6	19.7	3.1
1983-84	118.5	20.5	3.0

1. Information collected in terms of litres of alcohol converted from litres of alcohol to litres of product assuming an average alcoholic content of 38 per cent.

From the Australian Bureau of Statistics

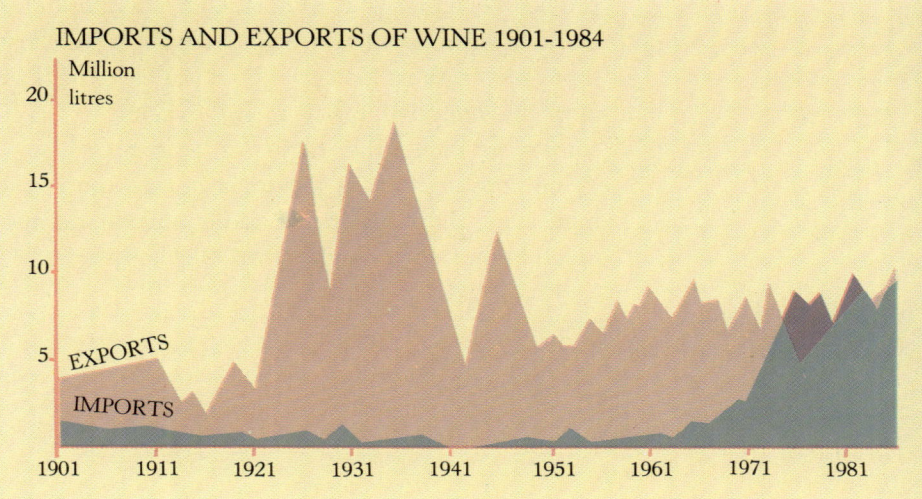

IMPORTS AND EXPORTS OF WINE 1901-1984

From the Australian Bureau of Statistics; compiled by Australian Wine & Brandy Producers' Association

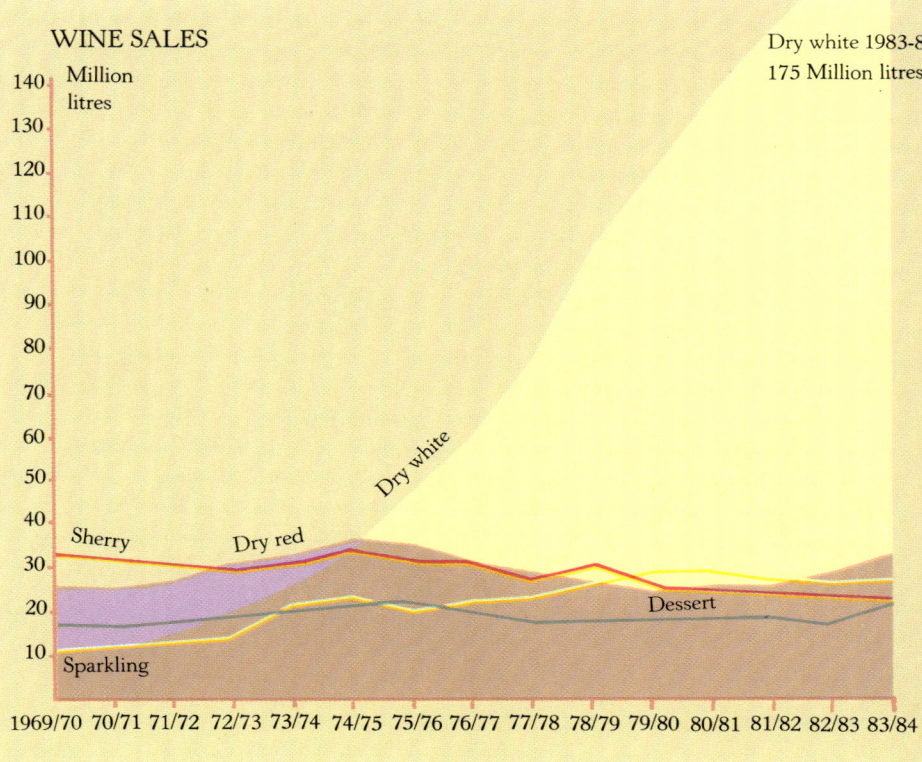

WINE SALES

From Australian Bureau of Statistics; compiled by Australian Wine and Brandy Corporation

The Sunraysia district, in north-western Victoria, source of a large slice of Australia's wine grapes.

AUSTRALIAN WINE TODAY

A global perspective: the accompanying table should provide benchmarks as to how Australia rates in the world of wine. As vineyards go, Australia is small fry; though even West Germany does not have the huge areas in vineyards many might imagine. As consumers we rank rather higher on a per capita basis. Wine consumption in Australia per person is the highest of the developed nations outside Europe; much higher, for example, than North America. As far as exports are concerned we hardly register. By the time our wine is transported to export markets on the other side of the world, overcomes the various barriers to wine trade (quotas, licences, labelling), and we pay the various customs duties and taxes, it is far from the inexpensive beverage that left Australia.

Australian wines are exported all around the world, but we really only have a significant presence in nearby markets such as New Zealand, Fiji, and Papua New Guinea. Major but fluctuating shipments are made to North America, Japan and Europe but their impact is limited: it is still hard to find Australian wine on many overseas trips. The largest volume of wine exports originate from South Australia, though they are usually shipped through Melbourne.

HOW WE RATE[1]

PRODUCTION (millions of litres)	Australia	396
	West Germany	1 304
	South Africa	917
	Portugal	8 303
	France	6 812
	Italy	8 220
	World	34 450
VINEYARD AREA (thousands of hectares)	Australia	66
	West Germany	120
	South Africa	100
	France	1 096
	Italy	1 135
	World	9 750
EXPORTS (millions of litres)	Australia	8.4
	West Germany	11.5
	Italy	1 47.4
	France	1 05.1
	United States	34.5
	World	4 83.2
PER CAPITA CONSUMPTION (litres)	Australia	19.7
	West Germany	26.5
	South Africa	9.5
	United States	8.5
	United Kingdom	8.3
	France	85.0
	Italy	91.0

1. These are total wine figures, including fortified.

From the International Office of Wine, 1983 figures.

GRAPE VARIETIES

Principal grape varieties used in winemaking in descending order based on tonnage are as follows.

RED	Per cent
Shiraz	41
Grenache	26
Cabernet sauvignon	17
Mataro	8
Malbec	2.2
Other	5.8

WHITE	Per cent
Sultana	21
Muscat gordo blanco	20
Rhine riesling	10
Semillon	9
Doradillo	8
Other (including chardonnay, 2.4)	32

So although Australia does not export large quantities of wine, our distinctive wine styles are sought by discerning importers, especially the red table wines. Usually these are of the shiraz or cabernet sauvignon/shiraz types. Australia has easily the largest vineyard area of shiraz in the world, a fact which more than anything else distinguishes our red wines from most other countries.

There is widespread confusion in Australia regarding the correct nomenclature of grape varieties on wine labels. Unfortunately this is not subject to any specific legislation, so the nearest to an official nomenclature is that promulgated by the Commonwealth Scientific and Industrial Research Organisation (CSIRO) which is reproduced here – a handy reference for wine drinkers. Among common misnomers are hermitage (actually shiraz), Hunter River riesling (actually semillon), Clare riesling (actually crouchen), frontignac (actually muscat gordo blanco) and petite sirah (actually durif).

You will find the rarer varieties on the list. Generic terms such as 'claret', 'burgundy', 'riesling' (as used in Australia), and 'sauternes' have been appropriated from Europe and are not grape varieties.

WINE GRAPE VARIETIES IN USE IN AUSTRALIA

PREFERRED NAME	VALID SYNONYMS	INVALID SYNONYMS
Aleatico		
Alicante bouschet		
Alvarelhao		
Barbera		
Bastardo	Trousseau	Cabernet gros (S.A.), touriga (N.S.W.)
Biancone		White grenache (W.A., S.A.), green doradillo
Bonvedro		False carignan (S.A.)
Cabernet franc		
Cabernet sauvignon		
Canocazo		False pedro (S.A.), common palomino (Vic.)
Carignan	Carignane	
Chardonnay	Pinot chardonnay	
Chasselas	Chasselas doré, golden chasselas	
Chenin blanc		Albillo, stein, sherry
Cinsaut	Blue imperial	Ulliade, oeillade, black prince (Great Western)
Clairette	Blanquette (Hunter Valley)	
Colombard		French colombard
Cornifesto		
Crouchen		Clare riesling
Dolcetto		Malbec (Great Western)
Doradillo		Blanquette (S.A.)
Dourado		Rutherglen pedro
Durif		Petite sirah and serine (California)
Emerald riesling		
Farana	Planta pedralba	False trebbiano (S.A.)
Gouais		
Graciano	Morrastel (France)	Xeres (California)
Grenache		
Grey grenache		White grenache (Vic., N.S.W.)
Malbec	Cot	
Malvasia bianca		
Mammolo		
Marsanne		
Mataro	Balzac, esparte, mourvèdre	Morrastel (S.A.)

Melon	Muscadet	Pinot blanc (California)
Merlot		
Meunier	Pinot meunier	Miller's burgundy
Monbadon		Burger (California)
Mondeuse	Refosco	
Montils		
Muller-Thurgau		
Muscadelle		Tokay (Australia), sauvignon vert (California)
Muscat à petits grains blanc	White frontignac	
Muscat à petits grains rose	Red frontignac	Frontignan (for Europe)
Muscat à petits grains rouge	Brown muscat, brown frontignac	
Muscat gordo blanco	Gordo, muscat of Alexandria	
Nebbiolo		
Ondenc		Sercial, Irvine's white
Orange muscat	Muscat fleur d'oranger	
Palomino	Listan	
Pedro ximinez		
Peloursin		Durif (Vic. part)
Petit verdot		Gros manseng (Califorinia)
Pinot gris	Rulander	
Pinot noir		Gamay beaujolais (California)
Riesling	Rhine riesling	Johannesburg riesling
Rkaziteli		
Ruby cabernet		
Saint macaire	Moustère	Saint macaire (for Europe)
Sangiovese		Canaiolo (N.S.W.)
Sauvignon blanc		Savagnin musqué (California)
Semillon		Hunter River Riesling (N.S.W.) madeira (S.A.)
Shiraz	Syrah	Caracosa, xeres (Vic.), hermitage
Siegerrebe		
Souzao		
Sultana	Sultanina, Thompson seedless	
Sylvaner		
Tempranillo		Valdepenas (California)
Terret noir		Auldana No. 2, claret (S.A.)
Tinta amarella		Malbec (Wilksch), Portugal
Tinta cao		Mourisco preto (California)
Tinta madeira		
Touriga		Alvarelhao (California)
Traminer	Gewurztraminer	
Trebbiano	Ugni blanc	Saint Emilion, white hermitage, white shiraz
Trousseau gris		Grey riesling (California)
Valdiguié		Gamay (California)
Veltliner green		
Veltliner red		
Verdelho		Madeira (N.S.W.)
Waltham cross	Rosaki	Malaga (S.A.)
Zinfandel		

HYBRIDS
Jacquez		Troya (M.I.A.)
Royalty		
Rubired		

A. J. Antcliff, C.S.I.R.O., Division of Horticultural Research.

GROWING AREAS

The largest winegrape-producing areas are not the 'better known' regions such as the Barossa Valley or Hunter Valley, but the Riverland in South Australia, Riverina in New South Wales, and the Sunraysia/Swan Hill regions of Victoria. Smaller grape-growing districts can be highly significant because of the special wine styles and quality of wine they produce. Their importance may also stem from historical significance and their proximity to population centres or the concentration of wine-producing facilities; the Barossa Valley is a good example. The diagrams portray the size of the wine regions of Australia, distinguishing between where the grapes are grown and where the grapes are crushed. One complicating factor is large bulk tanker movements of grape juice and wine between wine-producing areas and interstate. This is difficult to track but it could be in the order of half a million litres a week. It is therefore difficult to accurately compare the significance of one wine region with another. Modern technology has clouded the issue.

The river areas owe their dominance to historical factors which saw them established as bulk fortified wine-producing areas. That their prominence as the backbone of Australian wine production has continued into the table wine era of today is a reflection of the economies of grape production in these regions and the technical skills of Australian winemakers. Abundant sunshine, water and fertile land deliver

RELATIVE SIZE OF AUSTRALIAN WINEGROWING REGIONS
(Based on origin of grapes)

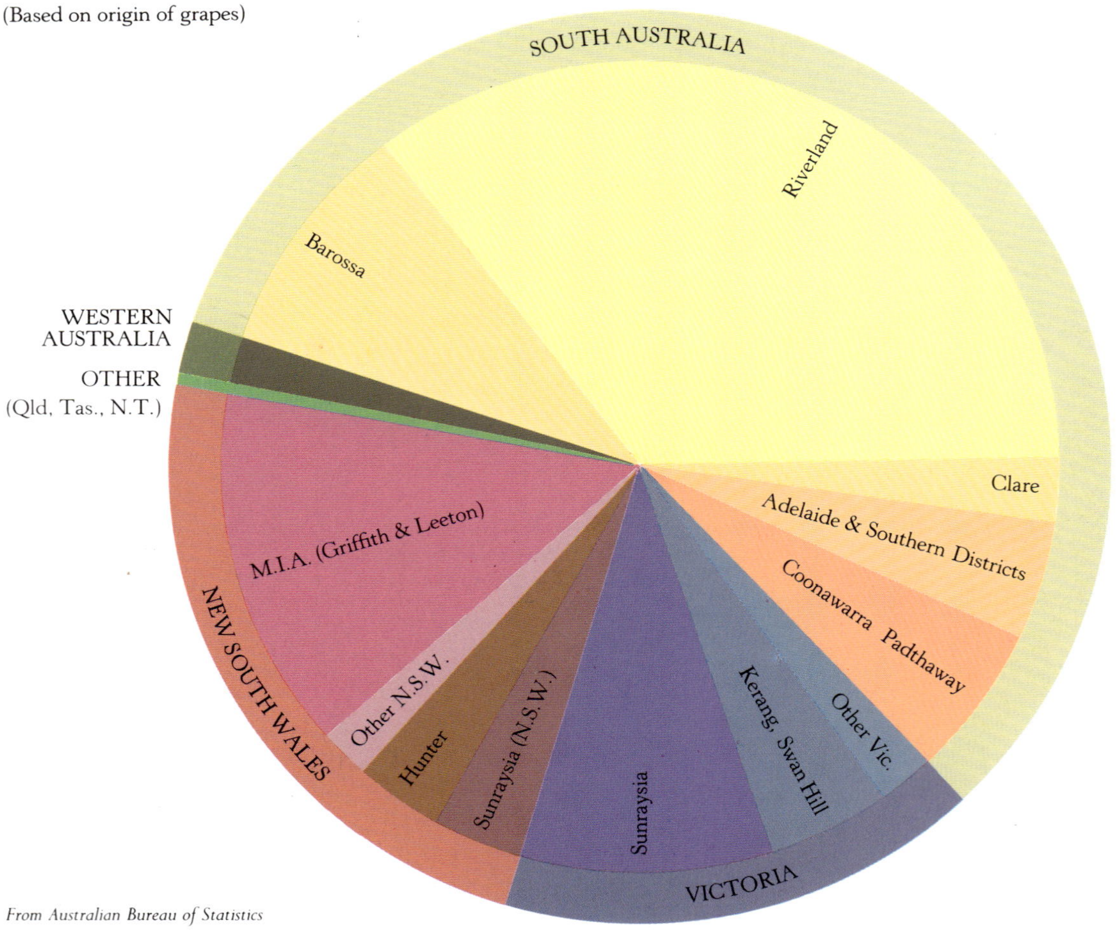

SOUTH AUSTRALIA

Riverland

Barossa

WESTERN AUSTRALIA

OTHER (Qld, Tas., N.T.)

M.I.A. (Griffith & Leeton)

NEW SOUTH WALES

Other N.S.W.

Hunter

Sunraysia (N.S.W.)

Sunraysia

Kerang, Swan Hill

Other Vic.

Coonawarra Padthaway

Adelaide & Southern Districts

Clare

VICTORIA

From Australian Bureau of Statistics

yields per hectare that are around double the comparable yields from so-called 'dry' areas. Few wine areas in Australia are not irrigated in some way, be it from bores, dams or rivers via furrow, spray or drip irrigation. Supplementary watering is the term, which somehow, to many, sounds better than 'irrigated wines'. Australian viticulture research indicates wine quality is influenced more by climate (and certainly by winemaking skills) than by irrigation, or lack of it.

The high-yielding grape varieties and regions will continue to be the backbone of Australian wine production while quaffing wine styles remain the mainstay of wine drinkers in this country. The success of casks indicates this will be so for a long time.

RELATIVE SIZE OF AUSTRALIAN WINEGROWING AREAS
(Based on location where grapes are processed)

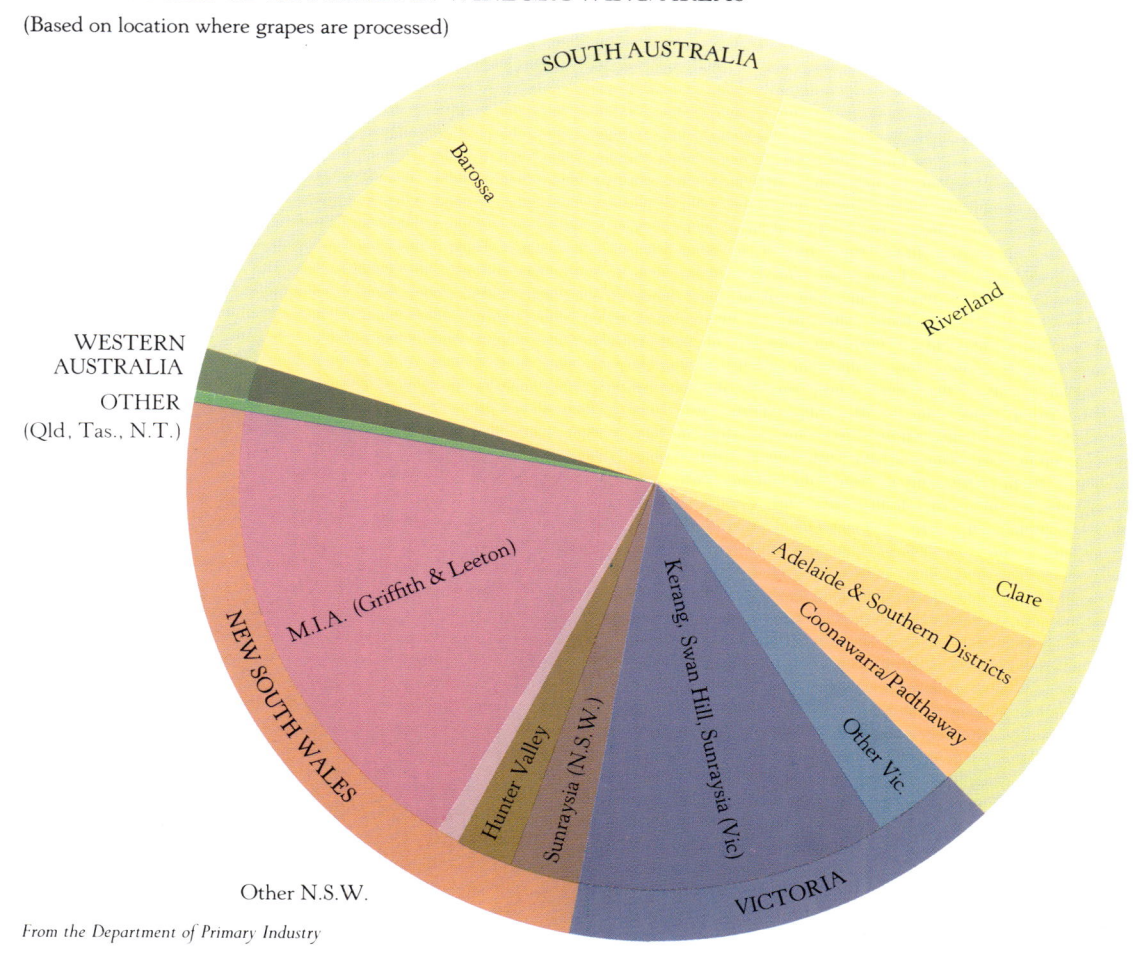

From the Department of Primary Industry

Red grapes coming through a mechanical harvester at Coonawarra.

The two 'pie' diagrams show some interesting points. For example, the South Australian Riverland produces more grapes than would normally translate to wine. A comparison of grape production (far left) and wine production (near left) would seem to indicate that quite a proportion of those Riverland grapes are made into wine in the Barossa Valley. And note what a small proportion of Australia's wine is made in, say, the Hunter Valley.

BOTTLES, FLAGONS AND CASKS

The fortunes of the wine industry have been much influenced by its usage of alternative forms of packaging. Wine allows itself to be packaged in more forms than most other beverages, a distinct advantage in a competitive consumer market because the alternative forms of packaging have brought about new consumption patterns and growth... witness the success of the ubiquitous cask, soft pack or bag-in-box (as the industry calls it).

In the 1960s the wine industry successfully popularised the flagon (then half gallon, now 2 litres). By the early Seventies flagons accounted for around one quarter of the wine market. It wasn't until 1973/74 that casks began making significant inroads. By 1976/ 77 flagons and casks accounted for some 40 per cent of the wine market; today it is about 80 per cent.

The wine cask is an Australian innovation. While they have more recently caught on in other countries there has been nowhere near the market penetration experienced in Australia. There appears to be no one reason why this is so, rather a combination of circumstances. First, in Australia wine is cheap, partly because table wine historically has seldom carried sales or excise taxes, so we can reasonably afford to pay for 4 litres at a time. Second, the wine cask is a take-home convenience pack which hit the market at a time when packaged beverage sales through discount outlets, as opposed to consumption on licensed premises, developed rapidly. Third, our climate and casual lifestyle led to acceptance of this radical packaging concept for wine.

The diagram shows the split of white and red table wine by type of package. Casks dominate white wine sales, while bottle sales are relatively strong for red wine. It is interesting to note the different State preferences for bottles, flagons and casks. Cask volumes in all States dominate other packaging types, particularly in Victoria and New South Wales. More Victorians prefer casks and bottles. South Australians have a particular affinity for flagons and New South Welshman also lean towards the flagon (although in both cases casks are still the volume leaders).

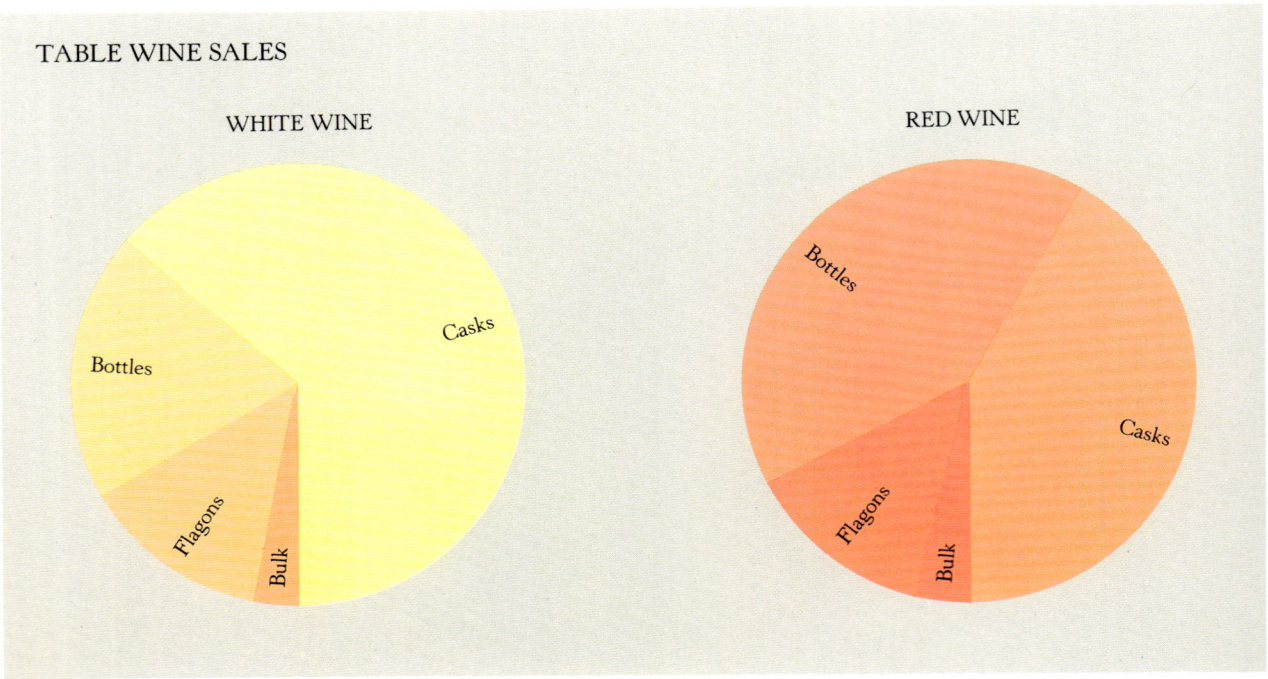

TABLE WINE SALES

WHITE WINE

RED WINE

From the Australian Bureau of Statistics

LABELLING

Certain information on wine labels sets it apart from the labelling of other beverages: the year it was made, grape variety and geographical region. The rules governing wine production and labelling are embodied in State legislation but in typical style, they differ slightly from State to State. However the basics are invariably the same.

* 'Wine' has to be made only from grapes and, with few and narrow exceptions, the addition of sugar and water is prohibited (this is not so in many other wine-producing nations).

* Vintage year: for a wine to be described as of a particular vintage 100 per cent of the wine must come from that year's vintage. This requirement is quite

unambiguous and, by world standards, strict.

* Grape variety: for a wine to be described as of a particular variety (or varieties) at least 80 per cent of the wine must be of the nominated variety. Where more than one variety is named they must appear in descending order of their volume in the blend. Again the requirement is clear, and on a par with, or better than, world standards. (In the United States, for example, the requirement for a varietal wine is 75 per cent, and until recently it was 50 per cent.)

* Geographical region: for a wine to be described as of a particular region at least 80 per cent of the wine must have come from grapes grown in that region, or have been made or blended in that region. The 80 per cent is level with world standards, but the detail is more than a little ambiguous, leading to some controversy in recent years.

Labelling has changed a lot since these labels were produced over a century ago. Note the spelling of 'Reisling'. It still happens in some places!

WEIGHTS AND MEASURES

750 millilitres = 1.32 imperial pints = 1.58 U.S. pints
1 litre = 35.19 imperial fluid ounces = 33.78 U.S. fluid ounces
1 dozen 750 millilitre bottles = 1.98 imperial gallons = 9 litres = (approximately) 18 kilograms gross

CASKS
Octave = 95 litres = 21 imperial gallons
Quarter cask = 160 litres = 35 imperial gallons
Australian hogshead = 295 litres = 65 imperial gallons
French hogshead = 225 litres = 50 imperial gallons
Puncheon = 495 litres = 109 imperial gallons

ALCOHOL STRENGTHS IN AUSTRALIA

Brandy and most other spirits:	minimum 37 per cent alcohol by volume except in W.A. (minimum 43 per cent)
Wine: table wine:	minimum 8 per cent, in practice usually between 10 and 13 per cent alcohol by volume
fortified wine:	minimum 18 per cent
Boiling point of alcohol:	78.5°C (173.3°F)
1 litre of alcohol (lal) =	3.6 x 750-millilitre bottles of brandy at 37 per cent alcohol by volume
1 litre of alcohol =	0.386 imperial proof gallon = 0.5283 U.S. proof gallon
100° U.S. proof =	50 per cent alcohol by volume
100° imperial proof =	57 per cent alcohol by volume

Hunter Valley vineyards. There are more than 5000 vineyards and some 400-plus wineries in Australia today.

THE WINE INDUSTRY

The grape-growing side of the wine industry is spread out relatively widely, with 5000 enterprises whose principal activity is grape-growing. There are many more properties with vineyards but where grape-growing is not the main business. Wineries obtain 80 per cent of their source material from these independent grape-growers, the remainder from their own vineyards. However wineries do grow a higher proportion of their own requirements of premium grapes, such as cabernet sauvignon, Rhine riesling and chardonnay.

The winemaking side of the wine industry is more concentrated and becoming even more so. Over 400 companies operate wineries throughout Australia; less than 5 per cent of these account for over 80 per cent of the vintage. The larger wine companies now crush over 20 000 tonnes a vintage. The top eight wine companies account for 52 per cent of industry turnover, 38 per cent of industry employment and 44 per cent of industry investment expenditure. (Recent acquisitions and mergers have pushed these figures much higher.)

The rapid development over the last twenty years has seen much restructuring of the wine industry as companies scramble for strategic positions in the market. The major realignments over the last twenty years have strongly influenced what we are drinking today and will drink tomorrow.

CONSOLIDATED WINERIES AND DISTILLERY
Formed in 1982/83 from an amalgamation of Renmano and Berri Co-Operative Wineries.

G. GRAMP & SONS (Orlando) and Morris Wines
Taken over in 1970 by Reckitt & Colman, the U.K.-based multinational manufacturer of household goods.

THOMAS HARDY & SONS
Hardy took over the Emu Wine Company in 1976 including Houghton and Valencia; Rhinecastle Wines (1982); and Reynella (late 1982).

KAISER STUHL AND PENFOLDS
Penfolds was taken over by Tooths in 1976 which in turn was acquired by the Adsteam group which then acquired Kaiser Stuhl in 1982. Wynn (Allied Vintners) was acquired by Penfolds/Kaiser Stuhl in May 1985.

LINDEMANS
Lindemans took over both Leo Buring and Rouge Homme in the 1960s, but was itself the subject of takeover in 1971 by Philip Morris, the U.S.-based tobacco multinational.

MILDARA
Mildara bought out Hamiltons in 1979. At the same time Grants, the Scottish distilling group, obtained a significant interest in Mildara. Mildara took over Yellowglen in 1984, and Balgownie (Victoria) in 1985.

QUELLTALER
Originally Buring and Sobels Ltd, taken over by Vignerons, Distillers and Vintners Ltd in 1970 whose parent company, Nathan and Wyeth, was taken over by Remy Martin (of France) in 1979.

SEAGRAMS
Saltram, Stonyfell, Falkenburg and Roxton were bought by Dalgety Australia in the early 1970s who later sold Saltram and Stonyfell to Seagrams. Falkenburg is now Krondorf while Roxton under David Hardy started out as Benelen but changed to Middlebrook after a legal challenge by Lindemans who claimed the name was too similar to their brand name, Ben Ean.

SEPPELT
Diverse Products (the Coca Cola bottlers in Adelaide), the State Government Insurance Commission and other institutional investors gained significant shareholdings in the 1982-84 period.

After a legal battle with the Adsteam group, Seppelt succumbed to a takeover from the South Australian Brewing Company.

STANLEY WINE CO.
Taken over by H. J. Heinz in 1971; expanded by buying Buronga Winery from Hungerford Hill in 1984.

TOLLANA WINES
Originally Tolley, Scott & Tolley, taken over by United Distillers (U.K.) in the 1950s. United Distillers is now part of the Distillers Company.

TOOHEYS
Tooheys took over Seaview, Wynn and Glenloth in the early 1970s.

WYNDHAM ESTATE
Dalwood, Hollydene, Hermitage Wines and Elliotts are now all part of Wyndham Estate which itself has been substantially owned by AGC and Anglo Thai Ltd. AGC relinquished its interest in 1983/84. Now largely a family (McGuigan and Hamley) controlled and operated enterprise, reversing the general trend.

At work in one of Lindemans' wineries. The company controls Leo Buring and Rouge Homme, and was itself taken over by a large multinational, Philip Morris, in 1971.

THE LAST SIP

Robert Mayne

ACETIC ACID

Acetic acid (CH_3COOH) turns wine into vinegar, so is not considered a good thing. An excess of acetic acid in a wine makes the wine VOLATILE.

ACID

The presence of acids in wine is essential to your enjoyment and their longevity. Too much however can spoil the wine – even turn it to vinegar; too little also affects wine quality.

AFTERTASTE

Flavour which lingers after tasting or swallowing, and which can be pleasant or unpleasant – or non-existent, which would indicate a neutral flavoured wine. Harsh or unpleasant aftertaste may indicate the presence of ACETIC ACID in the wine.

ALCOHOL

The substance that makes the difference between grape juice and wine. In this context, alcohol (C_2H_5OH) means ethyl alcohol, produced by the action of yeasts on grape sugars during fermentation. 'Alcoholic' usually means high in alcohol. Its ability to intoxicate is fairly well appreciated, but it also has an important bearing on the taste perceptions of wine. High levels of alcohol can leave a 'hot' taste in the mouth; brandies, ports and fortified wines demonstrate this characteristic.

ALL SAINTS

Winery at Wahgunyah, north-east Victoria, of spectacular construction. Known for its fortified wines.

ALLANDALE

Small Hunter Valley winemaker producing extremely good white and red table wines.

AMONTILLADO

A wood matured fino sherry. Dry, often with a 'nutty' flavour.

AMPELOGRAPHY

The science of classifying vine varieties, which is not as simple as it sounds, since there are thousands. The shape of leaves is one of the key ways of identifying them (for example, distinguishing cabernet sauvignon from cabernet franc) and there are certainly still many mis-identified varieties planted in Australia.

ANGOVE

Winery of middling to large size in the South Australian Riverland producing excellent brandies and some very good value-for-money VARIETAL wines.

APERITIF

French term for appetiser, here often meaning a pre-dinner glass of wine. I find a dry sherry an excellent aperitif, often served chilled.

APPELLATION

A system of guaranteeing the origin of a wine. From the French Government controlled *Appellation d'origine*. The word is being more widely used in Australia as various areas (parts of Western Australia, Tasmania and Mudgee in New South Wales) adopt 'guarantee of origin' schemes of different types. They are usually honest attempts to guide and attract wine drinkers, though whether the consumer really benefits is questionable.

AROMA

The smell of a wine, usually used to mean pleasant scents, rather than 'OFF' ODOURS. Young wines have more obvious aromas, normally associated with grape varieties, than older wines.

ARROWFIELD

Large mid-Hunter winery which has had varied fortunes. Has made some very good whites.

ASTRINGENT

Tannins in wine produce astringency. The best known way of detecting astringency is the involuntary 'puckering' of the mouth as these tannins hit the taste buds. Tannins are produced from skins and seeds of grapes and from wood.

AUSLESE

German term meaning selection of grapes riper than normal for winemaking. Its use on Australian labels normally indicates a white wine of greater than normal sweetness.

AUSTERE

Different things to different palates, though usually indicating a wine which has recognisably strong flavours with nothing too dominant.

BAILEY'S

The family of this name sold the Bundarra winery some years ago to Davis Gelatine. Located in Ned Kelly country in north-eastern Victoria. Makes excellent reds plus muscats and other fortified dessert wines which would make any bushranger lay down his guns.

BALANCE

The assessment that a wine being tasted has its flavour components in complete harmony, no one being dominant.

BALGOWNIE

Small winery in central Victoria, producing fine red wines. The winery was bought by another Victorian company, Mildara Wines, in early 1985.

BAUMÉ

Measurement of grape sugar. Approximately translates to alcohol level by volume in per cent. For example, grapes at 10 Baume ripeness will yield a wine of around 10 per cent alcohol by volume.

BEERENAUSLESE

German term one level up the ripeness scale from AUSLESE. Very ripe grapes help make very sweet wine.

BEN EAN

One of Australia's biggest selling wines, a 'moselle' from Lindemans Wines first made in 1956 by Ray Kidd. The name was taken from the company's Hunter Winery, though the wine has had little to do with that winery for many years (the winery is now Lindemans' Hunter Valley Winery). The wine itself is clean, fresh and fruity – an excellent wine with which to play tricks on wine buffs!

BERRI

Very large co-operative winery (owned by grape-growers) in the South Australian Riverland town of the same name. Merged with Renmano, another big co-op, several years ago to vie with Penfolds/Kaiser Stuhl as Australia's largest winery. Makes large volumes of cask and quaffing wines, but also makes a number of good bottled red wines.

BEST'S

Family winery near Great Western in central Victoria.

BIG

Powerful in flavours or bouquet.

BILGY

Bilgy or bilginess are accurately descriptive words to describe unpleasant characteristics of a wine emanating from slime bacteria caused by waterlogged wood casks.

BITTERNESS

Unpleasant characteristic in wine, usually detected on the aftertaste. Don't confuse with acidity.

BLANC

White, as in sauvignon blanc, the white grape variety. Its use otherwise by enthusiastic marketing managers produces nonsense labels such as 'blanc de blanc' in Australia.

BLAND

Winetasting term denoting a wine without character, though not necessarily having wine faults.

BLASS

Wolf Blass controls a highly successful middle-sized winery, Bilyara, based at Nuriootpa, at the eastern end of the Barossa Valley in South Australia. Maker and marketer of some good white wines and some superb red wines, especially blended reds.

BLEASDALE

Small family owned winery at Langhorne Creek, South Australia, noted for red wines.

BLEND

Mixing of two or more wines or grape varieties to increase quality or maintain consistency. Ben Ean Moselle, for example, is blended from various grapes and areas, and possibly different vintages. Blending is thought by some to be a dirty word but in fact has helped produce some of Australia's greatest wines, especially reds.

Grapes infected by botrytis.
They look worse as the
fungus sucks them almost dry.

BODY

Full bodied means with fullness of flavour in the mouth; conversely 'light bodied' means the reverse. For example, Penfolds Grange Hermitage would be considered a red wine with full bodied character.

BOTOBOLAR

Small winery outside Mudgee, New South Wales.

BOTRYTIS CINEREA

A parasitic fungus which attacks ripe grape berries, removing water and concentrating flavour constituents. Helps make some of the world's great sweet wines (for example, the wine of Sauternes in France). It is becoming increasingly common in Australia either because the mould has been artificially induced in some areas or has not been encouraged or noticed in the past.

BOTTLE

Usually a 750-millilitre glass container to hold wine. Various shapes, for example, champagne, burgundy, riesling, hock, etc.

BOTTLE AGE

Time spent in bottle after making and possible wood maturation. 'Will improve with bottle age' means the winemaker thinks it will get better if you keep it for a few years. Take most claims like this with a grain of salt, and taste ageing wines regularly!

BOTTLE VARIATION

Difference in character of a wine from bottle to bottle of the same wine. Can be caused by storage conditions, cork difference (and faults) or other factors which may be beyond the winemaker's control.

BOUQUET

The smell of the finished wine. May be affected by time spent in bottle.

BRANDY

The spirit of wine (although of course there are also fruit brandies). By Australian law brandy must be made only from the product of the grape and after distillation must be stored in wood for a minimum of two years. Most Australian brandies come from the Riverland areas of north-western Victoria and, especially, South Australia, and are used for mixing purposes (with soda, ginger ale or water), although some high quality 'liqueur' brandies are made by companies such as Angove and Hardy.

BREATHING

Allowing a wine to come in contact with air by opening some time before serving. There is little agreement between wine enthusiasts over whether it enhances wine flavours, only that sometimes it can allow some 'off' odours, for example, sulphur, to dissipate.

BRIGHT

Perfectly clear wine with no suspended particles. Bright colour is an important guide to wine quality.

BROKENWOOD

Small to middling Hunter Valley producer of esteemed reds and more recently some good white wines.

BROWN BROTHERS

Medium-sized family owned winemaker based at Milawa in northern Victoria. Producer of a wide range of excellent varietal table wines and some fortified wines.

BRUT

Dry, usually as the term applies to champagne. Commercial brut styles now usually have a very small amount of liqueuring added to sweeten the wine somewhat. Hence the growth of wines labelled 'brut de brut', meaning fully dry.

BURGUNDY

Great wine-producing area of eastern France. In Australia the term has been rendered almost meaningless, other than to signify a red wine, probably of a softer style.

BURING, LEO

Large wine company, owned by Lindemans Wines, in turn a subsidiary of Philip Morris. Named after the late Leo Buring, Sydney wine merchant. High quality across-the-board maker all the way from large selling Leibfrauwine to top quality aged Rhine rieslings. Main winery at Chateau Leonay in the Barossa Valley.

CABERNET FRANC

Relative of cabernet sauvignon and a red grape used in the blend of some Bordeaux reds. Little grown in Australia so far.

CABERNET SAUVIGNON

Red (or black) grape variety. Widely considered to produce the finest red wines in the world, sometimes with the blending of other varieties. Classic grape variety of Bordeaux. Widely grown in most Australian areas and while not the dominant variety by any means, becoming more popular with winemakers and drinkers alike.

CAMPBELL'S

Family owned winery not far from Rutherglen, north-east Victoria. Produce good quality table wines and fortified wines at fair prices.

CAPSULE

In wine, usually a reference to the cylinder of plastic, foil or lead used to wrap the top of the neck of a wine bottle.

CARBON DIOXIDE

CO_2. This gas is a by-product of fermentation and with still wines is dissipated into the atmosphere. However when a secondary fermentation is induced inside a champagne bottle the CO_2 which is produced dissolves in the wine, producing the famous bubbles. CARBONATED wines are wines into which CO_2 is injected directly, and they are both cheaper and coarser on the palate.

CARBONATED

Sparkling wines made cheaply by the direct injection of carbon dioxide into the liquid.

CARIGNAN

Red grape variety grown in south-eastern France but not widely used (or acknowledged) in Australia.

CASSIS

A liqueur made from blackcurrants. If you walk into a restaurant and they give you a glass of champagne with a dash of cassis in it, it's probably the sort of place you'll need a wheelbarrow full of money to pay the bill.

CHABLIS

Famous dry white wine area of France. Australian winemakers cannot decide what constitutes a 'chablis' style wine, so you are likely to get anything that is full flavoured, dry or both.

CHAMPAGNE

The famous sparkling wines of the region of this name, north of Paris. Australian sparkling wines fermented in the bottle can be so labelled domestically. (*See* MÉTHODE CHAMPENOISE.) The various sizes of champagne bottles are:

Bottle	750 millilitres	
Magnum	1.5 litres	Two bottles
Jeroboam	3.2 litres	Four bottles
Rheoboam	4.8 litres	Six bottles
Methuselah	6.4 litres	Eight bottles
Salmanazar	9.6 litres	12.8 bottles
Balthazar	12.8 litres	17 bottles
Nebuchadnezzar	20 litres	26.6 bottles

CHAPTALISATION

Adding sugar to fermenting wine, widely practised in Europe, where low sunlight levels sometimes mean grapes will not ripen to provide enough grape sugar for wine production. Illegal in Australia.

CHARDONNAY

White grape variety producing some of the most famous dry white wines in the world, notably from Burgundy and, more latterly, California.

503

CHARMAT

Monsieur Eugène Charmat was a Frenchman who, earlier this century, developed a way of making sparkling wines in large sealed containers in bulk. Produces very drinkable sparkling wines which cannot by law in Australia be labelled 'champagne' though they have many of the virtues of the product of that name, but are much cheaper.

CHASSELAS

White grape variety, grown in parts of France and the United States. Of no great distinction in Australia.

CHATEAU REYNELLA

Historic (1838) winery established by John Reynell. After most of the Reynell family died out it passed on to various companies, including Rothman's of Pall Mall. Finally Thomas HARDY and Sons bought it in late 1982 and restored it magnificently, to become their head office and white winemaking centre. Superb red and fortified wines still made separately under the REYNELLA label.

CHATEAU TAHBILK

Historic winery near Nagambie, north of Melbourne in the Goulburn Valley, owned by the Purbrick family. Noted for red wines, especially powerful cabernets and shiraz wines, and some interesting whites, such as marsanne.

CHATEAU YALDARA

Large and unusual winery at the southern mouth of the Barossa Valley.

CHATEAU YARRINYA

Small winery in Victoria's Yarra Valley making excellent reds.

CHENIN BLANC

White grape variety which makes the wines of the Loire area of France. In Australia it tends to make rather neutral white wines, though some good chenins have been made in Western Australia, notably Houghton.

CIGAR BOX

Aroma akin to the smell it describes, it is not as unpleasant in a wine as it may sound. Combination of fruit, wood and other constituents of well-made red wines, notably the great reds of Bordeaux.

CINSAUT

Red grape variety which makes 'so-so' wines in Australia. Sometimes incorrectly called oeillade.

CINZANO

Large Italian wine company famous for its vermouths. Cinzano Australia is a wholly owned subsidiary and makes wines in Australia, at Griffith, New South Wales.

CLARET

Originally the English word (probably derived from 'Clairette' or light red) for the wines of Bordeaux.

Like 'burgundy', it is somewhat meaningless in Australia today, other than to signify a red wine of medium body aimed at the commercial end of the market. There are, however, some excellent value wines made and sold bearing this generic description.

CLIMATE

Should be the subject of another wine book, because climate has enormous influence on grape quality and hence wine quality. 'Cool climate' are new rage words for growing grapes in areas which are allegedly more European (that is, colder) in growing conditions.

'Microclimate' refers to variations in climate in a small vineyard area, for example, between the top and bottom slopes of a vineyard.

CLOUDY

A cloudy wine has suspended particles in it, obscuring the colour. Indicative of wine problems.

COGNAC

French brandy, generally acknowledged to be the finest in the world. V.S.O.P. is one style, meaning 'very special old pale'. It is distilled wine aged in wood for lengthy periods, and coming from the Cognac region in the west of France. Cognac is generally a 'liqueur' wine, as distinct from a 'mixer' brandy. Australian brandies are generally mixers, though there are several (such as, Angove's Very Old and Hardy's V.S.O.P.) which approach French quality.

COLOUR

In wine an extremely important indicator of wine quality and condition

COONAWARRA

Australian wine region, near Mount Gambier, in south-eastern South Australia, famous for its *terra rossa* soils and somewhat cooler climate. Considered by many to be the greatest red wine area of the country, especially for cabernet sauvignon. Recent good vintages for reds include 1976, 1977, 1978, 1979, (notably) 1980, 1982, 1984 and 1985. Whites were good in 1978, 1979, 1980, 1982 and 1984. (1983 was a terrible year for both.)

CORIOLE

Small winery near McLaren Vale, South Australia, noted for reds.

CORK

Bark of a tree, generally grown around the Mediterranean end of Europe, used to close wine bottles. However *Quercus suber*'s bark is in great demand and good corks can cost between 10 and 20 cents each. It is not without its problems, failing every now and then, to give winemakers heartache and consumers vinegar. Winemakers who are vain enough to believe their wine will live for decades often use the long, European corks to better protect the wine.

CORKED

Term meaning that a wine has a problem which comes either from something in the cork itself, or a fault in the cork which allows air or other foreign elements in. Does not happen a lot these days, but when it does it means trouble.

CORKSCREWS

They come in many and varied shapes and sizes, but the best all rounder is the 'waiter's friend', the indispensable tool with a blade to cut the neck capsule, a screw and a levering mechanism to help you extract the cork from the bottle mouth. Simple to use (if well made), they must be lifted properly to get the cork out cleanly. The American designed Screwpull is more expensive but excellent.

CRAIGMOOR

Small and historic winery near Mudgee in New South Wales, now owned by Montrose. Wines have been mediocre but the new owners should improve quality considerably.

CRUSH

To free grape juice from within the grape berries. Sometimes used to denote the size of a winery, for example, 'They have a crush of 20 000 tonnes.' The crusher is the area of a winery where grapes are dumped for initial extraction of the juice.

CRUST

Deposit sometimes found in red wines and ports, particularly vintage ports. Comes from grape solids and, while it may not look terribly inviting, is harmless and can be removed by decanting or straining.

CRYSTALS

Tiny crystals which can sometimes be seen in both red and white wines, in the wine or on the bottom of the cork. They are tartrates which, for one reason or another, have not been removed by the winemaker from the wine. Only occasionally found in the wines of major makers with the expertise and the technology to remove them from a finished wine before bottling. Jokingly referred to by some as 'wine diamonds'. Harmless.

CULLENS' WILLYABRUP

Small winery in Margaret River area of Western Australia producing good wines.

CUVÉE

Most generally, a blend. Often used in relation to champagne.

d'ARENBERG

Medium-sized winery near McLaren Vale, South Australia, making a range of quality wines.

DECANT

Transfer of wine from the bottle into another container. Most recently made table wines do not need this rather ritualistic process, which was developed to isolate the grape deposits in bottles of wine and port. Nevertheless, it still has a certain magic in the right surroundings, especially with vintage ports, which are likely to have a 'crust' in the bottom. Easy to do, using a clear glass decanter, a clean strainer and (should you wish to go the full hog) a candle to show you when the sediment at the bottom of the bottle is about to pass through the bottle's neck.

DEGREE DAYS
See HEAT DEGREE DAYS.

DEMI SEC
French term meaning 'half dry'. Here, usually means 'half sweet'. Usually applied to sparkling wines of lesser quality.

DESSERT WINE
Wine suitable for consumption with sweeter foods. Usually a richer, sweeter style of wine such as sauternes, port, muscat, tokay.

DISTILLATION
Process by which most spirits (in the case of wine, brandy) are made. Heating up an alcoholic beverage vapourises the alcohol at a lower temperature than water, so the alcohol can be captured and concentrated. There are various 'stills' including pot stills and continuous stills.

DOSAGE
Also known as *liqueur d'expedition,* this is a small amount of sugar (usually cane sugar) added to sparkling wine before it is finally sealed and sold, to give it a slight extra touch of sweetness.

DRAYTON
Family owned and operated winery in the Hunter Valley, established in 1860. Makes whites and reds of considerable, if variable, character.

DRY
Absence of residual sugar in wine.

EARTHY
Wine-tasting term meaning the wine has the taste or odour of the soil. Hunter wines often have this sort of taste; it is not necessarily unpleasant.

ELLIOTT
Small winery in the Hunter Valley, New South Wales, established by the Elliott family in 1893 and with which they are still associated. Quality wines.

ENTERPRISE
Winery in Clare Valley, South Australia, operated by Tim Knappstein. Quality whites and reds.

ESTERY
Class of organic compounds formed by the reaction of acid with alcohol. This happens in ageing bottles of wine, such as vintage ports and old dry wines. 'Estery' means strong scents coming from esters derived from bottle maturation.

ETHYL ALCOHOL
See ALCOHOL.

EVANS AND TATE
Medium-sized quality winemaker based in the Swan Valley, Western Australia, noted for quality reds.

FERGUSSONS
Small winery owned by the Fergussons in the Yarra Valley, Victoria.

FERMENTATION
Process of converting grape sugar into alcohol by yeasts.

FILTERING
Modern winemaking calls for a good deal of filtering of wines, using various pieces of equipment to remove impurities, solids and other matter in the wine. Hence modern wines are seldom cloudy or unclear. It can reduce wine quality, however.

FINING
Way of clarifying young wine before it is bottled. Different to FILTERING.

FINISH
End taste of a wine after it has been swallowed or spat out. High tannin content might cause 'firm finish' or lack of flavour might be described as 'poor finish'.

FINO
A very dry style of sherry. *See also* FLOR.

FIRM
Wine-tasting term referring to taste experience at the back of the palate, caused by tannins.

FLABBY
Wine-tasting term (also 'fat') meaning the wine has unpleasantly voluptuous flavours on the back palate. High in glycerine character; soft and broad.

FLAGON
Glass container, usually holding 2 litres, referred to in the United States as a 'jug'. The term was probably derived from the contraction of 'half gallon' as the container originally held 2.25 litres or about half a gallon. Some reasonable quality wines, especially reds, can still be found in these containers in Australia.

FLAT
Uninteresting; little flavour. In sparkling wines, of course, no or little bubble.

FLAVOUR
The taste of wine.

FLINTY
Wine-tasting term usually applied to dry white wines, especially of the chablis style. Traces of gun flint on the palate.

FLOR
A yeast which grows on the surface of a wine, especially sherry, and gives it a 'nutty' character. Usually applied to flor fino sherries.

FLOWERY
An attractive scent reminiscent of flowers. 'Floral' and 'fragrant' are similar words often applied to whites, usually aromatic young wines.

FORTIFY
To add grape spirit to a wine. Increases alcoholic strength and preserves the wine. Fortified wines include ports, vermouths, sherries, muscats and tokays.

FOXY
One of the hard wine-tasting terms to define in words, but once you taste/smell it, you'll know it. Often applied to the scent and taste of the wines made from the *Vitis labrusca* strain of grapes, such as those grown in New York State. A sweetish smell and taste.

FREE RUN
The juice released from the grape berries when they are first crushed at the winery, before further pressing. Highest quality juice used for making best whites.

FUMÉ BLANC
Dry white wine, usually intended to mean 'smoky white' though whether the wine has actually seen any time in wood barrels is dubious. SAUVIGNON BLANC is the other suggestion implicit with wine labelled this way, but it isn't necessarily so these days.

GAMAY
Red grape grown in France (where it produces, among other things, Beaujolais wines) and elsewhere. Probably related to PINOT NOIR, it also produces wines of generally lighter style.

GEWURZTRAMINER
Spicy traminer (*see* TRAMINER).

GNANGARA
Brand name for Evans and Tate wines from Western Australia. Good reds.

GRANGE HERMITAGE
Red wine developed by Penfolds winemaker Max Schubert in the early 1950s, patterned on Bordeaux reds. Named after red grape variety (actually shiraz). The wines are strong on fruit flavours, wood treatment and tannins. Great vintages were 1955, 1962 and 1965, closely followed by 1966, 1971 and 1976.

GREEN
A wine not ready for drinking; or one which has malic acid content.

GRENACHE
Red variety widely grown in many parts of Australia for use in red and fortified wines, now somewhat unfashionable, perhaps unfairly. Can still make good reds, ports and rosé wines.

GROG
Australian abbreviation for an alcoholic drink. Admiral Vernon ordered the watering of the rum ration issued to the Royal Navy in 1740. He always wore a grogram cloak — the word is said to come from this.

505

HARD

Wine-tasting term which, with 'harsh', refers to bitter and dry tastes associated with tannins on the finish of some wines.

HARDY

Thomas Hardy and Sons is a large family owned wine and brandy producer, established in 1853 and based in South Australia. Premium bottled wines and brandies, notably Siegersdorf Rhine Riesling, Old Castle Riesling, Nottage Hill Claret, Eileen Hardy Red, and Black Bottle Brandy. Renowned for premium tawny and vintage ports. Owns Chateau Reynella, Houghton and Rhine Castle Wines.

HEAT DEGREE DAYS

The figure for heat degree days is derived from a viticulture formula to indicate the effect local climate has on speed of ripening, and hence the quality of resulting grapes. The lower the number the higher the fruit quality, as a rule.

HENSCHKE

Small to medium-sized family company based at Keyneton, in the Barossa Ranges. Excellent reds.

HERBACEOUS

Taste which can be related to herb flavours. Some reds, notably cabernet, and some whites (for example, sauvignon blanc) are sometimes described in this way.

HERMITAGE

Synonym used in some parts of Australia for SHIRAZ; a red grape. Also name of middle-sized Hunter maker, Hermitage Estate, associated with the Wyndham Estate.

HICKINBOTHAM

Small family winery at Geelong, Victoria. Quality wines.

HOCK

English name for dry white wine, now in little use in Australia. Comes from German town of Hochheim, where Rhine wines are made.

HOGSHEAD

Wooden barrel for storing wine and usually imparting oak flavours to it. Holds about 300 litres.

HONEYED

Wine-tasting term, often used with sauternes wines and some others, including older Hunter semillons.

HOT

Wine-tasting term referring to slightly burning feeling in the mouth. Usually means a high level of alcohol, as with port, etc.

HOUGHTON

Swan Valley (Western Australian) winery established 1836. Best known for quality whites, especially Houghton White Burgundy.

H₂S

H_2S
Hydrogen sulphide. Rotten egg smell in wine caused by winemaking or storage fault. *Big* trouble!

HUNGERFORD HILL

Medium-sized wine company based in the centre of the Hunter Valley, New South Wales. Excellent whites and reds, especially wines from their Coonawarra vineyards.

HUNTINGTON ESTATE

Small producer based in Mudgee, New South Wales. Some excellent whites (semillon) and reds (cabernet and merlot).

IDYLL

Small winemaker at Geelong, Victoria.

JAMMY

Wine-tasting term usually applied to red wines. Heavily pressed fruit from hot climate causes 'jammy' flavours. Less common now, with many Australian wineries picking at night and having temperature control equipment to avoid such tastes.

JEROBOAM

See CHAMPAGNE.

JIMMY WATSON TROPHY

Jimmy Watson was a Melbourne wine merchant (and his bar and bistro, now run by his son Alan, is still a well-frequented watering hole) who donated a trophy to be awarded each year to the best one-year-old wine judged at the Melbourne Wine Show. Wolf Blass made it famous (and himself as well) when he won it three years running, in 1974, 1975 and 1976.

KAISER STUHL

Large winemaker based in the Barossa Valley, South Australia. Was a grape-grower owned co-operative, bought by Penfolds/Adsteam. Wide range of products; notable wines include Green Ribbon Rhine rieslings and good Red Ribbon reds.

KATNOOK

Winery at Coonawarra, South Australia, operated by Coonawara Machine Co. High quality but pricey whites and reds.

KAY'S

Small family company near McLaren Vale, South Australia. Interesting reds.

KEROSENE

Wine-tasting term, sometimes applied to aged Australian Rhine rieslings; some petroleum compounds have a similar structure. Not as unpleasant as it sounds: try an old Leo Buring Rhine riesling, for example.

KRONDORF

Medium-sized South Australian company which makes good white and red varietal wines, and markets them aggressively. Wineries in the Barossa Valley and McLaren Vale.

LACTIC

An acid character evident on the palate of some wines, resulting from MALOLACTIC FERMENTATION.

LAKE'S FOLLY

Dr Max Lake's Hunter Valley winery, making small quantities of varietal wines.

LATE PICKED

Grapes picked later than most others, hence riper and with high levels of sugar. Can be used in production of SPÄTLESE and AUSLESE wines.

LEASINGHAM

The STANLEY Wine Company, owned by H. J. Heinz, makes the wines under this brand. Large company making very good whites (especially rieslings) and reds (such as cabernet/malbec) from wineries in the Clare Valley and Buronga, on the New South Wales side of Mildura.

LEEUWIN ESTATE

Magnificent winery at Margaret River, Western Australia. High quality – and expensive – whites and reds.

L.B.V.

Late Bottled Vintage – port term meaning a young port wine made in the vintage, given some wood treatment and designed for early drinking.

LEES

Deposits in cask or bottle. Notably the residue in champagne bottles from dead yeast cells after secondary fermentation, and before disgorging, which is called 'lying on lees' which helps give champagnes their yeasty flavour.

LEGS

Columns of wine, especially fortified wines, which run down the side of a glass after it is swirled.

LEO BURING

See BURING, LEO.

LINDEMANS

One of Australia's largest and best winemaking companies, a subsidiary of Philip Morris. Based in Sydney with wineries in the Hunter Valley, Karadoc (Victoria), the Barossa Valley, and Coonawarra. Noted for the skill with which they make premium wines and hold some back for later release when aged.

LUSCIOUS

Wine-tasting term meaning full, rich, ripe, fruity and sweet flavours.

McWILLIAM'S

Large family owned company based in New South Wales. Wineries in the Hunter Valley (Mount Pleasant), Griffith (three) and head office in Sydney. Wide range of quality table and fortified wines at very reasonable prices.

MADERISE

Character named after old wines of Madeira. Bottle developed character resulting from the oxidation of the alcohol to acetaldehyde, producing a oxidised, almond-like flavour in wine and fortified wines – gives brown colour.

MAGNUM
Large bottle containing equivalent of two bottles of wine, or 1.5 litres. Magnums will normally age longer than 750-millilitre bottles because of the higher ratio of wine to air between the top of the wine and the bottom of the cork.

MALBEC
Red grape variety grown in parts of France. Becoming more widely used in Australian red blends to soften reds for earlier drinking, for example, Jacob's Creek Claret.

MALOLACTIC FERMENTATION
Malolactic fermentation is the decomposition of malic acid by bacteria to give lactic acid and carbon dioxide. Malic acid is complex (COOH.CH$_2$CH[OH].COOH). A process which is still not fully understood by many. 'Malo' can cause winemakers great problems if it happens in the bottle (the cork can blow out) rather than in the cask.

MARC
Leftover solid material after pressing grapes – dry residue of grape skins and seeds.

MARIENBERG
Small winery operated by Ursula Pridham near Happy Valley in South Australia.

MARSANNE
White grape variety, grown in the Rhône Valley in France, and only a few Australian areas. Best known from Chateau Tahbilk in Victoria. Makes dry yet full flavoured whites.

MATARO
Lesser red grape variety.

MATURE
Mellow flavour/colour of aged wine. Attractive softness.

MENISCUS
Literally, the upper part of a liquid column made convex or concave by capillarity. In wine, the shallow part against the edge of a glass, where you can best see the colour of the wine.

MERCAPTAN
A chemical formed in wine and derived from H$_2$S. Its appeal can be judged from Len Evans' advice about how it smells: 'It is produced by yeast and combines with other natural ingredients of wine to produce a range of smelly compounds which have odours reminiscent of onion, garlic, burnt rubber, skunk, stale cabbage and asparagus.' See also H$_2$S.

MERLOT
Premium red variety, usually used blended with other varieties (cabernet, etc.). Widely grown in France, notably Bordeaux. At its best, it can give a wine a velvety texture.

MÉTHODE CHAMPENOISE
Authentic French method of making bottle fermented CHAMPAGNE.

METHUSELAH
See CHAMPAGNE.

MILDARA
Large winery based at Merbein, near Mildura, in the Victorian Riverland. Produces excellent fortified wines (sherries, ports) and many fine varietal and table wines, especially those from its Coonawarra vineyards.

MIRAMAR
Small winery near Mudgee, New South Wales. High quality wines, excellent rosé.

MISTELLE
Grape juice used as sweetening agent, for example, for VERMOUTH.

MITCHELTON
Medium-sized winery near Nagambie, in Victoria's Goulburn Valley, marked by unusual tall tower building. Makes fine varietal whites and reds.

MONDEUSE
Unusual red grape variety, normally used in blends with others (for example, in Brown Brothers Shiraz, Mondeuse and Cabernet).

MONTROSE
Medium-sized winery at Mudgee, New South Wales, owned by an Italian corporation. Producer of quality white and red wines. Also owns nearby Craigmoor winery.

MOORILLA ESTATE
Small winery near Hobart, Tasmania, owned by Claudio Alcorso.

MORRIS
Mick Morris still runs this Rutherglen (Victoria) winery, though it is now owned by Orlando (Reckitt and Colman). Famous for some of Australia's greatest fortified wines, especially liqueur muscats and tokays of opulent richness, but now also making excellent whites.

MOSELLE
Australian version of the wines of the River Mosel, Germany. For 'moselle', read: light, fresh, young, fruity, white wine which is fairly cheap.

MOSS WOOD
Small winery in Margaret River, Western Australia, run by Dr Bill Pannell. Fine cabernets and some other varietal wines.

MOUNT MARY
Tiny winery in the Yarra Valley, Victoria, making fine whites and reds.

MOUSY
Unpleasant smell and taste of acetic nature. Evidence of bacterial disease in wine.

MULLED WINE
Atrocity performed to wine by skiers and others who add herbs and spices, sweeteners and other odds and ends, then heat it up.

MULLER THURGAU
White grape variety, a cross between riesling and sylvaner, developed in Switzerland, but not yet much grown in Australia, though it is successfully grown in New Zealand.

MUSCADELLE
White grape apparently related to the MUSCAT family.

MUSCAT
Sweet and fruity white grape, one of the most important (in volume terms) in Australia. Comes in many different varieties and the name is derived from 'muscat of Alexandria' (hence 'Lexia' – a contraction from 'Alexandria' – as a term for some wines). Very broad flavoured and obvious, to the point of coarseness, it is the basis of many cask and flagon wines.

MUST
Grape juice, skins and seeds after the initial crushing process. Some winemakers crush in the field (vineyard) and transport the must to the winery – perhaps 400 kilometres or further away – to transform it into wine.

NEUTRAL
Little flavour, nothing bad but not much to taste.

NOBLE ROT
BOTRYTIS CINEREA – a fungus which attacks grapes and affects the resulting wine.

NOSE
The smell or bouquet of a wine.

NUTTY
Sherries sometimes smell like this.

OAK
Various types of wood are used to store wine and, more particularly, to impart oak flavours to it: mainly French oak, American oak and German oak. Oak chips (splintered barrels) and oak essence can be used to give oak flavour quicker and more cheaply, but the results are not the same.

OENOLOGY
The science of wine and winemaking. Two schools teach oenology in Australia (Roseworthy in South Australia and the Riverina College of Advanced Education at Wagga Wagga in New South Wales).

'OFF' ODOURS
Unpleasant smells or odours in a wine.

OILY
Oily flavours can be imparted to wine by errors in winemaking. They usually come from oils in the pips and stalks.

OLFACTORY
Relating to the sense of smell.

OLOROSO
Sherry style: old and semi-sweet to sweet sherry, matured in wood.

507

ORLANDO
Large winemaker, based in South Australia (with wineries in the Barossa Valley and in Griffith, New South Wales) owned by Reckitt and Colman. Producers of a wide range of bulk and premium wines (Coolabah casks, Jacob's Creek Claret, Carrington Champagne) of excellent quality. Also owns MORRIS Wines.

OVERRIPE
Wine made from grapes which were too ripe. *See also* JAMMY.

OXIDATION
Process by which presence of oxygen causes wine to decompose.

PALOMINO
Rather neutral white grape variety, used especially in sherry making.

PEDRO
Pedro ximinez (or P.X.) is a white grape variety used in sherry making.

PENFOLDS
One of the largest wine producers in Australia, owned by the Adsteam group, and which in turn controls KAISER STUHL. Established 1844 and famous for making red wines such as GRANGE HERMITAGE, St Henri Claret and Bin 389 Cabernet/Shiraz. Major marketer of a complete range of wine styles, though to date its white wines have been disappointing. Major winery in the Barossa Valley, South Australia. Also known for Minchinbury Champagne and Grandfather Port.

PEPPERY
Not entirely unpleasant 'spicy' characteristic sometimes found in young red wines (especially shiraz) and ports. Somewhat raw and biting characteristic reminiscent of black pepper.

PERFUMED
Reminiscent of certain perfume smells. Usually resulting from fermentation.

PETALUMA
Medium-sized high-technology winery in the Adelaide Hills at Piccadilly operated by winemaker/managing director Brian Croser, and involving Len Evans and Denis Horgan (who owns LEEUWIN ESTATE). High quality, cool climate grapes from the Adelaide Hills, Coonawarra and premium areas of New South Wales have gone into Rhine rieslings, chardonnays and reds. The wines are not cheap. Premium champagnes, in collaboration with Bollinger, are promised.

PETILLANT
French word for lightly carbonated wine.

pH
The measure of the acidity or alkalinity of a solution, in this case, wine. Of interest to winemakers and viticulturalists only. After ten years trying to fully understand the definition of pH, I have given up.

PHYLLOXERA
Phylloxera vastatrix is a vine louse, a parasitic disease which swept through Europe late last century and was transmitted to Australia and elsewhere shortly afterwards in vine cuttings. It devastated the Victorian wine industry, and swept through New South Wales, though it has apparently been kept out of South Australia by controls. The only known answer to it is to replant grapevines on resistant American rootstocks.

PINOT BLANC
One of the grape varieties of Alsace. Some is grown in Australia (for example, at Chateau Reynella) for interesting dry white wines.

PINOT NOIR
The red grape variety of Burgundy, also one of the varieties of Champagne in France. Produces lighter styles of red which, when well made from good vintages, have intense flavour. Australian winemakers and grape-growers are still coming to grips with pinot noir.

PIPER'S BROOK
Small winery established near Launceston in northern Tasmania by Dr Andrew Pirie. Good Rhine rieslings, and other wines coming on.

PLANTAGENET
Smallish winery at Mt Barker, south-east Western Australia. Winemaker Rob Bowen has produced fine whites, good reds and an excellent rosé wine.

PORT
Fortified red wine. Australia makes some excellent port style wines modelled on those of Oporto, Portugal. Vintage ports are those made from the grapes of a nominated year and usually need plenty of ageing to become enjoyable. Tawny ports are blended from various vintages, old, medium and recent, to be enjoyable on purchasing. Vintage ports often have a CRUST of grape sediments and need decanting. Other port styles include ruby port, a blended young sweet wine whose colour is ruby (it has not become 'tawny' with age). Best makers of vintage and tawny ports include Yalumba, Lindemans, Seppelt, McWilliam's, Hardy and Chateau Reynella. Tawny ports will keep for a short time after opening; vintage ports should be drunk quickly.

POT STILL
Old method of distillation of brandy, still considered the best.

PRESSINGS
After initial crushing the FREE RUN juice is pumped away and the residue is pressed heavily to obtain more juice; this is higher in tannins and acids, but can also be used to give lesser wines more flavour (for example, the pressings of chardonnay grapes can add more flavour to a more neutral, and cheaper, white wine (say a 'chablis' or 'white burgundy'). More colour, flavour and tannin can also be obtained from red wines in this way as the colour comes from the skins.

PRICKED
A wine which smells of ethyl acetate, which can be said to be becoming VOLATILE.

PUNCHEON
A larger type of wooden barrel – perhaps holding 500 litres of wine.

PUNGENT
Strong and aromatic, perhaps too much so.

PUNT
The concave bottom of a champagne bottle, to help resist the pressure. Now used on a number of European still wine bottles, and increasingly on premium Australian whites and reds. Add $5 to the price when you see a punted wine bottle!

QUELDINBURG
Small family winery outside Muswellbrook, in the Upper Hunter, New South Wales.

QUELLTALER
Medium-sized and picturesque winery near Watervale at the mouth of the Clare Valley, South Australia, owned by the French Remy group. Makes very good whites, good reds and some admirable fortified and sparkling wines. Another winery near Avoca, Victoria.

RACKING
Transferring wine from one cask to another, a process which enables the winemaker to move it away from a sediment or deposit. A wine that has been racked may temporarily lose some quality.

RANCIO
The oxidised character evident in older sweet wines and some sherries. In this context, not necessarily a fault.

REDMAN
Redman's family winery (called Redbank) in Coonawarra, South Australia. Bruce Redman is now the winemaker and they still make only two wines – a cabernet sauvignon and shiraz wine – each vintage.

RESIDUAL SUGAR
Grape sugar left in a wine after fermentation has been halted by the winemaker. One of the characteristics of modern white wines which wine drinkers obviously like.

REYNELLA
Southern suburb of Adelaide, given its name by John Reynell, who established CHATEAU REYNELLA in 1838. Two other wineries there are Wynn's Glenloth (specialising in champagne) and St Francis.

RHEOBOAM
See CHAMPAGNE.

RHINE RIESLING

Variant of the riesling grape of Germany, widely grown in Australia and made in different styles. The term 'riesling' usually means a dry or medium dry white wine made from a blend of white grape varieties, not necessarily including Rhine riesling. Some of Australia's best 'Rhines' come from makers including Lindemans, Leo Buring, Yalumba, Wynn, Hungerford Hill, Petaluma, Rosemount, Orlando, Hardy, Chateau Reynella, Quelltaler, Seppelt, Leasingham and Brown Brothers.

RICHMOND GROVE

Upper Hunter winery operated by Mark Cashmore which is linked with the Wyndham Estate. Good range of commercial wines, expertly marketed.

ROBSON

Murray Robson established his boutique winery at the southern end of the Hunter Valley, New South Wales, in 1972. The picturesque vineyard and winery produce some excellent red and white varietal wines.

ROSÉ

Light and fresh young red wine. Surprisingly, has not caught on in any meaningful way, perhaps because no really uniform style has been established. Commercial best seller is Kaiser Stuhl Rosé, and another excellent wine comes in a Mateus-style bottle from Tollana. Other top examples from Houghton and Plantagenet. The bright salmon pink colour should have no tinges of brown; the colour comes from the skins of the red grapes used for making the wine. Winemakers say they often sweat blood over making good rosé wines.

ROSEMOUNT

Medium-sized Upper Hunter Valley (New South Wales) winery owned by coffee millionaire Bob Oatley. Excellent whites (chardonnays, Rhine rieslings, etc.) and reds getting better, with Coonawarra vineyards planted.

ROTHBURY

The Rothbury Estate was established by Len Evans and a group of other wine enthusiasts in 1968. Through financial times thick and thin Rothbury has produced some notable whites, mainly semillons, and seems to be on the right road with reds and other wines. Superb location and winery, venue for some of the greatest wine, food and other entertainment spectacles held in Australia.

ROUGE HOMME

True to name, the Redman family established this winery in 1908, but sold out to LINDEMANS in 1965. Since then Lindemans have made some of the greatest red wines in Australia from these and nearby vineyards in COONAWARRA.

RUBBERY

An unhappy character in a wine, often in old whites, sometimes associated with MERCAPTAN.

ST HUBERT

Small Yarra Valley (Victoria) winemaker making top reds.

SALTRAM

Large Barossa Valley (South Australia) based winemaker owned by multi-national Seagram company. Good wines across the board, epecially varietal whites and Stoneyfell reds.

SANDALFORD

Second largest winery in Western Australia, based in the Swan Valley but with big vineyard interests in the Margaret River region. Interesting verdelho whites and Margaret River reds, plus old liqueur verdelho.

SAUVIGNON BLANC

White grape variety, makes wines in Bordeaux and the Loire areas of France. Its grassy/steely character is now making it a popular variety in Australia, though plantings are so far small. Descriptions such as FUMÉ BLANC and Blanc Fumé are intended to suggest that the wines are made from this variety, though this is not always so.

SEAVIEW

Famous winery north of McLaren Vale, South Australia, which gave its name to one of the brand leaders in the champagne market in Australia. Operated by the WYNN (Allied Vintners) group.

SEC

Dry.

SEMILLON

Another great French dry white variety, including the whites of Bordeaux. Quite widely grown in Australia, making whites which are usually dry.

SEPPELT

Large South Australian based winemaker, taken over by S.A. Brewing in 1985. Established by the Seppelt family in 1851. Wineries in the Barossa Valley and Victoria (Great Western). Remarkably successful maker of premium table wines, sparkling wines (Great Western Champagne) and fortified wines (Para Liqueur Port and sherries) plus vinegar.

SHARP

Acid taste on the palate. This may not be totally unpleasant.

SHERRY

Fortified wine from southern Spain, also widely made in Australia, though not as popular as it was several decades ago. Better makers include Lindemans, McWilliam's, Seppelt, Mildara, Hardy and Reynella. See AMONTILLADO and FINO.

SHIRAZ

One of the most heavily planted red grape varieties in Australia. Shiraz (or hermitage) grows in most winegrowing regions and makes just about every level of red wine from quaffing casks to Grange Hermitage.

SOFT

Wine-tasting term. No harsh sensation on the palate and after-palate.

SOLERA

Method of producing some fortified wines (sherries and some ports) by rotating wine through casks.

SPÄTLESE

Late picked style of fruity and/or sweet white wine.

SPICY

Some TRAMINER wines, among others, can have this character.

SPRITZIG

A small amount of CO_2 in a wine, such as a rosé. Leaves a slight fizzing sensation on the tongue.

SPUMANTE

Italian word for sparkling wine. Here it usually means sweet, sparkling and cheap.

STALKY

Tasting of grape stalks – rather like OILY.

STANLEY

Large wine company based in the Clare Valley, making LEASINGHAM wines. Owned by H.J. Heinz, but like most Australian wine companies, Stanley probably makes many more than 57 varieties of wine.

SULPHUR DIOXIDE

SO_2. Chemical used as an anti-oxidant in winemaking, also for sterilisation. The smell of sulphur can be present in a newly opened bottle of wine, but it should dissipate.

SULTANA

White, heavy bearing and large-berried grape. One of the most grown in Australia, it is dual purpose, that is, it can also be used for dried fruit and as a table grape. Makes rather coarse white wines and a lot of it goes into cask and flagon brands.

SWAN VALLEY

Western Australian wine-growing area just to the east of Perth, along the Swan River. Hot grape-growing area containing a number of historic and newer wineries.

SWEET

More than fruity – pertaining to sugar.

SYLVANER

White grape variety making 'so-so' aromatic whites.

SYRAH

Best red grape variety of the Rhône Valley of France. Similar if not the same variety as SHIRAZ. Also spelt sirah, but not the same variety known as petite sirah in the United States (which is actually the variety, durif).

TALTARNI

Small winemaker near Avoca in central Victoria. High quality reds and sparkling wines.

509

TANNIN

A vital ingredient (and preservative) in wines, especially red wines. It comes from the stalks, skins and pips on grapes. The taste of tannins on the palate when the wine is young give that bitter, puckering taste on the palate. A complex and important constituent of wine, enabling a red wine to last in the bottle for some time, perhaps decades or longer.

TART

Taste of acidity, of malic acid, in a noticeable way.

TAWNY

Blended PORT.

TAYLORS

Middle-sized, modern winery near Watervale, South Australia. Good red wines (especially the 1976 Cabernet) and commercial whites (Rhine riesling, white burgundy).

TIRAGE LIQUEUR

Sugar solution which is added to a base wine to turn it into champagne. The secondary fermentation converts this into a small amount of extra alcohol and CO_2 which is dissolved in the wine.

TISDALL

Medium-sized premium winemaker in central northern Victoria owned and established by Dr Peter Tisdall.

TOLLANA

Large Barossa Valley (South Australia) winemaker with impeccable winemaking skills. Operated by Tolley, Scott and Tolley. Across-the-board range of table, bulk and fortified wines including white burgundy, red blends and champagne.

TRAMINER

White grape variety, widely grown in various parts of the world, producing wines with abundant fruit flavours, though not necessarily sweet, and often with spicy overtones. 'Gewurztraminer' is often used to designate this spiciness.

TREBBIANO

White grape variety from Italy (also known as ugni blanc). Used in some parts of Australia for fairly ordinary medium to dry whites, sometimes blended with others.

TULLOCH

Premium Hunter Valley winemaker now owned by Allied Vintners. Makes excellent reds (shiraz) and whites (semillons).

TYRRELLS

Medium-sized family owned Hunter Valley winemaker. Reputation for top fine dry whites (semillon mainly), chardonnay and reds (mainly shiraz). Old winery was established 1858.

UGNI BLANC

Synonym for TREBBIANO white grape.

ULLAGE

The air space between the top of the wine in a bottle and the bottom of the cork. If excessive, the wine is 'ullaged'.

VARIETAL

Wine made from a particular grape variety (for example, Rhine riesling). Opposite to generic wines (for example, chablis).

VERDELHO

White grape variety used on the island of Madeira. Mainly grown in Western Australia for dry whites, but also used there for excellent fortified wines; some is used in the Hunter Valley for dry white wines.

VERMOUTH

Wine fortified and to which many flavour components are added, for example, herbs, flowers and roots.

VIGNERON

Grape-grower.

VIGOROUS

In wine, a lively taste or feel; in a grapevine, sometimes a bad thing.

VIN

Wine (French). As in *vin ordinaire*: ordinary wine.

VINEGAR

Wine spoilt by the vinegar bacteria – deliberately or otherwise. Not pleasant to drink, either way, and a major winemaking fault, easily spotted.

VINICULTURE

The skills of growing grapevines.

VINOSITY

Wine-tasting term pertaining to alcoholic strength of a wine and the grape character of the wine.

VINTAGE

The period of picking the grapes each year. Also the year a wine was made ('vintaged').

VINTAGE PORT

See PORT.

VINTNER

Winemaker.

VISCOUS

Thick appearance in a wine; showing the presence of glycerol.

VITIS

Vitis vinifera – the grape-bearing vine responsible for most of the world's quality wines. *Vitis labrusca*: North American native vine (*see* FOXY).

VOLATILE

A wine spoilt by the presence of ACETIC ACID is said to be volatile, or have volatile acidity (v.a.).

WINE

Fermented juice of grapes.

WINE SHOWS

The Royal Agricultural Societies in the various capital cities organise wine judging on a circuit which usually begins in Sydney (the judging is done before the Royal Easter Show) and runs Brisbane-Melbourne-Perth-Adelaide-Hobart-Canberra. The Canberra Show is open to entries which have won medals in the other shows. The experts seem to agree that the wine shows to watch (because standards are high) are Sydney, Adelaide and Canberra.

WIRRA WIRRA

Small, high quality winery at McLaren Vale, South Australia, specialising in varietal table wines.

WOLF BLASS

See BLASS.

WOODLEY'S

Large wine company owned by Industrial Equity Limited. Large marketer of commercial wines, for example, Queen Adelaide Rhine Riesling. Based in old cellars in Adelaide.

WOODY

Strong bouquet of wood (oak) in wine, not necessarily offensive, but possibly very obvious.

WYNDHAM ESTATE

Very successful winemakers and marketers under winemaker Brian McGuigan. Based at historic Dalwood in the Hunter Valley. Good whites and reds.

WYNN WINEGROWERS

Allied Vintners/Toohey's owned Wynn from the early 1970s until May 1985 when they were acquired by Penfolds/Kaiser Stuhl. They have large wineries in South Australia and make and market all styles of wine. High quality bottled wines, especially those from Coonawarra Estate and large volume Seaview Champagne from the Romalo cellars in Adelaide, and at Glenloth, Reynella.

XANADU

Chateau Xanadu is a small winery near Margaret River, Western Australia.

YALUMBA

Large, historic and beautiful winery owned by the Smith family near Angaston, in the Barossa Hills. Excellent range of all styles of wines, including 'Signature' series reds, Pewsey Vale and Heggies rieslings, ports, sherries and champagne.

YARRA YERING

Small winery, making premium reds, in the Yarra Valley near Melbourne, Victoria.

YEAST

Single cell organisms responsible for conversion of grape sugar into ethyl alcohol (fermentation).

ZINFANDEL

Red grape variety widely grown in California. Little grown in Australia, mainly grown in Western Australia, especially the Margaret River region.

INDEX

Best wishes
Val Everist.

Julie Schmedje

Best wishes for the future Jim
& Good luck in Australia. Roseen xx
Judy P xx

Kevin Moylan xx

All the best
Donna Spencer xxx

Jenny Johnston xxx
1987

Hope this brings back pleasant memories
Malcolm.

Very Pleasant to
work with Anne Red
xx

All the best for
the future. Sue T.

Pleasure to know you
Phil Z.

Best of luck
JJ

A pleasure to work with you
Jim, Best wishes,
Jonathon & Andrea

Graham King

I hope this helps you
remember Shepparton
in Sheptember
best wishes
Judy Bryant

Take care
Emily x+

Thanks for all you
have done. Best
wishes for the
future
Julie x+

You will
be missed
Love Helen.

Best wishes
R M Hogue
Jack Pool.

GOOD LUCK
DOWN ON THE
BEACH.
THANKS FOR YOUR
SUPPORT.
Meredith.

lovely working
with you
Michael Gibson

22nd September
1987

AUSTRALIA

Darwin

ALICE SPRINGS

ROMA

STANTHORPE   *Brisbane*

                                        MUDGEE   UPPER HUNTER
                                                  LOWER HUNTER
Perth • SWAN VALLEY   CLARE   RIVERLAND
                      BAROSSA VALLEY   *Sydney*
SOUTH-WEST COASTAL REGION   ADELAIDE   MILDURA   GRIFFITH/LEETON M.I.A.
MARGARET RIVER   McLAREN VALE   RUTHENGLEN
                      LANGHORNE CREEK   SWAN HILL   GLENROWAN/MILAWA
MT BARKER-FRANKLAND REGION
                         COONAWARRA   *Melbourne*
                         GREAT WESTERN   YARRA VALLEY
                      CENTRAL VICTORIA
                      GOULBURN VALLEY   LAUNCESTON
                         GEELONG
                                                        HOBART